ORGANIZATIONAL BEHAVIOR

FOURTH EDITION

ORGANIZATIONAL BEHAVIOR

CONCEPTS, CONTROVERSIES, AND APPLICATIONS

Stephen P. Robbins

Southern Illinois University at Edwardsville
and
San Diego State University

PRENTICE HALL, Englewood Cliffs, New Jersey 07632

Library of Congress Cataloging-in-Publication Data

ROBBINS, STEPHEN P.
    Organizational behavior : concepts, controversies, and
applications / Stephen P. Robbins.—4th ed.
        p.   cm.

    Includes bibliographies and indexes.
    ISBN 0-13-641762-0
    1. Organizational behavior.   I. Title.
HD58.7.R62   1989   88-15696
158.7—dc 19   CIP

Editorial/production supervision: **Eleanor Ode Walter**
Interior design: **Linda J. Conway**
Cover design: **Linda J. Conway**
Manufacturing buyer: **Ed O'Dougherty**

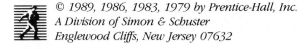 *© 1989, 1986, 1983, 1979 by Prentice-Hall, Inc.*
A Division of Simon & Schuster
Englewood Cliffs, New Jersey 07632

Printed in the United States of America

10   9   8   7   6   5   4   3

ISBN 0-13-641762-0

Prentice-Hall International (UK) Limited, London
Prentice-Hall of Australia Pty. Limited, Sydney
Prentice-Hall Canada Inc., Toronto
Prentice-Hall Hispanoamericana, S.A., Mexico
Prentice-Hall of India Private Limited, New Delhi
Prentice-Hall of Japan, Inc., Tokyo
Simon & Schuster Asia Pte. Ltd., Singapore
Editora Prentice-Hall do Brasil, Ltda., Rio de Janeiro

For Joan G. Rapp—
my "in-house" library resource.

Contents

3 Foundations of Individual Behavior *42*

4 Perception and Individual Decision Making *81*

5 Values, Attitudes, and Job Satisfaction *116*

6 Basic Motivation Concepts *146*

10 Leadership *301*

11 Power and Politics *338*

PART FOUR / THE ORGANIZATION SYSTEM

14 Human Resource Policies and Practices *429*

15 Cultural Systems *464*

PART FIVE / ORGANIZATIONAL DYNAMICS

Preface

Many years ago, I was watching a television interview of a famous novelist. During that interview, the novelist said, "A writer can never forget who his audience is." As this text has evolved over its four editions, I think I've replayed that statement in my mind at least a thousand times, because I never want to lose sight that I'm writing this book for students, and not for faculty or researchers. From this perspective, I think a good text should be designed and written to hold a student's attention. That means it has to be organized in a logical way, written in a lively style, and include examples with which students can readily identify. Because it is not being written for academics, detailed discussions of esoteric topics or trivial methodological debates need to be excluded. But, of course, a good text must also be true to its discipline. It must reflect the most current thinking and research in its field.

I've worked hard on this edition, as well as on the previous ones, to write an introductory organizational behavior book that meets the needs of students and also provides an accurate review of the field. Using the previously mentioned guideposts for a "good text," I will summarize briefly what I've done to make this text a valuable resource for students studying organizational behavior.

ORGANIZATION OF TOPICS

To be an effective learning tool, a text should cover more than just fifteen to twenty subjects, each called a "chapter," randomly shuffled together. It must provide some logical framework that can guide readers through its maze of subjects. I was particularly sensitive to this concern in the mid-1970s, when I began planning the first edition of this book. What I came up with at that time was a building block model of OB. This model describes OB as focusing on three levels—the individual, the group, and the organization system—and defines the objectives of OB as explaining and predicting four outcomes— employee productivity, absence, turnover, and satisfaction. This model has stood the test of time. It has proven to be an effective structure for overviewing the field of organizational behavior and for helping students to integrate concepts. In Chapter 2, the building block model is introduced, as well as the key topics that make up OB and the interrelationships between them. This model, then, becomes the framework upon which the rest of the text is built.

WRITING STYLE

I don't know where it's written, but a number of my colleagues tell me that textbooks are not meant to be interesting. They're supposed to be serious and intellectually rigorous. I agree that a textbook should be serious and intellectually demanding, but that shouldn't preclude it from being lively and interesting; especially a text in organizational behavior.

Few people voluntarily put down a Stephen King or Danielle Steel novel to read a textbook. In most cases, the reason is obvious: the subject matter. Horror stories and romances are typically more interesting than calculus or geology. But OB is about people. It's about life at work. It's about what motivates people, why some people are leaders and others aren't, and how people politic in organizations to get ahead. These are interesting issues. So OB, at least in contrast to some academic subjects, doesn't necessarily suffer from being bland or irrelevant.

On the contrary, I think the subject matter of OB is inherently interesting and relevant, and I've tried to convey that in this text. I use a conversational style. I talk *to* you, the reader, rather than *at* you. I rely heavily on the use of examples to explain and amplify concepts. Moreover, the examples are drawn from the life experiences of students as well as from the world of business. For instance, you'll find a lot of examples that relate to the classroom and student-teacher interactions, with the result that students and instructors have consistently described earlier editions of this text as "extremely well-written," "engaging," and having a "lively style." I hope this edition will continue to generate such comments.

CONTENT ISSUES IN OB

The basic test that every textbook must pass is this: Does it adequately cover the subject matter? No matter how engaging the writing style, if a text fails this hurdle, it will fail in the marketplace.

You'll find that this text covers the concepts and theories that comprise the core of organizational behavior. But since the last edition, new issues have emerged and others have gained importance. I've tried to reflect these changes in the text. In this section, I want to review important issues from the previous edition that many other OB texts continue to overlook, and describe topics that have been revised in this edition as well as those topics that are new to this edition.

From the Previous Edition

I think the following issues are important in developing an understanding of organizational behavior, so I included them in the previous edition. However, many OB texts continue to overlook them:

- Biographical characteristics (age, sex, tenure, etc.) as predictors of behavior (Chapter 3)

- Ability's effect on performance (Chapters 3 and 6)
- Holland's personality-job fit theory (Chapter 3)
- Values (Chapter 5)
- Cognitive evaluation theory (Chapter 6)
- Integrating motivation theories (Chapter 6)
- Stages of group development (Chapter 8)
- Group demography (Chapter 8)
- Hersey and Blanchard's situational leadership theory (Chapter 10)
- Contrasting bases and sources of power (Chapter 11)
- Impact of unions on employee behavior (Chapter 14)
- OB in an international context (Chapter 15)

Revised Coverage

As I reviewed the OB literature since 1985, it became clear to me that several issues discussed in the third edition needed to be revised and/or elaborated upon. The following highlights those changes:

- Research in organizational behavior (Chapter 2)—I rewrote this section to better clarify research concepts and their relevance to understanding OB. The focus, however, still continues to be on helping the reader to be a more aware consumer, not on making him or her a researcher.
- Individual decision making (Chapter 4)—I've greatly expanded this material, especially alternatives to the optimizing perspective such as the satisficing and implicit favorite models.
- Group behavior (Chapter 8)—I've reorganized this chapter around an integrative group behavior model. This change improves the clarity and flow of the discussion.
- Work stress (Chapter 16)—This edition now has a full chapter on work stress.

New to This Edition

The following highlights topics that are completely new to this edition:

- How employees express dissatisfaction (Chapter 5)
- New chapter on applied motivation that links theory and application (Chapter 7)
- Graen's leader-member exchange theory (Chapter 10)
- Charismatic leadership (Chapter 10)
- Intergroup relations (Chapter 12)
- OD consultation process (Chapter 17)
- Implementation issues in OD (Chapter 17)

PEDAGOGICAL FEATURES

An effective textbook is a comprehensive learning system. It should be designed to facilitate understanding and application. I've included a number of features in this text to help readers better assimilate its contents.

- *Chapter outline and learning objectives*—Each chapter opens with a topic outline and a set of learning objectives that students should be able to answer after reading the material.
- *Implications for performance and satisfaction*—Each of the core chapters ends with a section where that chapter's concepts are summarized in terms of their relevance to explaining and predicting employee performance and satisfaction.
- *"OB Close-Up" boxes*—These are new to this edition. They are designed to help illustrate applications of concepts and elaborate on current issues in OB.
- *Chapter wrap-ups*—All chapters end with a set of discussion questions and references for further reading.
- *"Point–Counterpoint" debates*—A unique pedagogical component in this text is the inclusion of "Point–Counterpoint" debates at the end of each chapter. They present interesting and current controversies in OB. Additionally, they provide excellent vehicles for stimulating class discussion.
- *Exercises and cases*—To assist in the transition from theory to practice, an exercise and case incident is included at the end of each chapter. This represents a reorganization from the third edition, where cases and exercises were placed at the end of the sections.

SUPPLEMENTARY MATERIALS

A textbook is, today, only part of an overall teaching *package*. Instructors are looking for supportive materials to make their teaching more effective. In response to this need, Prentice Hall and I have put together a comprehensive package of supplements for this book.

Annotated Instructor's Edition

This special edition of the text contains course outlines, extensive lecture enrichments, answers to end-of-chapter discussion questions, point-counterpoint summaries and analyses, and answers to case incidents. Additionally, it offers film and video suggestions to enhance specific topics, and cross-references interpersonal skill behaviors to various OB concepts (see discussion of TIPS that follows).

Transparency Masters

Text figures, tables, and chapter outlines are provided as transparency masters for duplication.

Test-Item File

Trina Redford and I have carefully prepared the test-item file to provide questions that accurately and fairly assess student competence in the text material. The questions have been reviewed to ensure the highest quality, and are organized by the chapter outline. Each question has been rated for difficulty, and is designated as either factual or applied, so that instructors can provide a balanced set of questions for student exams. Prentice Hall offers its telephone test preparation service with this text and it is also available in a computerized software package called Diploma.

TIPS

Adopters may, at a special price, choose to have their students receive my *Training in InterPersonal Skills* (TIPS) book along with this text. TIPS provides students with an opportunity to learn and practice ten key interpersonal skills: listening, goal setting, providing feedback, appraising performance, disciplining, delegating, using oral persuasion, politicking, running a group meeting, and resolving conflicts. Instructors who use TIPS will also be provided with its accompanying manual, *Teaching TIPS*.

ACUMEN

This is an educational version of HUMAN FACTORS Advanced Technology Group's sophisticated and highly popular managerial assessment program. Based on fifteen years of research on more than 250,000 managers in over 6,000 companies, ACUMEN provides each student with a comprehensive personal management style profile. This software program is available shrinkwrapped to this text in a special edition package at a price substantially lower than if the two were purchased separately.

Videos

For large adoptions of this text, over forty videos from the *Enterprise* series and five from the *In Search of Excellence* series are available.

ACKNOWLEDGMENTS

Every author has a long list of individuals to whom he or she is indebted. My list includes colleagues and friends, as well as the people at Prentice Hall.

I appreciate the comments and suggestions made by outside reviewers: R. E. Kelley, Governors State University; Irene Devine, Concordia University,

Montreal; James L. Hall, University of Santa Clara; Charles R. Kuehl, University of Missouri-St. Louis. I am also appreciative of the ideas offered by my colleagues at San Diego State, particularly Alan Omens and Mark Butler. Of course, I solely accept full responsibility for any errors or omissions. My department chair in San Diego, Penny Wright, deserves a special thanks for providing physical resources and moral support.

Books aren't books without publishers and I'm fortunate to have the number one college textbook publisher—Prentice Hall—in my corner. Their acquisition, production, design, marketing, and sales personnel are, without question, the brightest and most talented in the business. There isn't enough space to personally acknowledge all the people at Prentice Hall, past and present, who have contributed to this text. But let me single out a dozen or so: Alison Reeves, Fran Falk, Eleanor Walter, Jayne Maerker, Earl Kivett, Linda Albelli, Nan Fausnaugh, Mary Adam, Gerry Johnson, Dennis Hogan, and John Isley.

Finally, I want to acknowledge my "significant other," Joan Rapp. She is one of the few people I know who doesn't think my seven day workweek schedule is "weird." She actually believes obsessive-compulsive behavior is a positive quality! There are not many like her around, and I value her support.

Stephen P. Robbins
St. Louis, Missouri

ORGANIZATIONAL BEHAVIOR

1

What Is Organizational Behavior?

■ *Learning objectives*

Explain the value of the systematic study of OB
Identify the contributions made by major behavioral science disciplines to OB
Distinguish between OB and management
State why managers require a knowledge of OB
Explain the need for a contingency approach for studying OB

I'm not smart. I try to observe. Millions saw the apple fall but Newton was the one who asked why.

———— B. BARUCH

Each of us is a student of behavior. Since our earliest years, we have watched the actions of others and have attempted to interpret what we see. Whether or not you have explicitly thought about it before, you have been "reading" people almost all your life. You watch what others do and try to explain why they have engaged in their behavior. Additionally, you've attempted to predict what they might do under different sets of conditions.

You have already developed some generalizations that you find helpful in explaining and predicting what people do and will do. But how did you arrive at these generalizations? You did so by observing, sensing, asking, listening, and reading. That is, your understanding comes either directly from your own experience with things in the environment, or secondhand, through the experience of others.

How accurate are the generalizations that you hold? Some may represent extremely sophisticated appraisals of behavior and may prove highly effective in explaining and predicting the behavior of others. However, most of us also carry with us a number of beliefs that frequently fail to explain why people do what they do. To illustrate, consider the following statements about work-related behavior:

1. Happy workers are productive workers.
2. All individuals are most productive when their boss is friendly, trusting, and approachable.
3. Interviews are effective selection devices for separating job applicants who would be high-performing employees from those who would be low performers.
4. Everyone wants a challenging job.
5. You have to scare people a little to get them to do their job.
6. Everyone is motivated by money.
7. Most individuals are much more concerned with the size of their salary than with others' salaries.
8. The most effective work groups are devoid of conflict.

How many of these statements are true? For the most part, they are all false, and we shall touch on each later in this text. But whether these statements are true or false is not really important at this time. What is important is to be aware that many of the views you hold concerning human behavior are based on intuition rather than fact. As a result, a systematic approach to the study of behavior can improve your explanatory and predictive abilities.

REPLACING INTUITION WITH SYSTEMATIC STUDY

Casual or commonsense approaches for obtaining knowledge about human behavior are inadequate. In reading this text you will discover that a systematic approach will uncover important facts and relationships, and provide a base from which more accurate predictions of behavior can be made.

Underlying this systematic approach is the belief that **behavior** is not random. It is **caused** and directed toward some end that the individual believes, rightly or wrongly, is in his or her best interest.

> Behavior generally is predictable if we know how the person perceived the situation and what is important to him or her. While people's behavior may not appear to be rational to an outsider, there is reason to believe it usually is *intended* to be rational and it is seen as rational by them. An observer often sees behavior as nonrational because the observer does not have access to the same information or does not perceive the environment in the same way.[1]

Certainly there are differences between individuals. Placed in similar situations, all people do not act alike. However, there are certain fundamental consistencies underlying the behavior of all individuals that can be identified and used to alter conclusions based on individual differences.

These fundamental consistencies are very important. Why? Because they allow predictability. When you get into your car, you make some definite and usually highly accurate predictions about how other people will behave. You predict that other drivers will stop at stop signs and red lights, drive on the right side of the street, pass on your left, and not cross the solid double line on mountain roads. Notice that your predictions about the behavior of people behind the wheel of their cars is almost always correct. Obviously, the rules of driving make predictions about driving behavior fairly easy. What may be less obvious is that there are rules (written and unwritten) in every setting. Therefore, it can be argued that it is possible to predict behavior (obviously, not always with 100 percent accuracy) in supermarkets, classrooms, doctors' offices, elevators, and in most structured situations. To illustrate further, do you turn around and face the doors when you get into an elevator? Almost everyone does, yet did you ever read that you're supposed to do this? Probably not! Just as I make predictions about automobile drivers (where there are definite rules of the road), I can make predictions about the behavior of people in elevators (where there are few written rules). In a class of sixty students, if you wanted to ask a question of the instructor, I would predict that you would raise your hand. Why don't you clap, stand up, raise your leg, cough, or yell "Hey, over here!" The reason is that you have learned that raising your hand is appropriate behavior in school. These examples support a major contention

Caused behavior

Behavior that is directed toward some end; not random.

[1] E. E. Lawler III and J. G. Rhode, *Information and Control in Organizations* (Pacific Palisades, CA: Goodyear, 1976), p. 22.

Systematic study

Looking at relationships, attempting to attribute causes and effects, and drawing conclusions based on scientific evidence.

Intuition

A feeling not necessarily supported by research.

in this text. Behavior is generally predictable, and the **systematic study** of behavior is a means to making reasonably accurate predictions.

When we use the phrase "systematic study," we mean looking at relationships, attempting to attribute causes and effects, and basing our conclusions on scientific evidence, that is, on data gathered under controlled conditions and measured and interpreted in a reasonably rigorous manner.

Systematic study replaces **intuition** or those "gut feelings" about "why I do what I do" and "what makes others tick." Of course, a systematic approach does not mean that those things you have come to believe in an unsystematic way are necessarily incorrect. Some of the conclusions we make in this text, based on reasonably substantive research findings, will only support what you always knew was true. But you will also be exposed to research evidence that runs counter to what you may have thought was common sense. In fact, one of the challenges to teaching a subject like organizational behavior is to overcome the notion, held by many, that "it's *all* common sense."[2] You will find that many of the so-called "commonsense" views you hold about human behavior are, on closer examination, wrong. Moreover, what one person considers "common sense" frequently runs counter to another's version of "common sense." Are leaders born or made? Is conflict in a group always a bad sign, or can conflict increase group performance? You probably have answers to such questions, and individuals who have not reviewed the research are likely to differ on their answers. Our point is that one of the objectives of this text is to encourage you to move away from your intuitive views of behavior toward a systematic analysis, in the belief that the latter will enhance your effectiveness in accurately explaining and predicting behavior.

PUTTING THE "ORGANIZATION" INTO ORGANIZATIONAL BEHAVIOR

Organization

A consciously coordinated social unit, composed of two or more people, that functions on a relatively continuous basis to achieve a common goal or set of goals.

This chapter's title asks, "What is organizational behavior?" To this point, we have addressed only the general subject of behavior, which concerns itself with people's actions that can be observed or measured. Now, let us turn our attention to the "organizational" context.

First, what is an **organization**? An organization is a consciously coordinated social unit, composed of two or more people, that functions on a relatively continuous basis to achieve a common goal or set of goals. Manufacturing and service firms clearly meet this definition, as do schools, hospitals, churches, military units, retail stores, police departments, and local, state, and federal government agencies.

What, then, is **organizational behavior?** Organizational behavior (frequently abbreviated as OB) is a *a field of study that investigates the impact that individuals,*

Organizational behavior (OB)

A field of study that investigates the impact that individuals, groups, and structure have on behavior within organizations, for the purpose of applying such knowledge toward improving an organization's effectiveness.

[2] R. Weinberg and W. Nord, "Coping with 'It's All Common Sense,' " *Exchange*, Vol. 7, No. 2 (1982), pp. 29–33; R. P. Vecchio, "Some Popular (But Misguided) Criticisms of the Organizational Sciences," *Organizational Behavior Teaching Review*, Vol. 10, No. 1 (1986–87), pp. 28–34; and M. L. Lynn, "Organizational Behavior and Common Sense: Philosophical Implications for Teaching and Thinking," paper presented at the 14th Annual Organizational Behavior Teaching Conference; Waltham, MA; May 1987.

groups, and structure have on behavior within organizations, for the purpose of applying such knowledge toward improving an organization's effectiveness. That's a lot of words, so let's break it down.

Organizational behavior is a field of study. This means that it is a distinct area of expertise with a common body of knowledge. What does it study? It studies three determinants of behavior in organizations: individuals, groups, and structure. Additionally, OB is an applied field. It applies the knowledge gained about individuals, groups, and the effect of structure on behavior toward the end of making organizations work more effectively.

To sum up our definition, OB is concerned with the study of what people do in an organization and how that behavior affects the performance of the organization. And because OB is specifically concerned with employment-related environments, you should not be surprised to find that it emphasizes behavior as related to jobs, work, absenteeism, employment turnover, productivity, human performance, and management.

In addition to our definition, OB has been characterized in the broad sense as a way of thinking, and in a narrower sense as a body of knowledge covering a relatively specific set of core topics. Let us briefly elaborate on these two points.

When we view OB as a way of thinking, we acknowledge that it can be systematically studied. Organizational behavior can be conceptualized as the systematic study of nonrandom cause and effect phenomena. It also directs one's thinking toward viewing behavior in a performance-related context; that is, as it leads to effectiveness or success in achieving organizationally desirable outcomes.

There is increasing agreement as to the components or topics that comprise the subject area of OB. While there continues to be considerable debate as to the relative importance of each, there appears to be general agreement that OB includes the core topics of motivation, leader behavior and power, interpersonal communication, group structure and process, learning, attitude development and perception, change processes, conflict, job design, and work stress.

IS OB WORTH STUDYING?

So far, we have only *assumed* that there is value in being able to explain and predict behavior in an organizational setting. Therefore, we need to consider some specific reasons why the study of OB deserves your attention and effort.

Many people are interested in learning about OB for the sake of curiosity alone. They seek to understand behavior. They have no intention of ever applying their knowledge; rather, they merely seek an answer to why people behave the way they do in organizations with which they are familiar.

Beyond this understanding lies a desire to be able to predict what others will do. You may want to develop your skills to make valid predictions; that is, if X, then Y. The study of OB will help you to develop this predictive skill as it relates to behavior within organizations.

Probably the most popular reason for studying OB is that the reader is interested in pursuing a career in management and wants to learn how to

OB Close-Up

People Skills: A Primary Deficiency of Today's Business School Graduates

A recent study prepared by the major accrediting body of collegiate business schools reported that a primary deficiency of business school graduates is not their inability to write, perform analytical studies, or make decisions. It's their people or interpersonal skills.[3]

Schools of business are preparing tomorrow's managers. But managers fail more often because they lack solid interpersonal skills than because of inadequate technical competencies. Successful managers must be able to lead, motivate, communicate, work as part of a team, resolve conflicts, and engage in similar interpersonal activities. Unfortunately, until very recently, courses in organizational behavior, interpersonal processes, human relations, and applied psychology have taken a backseat to those in finance, accounting, and quantitative techniques. However, now that this weakness in the preparation of business students has been identified, actions are being planned to correct the problem. Colleges will be expanding their courses in the applied behavioral sciences, and making more of these courses required. Business, too, will respond by insuring that current managers, and those with management potential, receive training to improve their interpersonal skills. Some companies will send employees to workshops offered by universities and training firms. Others will offer in-house programs for employees.

predict behavior and apply it in some meaningful way to make organizations more effective. Having good "people skills"—which includes the ability to understand your employees and to use this knowledge to get them to work efficiently and effectively for you—is a vital requirement if you are going to succeed as a manager.

[3] L. W. Porter and L. E. McKibbin, *Future of Management Education and Development: Drift or Thrust into the 21st Century?* (New York: McGraw-Hill, 1988).

FIGURE 1–1

Source: Copyright 1960 by United Feature Syndicate, Inc. With permission.

Our final reason for studying OB may not be very exciting, but it is pragmatic—it may be a requirement for a particular degree or certificate you are seeking. In other words, you may be a captive in a required course, and learning OB in your opinion may offer no obvious end that has value to you. In that case, studying OB is only a means toward getting a degree or certificate. Hopefully one of our first three reasons holds more relevance to *you*.

CONTRIBUTING DISCIPLINES TO THE OB FIELD

Organizational behavior is an applied behavioral science and, as a result, is built upon contributions from a number of behavioral disciplines. The predominant areas are psychology, sociology, social psychology, anthropology, and political science.[4] As we shall learn, contributions of the psychologists have been mainly at the individual or micro level of analysis, while the latter disciplines have contributed to our understanding of macro concepts—group processes and organization. Figure 1–2 overviews the major contributions to the study of organizational behavior.

Psychology

Psychology is the science that seeks to measure, explain, and sometimes change the behavior of humans and other animals. Psychologists concern themselves with studying and attempting to understand *individual* behavior. Those who have contributed and continue to add to the knowledge of OB are learning theorists, personality theorists, counseling psychologists, and, most important, industrial and organizational psychologists.

Early industrial psychologists concerned themselves with problems of fatigue, boredom, and any other factor relevant to working conditions that could impede efficient work performance. More recently, their contributions have been expanded to include learning, perception, personality, training, leadership effectiveness, needs and motivational forces, job satisfaction, decision-making processes, performance appraisals, attitude measurement, employee selection techniques, job design, and work stress.

Sociology

Whereas psychologists focus their attention on the individual, sociologists study the social system in which individuals fill their roles; that is, sociology studies people in relation to their fellow human beings. Specifically, sociologists have made their greatest contribution to OB through their study of group behavior in organizations, particularly formal and complex organizations. Some of the areas within OB that have received valuable input from sociologists include

[4] See, for example, M. J. Driver, "Cognitive Psychology: An Interactionist View;" R. H. Hall, "Organizational Behavior: A Sociological Perspective;" and C. Hardy, "The Contribution of Political Science to Organizational Behavior," all in J. W. Lorsch (ed.), *Handbook of Organizational Behavior* (Englewood Cliffs, NJ: Prentice Hall, 1987), pp. 62–108.

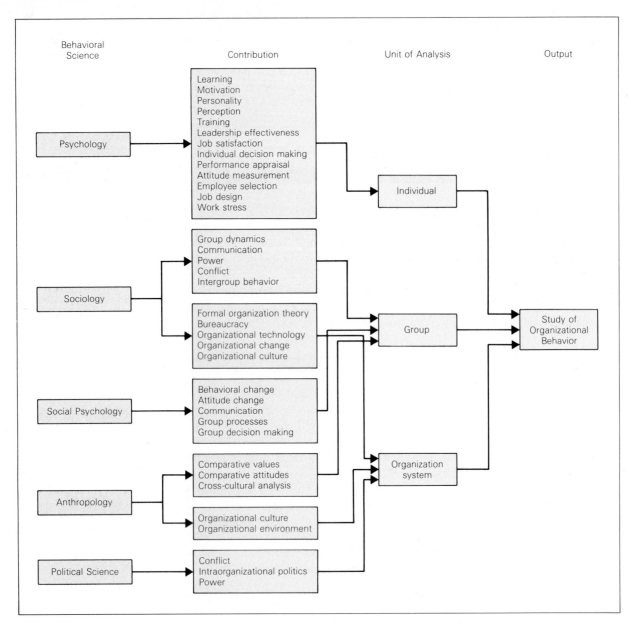

FIGURE 1–2
Toward an OB Discipline

group dynamics, organizational culture, formal organization theory and structure, organizational technology, bureaucracy, communications, power, conflict, and intergroup behavior.

Social Psychology

Social psychology focuses on interpersonal behavior. Whereas psychology and sociology attempt to explain individual and group behavior, respectively, social psychology seeks to explain how and why individuals behave as they do in

Viewing a Common Event Through Dissimilar Eyes

The diversity of training, interests, and perspective among members of the various behavioral disciplines has contributed to divergent approaches to the study of many OB topics. To illustrate, take the issue of conflict within organizations. If an industrial psychologist and an organizational sociologist look at the same conflict situation, they rarely see it in the same way. Psychologists tend to see the cause of most conflicts as lying in the motives and personalities of the parties involved. In contrast, sociologists tend to see the source of the conflict as the roles and structure that define the relationships between the parties. As a result, the psychologist's solution to conflict focuses on changing people, whereas the sociologist's solution is more likely to emphasize restructuring relationships.

This illustration dramatizes two important points that you should keep in mind as you read this text: The field of OB has clearly been broadened by the diverse inputs brought to it by psychologists, sociologists, social psychologists, anthropologists, and political scientists. However, each discipline molds issues of interest to fit into the perspective with which that discipline views the world.

group activities. One of the major areas receiving considerable investigation by social psychologists has been *change*—how to implement it and how to reduce barriers to its acceptance. Additionally, we find social psychologists making significant contributions in measuring, understanding, and changing attitudes, communication patterns, the ways in which group activities can satisfy individual needs, and group decision-making processes.

Anthropology

Anthropologists study societies to learn about human beings and their activities. Their work on cultures and environments, for instance, has helped us understand differences in fundamental values, attitudes, and behavior between people in different countries and within different organizations. Much of our current understanding of organizational culture, organizational environments, and differences between national cultures is the result of the work of anthropologists or those using their methodologies.

Political Science

Although frequently overlooked, the contributions of political scientists are significant to the understanding of behavior in organizations. Political scientists study the behavior of individuals and groups within a political environment. Specific topics of concern include structuring of conflict, allocation of power, and how people manipulate power for individual self-interest.

ARE "OB" AND "MANAGEMENT" SYNONYMOUS TERMS?

Management

A field of study devoted to determining how best to attain goals in organizations.

Many academics, practitioners, and students confuse the subject matter in OB with that in **management** or administration. While there is some overlap, management and OB have different means and ends.

Organizational behavior, as noted previously, is concerned with how people, individually and in groups, act in organizations. Management is concerned with the optimum attainment of organizational goals. However, since these goals are unattainable without human input, OB is a significant subset or segment of management.

The subject of OB is intended to support the knowledge necessary to be a manager. The understanding of individual and group behavior is important for what it can contribute toward the education and development of one's managerial talents. When managers perform managerial functions—planning, organizing, leading, and controlling—they need to know what impact their actions will have on people. Since managers work with and get things done through other people, an understanding of people is critical to being a successful manager. But, of course, since managers also work with physical inputs (for example, equipment and inventories) and financial inputs, a manager requires knowledge of subjects that go beyond human behavior to include, but not be limited to, accounting, finance, marketing, production systems, purchasing, forecasting, strategy and policy formation, economics, and computer science.

THERE ARE FEW ABSOLUTES IN OB

There are few, if any, simple and universal principles that explain organizational behavior. There are laws in the physical sciences—chemistry, astronomy, physics—that are consistent and apply in a wide range of situations. They allow scientists to generalize about the pull of gravity, or to confidently send astronauts into space to repair satellites. But as one noted behavioral researcher aptly concluded, "God gave all the *easy* problems to the physicists." Human beings are very complex. They are not alike, which limits the ability to make simple, accurate, and sweeping generalizations. Two people often act very differently in the same situation, and the same person's behavior changes in different situations. For instance, not everyone is motivated by money, and you behave differently at church on Sunday than you did at the beer party the night before.

That doesn't mean, of course, that we can't offer reasonably accurate explanations of human behavior or make valid predictions. It does mean, however, that OB concepts must reflect situational or contingency conditions. We can say that x leads to y, but only under conditions specified in z (the **contingency variables**). The science of OB was developed by using general concepts, and then altering their application to the particular situation. So, for example, OB scholars would avoid stating that effective leaders should always seek the ideas of their subordinates before making a decision. Rather, we shall find that in some situations a participative style is clearly superior, but in other situations, an autocratic decision style is more effective. In other words, the effectiveness of a particular leadership style is *contingent* upon the situation in which it is utilized.

As you proceed through this text, you'll encounter a wealth of research-based theories about how people behave in organizations. But don't expect to find a lot of straightforward cause-effect relationships. There aren't many! Organizational behavior theories mirror the subject matter with which they deal. People are complex and complicated, and so too must be the theories developed to explain their actions.

Consistent with the contingency philosophy, you'll find point-counterpoint debates at the conclusion of each chapter. These debates are included to reinforce that within the OB field there are many issues over which there is significant disagreement. By directly addressing some of the more controversial issues, using the point-counterpoint format, you get the opportunity to explore different points of view, discover how diverse perspectives complement and oppose each other, and gain insight into some of the debates currently taking place within the OB field.[5]

So, at the end of one chapter, you'll find an argument that projects leadership as playing an important role in an organization attaining its goals, followed by the argument that there is little evidence to support this claim. Similarly, at the end of other chapters, you'll read both sides of the debate on whether money is a motivator, clear communication is always desirable, bureaucracies have become obsolete, and the like. These arguments are meant to demonstrate that OB, like many disciplines, has disagreements over specific findings, methods, and theories. Some of the point-counterpoint arguments are more provocative than others, but each makes some valid points that you should find thought-provoking. The key is to be able to decipher under what conditions each argument may be right or wrong.

Contingency variables

Those variables that moderate the relationship between the independent and dependent variables and improve the correlation.

---

[5] D. Tjosvold, "Controversy for Learning Organizational Behavior," *Organizational Behavior Teaching Review*, Vol. XI, No. 3 (1986–87), pp. 51–59.

POINT

OB IS A SOCIAL SCIENCE

OB has grown out of at least two older fields in business schools: human relations and management. It also includes significant ideas from psychology and sociology, although other social sciences such as economics, anthropology, and political science have certainly contributed to OB's development. In the past fifteen years, OB has received substantial inputs from a younger generation of scholars who have received their training in business schools under the label of Organizational Behavior itself (or some related term). If one, however, were required to select a single discipline that has most influenced the content of OB and its research methodologies, there is little disagreement over the answer: psychology. In second place, and closing slowly on the leader, is sociology.

Any study of the OB field would be generally acknowledged as incomplete without a discussion of the following ten topics: attitudes, job satisfaction, personality, perception, motivation, learning, job design, leadership, communication, and group dynamics. With the exception of the last two, the major work on each of these topics has been done by individuals whose primary training has been in psychology. The study of groups has belonged to the social psychologist and the sociologist. The interest in the past decade in power and conflict in organizations has also generally been furthered by individuals with sociological training. But the topics of power, conflict, and other interests of sociologists—including organizational culture and structure—suffer in contrast to the previously mentioned psychologically-based concepts by failing to achieve unanimity among OB scholars as to their legitimacy.

Based on contributions from researchers in psychology, sociology, and other social sciences, we have made substantial progress in our search to be able to explain and predict the behavior of people at work. We have, for example, identified a number of factors that contribute to employees voluntarily quitting their jobs. More important, we have also developed models that show how these factors interact.

Does this imply that we now have a science of OB that can consistently and perfectly predict behavior? No! We have made substantial progress, but our knowledge is far from complete. There are many questions that remain unanswered. There is also considerable research that is inconsistent and, in some cases, even contradictory. Unfortunately, understanding human behavior is not as simple as the understanding of, say, polio. The latter led to a vaccine that effectively eliminated polio in North America. Further research on polio is not necessary. The understanding of human behavior, in contrast, will never be fully understood. Research will continue, leading old theories to be replaced with new ones. We have come a great distance in our understanding of human behavior, but the road is long and we still have distance to cover.

COUNTERPOINT
BEHAVIOR IS GENETICALLY DETERMINED

Harvard zoologist Edward O. Wilson has, for over a decade, been developing his argument that social behavior is substantially biologically based. He would claim that the study of human behavior is not the sole province of social scientists. Human beings are not born with a blank slate as social scientists claim, with their behavior being totally a response to their environment. Wilson views a large part of human behavior—why we organize ourselves as we do, act as we do, and perhaps even think as we do—as a result of a gene-culture coevolution. Genetic makeup helps to guide and create culture, whereas culture in turn operates directly on the genes. Wilson believes that the future of understanding and changing behavior may lie in sociobiology—the study of the biological basis of social behavior.

Sociobiology began innocently enough as an attempt to understand the social behavior of animals, in particular, insects. Wilson focused on their population structure, castes, and communication, together with all the physiology underlying the social adaptations. For instance, he found that the incest taboo, which prohibits sexual relations between close relatives, has been deterred in the animal world by natural selection. In some animal social systems, males are programmed to leave home and find a new colony or herd when they reach puberty. And in a specialized form of programmed learning known as "imprinting," many young animals, birds as well as mammals, memorize the appearance, voice, or odor of their siblings and parents and use the resulting image to make later mating decisions. They will go to great lengths in adulthood to avoid mating with a sibling with whom they have been raised.

Of course, it is one thing to talk about insects and another to talk about human beings. Not surprisingly, it's been Wilson's extension of sociobiological concepts to humans that has generated the most discussion and criticism. He is suggesting some interesting ideas—such as the possibility of social engineering—that touch the deepest level of human motivation and moral reasoning. By selectively controlling the gene makeup in our society, we could significantly increase SAT scores, produce employees with high internal motivation, and eradicate racial divisiveness and wars. But who would decide this "ideal" society?

Wilson is not proposing that sociobiology will replace the social sciences. Rather, he sees disciplines such as psychology and sociology in some future time—probably 100 or more years from now—being encompassed within the physical sciences. The study of topics like stress, perception, learning, and creativity would then be analyzed in physiological terms. Stress would be evaluated in terms of the neurophysiological perturbations and their relaxation times. Perception would be translated into brain circuitry. Learning and creativity would be defined as the alteration of specific portions of the cognitive machinery regulated by input from the motive centers.

If you deem Wilson's ideas too abstract, look at the progress made in this century in chemistry. Psychopharmacology currently provides us with a wealth of drugs that can change and control behavior. Have you taken a valium recently?

KEY TERMS

Caused Behavior

Contingency Variables

Intuition

Management

Organization

Organizational Behavior

Systematic Study

FOR DISCUSSION

1. Contrast an intuitive approach to studying behavior with a systematic approach. Is intuition always inaccurate?

2. What does the phrase "behavior is caused" mean?

3. Define organizational behavior. How does this compare with management?

4. What is an organization? Is the family unit an organization?

5. Give four reasons for studying OB.

6. In what areas has psychology contributed to OB? Sociology? Social psychology? Anthropology? Political science? What other academic disciplines may have contributed to OB?

7. "The best way to view OB is through a contingency approach." Build an argument to support this statement.

8. "Since behavior is generally predictable, there is no need to formally study OB." Why is this statement wrong?

9. Some authors have defined the purpose of OB as being "to explain, predict, and *control* behavior." Do you agree or disagree? Discuss.

10. Why do you think the subject of OB might be criticized as being "only common sense," when one would rarely hear such a criticism of a course in physics or statistics?

11. Can the behavioral sciences such as psychology, sociology, and organizational behavior ever reach the precision of predictability that exists in the physical sciences? Support your position.

12. Give some examples of problems a manager might face for which a knowledge of organizational behavior might prove beneficial for finding solutions.

FOR FURTHER READING

BOONE, L. E., and D. D. BOWEN, *The Great Writings in Management and Organizational Behavior*, 2nd edition. New York: Random House, 1987. Presents classic articles and essays by major names in management and organizational behavior.

LORSCH, J. W. (ed.), *Handbook of Organizational Behavior*. Englewood Cliffs, NJ: Prentice Hall, 1987. A collection of twenty-seven essays covering the history of OB, its underlying disciplines, methodologies, analysis at various systems levels, managerial issues, and applications in nonbusiness settings.

MOHR, L., *Explaining Organizational Behavior*. San Francisco: Jossey-Bass, 1982. Offers a critical appraisal of efforts to develop explanatory theories about organizational behavior.

MUCHINSKY, P. M., *Psychology Applied to Work*, 2nd Edition. Chicago: The Dorsey Press, 1987. An introduction to industrial and organizational psychology.

SCHNEIDER, B., "Organizational Behavior," in M. R. Rosenzweig and L. W. Porter (eds.), *Annual Review of Psychology*, Vol. 36. Palo Alto, CA: Annual Reviews, Inc., 1985, pp. 573–611. Reviews the contemporary journal literature in OB.

WHYTE, W. F., "From Human Relations to Organizational Behavior: Reflections on the Changing Scene," *Industrial and Labor Relations Review*, July 1987, pp. 487–500. Interprets the last fifty years of behavioral science research in industry.

WHAT DO YOU KNOW ABOUT HUMAN BEHAVIOR?

Much of what we "know" about the world is based on intuition. We have opinions, biases, hunches, and misinformation that we use both in making statements about others and in deciding what we do. The following twenty questions are designed to provide you with some feedback regarding what you "know" about human behavior. Read each statement and mark T (true) or F (false).

True or False?

_____ 1. People who graduate in the upper third of their college class tend to make more money during their careers than do average students.

_____ 2. Exceptionally intelligent people tend to be physically weak and frail.

_____ 3. Most great athletes are of below average intelligence.

_____ 4. All people in America are born equal in capacity for achievement.

_____ 5. On the average, women are slightly more intelligent than men.

_____ 6. People are definitely either introverted or extroverted.

_____ 7. After you learn something, you forget more of it in the next few hours than in the next several days.

_____ 8. In small doses, alcohol facilitates learning.

_____ 9. Women are more intuitive than men.

_____ 10. Smokers take more sick days per year than do nonsmokers.

_____ 11. Forty-year-old people are more intelligent than twenty-year-olds.

_____ 12. If you have to reprimand someone for a misdeed, it is best to do so immediately after the mistake occurs.

_____ 13. People who do poorly in academic work are superior in mechanical ability.

_____ 14. High-achieving people are high risk-takers.

_____ 15. Highly cohesive groups are also highly productive.

_____ 16. When people are frustrated, they frequently become aggressive.

_____ 17. Experiences as an infant tend to determine behavior in later life.

_____ 18. Successful top managers have a greater need for money than for power.

_____ 19. Most people who work for the federal government are low risk-takers.

_____ 20. Most managers are highly democratic in the way that they supervise their people.

Turn to page 560 for scoring directions and key.

Source: Adapted from *Organizational Behavior: Theory and Practice* by S. Altman, E. Valenzi, and R. M. Hodgetts, © 1985 by Harcourt Brace Jovanovich, Inc. Reprinted by permission of the publisher.

CASE INCIDENT 1

DO ACCOUNTANTS NEED PEOPLE SKILLS?

Martha Altus and Gene White were both in their junior year, majoring in accounting, at State College. They sat in a study corner of the business building on a late April afternoon with their college catalogs and next fall's class schedule spread out before them.

"You know," interrupted Martha, "we wouldn't have so much trouble getting a decent schedule if it weren't for this conflict between Advanced Accounting Problems and Organizational Behavior."

"I know," replied Gene, "my emphasis is auditing. What's yours?"

"Tax."

"All right," began Gene, "explain something to me. Why the devil do we have to waste our time taking a course in organizational behavior? I can understand the finance courses, the quantitative methods course, and the classes in information systems. But why do they load us down with courses like marketing and organizational behavior? I doubt we'll get anything out of them. Even if I give these courses the benefit of the doubt—maybe there's something of value in them for us—look at the opportunity costs. If we weren't required to take these classes, we could take more advanced courses in tax, cost, and auditing!"

"You're absolutely right," agreed Martha. "I want to take all the tax courses I can. It's a tough field. Lots of specialized laws to know. And how are we going to pass the CPA exam if they make us take irrelevent course work?

Accounting is a profession. It's based on technical skills, just like law and medicine. You don't see lawyers and doctors taking courses in marketing or organizational behavior! Of course not! Their faculty understands the need to develop a high level of specialization. But accounting programs somehow got intertwined with business degrees, so we have to take all these other courses."

As both struggled with finding an acceptable class schedule, Gene summed up his frustration: "I challenge the dean to explain how a course in organizational behavior is important to us. I expect to join a Big Eight accounting firm's auditing staff, and you will be in the tax department of some large corporation. What can this course offer us?"

QUESTIONS

1. What value, in general, could a course in OB be to accounting students?
2. What specific value could an OB course offer an auditor with a large accounting firm? A tax specialist with a large corporation?
3. Would an OB course be less relevant if these individuals' career goals were to run a one-person accounting practice offering advisory services to individuals and small businesses?
4. What value would a marketing course offer to accounting students?
5. How valid is the "opportunity costs" argument?

2

Toward Explaining and Predicting Behavior

■ *Learning objectives*

Explain the purpose of research
Summarize the criteria by which to evaluate research
Identify the research designs most used by OB researchers
List the individual advantages of laboratory and field settings
Define the three levels of analysis in OB
Describe the four key dependent variables in OB

Get your facts first, and then you can distort them as much as you please.

———— MARK TWAIN

The purpose of this chapter is essentially to answer two questions. This text will introduce hundreds of research studies in support of a number of behavioral theories. But theories are only as good as the research presented to support them. So our first question is: *How do you, as a consumer of OB theories, evaluate the individual research studies presented in this text?* Second, there are many topics that are included within the discipline of OB. If you're going to understand what OB is about, you need to understand how the topics fit together. Therefore, the other question to be answered in this chapter is: *How do you structure the topics within OB into an integrative whole?* These two questions may, at first glance, seem somewhat unrelated. However, by the time you get to the end of this chapter, it should become obvious that the answers to these questions form the foundation upon which the rest of this text is built.

RESEARCH IN ORGANIZATIONAL BEHAVIOR

A friend recently exclaimed that he had read about the findings from a research study that finally, once and for all, resolved the question of what it takes to make it to the top in a large corporation. I doubted there was any simple answer to this question but, not wanting to dampen his enthusiasm, I asked him to tell me what he had read. The answer, according to my friend, was: *participation in college athletics.* To say I was skeptical of his claim is a gross understatement, so I asked him to tell me more.

The study encompassed 1,700 successful senior executives at the 500 largest U.S. corporations. The researchers found that half of these executives had played varsity-level college sports.[1] My friend, who happens to be good with statistics, informed me that since fewer than 2 percent of all college students participate in intercollegiate athletics, the probability of this finding occurring by mere chance is less than one in 10,000,000! He concluded his analysis by telling me that, based on this research, I should encourage my management students to get into shape and to make one of the varsity teams.

My friend was somewhat perturbed when I suggested that his conclusions

[1] J. A. Byrne, "Executive Sweat," *Forbes*, May 20, 1985, pp. 198–200.

were likely to be flawed. These executives were all males who attended college in the 1940s and 1950s. Would his advice be meaningful to females in the 1980s or 1990s? These executives also weren't your typical college students. For the most part, they attended small, private colleges, where a large proportion of the student body participates in intercollegiate sports. Moreover, maybe the researchers had confused the direction of causality. That is, maybe individuals with the motivation and ability to make it to the top of a large corporation are drawn to competitive activities like college athletics.

My friend was guilty of misusing research data. Of course, he is not alone. We are all continually bombarded with reports of experiments that link certain substances to cancer in mice, and surveys that show changing attitudes toward sex among college students, for example. Many of these studies are carefully designed, with great caution taken to note the implications and limitations of the findings. But some studies are poorly designed, making their conclusions at best suspect, and at worst, meaningless.

Rather than attempting to make you a researcher, the purpose of this section is to increase your awareness as a consumer of behavioral research. A knowledge of research methods allows you to appreciate more fully the care in data collection that underlies the information and conclusions that will be presented in this text. Moreover, an understanding of research methods will make you a more skilled evaluator of those OB studies you will encounter in business and professional journals. So an appreciation of behavioral research is important because (1) it is the foundation upon which the theories in this text are built, and (2) it will benefit you in future years when you read reports of research and attempt to assess their value.

Purpose of Research

Research is concerned with the systematic gathering of information. Its purpose is to help us in our search for the truth. While we will never find ultimate truth—in our case, that would be to know precisely how any person would behave in any organizational context—ongoing research adds to our body of OB knowledge by supporting some theories, contradicting others, and suggesting new theories to replace those that fail to gain support.

Research
The systematic gathering of information.

Research Terminology

Researchers have their own vocabulary for communicating among themselves and with outsiders. The following briefly defines some of the more popular terms you're likely to encounter in behavioral science studies.[2]

Variable   A **variable** is any general characteristic that can be measured and that changes in either amplitude, intensity, or both. Some examples of OB variables you'll find in this text are job satisfaction, employee productivity, work stress, ability, personality, and group norms.

Variable
Any general characteristic that can be measured and that changes in either amplitude, intensity, or both.

[2] This discussion is based on material presented in E. Stone, *Research Methods in Organizational Behavior* (Santa Monica, CA: Goodyear, 1978).

Hypothesis

A tentative explanation about the relationship between two or more variables.

Hypothesis   A tentative explanation about the relationship between two or more variables is called a **hypothesis.** My friend's statement that participation in college athletics leads to a top executive position in a large corporation is an example of a hypothesis. Until confirmed by empirical research, a hypothesis remains only a *tentative* explanation.

Dependent variable

A response that is affected by an independent variable.

Dependent variable   A **dependent variable** is a response that is affected by an independent variable. In terms of the hypothesis, it is the variable that the researcher is interested in explaining. Referring back to the previous example, the dependent variable in my friend's hypothesis was executive succession. In behavioral research, the most popular dependent variables are productivity, absenteeism, turnover, job satisfaction, and organizational commitment.[3]

Independent variable

The presumed cause of some change in the dependent variable.

Independent variable   An **independent variable** is the presumed cause of some change in the dependent variable. Participating in varsity athletics was the independent variable in my friend's hypothesis. Popular independent variables studied by OB researchers include intelligence, personality, job satisfaction, experience, motivation, reinforcement patterns, leadership style, reward allocations, selection methods, and organization design. We have said that job satisfaction is frequently used by OB researchers as both a dependent and independent variable. This is not an error. It merely reflects that the label given to a variable depends on its place in the hypothesis. In the statement "Increases in job satisfaction lead to reduced turnover," job satisfaction is an independent variable. However, in the statement, "Increases in money lead to higher job satisfaction," job satisfaction becomes a dependent variable.

Moderating variable

Abates the effect of the independent variable on the dependent variable; also known as contingency variable.

Moderating variable   A **moderating variable** abates the effect of the independent variable on the dependent variable. It might also be thought of as the contingency variable: If X (independent variable), then Y (dependent variable) will occur, but only under conditions Z (moderating variable). To translate this into a real-life example, we might say that if we increase the amount of direct supervision in the work area (X), then there will be a change in worker productivity (Y), but this effect will be moderated by the complexity of the tasks being performed (Z).

Causality

The implication that the independent variable causes the dependent variable.

Causality   A hypothesis, by definition, implies a relationship. That is, it implies a presumed cause and effect. This direction of cause and effect is called **causality.** Changes in the independent variable are assumed to *cause* changes in the dependent variable. However, in behavioral research, even though relationships may be found, it is possible to make an incorrect assumption of causality. For example, as we'll show in a later chapter, early behavioral scientists found a relationship between employee satisfaction and productivity. They concluded that a happy worker was a productive worker. Follow-up research has supported

---

[3] B. M. Staw and G. R. Oldham, "Reconsidering Our Dependent Variables: A Critique and Empirical Study," *Academy of Management Journal,* December 1978, pp. 539–59; and B. M. Staw, "Organizational Behavior: A Review and Reformulation of the Field's Outcome Variables," in M. R. Rosenzweig and L. W. Porter (eds.), *Annual Review of Psychology,* Vol. 35 (Palo Alto, CA: Annual Reviews, 1984), pp. 627–66.

the relationship, but disconfirmed the direction of the arrow. The evidence more correctly suggests that high productivity leads to satisfaction, rather than the other way around.

Correlation coefficient It is one thing to know that there is a relationship between two or more variables. It is another to know the *strength* of that relationship. The term **correlation coefficient** is used to indicate that strength, and is expressed as a number between −1.00 (a perfect negative relationship) to +1.00 (a perfect positive correlation).

When two variables vary directly with one another, the correlation will be expressed as a positive number. When they vary inversely—that is, one increases as the other decreases—the correlation will be expressed as a negative number. If the two variables vary independently of each other, we say that the correlation between them is zero. For example, a researcher might survey a group of employees to determine the satisfaction of each with his or her job. Then, using company absenteeism reports, the researcher could correlate the job satisfaction scores against individual attendance records to determine whether employees who are more satisfied with their jobs have better attendance records than their counterparts who indicated lower job satisfaction. Let's suppose the researcher found a correlation coefficient between satisfaction and attendance of +0.50. Would that be a strong association? There is, unfortunately, no precise numerical cutoff separating strong and weak relationships. A standard statistical test would need to be applied to determine whether or not the relationship was a significant one. A final point needs to be made before we move on: A correlation coefficient measures only the strength of association between two variables. A high value does *not* imply causality. The length of women's skirts and stock market prices, for instance, have long been noted to be highly correlated, but one should be careful not to infer that a causal relationship between the two exists. In this instance, the high correlation is more happenstance than predictive.

Theory The final term we'll introduce in this section is **theory**. Theory describes a set of systematically interrelated concepts or hypotheses that purport to explain and predict phenomena. In OB, theories are also frequently referred to as *models*. We'll use the two terms interchangeably.

There are no shortages of theories in OB. For instance, we have theories to describe what motivates people, the most effective leadership styles, the best way to resolve conflicts, and how people acquire power. In some cases, we have half-a-dozen or more separate theories that purport to explain and predict a given phenomenon. In such cases, is one right and the others wrong? No! They tend to reflect science at work—researchers testing previous theories, modifying them, and, when appropriate, proposing new models that may prove to have higher explanatory and predictive powers. Multiple theories attempting to explain common phenomena merely attest that OB is an active discipline, still growing and evolving.

As we proceed through this text, we'll introduce and describe a great many theories. We'll also review the research evidence underlying them. In this way you'll see the present state of the field, and assess which theories, at least at the current time, provide the best explanations of OB phenomena.

Correlation coefficient

Indicates the strength of a relationship between two or more variables.

Theory

A set of systematically interrelated concepts or hypotheses that purport to explain and predict phenomena.

Evaluating Research

As a potential consumer of behavioral research, you should follow the dictum of *caveat emptor*—let the buyer beware! In evaluating any research study, you need to ask three questions:[4]

Is it valid? Is the study actually measuring what it claims to be measuring? Many psychological tests have been discarded by employers in recent years because they have not been found to be valid measures of the applicants' ability to successfully do a given job. But the **validity** issue is relevant to all research studies. So, if you find a study that links cohesive work groups with higher productivity, you want to know how each of these variables were measured and whether they are actually measuring what they are supposed to be measuring.

Is it reliable? **Reliability** refers to consistency of measurement. If you were to have your height measured every day with a wooden yardstick, you would get highly reliable results. On the other hand, if you were measured each day by an elastic tape measure, there would probably be considerable disparity between your height measurements from one day to the next. Your height, of course, does not change from day to day. The variability is due to the unreliability of the measuring device. Reliable measurement procedures are free from systematic sources of error.

Is it generalizable? Are the results of the research study **generalizable** to groups of individuals other than those who participated in the original study? Be aware, for example, of the limitations that might exist in research that uses college students as subjects. Are the findings in such studies generalizable to full-time employees in real jobs? Similarly, how generalizable to the overall work population are the results from a study that assesses job stress among ten nuclear power plant engineers in the hamlet of Mahone Bay, Nova Scotia?

Validity

The degree to which a research study is actually measuring what it claims to be measuring.

Reliability

Consistency of measurement.

Generalizability

The degree to which results of a research study are applicable to groups of individuals other than those who participate in the original study.

Research Design

Doing research is an exercise in trade-offs. Richness of information typically comes with reduced generalizability. The more a researcher seeks to control for confounding variables, the less realistic his or her results are likely to be. High precision, generalizability, and control almost always translate into higher costs. When researchers make choices about who they'll study, where their research will be done, the methods they'll use to collect data, etc., they must make some concessions. Good research designs are not perfect, but they are chosen to carefully reflect the questions being addressed. Keep these facts in mind as we review the strengths and weaknesses of four popular research designs: case studies, field surveys, laboratory experiments, and field experiments.

Case Study You pick up a copy of Lee Iacocca's autobiography. In it he describes how he moved up the management ladder at Ford Motor Co., eventually

[4] R. S. Blackburn, "Experimental Design in Organizational Settings," in J. W. Lorsch (ed.), *Handbook of Organizational Behavior* (Englewood Cliffs, NJ: Prentice Hall, 1987), pp. 127–28.

became president, was fired, took over as head of Chrysler Corp., and, in one of the most dramatic turnarounds in U.S. corporate history, took Chrysler from the brink of bankruptcy to billions in profits. Or, you're in a business class and the instructor distributes a fifty-page handout covering two companies: Apple Computer and Control Data Corporation. The handout details the two firms' histories, describes their product lines, production facilities, management philosophy, marketing strategies and includes copies of recent balance sheets and income statements from each. The instructor asks the class members to read the handout, analyze the data, and determine why Apple has been more successful in recent years than CDC.

Lee Iacocca's autobiography and the Apple and CDC handouts are **case studies**. Drawn from real-life situations, case studies represent an in-depth analysis of one setting. They are thorough descriptions, rich in details about an individual, group, or organization. The primary source of information in case studies is obtained through observation, occasionally backed up by interviews and a review of records and documents.

Case studies have their drawbacks. They're open to the perceptual bias and subjective interpretations of the observer. The reader of a case is captive to what the observer/case writer chooses to include and exclude. Cases also trade off generalizability for depth of information and richness of detail. Since it's always dangerous to generalize from a sample of one, case studies make it difficult to prove or reject a hypothesis. On the other hand, you can't ignore the in-depth analysis that cases often provide. They are an excellent device for initial exploratory research and for evaluating real-life problems in organizations.

Field Survey   A questionnaire was made up of approximately a dozen items, and sought to examine the content of supervisory training programs in billion-dollar corporations. Copies of the questionnaire, with a cover letter explaining the nature of the study, were mailed to the corporate training officers at 250 corporations randomly selected from the *Fortune 500* list. One-hundred-and-fifty-five officers responded to the questionnaire. The results of this survey found, among other things, that the most common training topic was providing performance evaluation feedback to employees (92 percent of the surveyed companies selected this topic as the most common aspect of their program). This was closely followed by developing effective delegation skills (90 percent) and listening skills (83 percent).[5]

The preceding study illustrates a typical **field survey**. A sample of respondents (in this case, 250 corporate training officers) were selected to represent a larger group which was under examination (corporate training officers in *Fortune* 500 firms). The respondents were then surveyed using a questionnaire or interviewed to collect data on particular characteristics (the content of supervisory training programs) of interest to the researcher. The standardization of response items allows for data to be easily quantified, analyzed, and summarized, and for the researcher to make inferences about the larger population from the representative sample.

The field survey provides economies for doing research. It's less costly

Case study

An in-depth analysis of one setting.

Field survey

Questionnaire or interview responses are collected from a sample, analyzed, and then references are made about the larger population from which the sample is representative.

---

[5] G. G. Alpander, "Supervisory Training Programmes in Major U.S. Corporations," *Journal of Management Development*, Vol. 5, No. 5, 1986, pp. 3–22.

to sample a population than to obtain data from every member of that population. Moreover, as the supervisory training program example illustrated, field surveys provide an efficient way to find how people feel about issues or how they say they behave. These data can then be easily quantified. But the field survey has a number of potential weaknesses. First, mailed questionnaires rarely obtain 100 percent returns. Low response rates call into question whether conclusions based on respondents' answers are generalizable to nonrespondents. Second, the format is better at tapping respondents' attitudes and perceptions than behaviors. Third, reponses can suffer from social desirability; that is, people saying what they think the researcher wants to hear. Fourth, since field surveys are designed to focus on specific issues, they're a relatively poor means of acquiring depth of information. Finally, the quality of the generalizations is largely a factor of the population chosen. Responses from executives at *Fortune 500* firms, for instance, tell us nothing about small- or medium-sized firms or not-for-profit organizations. In summary, even a well-designed field survey trades off depth of information for breadth, generalizability, and economic efficiencies.

Laboratory experiment

In an artificial environment, the researcher manipulates an independent variable under controlled conditions, and then concludes that any change in the dependent variable is due to the manipulation or change imposed on the independent variable.

Laboratory Experiment   The following study is a classic example of the **laboratory experiment**: A researcher wondered how far individuals would go in following commands. If subjects were placed in the role of a teacher in a learning experiment and told by an experimenter to administer a shock to a learner each time that learner made a mistake, would the subjects follow the commands of the experimenter? Would their willingness to comply decrease as the intensity of the shock was increased?

To test these hypotheses, the researcher hired a set of subjects. Each was led to believe that the experiment was to investigate the effect of punishment on memory. Their job was to act as a teacher, and administer punishment whenever the learner made a mistake on the learning test.

Punishment was administered by an electric shock. The subject sat in front of a shock generator with thirty levels of shock—beginning at zero and progressing in 15-volt increments to a high of 450 volts. The demarcations of these positions ranged from "Slight Shock" at 15 volts to "Danger: Severe Shock" at 450 volts. To increase the realism of the experiment, the subjects received a sample shock of 45 volts and saw the learner—a pleasant, mild-mannered man, about fifty years old—strapped into an "electric chair" in an adjacent room. Of course, the learner was an actor, and the electric shocks were phony, but the subjects didn't know this.

Taking his seat in front of the shock generator, the subject was directed to begin at the lowest shock level and to increase the shock intensity to the next level each time the learner made a mistake or failed to respond.

When the test began, the shock intensity rose rapidly because the learner made many errors. The subject got verbal feedback from the learner: at 75 volts the learner began to grunt and moan; at 150 volts he demanded to be released from the experiment; at 180 volts he cried out that he could no longer stand the pain; and at 300 volts he insisted that he be let out, yelled about his heart condition, screamed, and then failed to respond to further questions.

Most subjects protested and, fearful they might kill the learner if the increased shocks were to bring on a heart attack, insisted they could not go on with their job. Hesitations or protests by the subject were met by the experimenter's statement, "You have no choice, you must go on! Your job is to punish the learner's mistakes." Of course, the subjects did have a choice. All they had to do was stand up and walk out.

The majority of the subjects dissented. But dissension isn't synonymous with disobedience. Sixty-two percent of the subjects increased the shock level to the maximum of 450 volts. The average level of shock administered by the remaining 38 percent was nearly 370 volts.[6]

In a laboratory experiment, an artificial environment is created by the researcher. Then, the researcher manipulates an independent variable under controlled conditions. Finally, since all other things are held equal, the researcher is able to conclude that any change in the dependent variable is due to the manipulation or change imposed on the independent variable. Note that, because of the controlled conditions, the researcher is able to imply causation between the independent and dependent variables.

The laboratory experiment trades off realism and generalizability for precision and control. It provides a high degree of control over variables and precise measurement of those variables. But findings from laboratory studies are often difficult to generalize to the real world of work. This is because the artificial laboratory rarely duplicates the intricacies and nuances of real organizations. Additionally, many laboratory experiments deal with phenomena that cannot be reproduced or applied to real-life situations.

Field Experiment The following is an example of a **field experiment**: The management of a large company is interested in determining the impact that a four-day workweek would have on employee absenteeism. To be more specific, they want to know if employees working four ten-hour days have lower absence rates than similar employees working the traditional five-day week of eight hours each day. Because the company is large, it has a number of manufacturing plants that employ essentially similar work forces. Two of these are chosen for the experiment, both located in the greater Cleveland area. Obviously, it would not be appropriate to compare two similar-sized plants where one is in rural Mississippi and the other is in downtown Boston. Factors such as transportation and weather, in comparison, might more likely explain any differences found than changes in the number of days worked per week.

In one plant, the experiment was put into place—workers began the four-day week. At the other plant, which became the control group, no changes were made in the employees' five-day week. Absence data was gathered from the company's records at both locations for a period of eighteen months. This extended time period lessened the possibility that any results would be distorted by the mere novelty of changes being implemented in the experimental plant. After eighteen months, management found that absenteeism had dropped by 40 percent at the experimental plant, and only by 6 percent in the control plant. Because of the design of this study, management believed that the larger drop in absences at the experimental plant was due to the introduction of the compressed work week.

The field experiment is similar to the laboratory experiment, except it is conducted in a real organization. The natural setting is more realistic than the laboratory setting. Additionally, unless control groups are maintained, there

Field experiment

A controlled experiment conducted in a real organization.

---

[6] S. Milgram, *Obedience to Authority* (New York: Harper & Row, 1974).

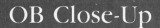

OB Close-Up

Is OB the "Science of the College Sophomore"?

A major determinant of the generalizability of any laboratory experiment are the characteristics of the study's subjects. If the subjects are all male managers, between the ages of forty-five and sixty, working in large corporations like General Motors and IBM, conclusions based on the study's findings need to be limited to reflect this.

This recognition of limiting generalizability to reflect characteristics of the subjects would not be a problem in OB if laboratory experiments tended to include all sizes, shapes, and kinds of subjects. After all, organizations come in all types, and so do their employees. But it has long been observed that the behavioral studies which compose a large part of the OB research literature rely heavily upon college students as experimental subjects.[7] Generations of college students have toiled in university laboratories solving problems they didn't create, working at "jobs" that only hours before they knew nothing about, selecting applicants for hire in nonexistent organizations, and the like. The results of these experiments then find their way into the behavioral literature and form the basis for current theories as well as sugges-

can be a loss of control if extraneous forces intervene—for example, an employee strike, a major layoff, or a corporate restructuring. Maybe the greatest concern with field studies has to do with organizational selection bias. Not all organizations are going to allow outside researchers to come in and study their employees and operations. This is especially true of organizations that have serious problems. Therefore, since most published studies in OB are done by outside researchers, the selection bias might work toward publication of studies conducted almost exclusively at successful and well-managed organizations.

Our general conclusion is that, of the four research designs we've discussed, the field experiment typically provides the most valid and generalizable findings and, except for its high cost, trades off the least to get the most.

Summary

The subject of organizational behavior is composed of a large number of theories that are research-based. Research studies, when cumulatively integrated, become

---

[7] This box is based on M. E. Gordon, L. A. Slade, and N. Schmitt, "The 'Science of the Sophomore' Revisited: From Conjecture to Empiricism," *Academy of Management Review*, January 1986, pp. 191–207; J. Greenberg, "The College Sophomore as Guinea Pig: Setting the Record Straight," *Academy of Management Review*, January 1987, pp. 157–59; and E. A. Locke (ed.), *Generalizing from Laboratory to Field Settings: Research Findings from Industrial–Organizational Psychology, Organizational Behavior, and Human Resource Management* (Lexington, MA: Lexington Books, 1986).

tions for improved practices. For instance, approximately 75 percent of published research in social psychology has involved college students.

Why has this occurred? The best answer is, probably for convenience. College students are a readily available resource to faculty researchers and a low-cost alternative to investigating full-time employees in work organizations.

Does this wide use of college students invalidate OB theories? This question is not easily answered. Clearly college students are not representative of the general work population. This is especially true where subjects are young college undergraduates with little or no substantive work experience. But for many research objectives, students are not unlike nonstudents. For example, studies dealing with perception, attitude change, learning processes, or communication are likely to be as generalizable with college students as with any other population. Additionally, *any* research population can be argued to be atypical. Homogeneously defined groups of subjects—be they college-educated, white-collar professionals, employees in high-tech industries, *or* college students—require the researcher to qualify his or her findings. And since no group can fully represent the complete diversity of employees in all types of organizations, in all countries of the world, all studies will have some limitations to their generalizability. The key is understanding what those limitations are.

theories; and theories are proposed and followed by research studies designed to validate them. The concepts that make up OB, therefore, are only as valid as the research that supports them.

As you review the topics and issues introduced in this text, keep in mind that they are—for the most part—largely research-derived. They represent the result of systematic information gathering rather than merely hunch, intuition, or opinion. But this does not mean that we have all the answers to OB issues. Many require far more corroborating evidence. The generalizability of others is limited by the research methods used. As we proceed through the topics in this text and as the research is reviewed, every effort will be made to point out limitations to the findings that relate to the quality or quantity of supporting research.

DEVELOPING AN OB MODEL

The second part of this chapter presents a general model that defines the field of OB, stakes out its parameters, and identifies its primary dependent and independent variables. The end result will be a "coming attraction" of the topics comprising the remainder of this book.

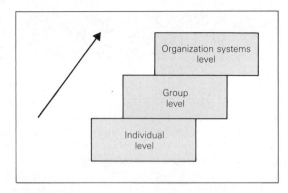

FIGURE 2–1
Basic OB Model, Stage I

An Overview

Model

Abstraction of reality; simplified representation of some real-world phenomenon.

A **model** is an abstraction of reality, a simplified representation of some real-world phenomenon. A mannequin in a retail store is a model. So, too, is the accountant's formula: Assets = Liabilities + Owner's Equity. Figure 2–1 presents a skeleton on which we will construct our OB model. It proposes that there are three levels of analysis in OB, and that as we move from the individual level to the organizational systems level, we add systematically to our understanding of behavior in organizations. The three basic levels are analogous to building blocks—each level is constructed upon the previous level. Group concepts grow out of the foundation laid in the individual section; we overlay structural constraints on the individual and group in order to arrive at organizational behavior.

The Dependent Variables

What are the primary dependent variables in OB? Scholars tend to emphasize productivity, absenteeism, turnover, and job satisfaction. Because of their wide acceptance, we shall use these four as the critical determinants of an organization's human resources effectiveness. However, there is nothing magic about these variables. They show that OB research has strongly reflected managerial interests over those of individuals or of society as a whole. Of course, in years to come, new dependent variables may be added to, or may replace, those that currently dominate the OB field. For instance, one author has argued for the growing importance of job stress, individual dissent, and innovation as dependent variables.[8] In defense of innovation, he argues, "As a greater percentage of work becomes highly skilled and professionalized, the criteria of performance will likely become more ambiguous and subject to change. Therefore, questions of [employee] productivity may become translated into inquiries about working smarter rather than harder. . . . Where there is rapid change or competition is fierce, innovation may be the organization's most important outcome

[8] B. M. Staw, "Organizational Behavior: A Review and Reformulation."

variable."[9] The fact remains, however, that productivity, absenteeism, turnover, and job satisfaction currently dominate the field. So let's review these terms to ensure that we understand what they mean and why they have achieved the distinction of being OB's primary dependent variables.

Productivity   An organization is productive if it achieves its goals, and does so by transferring inputs to outputs at the lowest cost. As such, **productivity** implies a concern for both **effectiveness** and **efficiency**.

A hospital, for example, is *effective* when it successfully meets the needs of its clientele. It is *efficient* when it can do this at a low cost. If a hospital manages to achieve higher output from its present staff by reducing the average number of days a patient is confined to a bed or by increasing the number of staff-patient contacts per day, we can say that the hospital has gained productive efficiency. Similarly, a school may be effective when a certain percentage of students achieve a specified score on standardized achievement tests. The school can improve its efficiency if these higher test scores can be secured by a smaller teaching and support staff. A business firm is effective when it attains its sales or market share goals, but its productivity also depends on achieving these goals efficiently. Measures of such efficiency may include return on investment, profit per dollar of sales, and output per hour of labor.

We can also look at productivity from the perspective of the individual employee. Take the cases of Mike and Al, who are both long-distance truckers. If Mike is supposed to haul his fully loaded rig from New York to its destination in Los Angeles in seventy-five hours or less, he is effective if he makes the 3,000-mile trip within this time period. But measures of productivity must take into account the costs incurred in reaching the goal. That is where efficiency comes in. Let us assume that Mike made the New York to Los Angeles run in sixty-eight hours and averaged seven miles per gallon. Al, on the other hand, made the trip in sixty-eight hours also but averaged nine miles per gallon (rigs and loads are identical). Both Mike and Al were effective—they accomplished their goal—but Al was more efficient than Mike because his rig consumed less gas and, therefore, he achieved his goal at a lower cost.

In summary, one of OB's major concerns is productivity. We want to know what factors will influence the effectiveness and efficiency of individuals, of groups, and of the overall organization.

Absenteeism   The annual cost of **absenteeism** to U.S. organizations has been estimated at nearly $40 billion a year. At the job level, a one-day absence by a clerical worker can cost an employer up to $100 in reduced efficiency and increased supervisory workload.[10] These figures indicate the importance to an organization of keeping absenteeism low.

It is obviously difficult for an organization to operate smoothly and to attain its objectives if employees fail to report to their jobs. The work flow is disrupted, and often important decisions must be delayed. In organizations that rely heavily upon assembly-line technology, absenteeism can be considerably more than a disruption—it can result in a drastic reduction in quality of output, or, in some cases, it can bring about a complete shutdown of the production

Productivity

A performance measure including effectiveness and efficiency.

Effectiveness

Achievement of goals.

Efficiency

The ratio of effective output to the input required to achieve it.

Absenteeism

Failure to report to work.

---

[9] Ibid, pp. 655–56.

[10] Cited in "Expensive Absenteeism," *Wall Street Journal*, July 29, 1986, p. 1.

facility. Examples abound, for example, of the problems that the major U.S. automobile manufacturers have with alarmingly large increases in absences on Mondays and Fridays, especially in summer months and at the onset of the hunting and fishing seasons. Certainly, levels of absenteeism beyond the normal range have a direct impact on an organization's effectiveness and efficiency.

Are *all* absences bad? Probably not! While most absences impact negatively on the organization, we can conceive of situations where the organization may benefit by an employee voluntarily choosing not to come to work. For instance, fatigue or excess stress can significantly decrease an employee's productivity. In jobs where an employee needs to be alert—surgeons and airline pilots are obvious examples—it may well be better for the organization if the employee does not report to work rather than show up and perform poorly. The cost of an accident in such jobs could be prohibitive. Even in managerial jobs, where mistakes are less spectacular, performance may be improved when incumbents absent themselves from work rather than make a poor decision under stress. But these examples are clearly atypical. For the most part, we can assume that organizations benefit when employee absenteeism is reduced.

Turnover

Voluntary and involuntary permanent withdrawal from the organization.

Turnover   A high rate of **turnover** in an organization means increased recruiting, selection, and training costs. It can also mean a disruption in the efficient running of an organization when knowledgeable and experienced personnel leave and replacements must be found and prepared to assume positions of responsibility. All organizations, of course, have some turnover. If the right people are leaving the organization—the marginal and submarginal employees—turnover can be positive. It may create theopportunity to replace an individual with someone with higher skills or motivation, open up increased opportunities for promotions, and add new and fresh ideas to the organization.[11] But when turnover is excessive or when it is confined to the superior performers, it can be a major disruptive factor, hindering the organization's effectiveness.

Job satisfaction

A general attitude toward one's job; the difference between the amount of rewards workers receive and the amount they believe they should receive.

Job Satisfaction   The final dependent variable we will look at is **job satisfaction,** which we'll define simply, at this point, as the difference between the amount of rewards workers receive and the amount they believe they should receive. (We'll expand considerably on this definition in Chapter 5.) Unlike the previous three variables, job satisfaction is unique because it represents an attitude rather than a behavior. Why is it then that it has become a primary dependent variable? This is probably due to its demonstrated relationship to performance factors, and the value preferences held by many OB researchers.

The belief that satisfied employees are more productive than dissatisfied employees has been a basic tenet among managers for years. While evidence questions this assumed causal relationship, it can be argued that a wealthy nation should not only be concerned with the quantity of life, but also with improving its quality. Those researchers with strong humanistic values argue that satisfaction should be a legitimate objective of an organization. Not only

---

[11] See, for example, D. R. Dalton and W. D. Todor, "Functional Turnover: An Empirical Assessment," *Journal of Applied Psychology*, December 1981, pp. 716–21; and G. M. McEvoy and W. F. Cascio, "Do Good or Poor Performers Leave? A Meta-Analysis of the Relationship Between Performance and Turnover," *Academy of Management Journal*, December 1987, pp. 744–62.

is satisfaction negatively related to absenteeism and turnover, but, they argue, organizations have a responsibility that goes beyond dollars and cents to provide employees with jobs that are challenging and intrinsically rewarding. Therefore, although job satisfaction represents an attitude rather than a behavior, OB researchers typically consider job satisfaction an important dependent variable.

The Independent Variables

What are the major determinants of productivity, absenteeism, turnover, and job satisfaction? Our answer to that question brings us to the independent variables. Consistent with our belief that organizational behavior can best be understood when viewed essentially as a set of increasingly complex building blocks, the base or first level of our model lies in understanding individual behavior.

Individual-Level Variables It has been said that "managers, unlike parents, must work with used, not new, human beings—human beings whom others have gotten to first."[12] When individuals enter an organization, they're a bit like used cars. Each is different. Some are "low mileage"—they have been treated carefully and have limited exposure to the realities of the elements. Others are "well worn," having experienced a number of rough roads. This metaphor indicates that people enter organizations with certain characteristics that will influence their behavior at work. The more obvious of these are personal or biographical characteristics such as one's age, sex, and marital status; one's personality characteristics; one's values and attitudes; and one's basic ability levels. These characteristics are essentially intact when an individual enters the work force, and, for the most part, there is little management can do to alter them. Yet, they have a very real impact on employee behavior. Therefore, each of these factors—biographical characteristics, personality, values and attitudes, and ability—will be discussed as independent variables in Chapters 3 and 5.

There are four other individual-level variables that have been shown to affect employee behavior: perception, individual decision making, learning, and motivation. These topics will be introduced and discussed in Chapters 3, 4, 6, and 7.

Figure 2–2 describes the individual level in our OB model. Note the dotted line around biographical characteristics, personality, values and attitudes, and ability. This is to dramatize that these variables, for the most part, are already in place when an employee joins an organization. The individual variables shown in Figure 2–2 are the subject matter of Chapters 3 through 7.

Group-Level Variables The behavior of people in groups is more than the sum total of each individual acting in his or her own way. The complexity of our model is increased when we acknowledge that people's behavior when they are in groups is different from their behavior when they are alone. Therefore, the next step in the development of an understanding of OB is the study of group behavior.

[12] H. J. Leavitt, *Managerial Psychology*, rev. ed. (Chicago: University of Chicago Press, 1964), p. 3.

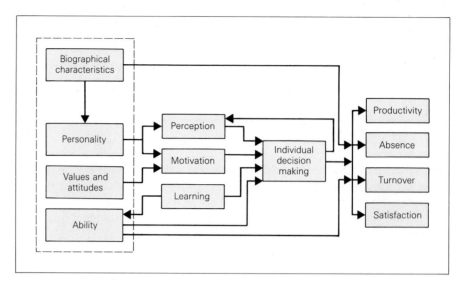

FIGURE 2–2
The Individual Level in the OB Model

Chapter 8 lays the foundation for an understanding of the dynamics of group behavior. This chapter discusses how individuals in groups are influenced by the patterns of behavior they are expected to exhibit, what the group considers to be acceptable standards of behavior, and the degree to which group members are attracted to each other. Chapters 9 through 12 demonstrate how communication patterns, group decision making processes, leadership styles, power and politics, intergroup relations, and levels of conflict affect group behavior. Figure 2–3 describes how these concepts interact and form the group level in our OB model.

FIGURE 2–3
The Group Level in the OB Model

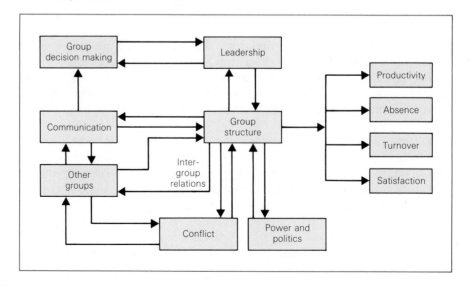

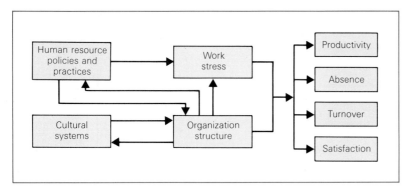

FIGURE 2–4
The Organization System Level in the OB Model

Organization System-Level Variables Organizational behavior reaches its highest level of sophistication when we add formal structure to our previous knowledge of individual and group behavior. Just as groups are more than the sum of their individual members, organizations are not necessarily merely the summation of the behavior of a number of groups. The structural design of the formal organization, the organization's human resource policies and practices (that is, selection processes, training programs, performance appraisal methods), levels of work stress, the national culture in which the organization operates, and the organization's internal culture all have an impact on the dependent variables.

Figure 2–4 describes the organization system-level variables in our model. These are discussed in detail in Chapters 13 through 16.

Toward a Contingency OB Model

Our final model is shown in Figure 2–5. It portrays the four key dependent variables, and a large number of independent variables that research suggests have varying impacts on the former. Of course, the model does not do justice to the complexity of the OB subject matter. But for the purpose of helping to explain and predict behavior, it should prove valuable.

Our model does not explicitly identify moderating variables because of the tremendous complexity that would be involved in such a diagram. Rather, throughout this text we shall introduce important moderating variables that will improve the explanatory linkage between the independent and dependent variables in our OB model. Thus, the text will follow a contingency approach— identifying independent variables, isolating moderating variables, and attempting to explain why in certain situations *A* causes *B*, yet in other situations *A* causes *C*.

Also note that we've added the concepts of change and development to Figure 2–5, acknowledging the dynamics of behavior and recognizing that there are ways for change agents or managers to modify many of the independent variables if they are having a negative impact on the key dependent variables. Specifically, in Chapter 17, we'll discuss techniques for changing employee

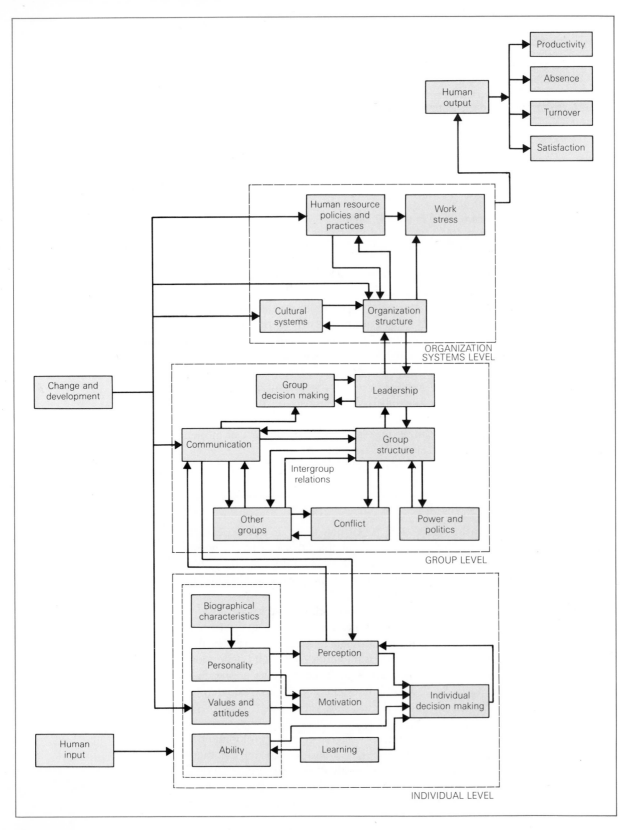

FIGURE 2–5
Basic OB Model, Stage II

attitudes, improving communication processes, modifying organization structures, and the like.

Finally, Figure 2–5 includes linkages between the three levels of analysis. For instance, organization structure is linked to leadership. This is meant to convey that authority and leadership are related—management exerts its influence on group behavior through leadership. Similarly, communication is the means by which individuals transmit information; thus, it is the link between individual and group behavior.

POINT

EMPLOYEE TURNOVER IS DYSFUNCTIONAL TO AN ORGANIZATION

This text presents employee turnover as one of the four primary dependent variables in OB. This is consistent with the view—held by executives, personnel managers, and researchers in OB—that turnover has negative consequences for organizational performance. When an employee quits and has to be replaced, the organization incurs some very real and tangible costs. These can range from a few hundred dollars to train a counter clerk at McDonald's, to several hundred thousand dollars for a nuclear power engineer or Air Force fighter pilot. Turnover costs to a firm for a typical job is probably at least several thousand dollars, as evidenced by research in a bank that found every instance of turnover by a teller costing approximately $2,800.

Every turnover incidence includes both direct and indirect costs. A review of these costs goes a long way in explaining why management should be concerned with minimizing employee turnover.

When an employee leaves, a replacement needs to be found. If inadequate notice is given, management will not have time to find and train the replacement, and a temporary employee will need to fill in. The result in this case is typically a drop in productivity. Where sufficient notice is given, the organization incurs the costs of recruiting, selecting, and training the replacement. In many cases, there may be a period of a few weeks or months where two people are on the payroll to do one job—the departing employee staying on to train his or her replacement.

The recruitment and training costs for almost any job quickly amount to a sizable dollar figure. These costs include advertisements, maintaining a college recruitment staff, employment agency fees, travel and accommodation expenses for recruits, screening tests, background investigations, and the time spent by executives in interviewing. The departure of a middle-level manager may result in replacement costs exceeding $50,000, as the following suggests:

Search fees and expenses	$20,000
Interviewing time and expenses	3,000
Administrative costs (reference checks, psychological tests, medical exams)	3,000
Reimbursement associated with selling old home and purchasing new one	15,000
Travel and temporary living expenses	6,000
Moving expenses	8,000
Signing bonus	10,000
	$65,000

This list considers only the direct costs attributable to employee turnover. To these we must add indirect costs such as training the replacement, loss in productivity incurred while the replacement develops his or her proficiency, loss in work group cohesiveness and morale, and the general organizational disruption caused by turnover (such as scheduling difficulties).

Given the direct and indirect costs associated with turnover, it is obvious that a management team that is concerned with maintaining effectiveness and efficiency will want to keep employee turnover to a minimum.

COUNTERPOINT

EMPLOYEE TURNOVER CAN BE FUNCTIONAL

All turnover is not bad for an organization. Discussions on the subject tend to stress the costs side of the ledger. But turnover also provides benefits to the organization. In fact, healthy levels of employee turnover may be a virtual windfall—in hard dollar terms—for the organization.

To consider all turnover negatively overstates its impact. Why? Well, first we need to look only at voluntary turnover. Involuntary turnover—where management initiates the departure—is functional, if we assume the decision is for a cause. Second, there are people who voluntarily leave the organization and in so doing benefit it. They may have been poor or, at best, marginal performers. But because of institutionalized employment security (labor unions, appeal boards, etc.), sympathetic bosses, the desire to maintain group morale, or similar factors, these people are not terminated. Finally, all voluntary quits are not controllable by management. That is, there are situations in which no reasonable action by management could have prevented it. It's a waste of organizational resources to try to reduce this element of turnover. In summary, any discussion of turnover should be concerned only with voluntary quits, and from that number we need to subtract all functional turnover plus the portion that, while dysfunctional, is unavoidable.

Now let's turn to a neglected issue: Turnover has a positive "dollar and cents" impact on the organization. In support of this position, we need to recognize that turnover may be reduced, but at a cost that exceeds its benefits, and new hires are not as costly to maintain in terms of salary and fringe benefits as are more senior employees.

A number of jobs have characteristically high levels of turnover—for instance, waitresses and bank clerks—that could be significantly reduced by merely raising their wage rates. But management has chosen not to pay the wages that would be necessary to keep these people. In cost-effectiveness terms, management's strategy has been to trade off higher turnover for lower labor costs.

An overlooked fact in organizations is that there are a number of jobs where wage rates increase with time, but there is no comparable increase in productivity. For instance, at one large public utility, entry-level employees receive $5.82 per hour and then move through the wage progression to $10.45 in their fifth year. The job remains the same, only the hourly wage cost nearly doubles. While employee productivity will increase over this five-year period, the increase is more likely to be in the 10 to 20 percent range. Additionally, given that fringe benefit costs tend to be a percentage of direct labor costs, these too go up significantly as employee seniority increases. The result: Recent hires cost the organization less.

There are relatively large economies to be realized by employee turnover. To the extent that turnover is not excessive, that is, its costs do not exceed its benefits, a large amount of money might be saved each year by reasonable levels of turnover. Vigorous programs by organizations to reduce the incidence of employee turnover may be thoroughly shortsighted. This caveat may be particularly appropriate for organizations in which training requirements are minimal and experience may not lead to appreciably higher levels of performance.

Based on D. R. Dalton, W. D. Todor, and D. M. Krackhardt, "Turnover Overstated: The Functional Taxonomy," *Academy of Management Review*, January 1982, pp. 117–23; Dalton and Todor, "Turnover: A Lucrative Hard Dollar Phenomenon," *Academy of Management Review*, April 1982, pp. 212–18; and J. R. Hollenbeck and C. R. Williams, "Turnover Functionality Versus Turnover Frequency: A Note on Work Attitudes and Organizational Effectiveness," *Journal of Applied Psychology*, November 1986, pp. 606–11.

KEY TERMS

Absenteeism	Job Satisfaction
Case Study	Laboratory Experiment
Causality	Model
Correlation Coefficient	Moderating Variable
Dependent Variable	Productivity
Effectiveness	Reliability
Efficiency	Research
Field Experiment	Theory
Field Survey	Turnover
Generalizability	Validity
Hypothesis	Variable
Independent Variable	

FOR DISCUSSION

1. Why should students of OB spend time to develop an elementary understanding of research design?

2. What factors might reduce the generalizability of a research study?

3. What are the advantages and disadvantages of a (a) case study, (b) field survey, (c) laboratory experiment, and (d) field experiment?

4. What is reliability? Validity? What is the relevance of each to research?

5. Define *independent*, *dependent*, and *moderating variables*. Explain their relationship.

6. It is well-documented that married men and women live longer than their unmarried counterparts. Does marriage cause longer life? Explain.

7. Statistics clearly show that college graduates earn substantially more money during their working lives than do individuals who have not attended college. Does the college experience cause higher earnings? Explain.

8. What are the three levels of analysis in our OB model? Are they related? If so, how?

9. If job satisfaction is not a behavior, why is it considered as an important dependent variable?

10. What are "effectiveness" and "efficiency," and how are they related to organizational behavior?

11. What are the four dependent variables in the OB model? Why have they been chosen over, for instance, percent return on investment?

12. Why are individual-, group-, and organization system-level behaviors each described as increasingly more complex?

FOR FURTHER READING

BLAIR, J. D., and J. G. HUNT, "Getting Inside the Head of the Management Researcher One More Time: Context-Free and Context-Specific Orientations in Research," *Journal of Management*, Summer 1986, pp. 147–66. Context-free versus context-specific research orientations are discussed as researchers' cognitive styles that influence the way in which management research is conducted.

DAFT, R. L., "Learning the Craft of Organizational Research," *Academy of Management Review*, October 1983, pp. 539–46. Proposes that scholarly research is a craft and that significant research outcomes are associated with the mastery of craft elements in the research process.

GOODMAN, P. S., R. S. ATKIN, and Associates, *Absenteeism*. San Francisco: Jossey-Bass, 1985. Presents contemporary approaches for understanding, measuring, and managing employee absence.

LOCKE, E. A. (ed.), *Generalizing from Laboratory to Field Setting*. Lexington, MA: Lexington Books, 1986. Presents behavioral research findings and seeks to answer the question of the generalizability of lab studies to real-life settings.

MCGUIRE, J. B., "Management and Research Methodology," *Journal of Management*, Spring 1986, pp. 5–17. Discusses the the generalizability of the literature on research methodology to linking theory and management practice.

PODSAKOFF, P. M., and D. R. DALTON, "Research Methodology in Organizational Studies," *Journal of Management*, Summer 1987, pp. 419–41. A content analysis of articles in key OB journals finds that a relatively limited set of research strategies and analytical procedures dominate the organizational sciences.

EXERCISE 2

HOW DO YOU FEEL ABOUT YOUR PRESENT JOB?

Some jobs are more interesting and satisfying than others. This exercise contains eighteen statements about jobs. Check the response next to each statement which best describes how you feel about your present job. There are no right or wrong answers.

	Strongly Agree	Agree	Undecided	Disagree	Strongly Disagree
1. My job is like a hobby to me.	___	___	___	___	___
2. My job is usually interesting enough to keep me from getting bored.	___	___	___	___	___
3. It seems that my friends are more interested in their jobs.	___	___	___	___	___
4. I consider my job rather unpleasant.	___	___	___	___	___
5. I enjoy my work more than my leisure time.	___	___	___	___	___
6. I am often bored with my job.	___	___	___	___	___
7. I feel fairly well satisfied with my present job.	___	___	___	___	___
8. Most of the time I have to force myself to go to work.	___	___	___	___	___
9. I am satisfied with my job for the time being.	___	___	___	___	___
10. I feel that my job is no more interesting than others I could get.	___	___	___	___	___
11. I definitely dislike my work.	___	___	___	___	___
12. I feel that I am happier in my work than most other people.	___	___	___	___	___
13. Most days I am enthusiastic about my work.	___	___	___	___	___
14. Each day of work seems like it will never end.	___	___	___	___	___
15. I like my job better than the average worker does.	___	___	___	___	___
16. My job is pretty uninteresting.	___	___	___	___	___
17. I find real enjoyment in my work.	___	___	___	___	___
18. I am disappointed that I ever took this job.	___	___	___	___	___

Turn to page 560 for scoring directions and key.

Source: Adapted from A. H. Brayfield and H. F. Rothe, "An Index of Job Satisfaction," *Journal of Applied Psychology*, October 1951, pp. 307–11.

Tom Peters and Robert Waterman's *In Search of Excellence* (Harper & Row, 1982), with sales in excess of 5,000,000 copies, has become one of the largest selling and most often quoted books in the popular management literature. The book describes what the authors have found to be the distinct cultural traits that lead to excellence in a company. Based on Peters and Waterman's research, they propose that there are eight cultural characteristics (the independent variables) that predict companies' excellence as defined in terms of financial performance and innovation (the dependent variables).

The authors make no mention of how their original population of firms was chosen. Nevertheless, they identified seventy-five firms which appeared, on the surface, to be excellent companies. Most or all of the European firms were eliminated to bring the sample down to sixty-two. These firms were then screened on the basis of seven criteria. Six criteria were measures of financial performance: compound asset growth, compound equity growth, ratio of market value to book value, average return on total capital, average return on equity, and average return on sales. If a firm was in the top half of its industry on at least four of these six financial criteria for each year over a twenty-year period, the authors considered them excellent and kept them in the research set. The seventh selection criterion was innovation. An informal group of businessmen, consultants, members of the press, and business academics were used to judge the remaining companies on the basis of innovativeness. This was a subjective assessment.

The result was a set of forty-three "excellent" firms.

These companies became the primary focus of Peters and Waterman's study. Some of the companies that were described as excellent included Avon, Boeing, Disney Productions, Dow Chemical, IBM, Johnson & Johnson, K-Mart, 3M Co., Marriot, Procter & Gamble, Texas Instruments, and Wang Labs. A few of the firms that didn't make the "cut" included General Electric, General Foods, Lockheed, Polaroid, and Xerox. The authors had extensive interviews in twenty-one of the firms, and briefer interviews in the remaining twenty-two. The description in the book of the structure and substance of the interviews is not clearly revealed.

The major conclusion from *In Search of Excellence* is that there is a strong link between culture and business performance. More specifically, excellent companies share eight common cultural characteristics: (1) a bias for action; (2) close to the customer; (3) autonomy and entrepreneurship; (4) productivity through people; (5) hands-on, value driven; (6) stick to the knitting; (7) simple form, lean staff; and (8) simultaneous loose-tight properties. It should be noted, however, that Peters and Waterman do not tell us if all forty-three firms had all eight characteristics or whether some had only six or seven.

QUESTIONS

1. What flaws can you find in the research upon which this book is based?
2. How generalizable do you think this study's findings are?
3. How do you explain the tremendous popularity of this book, given its questionable research base?

3

Foundations of Individual Behavior

■ *Chapter outline*

■ *Learning Objectives*

Define the key biographical characteristics
Identify two types of ability
Explain the factors that determine an individual's personality
Describe the impact of job typology on the personality-job performance relationship
Summarize how learning theories provide insights into changing behavior
Distinguish between the four schedules of reinforcement
Clarify the role of punishment in learning

I ain't much, baby—but I'm all I've got.

———J. LAIR

Are older workers more likely to remain with an organization than their younger counterparts? How do differences in ability affect job performance? Do certain personality types make better employees? Do employees learn better by having their desirable behaviors rewarded or their undesirable behaviors punished? These questions deal with four variables: biographical characteristics, ability, personality, and learning. In this chapter, we'll answer such questions and many more by reviewing how these four individual variables affect employee performance and satisfaction.

BIOGRAPHICAL CHARACTERISTICS

As discussed in the last chapter, this text is essentially concerned with finding and analyzing those variables that have an impact on employee productivity, absence, turnover, and satisfaction. The list of these variables—as was shown in Figure 2–5—is long and contains a number of complicated concepts. Many of these concepts—like motivation level, power relations, or organizational culture—are hard to assess. It might be valuable, then, to begin by looking at factors that are easily definable and readily available; data that can be obtained, for the most part, simply from information available in an employee's personnel file. What factors would this include? Obvious characteristics would be an employee's age, sex, marital status, number of dependents, and length of service with an organization. Fortunately, there is a sizable amount of research that has specifically analyzed many of these **biographical characteristics**.

Biographical characteristics
Personal characteristics—such as age, sex, and marital status—that are objective and easily obtained from personnel records.

Age

The older you get, the less likely you are to quit your job. That is the overwhelming conclusion based on studies of the age-turnover relationship.[1] Of course,

---

[1] L. W. Porter and R. Steers, "Organizational, Work and Personal Factors in Employee Turnover and Absenteeism," *Psychological Bulletin*, January 1973, pp. 151–76; W. H. Mobley, R. W. Griffeth, H. H. Hand, and B. M. Meglino, "Review and Conceptual Analysis of the Employee Turnover Process," *Psychological Bulletin*, May 1979, pp. 493–522; and S. R. Rhodes, "Age-Related Differences in Work Attitudes and Behavior: A Review and Conceptual Analysis," *Psychological Bulletin*, March 1983, pp. 328–67.

this conclusion should not be too surprising. As workers get older they have fewer alternative job opportunities. In addition, older workers are less likely to resign because their longer tenure tends to provide them with higher wage rates, longer paid vacations, and more attractive pension benefits.

It's tempting to assume that age would also be inversely related to absenteeism. After all, if older workers are less likely to quit, wouldn't they also demonstrate higher stability by coming to work more regularly? Not necessarily! Most studies *do* show an inverse relationship, but closer examination finds that the age-absence relationship is partially a function of whether the absence is avoidable or unavoidable.[2] Generally, older employees have lower rates of avoidable absence than do younger employees. However, they have higher rates of unavoidable absence. This is probably due to poorer health associated with aging and the longer recovery period that older workers need when injured.

How does age affect productivity? There is a widespread belief that productivity declines with age. It is often assumed that an individual's skills—particularly speed, agility, strength, and coordination—decay over time, and that prolonged job boredom and lack of intellectual stimulation all contribute to reduced productivity. The evidence, however, contradicts these beliefs and assumptions. A comprehensive analysis of the literature found that productivity actually *increases* as employees grow older.[3] The natural conclusion here is that the demands of most jobs are not extreme enough for potential declines in physical skill levels due to age to have an impact on productivity or, even if there is some decay due to age, it is more than offset by gains due to experience.[4]

Our final concern is the relationship between age and job satisfaction. There is overwhelming evidence indicating a positive association between age and satisfaction, at least up to age sixty.[5] However, current changes taking place in technology may alter this. In jobs where workers are subject to dramatic changes causing their skills to become obsolete, such as those affected by the computer, the satisfaction of older workers is likely to be lower than is that of younger employees.

Sex

Few issues initiate more debates, myths, and unsupported opinions than whether females perform as well on jobs as do males. In this section, we want to review the research on this issue.

The evidence suggests that the best place to begin is with the recognition that there are few, if any, important differences between males and females that will affect their job performance. There are, for instance, no consistent

[2] Rhodes, "Age-Related Differences," pp. 347–49.

[3] D. A. Waldman and B. J. Avolio, "A Meta-Analysis of Age Difference in Job Performance," *Journal of Applied Psychology*, February 1986, pp. 33–38.

[4] S. Giniger, A. Dispenzieri, and J. Eisenberg, "Age, Experience, and Performance on Speed and Skill Jobs in an Applied Setting," *Journal of Applied Psychology*, August 1983, pp. 469–75.

[5] A. L. Kalleberg and K. A. Loscocco, "Aging, Values, and Rewards: Explaining Age Differences in Job Satisfaction," *American Sociological Review*, February 1983, pp. 78–90; and R. Lee and E. R. Wilbur, "Age, Education, Job Tenure, Salary, Job Characteristics, and Job Satisfaction: A Multivariate Analysis," *Human Relations*, August 1985, pp. 781–91.

An Aging Work Force Is Good News for American Productivity

In the mid-1980s, about one in eight Americans was sixty-five or older. In forty years, it is estimated that that ratio will fall to nearly one in five.[6] The trend is clear: America is aging. Because couples are choosing to have smaller families and because people are living longer, our future population will have a higher proportion of older people. But does an older population translate into an older work force? The probable answer is "Yes."

At least three forces are likely to push up the average age of the American labor force. First, federal legislation has all but wiped out mandatory retirement rules. Most employees don't have to retire at sixty-five if they don't want to. Second, a large proportion of the work force can't afford to retire even if that were their preference. Their Social Security checks, other retirement benefits, and savings are inadequate for them to maintain their standard of living. The third factor is the growing scarcity, at least until the turn of the century, of workers to fill jobs in the fast-growing service industries.[7] Employers are looking to older Americans—those in the traditional post-retirement years—as part of the solution to tight labor markets. For instance, McDonald's has been aggressively advertising to reach retirees who might be potential job candidates, and Travelers Insurance regularly taps its retirees for temporary help.

Based on the research relating age and job performance, an aging work force should be viewed as good news for American productivity statistics. Older workers are more stable, have fewer avoidable absences, are more productive, and are more satisfied with their jobs. Given the graying of America, this should translate into higher productivity for the U.S. work force.

male-female differences in problem-solving ability, analytical skills, competitive drive, motivation, leadership, sociability, or learning ability.[8] While psychological studies[9] have found that women are more willing to conform to authority, and that men are more aggressive and more likely than women to have expectations of success, these differences are minor. Given the significant changes that have taken place in the last dozen years in terms of increasing female participation rates in the work force and rethinking of what constitutes male

[6] M. H. Ansley, "What's Ahead for a Gray America," *Chicago Tribune*, October 23, 1983, Sec. 7, p. 1.

[7] "Help Wanted," *Business Week*, August 10, 1987, pp. 48–53.

[8] See, for example, G. N. Powell, *Women and Men in Management* (Beverly Hills, CA: Sage Publications, 1988).

[9] E. Maccoby and C. Nagy Jacklin, *The Psychology of Sex Differences* (Stanford, CA: Stanford University Press, 1974), pp. 154, 211.

and female roles, you should operate from the assumption that there is no significant difference as to job productivity between males and females. Similarly, there is no evidence indicating that an employee's sex affects job satisfaction.[10]

But what about absence and turnover rates? Are females less stable employees than males? First, on the question of turnover, the evidence is mixed.[11] Some have found females to have higher turnover rates, while others have found no difference. There doesn't appear to be enough information from which to draw meaningful conclusions. The research on absence, however, is a different story. The evidence consistently indicates that women have higher rates of absenteeism than do men.[12] The most logical explanation for this finding is that our society has historically placed home and family responsibilities on the female. When a child is ill or someone needs to stay home to await the plumber, it has been the woman who has traditionally taken time off work. However, this research is undoubtedly time-bound. The historical role of the woman in child caring and as secondary breadwinner has definitely changed in the past decade.

Marital Status

There are not enough studies to draw any conclusions as to the effect of marital status on productivity. But consistent research indicates that married employees have fewer absences, undergo less turnover, and are more satisfied with their jobs.[13]

Marriage imposes increased responsibilities that may make a steady job more valuable and important. Of course, the results represent correlational studies; therefore, the causation issue is not clear. It may very well be that conscientious and satisfied employees are more likely to be married. Another offshoot of this issue is that research has not pursued other statuses besides single or married. Does being divorced have an impact on an employee's performance and satisfaction? What about couples who live together without being married? These are questions in need of investigation.

[10] R. P. Quinn, G. L. Staines, and M. R. McCullough, *Job Satisfaction: Is There a Trend?* (Washington, D.C.: U.S. Government Printing Office, Document 2900–00195, 1974).

[11] T. W. Mangione, "Turnover—Some Psychological and Demographic Correlates," in R. P. Quinn and T. W. Mangione (eds.), *The 1969–70 Survey of Working Conditions* (Ann Arbor: University of Michigan, Survey Research Center, 1973); and R. Marsh and H. Mannari, "Organizational Commitment and Turnover: A Predictive Study," *Administrative Science Quarterly*, March 1977, pp. 57–75.

[12] R. J. Flanagan, G. Strauss, and L. Ulman, "Worker Discontent and Work Place Behavior," *Industrial Relations*, May 1974, pp. 101–23; K. R. Garrison and P. M. Muchinsky, "Attitudinal and Biographical Predictors of Incidental Absenteeism," *Journal of Vocational Behavior*, April 1977, pp. 221–30; G. Johns, "Attitudinal and Nonattitudinal Predictors of Two Forms of Absence from Work," *Organizational Behavior and Human Performance*, December 1978, pp. 431–44; and R. T. Keller, "Predicting Absenteeism from Prior Absenteeism, Attitudinal Factors, and Nonattitudinal Factors," *Journal of Applied Psychology*, August 1983, pp. 536–40.

[13] Garrison and Muchinsky, "Attitudinal and Biographical Predictors"; C. J. Watson, "An Evaluation and Some Aspects of the Steers and Rhodes Model of Employee Attendance," *Journal of Applied Psychology*, June 1981, pp. 385–89; Keller, "Predicting Absenteeism"; J. M. Federico, P. Federico, and G. W. Lundquist, "Predicting Women's Turnover as a Function of Extent of Met Salary Expectations and Biodemographic Data," *Personnel Psychology*, Winter 1976, pp. 559–66; and Marsh and Mannari, "Organizational Commitment."

Number of Dependents

Again, we don't have enough information relating to employee productivity, but quite a bit of research has been done on the relationship between the number of dependents an employee has and absence, turnover, and satisfaction.

There is very strong evidence that the number of children an employee has is positively correlated with absence, especially among females.[14] Similarly, the evidence seems to point to a positive relationship between number of dependents and job satisfaction.[15] In contrast, studies relating number of dependents and turnover produce a mixed bag of results.[16] Some indicate that children increase turnover, while others show that they result in lower turnover. At this point, the evidence regarding turnover is just too contradictory to permit us to draw conclusions.

Tenure

The last biographical characteristic we'll look at is tenure. With the exception of the concern about male-female differences, there is probably no other issue that is more subject to myths and speculations than the impact of seniority on job performance.

Extensive reviews of the seniority-productivity relationship have been conducted.[17] While past performance tends to be related to output in a new position, seniority by itself is not a good predictor of productivity. In other words, holding all other things equal, there is no reason to believe that people who have been on a job longer are more productive than are those with less seniority.

The research relating tenure with absence is quite straightforward. Studies consistently demonstrate seniority to be negatively related to absenteeism.[18] In fact, in terms of both absence frequency and total days lost at work, tenure is the single most important explanatory variable.[19]

As with absence, tenure is also a potent variable in explaining turnover. "Tenure has consistently been found to be negatively related to turnover and

[14] Porter and Steers, "Organizational, Work, and Personal Factors"; N. Nicholson and P. M. Goodge, "The Influence of Social, Organizational and Biographical Factors on Female Absence," *Journal of Management Studies*, October 1976, pp. 234–54; P. M. Muchinsky, "Employee Absenteeism: A Review of the Literature," *Journal of Vocational Behavior*, June 1977, pp. 316–40; and R. M. Steers and S. R. Rhodes, "Major Influences on Employee Attendance: A Process Model," *Journal of Applied Psychology*, August 1978, pp. 391–407.

[15] Porter and Steers, "Organizational, Work, and Personal Factors"; Federico, Federico, and Lundquist, "Predicting Women's Turnover"; and Marsh and Mannari, "Organizational Commitments."

[16] A. S. Gechman and Y. Wiener, "Job Involvement and Satisfaction as Related to Mental Health and Personal Time Devoted to Work," *Journal of Applied Psychology*, August 1975, pp. 521–23.

[17] M. E. Gordon and W. J. Fitzgibbons, "Empirical Test of the Validity of Seniority as a Factor in Staffing Decisions," *Journal of Applied Psychology*, June 1982, pp. 311–19; and M. E. Gordon and W. A. Johnson, "Seniority: A Review of Its Legal and Scientific Standing," *Personnel Psychology*, Summer 1982, pp. 255–80.

[18] Garrison and Muchinsky, "Attitudinal and Biographical Predictors"; N. Nicholson, C. A. Brown, and J. K. Chadwick-Jones, "Absence from Work and Personal Characteristics," *Journal of Applied Psychology*, June 1977, pp. 319–27; and Keller, "Predicting Absenteeism."

[19] P. O. Popp and J. A. Belohlav, "Absenteeism in a Low Status Work Environment," *Academy of Management Journal*, September 1982, p. 681.

has been suggested as one of the single best predictors of turnover."[20] Moreover, consistent with research that suggests that past behavior is the best predictor of future behavior,[21] evidence indicates that tenure on an employee's previous job is a powerful predictor of future employee turnover.[22]

ABILITY

Contrary to what we were taught in grade school, we weren't all created equal. Most of us are to the left of the median on some normally distributed ability curve. Regardless of how motivated you are, it is unlikely that you can write as well as Stephen King, run as fast as Ben Johnson, act as well as Meryl Streep, or do improvisation as well as Robin Williams. Of course, just because we aren't all equal in abilities does not imply that some individuals are generally inferior to others. What we're acknowledging is that everyone has strengths and weaknesses in terms of ability that make him or her relatively superior or inferior to others in performing certain tasks or activities.[23] From management's standpoint, the issue isn't whether or not people differ in terms of their abilities. They do! The issue is *how* people differ in abilities and *using* that knowledge to increase the likelihood that an employee will perform his or her job well.

What does **ability** mean? As we'll use the term, ability refers to an individual's capacity to perform the various tasks in a job. It is a current assessment of what one *can* do. An individual's overall abilities are essentially made up of two sets of skills: intellectual and physical.

Ability

An individual's capacity to perform the various tasks in a job.

Intellectual Abilities

Intellectual ability

That required to do mental activities.

Intellectual abilities are those needed to perform mental activities. IQ tests, for example, are designed to ascertain one's intellectual abilities. So, too, are popular college admission tests like the SAT and ACT and graduate admission tests in business (GMAT), law (LSAT), and medicine (MCAT). Some of the more relevant dimensions making up intellectual abilities include number aptitude, verbal comprehension, perceptual speed, and inductive reasoning. Table 3–1 describes these dimensions.

Jobs differ in the demands they place on incumbents to use their intellectual abilities. Generally speaking, the higher an individual rises in an organization's hierarchy, the more general intelligence and verbal abilities will be necessary to perform the job successfully. A high IQ, for example, may not be a prerequisite

---

[20] H. J. Arnold and D. C. Feldman, "A Multivariate Analysis of the Determinants of Job Turnover," *Journal of Applied Psychology*, June 1982, p. 352.

[21] R. D. Gatewood and H. S. Feild, *Human Resource Selection* (Chicago: Dryden Press, 1987).

[22] J. A. Breaugh and D. L. Dossett, "The Effectiveness of Biodata for Predicting Turnover," paper presented at the National Academy of Management Conference, New Orleans, August 1987.

[23] L. E. Tyler, *Individual Differences: Abilities and Motivational Directions* (Englewood Cliffs, NJ: Prentice Hall, 1974).

TABLE 3–1
Dimensions of Intellectual Ability

Dimension	Description	Job Example
Number aptitude	Ability to do speedy and accurate arithmetic computations	Accountant: Determining the sales tax on a set of items
Verbal comprehension	Ability to understand what is read or heard and the relationship of words to each other	Plant Manager: Following corporate policies
Perceptual speed	Ability visually to identify similarities and differences quickly and accurately	Fire Investigator: Identifying clues to support a charge of arson
Inductive reasoning	Ability to identify a logical sequence in a problem and then solve the problem	Market Researcher: Forecasting demand for a product in the next time period

for all jobs. In fact, for many jobs—where employee behavior is highly routine and there are little or no opportunities to exercise discretion—a high IQ may be unrelated to performance. On the other hand, a careful review of the evidence demonstrates that tests that assess verbal, numerical, spatial, and perceptual abilities are valid predictors of job proficiency across all levels of jobs.[24] So tests that measure specific dimensions of intelligence have been found to be strong predictors of job performance.

The major dilemma faced by employers who use mental ability tests for selection, promotion, training, and similar personnel decisions is that they have a negative impact on racial and ethnic groups.[25] The evidence indicates that some minority groups score, on the average, as much as one standard deviation lower than whites on verbal, numerical, and spatial ability tests. The negative impact from these tests can be eliminated by either avoiding these types of tests or seeking racial and ethnic balance by hiring and promoting on the basis of ability within each ethnic group separately. This latter suggestion, incidentally, underlies legal efforts by the courts to eliminate employment discrimination through the use of targets and goals.

Physical Abilities

To the same degree that intellectual abilities play a larger role in performance as individuals move up the organizational hierarchy, specific **physical abilities** gain importance for successfully doing less skilled and more standardized jobs in the lower part of the organization. Jobs where success demands stamina, manual dexterity, leg strength, or similar talents require management to identify an employee's physical capabilities.

Research on the requirements needed in hundreds of jobs has identified

Physical ability

That required to do tasks demanding stamina, dexterity, strength, and similar skills.

---

[24] J. E. Hunter and R. F. Hunter, "Validity and Utility of Alternative Predictors of Job Performance," *Psychological Bulletin*, January 1984, pp. 72–98.

[25] Ibid., 73–74.

TABLE 3–2
Nine Basic Physical Abilities

Strength Factors

1. Dynamic strength	Ability to exert muscular force repeatedly or continuously over time
2. Trunk strength	Ability to exert muscular strength using the trunk (particularly abdominal) muscles
3. Static strength	Ability to exert force against external objects
4. Explosive strength	Ability to expend a maximum of energy in one or a series of explosive acts

Flexibility Factors

5. Extent flexibility	Ability to move the trunk and back muscles as far as possible
6. Dynamic flexibility	Ability to make rapid, repeated flexing movements

Other Factors

7. Body coordination	Ability to coordinate the simultaneous actions of different parts of the body
8. Balance	Ability to maintain equilibrium despite forces pulling off balance
9. Stamina	Ability to continue maximum effort requiring prolonged effort over time

---

Source: Reprinted from the June 1979 issue of *Personnel Administrator*, copyright 1979, The American Society for Personnel Administration; 606 North Washington Street; Alexandria, Virginia 22314, pp. 82–92.

nine basic abilities involved in the performance of physical tasks.[26] These are described in Table 3–2. Individuals differ in the amount to which they hold each of these abilities. Not surprisingly, there is also little relationship between them: A high score on one is no assurance of a high score on others. High employee performance is likely to be achieved when management has ascertained the extent to which a job requires each of the nine abilities and then ensures that employees in that job have those abilities.

The Ability-Job Fit

Our concern is with explaining and predicting the behavior of people at work. In this section, we have demonstrated that jobs make differing demands on people and that people differ in the abilities they possess. Employee performance, therefore, is enhanced when there is a high ability-job fit.

The specific intellectual or physical abilities required for adequate job performance depend on the ability requirements of the job. Directing attention at only the employee's abilities or the ability requirements of the job ignores that employee performance depends on the interaction of the two.

What predictions can we make when the fit is poor? As alluded to previously,

---

[26] E. A. Fleishman, "Evaluating Physical Abilities Required by Jobs," *Personnel Administrator*, June 1979, pp. 82–92.

if employees lack the required abilities, they are likely to fail. If you're hired as a typist and you can't meet the job's basic typing requirements, your performance is going to be poor irrespective of your positive attitude or your high level of motivation. When the ability-job fit is out of sync because the employee has abilities that far exceed the requirements of the job, our predictions would be very different. Job performance is likely to be adequate, but there will be organizational inefficiencies and possible declines in employee satisfaction. Given that employee pay tends to reflect the highest skill level that they possess, if their abilities far exceed those necessary to do the job, management will be paying them more than they need to. Abilities significantly above those required can also reduce the employee's job satisfaction when the employee's desire to use his or her ability is particularly strong but that desire is frustrated by the limitations of the job.

PERSONALITY

Why are some people quiet and passive, while others are loud and aggressive? Are certain personality types better adapted for certain job types? What do we know from theories of personality that can help us to explain and predict the behavior of individuals in organizations? In this section we will attempt to answer such questions.

What Is Personality?

When we talk of personality, we do not mean that a person has charm, a positive attitude toward life, a smiling face, or is a finalist for "Happiest and Friendliest" in this year's Miss America contest. When psychologists talk of personality, they mean a dynamic concept describing the growth and development of a person's whole psychological system. Rather than looking at parts of the person, personality looks at some aggregate whole that is greater than the sum of the parts.

The most frequently used definition of personality was produced by Gordon Allport more than fifty years ago. He said personality is "the dynamic organization within the individual of those psychophysical systems that determine his unique adjustments to his enviroment."[27] For our purposes, you should think of **personality** as the sum total of ways in which an individual reacts and interacts with others. This is most often described in terms of measurable personality traits that a person exhibits.

Personality

The sum total of ways in which an individual reacts and interacts with others.

Personality Determinants

An early argument in personality research was whether an individual's personality was the result of heredity or environment. Was the personality predetermined

---

[27] G. W. Allport, *Personality: A Psychological Interpretation* (New York: Holt, Rinehart and Winston, 1937), p. 48.

at birth, or was it the result of the individual's interaction with his or her environment? Clearly, there is no simple "black-or-white" answer. Personality appears to be a result of both influences. Additionally, there has recently been an increased interest in a third factor—the situation. Thus, an adult's personality is now generally considered to be made up of both hereditary and environmental factors, moderated by situational conditions.

Heredity   Heredity refers to those factors that were determined at conception. Physical stature, facial attractiveness, sex, temperament, muscle composition and reflexes, energy level, and biological rhythms are characteristics that are generally considered to be either completely or substantially influenced by who your parents were; that is, by their biological, physiological, and inherent psychological makeup. The heredity approach argues that the ultimate explanation of an individual's personality is the molecular structure of the genes, located in the chromosomes. "In fact, much of the early work in personality could be subsumed under the series: Heredity is transmitted through the genes; the genes determine the hormone balance; hormone balance determines physique; and physique shapes personality."[28]

The heredity argument can be used to explain why Veronica's nose looks like her father's or why her chin resembles her mother's. It may explain why Diane is a "gifted athlete" when both her parents were similarly gifted. More controversy would surround the conclusion, by those who advocate the heredity approach, that Michael is lethargic as a result of inheriting this characteristic from his parents.

If all personality characteristics were completely dictated by heredity, they would be fixed at birth and no amount of experience could alter them. If you were relaxed and easygoing, for example, that would be the result of your genes, and it would not be possible for you to change these characteristics. While this approach may be appealing to the bigots of the world, it is an inadequate explanation of personality.

Environment   Among the factors that exert pressures on our personality formation are the culture in which we are raised, our early conditioning, the norms among our family, friends, and social groups, and other influences that we experience. The environment we are exposed to plays a critical role in shaping our personalities.

For example, culture establishes the norms, attitudes, and values that are passed along from one generation to the next and create consistencies over time. An ideology that is fostered in one culture may have only moderate influence in another. For instance, we in North America have had the themes of industriousness, success, competition, independence, and Protestant ethic constantly instilled in us through books, the school system, family, and friends. North Americans, as a result, tend to be ambitious and aggressive relative to individuals raised in cultures that have emphasized getting along with others, cooperation, and the priority of family over work and career.

An interesting area of research linking environmental factors and personality has focused on the influence of birth order. It has been argued that sibling

---

[28] J. Kelly, *Organizational Behavior*, rev. ed. (Homewood, IL: Richard D. Irwin, 1974), p. 243.

position is an important psychological variable "because it represents a microcosm of the significant social experiences of adolescence and adulthood."[29] Those who see birth order as a predictive variable propose that while personality differences between children are frequently attributed to heredity, the environment in which the children are raised is really the critical factor that creates the differences. And the environment that a firstborn child is exposed to is different from that of later-born children.

The research indicates that firstborns are more prone to schizophrenia, more susceptible to social pressure, and more dependent than the later-born.[30] The firstborn are also more likely to experience the world as more orderly, predictable, and rational than later-born children. Of course, there is much debate as to the differing characteristics of first- versus later-born children, but the evidence does indicate that firstborns of the same sex "should be more concerned with social acceptance and rejection, less likely to break the rules imposed by authority, more ambitious and hard-working, more cooperative, more prone to guilt and anxiety, and less openly aggressive."[31]

Careful consideration of the arguments favoring either heredity or environment as the primary determinant of personality forces the conclusion that both are important. Heredity sets the parameters or outer limits, but an individual's full potential will be determined by how well he or she adjusts to the demands and requirements of the environment.

Situation   A third factor, the situation, further influences the effects of heredity and environment on personality. An individual's personality, while generally stable and consistent, does change in different situations. Different demands in different situations call forth different aspects of one's personality. We should not, therefore, look at personality patterns in isolation.

While it seems only logical to suppose that situations will influence an individual's personality, a neat classification scheme that would tell us the impact of various types of situations has so far eluded us. "Apparently we are not yet close to developing a system for clarifying situations so that they might be systematically studied."[32] However, we do know that certain situations are more relevant than others in influencing personality.

> What is of interest taxonomically is that situations seem to differ substantially in the constraints they impose on behavior, with some situations—e.g. church, an employment interview—constraining many behaviors and others—e.g. a picnic in a public park—constraining relatively few.[33]

Furthermore, although certain generalizations can be made about personality, there are significant individual differences. As we shall see, the study of individual differences has come to receive greater emphasis in personality research, which originally sought out more general, universal patterns.

[29] I. Janis, G. F. Mahl, J. Kagan, and R. P. Holt, *Personality: Dynamics, Development and Assessment* (New York: Harcourt, Brace & World, 1969), p. 555.

[30] J. R. Warren, "Birth Order and Social Behavior," *Psychological Bulletin*, January 1966, pp. 38–49.

[31] Janis et al., *Personality*, p. 552.

[32] L. Sechrest, "Personality," in M. R. Rosenzweig and L. W. Porter (eds.), *Annual Review of Psychology*, Vol. 27 (Palo Alto, CA: Annual Reviews, 1976), p. 10.

[33] Ibid.

FIGURE 3–1

Source: Copyright 1959 by United Feature Syndicate, Inc. With permission.

Personality Traits

Personality traits

Enduring characteristics that describe an individual's behavior.

The early work in the structure of personality revolved around attempts to identify and label enduring characteristics that describe an individual's behavior. Popular characteristics include shy, aggressive, submissive, lazy, ambitious, loyal, or timid. These characteristics, when they are exhibited in a large number of situations, are called **traits**. The more consistent the characteristic and the more frequently it occurs in diverse situations, the more important that trait is in describing the individual.

Efforts to isolate traits have been hindered because there are so many of them. In one study, 17,953 individual traits were identified.[34] However, it is virtually impossible to predict behavior when such a large number of traits must be taken into account. As a result, attention has been directed toward

TABLE 3–3
Sixteen Source Traits

1. Reserved	Outgoing
2. Less intelligent	More intelligent
3. Affected by feelings	Emotionally stable
4. Submissive	Dominant
5. Serious	Happy-go-lucky
6. Expedient	Conscientious
7. Timid	Venturesome
8. Tough-minded	Sensitive
9. Trusting	Suspicious
10. Practical	Imaginative
11. Forthright	Shrewd
12. Self-assured	Apprehensive
13. Conservative	Experimenting
14. Group-dependent	Self-sufficient
15. Uncontrolled	Controlled
16. Relaxed	Tense

[34] G. W. Allport and H. S. Odbert, "Trait Names, A Psycholexical Study," *Psychological Monographs*, No. 47 (1936).

	High anxiety	Low anxiety
Extrovert	Tense, excitable, unstable, warm, sociable, and dependent	Composed, confident, trustful, adaptable, warm, sociable and dependent
Introvert	Tense, excitable, unstable, cold, and shy	Composed, confident, trustful, adaptable, calm, cold, and shy

FIGURE 3–2
Four-Type Thesis

reducing these thousands to a more manageable number—to ascertain the source or primary traits.

One researcher isolated 171 surface traits but concluded that they were superficial and lacking in descriptive power.[35] What he sought was a reduced set of traits that would identify underlying patterns. The result was the identification of sixteen personality factors, which he called source or primary traits, that are the basic underlying causes of surface traits. They are shown in Table 3–3. These sixteen traits have been found to be generally steady and constant sources of behavior, allowing prediction of an individual's behavior in specific situations by weighing the characteristics for their situational relevance.

Traits can additionally be grouped to form personality types. Instead of looking at specific characteristics, we can group those qualities that go together into a single category. For example, ambition and aggression tend to be highly correlated. Efforts to reduce the number of traits into common groups tend to isolate introversion-extroversion and something approximating high anxiety-low anxiety as the underlying interconnecting characteristics.[36] As depicted in Figure 3–2, these dimensions suggest four personality types.[37] For example, an individual with high anxiety and extroversion would be tense, excitable, unstable, warm, sociable, and dependent.

Should you put a lot of weight on personality traits as explanatory devices or predictors of employee behavior across a broad spectrum of situations? Probably not! This is because traits ignore situational contexts. They are not contingency oriented and, therefore, largely ignore the dynamic interchange that occurs in an individual's personality as a result of interaction with his or her environment. As a result, personality traits tend to be most valuable only with individuals who hold a trait at its extreme (see Figure 3–3). We might be able to predict some common behaviors among *extreme* extroverts or individuals who are *highly* anxious. But since the majority of people are in the vast

---

[35] R. B. Cattell, "Personality Pinned Down," *Psychology Today*, July 1973, pp. 40–46.

[36] R. B. Cattell, *The Scientific Analysis of Personality* (Chicago: Aldine, 1965); and H. J. Eysenck, *The Structure of Human Personality* (London: Methuen, 1953).

[37] S. R. Maddi, *Personality Theories* (Homewood, IL: Dorsey, 1968).

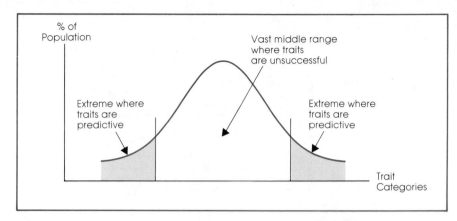

FIGURE 3–3
Predictive Validity of Personality Traits

middle range on most trait characteristics, personality traits must be considered in their situational context.

Major Personality Attributes Influencing OB

A number of specific personality attributes have been isolated as having potential for predicting behavior in organizations. The first of these is related to where one perceives the locus of control in one's life. The others are achievement orientation, authoritarianism, Machiavellianism, and propensity for risk taking. In this section, we shall briefly introduce these attributes and summarize what we know as to their ability to explain and predict employee behavior.

Locus of Control Some people believe that they are masters of their own fate. Other people see themselves as pawns of fate, believing that what happens to them in their lives is due to luck or chance. The first type, those who believe that they control their destinies, have been labeled **internals**, whereas the latter, who see their lives as being controlled by outside forces, have been called **externals**.[38]

A large amount of research comparing internals with externals has consistently shown that individuals who rate high in externality are less satisfied with their jobs, have higher absenteeism rates, are more alienated from the work setting, and are less involved on their jobs than are internals.[39]

Why are externals more dissatisfied? The answer is probably because they perceive themselves as having little control over those organizational outcomes that are important to them. Internals, facing the same situation, attribute

Internals

Individuals who believe that they control what happens to them.

Externals

Individuals who believe that what happens to them is controlled by outside forces such as luck or chance.

[38] J. B. Rotter, "Generalized Expectancies for Internal Versus External Control of Reinforcement," *Psychological Monographs*, Vol. 80, no. 609 (1966).

[39] P. E. Spector, "Behavior in Organizations as a Function of Employee's Locus of Control," *Psychological Bulletin*, May 1982, pp. 482–97.

OB Close-Up

Using Personality Tests to Improve Communication

The Myers-Briggs Type Indicator (MBTI) is a 100-question personality test that asks people how they usually feel or act in particular situations.[40] It is one of the most widely used personality tests in the U.S.—in one recent year alone, some 1.5 million people took it. Organizations using the MBTI include Allied-Signal, Apple Computer, AT&T, Citicorp, Exxon, GE, Honeywell, 3M Co., plus many hospitals, educational institutions, and even the U.S. Armed Forces.

The test labels people as extroverted or introverted (E or I), sensing or intuitive (S or N), thinking or feeling (T or F), and perceiving or judging (P or J). These are then combined into sixteen personality types. (These are different from the sixteen source traits in Table 3–3.) To illustrate, let's take several examples. INTJ's are visionaries. They usually have original minds and great drive for their own ideas and purposes. They're characterized as skeptical, critical, independent, determined, and often stubborn. ESTJ's are organizers. They're practical, realistic, matter-of-fact, with a natural head for business or mechanics. They like to organize and run activities. The ENTP-type is a conceptualizer. He or she is quick, ingenious, and good at many things. This person tends to be resourceful in solving challenging problems, but may neglect routine assignments.

Users of MBTI aren't using the test to screen job applicants. Rather, it is being used to improve employee self-awareness, and in management development programs to help executives understand how they come across to others who may see things differently. For instance, some users report that the results help explain behaviors of colleagues that have puzzled them for years. Proponents argue that when people are aware of their own and their coworkers' types, communication improves, and with it productivity. Whether the use of MBTI actually improves employee productivity is problematic. But the growing popularity of MBTI in organizations can't be ignored.

---

organizational outcomes to their own actions. If the situation is unattractive, they believe that they have no one else to blame but themselves. Also, the dissatisfied internal is more likely to quit a dissatisfying job.

The impact of **locus of control** on absence is an interesting one. Internals believe that health is substantially under their own control through proper habits, so they take more responsibility for their health and have better health habits. This leads to lower incidences of sickness and, hence, lower absenteeism.[41]

We shouldn't expect any clear relationship between locus of control and turnover. The reason is that there are opposing forces at work. "On the one

Locus of control

The degree to which people believe they are masters of their own fate.

[40] This is based on Thomas Moore, "Personality Tests Are Back," *Fortune*, March 30, 1987, pp. 74–82.

[41] Keller, "Predicting Absenteeism."

hand, internals tend to take action and thus might be expected to quit jobs more readily. On the other hand, they tend to be more successful on the job and more satisfied, factors associated with less individual turnover."[42]

The overall evidence indicates that internals generally perform better on their jobs, but that conclusion should be moderated to reflect differences in jobs. Internals search more actively for information before making a decision, are more motivated to achieve, and make a greater attempt to control their environment. Externals, however, are more compliant and willing to follow directions. Therefore, internals do well on sophisticated tasks—which includes most managerial and professional jobs—that require complex information processing and learning. Additionally, internals are more suited to jobs that require initiative and independence of action. In contrast, externals should do well on jobs that are well structured and routine and where success depends heavily on complying with the direction of others.

Achievement Orientation

We have noted that internals are motivated to achieve. This achievement orientation has also been singled out as a personality characteristic that varies among employees and that can be used to predict certain behaviors.

Research has centered around the need to achieve (**nAch**). People with a high need to achieve can be described as continually striving to do things better. They want to overcome obstacles, but they want to feel that their success (or failure) is due to their own actions. This means they like tasks of intermediate difficulty. If a task is very easy, it will lack challenge. High achievers receive no feeling of accomplishment from doing tasks that fail to challenge their abilities. Similarly, they avoid tasks that are so difficult that the probability of success is very low. Even if they succeed, it is more apt to be due to luck than ability. Given the high achiever's propensity for tasks where the outcome can be attributed directly to his or her efforts, the high-*nAch* person looks for challenges having approximately a 50–50 chance of success.

What can we say about high achievers on the job? In jobs that provide intermediate difficulty, rapid performance feedback, and allow the employee control over his or her results, the high *nAch* individual will perform well.[43] This implies, though, that high achievers will do better in sales, professional sports, or in management than on an assembly line or in clerical tasks. That is, those individuals with a high *nAch* will not always outperform those who are low or intermediate in this characteristic. The tasks that high achievers undertake must provide the challenge, feedback, and responsibility they look for if the high-*nAch* personality is to be positively related to job performance.

Authoritarianism

There is evidence that there is such a thing as an authoritarian personality, but its relevance to job behavior is more speculation than fact. With that qualification, let us examine **authoritarianism** and consider how it might be related to employee performance.

Authoritarianism refers to a belief that there should be status and power

nAch

Need to achieve or strive continually to do things better.

Authoritarianism

The belief that there should be status and power differences among people in organizations.

---

[42] Spector, "Behavior in Organizations," p. 493.

[43] J. B. Miner, *Theories of Organizational Behavior* (Hinsdale, IL: Dryden Press, 1980), pp. 46–75.

differences among people in organizations.[44] The extremely high-authoritarian personality is intellectually rigid, judgmental of others, deferential to those above and exploitative of those below, distrustful, and resistant to change. Of course, few people are extreme authoritarians, so conclusions must be guarded. It seems reasonable to postulate, however, that possessing a high-authoritarian personality would be related negatively to performance where the job demanded sensitivity to the feelings of others, tact, and the ability to adapt to complex and changing situations.[45] On the other hand, where jobs are highly structured and success depends on close conformance to rules and regulations, the high-authoritarian employee should perform quite well.

Machiavellianism   Closely related to authoritarianism is the characteristic of Machiavellianism (Mach), named after Niccolo Machiavelli who wrote in the sixteenth century on how to gain and manipulate power. An individual high in Machiavellianism is pragmatic, maintains emotional distance, and believes that ends can justify means. "If it works, use it" is consistent with a high-Mach perspective.

A considerable amount of research has been directed toward relating high- and low-Mach personalities to certain behavioral outcomes.[46] High Machs manipulate more, win more, are persuaded less, and persuade others more than do low Machs.[47] Yet these high-Mach outcomes are moderated by situational factors. It has been found that high Machs flourish (1) when they interact face to face with others rather than indirectly; (2) when the situation has a minimum number of rules and regulations, thus allowing latitude for improvisation; and (3) where emotional involvement with details irrelevant to winning distracts low Machs.[48]

Should we conclude that high Machs make good employees? That answer depends on the type of job and whether you consider ethical implications in evaluating performance. In jobs that require bargaining skills (such as labor negotiation) or where there are substantial rewards for winning (as in commissioned sales), high Machs will be productive. But if ends can't justify the means, if there are *absolute* standards of behavior, or if the three situational factors noted in the previous paragraph are not in evidence, our ability to predict a high Mach's performance will be severely curtailed.

Risk Taking   People differ in their willingness to take chances. This propensity to assume or avoid risk has been shown to have an impact on how long it takes managers to make a decision and how much information they require before making their choice. For instance, seventy-nine managers worked on simulated personnel exercises that required them to make hiring decisions.[49]

Machiavellianism

Degree to which an individual is pragmatic, maintains emotional distance, and believes that ends can justify means.

---

[44] T. Adorno et al., *The Authoritarian Personality* (New York: Harper & Brothers, 1950).

[45] H. Gough, "Personality and Personality Assessment," in M. D. Dunnette (ed.), *Handbook of Industrial and Organizational Psychology* (Chicago: Rand McNally, 1976), p. 579.

[46] R. G. Vleeming, "Machiavellianism: A Preliminary Review," *Psychological Reports*, February 1979, pp. 295–310.

[47] R. Christie and F. L. Geis, *Studies in Machiavellianism* (New York: Academic Press, 1970), p. 312.

[48] Ibid.

[49] R. N. Taylor and M. D. Dunnette, "Influence of Dogmatism, Risk-Taking Propensity, and Intelligence on Decision-Making Strategies for a Sample of Industrial Managers," *Journal of Applied Psychology*, August 1974, pp. 420–23.

High-risk-taking managers made more rapid decisions and used less information in making their choices than did the low-risk-taking managers. Interestingly, the decision accuracy was the same for both groups.

While it is generally correct to conclude that managers in organizations are risk aversive,[50] there are still individual differences on this dimension.[51] As a result, it makes sense to recognize these differences and even to consider aligning risk-taking propensity with specific job demands. For instance, a high-risk-taking propensity may lead to more effective performance for a stock trader in a brokerage firm. This type of job demands rapid decision making. On the other hand, this personality characteristic might prove a major obstacle to accountants performing auditing activities. This latter job might be better filled by someone with a low-risk-taking propensity.

Matching Personality and Jobs

In our discussion of locus of control, authoritarianism, Machiavellianism, and risk taking, our conclusions were qualified to recognize that the requirements of the job moderated the relationship between possession of the personality characteristic and job performance. This concern with matching the job requirements with personality characteristics has recently received increased attention. It is best articulated in John Holland's personality-job fit theory.[52] The theory is based on the notion of fit between a person's interests (taken to be an expression of personality) and his or her occupational environment. Holland presents six personality types and proposes that satisfaction and the propensity to leave a job depends on the degree to which individuals successfully match their personalities with a congruent occupational environment.

Each one of the six personality types has a matching occupational environment. Listed next is a description of the six types and examples of congruent occupations:

Type	*Occupations*
1. *Realistic*—involves aggressive behavior, physical activities requiring skill, strength, and coordination	Forestry, farming
2. *Investigative*—involves activities requiring thinking, organizing, and understanding rather than feeling or emotion	Biology, mathematics, news reporting
3. *Social*—involves interpersonal rather than intellectual or physical activities	Foreign service, social work, clinical psychology

[50] I. L. Janis and L. Mann, *Decision Making: A Psychological Analysis of Conflict, Choice, and Commitment* (New York: Free Press, 1977).

[51] N. Kogan and M. A. Wallach, "Group Risk Taking as a Function of Members' Anxiety and Defensiveness," *Journal of Personality*, March 1967, pp. 50–63.

[52] J. L. Holland, *Making Vocational Choices: A Theory of Vocational Personalities and Work Environments*, 2nd ed. (Englewood Cliffs, NJ: Prentice Hall, 1985).

Type	Occupations
4. *Conventional*—involves rule-regulated activities and sublimation of personal needs to an organization or person of power and status	Accounting, finance, corporate management
5. *Enterprising*—involves verbal activities to influence others, to attain power and status	Law, public relations, small-business management
6. *Artistic*—involves self-expression, artistic creation, or emotional activities	Art, music, writing

Holland has developed a Vocational Preference Inventory questionnaire that contains 160 occupational titles. Respondents indicate which of these occupations they like or dislike, and these answers are used to form personality profiles. Utilizing this procedure, research strongly supports the hexagonal diagram in Figure 3–4.[53] This figure shows that the closer two fields or orientations are

FIGURE 3–4
Relationships Among Occupational Personality Types

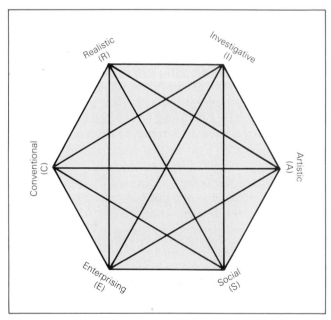

Source: J. L. Holland, *Making Vocational Choices: A Theory of Vocational Personalities and Work Environments*, 2nd ed. (Englewood Cliffs, NJ: Prentice Hall, 1985). Used by permission. This model originally appeared in J. L. Holland et al., "An Empirical Occupational Classification Derived from a Theory of Personality and Intended for Practice and Research," ACT Research Report No. 29 (Iowa City: The American College Testing Program, 1969).

[53] See, for example, A. R. Spokane, "A Review of Research on Person-Environment Congruence in Holland's Theory of Careers," *Journal of Vocational Behavior*, June 1985, pp. 306–43.

in the hexagon, the more compatible they are. Adjacent categories are quite similar, while those diagonally opposite are highly dissimilar.

What does all this mean? The theory argues that satisfaction is highest and turnover lowest where personality and occupation are in agreement. Social individuals should be in social jobs, conventional people in conventional jobs, and so forth. A realistic person in a realistic job is in a more congruent situation than is a realistic person in an investigative job. A realistic person in a social job is in the most incongruent situation possible. The key points of this model are that (1) there do appear to be intrinsic differences in personality among individuals, (2) there are different types of jobs, and (3) people in job environments congruent with their personality types should be more satisfied and less likely to voluntarily resign than should people in incongruent jobs.

LEARNING

The last topic we will introduce in this chapter is learning. It is included for the obvious reason that almost all complex behavior is learned. If we want to explain and predict behavior, we need to understand how people learn.

A Definition of Learning

Learning

Any relatively permanent change in behavior that occurs as a result of experience.

What is **learning?** A psychologist's definition is considerably broader than the layperson's view that "it's what we did when we went to school." In actuality, each of us is continuously going "to school." Learning occurs all of the time. A generally accepted definition of learning is, therefore, *any relatively permanent change in behavior that occurs as a result of experience.* Ironically, we can say that changes in behavior indicate that learning has taken place and that learning is a change in behavior.

Obviously, the foregoing definition suggests that we shall never see someone "learning." We can see changes, but not the learning itself. The concept is theoretical and hence not directly observable:

> You have seen people in the process of learning, you have seen people who behave in a particular way as a result of learning and some of you (in fact, I guess the majority of you) have "learned" at some time in your life. In other words, we infer that learning has taken place if an individual behaves, reacts, responds as a result of experience in a manner different from the way he formerly behaved.[54]

Our definition has several components that deserve clarification. First, learning involves change. This may be good or bad from an organizational point of view. People can learn unfavorable behaviors—to hold prejudices or to restrict their output, for example—as well as favorable behaviors. Second, the change must be relatively permanent. Temporary changes may be only reflexive and fail to represent any learning. Therefore, this requirement rules

---

[54] W. McGehee, "Are We Using What We Know About Training?—Learning Theory and Training," *Personnel Psychology*, Spring 1958, p. 2.

out behavioral changes caused by fatigue or temporary adaptations. Third, our definition is concerned with behavior. Learning takes place where there is a change in actions. A change in an individual's thought processes or attitudes, if accompanied by no change in behavior, would not be learning. Finally, some form of experience is necessary for learning. This may be acquired directly through observation or practice. Or it may result from indirect experiences, such as that acquired through reading. The crucial test still remains: Does this experience result in a relatively permanent change in behavior? If the answer is "Yes," we can say that learning has taken place.

Theories of Learning

How do we learn? Three theories have been offered to explain the process by which we acquire patterns of behavior. These are classical conditioning, operant conditioning, and social learning.

Classical Conditioning   **Classical conditioning** grew out of experiments to teach dogs to salivate in response to the ringing of a bell, conducted at the turn of the century by a Russian physiologist, Ivan Pavlov.[55]

Classical conditioning

A type of conditioning where an individual responds to some stimulus that would not invariably produce such a response.

A simple surgical procedure allowed Pavlov to measure accurately the amount of saliva secreted by a dog. When Pavlov presented the dog with a piece of meat, the dog exhibited a noticeable increase in salivation. When Pavlov withheld the presentation of meat and merely rang a bell, the dog had no salivation. Then, Pavlov proceeded to link the meat and the ringing of the bell. After repeatedly hearing the bell before getting the food, the dog began to salivate as soon as the bell rang. After a while, the dog would salivate merely at the sound of the bell, even if no food was offered. In effect, the dog had learned to respond—that is, to salivate—to the bell. Let's review this experiment to introduce the key concepts in classical conditioning.

The meat was an *unconditioned stimulus*; it invariably caused the dog to react in a specific way. The reaction that took place whenever the unconditioned stimulus occurred was called the *unconditioned response* (or the noticeable increase in salivation, in this case). The bell was an artificial stimulus, or what we call the *conditioned stimulus*. While it was originally neutral, when the bell was paired with the meat (an unconditioned stimulus), it eventually produced a response when presented alone. The last key concept is the *conditioned response*. This describes the behavior of the dog salivating in reaction to the bell alone.

Using these concepts, we can summarize classical conditioning. Essentially, learning a conditioned response involves building up an association between a conditioned stimulus and an unconditioned stimulus. Using the paired stimuli, one compelling and the other one neutral, the neutral one becomes a conditioned stimulus and, hence, takes on the properties of the unconditioned stimulus.

Classical conditioning can be used to explain why Christmas carols often bring back pleasant memories of childhood—the songs being associated with

[55] I. P. Pavlov, *The Work of the Digestive Glands*, trans. W. H. Thompson (London: Charles Griffin, 1902).

the festive Christmas spirit and initiating fond memories and feelings of euphoria. In an organizational setting, we can also see classical conditioning operating. For example, at one manufacturing plant, every time the top executives from the head office would make a visit, the plant management would clean up the administrative offices and wash the windows. This went on for years. Eventually, employees would turn on their best behavior and look prim and proper whenever the windows were cleaned—even in those occasional instances when the cleaning was not paired with the visit from the top brass. People had learned to associate the cleaning of the windows with the visit from the head office.

Classical conditioning is passive. Something happens and we react in a specific way. It is elicited in response to a specific, identifiable event. As such it can explain simple reflexive behaviors. But most behavior—particularly the complex behavior of individuals in organizations—is emitted rather than elicited. It is voluntary rather than reflexive. For example, employees choose to arrive at work on time, ask their boss for help with problems, or "goof off" when no one is watching. The learning of these behaviors is better understood by looking at operant conditioning.

Operant conditioning

A type of conditioning in which desired voluntary behavior leads to a reward or prevents a punishment.

Operant Conditioning   Operant conditioning argues that behavior is a function of its consequences. People learn to behave so they get something they want or avoid something they don't want. Operant behavior means voluntary or learned behavior in contrast to reflexive or unlearned behavior. The tendency to repeat such behavior is influenced as a result of the reinforcement or lack of reinforcement brought about by the consequences of the behavior. Reinforcement, therefore, strengthens a behavior and increases the likelihood that it will be repeated.

What Pavlov did for classical conditioning, noted Harvard psychologist B. F. Skinner has done for operant conditioning.[56] Building on earlier work in the field, Skinner's research has extensively expanded our knowledge of operant conditioning. Even his staunchest critics, who represent a sizable group, admit that his operant concepts work.

Behavior is assumed to be determined from without—that is, learned—rather than from within (reflexive or unlearned). Skinner argues that by creating pleasing consequences to follow specific forms of behavior, the frequency of that behavior will increase. People will most likely engage in desired behaviors if they are positively reinforced for doing so. Rewards, for example, are most effective if they immediately follow the desired response. Additionally, behavior that is not rewarded, or is punished, is less likely to be repeated.

You see illustrations of operant conditioning everywhere. For example, any situation in which it is either explicitly stated or implicitly suggested that reinforcements are contingent on some action on your part involves the use of operant learning. Your instructor says that if you want a high grade in the course you must supply correct answers on the test. A commissioned salesperson wanting to earn a sizable income finds that this is contingent on generating high sales in her territory. Of course, the linkage can also work to teach the individual to engage in behaviors that work against the best interests of the

[56] B. F. Skinner, *Contingencies of Reinforcement* (East Norwalk, CT: Appleton-Century-Crofts, 1971).

organization. Assume your boss tells you that if you will work overtime during the next three-week busy season, you will be compensated for it at the next performance appraisal. However, when performance appraisal time comes, you find that you are given no positive reinforcement for your overtime work. The next time your boss asks you to work overtime, what will you do? You will probably decline! Your behavior can be explained by operant conditioning: If a behavior fails to be positively reinforced, the probability that the behavior will be repeated declines.

Social Learning   Individuals can also learn by observing what happens to other people and just by being told about something, as well as by direct experiences. So, for example, much of what we have learned comes from watching models— parents, teachers, peers, motion picture and television performers, bosses, and so forth. This view that we can learn both through observation and direct experience has been called **social learning theory.**[57]

While social learning theory is an extension of operant conditioning, that is, it assumes that behavior is a function of consequences, it also acknowledges the existence of observational learning and the importance of perception in learning. People respond to how they perceive and define consequences, not to the objective consequences themselves.

The influence of models is central to the social learning viewpoint. Four processes have been found to determine the influence that a model will have on an individual. As we'll show later in this chapter, the inclusion of the following processes when management sets up employee training programs will significantly improve the likelihood that the programs will be successful:

1. *Attentional processes.* People only learn from a model when they recognize and pay attention to its critical features. We tend to be most influenced by models that are attractive, repeatedly available, and we think are important, or we see as similar to us.

2. *Retention processes.* A model's influence will depend on how well the individual remembers the model's action, even after the model is no longer readily available.

3. *Motor reproduction processes.* After a person has seen a new behavior by observing the model, the watching must be converted to doing. This process then demonstrates that the individual can perform the modeled activities.

4. *Reinforcement processes.* Individuals will be motivated to exhibit the modeled behavior if positive incentives or rewards are provided. Behaviors that are reinforced will be given more attention, learned better, and performed more often.

Social learning theory

People can learn through observation and direct experience.

Shaping: A Managerial Tool

Because learning takes place on the job as well as prior to it, managers will be concerned with how they can teach employees to behave in ways that

[57] A. Bandura, *Social Learning Theory* (Englewood Cliffs, NJ: Prentice Hall, 1977).

Shaping behavior

Systematically reinforcing each successive step that moves an individual closer to the desired response.

most benefit the organization. When we attempt to mold individuals by guiding their learning in graduated steps, we are **shaping behavior**.

Consider the situation in which an employee's behavior is significantly different from that sought by management. If management only reinforced the individual when he or she showed desirable responses, there might be very little reinforcement taking place. In such a case, shaping offers a logical approach toward achieving the desired behavior.

We *shape* behavior by systematically reinforcing each successive step that moves the individual closer to the desired response. If an employee who has been chronically a half-hour late for work comes in only twenty minutes late, we can reinforce this improvement. Reinforcement would increase as responses more closely approximate the desired behavior.

Methods of Shaping Behavior There are four ways in which to shape behavior: through positive reinforcement, negative reinforcement, punishment, or extinction. When a response is followed with something pleasant, it is called *positive reinforcement*. This would describe, for instance, the boss who praises an employee for a job well done. When a response is followed by the termination or withdrawal of something unpleasant, it is called *negative reinforcement*. If your college instructor asks a question and you don't know the answer, looking through your lecture notes is likely to preclude your being called on. This is a negative reinforcement because you have learned that looking busily through your notes terminates being called on by the instructor. *Punishment* is causing an unpleasant condition in an attempt to eliminate an undesirable behavior. An employee who receives a two-day suspension from work, without pay, for showing up drunk is an example of punishment. Eliminating any reinforcement that is maintaining a behavior is called *extinction*. When the behavior is not reinforced, it tends to gradually be extinguished. College instructors who wish to discourage students from asking questions in class can eliminate this behavior in their students by ignoring those who raise their hands to ask questions. Hand-raising will become extinct when it is invariably met with an absence of reinforcement.

Both positive and negative reinforcement result in learning. They strengthen a desired response and increase the probability of repetition. In the preceding illustrations, praise strengthens and increases the behavior of doing a good job because praise is desired. The behavior of "looking busy" is similarly strengthened and increased by its terminating the undesirable consequence of being called on by the teacher. Both punishment and extinction, however, weaken behavior and tend to decrease its subsequent frequency.

Reinforcement, whether it is positive or negative, has an impressive record as a shaping tool. Our interest, therefore, is in reinforcement rather than punishment or extinction. A review of research findings on the impact of reinforcement upon behavior in organizations concluded that

1. Some type of reinforcement is necessary to produce a change in behavior.

2. Some types of rewards are more effective for use in organizations than others.

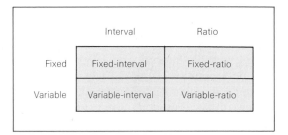

	Interval	Ratio
Fixed	Fixed-interval	Fixed-ratio
Variable	Variable-interval	Variable-ratio

FIGURE 3–5
Schedules of Reinforcement

3. The speed with which learning takes place and the lasting of its effects will be determined by the timing of reinforcement.[58]

Point 3 is extremely important and deserves considerable elaboration.

Schedules of Reinforcement The two major types of reinforcement schedules are *continuous* and *intermittent*. A **continuous** schedule reinforces the desired behavior each and every time it is demonstrated. For example, in the case of someone who has historically had trouble being at work on time, every time he is *not* tardy his manager might compliment him on his desirable behavior. In an intermittent schedule, on the other hand, not every instance of the desirable behavior is reinforced, but reinforcement is given often enough to make the behavior worth repeating. This latter schedule can be compared to the workings of a gambling slot machine, which people will continue to play even when they know that it is adjusted to give a considerable return to the gambling house. The intermittent payoffs occur just often enough to reinforce the behavior of slipping in quarters and pulling the handle. Evidence indicates that the intermittent or varied form of reinforcement tends to promote more resistance to extinction than does the continuous form.[59]

An **intermittent reinforcement** can be of a ratio or interval type. Ratio schedules depend upon how many responses the subject makes. The individual is reinforced after giving a certain number of specific types of behavior. Interval schedules depend upon how much time has passed since the last reinforcement. With interval schedules, the individual is reinforced on the first appropriate behavior after a particular time has elapsed. A reinforcement can also be classified as fixed or variable. Intermittent techniques for administering rewards can, therefore, be placed into four categories, as shown in Figure 3–5.

When rewards are spaced at uniform time intervals, the reinforcement schedule is of the **fixed-interval** type. The critical variable is time, and it is held constant. This is the predominant schedule for almost all salaried workers in North America. When you get your paycheck on a weekly, semi-monthly,

Continuous reinforcement

A desired behavior is reinforced each and every time it is demonstrated.

Intermittent reinforcement

A desired behavior is reinforced often enough to make the behavior worth repeating, but not every time it is demonstrated.

Fixed-interval schedule

Rewards are spaced at uniform time intervals.

[58] T. W. Costello and S. S. Zalkind, *Psychology in Administration* (Englewood Cliffs, NJ: Prentice Hall, 1963), p. 193.

[59] F. Luthans and R. Kreitner, *Organizational Behavior Modification and Beyond*, 2nd ed. (Glenview, IL: Scott, Foresman, 1985).

monthly, or other predetermined time basis, you are rewarded on a fixed-interval reinforcement schedule.

If rewards are distributed in time so that reinforcements are unpredictable, the schedule is of the **variable-interval** type. When an instructor advises her class that there will be a number of pop quizzes given during the term (the exact number of which is unknown to the students), and the quizzes will account for 20 percent of the term grade, she is using such a variable-interval schedule. Similarly, a series of randomly timed unannounced visits to a company office by the corporate audit staff is an example of a variable-interval schedule.

In a **fixed-ratio** schedule, after a fixed or constant number of responses are given, a reward is initiated. For example, a piece-rate incentive plan is a fixed-ratio schedule—the employee receives a reward based on the number of work pieces generated. If the piece rate for a zipper installer in a dressmaking factory is $5.00 a dozen, the reinforcement (money in this case) is fixed to the number of zippers sewn into garments. After every dozen is sewn in, the installer has earned another $5.00.

When the reward varies relative to the behavior of the individual, he or she is said to be reinforced on a **variable-ratio** schedule. Salespeople on commission represent examples of individuals on such a reinforcement schedule. On some occasions, they may make a sale after only two calls on potential customers. On other occasions, they might need to make twenty or more calls to secure a sale. The reward, then, is variable in relation to the number of successful calls the salesperson makes.

Reinforcement Schedules and Behavior Continuous reinforcement schedules can lead to early satiation, and, under this schedule, behavior tends to weaken rapidly when reinforcers are withheld. However, continuous reinforcers are appropriate for newly emitted, unstable, or low-frequency responses. In contrast, intermittent reinforcers preclude early satiation because they don't follow every response. They are appropriate for stable or high-frequency responses.

In general, variable schedules tend to lead to higher performance than fixed schedules. For example, as noted previously, most employees in organizations are paid on fixed-interval schedules. But such a schedule does not clearly link performance and rewards. The reward is given for time spent on the job rather than for a specific response (performance). In contrast, variable-interval schedules generate high rates of response and more stable and consistent behavior because of a high correlation between performance and reward and because of the uncertainty involved—the employee tends to be more alert since there is a surprise factor.

Some Specific Organizational Applications

We have alluded to a number of situations where learning theory could be helpful to managers. In this section, we will briefly look at five specific applications: reducing absenteeism through the use of lotteries, substituting well pay for sick pay, disciplining problem employees, developing effective employee training programs, and creating mentoring programs for new employees.

Variable-interval schedule

Rewards are distributed in time so that reinforcements are unpredictable.

Fixed-ratio schedule

Rewards are initiated after a fixed or constant number of responses.

Variable-ratio schedule

The reward varies relative to the behavior of the individual.

How Lufkin Industries Saved $805,000

Lufkin Industries is a Texas-based manufacturing company that has annual sales of approximately $215 million.[60] Up to 1985, absenteeism was relatively stable, an average of 5 to 7 percent. However, during 1985 absenteeism doubled to approximately 13 to 14 percent. Personnel records indicated that on an average day in 1985, 255 production workers were not on the job. The annual cost of this absenteeism to Lufkin was in excess of $3.2 million.

Lufkin's management had a problem. The company's absentee policy—with written warnings after two unexcused absences, a three day lay-off after the fourth, and possible termination after the sixth incident—had been unchanged for years but seemed not to be working any longer. So management tried a different approach—it would encourage attendance rather than discourage absenteeism. A certificate good for a book of trading stamps was awarded to every employee who had perfect attendance or no unexcused absences for the prior month. And the reward was cumulative—two months of perfect attendance resulted in two books of stamps—up to six books for six months. For months six to twelve, perfect attendance was rewarded with six books a month. An employee with a perfect attendance record in any calendar year could receive up to fifty-seven books of stamps, with a bonus of twenty-five books for going twelve months without a blemish. Of course, even one unexcused absence automatically meant that the employee had to start all over again. To make attendance even more attractive, Lufkin made every production employee with a perfect record for six or more months eligible for a bonus drawing that included color televisions, a boat, and a pick-up truck.

The reward program proved to be effective. Absenteeism among production workers during 1986 dropped 25 percent, or 191 absences per day. Lufkin calculated its savings in labor costs—after factoring in the costs of trading stamps, prizes, and administrative costs—as totalling $805,000.

Using Lotteries to Reduce Absenteeism Management can design programs to reduce absenteeism by utilizing learning theory. For example, one firm created a poker game lottery for part of its organization whereby employees who came to work on time got to choose a card from a deck of playing cards.[61] At the end of the five-day week, the employee whose five cards made up the highest poker hand won $20. Obviously, anyone who was late or absent didn't get a card and couldn't participate in that week's lottery. Eight departments

[60] J. Long and J. G. Ormsby, "Stamp Out Absenteeism," *Personnel Journal*, November 1987, pp. 94–96.

[61] E. Pedalino and V. U. Gamboa, "Behavior Modification and Absenteeism: Intervention in One Industrial Setting," *Journal of Applied Psychology*, December 1974, pp. 694–98.

were chosen to participate in the lottery experiment, and a $20 prize was given to the best poker hand in each department. Several other sections within the organization were used as control groups—their attendance was monitored, but no lottery was implemented.

The poker game lottery followed a variable-ratio schedule. Prompt attendance increased an employee's probability of winning, yet just because an employee obtained five cards was no assurance that he or she would be reinforced by winning the $20. Consistent with the research on reinforcement schedules, this lottery resulted in lower absence rates. Over a four-month period, attendance among employees who participated in the lottery improved by 18 percent, while the attendance rate for employees in the control group actually decreased a little.

Well Pay vs. Sick Pay   Most organizations provide their salaried employees with paid sick leave as part of the employee's fringe benefit program. But ironically, organizations with paid sick leave programs experience almost twice the absenteeism of organizations without such a program.[62] The reality is that sick leave reinforces the wrong behavior—absence from work. Organizations should have programs that encourage employees to be on the job by discouraging unnecessary absences. When an employee receives ten paid sick days a year, it is the unusual employee who doesn't make sure that all his or her days are consumed, regardless of whether he or she is sick or not. This suggests that organizations should reward attendance, not absence. As a case in point, one Midwest organization implemented a well-pay program that paid a bonus to employees who had no absence for any given four-week period and then only paid for sick leave after the first eight hours of absence.[63] Evaluation of the well-program found that it produced increased savings to the organization, reduced absenteeism, increased productivity, and improved employee satisfaction.

Employee Discipline   Every manager will, at some time, be faced with having to deal with an employee who drinks on the job, is insubordinate, steals company property, arrives consistently late for work, or engages in similar problem behaviors. Managers will respond with disciplinary actions such as verbal warnings, oral reprimands, or temporary suspensions. Research on discipline shows that the manager should act immediately to correct the problem, match the severity of the punishment to the severity of the "crime," and ensure that the employee sees the link between the punishment and the undesirable behavior.[64] But, in addition, our knowledge about punishment's effect on behavior indicates that the use of discipline carries costs. It may provide only a short-term solution and result in serious side effects.

Disciplining employees for undesirable behaviors only tells them what

[62] D. Willings, "The Absentee Worker," *Personnel and Training Management*, December 1968, pp. 10–12.

[63] B. H. Harvey, J. F. Rogers, and J. A. Schultz, "Sick Pay vs. Well Pay: An Analysis of the Impact of Rewarding Employees for Being on the Job," *Public Personnel Management Journal*, Summer 1983, pp. 218–24.

[64] J. A. Belohlav, *The Art of Disciplining Your Employees* (Englewood Cliffs, NJ: Prentice Hall, 1985).

not to do. It doesn't tell them what alternative behaviors are preferred. The result is that this form of punishment frequently leads to only short-term suppression of the undesirable behavior rather than its elimination. Continued use of punishment, rather than positive reinforcement, also tends to produce a conditional fear of the manager. As the punishing agent, the manager becomes associated in the employee's mind with adverse consequences. Employees respond by "hiding" from their boss. Hence, the use of punishment can undermine manager-employee relations.

The popularity of discipline undoubtedly lies in its ability to produce fast results in the short run. Managers are reinforced for using discipline because it produces an immediate change in the employee's behavior. But over the long run, when used without positive reinforcement of desirable behaviors, it is likely to lead to employee frustration, fear of the manager, reoccurrences of the problem behaviors, and increases in absenteeism and turnover.

Developing Training Programs   Most large organizations are actively involved with employee training. Can these organizations draw from our discussion of learning in order to improve the effectiveness of their training programs? Certainly.

Social learning theory offers such a guide. It tells us that training should provide a model; it needs to grab the trainee's attention; provide motivational properties; help the trainee to file away what he or she has learned for later use; provide opportunities to practice new behaviors; offer positive rewards for accomplishments; and if the training has taken place off the job, allow the trainee some opportunity to transfer what he or she has learned to the job.

Creating Mentoring Programs   It's the unusual senior manager who, early in his or her career, didn't have an older, more experienced mentor higher up in the organization. This mentor took the protégé under his or her wing and provided advice and guidance on how to survive and get ahead in the organization. Mentoring, of course, is not limited to the managerial ranks. Union apprenticeship programs, for example, do the same thing for preparing individuals to move from unskilled apprentice status to that of skilled journeyman. A young electrician apprentice typically works under an experienced electrician for several years to develop the full range of skills necessary to effectively execute his or her job.

A successful mentoring program will be built on modeling concepts from social learning theory. That is, a mentor's impact comes from more than merely what he or she explicitly tells a protégé. Mentors are role models. Protégés learn to convey the attitudes and behaviors that the organization wants by emulating the traits and actions of their mentors. They observe and then imitate. Top managers who are concerned with developing employees who will fit into the organization and in preparing young managerial talent for greater responsibilities should give careful attention to who takes on mentoring roles. The creating of formal mentoring programs—where young individuals are officially assigned a mentor—allows senior executives to manage the process and increases the likelihood that protégés will be molded the way top management desires.

Let's try to summarize what we've found in terms of what impact biographical characteristics, ability, personality, and learning have on an employee's performance and satisfaction.

Biographical Characteristics

Biographical characteristics are readily available to management. For the most part, they represent data that are contained in almost every employee's personnel file.

A review of the research allows some noteworthy conclusions. First, it is difficult to make accurate predictions about an employee's productivity based on biographical data. Perhaps the strongest statement we can make is that the belief that productivity declines with employee age is a myth. Older workers are actually likely to be more productive than their younger colleagues. However, absence rates, turnover, and job satisfaction *are* influenced by several biographical characteristics.

The strongest evidence supports an employee's age and seniority in the organization. Older workers are less likely to resign and tend to be more satisfied with their jobs. Similarly, tenure is negatively related to both absence and turnover; that is, employees with longer service have better attendance records and are less likely to quit. Moreover, the longer an employee held his or her previous job, the less likely he or she is to quit his or her current job.

Investigation of two other variables—sex and marital status—also produced significant findings. Women demonstrate poorer attendance records than do men. However, this statistic is undoubtedly dated. It tends to reflect the historical role of women in our culture. As more women work and pursue long-term careers in organizations, any difference between males and females in terms of absenteeism will undoubtedly disappear. Finally, the evidence indicates that married employees show greater stability and higher satisfaction than do their single counterparts.

Ability

Ability directly influences an employee's level of performance and satisfaction through the ability-job fit. Given management's desire to get a compatible fit, what can be done?

First, an effective selection process will improve the fit. A job analysis will provide information about jobs currently being done and the abilities that individuals need to perform the jobs adequately. Applicants can then be tested, interviewed, and evaluated as to the degree to which they possess the necessary abilities. Second, promotion and transfer decisions affecting individuals already in the organization's employment should reflect the abilities of candidates. As with new employees, care should be taken to assess critical abilities that incumbents will need in the job and matching those requirements with the organization's human resources. Third, the fit can be improved by fine-tuning the job to better match an incumbent's abilities. Often modifications can be made in the job that, while not having a significant impact on the job's basic activities, better adapts it to the specific talents of a given employee. Examples of this might include changing some of the equipment used or reorganizing tasks within a group of employees. A final alternative is to provide training for employees. This is applicable to both new workers and present job incumbents. For the latter, training can keep their abilities current or provide new skills as times and conditions change.

Personality

A review of the personality literature offers general guidelines that can lead to effective job performance. As such, it can improve hiring, transfer, and promotion decisions. Because personality characteristics create the parameters for people's behavior, they give us a framework for predicting behavior. For example, individuals who are shy, introverted, and uncomfortable in social situations would probably be illsuited as salespeople. Individuals who are submissive and conforming might not be effective as advertising "idea" people.

Can we predict which people will be high performers in sales, research, or assembly-line work based on their personality characteristics alone? The answer is: No. But a knowledge of an individual's personality can aid in reducing mismatches which, in turn, can lead to reduced turnover and higher job satisfaction.

We can look at certain personality characteristics that tend to be related to job success, test for these traits, and use these data to make selection more effective. A person who accepts rules, conformity, and dependence and rates high on authoritarianism is likely to feel more comfortable in a structured assembly-line job, as an admittance clerk in a hospital, or as an administrator in a large public agency than as a researcher or an employee whose job requires a high degree of creativity. Such selection matching is likely to lead to lower turnover rates.

There is strong evidence linking personality traits and job satisfaction. Individuals who, as adolescents, possess generally positive personality characteristics—they're cheerful, likable, giving—tend to be content with their jobs later in life.[65] This suggests that satisfaction may lie more in the person than in the characteristics of his or her job or the work environment, and reaffirms the value of personality tests as possible potent predictors of an applicant's later job satisfaction.

Learning

Any observable change in behavior is, by definition, prima facie evidence that learning has taken place. What we want to do, of course, is ascertain if learning concepts provide us with any insights that would allow us to explain and predict

---

[65] B. M. Staw, N. E. Bell, and J. A. Clausen, "The Dispositional Approach to Job Attitudes: A Lifetime Longitudinal Test," *Administrative Science Quarterly*, March 1986, pp. 56–77.

behavior. The evidence suggests that conditioning and shaping offer important tools for explaining levels of productivity, absenteeism rates, lateness, and the quality of employees' work. These concepts also can be valuable for giving insight into how undesirable work behaviors can be modified.

Positive reinforcement is a powerful tool for modifying behavior. By identifying and rewarding performance-related behaviors, management increases the likelihood that they will be repeated.

Our knowledge about learning further suggests that reinforcement is a more effective tool than punishment. Punished behavior tends to be only temporarily suppressed rather than permanently changed, and the recipients of punishment tend to become resentful of the punisher. Although punishment eliminates undesired behavior more quickly than negative reinforcement does, its effect is only temporary and it may later produce unpleasant side effects such as lower morale and higher absenteeism or turnover. Managers, therefore, are advised to use reinforcement rather than punishment.

POINT

MANAGEMENT IS WARY OF IQ TESTS

In the post-war period of the 1940s and 1950s, IQ tests were a popular means by which organizations identified and selected high performing workers. Today, few organizations use such general intelligence tests as measures of ability. The general argument is that these tests are not valid. That is, there is little relationship between performance scores on these tests and later job performance. Let's look at reasons managers might give for not using general intelligence tests as a selection tool.

IQ tests are racially and socioeconomically biased. The most popular IQ tests are designed for and validated against a white, middle-class population. Because the cultural experiences of minorities and the poor are typically different than those of this group, what is perceived to be a "right" answer has little to do with one's cognitive skills and a lot to do with what one reads (or doesn't read), family values, experiences shared with friends, and the like.

Test scores measure only test-taking skills. Some people are good at taking tests and others aren't. Unfortunately, test-taking skills and job performance are very different. Everyone knows someone who got high grades in school but never succeeded in the "real world." Their greatest claim to fame in school was that they knew how to take tests. And who doesn't know of someone else who was notorious for "choking" on tests? Everyone knew he or she was smart but suffered high test-anxiety.

High intelligence isn't necessary in a great many jobs. High intelligence may be necessary for complex jobs like physician, attorney, or research scientist, but many jobs are simple and routine. Performance on those latter jobs doesn't require a great deal of intelligence.

So while some basic, minimal level of intelligence may be necessary to perform a job well, high intelligence is relevant for only a small segment of jobs. If IQ tests have any value, therefore, it would be only to identify individuals with very low scores.

Job performance is based far more on motivation than intelligence. High performing employees stand out more for their willingness to work hard than for their intelligence. A high level of motivation can overcome inadequacies in mental abilities.

Differences in job performance depend more on training than intelligence. Organizations spend billions of dollars every year in training employees. Competent training can overcome weaknesses in intelligence. Similarly, the bright but poorly trained employee is likely to underperform his or her well-trained counterpart.

Even the experts disagree. Few areas of management and organizational practices are more controversial than the validity of intelligence tests as a selection device. Even the experts can't agree on key issues surrounding IQ tests. For example, a survey of over 600 professional psychologists published by the *American Psychologist* in February 1987 revealed the extent of these differences. When asked whether there was a consensus on the basic definition of "intelligence," 53 percent agreed, while 40 percent disagreed. More than half of the respondents believed that IQ tests didn't adequately measure important elements of intelligence such as adaptation to one's environment, creativity, goal-directedness, and achievement motivation. Further, these experts disagreed on the degree to which IQ test results suffer from racial, economic, and test-taker anxiety biases.

COUNTERPOINT

IQ TESTS ARE THE SINGLE BEST PREDICTOR OF WORKER PRODUCTIVITY

The validity of IQ tests is an emotionally-packed issue. A few well-substantiated results regarding these tests can illustrate why. The average gap in IQ scores between black and white Americans is fifteen points, while Japanese, Chinese, and Korean scores are between four and nine points higher than those of white Americans. Women have less variability than men on IQ scores, which results in men outnumbering women by a ratio of 7 to 5 at 140 IQ and above. If this were not incendiary enough, the evidence demonstrates that hereditary factors account for at least 60 percent of the variability in IQ and may explain up to 80 percent of differences. Moreover, like it or not, we should know that the following facts are well supported by research findings: Not all people are equally intelligent; general intelligence represents real and fundamental differences in how well individuals perform cognitive tasks; and the evidence demonstrates a high correlation between cognitive ability and performance on *all* jobs. The observable hierarchy in occupational status in North America is, in essence, an intelligence hierarchy. Only about 10 to 20 percent of the population has the intelligence to perform minimally as a doctor, but about 80 percent could make it as a licensed practical nurse. A 1988 survey of 120 corporate chief executive officers, reported in the *Wall Street Journal*, found that these executives averaged 121 on an intelligence test. That would place them, as a group, among the top 4 percent of the population.

A review of the massive evidence from hundreds of studies on intelligence shows unquestionably that general cognitive ability predicts performance on all jobs, including the so-called "manual" jobs as well as "mental" jobs. The path, too, is fairly straightforward. The correlation between general cognitive ability and job knowledge is 0.80. Similarly, job knowledge is correlated 0.80 with job performance as measured by objective work sample performance. So general cognitive ability predicts job performance in large part because it predicts learning and job mastery. Ability is highly correlated with job knowledge, and job knowledge is highly correlated with job performance. At the aggregate level, cognitive ability predicts performance with a correlation of 0.75. No other predictor is currently known to have similar validity. This means that tests of general cognitive ability (which is essentially what IQ tests are) are the single best predictor of worker productivity. They are better than tests that seek to measure specific job skills or motivation.

Why does cognitive ability correlate with performance in all jobs? One answer is that even simple jobs require far more learning than is evident to outsiders. Planning, judgment, and memory—all major cognitive processes—are used in day-to-day performance on all jobs. Since learning the job is the key to job performance, and general cognitive ability predicts learning, it is to be expected that general cognitive ability will be the key predictor of job performance. High ability workers are faster at cognitive operations on the job, are better able to prioritize between conflicting rules, are better able to adapt old procedures to altered situations, are better able to innovate to meet unexpected problems, and are better able to learn new procedures quickly as the job changes over time.

The evidence in this argument is drawn from J. E. Hunter, "Cognitive Ability, Cognitive Aptitudes, Job Knowledge, and Job Performance," *Journal of Vocational Behavior*, December 1986, pp. 340–62; L. S. Gottfredson, "Societal Consequences of the g Factor in Employment," *Journal of Vocational Behavior*, December 1986, pp. 379–410; and S. Itzkoff, *Why Humans Vary in Intelligence* (New York: Paideia, 1987).

KEY TERMS

Ability

Authoritarianism

Biographical Characteristics

Classical Conditioning

Continuous Reinforcement

Externals

Fixed-Interval Schedule

Fixed-Ratio Schedule

Intellectual Ability

Intermittent Reinforcement

Internals

Learning

Locus of Control

Machiavellianism

nAch

Operant Conditioning

Personality

Personality Traits

Physical Ability

Shaping Behavior

Social Learning Theory

Variable-Interval Schedule

Variable-Ratio Schedule

FOR DISCUSSION

1. Which biographical characteristics best predict *productivity*? *Absenteeism*? *Turnover*? *Satisfaction*?

2. Describe the specific steps you would take to ensure that an individual has the appropriate abilities to satisfactorily do a given job.

3. How does *heredity* influence personality? Environment? The situation?

4. What constrains the ability of personality traits to predict behavior?

5. What behavioral predictions might you make if you knew that an employee had (a) an external locus of control? (b) a high *nAch*? (c) a low Mach score?

6. "The type of job an employee does moderates the relationship between personality and job productivity." Do you agree or disagree with this statement? Discuss.

7. One day your boss comes in and he's nervous, edgy, and argumentative. The next day he is calm and relaxed. Does this suggest that personality traits aren't consistent from day to day?

8. "Everyone is a trait theorist. If one really believed that situations determined behavior, then there would be no reason to test or interview prospective employees for jobs—it would only be necessary to structure the situation properly." Do you agree or disagree? Discuss.

9. Contrast classical conditioning, operant conditioning, and social learning.

10. "Managers should never use discipline with a problem employee." Do you agree or disagree? Discuss.

11. Learning theory can be used to *explain* behavior and to *control* behavior. Can you distinguish between the two objectives? Can you give any ethical or moral arguments why managers should not seek control over others' behavior? How valid do you think these arguments are?

12. What have you learned about "learning" that could help you to explain the behavior of students in a classroom if (a) the instructor gives only one test—a final examination at the end of the course? (b) the instructor gives four exams during the term, all of which are announced on the first day of class? (c) the student's grade is based on the results of numerous exams, none of which are announced by the instructor ahead of time?

FOR FURTHER READING

BRUSH, D. H., M. K. MOCH, and A. POOYAN, "Individual Differences and Job Satisfaction," *Journal of Occupational Behaviour*, April 1987, pp. 139–55. A review of studies covering over 10,000 employees found a significant correlation between two demographic factors—age and organizational tenure—and job satisfaction.

JACKSON, D. N., A. C. PEACOCK, and J. P. SMITH, "Impressions of Personality in the Employment Interview," *Journal of Personality and Social Psychology*, August 1980, pp. 294–307. Reports on a research study that supports the importance of congruence of personality to the job in ratings of suitability and expected performance.

O'HARA, K., C. M. JOHNSON, and T. A. BEEHR, "Organizational Behavior Management in the Private Sector: A Review of Empirical Research and Recommendations for Further Investigation," *Academy of Management Review*, October 1985, pp. 848–64. Reviews the results of studies that have investigated the impact of operant conditioning techniques on organizational behavior.

LUTHANS, F., and R. KREITNER, *Organizational Behavior Modification and Beyond*, 2nd ed. Glenview, IL: Scott, Foresman, 1985. Offers an excellent review of how learning theories can be used by managers.

RORER, L. G., and T. A. WIDIGER, "Personality Structure and Assessment," in M. R. Rosenzweig and L. W. Porter (eds.), *Annual Review of Psychology*, Vol. 34, pp. 431–63. Palo Alto, CA: Annual Reviews, 1983. Reviews recent research on personality.

WEISS, H. M., and S. ADLER, "Personality and Organizational Behavior," in B. M. Staw and L. L. Cummings (eds.), *Research in Organizational Behavior*, Vol. 6, pp. 1–50. Greenwich, CT: JAI Press, 1984. Argues for the positive value that the study of personality provides to an understanding of individual behavior in organizations.

Instructions: Read the following statements and indicate whether you agree more with choice A or choice B.

A	B	
1. Making a lot of money is largely a matter of getting the right breaks.	1. Promotions are earned through hard work and persistence.	_____
2. I have noticed that there is usually a direct connection between how hard I study and the grades I get.	2. Many times the reactions of teachers seem haphazard to me.	_____
3. The number of divorces indicates that more and more people are not trying to make their marriages work.	3. Marriage is largely a gamble.	_____
4. It is silly to think that one can really change another person's basic attitudes.	4. When I am right I can convince others.	_____
5. Getting promoted is really a matter of being a little luckier than the next person.	5. In our society a person's future earning power is dependent upon his or her ability.	_____
6. If one knows how to deal with people they are really quite easily led.	6. I have little influence over the way other people behave.	_____
7. The grades I make are the result of my own efforts; luck has little or nothing to do with it.	7. Sometimes I feel that I have little to do with the grades I get.	_____
8. People like me can change the course of world affairs if we make ourselves heard.	8. It is only wishful thinking to believe that one can readily influence what happens in our society at large.	_____
9. A great deal that happens to me is probably a matter of chance.	9. I am the master of my fate.	_____
10. Getting along with people is a skill that must be practiced.	10. It is almost impossible to figure out how to please some people.	_____

Turn to page 561 for scoring directions and key.

Source: Adapted from Julian B. Rotter, "External Control and Internal Control," *Psychology Today*, June 1971, p. 42. Copyright 1971 by the American Psychological Association. Adapted with permission.

CASE INCIDENT 3

IS THERE AN ACCOUNTING PERSONALITY?

Dana Maher was in the last semester of her senior year at California State University. Mindful that her father was planning to discontinue her $600-a-month allowance upon her graduation, and that she did like to eat regularly, Dana began to search for a full-time job.

The market for accounting majors, such as Dana, seemed favorable. A number of companies were visiting the university's placement center and were looking for young graduates like Dana. She signed up for campus interviews, sent out a couple of dozen résumés to major companies, and began spreading the word through friends and relatives that she was soon to be "available."

Dana's friends had frequently teased her about her choice of an accounting major. The standard line was, "Dana, you just don't strike me as an accountant." Dana seemed different from most of her peers. She was extremely outgoing, talkative, and always in motion. She was active in her sorority and had at least two hundred "best" friends. Her mother frequently described her as having the "metabolism of a hummingbird." Her friends stereotyped her as being in a sales or personnel job rather than sitting quietly in some isolated office preparing accounting reports.

About six weeks prior to graduation, the job offers began to crystallize. Dana narrowed her choices to a trainee position with a San Francisco mortgage broker, and a staff accounting job in Los Angeles with a prestigious national hotel chain. She accepted the accounting position, excited about the opportunity to work in the hotel business.

After six months on the job, Dana looked back on her experience. "I really enjoy my job. I spent the first six weeks in a general training program doing all kinds of different activities. I worked in the kitchen, in housekeeping, behind the check-in desk, and as a night auditor. Then I settled into the controller's office as a general accountant. I'm involved with accounts payable, preparing monthly financial statements, and doing special projects as they're needed. I think I'm doing a good job; at least everything Jim [her boss] has told me is positive. Yet I can't ignore the constant comments by the people I work with in accounting, and some of my friends in other areas of the hotel, that I'd be happier and have better career opportunities if I was in marketing or operations. They say I'm too outgoing for being an accountant. I think that's nonsense! Sure, I'd be interested in getting into operations. It would be a real challenge to someday be running my own hotel. But the job vacancy was in accounting and that's what I studied in school."

QUESTIONS

1. Using the six personality types model, is there any discrepancy between Dana's personality and her job?
2. Is there such a thing as an "accounting personality" or a "marketing personality"?
3. Can you relate this case to learning theory?
4. If you had been Jim, would you have hired Dana? Support your position.

4

Perception and Individual Decision Making

■ *Learning objectives*

Distinguish between perception and reality in determining behavior

Explain how two people can see the same thing and interpret it differently

List the three determinants of attribution

Describe how shortcuts can assist in or distort our judgment of others

Explain how perception affects the decision process

Outline the six steps in the optimizing decision model

List the assumptions of the optimizing model

Explain how individuals satisfice

Describe the decision confirmation process

First umpire: "Some's balls and some's strikes and I calls 'em as they is."
Second umpire: "Some's balls and some's strikes and I calls 'em as I sees 'em."
Third umpire: "Some's balls and some's strikes but they ain't nothin' till I calls 'em."

—— H. CANTRIL

The way we see the outside world need not be the same as the world really is. We tend to see the world as we want to perceive it. For supporting evidence, we need go no farther than the perception of how effective a college instructor is in the classroom. It is not unusual for an instructor to be rated "excellent" by some students and "unsatisfactory" by other students in the same class. The instructor's teaching behavior, of course, is a constant. Even though all the students see the same instructor, they perceive his or her effectiveness differently. This illustration confirms that we do not see reality; rather, we interpret what we see and call it reality.

When distortions are low—for example, when you and I both agree that the bank robbery we just witnessed was carried out by a Caucasian male, approximately five feet, ten inches tall, 170 pounds, with dark brown hair, and wearing jeans and a light blue nylon jacket with a white patch on the right shoulder—it means that we not only saw the same thing but that our base of interpretation was similar.

A frequently cited case of how perceptions distort reality derives from a study conducted with representatives from both management and labor.[1] Each group was given a photograph of an ordinary-looking man and was asked to describe the individual in the photograph using a long list of personality characteristics. The only difference was that for half the cases the man in the photograph was labeled a plant manager and for the other half he was described as a union official. The results confirmed that impressions were radically different and depended on whether the man in the photograph was seen as "union" or "management" and, of course, whether the evaluator represented "union" or "management." Management and labor representatives formed significantly different impressions, each viewing the other as less dependable, and more intolerant of diverse points of view than members of their own group. Apparently, perception is like beauty, in that it lies "in the eye of the beholder."

[1] M. Haire, "Role Perceptions in Labor-Management Relations: An Experimental Approach," *Industrial and Labor Relations Review*, January 1955, pp. 204–16.

Perception can be defined as a process by which individuals organize and interpret their sensory impressions in order to give meaning to their environment. However, as we have noted, what one perceives can be substantially different from objective reality. It need not be, but there is often disagreement. For example, it is possible that all employees in a firm may view it as a great place to work—favorable working conditions, interesting job assignments, good pay, an understanding and responsible management—but, as most of us know, it is very unusual to find such circumstances.

Why is perception important in the study of OB? Simply, because people's behavior is based on their perception of what reality is, not reality itself. The world as it is perceived is the world that is behaviorally important.

Perception

A process by which individuals organize and interpret their sensory impressions in order to give meaning to their environment.

How do we explain that individuals may look at the same thing, yet perceive it differently? A number of factors operate to shape and sometimes distort perception. These factors can reside in the *perceiver*, in the object or *target* being perceived, or in the context of the *situation* in which the perception is made.

The Perceiver

When an individual looks at a target and attempts to interpret what he or she sees, that interpretation is heavily influenced by personal characteristics of the individual perceiver. Have you ever bought a new car and then suddenly noticed a large number of cars like yours on the road? It's unlikely that the number of such cars suddenly expanded. Rather, your own purchase has influenced your perception so that you are now more likely to notice them. This is an example of how factors related to the perceiver influence what he or she perceives. Among the more relevant personal characteristics affecting perception are attitudes, motives, interests, past experience, and expectations.

Sandy likes small classes because she enjoys asking a lot of questions of her teachers. Scott, on the other hand, prefers large lectures. He rarely asks questions and likes the anonymity that goes with being lost in a sea of bodies. On the first day of classes this term, Sandy and Scott find themselves walking into the university auditorium for their introductory course in psychology. They both recognize that they will be among some eight hundred students in this class. But given the different attitudes held by Sandy and Scott, it shouldn't surprise you to find that they interpret what they see differently. Sandy sulks, while Scott's smile does little to hide his relief in being able to blend unnoticed into the large auditorium. They both see the same thing, but they interpret it differently. A major reason is that they hold divergent *attitudes* concerning large classes.

Unsatisfied needs or *motives* stimulate individuals and may exert a strong influence on their perceptions. This was dramatically demonstrated in research on hunger.[2] Individuals in the study had not eaten for varying numbers of hours. Some had eaten an hour earlier, while others had gone as long as sixteen hours without food. These subjects were shown blurred pictures, and the results indicated that the extent of hunger influenced the interpretation of the blurred pictures. Those who had not eaten for sixteen hours perceived the blurred images as pictures of food far more frequently than did those subjects who had eaten only a short time earlier.

This same phenomenon has application in an organizational context as well. It would not be surprising, for example, to find that a boss who is insecure perceives a subordinate's efforts to do an outstanding job as a threat to his or her own position. Personal insecurity can be transferred into the perception that others are out to "get your job," regardless of the intention of the subordinates. Likewise, people who are devious are prone to see others in the same context.

It should not surprise you that a plastic surgeon is more likely to notice an imperfect nose than is a plumber. The supervisor who has just been reprimanded by her boss for the high level of lateness among her staff is more likely to notice lateness by an employee tomorrow than she was last week. If you are preoccupied with a personal problem, you may find it hard to be attentive in class. These examples illustrate that the focus of our attention appears to be influenced by our *interests*. Because our individual interests differ considerably, what one person notices in a situation can differ from what others perceive.

Just as interests narrow one's focus, so do one's *past experiences*. You perceive those things to which you can relate. However, in many instances, your past experiences will act to nullify an object's interest.

Those objects or events that have been experienced are less unusual or unique than are new experiences. As a result, you are more likely to notice a machine that you have never observed before than a standard typewriter that is exactly like a thousand others you have previously seen. Similarly, you are more likely to notice the operations along an assembly line if this is the first time you have seen an assembly line. In the late 1960s and early 1970s, women and minorities in managerial positions were highly visible, if for no other reason than historically these positions were the province of white males. Today, these groups are more widely represented in the managerial ranks, so we are less likely to take notice that a manager is female, black, or Chicano.

Finally, *expectations* can distort your perceptions in that you will see what you expect to see. If you expect police officers to be authoritative, young people to be unambitious, personnel directors to "like people," or individuals holding public office to be "power hungry," you may perceive them this way regardless of their actual traits.

[2] D. C. McClelland and J. W. Atkinson, "The Projective Expression of Needs: The Effect of Different Intensities of the Hunger Drive on Perception," *Journal of Psychology*, Vol. 25 (1948), pp. 205–22.

The Target

Characteristics in the target that is being observed can affect what is perceived. Loud people are more likely to be noticed in a group than are quiet ones. So, too, are extremely attractive or unattractive individuals. Motion, sounds, size, and other attributes of a target shape the way we see it.

Because targets are not looked at in isolation, the relationship of a target to its background influences perception, as does our tendency to group close things and similar things together.

What we see is dependent on how we separate a figure from its general background. For instance, what you see as you read this sentence is black letters on a white page. You do not see funny-shaped patches of black and white because you recognize these shapes and organize the black shapes against the white background. Figure 4–1 dramatizes this effect. The figure on the left may at first look like a white vase. However, if white is taken as the background, we see two gray profiles. At first observation, the figure on the right appears to be some gray modular figures against a white background. Closer inspection will reveal the word "FLY" once the background is defined as gray.

Objects that are close to each other will tend to be perceived together rather than separately. As a result of physical or time proximity, we often put together objects or events that are unrelated. Employees in a particular department are seen as a group. If, in a department of four members, two suddenly resign, we tend to assume that their departures were related when, in fact, they may be totally unrelated. Timing may also imply dependence when, for example, a new sales manager is assigned to a territory and, soon after, sales in that territory skyrocket. The assignment of the new sales manager and the increase in sales may not be related—the increase may be due to an introduction of a new product line or to one of many other reasons—but there is a tendency to perceive the two occurrences as related.

Persons, objects, or events that are similar to each other also tend to be grouped together. The greater the similarity, the greater the probability that

FIGURE 4–1
Figure-Ground Illustrations

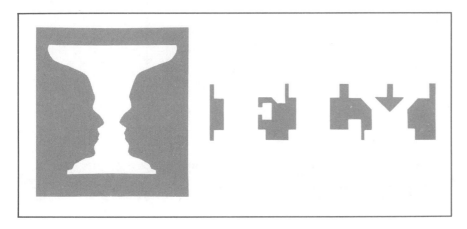

we will tend to perceive them as a common group. Women, blacks, or any other group that has clearly distinguishable characteristics in terms of features or color will tend to be perceived as alike in other, unrelated characteristics as well.

The Situation

The context in which we see objects or events is important. Elements in the surrounding environment influence our perceptions.

I may not notice a twenty-five-year-old female in an evening gown and heavy makeup at a nightclub on Saturday night. Yet that same woman, so attired for my Monday morning management class, would certainly catch my attention (and that of the rest of the class). Neither the perceiver nor the target changed between Saturday night and Monday morning, but the situation is different. Similarly, you are more likely to notice your employees goofing off if your boss from head office happens to be in town. Again, the situation affects your perception. The time at which an object or event is seen can influence attention, as can location, light, heat, or any number of situational factors. Figure 4–2 summarizes the factors influencing perception.

FIGURE 4–2
Factors That Influence Perception

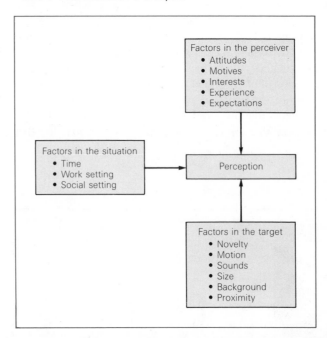

PERSON PERCEPTION: MAKING JUDGMENTS ABOUT OTHERS

Now we turn to the most relevant application of perception concepts to OB. This is the issue of person perception.

Attribution Theory

Our perceptions of people differ from our perceptions of inanimate objects like desks, machines, or buildings because we make inferences about the actions of people that we don't make about inanimate objects. Nonliving objects are subject to the laws of nature, but they have no beliefs, motives, or intentions. People do. The result is that when we observe people, we attempt to develop explanations of why they behave in certain ways. Our perception and judgment of a person's actions, therefore, will be significantly influenced by the assumptions we make about the person's internal state.

Attribution theory has been proposed to develop explanations of how we judge people differently depending on what meaning we attribute to a given behavior.[3] Basically, the theory suggests that when we observe an individual's behavior, we attempt to determine whether it was internally or externally caused. That determination, however, depends largely on three factors: (1) distinctiveness, (2) consensus, and (3) consistency. First, let's clarify the differences between internal and external causation and then elaborate on each of the three determining factors.

> **Attribution theory**
> When individuals observe behavior, they attempt to determine whether it is internally or externally caused.

Internally caused behaviors are those that are believed to be under the personal control of the individual. Externally caused behavior is seen as resulting from outside causes; that is, the person is seen as forced into the behavior by the situation. If one of your employees were late for work, you might attribute his lateness to his partying into the wee hours of the morning and then oversleeping. This would be an internal interpretation. But if you attributed his arriving late to a major automobile accident that tied up traffic on the road that your employee regularly uses, then you are making an external attribution.

Distinctiveness refers to whether an individual displays different behaviors in different situations. Is the employee who arrives late today also the source of complaints by co-workers for being a "goof-off"? What we want to know is if this behavior is unusual or not. If it is, the observer is likely to give the behavior an external attribution. If this action is not unique, it will probably be judged as internal.

If everyone who is faced with a similar situation responds in the same way, we can say the behavior shows *consensus*. Our late employee's behavior would meet this criterion if all employees who took the same route to work were also late. From an attribution perspective, if consensus is high you would be expected to give an external attribution to the employee's tardiness, whereas if other employees who took the same route made it into work on time, your conclusion as to causation would be internal.

Finally, an observer looks for *consistency* in a person's actions. Does the person respond the same way over time? Coming in ten minutes late for work is not perceived in the same way if for one employee it represents an unusual case (she hasn't been late for several months), while for another it is part of a routine pattern (she is regularly late two or three times a week). The more consistent the behavior, the more the observer is inclined to attribute it to internal causes.

Figure 4–3 summarizes the key elements in attribution theory. It would

---

[3] H. H. Kelley, "Attribution in Social Interaction," in E. Jones et al. (eds.), *Attribution: Perceiving the Causes of Behavior* (Morristown, NJ: General Learning Press, 1972).

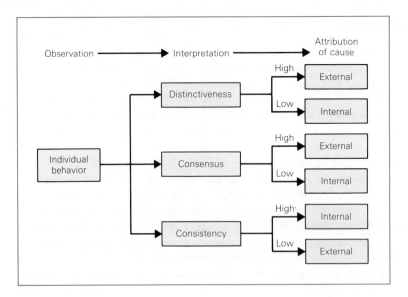

FIGURE 4–3
Attribution Theory

tell us, for instance, that if an employee—let's call her Ms. Smith—generally performs at about the same level on other related tasks as she does on her current task (low distinctiveness), if other employees frequently perform differently—better or worse—than Ms. Smith does on that current task (low consensus), and if Ms. Smith's performance on this current task is consistent over time (high consistency), her manager or anyone else who is judging Ms. Smith's work is likely to hold her primarily responsible for her task performance (internal attribution).

Attribution theory explains what you've seen operating for years. All similar behaviors are not perceived similarly. We look at actions and judge them within their situational context. If you have a reputation as a good student yet fail one test in a course, the instructor is more likely to disregard the poor exam. Why? He or she will attribute the cause of this unusual performance to external conditions. It may not be your fault. But for the student who has a consistent record of being a poor performer, it is unlikely the teacher will ignore the low test score. Similarly, if everyone in class blew the test, the instructor may attribute the outcome to external causes (maybe the questions were poorly written, the room was too warm, students didn't have the prerequisites that he assumed) rather than to causes under the students' own control.

One of the more interesting findings from attribution theory is that there are errors or biases that distort attributions. For instance, there is substantial evidence to support that when we make judgments about the behavior of other people, we have a tendency to underestimate the influence of external factors and overestimate the influence of internal or personal factors. This is called the **fundamental attribution error** and can explain why a sales manager may be prone to attribute the poor performance of her sales agents to laziness rather than the innovative product line introduced by a competitor. There is also a tendency for individuals to attribute their successes to internal factors like ability or effort while putting the blame for failure on external factors

Fundamental attribution error

The tendency to underestimate the influence of external factors and overestimate the influence of internal factors when making judgments about the behavior of others.

like luck. This is called **self-serving bias** and suggests that feedback provided to employees in performance reviews will be predictably distorted by recipients depending on whether it is positive or negative.

Self-serving bias

The tendency for individuals to attribute their successes to internal factors while putting the blame for failures on external factors.

Frequently Used Shortcuts in Judging Others

We use a number of shortcuts when we judge others. Perceiving and interpreting what others do is burdensome. As a result, individuals develop techniques for making the task more manageable. These techniques are frequently valuable—they allow us to make accurate perceptions rapidly and provide valid data for making predictions. However, they are not foolproof. They can and do get us into trouble. An understanding of these shortcuts can be helpful toward recognizing when they can result in significant distortions.

Selective Perception   Any characteristic that makes a person, object, or event stand out will increase the probability that it will be perceived. Why? Because it is impossible for us to assimilate everything we see—only certain stimuli can be taken in. This explains why, as we noted earlier, you're more likely to notice cars like your own or why some people may be reprimanded by their boss for doing something that when done by another employee goes unnoticed. Since we can't observe everything going on about us, we engage in **selective perception**. A classic example shows how vested interests can significantly influence what problems we see.

Selective perception

People selectively interpret what they see based on their interests, background, experience, and attitudes.

Dearborn and Simon[4] performed a perceptual study in which twenty-three business executives read a comprehensive case describing the organization and activities of a steel company. Six of the twenty-three executives were in the sales function, five in production, four in accounting, and eight in miscellaneous functions. Each manager was asked to write down the most important problem he found in the case. Eighty-three percent of the sales executives rated sales important, while only 29 percent of the others did so. This, along with other results of the study, led the researchers to conclude that the participants perceived aspects in a situation that related specifically to the activities and goals of the unit to which they were attached. A group's perception of organizational activities is selectively altered to align with the vested interests they represent. In other words, where the stimuli are ambiguous, as in the steel company case, perception tends to be influenced more by an individual's base of interpretation (that is, attitudes, interests, and background) than by the stimulus itself.

But how does selectivity work as a shortcut in judging other people? Simply, since we cannot assimilate all that we observe, we take in bits and pieces. But these bits and pieces are not chosen randomly; rather, they are selectively chosen depending on the interests, background, experience, and attitudes of the observer. Selective perception allows us to "speed read" others, but not without the risk of drawing an inaccurate picture. Because we see what we want to see, we can draw unwarranted conclusions from an ambiguous situation. If there is a rumor going around the office that your company's

[4] D. C. Dearborn and H. A. Simon, "Selective Perception: A Note on the Departmental Identification of Executives," *Sociometry*, June 1958, pp. 140–44.

OB Close-Up

The Pervasiveness of Sex-Role Stereotypes

Tim Ganter received a report from the corporate engineering research office. The report was signed by the office's director, Dr. L. L. Stockton. Tim has never met Dr. Stockton, but had a question about the report. So he called Stockton's office. The phone rang. A woman answered, "Engineering research. Can I help you?" Tim replied, "Yes. I'm trying to reach Dr. Stockton. Are you his secretary?" The voice replied, "No, I'm Dr. Stockton!"

Tim Ganter had made a mistake. He was embarrassed, and rightly so. He was guilty of sex-role stereotyping. Managers are not all males; nor are all engineers with doctoral degrees. Yet sex-role stereotypes are widespread in organizations.

sales are down and that large layoffs may be coming, a routine visit by a senior executive from headquarters might be interpreted as the first step in management's identification of people to be fired, when in reality such an action may be the farthest thing from the mind of the senior executive.

Projection

Attributing one's own characteristics to other people.

Projection   It is easy to judge others if we assume they are similar to us. For instance, if you want challenge and responsibility in your job, you assume that others want the same. This tendency to attribute one's own characteristics to other people—which is called **projection**—can distort perceptions made about others. When managers engage in projection, they compromise their ability to respond to individual differences. They tend to see people as more homogeneous than they really are.

What this means in practice is that among people who engage in projection, their perception of others is influenced more by what the observer is like than by what the person being observed is like. When observing others who actually are like them, these observers are quite accurate—not because they are more perceptive, but only because they judge people as being similar to themselves, so when they finally find someone who is, they are naturally correct.

Stereotyping

Judging someone on the basis of the perception of the group to which that person belongs.

Stereotyping   When we judge someone on the basis of our perception of the group to which he or she belongs, we are using the shortcut called **stereotyping**. William Faulkner engaged in stereotyping in his reported conversation with Ernest Hemingway, when he said, "The rich are different from you and me." Hemingway's reply, "Yes, they have more money," indicated that other than the required difference (you need money to be rich), he refused to stereotype or generalize characteristics about people based on their wealth.

Generalizations, of course, are not without their advantages. It makes assimilating easier since it permits us to maintain consistency. It is less difficult

This is especially true for women managers. Studies indicate that male and female managers alike hold negative stereotypes about the ability of women to manage effectively.[5] Successful managers—whether male or female—tend to be perceived as having personality traits and skills associated with men. But, unfortunately, the same aggressive behavior that is judged positively when exhibited by a male manager is often appraised negatively when exhibited by a female manager. As one female executive confided, "When I'm forceful and direct, I'm accused of being too aggressive. When I'm thoughtful or considerate, I'm told that I'm too weak. No matter what I do, I can't win!" Such negative stereotypes create conflicts for women in, and aspiring to, managerial positions. And, of course, they suboptimize the organization's effectiveness when they prevent the selection or promotion of the most qualified applicant.

to deal with an unmanageable number of stimuli if we use stereotypes. But the problem occurs when we inaccurately stereotype. All accountants are *not* quiet and introspective in the same way that all salespeople are *not* aggressive and outgoing.

In an organizational context, we frequently hear comments that represent stereotyped representation of certain groups: "Managers don't give a damn about their people, only getting the work out"; or "Union people expect something for nothing." Clearly, these phrases represent stereotypes, but if people expect these perceptions, that is what they will see, whether it represents reality or not.

Obviously, one of the problems of stereotypes is that they are so widespread, despite the fact that they may not contain a shred of truth, or may be irrelevant. Their being widespread may only mean that many people are making the same, inaccurate perception based on a false premise about a group.

Halo effect   When we draw a general impression about an individual based on a single characteristic such as intelligence, sociability, or appearance, a **halo effect** is operating. This phenomenon frequently occurs when students appraise their classroom instructor. Students may isolate a single trait such as enthusiasm and allow their entire evaluation to be tainted by how they judge the instructor on this one trait. Thus, an instructor may be quiet, assured, knowledgeable, and highly qualified, but if his style lacks zeal, he will be rated lower on a number of other characteristics.

Halo effect

Drawing a general impression about an individual based on a single characteristic.

[5] See, for example, G. E. Stephens and A. S. Denisi, "Women as Managers: Attitudes and Attributions for Performance by Men and Women," *Academy of Management Journal*, June 1980, pp. 355–61; and A. S. Baron and K. Abrahamsen, "Will He—Or Won't He—Work with a Female Manager?" *Management Review*, November 1981, pp. 48–53.

The reality of the halo effect was confirmed in a classic study where subjects were given a list of traits like intelligent, skillful, practical, industrious, determined, and warm and asked to evaluate the person to whom these traits applied.[6] Based on these traits, the person was judged to be wise, humorous, popular, and imaginative. When the same list was modified to substitute cold for warm in the trait list, a completely different set of perceptions was obtained. Clearly, the subjects were allowing a single trait to influence their overall impression of the person being judged.

The propensity for the halo effect to operate is not random. Research suggests that it is likely to be most extreme when the traits to be perceived are ambiguous or unclear in behavioral terms, when the traits have moral overtones, and when the perceiver is judging traits with which he or she has had limited experience.[7]

In organizations, the halo effect is important in understanding an individual's behavior, particularly when judgment and evaluation must be made. It is not unusual for the halo effect to occur in selection interviews or at performance appraisal time. A sloppily dressed candidate for a marketing research position may be perceived by an interviewer as an irresponsible person with an unprofessional attitude and marginal abilities, when in fact the candidate may be highly responsible, professional, and competent. What has happened is that a single trait—appearance—has overridden other characteristics in the interviewer's general perception about the individual. The halo effect can have a similarly distorting impact on performance evaluation, causing the full appraisal to be biased by a single trait.

Specific Applications in Organizations

People in organizations are always judging each other. Managers must appraise their subordinates' performance. We evaluate how much effort our co-workers are putting into their jobs. When a new person joins a department, he or she is immediately "sized up" by the other department members. In many cases, these judgments have important consequences for the organization. Let us briefly look at a few of the more obvious applications.

Employment interview   A major input into who is hired or rejected is the employment interview. It's fair to say that few people are hired without an interview. But the evidence indicates that interviewers make perceptual judgments that are often inaccurate. Additionally, interrater agreement among interviewers is often poor; that is, different interviewers see different things in the same candidate and thus arrive at different conclusions about the applicant.

Interviewers generally draw early impressions that become very quickly entrenched. If negative information is exposed early in the interview, it tends to be more heavily weighted than if that same information were conveyed

[6] S. E. Asch, "Forming Impressions of Personality," *Journal of Abnormal and Social Psychology*, July 1946, pp. 258–90.

[7] J. S. Bruner and R. Tagiuri, "The Perception of People," in E. Lindzey (ed.), *Handbook of Social Psychology* (Reading, MA: Addison-Wesley, 1954), p. 641.

later.[8] Studies indicate that most interviewers' decisions change very little after the first four or five minutes of the interview. As a result, information elicited early in the interview carries greater weight than does information elicited later, and a "good applicant" is probably characterized more by the absence of unfavorable characteristics than by the presence of favorable characteristics.

Importantly, who you think is a good candidate and who I think is one may differ markedly. Because interviews usually have so little consistent structure and interviewers vary in terms of what they consider a good candidate, judgments of the same candidate can vary widely. If the employment interview is an important input into the hiring decision, and it usually is, you should recognize that perceptual factors influence who is hired and eventually the quality of an organization's labor force.

Realistic job previews   Another perceptual issue related to hiring new employees is the problem of unrealistic expectations. Every applicant acquires, during the selection process, a set of expectations about the organization and about the specific job the applicant is hoping to be offered. It is not unusual for these expectations to be excessively inflated as a result of receiving almost uniformly positive information. There is evidence that now demonstrates these inaccurate perceptions lead to premature resignations, but that **realistic job previews** can lead to lower turnover rates.[9] More specifically, an organization that does *not* use realistic job previews will have, on average, 28.8 percent higher turnover than one that does use realistic job previews.[10] But what is a realistic job preview? It includes both unfavorable and favorable information about the job. Research leads us to conclude that applicants who have been given a realistic job preview hold lower and more realistic expectations about the job they'll be doing and are better prepared for coping with the job and its frustrating elements. The result is fewer unexpected resignations by new employees.

Realistic job previews
Job applicants receive both unfavorable and favorable information about the job.

Performance evaluation   Although the impact of performance evaluations on behavior will be discussed fully in Chapter 14, it should be pointed out here that an employee's performance appraisal is very much dependent on the perceptual process. An employee's future is closely tied to his or her appraisal—promotions, pay raises, and continuation of employment are among the most obvious outcomes. The performance appraisal represents an assessment of an employee's work. While this can be objective (for example, a salesperson is appraised on how many dollars of sales she generates in her territory), many jobs are evaluated in subjective terms. Subjective measures are easier to implement, they provide managers with greater discretion, and many jobs do not readily lend themselves to objective measures. Subjective measures are, by definition, judgmental. The evaluator forms a general impression of an employ-

[8] See, for example, E. C. Webster, *Decision Making in the Employment Interview* (Montreal: McGill University, Industrial Relations Center, 1964).

[9] S. L. Premack and J. P. Wanous, "A Meta-Analysis of Realistic Job Preview Experiments," *Journal of Applied Psychology*, November 1985, pp. 706–20.

[10] P. Popovich and J. P. Wanous, "The Realistic Job Preview as a Persuasive Communication," *Academy of Management Review*, October 1982, p. 572.

ee's work. To the degree that managers use subjective measures in appraising employees, what the evaluator perceives to be "good" or "bad" employee characteristics/behaviors will significantly influence the appraisal outcome.

Employee effort   An individual's future in an organization is usually not dependent on performance alone. In many organizations, the level of an employee's effort is given high importance. Just as teachers frequently consider how hard you try in a course as well as how you perform on examinations, so often do managers. And assessment of an individual's effort is a subjective judgment susceptible to perceptual distortions and bias. If it is true, as some claim, that "more workers are fired for poor attitudes and lack of discipline than for lack of ability,"[11] then appraisal of an employee's effort may be a primary influence on his or her future in the organization.

Employee loyalty   Another important judgment that managers make about employees is whether they are loyal to the organization. Few organizations appreciate employees, especially those in the managerial ranks, disparaging the firm. Further, in some organizations, if the word gets around that an employee is looking at other employment opportunities outside the firm, that employee may be labeled as disloyal, cutting off all future advancement opportunities. The issue is not whether organizations are right in demanding loyalty, but that many do, and that assessment of an employee's loyalty or commitment is highly judgmental. What is perceived as loyalty by one decision maker may be seen as excessive conformity by another. An employee who questions a top management decision may be seen as disloyal by some, yet caring and concerned by others. When evaluating a person's attitude, as in loyalty assessment, we must recognize that we are again involved with person perception.

THE LINK BETWEEN PERCEPTION AND INDIVIDUAL DECISION MAKING

Individuals in organizations make decisions. That is, they make choices from among two or more alternatives. Top managers, for instance, determine their organization's goals, what products or services to offer, how best to organize corporate headquarters, or where to locate a new manufacturing plant. Middle- and lower-level managers determine production schedules, select new employees, and decide how pay raises are to be allocated. Of course, making decisions is not the sole province of managers. Nonmanagerial employees also make decisions that affect their jobs and the organizations they work for. The more obvious of these decisions might include whether to come to work or not on any given day, how much effort to put forward once at work, and whether to comply with a request made by the boss. Individual decision making, therefore, is an important part of organizational behavior. But how individuals in organizations make decisions, and the quality of their final choices, are largely influenced by their perceptions.

---

[11] D. Kipnis, *The Powerholders* (Chicago: University of Chicago Press, 1976).

Decision making occurs as a reaction to a problem. There is a discrepancy between some *current* state of affairs and some *desired* state, requiring consideration of alternative courses of action. So, if your car breaks down and you rely on it to get to school, you have a problem that requires a decision on your part. Unfortunately, most problems don't come neatly packaged with a label "problem" clearly displayed on them. One person's *problem* is another person's *satisfactory state of affairs*. One manager may view her division's 2 percent increase in quarterly sales to be a serious problem requiring immediate action on her part. In contrast, her counterpart in another division of the same company, who also had a 2 percent sales increase, may consider that quite satisfactory. So the awareness that a problem exists and that a decision needs to be made is a perceptual issue.

Moreover, every decision requires interpretation and evaluation of information. Data is typically received from multiple sources and it needs to be screened, processed, and interpreted. What data, for instance, is relevant to the decision and what isn't? The perceptions of the decision maker will answer this question. Alternatives will be developed and the strengths and weaknesses of each will need to be evaluated. Again, because alternatives don't come with "red flags" identifying themselves as such or with their strengths and weaknesses clearly marked, the individual decision maker's perceptual process will have a large bearing on the final outcome.

THE OPTIMIZING DECISION MAKING MODEL

Let's begin by describing how individuals should behave in order to maximize some outcome. We will call this the **optimizing model** of decision making.[12]

Optimizing model

A decision making model that describes how individuals should behave in order to maximize some outcome.

Steps in the Optimizing Model

Table 4–1 outlines the six steps an individual should follow, either explicitly or implicitly, when making a decision.

TABLE 4–1
Steps in the Optimizing
Decision Model

---

1. Ascertain the need for a decision
2. Identify the decision criteria
3. Allocate weights to the criteria
4. Develop the alternatives
5. Evaluate the alternatives
6. Select the best alternative

---

[12] For a comprehensive review of the optimizing model and its assumptions, see E. F. Harrison, *The Managerial Decision-Making Process*, 2nd ed. (Boston: Houghton Mifflin, 1981), pp. 53–57 and 81–93.

Step 1: Ascertain the Need for a Decision   The first step requires recognition that a decision needs to be made. The existence of a problem, or as we stated previously, a disparity between some desired state and the actual condition, brings about this recognition. If you calculate your monthly expenses and find that you're spending $50 more than you allocated in your budget, you have ascertained the need for a decision. There is a disparity between your desired expenditure level and what you're actually spending.

Step 2: Identify the Decision Criteria   Once an individual has determined the need for a decision, the criteria that will be important in making the decision must be identified. For illustration purposes, let's consider the case of a high school senior confronting the problem of choosing a college. The concepts derived from this example may be generalized to any decision a person might confront.

For the sake of simplicity, let's assume that our high school senior has already chosen to attend college (versus other noncollege options). We know that the need for a decision is precipitated by graduation. Once she has recognized this need for a decision, the student should begin to list the criteria or factors that will be relevant to her decision. For our example, let's assume she has identified the following criteria about the school: annual cost, availability of financial aid, admission requirements, status or reputation, size, geographic location, curricula offering, male:female ratio, quality of social life, and the physical attractiveness of the campus. These criteria represent what the decision maker thinks is relevant to her decision. Note that, in this step, what is *not* listed is as important as what *is*. For example, our high school senior did not consider factors such as where her friends were going to school, availability of part-time employment, or whether freshmen are required to reside on campus. To someone else making a college selection decision, the criteria used might be considerably different.

This second step is important because it identifies only those criteria that the decision maker considers relevant. If a criterion is omitted from this list, we treat it as irrelevant to the decision maker.

Step 3: Allocate Weights to the Criteria   The criteria listed in the previous step are not all equally important. It's necessary, therefore, to weight the factors listed in Step 2 in order to prioritize their importance in the decision. All the criteria are relevant, but some are more relevant than others.

How does the decision maker weight criteria? A simple approach would merely be to give *the* most important criteria a number—say ten—and then assign weights to the rest of the criteria against this standard. So the result of Steps 2 and 3 is to allow decision makers to use their personal preferences both to prioritize the relevant criteria and to indicate their relative degree of importance by assigning a weight to each. Table 4–2 lists the criteria and weights our high school senior is using in her college decision.

Step 4: Develop the Alternatives   The fourth step requires the decision maker to list all the viable alternatives that could possibly succeed in resolving the problem. No attempt is made in this step to appraise the alternatives; only to list them. To return to our example, let us assume that our high schooler has identified eight potential colleges—Alpha, Beta, Delta, Gamma, Iota, Omega, Phi, and Sigma.

TABLE 4–2
Criteria and Weights in Selection of a College

Criteria	Weights
• Availability of financial aid	10
• School's reputation	10
• Annual cost	8
• Curricula offering	7
• Geographic location	6
• Admission requirements	5
• Quality of social life	4
• School size	3
• Male:female ratio	2
• Physical attractiveness of the campus	2

Step 5: Evaluate the Alternatives   Once the alternatives have been identified, the decision maker must critically evaluate each one. The strengths and weaknesses of each alternative will become evident when they are compared against the criteria and weights established in Steps 2 and 3.

The evaluation of each alternative is done by appraising it against the weighted criteria. In our example, the high school senior would evaluate each college using every one of the criteria. To keep our example simple we'll assume that a ten means that the college is rated as "most favorable" on that criterion. The results from evaluating the various alternative colleges are shown in Table 4–3.

TABLE 4–3
Evaluation of Eight Alternatives Against the Decision Criteria*

Criteria	ALTERNATIVES							
	Alpha College	Beta College	Delta College	Gamma College	Iota College	Omega College	Phi College	Sigma College
Availability of financial aid	5	4	10	7	7	8	3	7
School's reputation	10	6	6	6	9	5	9	6
Annual cost (low cost preferred)	5	7	8	8	5	10	5	8
Curricula offering	6	10	8	9	8	8	9	8
Geographic location	6	7	10	10	6	9	10	7
Admission requirements (in terms of likelihood of acceptance)	7	10	10	10	8	10	8	10
Quality of social life	10	5	7	7	3	7	10	8
School size	10	7	7	7	9	7	9	4
Male:female ratio	2	2	8	8	8	10	2	8
Physical attractiveness of the campus	8	10	6	3	4	10	5	9

* The colleges that achieved the highest rating for a criterion are given ten points.

Keep in mind that the ratings given the eight colleges shown in Table 4–3 are based on the assessment made by the decision maker. Some assessments can be made in a relatively objective fashion. If our decision maker prefers a small school, one with an enrollment of 1,000 is obviously superior to one with 10,000 students. Similarly, if a high male:female ratio is sought, 3:1 is clearly higher than 1.2:1. But the assessment of criteria such as reputation, quality of social life, or the physical attractiveness of the campus reflects the decision maker's values. The point is that most decisions contain judgments. They are reflected in the criteria chosen in Step 2, the weights given to these criteria, and the evaluation of alternatives. This explains why two people faced with a similar problem—such as selecting a college—may look at two totally different sets of alternatives or even look at the same alternatives but rate them very differently.

Table 4–3 represents an evaluation of only eight alternatives against the decision criteria. It does not reflect the weighting done in Step 3. If one choice had scored ten on every criterion, there would be no need to consider the weights. Similarly, if the weights were all equal, you could evaluate each alternative merely by summing up the appropriate column in Table 4–3. For instance, Omega College would be highest, with a total score of eighty-four. But our high school senior needs to multiply each alternative against its weight. The result of this process is shown in Table 4–4. The summation of these scores represents an evaluation of each college against the previously established criteria and weights.

Step 6: Select the Best Alternative The final step in the optimizing decision model is the selection of the best alternative from among those enumerated and evaluated. Since best is defined in terms of highest total score, the selection is quite simple. The decision maker merely chooses the alternative that generated the largest total score in Step 5. For our high school senior, that means Delta

TABLE 4–4
Evaluation of College Alternatives

Criteria (and weight)	ALTERNATIVES							
	Alpha College	Beta College	Delta College	Gamma College	Iota College	Omega College	Phi College	Sigma College
Availability of financial aid (10)	50	40	100	70	70	80	30	70
School's reputation (10)	100	60	60	60	90	50	90	60
Annual cost (8)	40	56	64	64	40	80	40	64
Curricula offering (7)	42	70	56	63	56	56	63	56
Geographic location (6)	36	42	60	60	36	54	60	42
Admission requirements (5)	35	50	50	50	40	50	40	50
Quality of social life (4)	40	20	28	28	12	28	40	32
School size (3)	30	21	21	21	27	21	27	12
Male:female ratio (2)	4	4	16	16	16	20	4	16
Physical attractiveness of the campus (2)	16	20	12	6	8	20	10	18
Totals	393	373	467	438	395	459	404	420

College. Based on the criteria identified, the weights given to the criteria, and the decision maker's evaluation of each college on each of the criteria, Delta College scored highest and thus becomes the best.

Assumptions of the Optimizing Model

The steps in the optimizing model contain a number of assumptions. It is important to understand these assumptions if we are to determine how accurately the optimizing model describes actual individual decision making.

The assumptions of the optimizing model are the same as those that underly the concept of **rationality**. Rationality refers to choices that are consistent and value maximizing. Rational decision making, therefore, implies that the decision maker can be fully objective and logical. The individual is assumed to have a clear goal, and all of the six steps in the optimizing model are assumed to lead toward the selection of the alternative that will maximize that goal. Let's take a closer look at the assumptions inherent in rationality and, hence, the optimizing model.

Rationality
Choices that are consistent and value maximizing.

Goal-oriented   The optimizing model assumes that there is no conflict over the goal. Whether the decision involves selecting a college to attend, determining whether or not to go to work today, or choosing the right applicant to fill a job vacancy, it is assumed that the decision maker has a single, well-defined goal that he or she is trying to maximize.

All Options Are Known   It is assumed that the decision maker can identify *all* the relevant criteria and can list *all* viable alternatives. The optimizing model portrays the decision maker as fully comprehensive in his or her ability to assess criteria and alternatives.

Preferences Are Clear   Rationality assumes that the criteria and alternatives can be assigned numerical values and ranked in a preferential order.

Preferences Are Constant   The same criteria and alternatives should be obtained every time because, in addition to the goal and preferences being clear, it is assumed that the specific decision criteria are constant and the weights assigned to them are stable over time.

Final Choice Will Maximize the Outcome   The rational decision maker, following the optimizing model, will choose the alternative that rates highest. This most preferred solution will, based on Step 6 of the process, give the maximum benefits.

Predictions from the Optimizing Model

Using the preceding assumptions, we would predict that the individual decision maker would have a clear and specific goal; a fully comprehensive set of criteria that determine the relevant factors in the decision; a precise ranking of the criteria, which will be stable over time; and that the decision maker will select the alternative that scores highest after all options have been evaluated. (See Figure 4–4.)

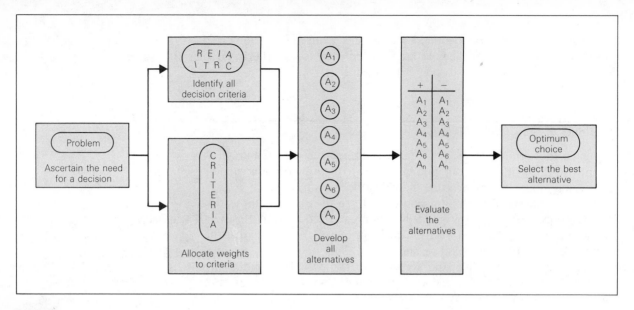

FIGURE 4–4
The Optimizing Model

In terms of the college selection decision introduced earlier, the optimizing model would predict that the high school student could identify every factor that might be important in her decision. Each of these factors would be weighted in terms of importance. All of the colleges that could possibly be viable options would be identified and evaluated against the criteria. Remember, because all alternatives are assumed to be considered, our decision maker might be looking at hundreds of colleges. Also, even if this activity took six months to complete, the criteria and weights would not vary over time. If the college's reputation was most important in September, it would still be so in March. Further, if Beta College was given a score of six on this criterion in September, six months later the assessment would be the same. Finally, since every factor that is important in the decision has been considered and given its proper weight, and since every alternative has been identified and evaluated against the criteria, the decision maker can be assured that the college that scores highest in the evaluation is the best choice. There are no regrets because all information has been obtained and evaluated in a logical and consistent manner.

ALTERNATIVE DECISION MAKING MODELS

Do individuals actually make their decisions the way the optimizing model predicts? Sometimes. When decision makers are faced with a simple problem having few alternative courses of action, and when the cost to search out and evaluate alternatives is low, the optimizing model provides a fairly accurate description of the decision process.[13] Buying a pair of shoes or a new personal computer might be examples of decisions where the optimizing model would

[13] D. L. Rados, "Selection and Evaluation of Alternatives in Repetitive Decision Making," *Administrative Science Quarterly*, June 1972, pp. 196–206.

apply. But many decisions, particularly important and difficult ones—the kind a person hasn't encountered before and for which there are no standardized or programmed rules to provide guidance—don't involve simple and well-structured problems. Rather, they're characterized by complexity, relatively high uncertainty (all the alternatives, for example, are unlikely to be known), and goals and preferences that are neither clear nor consistent. This latter category would include choosing a spouse, considering whether to accept a new job offer in a different city, selecting among job applicants for a vacancy in your department, developing a marketing strategy for a new product, deciding where to build an additional manufacturing plant, or determining the proper time to take your small company public by selling stock in it. In this section, we'll review two alternatives to the optimizing model: the satisficing or bounded rationality model and the implicit favorite model.

The Satisficing Model

The essence of the **satisficing model** is that, when faced with complex problems, decision makers respond by reducing the problems to a level at which they can be readily understood. This is because the information processing capability of human beings makes it impossible to assimilate and understand all the information necessary to optimize. Since the capacity of the human mind for formulating and solving complex problems is far too small to meet all the requirements for full rationality, individuals operate within the confines of **bounded rationality**. They construct simplified models that extract the essential features from problems without capturing all their complexity.[14] Individuals can then behave rationally within the limits of the simple model.

How does bounded rationality work for the typical individual? Once a problem is identified, the search for criteria and alternatives begins. But the list of criteria is likely to be far from exhaustive. The decision maker will identify a limited list made up of the more conspicuous choices. These are the choices that are easy to find and which tend to be highly visible. In most cases, they will represent familiar criteria and the tried and true solutions. Once this limited set of alternatives is identified, the decision maker will begin reviewing them. But the review will not be comprehensive. That is, not all the alternatives will be carefully evaluated. Instead, the decision maker will begin with alternatives that differ only in a relatively small degree from the choice currently in effect. Following along familiar and well-worn paths, the decision maker proceeds to review alternatives only until he or she identifies an alternative that satisfices—one that is satisfactory and sufficient. So the satisficer settles for the first solution that is "good enough," rather than continuing to search for the optimum. The first alternative to meet the "good enough" criteria ends the search, and the decision maker can then proceed toward implementing this acceptable course of action. This is illustrated in Figure 4–5.

One of the more interesting aspects of the satisficing model is that the order in which alternatives are considered is critical in determining which

Satisficing model

A decision making model where a decision maker chooses the first solution that is "good enough"; that is, satisfactory and sufficient.

Bounded rationality

Individuals make decisions by constructing simplified models that extract the essential features from problems without capturing all their complexity.

[14] See H. A. Simon, *Administrative Behavior*, 3rd ed. (New York: Free Press, 1976); and J. Forester, "Bounded Rationality and the Politics of Muddling Through," *Public Administration Review*, January-February 1984, pp. 23–31.

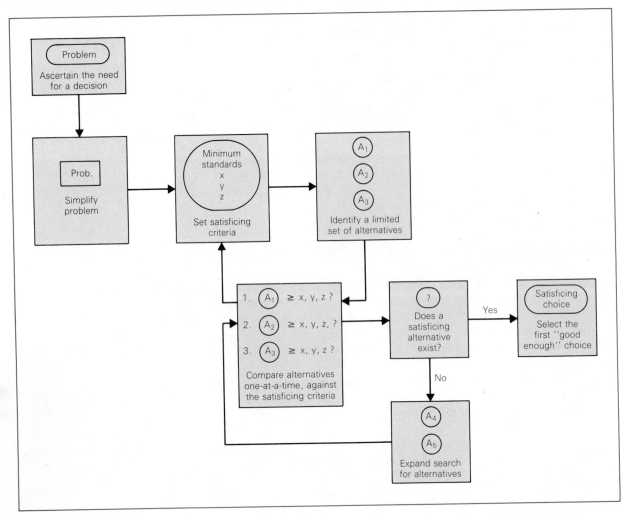

FIGURE 4–5
The Satisficing Model

alternative is selected. If the decision maker were optimizing, all alternatives would eventually be listed in a hierarchy of preferred order. Since all the alternatives would be considered, the initial order in which they would be evaluated is irrelevant. Every potential solution would get a full and complete evaluation. But this is not the case with satisficing. Assuming that a problem has more than one potential solution, the satisficing choice will be the first acceptable one the decision maker encounters. Since decision makers use simple and limited models, they typically begin by identifying alternatives that are obvious, ones with which they are familiar, and those not too far from the status quo. Those solutions that depart least from the status quo and meet the decision criteria are most likely to be selected. This may help to explain why many decisions that people make don't result in the selection of extremely different or radical solutions from those they have made before. A unique alternative may present an optimizing solution to the problem; however, it will rarely be chosen. An acceptable solution will be identified well before the decision maker is required to search very far beyond the status quo.

Using the satisficing model, how might we predict that the high school senior, introduced earlier, would make her college choice? Obviously, she will not consider all of the more than 2,000 colleges in the U.S. or the multitude of others in foreign countries. Based on schools that she's heard about from friends and relatives, plus possibly a quick look through a guide to colleges, she would typically select a half-a-dozen or a dozen colleges to which she will send for catalogs, brochures, and applications. Based on a cursory appraisal of the materials she receives from the colleges, and using her rough decision criteria, she will look for a school that meets her minimal requirements. When she finds one, the decision search will be over. If none of the colleges in this initial set meet the "good enough" standards, she will expand her search to include more diverse colleges. But even following this extended search, the first college she uncovers that meets her minimal requirements will become the alternative of choice.

The Implicit Favorite Model

Another model designed to deal with complex and nonroutine decisions is the **implicit favorite model**.[15] Like the satisficing model, it argues that individuals solve complex problems by simplifying the process. However, simplification in the implicit favorite model means not entering into the difficult "evaluation of alternatives" stage of decision making until one of the alternatives can be identified as an implicit "favorite." In other words, the decision maker is neither rational nor objective. Instead, early in the decision process, he or she implicitly selects a preferred alternative. Then the rest of the decision process is essentially a decision confirmation exercise, where the decision maker makes sure that his or her implicit favorite is indeed the "right" choice.

Implicit favorite model

A decision making model where the decision maker implicitly selects a preferred alternative early in the decision process and biases the evaluation of all other choices.

The implicit favorite model evolved from research on job decisions by graduate management students at the Massachusetts Institute of Technology. Clearly, these students knew and understood the optimizing model. They had spent several years repeatedly using it for solving problems and analyzing cases in accounting, finance, management, marketing, and quantitative methods courses. Moreover, the job choice decision was an important one. If there was a decision where the optimizing model should be used, and a group experienced in using it, this should be it. But the researcher found that the optimizing model was not followed. Rather, the implicit favorite model provided an accurate description of the actual decision process.

The implicit favorite model is outlined in Figure 4–6. Once a problem is identified, the decision maker implicitly identifies an early favorite alternative. But the decision maker doesn't end the search at this point. In fact, the decision maker is often unaware that he or she has already identified an implicit favorite and that the rest of the process is really an exercise in prejudice. So more alternatives will be generated. This is important, for it gives the appearance of

---

[15] See P. O. Soelberg, "Unprogrammed Decision Making," *Industrial Management Review*, Spring 1967, pp. 19–29; and D. J. Power and R. J. Aldag, "Soelberg's Job Search and Choice Model: A Clarification, Review, and Critique," *Academy of Management Review*, January 1985, pp. 48–58.

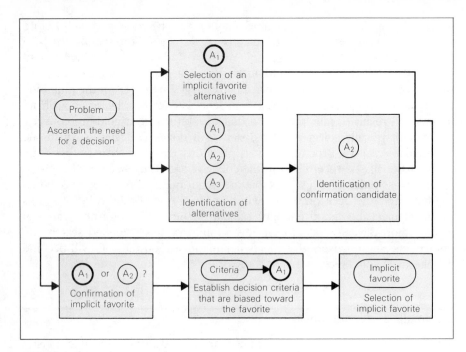

FIGURE 4–6
The Implicit Favorite Model

objectivity. Then the confirmation process begins. The alternative set will be reduced to two—the choice candidate and a confirmation candidate. If the choice candidate is the only viable option, the decision maker will try to obtain another acceptable alternative to become the confirmation candidate, and so he or she will have something to compare against. At this point, the decision maker establishes the decision criteria and weights. A great deal of perceptual and interpretational distortion is taking place, with the selection of criteria and their weight being "shaped" to insure victory for the favored choice. And, of course, that's exactly what transpires. The evaluation demonstrates unequivocally the superiority of the choice candidate over the confirmation candidate.

If the implicit favorite model is at work, the search for new alternatives ends well before the decision maker is willing to admit having made his or her decision. In the job search with MIT students, the researcher found that he was able to accurately predict 87 percent of the career jobs taken two to eight weeks before the students would admit that they had reached a decision.[16] This argues to a decision process that is influenced a lot more by intuitive feelings than by rational objectivity.

Using the implicit favorite model, let's look at how our high school senior might go about choosing which college to attend. Early on in the process, she will find that one of the colleges seems intuitively right for her. However, she may not reveal this to others, nor be aware of it herself. She'll review

---

[16] Soelberg, "Unprogrammed Decision Making."

catalogs and brochures on a number of schools, but eventually reduce the set to two. One of these two, of course, will be her implied favorite. She'll then focus in on the relevant factors in her decision. Which college has the best reputation? Where will she have the better social life? Which campus is more attractive? Her evaluation of criteria such as these are subjective judgments. Her assessment, though, won't be fair and impartial. Rather, she'll distort her judgments to align with her intuitive preference. Since "the race is fixed," the winner is a foregone conclusion. Our high school student won't necessarily choose the optimum alternative, nor can we say that her choice will satisfice. Remember, she distorted her evaluations to get the results she wanted, so there is no guarantee that her final selection will reflect the assumptions of bounded rationality. What we can say is that, if she follows the implicit favorite model, she'll choose the college that was her early preference, regardless of any relevant facts that may have surfaced later in the decision process.

IMPLICATIONS FOR PERFORMANCE AND SATISFACTION

Perception

Individuals behave in a given way based not on the way their external environment actually is but, rather, on what they see or believe it to be. Because individuals act on their interpretations of reality rather than reality itself, it is clear that perception must be a critical determinant of our dependent variables.

An organization may spend millions of dollars to create a pleasant work environment for its employees. However, in spite of these expenditures, if an employee believes that his or her job is lousy, he or she will behave accordingly. It is the employee's perception of a situation that becomes the basis on which he or she behaves. The employee who perceives his or her supervisor as a hurdle-reducer and an aid to help him or her do a better job and the employee who sees the same supervisor as "big brother, closely monitoring every motion, to ensure that I keep working" will differ in their behavioral responses to their supervisor. The difference has nothing to do with the reality of the supervisor's role; the difference in behavior is due to different perceptions.

The evidence suggests that what individuals *perceive* from their work situation will influence their productivity more than will the situation itself. Whether a job is actually interesting or challenging is irrelevant. Whether a manager successfully plans and organizes the work of his or her subordinates and actually helps them to structure their work more efficiently and effectively is far less important than how subordinates perceive his or her efforts. Similarly, issues like fair pay for work performed, the validity of performance appraisals, and the adequacy of working conditions are not judged by employees in a way that assures common perceptions, nor can we be assured that individuals will interpret conditions about their jobs in a favorable light. Therefore, to be able to influence productivity, it is necessary to assess how workers perceive their jobs.

It is unacceptable for a sales manager to argue that "John should be selling far more of our products in his territory. His territory is a gold mine. It has unlimited potential." When John is interviewed, we find that he believes he is getting as much as possible out of his territory. Whether the salesman is right or wrong is irrelevant. He *perceives his view to be right*. If the manager hopes to improve sales in John's territory, he or she must first succeed in changing John's perceptions.

As with productivity, absenteeism, turnover, and job satisfaction are reactions to the individual's perceptions. Dissatisfaction with working conditions or the belief that there is a lack of promotion opportunities in the organization are judgments based on attempts to make some meaning out of one's job. Since there can be no such thing as a "bad job," only the perception that the job is bad, managers must spend time to understand how each individual interprets reality and, where there is a significant difference between what is seen and what exists, try to eliminate the distortions. Failure to deal with the differences when individuals perceive the job in negative terms will result in increased absenteeism and turnover and lower job satisfaction.

Individual Decision Making

Individuals think and reason before they act. It is because of this that an understanding of how people make decisions can be helpful if we are to explain and predict their behavior.

Under some decision situations, people follow the optimizing model. But for most people, and most nonroutine decisions, this is probably more the exception than the rule. Few important decisions are simple or unambiguous enough for the optimizing model's assumptions to apply. So we find individuals looking for solutions that satisfice rather than optimize, and injecting biases and prejudices into the decision process.

The alternative decision models we presented can help us explain and predict behaviors that would appear irrational or arbitrary if viewed under optimizing assumptions. Let's look at a couple of examples.

Employment interviews are complex decision activities. The interviewer finds himself or herself inundated with information. Research indicates that interviewers respond by simplifying the process.[17] Most interviewers' decisions change very little after the first four or five minutes of the interview. In a half-hour interview, the decision maker tends to make a decision about the suitability of the candidate in the first few minutes and then uses the rest of the interview time to select information that supports the early decision. In so doing, interviewers reduce the probability of identifying the highest performing candidate. They bias their decision toward individuals who make favorable first impressions.

Evaluating an employee's performance is a complex activity. Decision makers simplify the process by focusing on visible and easy to measure criteria.[18]

[17] E. C. Mayfield in N. Schmitt's "Social and Situational Determinants of Interview Decisions: Implications for Employment Interviews," *Personnel Psychology*, Spring 1976, p. 81.

[18] G. P. Huber, *Managerial Decision Making* (Glenview, IL: Scott, Foresman, 1980), p. 215.

This may explain why factors such as neatness, promptness, enthusiasm, and a positive attitude are often related to good evaluations. It also explains why quantity measures typically override quality measures. The former category is easier to appraise. This effort at satisficing encourages individuals to take on visible problems rather than important ones.

POINT

IN SUPPORT OF THE RATIONAL DECISION MAKER

The rational model is the classical approach in the field of decision theory. It provides the foundation for the quantitative disciplines of economics, mathematics, and statistics. Indeed, the rational model is the reason why many people regard decision making as quantitative. The rational model explicitly presumes that if a given variable cannot be assigned a numerical value, it should be disregarded or assumed away as a constant or given value. It is a model that operates within a closed environment with a rather precise number of variables. Consequently, the rational model is most applicable to routine or programmed decisions, although decision theorists use it with all types of decisions.

The rational model assumes that the decision maker is aware of all the options, that is, available courses of action, and that the effects of all possible futures can be determined—at least in the short run. One rather common variation of the rational model assumes that:

1. There is only one decision maker.

2. The decision maker has only one objective.

3. The objective can be written in quantitative terms.

4. The potential states of nature and courses of action are finite and have been identified.

5. The decision problem consists simply of choosing the best course of action.

More comprehensively, the rational model translates the objectives of the decision maker into a preference function that represents in numerical terms the value or utility of a given set of alternatives. A set of the consequences of a particular choice is attached to each alternative. Variations are generated at this point by making different assumptions about the accuracy of the decision maker's knowledge of the consequences. A choice in the rational model consists of selecting the alternative whose consequences rank highest in the decision maker's payoff function—that is, the alternative with the highest positive utility for the decision maker.

The rational model assumes that the decision maker must meet two principal requirements. First, given any two alternatives, A and B, the decision maker must always be able to tell whether A is preferred to B; B is preferred to A; or there is no particular preference for either A or B. This requirement is the so-called *closure axiom*. The second requirement is that all preferences must be transitive. For example, if A is preferred to B, and B is preferred to C, then A is preferred to C. This is the *transitivity axiom*.

This rational view of decision making is widely accepted by economists, mathematicians, and statisticians. It is the foundation upon which their research and predictions are made, probably because it permits a rigorous intellectual reasoning process. It allows for a complete and completely consistent package of rules for making decisions. It also has advantages for practicing managers. It can, for instance, facilitate arriving at a choice by:

1. combining estimates of outcome uncertainty, expressed as subjective probabilities, with measures of possible outcome consequences to obtain an overall measure of each alternative's desirability in terms of a specific decision making criterion;

2. providing an explicit basis for guiding the search activity, particularly in evaluating the desirability of gathering additional information prior to making a decision; and

3. providing a basis for reducing the number of relevant alternatives.

Source: Adapted from E. F. Harrison, *The Managerial Decision-Making Process*, 2nd ed. (Boston: Houghton Mifflin, 1981), pp. 53–57. Used with permission.

COUNTERPOINT
THE MYTH OF THE RATIONAL DECISION MAKER

The idea of a manager gathering all pertinent facts, weighing them carefully, and then making a decision in the best interests of his or her organization is largely a myth.

A more realistic and accurate statement would be: *In any complex decision where personal or behavioral factors apply, the individual preference will dominate the results.* There are also two corollaries to this statement. The first is: *A single factor usually forms the basis for a personal preference decision.* The second states: *While a decision is often based on personal preference, the analysis is usually a rational process.*

Examples abound to support this thesis. A purchasing agent awards a contract to the supplier who wines and dines him on a lavish scale. He explains that he rejected lower bids in order to ensure better quality and service.

An executive hires an old school mate, in preference to a proven manager with much more experience, on the grounds that "he'll fit in better around here."

A controller is concerned that a plan to decentralize the company will reduce her authority. So she hires a consultant to "prove" that the costs of such a move would outweigh the benefits.

Perhaps one of the strongest cases against the belief in rational decision making emerged from an international survey conducted among 496 managers. The managers were asked to rank ten characteristics in order of importance to the decision maker. Rationality appeared eighth on the list.

This low regard for rational thinking may be disturbing to executives who believe managers have progressed a long way since management was first formulated as a set of principles, but it reflects the conclusions of a number of behavioral scientists. Based on their research, there is convincing evidence that managers typically apply "subjective rationality" in decision situations.

This is not to say that all decisions are purely subjective. Rational decision making does exist, and its survival and propagation should be encouraged. Nor should it be suggested that a subjective decision is necessarily a bad one. If an individual has a high personal stake in a decision, he or she is more likely to carry it through successfully. And the chairman's son-in-law might even turn out to be the one person with the managerial skills to salvage the company.

But as long as one persists in the belief that choices are made on the basis of a rational thought process, one has little chance of predicting or understanding most organizational decisions.

Source: Reprinted with special permission from *International Management*, August 1974. Copyright © McGraw Hill Publications Co. All rights reserved.

KEY TERMS

Attribution Theory

Bounded Rationality

Fundamental Attribution Error

Halo Effect

Implicit Favorite Model

Optimizing Model

Perception

Projection

Rationality

Realistic Job Previews

Satisficing Model

Selective Perception

Self-Serving Bias

Stereotyping

FOR DISCUSSION

1. Define perception.

2. "That you and I agree on what we see suggests we have similar backgrounds and experiences." Do you agree or disagree? Discuss.

3. What is attribution theory? What are its implications for explaining organizational behavior?

4. What factors do you think might create the fundamental attribution error?

5. How might perceptual factors be involved when an employee receives a poor performance appraisal?

6. How does selectivity affect perception? Give an example of how selectivity can create perceptual distortion.

7. What is stereotyping? Give an example of how stereotyping can create perceptual distortion.

8. Give some positive results from using shortcuts when judging others.

9. What is the optimizing decision making model? Under what conditions is it applicable?

10. Explain the satisficing model. How widely applicable do you think this model is?

11. Contrast the implicit favorite model to the satisficing model.

12. "For the most part, individual decision making in organizations is an irrational process." Do you agree or disagree? Discuss.

FOR FURTHER READING

HARRISON, E. F., *The Managerial Decision-Making Process*, 2nd ed. Boston: Houghton Mifflin, 1981. A comprehensive review of the major decision making models.

JAMES, L. R., and L. E. TETRICK, "Confirmatory Analytic Tests of Three Causal Models Relating Job Perceptions to Job Satisfaction," *Journal of Applied Psychology*, February 1986, pp. 77–82. Demonstrates support for the argument that job satisfaction occurs after job perceptions in the causal order and job perceptions and job satisfaction are reciprocally related.

JANIS, I. L., and L. MANN, *Decision Making: A Psychological Analysis of Conflict, Choice and Commitment*. New York: The Free Press, 1977. Excellent analysis of psychological properties that limit applicability of the optimizing model.

McK. AGNEW, N., and J. L. BROWN, "Bounded Rationality: Fallible Decisions in Unbounded Decision Space," *Behavioral Science*, July 1986, pp. 148–61. Reviews assumptions of the satisficing model.

McCauley, C., C. L. Stitt, and M. Segal, "Stereotyping: From Prejudice to Prediction," *Psychological Bulletin*, January 1980, pp. 195–208. Presents counterpoints to the common arguments made against stereotypes.

Rowe, A. J., J. D. Boulgarides, and M. R. McGrath, *Managerial Decision Making*. Chicago: Science Research Associates, Inc., 1984. Reviews the decision making process, with particular attention given to the role of decision "style" on decision outcomes.

EXERCISE 4

ASSUMPTIONS ON PERCEPTIONS

Objectives: (1) To gain awareness of the influence of our assumptions on perceptions and evaluations of others. (2) To compare our perceptions with others and to find similarities and differences.

Directions:

(1) Read the descriptions of the four individuals provided in the *Personal Descriptions*.

(2) Decide which occupation is most likely for each person, and place the name by the corresponding *Occupations* list which follows. Each person is in a different occupation and no two people hold the same position.

(3) After completing step two, divide into groups of five to seven. Share and compare your choices. What assumptions were made about each person? Each occupation? How could such assumptions influence evaluations?

Personal Descriptions

R. B. Red is a trim, attractive woman in her early thirties. She holds an undergraduate degree from an eastern woman's college, and is active in several professional organizations. She is an officer (on the national level) of Toastmistress International.

Her hobbies include classical music, opera, and jazz. She is an avid traveler, and is planning a sojourn to China next year.

W. C. White is a quiet, meticulous person. W. C. is tall and thin with blond hair and wire-framed glasses. Family, friends, and church are very important, and W. C. devotes any free time to community activities.

W. C. is a wizard with figures but can rarely be persuaded to demonstrate this ability to do mental calculations.

G. A. Green grew up on a small farm in rural Indiana. He is an avid hunter and fisherman. In fact, he and his wife joke about their "deer-hunting honeymoon" in Colorado.

One of his primary goals is to "get back to the land," and he hopes to be able to buy a small farm before he is fifty. He drives a pickup truck and owns several dogs.

B. E. Brown is the child of wealthy professionals who reside on Long Island. Mr. Brown, B. E.'s father, is a "self-made" financial analyst, who made it a point to stress the importance of financial security as B. E. grew up.

B. E. values the ability to structure one's use of time, and can often be found on the golf course on Wednesday afternoons. B. E. dresses in a conservative upper-class manner and professes to be "allergic to polyester."

Occupations

Choose the occupation which seems most appropriate for each person described. Place the names in the spaces next to the corresponding occupations.

_____ Banker

_____ Labor negotiator

_____ Production manager

_____ Travel agent

_____ Accountant

_____ Teacher

_____ Computer operations manager
_____ Clerk
_____ Army general
_____ Salesperson
_____ Physician
_____ Truck driver
_____ Financial analyst

After you have completed this exercise, you can turn to page 561 and compare your choices to the actual occupations.

Source: Adapted from J. L. Frantzve, *Behaving in Organizations: Tales from the Trenches*. Copyright © 1983 by Allyn & Bacon. Used with permission.

CASE INCIDENT 4

"I DON'T MAKE DECISIONS"

I met Ted Kelly for the first time at a cocktail party. As things happen, we got to talking about our work. When he found out I taught organizational behavior, he understood my interest in his job. Ted was the plant manager at a large chemical refinery in town. About ten minutes or so into our conversation, I asked him what type of leadership style he used.

Ted: "I don't make decisions at my plant."

Author: "You mean you use democratic leadership?"

Ted: "No. I said I don't make decisions! My subordinates are paid to make decisions. No point in my doing their jobs."

Ted went on to say that about five years ago he decided that his subordinate managers had become too dependent on him. After some deliberation, he made a decision—as he tells it, it was the last one he made on his job. He decided never to make a decision again.

I didn't really believe what I was hearing. I guess Ted sensed that, so he offered me an invitation to visit his plant. I wasn't going to miss the opportunity. I asked him when I could come over. "Any time you like, except Mondays between 1 and 3 P.M." "Any time?" I questioned. "Yeah," he replied. "Ever since I decided not to decide, I've got nothing to keep me busy."

The middle of the next week, I popped in on Ted unannounced. I found his office by following the signs. He had no secretary. He was lying on his sofa, half asleep. My arrival seemed to jar him awake. He seemed glad to see me. He offered me a seat.

Our conversation began by my inquiring exactly what he did every day. "You're looking at it. I sleep a lot. Oh yeah, I read the four or five memos I get from the head office every week." I couldn't believe what I was hearing. Here was a fifty-year-old, obviously successful, executive, probably earning better than $100,000 a year, telling me he doesn't do anything. He could tell, however, that I wasn't buying his story.

"If you don't believe what I'm saying, check with my subordinates," he told me. He said he had six department managers working for him. I asked him to choose one I could talk with.

"No, I can't do that. First, I don't make decisions. Second, when the one I chose confirmed what I've been telling you, you'd think it was a setup. Here—these are the names and numbers of my department managers. You call them."

I did just that. I picked Peter Chandler, who headed up quality control. I dialed his number. He answered on the first ring. I told him that I wanted to talk to him about

his boss's leadership style. He said "Come on over. I've got nothing to do anyway."

When I arrived at Pete's office, he was staring out the window. We sat down and he began to laugh. "I'll bet Ted's been telling you about how he doesn't make decisions." I concurred. "It's all true," he injected. "I've been here for almost three years and I've never seen him make a decision."

I couldn't figure out how this could be. "How many people do you have working here?" I asked.

Peter: "About 200."

Author: "How does this plant's operating efficiency stack up against the others?"

Peter: "Oh, we're number one out of the eighteen refineries. Been that way for years and years. Interesting thing is that this is the oldest refinery in the company, too. Our equipment may be outdated, but we're as efficient as they come."

Author: "What does Ted Kelly do?"

Peter: "Beats me. He attends the staff meetings on Monday afternoons from 1 to 3, but other than that, I don't know."

Author: "I get it. He makes all the decisions at that once-a-week staff meeting?"

Peter: "No. Each department head tells what key decisions he made last week. We then critique each other. Ted says nothing. The only thing he does at those meetings is listen and pass on any happenings up at headquarters."

I wanted to learn more, so I went back to Ted's office. I found him clipping his fingernails.

"I told you I was telling the truth," was the first thing he said. What followed was a long conversation in which I learned the following facts:

The two-hour weekly staff meeting is presided over by one of the department heads. They choose among themselves who will be their leader. It's a permanent position. Any problem that has come up during the week, if it can't be handled by a manager, will first be considered by several of the managers together. Only if the problem is still unresolved will it be taken to the leader. All issues are resolved at that level. They are never taken to Ted Kelly's level.

The performance record at Kelly's plant is well known in the company. Three of the last four plant managers have come out of Kelly's plant. When asked by the head office to recommend candidates for a plant management vacancy, Ted always selects the department head who presides over the staff meetings. The result is that there is a great deal of competition to lead the staff meetings. Additionally, because of Kelly's plant record for breeding management talent, whenever there is a vacancy for a department manager at Kelly's plant, the best people in the company apply for it. Of course, the decision as to who is hired is made by the existing heads at their weekly staff meeting.

The three plant managers who previously worked under Kelly have instituted a similar leadership style. Their plants have also shown significant improvement as measured by the companywide efficiency reports.

Even the department managers are practicing the Kelly method. They are forcing decision making down to their supervisors.

QUESTIONS

1. Why does Ted Kelly's decision making style work?
2. Is Ted Kelly abrogating his decision making responsibilities? Are his department managers?
3. What decision making model is Ted Kelly using?
4. Would you like to work for Ted Kelly? Why?
5. Would you want Ted Kelly working for you? Why?
6. If Kelly's plant performance suddenly dropped off, what predictions would you make?

Source: Based on A. E. Carlisle, "MacGregor," *Organizational Dynamics*, 1976, pp. 50–62.

5

Values, Attitudes, and Job Satisfaction

■ *Chapter outline*

■ *Learning objectives*

Explain the source of an individual's value system
List the dominant values in today's work force
Describe the three primary job-related attitudes
Summarize the relationship between attitudes and behavior
Identify the role consistency plays in attitudes
Clarify how individuals reconcile inconsistencies
Describe how to measure job satisfaction
Explain what determines job satisfaction
State the relationship between job satisfaction and behavior
Describe the current level of job satisfaction in the workplace

When you prevent me from doing anything I want to do, that is persecution; but when I prevent you from doing anything you want to do, that is law, order and morals.

—— G. B. SHAW

"Managers should never socialize with their employees." "A little conflict in this place is good—it keeps everyone on their toes." "I don't think there's any justification for the president of this company to make a million dollars a year." "To me, the best boss is one who just leaves me alone!"

Statements such as these are regularly expressed by people at work. Importantly, these opinions—which we call values and attitudes—are not meaningless. They are often related to behavior. In this chapter, we will discuss values and attitudes and then look closely at the topic of job satisfaction.

VALUES

Is capital punishment right or wrong? How about engaging in sexual relations before marriage—is it right or wrong? If a person likes power, is that good or bad? The answers to these questions are value laden. Some might argue, for example, that capital punishment is right because it is an appropriate retribution for crimes like murder or treason. However, others may argue, just as strongly, that no government has the right to take anyone's life.

Values represent basic convictions that "a specific mode of conduct or end-state of existence is personally or socially preferable to an opposite or converse mode of conduct or end-state of existence."[1] They contain a judgmental element in that they carry an individual's ideas as to what is right, good, or desirable. Values have both content and intensity attributes. The content attribute says that a mode of conduct or end-state of existence is *important*. The intensity attribute specifies *how important* it is. When we rank an individual's values in terms of their intensity, we obtain that person's **value system**. All of us have a hierarchy of values that forms our value system. This system is identified by the relative importance we assign to such objects of values as freedom, pleasure, self-respect, honesty, obedience, equality, and so forth.

Values

Basic convictions that a specific mode of conduct or end-state of existence is personally or socially preferable to an opposite or converse mode of conduct or end-state of existence.

Value system

A ranking of individual values according to their relative importance.

[1] M. Rokeach, *The Nature of Human Values* (New York: Free Press, 1973), p. 5.

Importance of Values

Values are important to the study of organizational behavior because they lay the foundation for the understanding of attitudes and motivation as well as influencing our perceptions. Individuals enter an organization with preconceived notions of what "ought" and what "ought not" to be. Of course, these notions are not value free. On the contrary, they contain interpretations of right and wrong. Further, they imply that certain behaviors or outcomes are preferred over others. As a result, values cloud objectivity and rationality.

Values generally influence attitudes and behavior. Suppose that you enter an organization with the view that allocating pay on the basis of performance is right, whereas allocating pay on the basis of seniority is wrong or inferior. How are you going to react if you find that the organization you have just joined rewards seniority and not performance? You're likely to be disappointed—and this can lead to job dissatisfaction and the decision not to exert a high level of effort since "it's probably not going to lead to more money, anyway." Would your attitudes and behavior be different if your values aligned with the organization's pay policies? Most likely.

Sources of Our Value Systems

When we were children, why did many of our mothers tell us "you should always clean your dinner plate"? Why is it that, at least historically in our society, achievement has been considered good and being lazy has been considered bad? The answer is that, in our culture, certain values have developed over time and are continuously reinforced. Achievement, peace, cooperation, equity, and democracy are societal values that are considered desirable in our culture. These values are not fixed, but when they change, they do so very slowly.

The values we hold are essentially established in our early years—from parents, teachers, friends, and others. Your early ideas of what is right and wrong were probably formulated from the views expressed by your parents. Think back to your early views on such topics as education, sex, and politics. For the most part, they were the same as those expressed by your parents. As you grew up, and were exposed to other value systems, you may have altered a number of your values. For example, in high school, if you desired to be a member of a social club whose values included the conviction that "every person should carry a knife," there is a good probability that you changed your value system to align with members of the club, even if it meant rejecting your parents' value that "only hoodlums carry knives, and hoodlums are bad."

Interestingly, values are relatively stable and enduring. This has been explained as a result of the way in which they are originally learned.[2] As children, we are told that a certain behavior or outcome is *always* desirable or *always* undesirable. There are no gray areas. You were told, for example, that you should be honest and responsible. You were never taught to be just a little bit honest or a little bit responsible. It is this absolute or "black-or-white" learning of values that more or less assures their stability and endurance.

[2] Ibid., p. 6.

The process of questioning our values, of course, may result in a change. We may decide that these underlying convictions are no longer acceptable. More often, our questioning merely acts to reinforce those values we hold.

Types of Values

At this point, we might rightfully inquire if it is possible to identify certain value "types." The most important early work in categorizing values was done by Allport and his associates.[3] They identified six types of values:

1. *Theoretical*—places high importance on the discovery of truth through a critical and rational approach
2. *Economic*—emphasizes the useful and practical
3. *Aesthetic*—places the highest value on form and harmony
4. *Social*—assigns the highest value to the love of people
5. *Political*—places emphasis on acquisition of power and influence
6. *Religious*—is concerned with the unity of experience and understanding of the cosmos as a whole

Allport and his associates developed a questionnaire that describes a number of different situations and asks respondents to preference rank a fixed set of answers. Based on the respondents' replies, the researchers can rank individuals in terms of the importance they give to each of the six types of values. The result is a value system for a specific individual.

Using this approach, it has been found, not surprisingly, that people in different occupations place different importance on the six value types.

Table 5–1 shows the responses from ministers, purchasing agents, and industrial scientists. As expected, religious leaders consider religious values most important and economic values least important. Economic values, on the other hand, are of highest importance to the purchasing executives.

TABLE 5–1
Ranking of Values by Importance Among Three Groups

Ministers	Purchasing Executives	Scientists in Industry
1. Religious	1. Economic	1. Theoretical
2. Social	2. Theoretical	2. Political
3. Aesthetic	3. Political	3. Economic
4. Political	4. Religious	4. Aesthetic
5. Theoretical	5. Aesthetic	5. Religious
6. Economic	6. Social	6. Social

Source: R. Tagiuri, "Purchasing Executive: General Manager or Specialist?" *Journal of Purchasing*, August 1967, pp. 16–21.

[3] G. W. Allport, P. E. Vernon, and G. Lindzey, *Study of Values* (Boston: Houghton Mifflin, 1951).

TABLE 5–2
Dominant Values in Today's Work Force

Stage Category	Entered the Work Force	Approximate Current Age	Dominant Work Values	Level in the Value Hierarchy
I. Protestant Work Ethic	1940s–1950s	45–70	Hard work, conservative, loyalty to the organization.	Levels 2 and 4
II. Existentialism	1960s–1970s	30–45	Quality of life. Nonconforming. Seeks autonomy. Loyalty to self.	Levels 6 and 7
III. Pragmatism	1980s	Under 30	Success, achievement, ambition, hard work. Loyalty to career.	Level 5

More recent research suggests that there is a hierarchy of levels that are descriptive of personal values and life-styles. One such study identified seven levels:[4]

Reactive values

Individuals who value basic physiological needs and are unaware of themselves or others as human beings.

Level 1. Reactive. These individuals are unaware of themselves or others as human beings, and react to basic physiological needs. Such individuals are rarely found in organizations. This is most descriptive of newborn babies.

Level 2. Tribalistic. These individuals are characterized by high dependence. They are strongly influenced by tradition and the power exerted by authority figures.

Tribalistic values

The belief in tradition and power exerted by authority figures.

Level 3. Egocentrism. These persons believe in rugged individualism. They are aggressive and selfish. They respond primarily to power.

Egocentrism values

The belief in rugged individualism and selfishness.

Level 4. Conformity. These individuals have a low tolerance for ambiguity, have difficulty in accepting people whose values differ from their own, and desire that others accept their values.

Conformity values

A low tolerance for ambiguity, having difficulty in accepting people with different values, and a desire that others accept one's values.

Level 5. Manipulative. These individuals are characterized by striving to achieve their goals by manipulating things and people. They are materialistic and actively seek higher status and recognition.

Level 6. Sociocentric. These individuals consider it more important to be liked and to get along with others than to get ahead. They are repulsed by materialism, manipulation, and conformity.

Manipulative values

The striving to achieve goals by manipulating things and people.

Level 7. Existential. These individuals have a high tolerance for ambiguity and people with differing values. They are outspoken on inflexible systems, restrictive policies, status symbols, and arbitrary use of authority.

Sociocentric values

The belief that it is more important to be liked and to get along with others than to get ahead.

This value hierarchy can be used to analyze the problem of disparate values in organizations. Table 5–2 proposes that employees can be segmented by the era in which they entered the work force. Because most people start

Existential values

A high tolerance for ambiguity and individuals with differing values.

[4] C. W. Graves, "Levels of Existence: An Open Systems Theory of Values," *Journal of Humanistic Psychology*, Fall 1970, pp. 131–55; and M. S. Myers and S. S. Myers, "Toward Understanding the Changing Work Ethic," *California Management Review*, Spring 1974, pp. 7–19.

work between the ages of eighteen and twenty-three, the eras also correlate closely with the chronological age of employees.[5]

Workers who grew up during the Great Depression and World War II entered the work force in the 1940s and 1950s, believing in the Protestant Work Ethic. Once hired, they tended to be loyal to their employer. Levels 2 and 4 in the value hierarchy characterize these older workers in today's work force.

Employees who entered the work force during the 1960s and 1970s brought with them a large measure of the "Hippie ethic" and existential philosophy. They were more concerned with the quality of life than with the material quantity of money and possessions. Their desire for autonomy directed their loyalty toward themselves rather than any organization that employed them. These values align well with levels 6 and 7.

Finally, individuals who entered the work force in the 1980s reflect a return to more traditional values, but with far greater emphasis on achievement and material success. Today's younger worker is a pragmatist. He or she believes that ends can justify means. These workers see the organizations that employ them merely as vehicles that will propel their careers. The manipulative values of level 5 appear to most closely match this group of employees.

An understanding that people's values differ but tend to reflect the times and societal values of when they grew up can be a valuable aid for explaining and predicting behavior. Employees in their twenties and fifties, for instance, are more likely to be conservative and accepting of authority than their existential peers. Yet, when workers under thirty perceive that their contributions are not being immediately rewarded by their employer, they are more likely to quit their jobs and seek bigger and quicker payoffs somewhere else.

ATTITUDES

Attitudes are evaluative statements—either favorable or unfavorable—concerning objects, people, or events. They reflect how one feels about something. When I say "I like my job," I am expressing my attitude about work.

Attitudes are not the same as values. Values are the broader and more encompassing concept. So attitudes are more specific than values. Values also contain a moral flavor of rightness or desirability. The statement that "discrimination is bad" reflects one's values. "I favor the implementation of an affirmative action program to recruit and develop women for managerial positions in our organization" is an attitude.

While attitudes and values are different, they are closely related. One comprehensive study took a cross section of heterogeneous value issues—including rights of blacks and the poor, family security, salvation, cleanliness,

Attitudes

Evaluative statements or judgments concerning objects, people, or events.

---

[5] This three stage chronological model of values is based on ideas presented in R. J. Aldag and A. P. Brief, "Some Correlates of Work Values," *Journal of Applied Psychology*, December 1975, pp. 757–60; D. J. Cherrington, S. J. Condie, and J. L. England, "Age and Work Values," *Academy of Management Journal*, September 1979, pp. 617–23; T. Carson, "Fast-Track Kids," *Business Week*, November 10, 1986, pp. 90–92; and J. A. Raelin, "The '60s Kids in the Corporation: More Than Just 'Daydream Believers,'" *Academy of Management Executive*, February 1987, pp. 21–30.

imaginativeness, obedience—and found values and attitudes to be significantly correlated.[6] The researcher concluded that virtually any attitude will be significantly associated with some value set. The evidence allows us to say that the values people hold can explain their attitudes and, in many cases, the behaviors they engage in, but unfortunately, we cannot yet say which values underlie which attitudes and behaviors.

Sources of Attitudes

Attitudes, like values, are acquired from parents, teachers, and peer group members. In our early years, we begin modeling our attitudes after those we admire, respect, or maybe even fear. We observe the way family and friends behave, and we shape our attitudes and behavior to align with theirs. People imitate the attitudes of popular individuals or those they admire and respect. If the "right thing" is to favor eating at McDonald's, you are likely to hold that attitude. If it is popular to oppose busing, you may express that view.

In contrast to values, your attitudes are less stable. Advertising messages, for example, attempt to alter your attitudes toward a certain product or service: If the people at Ford can get you to hold a favorable opinion toward their cars, that attitude may lead to a desirable behavior (for them)—the purchase of a Ford product.

In organizations, attitudes are important because they affect job behavior. If workers believe, for example, that supervisors, auditors, bosses, and time and motion engineers are all in conspiracy to make the employee work harder for the same or less money, then it makes sense to try to understand how these attitudes were formed, their relationship to actual job behavior, and how they can be made more favorable.

Types of Attitudes

A person can have thousands of attitudes, but OB focuses our attention on a very limited number of job-related attitudes. These job-related attitudes tap positive or negative evaluations that employees hold about aspects of their work environment. Most of the research in OB has been concerned with three attitudes: job satisfaction, job involvement, and organizational commitment.

Job Satisfaction   The term job satisfaction refers to an individual's general attitude toward his or her job. A person with a high level of job satisfaction holds positive attitudes toward the job, while a person who is dissatisfied with his or her job holds negative attitudes about the job. When people speak of employee attitudes, more often than not they mean job satisfaction. In fact, the two are frequently used interchangeably. Because of the high importance OB researchers have given to job satisfaction, we'll review this attitude in considerable detail later in this chapter.

[6] Rokeach, *Human Values*, pp. 95–121.

② Job Involvement The term **job involvement** is a more recent addition to the OB literature.[7] While there is no complete agreement over what the term means, a workable definition states that job involvement measures the degree to which a person identifies psychologically with his or her job and considers his or her perceived performance level important to his or her self-worth.[8] Employees with a high level of job involvement strongly identify with and really care about the kind of work they do on their job.

High levels of job involvement have been found to be related to fewer absences and lower resignation rates.[9] However, it seems to more consistently predict turnover than absenteeism, accounting for as much as 16 percent of the variance in the former.[10]

③ Organizational Commitment The third job attitude we shall discuss is **organizational commitment**. It's defined as a state in which an employee identifies with a particular organization and its goals, and wishes to maintain membership in the organization.[11] So, high *job involvement* means identifying with one's specific job, while high *organizational commitment* means identifying with one's employing organization.

As with job involvement, the research evidence demonstrates negative relationships between organizational commitment and both absenteeism and turnover.[12] In fact, studies demonstrate that an individual's level of organizational commitment is a better indicator of turnover than the far more frequently used job satisfaction predictor, explaining as much as 34 percent of the variance.[13] Organizational commitment is probably a better predictor because it is a more global and enduring response to the organization as a whole than is job satisfaction.[14] An employee may be dissatisfied with his or her particular job, consider it a temporary condition, and not be dissatisfied with the organization

Job involvement

The degree to which a person identifies with his or her job, actively participates in it, and considers his or her performance important to his or her sense of self-worth.

Organizational commitment

An individual's orientation toward the organization in terms of loyalty, identification and involvement.

---

[7] See, for example, S. Rabinowitz and D. T. Hall, "Organizational Research in Job Involvement," *Psychological Bulletin*, March 1977, pp. 265–88; G. J. Blau, "A Multiple Study Investigation of the Dimensionality of Job Involvement," *Journal of Vocational Behavior*, August 1985, pp. 19–36; and N. A. Jans, "Organizational Factors and Work Involvement," *Organizational Behavior and Human Decision Processes*, June 1985, pp. 382–96.

[8] Based on G. J. Blau and K. R. Boal, "Conceptualizing How Job Involvement and Organizational Commitment Affect Turnover and Absenteeism," *Academy of Management Review*, April 1987, p. 290.

[9] G. J. Blau, "Job Involvement and Organizational Commitment as Interactive Predictors of Tardiness and Absenteeism," *Journal of Management*, Winter 1986, pp. 577–84; and K. Boal and R. Cidambi, "Attitudinal Correlates of Turnover and Absenteeism: A Meta Analysis." Paper presented at the meeting of the American Psychological Association; Toronto, Canada, 1984.

[10] G. Farris, "A Predictive Study of Turnover," *Personnel Psychology*, Summer 1971, pp. 311–28.

[11] Blau and Boal, "Conceptualizing," p. 290.

[12] See, for instance, P. W. Hom, R. Katerberg, and C. L. Hulin, "Comparative Examination of Three Approaches to the Prediction of Turnover," *Journal of Applied Psychology*, June 1979, pp. 280–90; H. Angle and J. Perry, "Organizational Commitment: Individual and Organizational Influence," *Work and Occupations*, May 1983, pp. 123–46; and J. L. Pierce and R. B. Dunham, "Organizational Commitment: Pre-Employment Propensity and Initial Work Experiences," *Journal of Management*, Spring 1987, pp. 163–78.

[13] P. W. Hom, R. Katerberg, and C. L. Hulin, "Comparative Examination"; and R. T. Mowday, L. W. Porter, and R. M. Steers, *Employee Organization Linkages: The Psychology of Commitment, Absenteeism, and Turnover* (New York: Academic Press, 1982).

[14] L. W. Porter, R. M. Steers, R. T. Mowday, and P. V. Boulian, "Organizational Commitment, Job Satisfaction, and Turnover Among Psychiatric Technicians," *Journal of Applied Psychology*, October 1974, pp. 603–09.

as a whole. But when dissatisfaction spreads to the organization itself, individuals are more likely to consider resigning.

Attitudes and Consistency

Did you ever notice how people change what they say so it doesn't contradict what they do? Perhaps a friend of yours has consistently argued that American cars are poorly built and that he'd never own anything but a foreign import. But his dad gives him a late-model American-made car, and suddenly they're not so bad. Or, when going through sorority rush, a new freshman believes that sororities are good and that pledging a sorority is important. If she fails to make a sorority, however, she may say: "I recognized that sorority life isn't all it's cracked up to be, anyway!"

Research has generally concluded that people seek consistency among their attitudes and between their attitudes and behavior. This means that individuals seek to reconcile divergent attitudes and align their attitudes and behavior so they appear rational and consistent. When there is an inconsistency, forces are initiated to return the individual to an equilibrium state where attitudes and behavior are again consistent. This can be done by altering either the attitudes or the behavior or by developing a rationalization for the discrepancy.

For example, a recruiter for the ABC Company, whose job it is to visit college campuses, identify qualified job candidates, and sell them on the advantages of ABC as a place to work, would be in conflict if he personally believes the ABC Company has poor working conditions and few opportunities for new college graduates. This recruiter could, over time, find his attitudes toward the ABC Company becoming more positive. He may, in effect, brainwash himself by continually articulating the merits of working for ABC. Another alternative would be for the recruiter to become overtly negative about ABC and the opportunities within the firm for prospective candidates. The original enthusiasm that the recruiter may have shown would dwindle, probably to be replaced by open cynicism toward the company. Finally, the recruiter might acknowledge that ABC is an undesirable place to work, but as a professional recruiter his obligation is to present the positive sides of working for the company. He might further rationalize that no place is perfect to work at; therefore, his job is not to present both sides of the issue, but rather to present a "rosy" picture of the company.

Cognitive Dissonance Theory

Can we additionally assume from this consistency principle that an individual's behavior can always be predicted if we know his or her attitude on a subject? If Mr. Jones views the company's pay level as too low, will a substantial increase in his pay change his behavior; that is, make him work harder? The answer to this question is, unfortunately, more complex than merely a "Yes" or "No."

Leon Festinger, in the late 1950s, proposed the theory of **cognitive dissonance.**[15] This theory sought to explain the linkage between attitudes and

Cognitive dissonance

Any incompatibility between two or more attitudes or between behavior and attitudes.

[15] L. Festinger, *A Theory of Cognitive Dissonance* (Stanford, CA: Stanford University Press, 1957).

behavior. Dissonance means an inconsistency. Cognitive dissonance refers to any incompatibility that an individual might perceive between two or more of his or her attitudes, or between his or her behavior and attitudes. Festinger argued that any form of inconsistency is uncomfortable and that individuals will attempt to reduce dissonance and, hence, the discomfort. Therefore, individuals will seek a stable state where there is a minimum of dissonance.

Of course, no individual can completely avoid dissonance. You know that cheating on your income tax is wrong, but you "fudge" the numbers a bit every year, and hope you're not audited. Or you tell your children to brush after every meal, but *you* don't. So how do people cope? Festinger would propose that the desire to reduce dissonance would be determined by the importance of the elements creating the dissonance, the degree of influence the individual believes he or she has over the elements, and the rewards that may be involved in dissonance.

If the elements creating the dissonance are relatively unimportant, the pressure to correct this imbalance will be low. However, say that a corporate manager—Mrs. Smith, who has a husband and several children—believes strongly that no company should pollute the air or water. Unfortunately, Mrs. Smith, because of the requirements of her job, is placed in the position of having to make decisions that would trade off her company's profitability against her attitudes on pollution. She knows that dumping the company's sewage into the local river (which we shall assume is legal) is in the best economic interest of her firm. What will she do? Clearly, Mrs. Smith is experiencing a high degree of cognitive dissonance. Because of the importance of the elements in this example, we cannot expect Mrs. Smith to ignore the inconsistency. There are several paths that she can follow to deal with her dilemma. She can change her behavior (stop polluting the river). Or she can reduce dissonance by concluding that the dissonant behavior is not so important after all ("I've got to make a living, and in my role as a corporate decision maker, I often have to place the good of my company above that of the environment or society"). A third alternative would be for Mrs. Smith to change her attitude ("There is nothing wrong in polluting the river"). Still another choice would be to seek out more consonant elements to outweigh the dissonant ones ("The benefits to society from our manufacturing our products more than offset the cost to society of the resulting water pollution").

The degree of influence that individuals believe they have over the elements will have an impact on how they will react to the dissonance. If they perceive the dissonance to be an uncontrollable result—something over which they have no choice—they are less likely to be receptive to attitude change. If, for example, the dissonance-producing behavior was required as a result of the boss's directive, the pressure to reduce dissonance would be less than if the behavior was performed voluntarily. While dissonance exists, it can be rationalized and justified.

Rewards also influence the degree to which individuals are motivated to reduce dissonance. High dissonance, when accompanied by high rewards, tends to reduce the tension inherent in the dissonance. The reward acts to reduce dissonance by increasing the consistency side of the individual's balance sheet. Since people in organizations are given some form of reward or remuneration for their services, employees often can deal with greater dissonance on their jobs than off their jobs.

OB Close-Up

When Consistency Is Dysfunctional

Cognitive dissonance theory argues that an individual's motivation to change his or her attitudes is based on his or her desire to appear consistent to himself or herself. Put in terms of the optimizing model presented in the previous chapter, individuals seek to appear rational.

But this desire for consistency isn't always a positive attribute in decision makers, because consistency can lead to inflexibility. If conditions change so that previous solutions no longer work, but the decision maker digs in his or her heels and refuses to acknowledge this fact, then this search for consistency can be counterproductive for the organization.

The desire to reduce dissonance has been shown to be dysfunctional when it leads to an *escalation of commitment*; that is, an increased commitment to a previous decision in spite of negative information. This is the proverbial situation where one "throws good money after bad." It has been well-documented that individuals escalate commitment to a failing course of action when they view themselves responsible for the failure.[16] Congruent with cognitive dissonance theory, they want to demonstrate that the initial decision was not wrong.

Maybe the most frequently cited example of the escalation of commitment phenomenon was President Lyndon Johnson's decisions regarding the Vietnam War. Despite continued information that bombing North Vietnam was not bringing the war any closer to conclusion, his solution was to increase the tonnage of bombs dropped. Of course, escalation of commitment doesn't apply only to presidential decisions. Many business firms have suffered large losses as a result of managers who were determined to prove their original decisions were right by continuing to commit resources to what was a lost cause from the beginning.

These moderating factors suggest that just because individuals experience dissonance does not necessarily mean that they will directly move toward consistency; that is, toward reduction of this dissonance. If the issues underlying the dissonance are of minimal importance, if an individual perceives that the dissonance is externally imposed and is substantially uncontrollable by him or her, or if rewards are significant enough to offset the dissonance, the individual will not be under great tension to reduce the dissonance.

What are the organizational implications of the theory of cognitive dissonance? It can help to predict the propensity to engage in attitude and behavioral change. If individuals are required, for example, by the demands of their job, to say or do things that contradict their personal attitude, they will tend to

---

[16] B. M. Staw, "The Escalation of Commitment to a Course of Action," *Academy of Management Review*, October 1981, pp. 577–87.

modify their attitude in order to make it compatible with the cognition of what they have said or done. Additionally, the greater the dissonance—after it has been moderated by importance, choice, and reward factors—the greater the pressures to reduce the dissonance.

Measuring the A-B Relationship

We have maintained throughout this chapter that attitudes affect behavior. The early research work on attitudes assumed that they were causally related to behavior; that is, the attitudes that people hold determine what they do. Common sense, too, suggests a relationship. Is it not logical that people watch television programs that they say they like or that employees try to avoid assignments they find distasteful?

However, in the late 1960s, this assumed relationship between attitudes and behavior (A-B) was challenged by a review of the research.[17] Based on an evaluation of a number of studies that investigated the A-B relationship, the reviewer concluded that attitudes were unrelated to behavior or, at best, only slightly related.[18] More recent research has demonstrated that the A-B relationship can be improved by taking into consideration moderating contingency variables.

Moderating Variables   One thing that improves our chances of finding significant A-B relationships is the use of both specific attitudes and specific behaviors.[19] It is one thing to talk about a person's attitude toward "preserving the environment" and another to speak of his or her attitude toward "purchasing unleaded gasoline" (which generates less air pollution in the environment). The more specific the attitude we are measuring and the more specific we are in identifying a related behavior, the greater the probability that we can show a relationship between A and B. As a case in point, in the early 1970s, the laws did not yet require late-model cars to operate only on unleaded gas. In those days, people were free to choose between regular and unleaded gas. The unleaded variety typically cost a few cents more, but it did less environmental damage. Several researchers drew samples of drivers using unleaded and regular gas and then asked the drivers four levels of questions ranging from items about general interest in the environment issues to a specific question about the degree of personal obligation the individual felt to buy unleaded gasoline. The A-B relationship increased from +0.12 to +0.59 as the questions went from the least to the most specific level.[20] That is, the more specific the question, the closer the response related to actual gasoline purchasing behavior.

Another moderator is social constraints on behavior. Discrepancies between attitudes and behavior may occur because the social pressures on the

---

[17] A. W. Wicker, "Attitude Versus Action: The Relationship of Verbal and Overt Behavioral Responses to Attitude Objects," *Journal of Social Issues*, Autumn 1969, pp. 41–78.

[18] Ibid., p. 65.

[19] T. A. Heberlein and J. S. Black, "Attitudinal Specificity and the Prediction of Behavior in a Field Setting," *Journal of Personality and Social Psychology*, April 1976, pp. 474–79.

[20] Ibid.

individual to behave in a certain way may hold exceptional power.[21] Group pressures, for instance, may explain why an employee who holds strong anti-union attitudes attends pro-union organizing meetings.

Still another moderating variable is experience with the attitude in question.[22] The A-B relationship is likely to be much stronger if the attitude being evaluated refers to something about which the individual has experience. For instance, most of us will respond to a questionnaire on most any issue. But is my attitude toward starving fish in the Amazon any indication of whether I'd donate to a fund to save these fish? Probably not! Asking college students, with no work experience, their views on job factors that are important in determining whether they would stay put in a job is an example of an attitude response that is unlikely to predict much in terms of actual turnover behavior.

Self-perception theory

Attitudes are used, after the fact, to make sense out of action that has already occurred.

Self-Perception Theory While most A-B studies yield positive results[23] —that attitudes do influence behavior—the relationship tends to be weak before adjustments are made for moderating variables. But requiring specificity, an absence of social constraints, and experience in order to get a meaningful correlation imposes severe limitations on making generalizations about the A-B relationship. This has prompted some researchers to take another direction—to look at whether behavior influences attitudes. This view, called **self-perception theory**, has generated some encouraging findings.[24] Let's briefly review the theory.

When asked about an attitude toward some object, individuals recall their behavior relevant to that object and then infer their attitude from the past behavior. So if an employee were asked about her feelings about being a payroll clerk at Exxon, she would likely think, "I've had this same job at Exxon as a payroll clerk for ten years, so I must like it!" Self-perception theory, therefore, argues that attitudes are used, after the fact, to make sense out of the action that has already occurred rather than as devices that precede and guide action.

Self-perception theory has been well supported.[25] While the traditional attitude-behavior relationship is generally positive, it is also weak. In contrast, the behavior-attitude relationship is quite strong. So what can we conclude? It seems that we are very good at finding reasons for what we do, but not so good at doing what we find reasons for.[26]

[21] H. Schuman and M. P. Johnson, "Attitudes and Behavior," in A. Inkeles (ed.), *Annual Review of Sociology*, (Palo Alto, CA: Annual Reviews, 1976), pp. 161–207.

[22] R. H. Fazio and M. P. Zanna, "Direct Experience and Attitude-Behavior Consistency," in L. Berkowitz (ed.), *Advances in Experimental Social Psychology*, (New York: Academic Press, 1981), pp. 161–202.

[23] L. R. Kahle and H. J. Berman, "Attitudes Cause Behaviors: A Cross-Lagged Panel Analysis," *Journal of Personality and Social Psychology*, March 1979, pp. 315–21; and C. L. Kleinke, "Two Models for Conceptualizing the Attitude-Behavior Relationship," *Human Relations*, April 1984, pp. 333–50.

[24] D. J. Bem, "Self-Perception Theory," in L. Berkowitz (ed.), *Advances in Experimental Social Psychology*, Vol. 6 (New York: Academic Press, 1972), pp. 1–62.

[25] See, for example, C. A. Kiesler, R. E. Nisbett, and M. P. Zanna, "On Inferring One's Belief from One's Behavior," *Journal of Personality and Social Psychology*, April 1969, pp. 321–27.

[26] R. Abelson, "Are Attitudes Necessary?" in B. T. King and E. McGinnies (eds.), *Attitudes, Conflicts, and Social Change* (New York: Academic Press, 1972), p. 25.

An Application: Attitude Surveys

The preceding review should not discourage us from using attitudes to predict behavior. In an organizational context, most of the attitudes management would seek to inquire about would be ones with which employees have some experience. If the attitudes in question are specifically stated, management should obtain information that can be valuable in guiding their decisions relative to these employees. But how does management get information about employee attitudes? The most popular method is through the use of **attitude surveys.**[27]

Table 5–3 illustrates what an attitude survey might look like. Typically, attitude surveys present the employee with a set of statements or questions. Ideally, the items will be tailor-made to obtain the specific information that management desires. An attitude score is achieved by summing up responses to individual questionnaire items. These scores can then be averaged for job groups, departments, divisions, or the organization as a whole.

Results from attitude surveys frequently surprise management. Why? Consistent with our discussion of perceptions in the previous chapter, the policies and practices that management views as objective and fair may be seen as inequitable by employees in general or among certain groups of employees. That these distorted perceptions have led to negative attitudes about the job and organization should be important to management. This is because employee behaviors are based on perceptions, not reality. Remember, the employee who quits because she believes she is underpaid—when in fact management has

Attitude surveys

Eliciting responses from employees through questionnaires about how they feel about their jobs, work groups, supervisors, and/or the organization.

TABLE 5–3
Sample Attitude Survey

Please answer each of the following statements using the following rating scale:
    5 = Strongly agree
    4 = Agree
    3 = Undecided
    2 = Disagree
    1 = Strongly disagree

Statement	Rating
1. This company is a pretty good place to work.	_____
2. I can get ahead in this company if I make the effort.	_____
3. This company's wage rates are competitive with those of other companies.	_____
4. Employee promotion decisions are handled fairly.	_____
5. I understand the various fringe benefits the company offers.	_____
6. My job makes the best use of my abilities.	_____
7. My work load is challenging but not burdensome.	_____
8. I have trust and confidence in my boss.	_____
9. I feel free to tell my boss what I think.	_____
10. I know what my boss expects of me.	_____

[27] See, for example, L. Reibstein, "A Finger on the Pulse: Companies Expand Use of Employee Surveys," *Wall Street Journal*, October 27, 1986, p. 27.

objective data to support that her salary is highly competitive—is just as gone as if she had actually been underpaid. The use of regular attitude surveys can alert management to potential problems and employees' intentions early so that action can be taken to prevent repercussions.[28]

JOB SATISFACTION

We have already discussed job satisfaction briefly—earlier in this chapter as well as in Chapter 2. In this section we want to dissect the concept more carefully. How do we measure job satisfaction? Are most workers today satisfied with their jobs? What determines job satisfaction? What is its effect on employee productivity, absenteeism, and turnover rates? We'll answer each of these questions in this section.

Measuring Job Satisfaction

We've previously defined job satisfaction as an individual's general attitude toward his or her job. This definition is clearly a very broad one. Yet this is inherent in the concept. Remember, a person's job is more than just the obvious activities of shuffling papers, waiting on customers, or driving a truck. Jobs require interaction with co-workers and bosses, following organizational rules and policies, meeting performance standards, living with working conditions that are often less than ideal, and the like. This means that an employee's assessment of how satisfied or dissatisfied he or she is with his or her job is a complex summation of a number of discrete job elements. So how then do we measure the concept?

The two most widely used approaches are a single global rating and a summation score made up of a number of job facets. The single global rating method is nothing more than asking individuals to respond to one question, such as "All things considered, how satisfied are you with your job?" Respondents then reply by circling a number between one and five that corresponds with answers from "Highly Satisfied" to "Highly Dissatisfied." The other approach—a summation of job facets—is more sophisticated. It identifies key elements in a job and asks for the employee's feelings about each. Typical factors that would be included are the nature of the work, supervision, present pay, promotion opportunities, and relations with co-workers.[29] These factors are rated on a standardized scale and then added up to create an overall job satisfaction score.

Is one of the foregoing approaches superior to the other? Intuitively, it would seem that summing up responses to a number of job factors would

---

[28] G. A. Kesselman, "The Attitude Survey: Does It Have a Bearing on Productivity?," *S.A.M. Advanced Management Journal*, Winter 1984, pp. 18–24; and D. R. York, "Attitude Surveying," *Personnel Journal*, May 1985, pp. 70–73.

[29] See J. L. Price and C. W. Mueller, *Handbook of Organizational Measurement* (Marshfield, MA: Pitman Publishing, 1986), pp. 223–27.

achieve a more accurate evaluation of job satisfaction. The research, however, doesn't support such intuition.[30] This is one of those rare instances in which simplicity wins out over complexity. Comparisons of one-question global ratings with the more lengthy summation of job factors method indicate that the former is more valid. The best explanation for this outcome is that the concept of job satisfaction is inherently so broad that the single question actually becomes a more inclusive measure.

Job Satisfaction as a Dependent Variable

We now turn to considering job satisfaction as a dependent variable. That is, we seek an answer to the question: *What* work-related variables determine job satisfaction? An extensive review of the literature indicates that the more important factors conducive to job satisfaction include mentally challenging work, equitable rewards, supportive working conditions, and supportive colleagues.[31]

Mentally Challenging Work   Employees tend to prefer jobs that give them opportunities to use their skills and abilities and offer a variety of tasks, freedom, and feedback on how well they are doing. These characteristics make work mentally challenging. Jobs that have too little challenge create boredom. But too much challenge creates frustration and feelings of failure. Under conditions of moderate challenge, most employees will experience pleasure and satisfaction.

Equitable Rewards   Employees want pay systems and promotion policies that they perceive as being just, unambiguous, and in line with their expectations. When pay is seen as fair based on job demands, individual skill level, and community pay standards, satisfaction is likely to result. Of course, not everyone seeks money. Many people willingly accept less money to work in a preferred location or in a less demanding job or to have greater discretion in the work they do and the hours they work. But the key in linking pay to satisfaction is not the absolute amount one is paid; rather, it is the perception of fairness. Similarly, employees seek fair promotion policies and practices. Promotions provide opportunities for personal growth, more responsibilities, and increased social status. Individuals who perceive that promotion decisions are made in a fair and just manner, therefore, are likely to experience satisfaction from their job.

Supportive Working Conditions   Employees are concerned with their work environment for both personal comfort and facilitating doing a good job. Studies demonstrate that employees prefer physical surroundings that are not dangerous or uncomfortable. Temperature, light, noise, and other environmental factors should not be at either extreme—for example, having too much heat or too little light. Additionally, most employees prefer working relatively close to home, in clean and relatively modern facilities, and with adequate tools and equipment.

[30] V. Scarpello and J. P. Campbell, "Job Satisfaction: Are All the Parts There?," *Personnel Psychology*, Autumn 1983, pp. 577–600.

[31] E. A. Locke, "The Nature and Causes of Job Satisfaction," in M. D. Dunnette (ed.), *Handbook of Industrial and Organizational Psychology* (Chicago: Rand McNally, 1976), pp. 1319–28.

OB Close-Up

Job Satisfaction in the Workplace Today

Are American workers satisfied with their jobs? The answer to this question, based on numerous studies, is a resounding "Yes!" Moreover, the numbers are surprisingly constant over time. Let's take a closer look at what we know.

Regardless of what studies you choose to look at, when employees are asked if they are satisfied with their jobs, the results tend to be very similar: Around 80 percent of American workers report they are *satisfied* with their jobs.[32] Or, from the negative perspective, only 10 to 15 percent report being *dissatisfied*.[33] Older workers report the highest satisfaction (92 percent for those age sixty-five and over), but even young people—under age twenty-five—report high levels of satisfaction (73 percent).[34]

While there was some concern in the late 1970s that satisfaction was declining across almost all occupational groups,[35] recent reinterpretations of these data and additional longitudinal studies indicate that job satisfaction levels have held steady for decades—through economic recessions as well as prosperous times.[36]

How does one explain these results? Taken literally, we can say that whatever it is that people want from their jobs, they seem to be getting it and have been for

Supportive Colleagues People get more out of work than merely money or tangible achievements. For most employees, work also fills the need for social interaction. Not surprisingly, therefore, having friendly and supportive co-workers leads to increased job satisfaction. The behavior of one's boss also is a major determinant of satisfaction. Studies generally find that employee satisfaction is increased when the immediate supervisor is understanding and friendly, offers praise for good performance, listens to the employee's opinions, and shows a personal interest in his or her employees.

---

[32] See, for instance, studies cited in A. F. Chelte, J. Wright, and C. Tausky, "Did Job Satisfaction Really Drop During the 1970s?," *Monthly Labor Review*, November 1982, pp. 33–36; "Job Satisfaction High in America, Says Conference Board Study," *Monthly Labor Review*, February 1985, p. 52; and C. Hartman and S. Pearlstein, "The Joy of Working," *Inc.*, November 1987, pp. 61–66.

[33] H. L. Sheppard and N. Q. Herrick, *Where Have All the Robots Gone?* (New York: Free Press, 1972); R. B. Freeman, "Job Satisfaction as an Economic Variable," *American Economic Review*, January 1978, pp. 135–41.

[34] "Job Satisfaction High in America," p. 52.

[35] G. L. Staines and R. P. Quinn, "American Workers Evaluate the Quality of Their Jobs," *Monthly Labor Review*, January 1979, pp. 3–12.

[36] Chelte, Wright, Tausky, "Did Job Satisfaction Really Drop?" and B. M. Staw, N. E. Bell, and J. A. Clausen, "The Dispositional Approach to Job Attitudes: A Lifetime Longitudinal Test," *Administrative Science Quarterly*, March 1986, pp. 56–77.

quite some time, at least if we believe what people say in job satisfaction surveys. But if we dig a little deeper, we might question this literal interpretation. For instance, based on our knowledge of cognitive dissonance theory, we might expect employees to resolve inconsistencies between dissatisfaction with their jobs and their staying with those jobs by not reporting the dissatisfaction. Also, when employees are asked whether they would again choose the same work or whether they would want their children to follow in their footsteps, typically less than half answer in the affirmative.[37] So maybe employees aren't as satisfied with their jobs as the numbers would suggest.

An interesting explanation has also been proposed for the stability of job satisfaction findings over time. Satisfaction may lie more in the employee's personality than in the job.[38] Analysis of satisfaction data for a selected sample of individuals over a fifty-year period found that individual results were consistently stable over time, even when these people changed the employer for whom they worked and their occupation. It may well be that many of the work-related variables that we think *cause* job satisfaction aren't that important. Rather, most individuals' disposition toward life—positive or negative—is established by adolescence, holds over time, carries over into their disposition toward work, and—at least among Americans—is generally upbeat.

Don't Forget the Personality-Job Fit! In Chapter 3, we presented Holland's personality-job fit theory. As you remember, one of Holland's conclusions was that high agreement between an employee's personality and occupation results in a more satisfied individual. His logic was essentially this: People with personality types congruent with their chosen vocations should find that they have the right talents and abilities to meet the demands of their jobs; are thus more likely to be successful on those jobs; and, because of this success, have a greater probability of achieving high satisfaction from their work. Studies to replicate Holland's conclusions have been almost universally supportive.[39] It's important, therefore, to add this to our list of factors that determine job satisfaction.

[37] R. L. Kahn, "The Meaning of Work: Interpretation and Proposals of Measurement," in A. Campbell and P. E. Converse (eds.), *The Human Meaning of Social Change* (New York: Russell Sage Foundation, 1972).

[38] Staw, Bell, and Clausen, 'The Dispositional Approach to Job Attitudes." This conclusion, however, has been challenged in B. Gerhart, "How Important Are Dispositional Factors as Determinants of Job Satisfaction? Implications for Job Design and Other Personnel Programs," *Journal of Applied Psychology*, August 1987, pp. 366–73.

[39] See, for example, D. C. Feldman and H. J. Arnold, "Personality Types and Career Patterns: Some Empirical Evidence on Holland's Model," *Canadian Journal of Administrative Science*, June 1985, pp. 192–210.

Job Satisfaction as an Independent Variable

Managers' interest in job satisfaction tends to center on its effect on employee performance. Researchers have recognized this interest—so we find a large number of studies that have been designed to assess the impact of job satisfaction on employee productivity, absenteeism, and turnover. Let's look at the current state of our knowledge.

Satisfaction and Productivity   A number of reviews were done in the 1950s and 1960s, covering dozens of studies that sought to establish the relationship between satisfaction and productivity.[40] These reviews could find no consistent relationship. In the late 1980s, though the studies are far from unambiguous, we can make some sense out of the evidence.

The early views on the satisfaction-performance relationship can be essentially summarized in the statement "a happy worker is a productive worker." Much of the paternalism shown by managers in the 1930s, 1940s, and 1950s—forming company bowling teams and credit unions, having company picnics, providing counseling services for employees, training supervisors to be sensitive to the concerns of subordinates—was done to make workers happy. But belief in the happy worker thesis was based more on wishful thinking than hard evidence. A careful review of the research indicates that if there is a positive relationship between satisfaction and productivity, the correlations are consistently low—in the vicinity of 0.14.[41] However, introduction of moderating variables has improved the relationship.[42] For example, the relationship is stronger when the employee's behavior is not constrained or controlled by outside factors. An employee's productivity on machine-paced jobs, for instance, is going to be much more influenced by the speed of the machine than his or her level of satisfaction. Similarly, a stockbroker's productivity is largely constrained by the general movement of the stock market. When the market is moving up and volume is high, both satisfied and dissatisfied brokers are going to ring up lots of commissions. Conversely, when the market is in the doldrums, the level of broker satisfaction is not likely to mean much. Job level also seems to be an important moderating variable. The performance-satisfaction correlations are stronger for higher-level employees. Thus, we might expect the relationship to be more relevant for individuals in professional, supervisory, and managerial positions.

Another point of concern in the satisfaction-productivity issue is the direction of the causal arrow. Most of the studies on the relationship used research

---

[40] A. H. Brayfield and W. H. Crockett, "Employee Attitudes and Employee Performance," *Psychological Bulletin*, September 1955, pp. 396–428; F. Herzberg, B. Mausner, R. O. Peterson, and D. F. Capwell, *Job Attitudes: Review of Research and Opinion* (Pittsburgh: Psychological Service of Pittsburgh, 1957); V. H. Vroom, *Work and Motivation* (New York: John Wiley, 1964); G. P. Fournet, M. K. Distefano, Jr., and M. W. Pryer, "Job Satisfaction: Issues and Problems," *Personnel Psychology*, Summer 1966, pp. 165–83.

[41] Vroom, *Work and Motivation*; and M. T. Iaffaldano and P. M. Muchinsky, "Job Satisfaction and Job Performance: A Meta-Analysis," *Psychological Bulletin*, March 1985, pp. 251–73.

[42] See, for example, J. B. Herman, "Are Situational Contingencies Limiting Job Attitude–Job Performance Relationship?," *Organizational Behavior and Human Performance*, October 1973, pp. 208–24; and M. M. Petty, G. W. McGee, and J. W. Cavender, "A Meta-Analysis of the Relationship Between Individual Job Satisfaction and Individual Performance," *Academy of Management Review*, October 1984, pp. 712–21.

designs that could not prove cause and effect. Studies that have controlled for this possibility indicate that the more valid conclusion is that productivity leads to satisfaction rather than the other way around.[43] If you do a good job, you intrinsically feel good about it. Additionally, assuming that the organization rewards productivity, your higher productivity should increase verbal recognition, your pay level, and probabilities for promotion. These rewards, in turn, increase your level of satisfaction with the job.

Satisfaction and Absenteeism   We find a consistent negative relationship between satisfaction and absenteeism, but the correlation isn't high—usually less than 0.40.[44] While it certainly makes sense that dissatisfied employees are more likely to miss work, other factors have an impact on the relationship and reduce the correlation coefficient. For example, remember our discussion of sick pay versus well pay in Chapter 3. Organizations that provide liberal sick leave benefits are encouraging all their employees—including those who are highly satisfied—to take days off. Assuming that you have a reasonable degree of varied interests, you can find work satisfying and yet still take off work to enjoy a three-day weekend, tan yourself on a warm summer day, or watch the World Series on television if those days come free with no penalties. Also, as with productivity, outside factors can act to reduce the correlation.

An excellent illustration of how satisfaction directly leads to attendance, where there is a minimum impact from other factors, is a study done at Sears, Roebuck.[45] Satisfaction data were available on employees at Sears' two headquarters in Chicago and New York. Additionally, it is important to note that Sears' policy was not to permit employees to be absent from work for avoidable reasons without penalty. The occurrence of a freak April 2 snowstorm in Chicago created the opportunity to compare employee attendance at the Chicago office with personnel in New York where the weather was quite nice. The interesting dimension in this study is that the snowstorm gave the Chicago employees a built-in excuse not to come to work. The storm crippled the city's transportation, and individuals knew they could miss work this day with no penalty. This natural experiment permitted the comparison of attendance records for satisfied and dissatisfied employees at two locations—one where you were expected to be at work (with normal pressures for attendance) and the other where you were free to choose with no penalty involved. If satisfaction leads to attendance, where there is an absence of outside factors, the more satisfied employees should have come to work in Chicago, while dissatisfied employees should have stayed home. The study found that, on this April 2 day, absenteeism rates

[43] C. N. Greene, "The Satisfaction-Performance Controversy," *Business Horizons*, February 1972, pp. 31–41; E. E. Lawler III, *Motivation in Organizations* (Monterey, CA: Brooks/Cole, 1973); and Petty, McGee, and Cavender, "A Meta-Analysis of the Relationship Between Individual Job Satisfaction and Individual Performance."

[44] Locke, "The Nature and Causes of Job Satisfaction," p. 1331; S. L. McShane, "Job Satisfaction and Absenteeism: A Meta-Analytic Re-Examination," *Canadian Journal of Administrative Science*, June 1984, pp. 61–77; R. D. Hackett and R. M. Guion, "A Reevaluation of the Absenteeism-Job Satisfaction Relationship," *Organizational Behavior and Human Decision Processes*, June 1985, pp. 340–81; and K. D. Scott and G. S. Taylor, "An Examination of Conflicting Findings on the Relationship Between Job Satisfaction and Absenteeism: A Meta-Analysis," *Academy of Management Journal*, September 1985, pp. 599–612.

[45] F. J. Smith, "Work Attitudes as Predictors of Attendance on a Specific Day," *Journal of Applied Psychology*, February 1977, pp. 16–19.

in New York (the control group) were just as high for satisfied groups of workers as for dissatisfied groups. But in Chicago, the workers with high satisfaction scores had much higher attendance than did those with lower satisfaction levels. These findings are exactly what we would have expected if satisfaction is negatively correlated with absenteeism.

Satisfaction and Turnover   Satisfaction is also negatively related to turnover, but the correlation is stronger than what we found for absenteeism.[46] Yet, again, other factors such as labor market conditions, expectations about alternative job opportunities, and length of tenure with the organization are important constraints on the actual decision to leave one's current job.[47]

Evidence indicates that an important moderating variable on the satisfaction-turnover relationship is the employee's level of performance.[48] Specifically, level of satisfaction is less important in predicting turnover for superior performers. Why? The organization typically makes considerable efforts to keep these people. They get pay raises, praise, recognition, increased promotional opportunities, and so forth. Just the opposite tends to apply to poor performers. Few attempts are made by the organization to retain them. There may even be subtle pressures to encourage them to quit. We would expect, therefore, that job satisfaction is more important in influencing poor performers to stay than for superior performers. Regardless of level of satisfaction, the latter are more likely to remain with the organization because the receipt of recognition, praise, and other rewards gives them more reasons for staying.

How Employees Can Express Dissatisfaction

One final point before we leave the issue of job satisfaction: Employee dissatisfaction can be expressed in a number of ways. For example, employees can choose to complain rather than quit. Figure 5–1 offers four responses that differ from one another along two dimensions: constructiveness/destructiveness and activity/passivity. They are defined as follows:[49]

- **Exit** - Behavior directed toward leaving the organization. Includes looking for a new position as well as resigning.

Exit

Dissatisfaction expressed through behavior directed toward leaving the organization.

[46] Brayfield and Crockett, "Employee Attitudes"; Vroom, *Work and Motivation*; J. Price, *The Study of Turnover* (Ames: Iowa State University Press, 1977); and W. H. Mobley, R. W. Griffeth, H. H. Hand, and B. M. Meglino, "Review and Conceptual Analysis of the Employee Turnover Process," *Psychological Bulletin*, May 1979, pp. 493–522.

[47] See, for example, C. L. Hulin, M. Roznowski, and D. Hachiya, "Alternative Opportunities and Withdrawal Decisions: Empirical and Theoretical Discrepancies and an Integration," *Psychological Bulletin*, July 1985, pp. 233–50; and J. M. Carsten and P. E. Spector, "Unemployment, Job Satisfaction, and Employee Turnover: A Meta-Analytic Test of the Muchinsky Model," *Journal of Applied Psychology*, August 1987, pp, 374–81.

[48] D. G. Spencer and R. M. Steers, "Performance as a Moderator of the Job Satisfaction-Turnover Relationship," *Journal of Applied Psychology*, August 1981, pp. 511–14.

[49] D. Farrell, "Exit, Voice, Loyalty, and Neglect as Responses to Job Dissatisfaction: A Multidimensional Scaling Study," *Academy of Management Journal*, December 1983, pp. 596–606; and C. Rusbult and D. Lowery, "When Bureaucrats Get the Blues: Responses to Dissatisfaction Among Federal Employees," *Journal of Applied Social Psychology*, Vol. 15, No. 1, 1985, pp. 80–103.

- **Voice** - Actively and constructively attempting to improve conditions. Includes suggesting improvements, discussing problems with one's boss, and some forms of union activity.
- **Loyalty** - Passively but optimistically waiting for conditions to improve. Includes speaking up for the organization in the face of external criticism and trusting the organization and its management to "do the right thing."
- **Neglect** - Passively allowing conditions to worsen. Includes chronic absenteeism or lateness, reduced effort, and increased error rate.

Voice

Dissatisfaction expressed through active and constructive attempts to improve conditions.

Loyalty

Dissatisfaction expressed by passively waiting for conditions to improve.

Neglect

Dissatisfaction expressed through allowing conditions to worsen.

FIGURE 5–1
Responses to Job Dissatisfaction

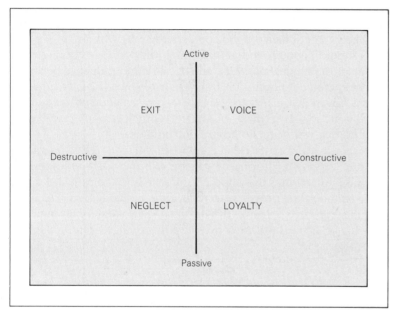

Source: C Rusbult and D. Lowery, "When Bureaucrats Get the Blues," *Journal of Applied Social Psychology*, Vol. 15, No. 1, 1985, p. 83. With permission.

Exit and neglect behaviors encompass our performance variables—productivity, absenteeism, and turnover. But this model expands employee response to include voice and loyalty—constructive behaviors that allow individuals to tolerate unpleasant situations or to revive satisfactory working conditions. It helps us to understand situations, such as those sometimes found among unionized workers, where low job satisfaction is coupled with low turnover.[50] Union members often express dissatisfaction through the grievance procedure or through formal contract negotiations. These voice mechanisms allow the union members to continue in their jobs while convincing themselves that they are acting to improve the situation.

[50] R. B. Freeman, "Job Satisfaction as an Economic Variable."

What is the importance of knowing about an individual's values? Although they don't have a direct impact on behavior, values strongly influence a person's attitudes. So knowledge of an individual's value system can provide insight into his or her attitudes.

Given that people's values differ, managers can use the seven-level hierarchy to characterize potential employees and determine if their values align with the dominant values of the organization. An employee's performance and satisfaction are likely to be higher if his or her values fit well with the organization. For instance, the egocentric individualist is poorly matched with an organization that seeks conformity from its employees. Managers are more likely to appreciate, evaluate positively, and allocate rewards to employees who "fit in," and employees are more likely to be satisfied if they perceive that they "fit in."

Managers should be interested in their employees' attitudes because attitudes give warnings of potential problems and because they influence behavior. Satisfied and committed employees, for instance, have lower rates of turnover and absenteeism. Given that managers want to keep resignations and absences down—especially among their more productive employees—they will want to do those things that will generate positive job attitudes.

Managers should also be aware that employees will try to reduce cognitive dissonance. More important, dissonance can be managed. If employees are required to engage in activities that appear inconsistent to them or that are at odds with their attitudes, the pressures to reduce the resulting dissonance are lessened when the employee perceives that the dissonance is externally imposed and is beyond his or her control or if the rewards are significant enough to offset the dissonance.

POINT

THE IMPORTANCE OF HIGH JOB SATISFACTION

The importance of job satisfaction is obvious. Managers should be concerned with the level of job satisfaction in their organizations for at least three reasons: (1) there is clear evidence that dissatisfied employees skip work more often and are more likely to resign; (2) it has been demonstrated that satisfied employees have better health and live longer; and (3) satisfaction on the job carries over to the employee's life outside the job.

We reviewed the evidence between satisfaction and withdrawal behaviors in this chapter. That evidence was fairly clear: satisfied employees have lower rates of both turnover and absenteeism. If we consider the two withdrawal behaviors separately, however, we can be more confident about the influence of satisfaction on turnover. Specifically, satisfaction is strongly and consistently negatively related to an employee's decision to leave the organization. Although satisfaction and absence are also negatively related, conclusions regarding the relationship should be more guarded.

An often overlooked dimension of job satisfaction is its relationship to employee health. Several studies have shown that employees who are dissatisfied with their jobs are prone to health setbacks—ranging from headaches to heart disease. Some research even indicates that job satisfaction is a better predictor of length of life than is physical condition or tobacco use. These studies suggest that dissatisfaction is not solely a psychological phenomenon. The stress that results from dissatisfaction apparently increases one's susceptibility to heart attacks and the like. For managers, this means that even if satisfaction didn't lead to less voluntary turnover and absence, the goal of a satisfied work force might be justifiable because it would reduce medical costs and the premature loss of valued employees by way of heart disease or strokes.

Our final point in support of job satisfaction's importance is the spin-off effect that job satisfaction has for society as a whole. When employees are happy with their jobs, it improves their lives off the job. In contrast, the dissatisfied employee carries that negative attitude home. In wealthy countries, such as the United States, doesn't management have a responsibility to provide jobs from which employees can receive high satisfaction? There are benefits, after all, that accrue to every citizen in our society. Satisfied employees contribute toward being satisfied citizens. These people will hold a more positive attitude toward life in general and make for a society of more psychologically healthy people.

The evidence is impressive. Job satisfaction is important. For management, a satisfied work force translates into higher productivity due to fewer disruptions caused by absenteeism or good employees quitting; and lower medical and life insurance costs. Additionally, there are benefits for society in general. Satisfaction on the job carries over to the employee's off-the-job hours. So the goal of high job satisfaction for employees can be defended in terms of both dollars and cents and social responsibility.

COUNTERPOINT

JOB SATISFACTION HAS BEEN OVEREMPHASIZED

Few issues have been more blown out of proportion than the importance of job satisfaction at work. Let's look closely at the evidence.

There is no consistent relationship indicating that satisfaction leads to productivity. And, after all, isn't productivity the name of the game? Organizations are not altruistic institutions. Management's obligation is to efficiently use the resources that it has available. It has no obligation to create a satisfied work force if the costs exceed the benefits. As one executive put it, "I don't care if my people are happy or not! Do they produce?"

It would be naive to assume that satisfaction alone would be a major impact on employee behavior. As a case in point, consider the issue of turnover. Certainly there are a number of other factors that have an equal or greater impact on whether an employee decides to remain with an organization or take a job somewhere else—length of time on the job, one's financial situation, availability of other jobs, and so on. If I'm fifty-five years old, have been with my company twenty-five years, perceive few other opportunities in the job market, and have no other source of income other than my job, does my unhappiness have much impact on my decision to stay with the organization? No!

Did you ever notice who seems to be most concerned with improving employee job satisfaction? It's usually college professors and researchers! They've chosen careers that provide them considerable freedom and opportunities for personal growth. They place a very high value on job satisfaction. The problem is that they also impose their values on others. Because job satisfaction is important to them, they suppose that it's important to everyone. To a lot of people, a job is merely a means by which to get the money they want to do the things they desire during their nonworking hours. Assuming you work forty hours a week and sleep eight hours a night, you still have seventy hours or more a week to achieve fulfillment and satisfaction in off-the-job activities. So the importance of job satisfaction may be oversold when you recognize that there are other sources—outside the job—where the dissatisfied employee can find satisfaction.

A final point against overemphasizing job satisfaction is to consider the issue in a contingency framework. Even if satisfaction were significantly related to performance, it is unlikely that the relationship would hold consistently across all segments of the work force. In fact, evidence demonstrates that people differ in terms of the importance that work plays in their lives. To some, the job is their central life interest. But for the majority of people, their primary interests are off the job. Nonjob-oriented people tend not to be emotionally involved with their work. This relative indifference allows them to accept frustrating conditions at work more willingly. Importantly, the majority of the work force probably falls into this nonjob-oriented category. So while job satisfaction might be important to lawyers, surgeons, and other professionals, it may be irrelevant to the average worker because he or she is generally apathetic toward the job's frustrating elements.

KEY TERMS

Attitudes

Attitude Surveys

Cognitive Dissonance

Conformity Values

Egocentrism Values

Escalation of Commitment

Existential Values

Exit

Job Involvement

Loyalty

Manipulative Values

Neglect

Organizational Commitment

Reactive Values

Self-perception Theory

Sociocentric Values

Tribalistic Values

Values

Value System

Voice

FOR DISCUSSION

1. "Thirty years ago, young employees we hired were ambitious, conscientious, hard-working, and honest. Today's young workers don't have the same values." Do you agree or disagree with this manager's comments? Support your position.

2. "Job candidates for a sales position are more likely to be successful if they hold egocentric values." Discuss.

3. Do you think there might be any positive and significant relationship between the possession of certain personal values and successful career progression in organizations like E. F. Hutton & Co., the AFL-CIO, or the City of Cleveland's Police Department? Discuss.

4. What is cognitive dissonance and how is it related to attitudes?

5. What is self-perception theory? Does it increase our ability to predict behavior?

6. What contingency factors can improve the statistical relationship between attitudes and behavior?

7. Why does job satisfaction receive so much attention by OB researchers? Do you think this interest is shared by practicing managers?

8. What determines job satisfaction?

9. What is the relationship between job satisfaction and productivity?

10. What is the relationship between job satisfaction and absenteeism? Turnover? Which is the stronger relationship?

11. What actions might management take if it wanted to change a specific employee attitude—for example, a negative view toward introduction of a new information system that requires many of the office personnel to make significant changes in the forms they use and the reports they fill out?

12. Contrast exit, voice, loyalty, and neglect as employee responses to job dissatisfaction.

FOR FURTHER READING

BERGER, C. J., C. A. OLSON, and J. W. BOUDREAU, "Effects of Unions on Job Satisfaction: The Role of Work-Related Values and Perceived Rewards," *Organizational Behavior and Human Performance*, December 1983, pp. 289–324. Examines the effects of unions on five facets of job satisfaction.

CALDER, B. J., and P. H. SCHURR, "Attitudinal Processes in Organizations," in L. L. CUMMINGS and B. M. STAW (eds.), *Research in Organizational Behavior*, Vol. 3, pp. 283–302. Greenwich, CT: JAI Press, 1981. Presents an information processing view of attitudes that reconciles the attitude-guides-behavior position versus the situational position.

CHAIKEN, S., and C. STANGOR, "Attitudes and Attitude Change," in M. R. Rosenzweig and L. W. Porter (eds.), *Annual Review of Psychology*, Vol. 38, pp. 575–630. Palo Alto, CA: Annual Reviews, 1987. Updates the research on the attitude-behavior relationship and other advances in the literature on attitudes.

COOPER, M. R., B. S. MORGAN, P. M. FOLEY, and L. B. KAPLAN, "Changing Employee Values: Deepening Discontent?" *Harvard Business Review*, January–February 1979, pp. 117–25. Presents survey data over twenty-five years that indicate that there has been a major shift in the attitudes and values of the U.S. work force.

FAZIO, R. H., M. C. POWELL, and P. M. HERR, "Toward a Process Model of the Attitude-Behavior Relation: Assessing One's Attitude upon Mere Observation of the Attitude Object," *Journal of Personality and Social Psychology*, July 1983, pp. 724–35. Presents a model that demonstrates how and when particular attitudes are brought into play.

RAVLIN, E. C., and B. M. MEGLINO, "Effect of Values on Perception and Decision Making: A Study of Alternative Work Values Measures," *Journal of Applied Psychology*, November 1987, pp. 666–73. Values were found to affect perceptual organization and act as a guide to decision making.

EXERCISE 5

VALUE ASSESSMENT TEST

Directions. Read each statement in turn, then circle both the number and letter appearing next to either Yes or No that best indicate your feeling of like or dislike for the activity described. *Be sure to answer each question.* A sample response is as follows:

"Enjoy eating ice cream"	(2A)	Yes	2A	No

1. Meet new people and get acquainted with them.	5D	Yes	5D	No
2. Take a carload of children for an outing.	6D	Yes	6D	No
3. Serve as a companion to an elderly person.	7D	Yes	7D	No
4. Like to be with people despite their physical deformities.	8D	Yes	8D	No
5. Work with a group to help the unemployed.	9D	Yes	9D	No
6. Work with labor and management to help solve their conflicts.	10D	Yes	10D	No
7. Go with friends to a movie.	4D	Yes	4D	No
8. Help distribute food at a picnic.	3D	Yes	3D	No
9. Play checkers with members of your family.	2D	Yes	2D	No
10. Make a phone call for movie reservations.	1D	Yes	1D	No
11. Collect specimens of small animals for a zoo or museum.	5A	Yes	5A	No
12. Do algebra problems.	6A	Yes	6A	No
13. Develop a foreign language.	7A	Yes	7A	No
14. Do an experiment with the muscle and nerve of a frog.	8A	Yes	8A	No
15. Study the various methods used in scientific investigations.	9A	Yes	9A	No
16. Do research on the relation of brainwaves to thinking.	10A	Yes	10A	No
17. Visit a research laboratory in which small animals are being tested in a maze.	4A	Yes	4A	No
18. Plan the defense and offense you are to use before a tennis game.	3A	Yes	3A	No
19. Read the biography of Louis Pasteur.	2A	Yes	2A	No
20. See moving pictures in which scientists are heroes.	1A	Yes	1A	No
21. Judge entries in a photo contest.	5C	Yes	5C	No
22. Sketch action scenes on a drawing pad.	6C	Yes	6C	No
23. Participate in a summer theater group.	7C	Yes	7C	No
24. Compare the treatment of a classical work as given by two fine musicians.	8C	Yes	8C	No
25. Mold a statue in clay.	9C	Yes	9C	No
26. Be a ballet dancer.	10C	Yes	10C	No
27. Be a sign painter.	4C	Yes	4C	No
28. Plant flowers and shrubbery around a home.	3C	Yes	3C	No
29. Listen to jazz records.	2C	Yes	2C	No
30. Play the jukebox.	1C	Yes	1C	No
31. Lead a round-table discussion.	5B	Yes	5B	No
32. Be chairman of an organizing committee.	6B	Yes	6B	No
33. Buy a run-down business and make it grow.	7B	Yes	7B	No
34. Borrow money in order to put over a business deal.	8B	Yes	8B	No

35.	Run for political office.	9B	Yes	9B	No
36.	Own and operate a bank.	10B	Yes	10B	No
37.	Be a bank teller.	4B	Yes	4B	No
38.	Take a course in Business English.	3B	Yes	3B	No
39.	Major in business subjects in school.	2B	Yes	2B	No
40.	Collect lunch money at the end of a school cafeteria line.	1B	Yes	1B	No
41.	Send a letter of condolence to a neighbor.	5D	Yes	5D	No
42.	Help people to be comfortable when traveling.	6D	Yes	6D	No
43.	Belong to several social agencies.	7D	Yes	7D	No
44.	Treat wounds to help people get well.	8D	Yes	8D	No
45.	Help an agency locate living places for evicted families.	9D	Yes	9D	No
46.	Be a medical missionary to a foreign country.	10D	Yes	10D	No
47.	Attend a dance.	4D	Yes	4D	No
48.	Dine with classmates in the school cafeteria.	3D	Yes	3D	No
49.	Play checkers.	2D	Yes	2D	No
50.	Ride in a bus to San Francisco or a neighboring city.	1D	Yes	1D	No
51.	Be a laboratory technician.	5A	Yes	5A	No
52.	Be a scientific farmer.	6A	Yes	6A	No
53.	Develop new kinds of flowers in a small greenhouse.	7A	Yes	7A	No
54.	Solve knotty legal problems.	8A	Yes	8A	No
55.	Develop improved procedures in a scientific experiment.	9A	Yes	9A	No
56.	Develop new mathematical formulas for research.	10A	Yes	10A	No
57.	Look at the displays on astronomy in an observatory exhibit.	4A	Yes	4A	No
58.	Visit the fossil display at a museum.	3A	Yes	3A	No
59.	Keep a chemical storeroom or physical laboratory.	2A	Yes	2A	No
60.	Sell scientific books.	1A	Yes	1A	No
61.	Judge window displays in a contest.	5C	Yes	5C	No
62.	Collect rare and old recordings.	6C	Yes	6C	No
63.	Be an interior decorator.	7C	Yes	7C	No
64.	Make a comparative study of architecture.	8C	Yes	8C	No
65.	Write a new arrangement for a musical theme.	9C	Yes	9C	No
66.	Paint a mural.	10C	Yes	10C	No
67.	Visit a flower show.	4C	Yes	4C	No
68.	Make and trim household accessories like lamp shades, etc.	3C	Yes	3C	No
69.	Dance to a fast number.	2C	Yes	2C	No
70.	Paint the kitchen with colors of your choice.	1C	Yes	1C	No
71.	Install improved office procedures in a big business.	5B	Yes	5B	No
72.	Plan business and commercial investments.	6B	Yes	6B	No
73.	Be an active member of a political group.	7B	Yes	7B	No
74.	Address a political convention.	8B	Yes	8B	No
75.	Operate a race track.	9B	Yes	9B	No
76.	Become a U.S. senator.	10B	Yes	10B	No
77.	Purchase supplies for a picnic.	4B	Yes	4B	No
78.	Live in a large city rather than a small town.	3B	Yes	3B	No
79.	Work at an information desk.	2B	Yes	2B	No
80.	Be a private secretary.	1B	Yes	1B	No

Turn to page 561 for scoring directions and key.

Source: J. Shorr, "The Development of a Test to Measure Intensity of Values," *Journal of Educational Psychology*, Vol. 44 (1953), pp. 266–74.

dogmatic — opinionated, positive

Frank Doherty is sixty-two years old. He dropped out of high school in the tenth grade to support his widowed mother and three younger brothers. At nineteen, he borrowed $200 from his uncle to buy a couple of used cars, which he hoped to resell at a profit. The rest is history. Today, Frank owns eight new car dealerships. A recent article in *Automotive News* described Frank Doherty as the largest new car dealer in Texas and among the top ten in the United States. It's estimated that his eight dealerships sell better than 2,500 cars a month.

John Doherty, Frank's son, has been in the business with his dad for less than a year. A recent graduate of the University of Texas, John hoped to put what he learned while earning his B.S. and M.B.A. to work in the car business. But it was obvious to Frank that he and John had some definite differences of opinion on a number of issues. John told this case writer that the root of the problem is that "My dad is so damn dogmatic. He's been extremely successful. I mean, hell, it's hard to criticize someone who started with nothing and was a millionaire at age thirty. But, you gotta admit a lot of his success was due to being in the right place at the right time. It would have been pretty hard to lose money in Dallas with a Chevy dealership in the 1950s. And getting the VW franchise in 1961, the Honda dealership in 1976, and the Hyundai franchise in 1986 wasn't exactly bad timing! Sure, Dad had the foresight to see what the customer wanted, but that's part of the problem. Everything he's touched has turned to gold. He thinks he's infallible. You name the problem and he's instantly got the answer. Nothing burns me up more than his ideas on managing our staff.

"You know we've got about 120 salespeople working for us. We've got another 150 in the shop, and our office staff numbers better than 35. I mean, we're a pretty big operation. But Dad makes personnel decisions based on a bunch of his notions about people.

"For instance, he won't hire college graduates. He says college kids expect too much, too fast. He says they don't have patience and that they want to run the show right out of school. When that doesn't happen, they get frustrated and quit.

"Go out on the sales floor of any of our dealerships. Notice anything unusual? Did our salesmen all look like linebackers for the Dallas Cowboys? That's the result of another of Dad's crazy beliefs. He says the best salesmen are big. There's no use trying to argue with him. He thinks big guys are more aggressive and self-confident. And that results in more sales. As I said, you can't argue with him. All he says is, 'Look at my track record.'

"In the office, Dad demands that the office manager keep a close eye on everybody. Dad says people are basically goof-offs. 'You leave them alone for a few minutes and they'll stop working and start playing.' The result is that our office looks like a Gestapo camp. Employees are always under close supervision.

"Every time I try to talk with Dad about his attitudes, I get the same response. 'Listen, John. Maybe my ideas aren't *always* right, but they're right *most* of the time. You may not agree with the way I run the dealerships, but you can't argue with the fact that it works.' "

QUESTIONS

1. What factors could explain the radical differences between father and son in their attitudes and approaches to dealing with people?
2. Do you think John can change his father's style of management? Discuss.
3. "Frank's right. College kids *do* expect too much! The best salesmen *are* big! People *are* basically goof-offs! It is just this type of generally valid insights that have made Frank the success that he is." Discuss.
4. What do you think the impact of Frank's attitudes are on (a) employee selection, and (b) effectiveness of his dealerships?
5. Only three of Frank's 120 salespeople are women, but these three are consistently among the top ten sales performers. How is Frank likely to deal with this fact?

6

Basic Motivation Concepts

■ *Learning objectives*

Outline the motivation process
Describe the best known theories of motivation
List the characteristics that high achievers prefer in a job
Explain why high achievers don't make good managers
Summarize the types of goals that increase performance
State the impact from underrewarding employees
Clarify the key relationships in expectancy theory

Money is what you'd get on beautifully without if only other people weren't so crazy about it.

— M. C. HARRIMAN

In the study of individual behavior, probably no concept has received more attention than motivation. A cursory look at any organization quickly suggests that some people work harder than others. An individual with outstanding abilities may consistently be outperformed by someone with obviously inferior talents. Why do people exert different levels of effort in different activities? Why do some people appear to be "highly motivated," whereas others are not? These are questions we wish to answer in this section.

WHAT IS MOTIVATION?

Maybe the place to begin is to say what motivation isn't. Many people incorrectly view motivation as a personal trait—that is, some have it and others don't. In practice, this would characterize the manager who labels a certain employee as lazy. Such a label assumes that an individual is always lazy or is lacking in motivation. Our knowledge of motivation tells us that this just isn't true. What we know is that motivation is the result of the interaction of the individual and the situation. Certainly, individuals differ in their basic motivational drive. But the same employee who is quickly bored when pulling the lever on his drill press may pull the lever on a slot machine in Las Vegas for hours on end without the slightest hint of boredom. You may read a complete novel at one sitting, yet find it difficult to stay with a textbook for more than twenty minutes. It's not necessarily you—it's the situation. So as we analyze the concept of motivation, keep in mind that level of motivation varies both between individuals and within individuals at different times.

We'll define **motivation** as the willingness to exert high levels of effort toward organizational goals, conditioned by the effort's ability to satisfy some individual need. While general motivation is concerned with effort toward *any* goal, we'll narrow the focus to *organizational* goals in order to reflect our singular interest in work-related behavior. The three key elements in our definition are effort, organizational goals, and needs.

The effort element is a measure of intensity. When someone is motivated, he or she tries hard. But high levels of effort are unlikely to lead to favorable job performance outcomes unless the effort is channeled in a direction that

Motivation
The willingness to exert high levels of effort toward organizational goals, conditioned by the effort's ability to satisfy some individual need.

Chapter 6   Basic Motivation Concepts   **147**

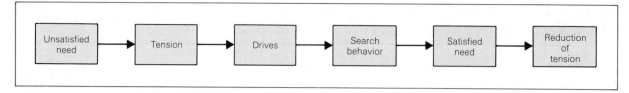

FIGURE 6–1
The Motivation Process

benefits the organization.[1] Therefore, we must consider the quality of the effort as well as its intensity. Effort that is directed toward, and consistent with, the organization's goals is the kind of effort that we should be seeking. Finally, we will treat motivation as a need-satisfying process. This is depicted in Figure 6–1.

A need, in our terminology, means some internal state that makes certain outcomes appear attractive. An unsatisfied need creates tension that stimulates drives within the individual. These drives generate a search behavior to find particular goals that, if attained, will satisfy the need and lead to the reduction of tension.

So we can say that motivated employees are in a state of tension. To relieve this tension, they exert effort. The greater the tension, the higher the effort level. If this effort successfully leads to the satisfaction of the need, tension is reduced. But since we are interested in work behavior, this tension-reduction effort must also be directed toward organizational goals. Therefore, inherent in our definition of motivation is the requirement that the individual's needs are compatible and consistent with the organization's goals. Where this does not occur, we can have individuals exerting high levels of effort that actually run counter to the interests of the organization. This, incidentally, is not so unusual. For example, some employees regularly spend a lot of time talking with friends at work in order to satisfy their social needs. There is a high level of effort, only it's being unproductively directed.

EARLY THEORIES OF MOTIVATION

The 1950s were a fruitful period in the development of motivation concepts. Three specific theories were formulated during this period, which, though heavily attacked and now questionable in terms of validity, are probably the best known explanations for employee motivation. These are the hierarchy of needs theory, Theories X and Y, and the motivation-hygiene theory. As you'll see later in this chapter, we have since developed more valid explanations of motivation, but you should know these early theories for at least two reasons: (1) they represent a foundation from which contemporary theories have grown,

[1] R. Katerberg and G. J. Blau, "An Examination of Level and Direction of Effort and Job Performance," *Academy of Management Journal*, June 1983, pp. 249–57.

and (2) practicing managers regularly use these theories and their terminology in explaining employee motivation.

Hierarchy of Needs Theory

It's probably safe to say that the most well-known theory of motivation is Abraham Maslow's **hierarchy of needs**.[2] He hypothesized that within every human being there exists a hierarchy of five needs. These needs are:

1. *Physiological*—includes hunger, thirst, shelter, sex, and other bodily needs
2. *Safety*—includes security and protection from physical and emotional harm
3. *Love*—includes affection, belongingness, acceptance, and friendship
4. *Esteem*—includes internal esteem factors such as self-respect, autonomy, and achievement; and external esteem factors such as status, recognition, and attention
5. *Self-actualization*—is represented by the drive to become what one is capable of becoming; includes growth, achieving one's potential, and self-fulfillment

As each of these needs becomes substantially satisfied, the next need becomes dominant. In terms of Figure 6–2, the individual moves up the hierarchy. From the standpoint of motivation, the theory would say that although no need is ever fully gratified, a substantially satisfied need no longer motivates. So if you want to motivate someone, according to Maslow, you need to understand where that person currently is on the hierarchy and focus on satisfying those needs at or above that level.

Maslow separated the five needs into higher and lower levels. Physiological and safety needs were described as **lower-order** and love, esteem, and self-actualization as **higher-order** needs. The differentiation between the two orders was made on the premise that higher-order needs are satisfied internally to the person, whereas lower-order needs are predominantly satisfied externally (by such things as money wages, union contracts, and tenure). In fact, the natural conclusion to be drawn from Maslow's classification is that in times of economic plenty, almost all permanently employed workers have their lower-order needs substantially met.

Maslow's need theory has received wide recognition, particularly among practicing managers. This can be attributed to the theory's intuitive logic and ease of understanding. Unfortunately, however, research does not generally validate the theory. Maslow provided no empirical substantiation, and several studies that sought to validate the theory found no support.[3]

Hierarchy of needs theory

There is a hierarchy of five needs—physiological, safety, love, esteem, and self-actualization—and as each need is sequentially satisfied, the next need becomes dominant.

Self-actualization

The drive to become what one is capable of becoming.

Lower-order needs

Needs that are satisfied externally; physiological and safety needs.

Higher-order needs

Needs that are satisfied internally; needs for love, esteem, and self-actualization.

[2] A. Maslow, *Motivation and Personality* (New York: Harper & Row, 1954).
[3] See for example, E. E. Lawler III and J. L. Suttle, "A Causal Correlational Test of the Need Hierarchy Concept," *Organizational Behavior and Human Performance*, April 1972, pp. 265–87; D. T. Hall and K. E. Nougaim, "An Examination of Maslow's Need Hierarchy in an Organizational Setting," *Organizational Behavior and Human Performance*, February 1968, pp. 12–35; and J. Rauschenberger, N. Schmitt, and J. E. Hunter, "A Test of the Need Hierarchy Concept by a Markov Model of Change in Need Strength," *Administrative Science Quarterly*, December 1980, pp. 654–70.

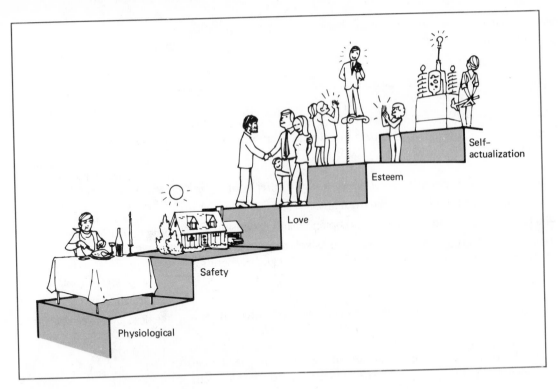

FIGURE 6–2
Maslow's Hierarchy of Needs

Source: By permission of the Modular Project of Organizational Behavior and Instructional Communications Centre. McGill University, Montreal, Canada.

Old theories, especially ones that are intuitively logical, apparently die hard. One researcher reviewed the evidence and concluded that "although of great societal popularity, need hierarchy as a theory continues to receive little empirical support."[4] Further, the researcher stated that the "available research should certainly generate a reluctance to accept unconditionally the implication of Maslow's hierarchy."[5] Another review came to the same conclusion.[6] Little support was found for the prediction that need structures are organized along the dimensions proposed by Maslow, the prediction of a negative relationship between the level of need gratification and the activation of that need, or the prediction of a positive relationship between the level of need gratification and the activation level of the next higher need.

[4] A. K. Korman, J. H. Greenhaus, and I. J. Badin, "Personnel Attitudes and Motivation," in M. R. Rosenzweig and L. W. Porter (eds.), *Annual Review of Psychology* (Palo Alto, CA: Annual Reviews, 1977), p. 178.

[5] Ibid., p. 179.

[6] M. A. Wahba and L. G. Bridwell, "Maslow Reconsidered: A Review of Research on the Need Hierarchy Theory," *Organizational Behavior and Human Performance*, April 1976, pp. 212–40.

Theory X and Theory Y

Douglas McGregor proposed two distinct views of human beings: one basically negative, labeled **Theory X**, and the other basically positive, labeled **Theory Y**.[7] After viewing the way in which managers dealt with employees, McGregor concluded that a manager's view of the nature of human beings is based on a certain grouping of assumptions and that he or she tends to mold his or her behavior toward subordinates according to these assumptions.

Under Theory X, the four assumptions held by managers are:

1. Employees inherently dislike work and, whenever possible, will attempt to avoid it.
2. Since employees dislike work, they must be coerced, controlled, or threatened with punishment to achieve goals.
3. Employees will shirk responsibilities and seek formal direction whenever possible.
4. Most workers place security above all other factors associated with work and will display little ambition.

In contrast to these negative views toward the nature of human beings, McGregor listed four other positive assumptions that he called Theory Y:

1. Employees can view work as being as natural as rest or play.
2. People will exercise self-direction and self-control if they are committed to the objectives.
3. The average person can learn to accept, even seek, responsibility.
4. The ability to make innovative decisions is widely dispersed throughout the population and is not necessarily the sole province of those in management positions.

What are the motivational implications if you accept McGregor's analysis? The answer is best expressed in the framework presented by Maslow. Theory X assumes that lower-order needs dominate individuals. Theory Y assumes that higher-order needs dominate individuals. McGregor, himself, held to the belief that Theory Y assumptions were more valid than Theory X. Therefore, he proposed such ideas as participation in decision making, responsible and challenging jobs, and good group relations as approaches that would maximize an employee's job motivation.

Unfortunately, there is no evidence to confirm that either set of assumptions is valid or that acceptance of Theory Y assumptions and altering one's actions accordingly will lead to more motivated workers. As will become evident later in this chapter, either Theory X or Theory Y assumptions may be appropriate in a particular situation.

Theory X

Assumes that employees dislike work, are lazy, dislike responsibility, and must be coerced to perform.

Theory Y

Assumes that employees like work, are creative, seek responsibility, and can exercise self-direction.

---

[7] D. McGregor, *The Human Side of Enterprise* (New York: McGraw-Hill, 1960).

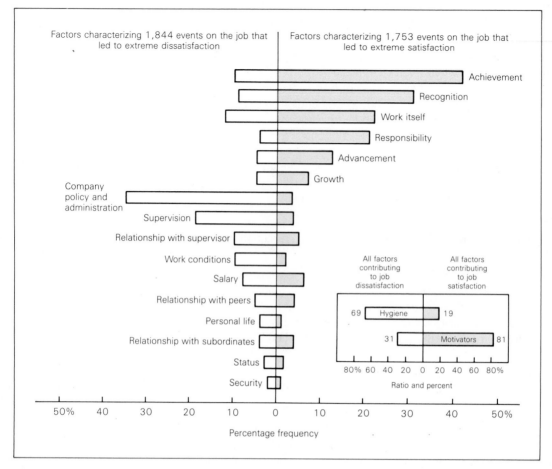

FIGURE 6–3

Comparison of Satisfiers and Dissatisfiers

Source: Frederick Herzberg, "One More Time: How Do You Motivate Employees?" *Harvard Business Review*, January-February 1968, p. 57. With permission. Copyright © 1967 by the President and Fellows of Harvard College; all rights reserved.

Motivation-Hygiene Theory

Motivation-hygiene theory

Intrinsic factors are related to job satisfaction, while extrinsic factors are associated with dissatisfaction.

The **motivation-hygiene theory** was proposed by psychologist Frederick Herzberg.[8] In the belief that an individual's relation to his or her work is a basic one and that his or her attitude toward this work can very well determine the individual's success or failure, Herzberg investigated the question, "What do people want from their jobs?" He asked people to describe, in detail, situations when they felt exceptionally good or bad about their jobs. These responses were tabulated and categorized. Factors affecting job attitudes as reported in twelve investigations conducted by Herzberg are illustrated in Figure 6–3.

[8] F. Herzberg, B. Mausner, and B. Snyderman, *The Motivation to Work* (New York: John Wiley, 1959).

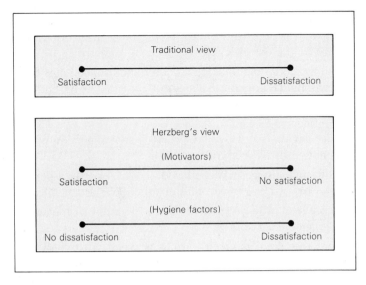

FIGURE 6–4
Contrasting Views of Satisfaction-Dissatisfaction

From the categorized responses, Herzberg concluded that the replies people gave when they felt good about their jobs were significantly different from the replies given when they felt bad. As seen in Figure 6–3, certain characteristics tend to be consistently related to job satisfaction (factors on the right side of the figure), and others to job dissatisfaction (the left side of the figure). Intrinsic factors, such as achievement, recognition, the work itself, responsibility, advancement, and growth seem to be related to job satisfaction. When those questioned felt good about their work, they tended to attribute these characteristics to themselves. On the other hand, when they were dissatisfied, they tended to cite extrinsic factors, such as company policy and administration, supervision, interpersonal relations, and working conditions.

The data suggest, says Herzberg, that the opposite of satisfaction is not dissatisfaction, as was traditionally believed. Removing dissatisfying characteristics from a job does not necessarily make the job satisfying. As illustrated in Figure 6–4, Herzberg proposes that his findings indicate the existence of a dual continuum: The opposite of "Satisfaction" is "No Satisfaction," and the opposite of "Dissatisfaction" is "No Dissatisfaction."

According to Herzberg, the factors leading to job satisfaction are separate and distinct from those that lead to job dissatisfaction. Therefore, managers who seek to eliminate factors that create job dissatisfaction can bring about peace, but not necessarily motivation. They will be placating their work force rather than motivating them. As a result, such characteristics as company policy and administration, supervision, interpersonal relations, working conditions, and salary have been characterized by Herzberg as **hygiene factors**. When they are adequate, people will not be dissatisfied; however, neither will they be satisfied. If we want to motivate people on their jobs, Herzberg suggests emphasizing achievement, recognition, the work itself, responsibility, and growth. These are the characteristics that people find intrinsically rewarding.

The motivation-hygiene theory is not without its detractors. The criticisms of the theory include the following:

Hygiene factors

Those factors—such as company policy and administration, supervision, and salary—that, when present in a job, placate workers. When these factors are present, people will not be dissatisfied.

1. The procedure that Herzberg used is limited by its methodology. When things are going well, people tend to take credit themselves. Contrarily, they blame failure on the extrinsic environment.

2. The reliability of Herzberg's methodology is questioned. Since raters have to make interpretations, it is possible that they may contaminate the findings by interpreting one response in one manner while treating another similar response differently.

3. The theory, to the degree that it is valid, provides an explanation of job satisfaction. It is not really a theory of motivation.

4. No overall measure of satisfaction was utilized. In other words, a person may dislike part of his or her job, yet still think the job is acceptable.

5. The theory is inconsistent with previous research. The motivation-hygiene theory ignores situational variables.

6. Herzberg assumes that there is a relationship between satisfaction and productivity. But the research methodology he used looked only at satisfaction, not at productivity. To make such research relevant, one must assume a high relationship between satisfaction and productivity.[9]

Regardless of criticisms, Herzberg's theory has been widely read and few managers are unfamiliar with his recommendations. The increased popularity since the mid-1960s of vertically expanding jobs to allow workers greater responsibility in planning and controlling their work can probably be largely attributed to Herzberg's findings and recommendations.

From another perspective, Herzberg's findings appear consistent with general surveys made of workers' opinions about what they want from their job. Nationwide polls conducted by the National Opinion Research Center, for example, indicate that "more than half of the white, male work force in the United States believes that the most important characteristic of a job is that it involve work that is important and provides a sense of accomplishment."[10] Meaningful work is rated "most important" three times more frequently than "high income" and seven times more frequently than is the desire for "shorter work hours and much free time."

CONTEMPORARY THEORIES OF MOTIVATION

The previous theories are well known but, unfortunately, have not held up well under close examination. However, all is not lost.[11] There are a number of contemporary theories that have one thing in common—each has a reasonable

---

[9] R. J. House and L. A. Wigdor, "Herzberg's Dual-Factor Theory of Job Satisfaction and Motivations: A Review of the Evidence and Criticism," *Personnel Psychology*, Winter 1967, pp. 369–89; D. P. Schwab and L. L. Cummings, "Theories of Performance and Satisfaction: A Review," *Industrial Relations*, October 1970, pp. 403–30; and R. J. Caston and R. Braito, "A Specification Issue in Job Satisfaction Research," *Sociological Perspectives*, April 1985, pp. 175–97.

[10] C. N. Weaver, "What Workers Want from Their Jobs," *Personnel*, May–June 1976, p. 49.

[11] D. Guest, "What's New in Motivation," *Personnel Management*, May 1984, pp. 20–23.

degree of valid supporting documentation. Of course, this doesn't mean that the theories we are about to introduce are unquestionably "right." What they do represent is the current "state of the art" in explaining employee motivation.

ERG Theory

Clayton Alderfer of Yale University has reworked Maslow's need hierarchy to align it more closely with the empirical research. His revised need hierarchy is labeled **ERG theory**.[12]

ERG theory

There are three groups of core needs: existence, relatedness, and growth.

Alderfer argues that there are three groups of core needs—existence, relatedness, and growth—hence the label: ERG theory. The existence group is concerned with providing our basic material existence requirements. They include the items that Maslow considered as physiological and safety needs. The second group of needs are those of relatedness—the desire we have for maintaining important interpersonal relationships. These social and status desires require interaction with others if they are to be satisfied, and they align with Maslow's love need and the external component of Maslow's esteem classification. Finally, Alderfer isolates growth needs—an intrinsic desire for personal development. These include the intrinsic component from Maslow's esteem category and the characteristics included under self-actualization.

Besides substituting three needs for five, how does Alderfer's ERG theory differ from Maslow? In contrast to Maslow, the ERG theory demonstrates that (1) more than one need may be operative at the same time and (2) if the gratification of a higher-level need is stifled, the desire to satisfy a lower-level need increases.

Maslow's need hierarchy is a rigid steplike progression. ERG theory does not assume that there exists a rigid hierarchy where a lower need must be substantially gratified before one can move on. A person can, for instance, be working on growth even though existence or relatedness needs are unsatisfied; or all three need categories could be operating at the same time.

ERG theory also contains a frustration-regression dimension. Maslow, you'll remember, argued that an individual would stay at a certain need level until that need was satisfied. ERG theory counters by noting that when a higher-order need level is frustrated, the individual's desire to increase a lower-level need takes place. Inability to satisfy a need for social interaction, for instance, might increase the desire for more money or better working conditions. So frustration can lead to a regression to a lower need.

In summary, ERG theory argues, like Maslow, that satisfied lower-order needs lead to the desire to satisfy higher-order needs; but multiple needs can be operating as motivators at the same time, and frustration in attempting to satisfy a higher-level need can result to regression to a lower-level need.

ERG theory is more consistent with our knowledge of individual differences among people. Variables such as education, family background, and cultural environment can alter the importance or driving force that a group of needs holds for a particular individual. The evidence demonstrating that people in other cultures rank the need categories differently—for instance, natives of

[12] C. P. Alderfer, "An Empirical Test of a New Theory of Human Needs," *Organizational Behavior and Human Performance*, May 1969, pp. 142–75.

Spain and Japan place social needs before their physiological requirements[13] —would be consistent with the ERG theory. Several studies have supported the ERG theory,[14] but there is also evidence that it doesn't work in some organizations.[15] Overall, however, ERG theory represents a more valid version of the need hierarchy.

Three Needs Theory

You've got one beanbag and there are five targets set up in front of you. Each one is progressively farther away and, hence, more difficult to hit. Target A is a cinch. It sits almost within arm's reach of you. If you hit it, you get $2. Target B is a bit farther out, but about 80 percent of the people who try can hit it. It pays $4. Target C pays $8, and about half the people who try can hit it. Very few people can hit Target D, but the payoff is $16 if you do. Finally, Target E pays $32, but it's almost impossible to achieve. Which target would you try for? If you selected C, you're very likely to be a high achiever. Why? Read on.

In Chapter 3, we introduced the need to achieve as a personality characteristic. It is also one of **three needs** proposed by David McClelland and others as being important in organizational settings for understanding motivation.[16] These three needs are achievement, power, and affiliation. They are identified as follows:

Three needs theory

Achievement, power, and affiliation are three important needs that help to understand motivation.

Power need

The desire to make others behave in a way that they would not otherwise have behaved.

Affiliation need

The desire for friendly and close interpersonal relationships.

- **Need for achievement**—the drive to excel, to achieve in relation to a set of standards, to strive to succeed
- **Need for power**—the need to make others behave in a way that they would not have behaved otherwise
- **Need for affiliation**—the desire for friendly and close interpersonal relationships

As described previously, some people who have a compelling drive to succeed are striving for personal achievement rather than the rewards of success per se. They have a desire to do something better or more efficiently than it has been done before. This drive is the achievement need (*nAch*). From research into the achievement need, McClelland found that high achievers differentiate themselves from others by their desire to do things better.[17] They seek situations where they can attain personal responsibility for finding solutions to problems, where they can receive rapid feedback on their performance so they can tell

---

[13] M. Haire, E. E. Ghiselli, and L. W. Porter, "Cultural Patterns in the Role of the Manager," *Industrial Relations*, February 1963, pp. 95–117.

[14] C. P. Schneider and C. P. Alderfer, "Three Studies of Measures of Need Satisfaction in Organizations," *Administrative Science Quarterly*, December 1973, pp. 489–505.

[15] J. P. Wanous and A. Zwany, "A Cross-Sectional Test of Need Hierarchy Theory," *Organizational Behavior and Human Performance*, May 1977, pp. 78–97.

[16] D. C. McClelland, *The Achieving Society* (New York: Van Nostrand Reinhold, 1961); J. W. Atkinson and J. O. Raynor, *Motivation and Achievement* (Washington, D.C.: Winston, 1974); and D. C. McClelland, *Power: The Inner Experience* (New York: Irvington, 1975).

[17] McClelland, *The Achieving Society*.

easily whether they are improving or not, and where they can set moderately challenging goals. High achievers are not gamblers; they dislike succeeding by chance. They prefer the challenge of working at a problem and accepting the personal responsibility for success or failure rather than leaving the outcome to chance or the actions of others. Importantly, they avoid what they perceive to be very easy or very difficult tasks.

Again as noted in Chapter 3, high achievers perform best when they perceive their probability of success as being 0.5, that is, where they estimate that they have a 50–50 chance of success. They dislike gambling with high odds because they get no achievement satisfaction from happenstance success. Similarly, they dislike low odds (high probability of success) because then there is no challenge to their skills. They like to set goals that require stretching themselves a little. When there is an approximately equal chance of success or failure, there is the optimum opportunity to experience feelings of accomplishment and satisfaction from their efforts.

The need for power (*nPow*) is the desire to have impact, to be influential, and to control others. Individuals high in *nPow* enjoy being "in charge," strive for influence over others, prefer to be placed into competitive and status-oriented situations, and tend to be more concerned with gaining influence over others and prestige than with effective performance.

The third need isolated by McClelland is affiliation (*nAff*). This need has received the least attention from researchers. Affiliation can be viewed as a Dale Carnegie-type of need—the desire to be liked and accepted by others. Individuals with a high affiliation motive strive for friendship, prefer cooperative situations rather than competitive ones, and desire relationships involving a high degree of mutual understanding.

Based on an extensive amount of research, some reasonably well-supported predictions can be made based on the relationship between achievement need and job performance. Although less research has been done on power and affiliation needs, there are consistent findings here, too.

First, as shown in Figure 6–5, individuals with a high need to achieve prefer job situations with personal responsibility, feedback, and an intermediate degree of risk. When these characteristics are prevalent, high achievers will be strongly motivated. The evidence consistently demonstrates, for instance, that high achievers are successful in entrepreneurial activities such as running their own businesses, managing a self-contained unit within a large organization, and serving in a variety of sales positions.[18]

Second, a high need to achieve does not necessarily lead to being a good manager, especially in large organizations. People with a high achievement need are interested in how well they do personally and not in influencing others to do well. High-*nAch* sales people do not necessarily make good sales managers, and the good general manager in a large organization does not typically have a high need to achieve.[19]

---

[18] D. C. McClelland and D. G. Winter, *Motivating Economic Achievement* (New York: Free Press, 1969).

[19] McClelland, *Power*; McClelland and D. H. Burnham, "Power Is the Great Motivator," *Harvard Business Review*, March–April 1976, pp. 100–10; and R. E. Boyatzis, "The Need for Close Relationships and the Manager's Job," in D. A. Kolb, I. M. Rubin, and J. M. McIntyre, *Organizational Psychology: Readings on Human Behavior in Organizations*, 4th ed. (Englewood Cliffs, NJ: Prentice Hall, 1984), pp. 81–86.

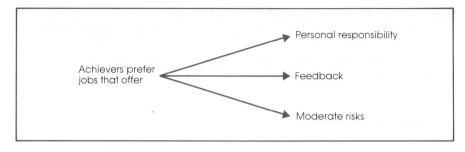

FIGURE 6–5
Matching Achievers and Jobs

Third, the needs for affiliation and power tend to be closely related to managerial success. The best managers are high in their need for power and low in their need for affiliation.[20] In fact, a high power motive may be a requirement for managerial effectiveness.[21] Of course, what is the cause and what is the effect is arguable. It has been suggested that a high power need may occur simply as a function of one's level in a hierarchical organization.[22] This latter argument proposes that the higher the level an individual rises to in the organization, the greater is the incumbent's power motive. As a result, powerful positions would be the stimulus to a high power motive.

Lastly, employees have been successfully trained to stimulate their achievement need. If the job calls for a high achiever, management can select a person with a high *nAch* or develop its own candidate through achievement training.[23]

Cognitive Evaluation Theory

Cognitive evaluation theory

Extrinsic rewards allocated for behavior that had been previously intrinsically rewarded tends to decrease the overall level of motivation.

In the late 1960s, one researcher proposed that the introduction of extrinsic rewards, such as pay, for work effort that had been previously intrinsically rewarding due to the pleasure associated with the content of the work itself, would tend to decrease the overall level of motivation.[24] This proposal—which has come to be called the **cognitive evaluation theory**—has been extensively researched, and a large number of studies have been supportive.[25] The importance of this theory cannot be overstated because, as we'll show, it has major implications for the way in which people are paid in organizations.

---

[20] Ibid.

[21] J. B. Miner, *Studies in Management Education* (New York: Springer, 1965).

[22] D. Kipnis, "The Powerholder," in J. T. Tedeschi (ed.), *Perspectives in Social Power* (Chicago: Aldine, 1974), pp. 82–123.

[23] D. Miron and D. C. McClelland, "The Impact of Achievement Motivation Training on Small Businesses," *California Management Review*, Summer 1979, pp. 13–28.

[24] R. de Charms, *Personal Causation: The Internal Affective Determinants of Behavior* (New York: Academic Press, 1968).

[25] E. L. Deci, *Intrinsic Motivation* (New York: Plenum, 1975); R. D. Pritchard, K. M. Campbell, and D. J. Campbell, "Effects of Extrinsic Financial Rewards on Intrinsic Motivation," *Journal of Applied Psychology*, February 1977, pp. 9–15; E. L. Deci, G. Betly, J. Kahle, L. Abrams, and J. Porac, "When Trying to Win: Competition and Intrinsic Motivation," *Personality and Social Psychology Bulletin*, March 1981, pp. 79–83; and P. C. Jordan, "Effects of an Extrinsic Reward on Intrinsic Motivation: A Field Experiment," *Academy of Management Journal*, June 1986, pp. 405–12.

OB Close-Up

Teaching People to Be Achievers

Successful achievement training is essentially a five step process conducted by professional trainers with groups of nine to twenty-five participants.[26]

The first step introduces the idea of achievement motivation. Participants are introduced to the idea that motives can be changed, and to results of research on achievement motivation.

The meaning of the achievement motive is taught in the second step. Participants learn how to measure the achievement motive by writing stories about pictures they're shown. As an example, the picture might show a male, in a suit, sitting at a desk in a relaxed position, staring out toward one of the walls in his office. Participants will write a story describing what they think is going on, what preceded this situation, and what will happen in the future. Participants will compare their stories to one written by a high achiever. The high achiever's story will contain references to accomplishments, winning, success, and the like. So, in our example, the high achiever might say that the person in the picture is the president of a large corporation who wants to get a major contract for his company. The bidding competition will be tough. But victory will enhance his company's position in the industry and probably result in a large bonus for him. He is, at the moment, feeling optimistic about getting the contract. He has just reviewed his company's proposal and he is confident that his production costs are lower than the competition, allowing him to be able to submit the lowest cost bid.

In the third step, participants learn how to *act* in a "high achievement" way. Specifically, they learn that achievers prefer situations where they have personal responsibility, feedback, and moderate risks. The trainer will use case studies and draw on the participants' own experiences to illustrate these concepts.

Next, the trainer provides feedback to the individual participants on their achievement-oriented behavior. This allows participants to compare their actions with achievement behavior.

Finally, the course concludes with each participant setting goals about how he or she will behave in an achievement-oriented fashion. These goals are written down, as are specific action plans for executing them, and a basis for evaluating progress toward attaining the goals is defined.

Historically, motivation theorists have generally assumed that intrinsic motivators such as achievement, responsibility, and competence were independent from extrinsic motivators like high pay, promotions, good supervisor relations, and pleasant working conditions. That is, the stimulation of one would not affect the other. But the cognitive evaluation theory suggests otherwise. It

---

[26] D. McClelland, "Toward a Theory of Motive Acquisition," *American Psychologist*, May 1965, pp. 321–33; and J. B. Miner, *Theories of Organizational Behavior* (Hinsdale, IL: Dryden Press, 1980), pp. 67–69.

argues that when extrinsic rewards are used by organizations as payoffs for superior performance, the intrinsic rewards, which are derived from individuals doing what they like, are reduced. In other words, when extrinsic rewards are given to someone for performing an interesting task, it causes intrinsic interest in the task itself to decline.

Why would such an outcome occur? The popular explanation is that the individual experiences a loss of control over his or her own behavior so that the previous intrinsic motivation diminishes. Further, the elimination of extrinsic rewards can produce a shift—from an external to an internal explanation—in an individual's perception of causation of why he or she works on a task. If you're reading a novel a week because your English literature instructor requires you to, you can attribute your reading behavior to an external source. However, after the course is over, if you find yourself continuing to read a novel a week, your natural inclination is to say, "I must enjoy reading novels, because I'm still reading one a week!"

If the cognitive evaluation theory is valid, it should have major implications for managerial practices. It has been a truism among compensation specialists for years that if pay or other extrinsic rewards are to be effective motivators, they should be made contingent on an individual's performance. But, cognitive evaluation theorists would argue, this will only tend to decrease the internal satisfaction that the individual receives from doing the job. We have substituted an external stimulus for an internal stimulus. In fact, if cognitive evaluation theory is correct, it would make sense to make an individual's pay *non*contingent on performance in order to avoid decreasing intrinsic motivation.

We noted earlier that the cognitive evaluation theory has been supported in a number of studies. Yet it has also met with attacks, specifically on the methodology used in these studies[27] and in the interpretation of the findings.[28] But where does this theory stand today? Can we say that when organizations use extrinsic motivators like pay and promotions to stimulate workers' performance that they do so at the expense of reducing intrinsic interest and motivation in the work being done? The answer is not a simple "Yes" or "No."

While further research is needed to clarify some of the current ambiguity, the evidence does lead us to conclude that the nonadditivity of extrinsic and intrinsic rewards is a real phenomenon.[29] But its impact on employee motivation at work, in contrast to motivation in general, may be considerably less than originally thought. First, many of the studies testing the theory were done with students, not paid organizational employees. The researchers would observe what happens to a student's behavior when a reward that had been allocated is stopped. This is interesting, but it does not represent the typical work situation.

[27] W. E. Scott, "The Effects of Extrinsic Rewards on 'Intrinsic Motivation': A Critique," *Organizational Behavior and Human Performance*, February 1976, pp. 117–19; B. J. Calder and B. M. Staw, "Interaction of Intrinsic and Extrinsic Motivation: Some Methodological Notes," *Journal of Personality and Social Psychology*, January 1975, pp. 76–80; and K. B. Boal and L. L. Cummings, "Cognitive Evaluation Theory: An Experimental Test of Processes and Outcomes," *Organizational Behavior and Human Performance*, December 1981, pp. 289–310.

[28] G. R. Salancik, "Interaction Effects of Performance and Money on Self-Perception of Intrinsic Motivation," *Organizational Behavior and Human Performance*, June 1975, pp. 339–51; and F. Luthans, M. Martinko, and T. Kess, "An Analysis of the Impact of Contingency Monetary Rewards on Intrinsic Motivation," *Proceedings of the Nineteenth Annual Midwest Academy of Management*, St. Louis, 1976, pp. 209–21.

[29] Miner, *Theories of Organizational Behavior*, p. 157.

In the real world, when extrinsic rewards are stopped it usually means the individual is no longer part of the organization. Second, evidence indicates that very high intrinsic motivation levels are strongly resistant to the detrimental impacts of extrinsic rewards.[30] Even when a job is inherently interesting, there still exists a powerful norm for extrinsic payment.[31] At the other extreme, on dull tasks extrinsic rewards appear to increase intrinsic motivation.[32] Therefore, the theory may have limited applicability to work organizations because most low-level jobs are not inherently satisfying enough to foster high intrinsic interest and many managerial and professional positions offer intrinsic rewards. Cognitive evaluation theory may be relevant to that set of organizational jobs that falls in between—those that are neither extremely dull nor extremely interesting.

Goal-Setting Theory

Gene Broadwater, coach of the Hamilton High School cross-country team, gave his squad these last words before they approached the line for the league championship race: "Each one of you is physically ready. Now, get out there and do your best. No one can ever ask more of you than that."

You've heard the phrase a number of times yourself: "Just do your best. That's all anyone can ask for." But what does "do your best" mean? Do we ever know if we've achieved that vague goal? Would the cross-country runners have recorded faster times if Coach Broadwater had given each a specific goal to shoot for? Might you have done better in your high school English class if your parents had said, "You should strive for 85 percent or higher on all your work in English" rather than telling you to "do your best"? The research on **goal setting** addresses these issues, and the findings, as you will see, are impressive in terms of the impact specific and challenging goals have on performance.

In the late 1960s, Edwin Locke proposed that intentions to work toward a goal are a major source of work motivation.[33] That is, goals tell an employee what needs to be done and how much effort will need to be expended.[34] The evidence strongly supports the value of goals. More to the point, we can say that specific goals increase performance; that difficult goals, when accepted, result in higher performance than do easy goals; and that feedback leads to higher performance than does nonfeedback.[35]

Goal-setting theory

The theory that specific and difficult goals lead to higher performance.

---

[30] H. J. Arnold, "Effects of Performance Feedback and Extrinsic Reward upon High Intrinsic Motivation," *Organizational Behavior and Human Performance*, December 1976, pp. 275–88.

[31] B. M. Staw, "Motivation in Organizations: Toward Synthesis and Redirection," in B. M. Staw and G. R. Salancik (eds.), *New Directions in Organizational Behavior* (Chicago: St. Clair, 1977), p. 76.

[32] B. J. Calder and B. M. Staw, "Self-Perception of Intrinsic and Extrinsic Motivation," *Journal of Personality and Social Psychology*, April 1975, pp. 599–605.

[33] E. A. Locke, "Toward a Theory of Task Motivation and Incentives," *Organizational Behavior and Human Performance*, May 1968, pp. 157–89.

[34] P. C. Earley, P. Wojnaroski, and W. Prest, "Task Planning and Energy Expended: Exploration of How Goals Influence Performance," *Journal of Applied Psychology*, February 1987, pp. 107–14.

[35] G. P. Latham and G. A. Yukl, "A Review of Research on the Application of Goal Setting in Organizations," *Academy of Management Journal*, December 1975, pp. 824–45; E. A. Locke, K. N. Shaw, L. M. Saari, and G. P. Latham, "Goal Setting and Task Performance," *Psychological Bulletin*, January 1981, pp. 125–52; A. J. Mento, R. P. Steel, and R. J. Karren, "A Meta-Analytic Study

Specific hard goals produce a higher level of output than does a generalized goal of "do your best." The specificity of the goal itself acts as an internal stimulus. For instance, when a trucker commits to making eighteen round-trip hauls between Baltimore and Washington, D.C., each week, this intention gives him a specific objective to reach for. We can say that, all things being equal, the trucker with a specific goal will outperform his counterpart operating with no goals or the generalized goal of "do your best."

If factors like ability and acceptance of the goals are held constant, we can also state that the more difficult the goals, the higher the level of performance. However, it's logical to assume that easier goals are more likely to be accepted. But once an employee accepts a hard task, he or she will exert a high level of effort until it is achieved, lowered, or abandoned.

People will do better when they get feedback on how well they are progressing toward their goals, because feedback helps to identify discrepancies between what they have done and what they want to do; that is, feedback acts to guide behavior. But all feedback is not equally potent. Self-generated feedback—where the employee is able to monitor his or her own progress—has been shown to be a more powerful motivator than externally generated feedback.[36]

If employees have the opportunity to participate in the setting of their own goals, will they try harder? The evidence is mixed regarding the superiority of participation over assigned goals.[37] In some cases, participatively set goals elicit superior performance, while in other cases individuals performed best when assigned goals by their boss. But a major advantage of participation may be in increasing acceptance of the goal, itself, as a desirable one to work toward.[38] As we noted, resistance is greater when goals are difficult. If people participate in goal setting, they are more likely to accept even a difficult goal than if they are arbitrarily assigned it by their boss. The reason is that individuals are more committed to choices in which they have a part. Thus, although participative goals may have no superiority over assigned goals when acceptance is taken as a given, participation does increase the probability that more difficult goals will be agreed to and acted upon.

Our overall conclusion is that intentions—as articulated in terms of hard and specific goals—are a potent motivating force. They do lead to higher performance. However, there is no evidence that such goals are associated with increased job satisfaction.[39]

---

of the Effects of Goal Setting on Task Performance: 1966–1984," *Organizational Behavior and Human Decision Processes*, February 1987, pp. 52–83; and M. E. Tubbs "Goal Setting: A Meta-Analytic Examination of the Empirical Evidence," *Journal of Applied Psychology*, August 1986, pp. 474–83.

[36] J. M. Ivancevich and J. T. McMahon, "The Effects of Goal Setting, External Feedback, and Self-Generated Feedback on Outcome Variables: A Field Experiment," *Academy of Management Journal*, June 1982, pp. 359–72.

[37] Latham and Yukl, "A Review of Research"; Locke, Shaw, Saari, and Latham, "Goal Setting"; and G. Shing-Yung Chang and P. Lovenzi, "The Effects of Participative Versus Assigned Goal Setting on Intrinsic Motivation," *Journal of Management*, Spring–Summer 1983, pp. 55–64.

[38] M. Erez, P. C. Earley, and C. L. Hulin, "The Impact of Participation on Goal Acceptance and Performance: A Two-Step Model," *Academy of Management Journal*, March 1985, pp. 50–66.

[39] J. C. Anderson and C. A. O'Reilly, "Effects of an Organizational Control System on Managerial Satisfaction and Performance," *Human Relations*, June 1981, pp. 491–501.

Reinforcement Theory

A counterpoint to goal-setting theory is **reinforcement theory**. The former is a cognitive approach, proposing that an individual's purposes direct his or her action. In reinforcement theory we have a behavioristic approach, which argues that reinforcement conditions behavior. The two are clearly at odds philosophically. Reinforcement theorists see behavior as being environmentally caused. You need not be concerned, they would argue, with internal cognitive events; what controls behavior are reinforcers—any consequence that, when immediately following a response, increases the probability that the behavior will be repeated.

Reinforcement theory ignores the inner state of the individual and concentrates solely on what happens to a person when he or she takes some action. Because it does not concern itself with what initiates behavior, it is not, strictly speaking, a theory of motivation. But it does provide a powerful means of analysis of what controls behavior, and it is for this reason that it is typically considered in discussions of motivation.[40]

We discussed the reinforcement process in detail in Chapter 3. We showed how using reinforcers to condition behavior gives us considerable insight into how people learn. Yet we cannot ignore the fact that reinforcement has a wide following as a motivational device. In its pure form, however, reinforcement theory ignores feelings, attitudes, expectations, and other cognitive variables that are known to impact behavior. In fact, some researchers look at the same experiments that reinforcement theorists use to support their position and interpret the findings in a cognitive framework.[41]

Reinforcement is undoubtedly an important influence on behavior, but few scholars are prepared to argue that it is the *only* influence. The behaviors you engage in at work and the amount of effort you allocate to each task *is* affected by the consequences that follow from your behavior. If you are consistently reprimanded for outproducing your colleagues, you will likely reduce your productivity. But your lower productivity may also be explained in terms of goals, inequity, or expectancies.

Reinforcement theory

Behavior is a function of its consequences.

Equity Theory

Jane Pearson graduated last year from the State University with a degree in accounting. After interviews with a number of organizations on campus, she accepted a position with one of the nation's largest public accounting firms and was assigned to their Boston office. Jane was very pleased with the offer she received: challenging work with a prestigious firm, an excellent opportunity to gain important experience, and the highest salary any accounting major at State was offered last year—$2,400 a month. But Jane was the top student in her class; she was ambitious and articulate and fully expected to receive a commensurate salary.

[40] R. M. Steers and L. W. Porter, *Motivation and Work Behavior*, 2nd ed. (New York: McGraw-Hill, 1979), p. 13.

[41] E. A. Locke, "Latham vs. Komaki: A Tale of Two Paradigms," *Journal of Applied Psychology*, February 1980, pp. 16–23.

Chapter 6 Basic Motivation Concepts **163**

TABLE 6–1
Equity Theory

Ratio Comparisons	Perception
$\dfrac{O}{I_A} < \dfrac{O}{I_B}$	Inequity due to being underrewarded
$\dfrac{O}{I_A} = \dfrac{O}{I_B}$	Equity
$\dfrac{O}{I_A} > \dfrac{O}{I_B}$	Inequity due to being overrewarded

where $\dfrac{O}{I_A}$ represents the employee and

$\dfrac{O}{I_B}$ represents relevant others

Twelve months have passed since Jane joined her employer. The work has proved to be as challenging and satisfying as she had hoped. Her employer is extremely pleased with her performance; in fact she recently received a $200-a-month raise. However, Jane's motivational level has dropped dramatically in the past few weeks. Why? Her employer has just hired a fresh college graduate out of State University, who lacks the one-year experience Jane has gained, for $2,650 a month—$50 more than Jane now makes! It would be an understatement to describe Jane in any other terms than livid. Jane is even talking about looking for another job.

Jane's situation illustrates the role that equity plays in motivation. Employees make comparisons of their job inputs and outcomes relative to those of others. We perceive what we get from a job situation (outcomes) in relation to what we put into it (inputs), and then we compare our input-outcome ratio with the input-outcome ratio of relevant others. This is shown in Table 6–1. If we perceive our ratio to be equal to the relevant others with whom we compare ourselves, a state of equity is said to exist. We perceive our situation as fair—that justice prevails. If the ratios are unequal, inequity exists; that is, we tend to view ourselves as underrewarded or overrewarded. J. Stacy Adams proposed that an equity process takes place in which people who view any inequity as aversive will attempt to correct it.[42]

The referent that an employee selects adds to the complexity of **equity theory**. Evidence indicates that the referent chosen is an important variable in equity theory.[43] There are four referent comparisons that an employee can use:

1. *Self-inside*—An employee's experiences in a different position inside his or her current organization

Equity theory

Individuals compare their job inputs and outcomes with those of others and then respond so as to eliminate any inequities.

[42] J. S. Adams, "Inequity in Social Exchanges," in L. Berkowitz (ed.), *Advances in Experimental Social Psychology* (New York: Academic Press, 1965), pp. 267–300.

[43] P. S. Goodman, "An Examination of Referents Used in the Evaluation of Pay," *Organizational Behavior and Human Performance*, October 1974, pp. 170–95; S. Ronen, "Equity Perception in Multiple Comparisons: A Field Study," *Human Relations*, April 1986, pp. 333–46; and R. W. Scholl, E. A. Cooper, and J. F. McKenna, "Referent Selection in Determining Equity Perception: Differential Effects on Behavioral and Attitudinal Outcomes," *Personnel Psychology*, Spring 1987, pp. 113–27.

2. *Self-outside*—An employee's experiences in a situation or position outside his or her current organization

3. *Other-inside*—Another individual or group of individuals inside the employee's organization

4. *Other-outside*—Another individual or group of individuals outside the employee's organization

So employees might compare themselves to friends, neighbors, co-workers, colleagues in other organizations, or past jobs they themselves have had. Which referent an employee chooses will be influenced by the information the employee holds about referents as well as the attractiveness of the referent. This has led to focusing on three moderating variables—the employee's salary level, amount of education, and length of tenure.[44] Employees with higher salaries and more education tend to be more cosmopolitan and have better information; thus, they're more likely to make comparisons with outsiders. Employees with short tenure in their current organization tend to have little information about others inside the organization, so they rely on their own personal experiences. On the other hand, employees with long tenure rely more heavily on co-workers for comparisons.

Based on equity theory, when employees perceive an inequity they can be predicted to make one of six choices:

1. Change their inputs (for example, don't exert as much effort)

2. Change their outcomes (for example, individuals paid on a piece-rate basis can increase their pay by producing a higher quantity of units of lower quality)

3. Distort perceptions of self (for example, "I used to think I worked at a moderate pace but now I realize that I work a lot harder than everyone else.")

4. Distort perceptions of others (for example, "Mike's job isn't as desirable as I previously thought it was.")

5. Choose a different referent (for example, "I may not make as much as my brother-in-law, but I'm doing a lot better than my Dad did when he was my age.")

6. Leave the field (for example, quit the job)

Equity theory recognizes that individuals are concerned not only with the absolute amount of rewards they receive for their efforts, but also with the relationship of this amount to what others receive. They make judgments as to the relationship between their inputs and outcomes and the inputs and outcomes of others. Based on one's inputs, such as effort, experience, education, and competence, one compares outcomes such as salary levels, raises, recognition, and other factors. When people perceive an imbalance in their input-outcome ratio relative to others, tension is created. This tension provides the

---

[44] P. S. Goodman, "An Examination of Referents"; and G. R. Oldham, C. T. Kulik, L. P. Stepina, and M. L. Ambrose, "Relations Between Situational Factors and the Comparative Referents Used by Employees," *Academy of Management Journal*, September 1986, pp. 599–608.

basis for motivation, as people strive for what they perceive as equity and fairness.

Specifically, the theory establishes four propositions relating to inequitable pay:

1. *Given payment by time, overrewarded employees will produce more than will equitably paid employees.* Hourly and salaried employees will generate high quantity or quality of production in order to increase the input side of the ratio and bring about equity.

2. *Given payment by quantity of production, overrewarded employees will produce fewer, but higher-quality, units than will equitably paid employees.* Individuals paid on a piece-rate basis will increase their effort to achieve equity, which can result in greater quality or quantity. However, increases in quantity will only increase inequity since every unit produced results in further overpayment. Therefore, effort is directed toward increasing quality rather than increasing quantity.

3. *Given payment by time, underrewarded employees will produce less or poorer quality of output.* Effort will be decreased, which will bring about lower productivity or poorer-quality output than equitably paid subjects.

4. *Given payment by quantity of production, underrewarded employees will produce a large number of low-quality units in comparison with equitably paid employees.* Employees on piece-rate pay plans can bring about equity because trading off quantity of output for quality will result in an increase in rewards with little or no increase in contributions.

These propositions have generally been supported, with two interesting qualifications.[45] First, inequities created by overpayment do not seem to have a very significant impact on behavior in most work situations. Apparently, people have a great deal more tolerance of overpayment inequities or are better able to rationalize them than of underpayment inequities. Second, not everyone equally appreciates the concept of fairness, yet the search for fairness is a central theme in equity theory. Equity predictions, therefore, are more likely to apply to people who are morally mature—that is, individuals guided by a moral system in which the fair distribution of rewards is a fundamental tenet.

In conclusion, equity theory demonstrates that employee motivation is influenced significantly by relative rewards as well as by absolute rewards. But some key issues are still unclear.[46] For instance, how do employees handle conflicting equity signals, such as when unions point to other employee groups who are substantially *better off*, while management argues how much things have *improved*? How do employees define inputs and outcomes? How do they combine and weigh their inputs and outcomes to arrive at totals? When and how do the factors change over time? Yet, regardless of these problems, equity theory continues to offer us some important insights into employee motivation.

[45] P. S. Goodman and A. Friedman, "An Examination of Adams' Theory of Inequity," *Administrative Science Quarterly*, September 1971, pp. 271–88; and R. P. Vecchio, "An Individual-Differences Interpretation of the Conflicting Predictions Generated by Equity Theory and Expectancy Theory," *Journal of Applied Psychology*, August 1981, pp. 470–81.

[46] P. S. Goodman, "Social Comparison Process in Organizations," in B. M. Staw and G. R. Salancik (eds.), *New Directions in Organizational Behavior* (Chicago: St. Clair, 1977), pp. 97–132.

Why Pro Athletes "Lack Motivation"

Tony Dorsett, a veteran star half-back formerly with the Dallas Cowboys, earned $700,000 a year but complained that he was demotivated when his team signed another half-back, Herschel Walker, to a million dollar a year contract. Eric Dickerson made $680,000 a year as a running back with the Los Angeles Rams. In his first four years in the pros, he led the NFL three times in rushing yardage. But when the Los Angeles Raiders signed rookie Bo Jackson, who plays the same position as Dickerson, to a $1.5 million a year contract, Dickerson said he was not motivated, had lost the spirit to compete, and wanted the Rams to either renegotiate his contract or trade him to a team that would pay him what he was worth. He was reluctantly traded by the Rams to the Indianapolis Colts, who met his financial demands.

No early season in professional sports would be complete without a few athletes "holding out" for more money. Do these athletes argue that they can't make ends meet on their half-million or million dollar a year salaries? Not very often! Their arguments are almost always couched in terms of equity.

Even though you and I might be euphoric over the opportunity to work six months a year for a couple of hundred thousand dollars a month—exclusive of earnings from endorsements and other promotional activities—these athletes are rarely concerned with the absolute dollars they receive. What they are doing is comparing themselves to other athletes who play a similar position and who have comparable or less impressive statistics. When they see a pay discrepancy, they seek equity. And when the management of these professional franchises fail to correct these inequities, they frequently find themselves with disgruntled and demotivated athletes.

Expectancy Theory

Currently, one of the most widely accepted explanations of motivation is Victor Vroom's **expectancy theory**.[47] Although it has its critics,[48] most of the research evidence is supportive of the theory.[49]

Expectancy theory

The strength of a tendency to act in a certain way depends on the strength of an expectation that an act will be followed by a given outcome and on the attractiveness of that outcome to the individual.

[47] V. H. Vroom, *Work and Motivation* (New York: John Wiley, 1964).

[48] See, for example, H. G. Heneman III and D. P. Schwab, "Evaluation of Research on Expectancy Theory Prediction of Employee Performance," *Psychological Bulletin*, July 1972, pp. 1–9; T. R. Mitchell, "Expectancy Models of Job Satisfaction, Occupational Preference and Effort: A Theoretical, Methodological and Empirical Appraisal," *Psychological Bulletin*, November 1974, pp. 1053–77; and L. Reinharth and M. A. Wahba, "Expectancy Theory as a Predictor of Work Motivation, Effort Expenditure, and Job Performance," *Academy of Management Journal*, September 1975, pp. 502–37.

[49] See, for example, L. W. Porter and E. E. Lawler III, *Managerial Attitudes and Performance* (Homewood, IL: Richard D. Irwin, 1968); D. F. Parker and L. Dyer, "Expectancy Theory as a Within-Person Behavioral Choice Model: An Empirical Test of Some Conceptual and Methodological Refine-

Essentially, the expectancy theory argues that the strength of a tendency to act in a certain way depends on the strength of an expectation that the act will be followed by a given outcome and on the attractiveness of that outcome to the individual. It includes three variables or relationships.[50]

1. *Attractiveness*—the importance that the individual places on the potential outcome or reward that can be achieved on the job. This considers the unsatisfied needs of the individual.

2. *Performance-reward linkage*—the degree to which the individual believes that performing at a particular level will lead to the attainment of a desired outcome.

3. *Effort-performance linkage*—the perceived probability by the individual that exerting a given amount of effort will lead to performance.

While this may sound pretty complex, it really is not that difficult to visualize. Whether one has the desire to produce at any given time depends on one's particular goals and one's perception of the relative worth of performance as a path to the attainment of these goals.

Figure 6–6 is a considerable simplification of expectancy theory, but it expresses its major contentions. The strength of a person's motivation to perform (effort) depends on how strongly he or she believes that he or she can achieve attempted tasks. If the person achieves this goal (performance), will he or she be adequately rewarded and, if rewarded by the organization, will the reward satisfy the person's individual goals? Let us consider the four steps inherent in the theory and then attempt to apply it.

First, what perceived outcomes does the job offer the employee? Outcomes may be positive: pay, security, companionship, trust, fringe benefits, a chance to use talent or skills, congenial relationships. On the other hand, employees may view the outcomes as negative: fatigue, boredom, frustration, anxiety, harsh supervision, threat of dismissal. Importantly, reality is not relevant here; the critical issue is what the individual employee *perceives* the outcome to be, regardless of whether or not his or her perceptions are accurate.

Second, how attractive do employees consider these outcomes? Are they valued positively, negatively, or neutrally? This obviously is an internal issue to the individual and considers his or her personal values, personality, and needs. The individual who finds a particular outcome attractive—that is, positively valued—would prefer attaining it to not attaining it. Others may find it negative and, therefore, prefer not attaining it to attaining it. Still others may be neutral.

Third, what kind of behavior must the employee produce in order to achieve these outcomes? The outcomes are not likely to have any effect on the individual employee's performance unless the employee knows, clearly and unambiguously, what he or she must do in order to achieve them. For example, what is "doing well" in terms of performance appraisal? What are the criteria the employee's performance will be judged on?

---

ments," *Organizational Behavior and Human Performance*, October 1976, pp. 97–117; and H. J. Arnold, "A Test of the Multiplicative Hypothesis of Expectancy-Valence Theories of Work Motivation," *Academy of Management Journal*, April 1981, pp. 128–41.

[50] Vroom refers to these three variables as *valence, instrumentality*, and *expectancy*, respectively.

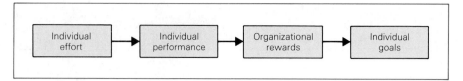

FIGURE 6–6
Simplified Expectancy Model

Fourth and last, how does the employee view his or her chances of doing what is asked? After the employee has considered his or her own competencies and ability to control those variables that will determine success, what probability does he or she place on successful attainment?[51]

Let us use the classroom organization as an illustration of how one can use expectancy theory to explain motivation.

Most students prefer an instructor who tells them what is expected of them in the course. They want to know what the assignments and examinations will be like, when they are due or to be taken, and how much weight each carries in the final term grade. They also like to think that the amount of effort they exert in attending classes, taking notes, and studying will be reasonably related to the grade they will make in the course. If we assume that the above describes you, consider that five weeks into a class you are really enjoying (we'll call it B.A. 301), an exam is given back. You have studied hard for this exam. You have consistently scored A's and B's on exams in other courses where you have expended similar effort. And the reason you work so hard is to make top grades, which you believe are important for getting a good job upon graduation. Also, you are not sure, but you may want to go on to graduate school. Again, you think grades are important for getting into a good graduate school.

The results of that five-week exam are in. The class median was 72. Ten percent of the class scored an 85 or higher and got an A. Your grade was 46; the minimum passing mark was 50. You're mad. You're frustrated. Even more, you're perplexed. How could you have possibly done so poorly on the exam when you usually score among the top grades in other classes by preparing as you had for this exam? Several interesting things are immediately evident in your behavior. Suddenly, you no longer are driven to attend B.A. 301 classes regularly. You find you do not study for the course either. When you do attend classes, you daydream a lot—the result is an empty notebook instead of several pages of notes. One would probably be correct in describing you as "lacking motivation" in B.A. 301. Why did your motivational level change? You know and I know, but let's explain it in expectancy terms.

If we use Figure 6–6 to understand this situation, we might say the following: Studying and preparation in B.A. 301 (effort) is conditioned by its resulting in answering the questions on the exam correctly (performance), which will produce a high grade (reward), which you believe will lead to the security, prestige, and other benefits that accrue from obtaining a good job (individual goal).

---

[51] This four-step discussion was adapted from K. F. Taylor, "A 'Valence-Expectancy' Approach to Work Motivation," *Personnel Practice Bulletin*, June 1974, pp. 142–48.

OB Close-Up

Different Strokes for Different Folks

What motivates me doesn't necessarily motivate you. Expectancy theory recognizes this by proposing that rewards be tailored to the individual. But can we generalize among subgroups of employees as to what they might place greater importance upon? A recent study of 1,000 employees asked them to rank order ten work-related factors.[52] Their answers were then tabulated by subgroups on the basis of sex, age, income level, job type, and organization level. The results are shown in Table 6–2.

While the results suggest that there is a great deal of similarity in preferences, especially between men and women, there are a few important differences. For instance, younger workers, those with low incomes, and those in lower, nonsupervisory positions are most concerned with money. Job security also is significantly less important to older workers and to those higher in the organization. If nothing else, these results challenge those who might simplistically assume that *everybody* considers factors such as good pay and promotion in the organization to be a high priority.

The attractiveness of the outcome—which in this case is a good grade—is high. But what about the performance-reward linkage? Do you feel that the grade you received truly reflects your knowledge of the material? In other words, did the test fairly measure what you know? If the answer is "Yes," then this linkage is strong. If the answer is "No," then at least part of the reason for your reduced motivational level is your belief that the test was not a fair measure of your performance. If the test was of an essay type, maybe you believe the instructor's grading method was poor. Was too much weight placed on a question that you thought was trivial? Maybe the instructor does not like you and was biased in grading your paper. These are examples of perceptions that influence the performance-reward linkage and your level of motivation.

Another possible demotivating force may be the effort-performance relationship, If, after you took the exam, you believed that you could not have passed it regardless of the amount of preparation you had done, then your desire to study will drop. Possibly the instructor wrote the exam under the assumption that you had had a considerably broader background in the course's

[52] K. A. Kovach, "What Motivates Employees? Workers and Supervisors Give Different Answers," *Business Horizons*, September-October 1987, pp. 58–65.

TABLE 6–2   What Workers Want, Ranked by Subgroups[1]

	Sex		Age				Income Level				Job Type				Organization Level		
	Men	Women	Under 30	31–40	41–50	Over 50	Under $12,000	$12,001–$18,000	$18,001–$25,000	Over $25,000	Blue-Collar Unskilled	Blue-Collar Skilled	White-Collar Unskilled	White-Collar Skilled	Lower Nonsupervisory	Middle Nonsupervisory	Higher Nonsupervisory
Interesting work	2	2	4	2	3	1	5	2	1	1	2	1	1	2	3	1	1
Full appreciation of work done	1	1	5	3	2	2	4	3	3	2	1	6	3	1	4	2	2
Feeling of being in on things	3	3	6	4	1	3	6	1	2	4	5	2	5	4	5	3	3
Job security	5	4	2	1	4	7	2	4	4	3	4	3	7	5	2	4	6
Good wages	4	5	1	5	5	8	1	5	6	8	3	4	6	6	1	6	8
Promotion and growth in organization	6	6	3	6	8	9	3	6	5	7	6	5	4	3	6	5	5
Good working conditions	7	7	7	7	7	4	8	7	7	6	9	7	2	7	7	7	4
Personal loyalty to employees	8	8	9	9	6	5	7	8	8	5	8	9	9	8	8	8	7
Tactful discipline	9	9	8	10	9	10	10	9	9	10	7	10	10	9	9	9	10
Sympathetic help with personal problems	10	10	10	8	10	6	9	10	10	9	10	8	8	10	10	10	9

[1] Ranked from 1 (highest) to 10 (lowest).

Source: Adapted from K. A. Kovach, "What Motivates Employees? Workers and Supervisors Give Different Answers," *Business Horizons*, September-October 1987, p. 61.

subject matter. Maybe the course had several prerequisites that you did not know about, or possibly you had the prerequisites but took them several years ago. The end result is the same: You place a low value on your effort leading to answering the exam questions correctly, and hence there is a reduction in your motivational level, and you lessen your effort.

The key to expectancy theory, therefore, is the understanding of an individual's goals and the linkage between effort and performance, between performance and rewards, and, finally, between the rewards and individual goal satisfaction. As a contingency model, expectancy theory recognizes that there is no universal principle for explaining everyone's motivations. Additionally, just because we understand what needs a person seeks to satisfy does not ensure that the individual himself perceives high performance as necessarily leading to the satisfaction of these needs. If you desire to take B.A. 301 in order to meet new people and make social contacts, but the instructor organizes the class on the assumption that you want to make a good grade in the course, the instructor may be personally disappointed should you perform poorly on the exams. Unfortunately, most instructors assume that their ability to allocate grades is a potent force in motivating students. But it will only be so if students place a high importance on grades, if students know what they must do to achieve the grade desired, and if the students consider there is a high probability of their performing well should they exert a high level of effort.

Let us summarize some of the issues expectancy theory has brought forward. First, it emphasizes payoffs or rewards. As a result, we have to believe that the rewards the organization is offering align with what the employee wants. It is a theory based on self-interest wherein each individual seeks to maximize his or her expected satisfaction: "Expectancy theory is a form of calculative, psychological *hedonism* in which the ultimate motive of every human act is asserted to be the maximization of pleasure and/or the minimization of pain."[53] Second, we have to be concerned with the attractiveness of rewards, which requires an understanding and knowledge of what value the individual puts on organizational payoffs. We want to reward the individual with those things he or she values positively. Third, expectancy theory emphasizes expected behaviors. Does the person know what is expected and how he or she will be appraised? Finally, the theory is concerned with expectations. It is irrelevant what is realistic or rational. An individual's own expectations of performance, reward, and goal satisfaction outcomes will determine his or her level of effort, not the objective outcomes themselves.

Does the expectancy theory work? The space we have devoted to it suggests that it is important; yet, as we have seen before, few theories are irrefutable, without critics, or devoid of contradictory findings. The expectancy theory is no exception. Attempts to validate the theory have been complicated by methodological, criterion, and measurement problems. As a result, many published studies that purport to support or negate the theory must be viewed with caution. Importantly, most studies have failed to replicate the methodology as it was originally proposed. For example, the theory proposes to explain different levels of effort within the same person under different circumstances, but almost all replication studies have looked at different people. By correcting for this flaw, support for the validity of the expectancy theory has been greatly improved.[54] Some critics suggest that the theory has only limited use, arguing that it tends to be more valid for predicting in situations where effort-performance and performance-reward linkages are clearly perceived by the individual.[55] Since few individuals perceive a high correlation between performance and rewards in their jobs, the theory tends to be idealistic. If organizations actually rewarded individuals for performance, rather than criteria such as seniority, effort, skill level, or job difficulty, then the theory's validity might be considerably greater. However, rather than invalidating expectancy theory, this criticism can be used in support of the theory and for explaining why a large segment of the work force exerts a minimal level of effort in carrying out their job responsibilities.

---

[53] E. A. Locke, "Personnel Attitudes and Motivation," in M. R. Rosenzweig and L. W. Porter (eds.), *Annual Review of Psychology*, (Palo Alto, CA: Annual Reviews, 1975), p. 459.

[54] P. M. Muchinsky, "A Comparison of Within- and Across-Subjects Analyses of the Expectancy-Valence Model for Predicting Effort," *Academy of Management Journal*, March 1977, pp. 154–58.

[55] R. J. House, H. J. Shapiro, and M. A. Wahba, "Expectancy Theory as a Predictor of Work Behavior and Attitudes: A Re-evaluation of Empirical Evidence," *Decision Sciences*, January 1974, pp. 481–506.

Don't Forget Ability and Opportunity

Robin and Chris both graduated from college a couple of years ago with their degrees in elementary education. They each took jobs as first-grade teachers, but in different school districts. Robin immediately confronted a number of obstacles on the job: a large class (forty-two students), a small and dingy class-room, and inadequate supplies. Chris' situation couldn't have been more differ-ent. He had only fifteen students in his class, plus a teaching aide for fifteen hours each week, a modern and well-lighted room, a well-stocked supply cabinet, the unlimited use of a personal computer for class planning, and a highly supportive principal. Not surprisingly, at the end of their first school year, Chris had been considerably more effective as a teacher than had Robin.

The preceding episode illustrates an obvious but often overlooked fact. Success on a job is facilitated or hindered by the existence or absence of support resources.

A popular, although arguably simplistic, way of thinking about employee performance is as a function of the interaction of ability and motivation; that is, performance $= f(A \times M)$. If either is inadequate, performance will be negatively affected. This helps to explain, for instance, the hardworking athlete or student with modest abilities who consistently outperforms his or her more gifted, but lazy, rival. So, as we noted in Chapter 3, an individual's intelligence and skills (subsumed under the label "ability") must be considered in addition to motivation if we are to be able to accurately explain and predict employee performance. But a piece of the puzzle is still missing. We need to add **opportunity to perform** to our equation—performance $= f(A \times M \times O)$.[56] Even though an individual may be willing and able, there may be obstacles that constrain performance. This is shown in Figure 6–7.

Opportunity to perform

High levels of performance are partially a function of an absence of obstacles that constrain the employee.

When you attempt to assess why an employee may not be performing to the level that you believe he or she is capable of, take a look at the work environment to see if it's supportive. Does the employee have adequate tools, equipment, materials, and supplies; does the employee have favorable working conditions, helpful co-workers, supportive rules and procedures to work under, adequate time to do a good job, and the like? If not, performance will suffer.

INTEGRATING CONTEMPORARY THEORIES OF MOTIVATION

We've looked at a lot of motivation theories in this chapter. The fact that a number of these theories have been supported only complicates the matter. How simple it would have been if, after presenting half-a-dozen theories, only

[56] L. H. Peters, E. J. O'Connor, and C. J. Rudolf, "The Behavioral and Affective Consequences of Performance-Relevant Situational Variables," *Organizational Behavior and Human Performance*, February 1980, pp. 79–96; and M. Blumberg and C. D. Pringle, "The Missing Opportunity in Organiza-tional Research: Some Implications for a Theory of Work Performance," *Academy of Management Review*, October 1982, pp. 560–69.

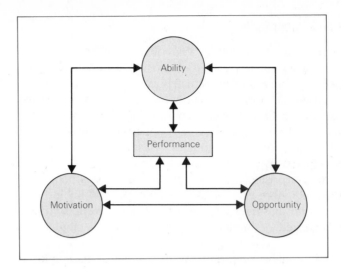

FIGURE 6–7
Performance Dimensions

Source: Adapted from M. Blumberg and C. D. Pringle, "The
Missing Opportunity in Organizational Research: Some
Implications for a Theory of Work Performance," *Academy
of Management Review*, October 1982, p. 565.

one was found valid. So the challenge is now to tie these theories together to
help you understand their interrelationship.

Figure 6–8 presents a model that integrates much of what we know about
motivation. Its basic foundation is the simplified expectancy model shown in
Figure 6–6. Let's work through Figure 6–8, beginning at the extreme left.

We begin by explicitly recognizing that opportunities can aid or hinder
individual effort. The individual effort box also has another arrow leading into
it. This arrow flows out of the individual's goals. Consistent with goal-setting
theory, this goals-effort loop is meant to remind us that goals direct behavior.

Expectancy theory predicts that an employee will exert a high level of
effort if he or she perceives that there is a strong relationship between effort
and performance, performance and rewards, and rewards and satisfaction of
personal goals. Each of these relationships, in turn, is influenced by certain
factors. For effort to lead to good performance, the individual must have the
requisite ability to perform, and the performance evaluation system that measures
the individual's performance must be perceived as being fair and objective.
The performance-reward relationship will be strong if the individual perceives
that it is performance (rather than seniority, personal favorites, or other criteria)
that is rewarded. If cognitive evaluation theory were fully valid in the actual
workplace, we would predict here that basing rewards on performance should
decrease the individual's intrinsic motivation. The final link in expectancy theory
is the rewards-goals relationship. ERG theory would come into play at this
point. Motivation would be high to the degree that the rewards an individual

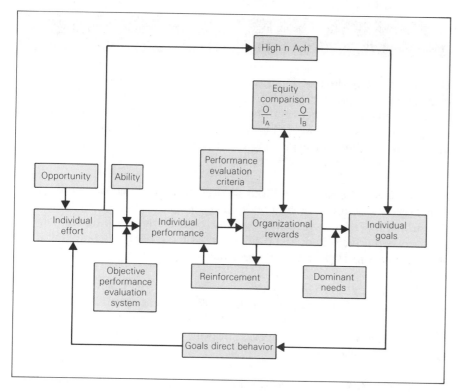

FIGURE 6–8
Integrating Contemporary Theories of Motivation

received for his or her high performance satisfied the dominant needs consistent with his or her individual goals.

A closer look at Figure 6–8 will also reveal that the model considers the achievement need and reinforcement and equity theories. The high achiever is not motivated by the organization's assessment of his or her performance or organizational rewards; hence, the jump from effort to individual goals for those with a high *nAch*. Remember, high achievers are internally driven as long as the jobs they are doing provide them with personal responsibility, feedback, and moderate risks. So they are not concerned with the effort-performance, performance-rewards, or rewards-goal linkages.

Reinforcement theory enters our model by recognizing that the organization's rewards reinforce the individual's performance. If management has designed a reward system that is seen by employees as "paying off" for good performance, the rewards will reinforce and encourage continued good performance.

Finally, rewards also play the key part in equity theory. Individuals will compare the rewards (outcomes) they receive from the inputs they make with the reward-input ratio of relevant others ($O/I_A : O/I_B$), and inequities may influence the effort expended.

The theories we've discussed in this chapter do not all address our four dependent variables. Some, for instance, are directed at explaining turnover, while others emphasize productivity. The theories also differ in their predictive strength. In this section, we'll (1) review the key motivation theories to determine their relevance in explaining our dependent variables, and (2) assess the predictive power of each.[57]

Need Theories   We introduced four theories which focused on needs. These were Maslow's hierarchy, motivation-hygiene, ERG, and the three-needs theories. The strongest of these is probably the latter, particularly regarding the relationship between achievement and productivity. If the other three have any value at all, it relates to explaining and predicting job satisfaction.

Maslow

Goal-setting Theory   There is little dispute that clear and difficult goals lead to higher levels of employee productivity. This evidence leads us to conclude that goal-setting theory provides one of the more powerful explanations of this dependent variable. The theory, however, does not address absenteeism, turnover, or satisfaction.

Reinforcement Theory   This theory has an impressive record for predicting factors like quality and quantity of work, persistence of effort, absenteeism, tardiness, and accident rates. It does not offer much insight into employee satisfaction or the decision to quit.

Equity Theory   Equity theory deals with all four dependent variables. However, it is strongest when predicting absence and turnover behaviors and weak when predicting differences in employee productivity.

Expectancy Theory   Our final theory focused on performance variables. It has proven to offer a relatively powerful explanation of employee productivity, absenteeism, and turnover. But expectancy theory assumes that employees have few constraints on their decision discretion. It makes many of the same assumptions that the optimizing model makes about individual decision making (see Chapter 4). This acts to restrict its applicability.

For major decisions, like accepting or resigning from a job, expectancy theory works well, because people don't rush into decisions of this nature. They're more prone to take the time to carefully consider the costs and benefits of all the alternatives. So expectancy theory is *not* a very good explanation for more typical types of work behavior, especially for individuals in lower-level jobs, because such jobs come with considerable limitations imposed by work methods, supervisors, and company policies. We would conclude, therefore, that expectancy theory's power in explaining employee productivity in-

---

[57] This section is based on F. J. Landy and W. S. Becker, "Motivation Theory Reconsidered," in L. L. Cummings and B. M. Staw (eds.), *Research in Organizational Behavior*, Vol. 9 (Greenwich, CT: JAI Press, 1987), pp. 24–35.

TABLE 6–3
Power of Motivation Theories[a]

Variable	THEORIES				
	Need	Goal-setting	Reinforce-ment	Equity	Expectancy
Productivity	3[b]	5	3	3	4[c]
Absenteeism			4	4	4
Turnover				4	5
Satisfaction	2			2	

[a] Theories are rated on a scale of 1 to 5, 5 being highest.
[b] Applies to individuals with a high need to achieve.
[c] Limited value in jobs where employees have little discretionary choice.

Source: Based on F. J. Landy and W. S. Becker, "Motivation Theory Reconsidered," in L. L. Cummings and B. M. Staw (eds.), *Research in Organizational Behavior*, Vol. 9 (Greenwich, CT: JAI Press, 1987), p. 33.

creases where the jobs being performed are more complex and higher in the organization where discretion is greater.

Summary   Table 6–3 attempts to summarize what we know about the power of the more well-known motivation theories to explain and predict our four dependent variables. While based on a wealth of research, it also includes some subjective judgments. However, it does provide a reasonable guide through the motivation theory maze.

POINT

MONEY MOTIVATES!

The importance of money as a motivator has been consistently downgraded by most behavioral scientists. They prefer to point out the value of challenging jobs, goals, participation in decision making, feedback, cohesive work groups, and other nonmonetary factors as stimulants to employee motivation. We will argue otherwise here—that money is *the* crucial incentive to work motivation. As a medium of exhange, it is the vehicle by which employees can purchase the numerous need-satisfying "things" they desire. Further, money also performs the function of a "scorecard" by which employees assess the value that the organization places on their services and by which employees can compare their "value" to others.

Money's value as a medium of exchange is obvious. People may not work *only* for money, but take the money away and how many people would come to work? For the vast majority of the work force, a regular paycheck is absolutely necessary in order to meet their basic physiological and safety needs.

As equity theory suggests, money has symbolic value in addition to its exchange value. We use pay as the primary outcome against which we compare our inputs to determine if we are being treated equitably. That an organization pays one executive $60,000 a year and another $75,000 means more than the latter's merely earning $15,000 a year more. It is a message, from the organization to both employees, of how much it values the contribution of each.

In addition to equity theory, both reinforcement and expectancy theories attest to the value of money as a motivator. In the former, if pay is contingent on performance, it will encourage workers to high levels of effort. Consistent with expectancy theory, money will motivate to the extent that it is seen as being able to satisfy an individual's personal goals and is perceived as being dependent upon performance criteria.

The best case for money as a motivator is a review of studies done by Edwin Locke of the University of Maryland.[1] Locke looked at four methods of motivating employee performance: money, goal setting, participation in decision making, and redesigning jobs to give workers more challenge and responsibility. He found that the average improvement from money was 30 percent; goal setting increased performance 16 percent; participation improved performance by less than 1 percent; and job redesign positively impacted performance by an average of 17 percent. Moreover, every study Locke reviewed that used money as a method of motivation resulted in some improvement in employee performance. Such evidence demonstrates that money may not be the *only* motivator, but it is difficult to argue that it *doesn't* motivate!

---

[1] E. A. Locke et al., "The Relative Effectiveness of Four Methods of Motivating Employee Performance," in *Changes in Working Life*, eds. K. D. Duncan, M. M. Gruneberg, and D. Wallis (London: John Wiley, Ltd., 1980), pp. 363–83.

COUNTERPOINT

MONEY DOESN'T MOTIVATE MOST EMPLOYEES TODAY!

Money can motivate *some* people under *some* conditions. So the issue isn't really whether or not money *can* motivate. The answer to that is: It can! The more relevant question is: Does money motivate most employees in the work force today to higher performance? The answer to this question, we'll argue, is "No."

For money to motivate an individual's performance, certain conditions must be met. First, money must be important to the individual. Second, money must be perceived by the individual as being a direct reward for performance. Third, the marginal amount of money offered for the performance must be perceived by the individual as being significant. Finally, management must have the discretion to reward high performers with more money. Let's take a look at each of these conditions.

Money is not important to all employees. High achievers, for instance, are intrinsically motivated. Money should have little impact on these people. Similarly, money is relevant to those individuals with strong lower-order needs; but for most of the work force, their lower-order needs are substantially satisfied.

Money would motivate if employees perceived a strong linkage between performance and rewards in organizations. Unfortunately, pay increases are far more often determined by community pay standards, the national cost-of-living index, and the organization's current and future financial prospects than by each employee's level of performance.

For money to motivate, the marginal difference in pay increases between a high performer and an average performer must be significant. In practice, it rarely is. For instance, a high-performing employee who currently is earning $30,000 a year is given a $200 a month raise. After taxes, that amounts to about $35 a week. But this employee's $30,000 a year co-worker, who is an average performer, is rarely passed over at raise time. Instead of getting an 8 percent raise, he or she is likely to get half of that. The net difference in their weekly paychecks is probably less than $20. How much motivation is there in knowing that if you work really hard you're going to end up with $20 a week more than someone who is doing just enough to get by? For a large number of people, not much!

Our last point relates to the degree of discretion that managers have in being able to reward high performers. Where unions exist, that discretion is almost zero. Pay is determined through collective bargaining and is allocated by job title and seniority, not level of performance. In nonunionized environments, the organization's compensation policies will constrain managerial discretion. Each job typically has a pay grade. So a systems analyst III can earn between $2,725 and $3,140 a month. No matter how good a job that analyst does, her boss cannot pay her more than $3,140 a month. Similarly, no matter how poorly someone does in that job, he will earn at least $2,725 a month. In most organizations, managers have a very small area of discretion within which they can reward their higher-performing employees. So money might be theoretically capable of motivating employees to higher levels of performance, but most managers aren't given enough flexibility to do much about it.

KEY TERMS

Affiliation Need

Cognitive Evaluation Theory

Equity Theory

ERG Theory

Expectancy Theory

Goal-Setting Theory

Hierarchy of Needs Theory

Higher-Order Needs

Hygiene Factors

Lower-Order Needs

Motivation

Motivation-Hygiene Theory

Opportunity to Perform

Power Need

Reinforcement Theory

Self-Actualization

Theory X

Theory Y

Three Needs Theory

FOR DISCUSSION

1. Define motivation. Describe the motivation process.

2. What are the implications of Theories X and Y to motivation practices?

3. Compare and contrast Maslow's hierarchy of needs theory with (a) Alderfer's ERG theory, and (b) Herzberg's motivation-hygiene theory.

4. Describe the three needs isolated by McClelland. How are they related to worker behavior?

5. "The cognitive evaluation theory is contradictory to reinforcement and expectancy theories." Do you agree or disagree? Explain.

6. "Goal setting is part of both reinforcement and expectancy theories." Do you agree or disagree? Explain.

7. Reconcile equity and expectancy theories.

8. Do you think workaholics and high achievers are the same thing? Discuss.

9. Explain Figure 6–8 in your own words.

10. Can an individual be *too* motivated, so that his or her performance declines as a result of excessive effort? Discuss.

11. Explain the formula: Performance $= f(A \times M \times O)$ and give an example.

12. Identify three activities you *really enjoy* (for example, playing tennis, reading a novel, going shopping). Next, identify three activities you *really dislike* (for example, going to the dentist, cleaning the house, staying on a restricted calorie diet). Using the expectancy model, analyze each of your answers to assess why some activities stimulate your effort while others don't.

FOR FURTHER READING

EVANS, M. G., "Organizational Behavior: The Central Role of Motivation," *Yearly Review of Management of the Journal of Management*, Summer 1986, pp. 203–22. Discusses individual behavior in terms of motivation theory, with emphasis on goals, feedback, attributions, and consequences of performance.

LOCKE, E. A., and D. HENNE, "Work Motivation Theories," in C. L. COOPER and I. ROBERTSON (eds.), *International Review of Industrial and Organizational Psychology, 1986* (Sussex, England: John Wiley & Sons, 1986). Comprehensive review of the work motivation literature.

PINDER, C. C., *Work Motivation: Theory, Issues, and Applications* (Glenview, IL: Scott, Foresman, 1984). Well-regarded review and analysis of basic motivation theories.

PRICE, J. L., and C. W. MUELLER, *Handbook of Organizational Measurement* (Marshfield, MA: Pitman Publishing, 1986), pp. 172–82. Defines motivation and presents two different approaches to its measurement.

SIEVERS, B., "Beyond the Surrogate of Motivation," *Organization Studies*, Vol. 7, No. 4, 1986, pp. 335–51. Critiques the concept of motivation and argues that the theories don't align with the reality of people in organizations.

STEERS, R. M., and L. W. PORTER, *Motivation and Work Behavior*, 4th ed. (New York: McGraw-Hill, 1987). Reprints some of the major articles in the study of work motivation.

EXERCISE 6

NEEDS TEST

Indicate how important each of the following is in the job you would like to get. Write the numbers 1, 2, 3, 4, or 5 on the line after each item.

> 1 = Not important
> 2 = Slightly important
> 3 = Moderately important
> 4 = Very important
> 5 = Extremely important

1. Cooperative relations with my co-workers. ____
2. Developing new skills and knowledge at work. ____
3. Good pay for my work. ____
4. Being accepted by others. ____
5. Opportunity for independent thought and action. ____
6. Frequent raises in pay. ____
7. Opportunity to develop close friendships at work. ____
8. A sense of self-esteem. ____
9. A complete fringe benefit program. ____
10. Openness and honesty with my co-workers. ____
11. Opportunities for personal growth and development. ____
12. A sense of security from bodily harm. ____

Turn to page 563 for scoring directions and key.

Source: Adapted from C. P. Alderfer, *Existence, Relatedness, and Growth: Human Needs in Organizational Settings*. Copyright © 1972 by The Free Press, a Division of Macmillan Publishing Co., Inc.

Stacey Friedman has been a literary agent with one of the largest literary agencies in New York for four years. Her job entails matching up authors and their manuscripts with book publishers. She has about two dozen established authors whom she represents in negotiations with the publishing houses. Stacey also regularly reviews manuscripts of new or less established authors who want her firm to represent them.

"I live and breathe this job. I'm up at 5:30 in the morning and in the office by 7:00. I either skip lunch or use lunch as an excuse to meet with publishing editors, with one of my established authors, or to talk with a prospective client. I'm never out of the office before 7:30 P.M., and it's usually closer to 9:00. When I get home, I spend an hour or two lying in bed reading manuscripts. I only wish I could find another five hours a day so I could squeeze in more things. God, I love my work."

You might be correct in calling Stacey a workaholic. She approaches her work almost compulsively. In college, she was in a sorority, played on her school's soccer team, and dated regularly. But Stacey's job is now her whole life. She told me she hadn't been on a date in five months, although she had had several dozen offers. She had no social life, except for that which rotated around her work. Stacey even admitted that she hadn't had time to dust or run the vacuum cleaner over the rugs in her apartment in six weeks.

"But don't get the wrong impression when I say my apartment is a mess," interjected Stacey. "I don't care. Every morning I pop out of bed and just thank the Lord for having a job that makes me so happy. When I run into people who complain about their work, I just shake my head. How lucky I am! I'd rather be negotiating with an editor, making manuscript suggestions, discussing strategy with one of my authors, or reading some unknown author's first book than be cleaning the house, jogging around Central Park, or for that matter, making love with Tom Selleck. I mean it when I say I've got a great job."

Stacey Friedman's enthusiasm appears to have had a very positive impact on her job performance. Her boss says she is the best young agent in the office. "She gives a hundred percent. But, of course, she's smart, too. Stacey has a bright future in this industry."

QUESTIONS

1. If you were to learn that Stacey made only $18,000 a year in her job, would you be surprised? Explain.
2. Since Stacey makes only $18,000, one can safely conclude that money is not her main source of motivation. What types of individual, organizational, and job-related factors might account for her high level of motivation?
3. Build a model showing the relationships among the factors that help explain Stacey's high level of performance and motivation.
4. Can you see any possible negative aspects of managing someone like Stacey?

7

Motivation: From Concepts to Applications

■ *Chapter outline*

MANAGEMENT BY OBJECTIVES
BEHAVIOR MODIFICATION
PARTICIPATIVE MANAGEMENT
PERFORMANCE-BASED
COMPENSATION
FLEXIBLE BENEFITS

TWO-TIER PAY SYSTEMS
ALTERNATIVE WORK SCHEDULES
JOB DESIGN
IMPLICATIONS FOR PERFORMANCE
AND SATISFACTION

■ *Learning objectives*

Identify the four ingredients common to MBO programs
Outline the typical five step problem-solving model in OB Mod
Explain why managers might want to use participative decision-making
Describe the link between performance-based compensation and expectancy theory
Explain how flexible benefits turn benefits into motivators
Summarize why two-tier pay systems are inconsistent with sound motivation theory
Describe how flextime schedules work
Outline the evolution of job design
Define the characteristics that make jobs different
Describe how to enrich a job
Clarify the trade-offs in selecting among job design approaches

Set me anything to do as a task, and it is inconceivable the desire I have to do something else.

_____ G. B. SHAW

A few years ago, I was teaching a class in OB. I had just spent two weeks reviewing, in detail, the theories covered in Chapter 6. As I wrapped up my discussion, I was acutely aware of one student. His look of puzzlement couldn't be ignored. "Do you have any questions?," I asked the class. The student with the puzzled look responded, "I've got the theories down cold. I can explain each one to you. Ask me any questions about them and I'm sure I could give you the right answer. But what's missing is the link between these theories and their application. As a manager, how would I use them?"

That student's dilemma was apparently shared by most of the class. This chapter responds to that concern by attempting to link motivation theories and applications. In the following pages, we'll review a large number of techniques and programs that have gained varying degrees of acceptance in practice. For example, there will be discussions on popular programs such as management by objectives, two-tier pay systems, and flexible work hours. Specific attention will be given to showing how these programs build on one or more of the motivation theories we covered previously.

MANAGEMENT BY OBJECTIVES

Goal-setting theory has an impressive base of research support. But as a manager, how do you make goal setting operational? The best answer to that question is: Install a management by objectives (MBO) program.

What Is MBO?

Management by objectives emphasizes participatively set goals that are tangible, verifiable, and measurable. It's not a new idea. In fact, it was originally proposed by Peter Drucker more than thirty years ago as a means of using goals to motivate people rather than to control them.[1] Today, no introduction to basic management concepts would be complete without a discussion of MBO.

Management by objectives (MBO)

A program that encompasses specific goals, participatively set, for an explicit time period, with feedback on goal progress.

[1] P. F. Drucker, *The Practice of Management* (New York: Harper & Row, 1954).

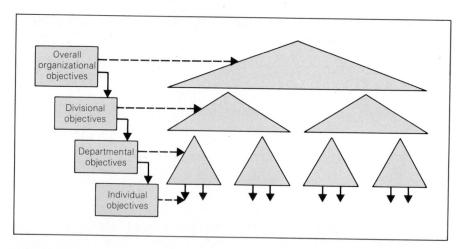

FIGURE 7–1
Cascading of Objectives

MBO's appeal undoubtedly lies in its emphasis on converting overall organizational objectives into specific objectives for organizational units and individual members. MBO operationalizes the concept of objectives by devising a process by which objectives cascade down through the organization. As depicted in Figure 7–1, the organization's overall objectives are translated into specific objectives for each succeeding level (that is, divisional, departmental, individual) in the organization. But because lower unit managers jointly participate in setting their own goals, MBO works from the "bottom up" as well as the "top down." The result is a hierarchy of objectives that link objectives at one level to those at the next level. And for the individual employee, MBO provides specific personal performance objectives. Each person, therefore, has an identified specific contribution to make to his or her unit's performance. If all the individuals achieve their goals, then their unit's goals will be attained and the organization's overall objectives become a reality.

There are four ingredients common to MBO programs. These are: goal specificity, participative decision making, an explicit time period, and performance feedback.[2]

Be Specific →

The objectives in MBO should be concise statements of expected accomplishments. It's not adequate, for example, to merely state a desire to cut costs, improve service, or increase quality. Such desires have to be converted into tangible objectives that can be measured and evaluated. To cut departmental costs *by 7 percent*, to improve service by ensuring that all telephone orders are processed *within twenty-four hours of receipt,* or to increase quality by keeping returns to *less than 1 percent of sales* are examples of specific objectives.

The objectives in MBO are not unilaterally set by the boss and then assigned to subordinates. MBO replaces imposed goals with participatively determined goals. The superior and subordinate jointly choose the goals and agree on how they will be measured.

---

[2] See, for instance, S. J. Carroll and H. L. Tosi, *Management by Objectives: Applications and Research* (New York, Macmillan, 1973).

Each objective has a concise time period in which it is to be completed. Typically the time period is three months, six months, or a year. So not only do managers and subordinates have specific objectives but stipulated time periods in which to accomplish them.

The final ingredient in an MBO program is feedback on performance. MBO seeks to give continuous feedback on progress toward goals. Ideally, this is accomplished by ongoing feedback to individuals so they can monitor and correct their own actions. This is supplemented by periodic managerial evaluations, when progress is reviewed. This applies at the top of the organization as well as at the bottom. The vice president of sales, for instance, has objectives for overall sales and for each of his or her major products. He or she will monitor ongoing sales reports to determine progress toward the sales division's objectives. Similarly, district sales managers have objectives, as does each salesperson in the field. Feedback in terms of sales and performance data is provided to let these people know how they are doing. Formal appraisal meetings also take place at which superiors and subordinates can review progress toward goals and further feedback can be provided.

Linking MBO and Goal-Setting Theory

Goal-setting theory demonstrates that hard goals result in a higher level of individual performance than do easy goals, that specific hard goals result in higher levels of performance than do no goals at all or the generalized goal of "do your best," and that feedback on one's performance leads to higher performance. Compare these findings with MBO.

MBO directly advocates specific goals and feedback. MBO implies, rather than explicitly states, that goals must be perceived as feasible. Consistent with goal setting, MBO would be most effective when the goals are difficult enough to require the person to do some stretching.

The only area of possible disagreement between MBO and goal-setting theory relates to the issue of participation—MBO strongly advocates it, while goal setting demonstrates that assigning goals to subordinates frequently works just as well. The major benefit to using participation, however, is that it appears to induce individuals to establish more difficult goals.

MBO in Practice

How widely used is MBO? Reviews of studies that have sought to answer this question suggest that it's a popular technique. Among large organizations—in business and in the public sector—probably half currently have a formal MBO program or had one at some time.[3]

[3] See, for instance, F. Schuster and A. F. Kendall, "Management by Objectives, Where We Stand—A Survey of the *Fortune* 500," *Human Resource Management*, Spring 1974, pp. 8–11; F. Luthans, "Management by Objectives in the Public Sector: The Transference Problem," unpublished paper presented at the 35th Annual Academy of Management Conference, New Orleans, Louisiana, 1975; R. C. Ford, F. S. MacLaughlin, and J. Nixdorf, "Ten Questions about MBO," *California Management Review*, Winter 1980, p. 89; and C. H. Ford, "MBO: An Idea Whose Time Has Gone?," *Business Horizons*, December 1979, p. 49.

MBO's popularity should not be construed to mean that it always works. There are a number of documented cases where MBO has been implemented but failed to meet management's expectations.[4] A close look at these cases, however, indicates that the problems rarely lie with MBO's basic components. Rather, the culprits tend to be factors such as unrealistic expectations regarding results, lack of top management commitment, or an inability or unwillingness by management to allocate rewards based on goal accomplishment. Nevertheless, MBO provides managers with the vehicle for implementing goal-setting theory.

BEHAVIOR MODIFICATION

There is a classic study that took place a few years ago with freight packers at Emery Air Freight.[5] Emery's management wanted packers to use freight containers for shipments, whenever possible, because of specific economic savings. When packers were queried as to the percentage of shipments containerized, the standard reply was 90 percent. An analysis by Emery found, however, that the container utilization rate was only 45 percent. In order to encourage employees to use containers, management established a program of feedback and positive reinforcements. Each packer was instructed to keep a checklist of his or her daily packings, both containerized and noncontainerized. At the end of each day, the packer computed his or her container utilization rate. Almost unbelievably, container utilization jumped to more than 90 percent on the first day of the program and held to that level. Emery reported that this simple program of feedback and positive reinforcements saved the company $2 million over a three-year period.

OB Mod

A program where managers identify performance-related employee behaviors and then implement an intervention strategy to strengthen desirable behaviors and weaken undesirable behaviors.

This program at Emery Air Freight illustrates the use of behavior modification, or what has become more popularly called **OB Mod**.[6] It represents the application of reinforcement theory to individuals in the work setting.

What Is OB Mod?

The typical OB Mod program, as shown in Figure 7–2, follows a five-step problem-solving model: (1) identification of performance-related behaviors; (2) measurement of the behaviors; (3) identification of behavioral contingencies; (4) development and implementation of an intervention strategy; and (5) evaluation of performance improvement.[7]

Everything an employee does on his or her job is not equally important in terms of performance outcomes. The first step in OB Mod, therefore, is to

[4] C. H. Ford, "MBO: An Idea Whose Time Has Gone?"

[5] "At Emery Air Freight: Positive Reinforcement Boosts Performance," *Organizational Dynamics*, Winter 1973, pp. 41–50.

[6] F. Luthans and R. Kreitner, *Organizational Behavior Modification and Beyond: An Operant and Social Learning Approach* (Glenview, IL: Scott, Foresman, 1985).

[7] F. Luthans and R. Kreitner, "The Management of Behavioral Contingencies," *Personnel*, July–August 1974, pp. 7–16.

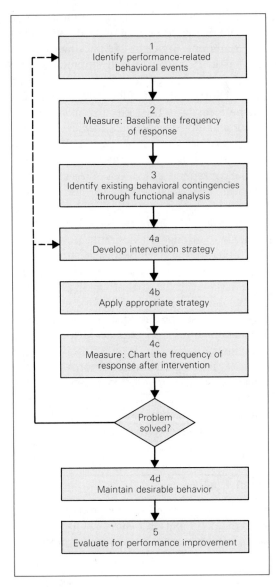

FIGURE 7–2
Steps in OB Mod

Source: Adapted by permission of the publisher
from "The Management of Behavioral
Contingencies," by F. Luthans and R. Kreitner,
Personnel, July-August 1974 by AMACOM, a
division of the American Management Association,
p. 13. All rights reserved.

identify the critical behaviors that make a significant impact on the employee's
job performance. These are those 5 to 10 percent of behaviors that may account
for up to 70 or 80 percent of each employee's performance. Using containers
whenever possible by freight packers at Emery Air Freight is an example of a
critical behavior.

The second step requires the manager to develop some baseline performance data. This is obtained by determining the number of times the identified behavior is occurring under present conditions. In our freight packing example at Emery, this would have revealed that 45 percent of all shipments were containerized.

The third step is to perform a functional analysis to identify the behavioral contingencies or consequences of performance. This tells the manager the antecedent cues that emit the behavior and the consequences that are currently maintaining it. At Emery Air Freight, social norms and the greater difficulty in packing containers were the antecedent cues. This encouraged the practice of packing items separately. Moreover, the consequences for continuing this behavior, prior to the OB Mod intervention, was social acceptance and escaping more demanding work.

Once the functional analysis is complete, the manager is ready to develop and implement an intervention strategy to strengthen desirable performance behaviors and weaken undesirable behaviors. The appropriate strategy will entail changing some element of the performance-reward linkage—structure, processes, technology, groups, or the task—with the goal of making high-level performance more rewarding. In the Emery example, the work technology was altered to require the keeping of a checklist. The checklist plus the computation, at the end of the day, of a container utilization rate, acted to reinforce the desirable behavior of using containers.

The final step in OB Mod is to evaluate performance improvement. In the Emery intervention, the immediate improvement in the container utilization rate demonstrated that behavioral change took place. That it rose to 90 percent and held at that level further indicates that learning took place. That is, the employees underwent a relatively permanent change in behavior.

Linking OB Mod and Reinforcement Theory

Reinforcement theory relies on positive reinforcement, shaping, and recognizing the impact of different schedules of reinforcement on behavior. OB Mod uses these concepts to provide managers with a powerful and proven means for changing employee behavior.

OB Mod in Practice

OB Mod has been used by a number of organizations to improve employee productivity, and to reduce errors, absenteeism, tardiness, and accident rates.[8] Organizations like Connecticut General Life, General Electric, Standard Oil of Ohio, Weyerhaeuser, B. F. Goodrich, Emerson Electronics, the City of Detroit, Collins Foods, and Dayton-Hudson report impressive results as a result of using OB Mod.[9] For instance, Collins Foods used it with clerical employees in its

[8] F. Luthans and R. Kreitner, *Organizational Behavior Modification and Beyond*, Chapter 8.

[9] W. C. Hamner and E. P. Hamner, "Behavior Modification on the Bottom Line," *Organizational Dynamics*, Spring 1976, pp. 12–24; and "Productivity Gains from a Pat on the Back," *Business Week*, January 23, 1978, pp. 56–62.

accounting department. Supervisors and employees first met to review the department's actual performance in such areas as billing error rates, and, based on this data, improvement goals were established. Employees were praised for reports containing fewer errors than the norm, and results were charted on a regular basis. Significant results were achieved; for example, the error rate in accounts payable fell from more than 8 percent to less than 0.2 percent. Dayton-Hudson used OB Mod in the men's department of one of its stores. The goal was to increase the average sale from $19 to $25. Employees were taught how to make extra sales and were congratulated by supervisors each time a sale went above $19. Within two months, department sales averaged $23. In addition, the philosophy behind OB Mod appears to be affecting many managers in the way they relate to their employees—in the kind and quantity of feedback they give, the content of performance appraisals, and the type and allocation of organizational rewards.

Despite the positive results that OB Mod has demonstrated, it is not without its critics.[10] Is it a technique for manipulating people? Does it decrease an employee's freedom? If so, is such action on the part of managers unethical? And do nonmonetary reinforcers like feedback, praise, and recognition get old after a while? Will employees begin to see these as ways for management to increase productivity without providing commensurate increases in their pay? There are no easy answers to questions such as these.

PARTICIPATIVE MANAGEMENT

At a General Electric lighting plant in Ohio, work teams perform many tasks and assume many of the responsibilities once handled by their supervisors. When the plant was faced with a recent decline in the demand for the tubes it produces, the workers decided first to slow production and eventually to lay themselves off. Eastern Air Lines implemented a program to allow operative employees a greater say in those decisions that directly affect their work. In the first six months of the program, Eastern's machinists alone came up with $50 million of productivity increases. Marketing people at USAA, a large insurance company, meet in a conference room for an hour every week to discuss ways they can improve the quality of their work and increase productivity. Management has listened and implemented many of their suggestions.[11]

What Is Participative Management?

The preceding are examples of **participative management**. The common thread through these examples is joint decision making. That is, subordinates actually share a significant degree of decision making power with their immediate

Participative management

A process where subordinates share a significant degree of decision making power with their immediate superiors.

[10] See, for example, E. Locke, "The Myths of Behavior Mod in Organizations," *Academy of Management Review*, October 1977, pp. 543–53.

[11] B. Saporito, "The Revolt Against 'Working Smarter,'" *Fortune*, July 21, 1986, pp. 58–65; and "Quality Circles: Rounding up Quality at USAA," *AIDE Magazine*, Fall 1983, p. 24.

superiors. But in actual practice, it's an umbrella term that encompasses such varied activities as goal setting, problem solving, direct involvement in work decisions, inclusion in consultation committees, representation on policy-making bodies, and selecting new coworkers.[12]

Participative management has, at times, been promoted as a panacea for poor morale and low productivity. One author has even argued that participative management is an ethical imperative.[13] But participative management is not appropriate for every organization or every work unit. For it to work, there must be adequate time to participate, the issues in which employees get involved must be relevant to their interests, employees must have the ability (intelligence, technical knowledge, communication skills) to participate, and the organization's culture must support employee involvement.[14]

Why would management want to share its decision making power with subordinates? There are a number of good reasons. As jobs have become more complex, managers often don't know everything their employees do. So participation allows those who know the most to contribute. The result can be better decisions. The interdependence in tasks that employees often do today also requires consultation with people in other departments and work units. This increases the need for committees and group meetings to resolve issues that affect them jointly. Participation additionally increases commitment to decisions. People are less likely to undermine a decision, at the time of its implementation, if they shared in making that decision. Finally, participation provides intrinsic rewards for employees. It can make their jobs more interesting and meaningful. This has become an increasing concern of younger and more highly educated workers.

Dozens of studies have been conducted on the participation-performance relationship. The findings, however, are mixed.[15] When the research is looked at carefully, it appears that participation typically has only a modest influence on variables such as employee productivity, motivation, and job satisfaction. Of course, that doesn't mean that the use of participative management can't be beneficial under the right conditions. What it says, however, is that the use of participation is no sure means for improving employee performance.

[12] J. L. Cotton, D. A. Vollrath, K. L. Froggatt, M. L. Lengnick-Hall, and K. R. Jennings, "Employee Participation: Diverse Forms and Different Outcomes," *Academy of Management Review*, January 1988, pp. 8–22.

[13] M. Sashkin, "Participative Management Is an Ethical Imperative," *Organizational Dynamics*, Spring 1984, pp. 5–22.

[14] R. Tannenbaum, I. R. Weschler, and F. Massarik, *Leadership and Organization: A Behavioral Science Approach* (New York: McGraw-Hill, 1961), pp. 88–100.

[15] E. Locke and D. Schweiger, "Participation in Decision Making: One More Look," in B. M. Staw (ed.), *Research in Organizational Behavior*, Vol. 1, Greenwich, CT: JAI Press, 1979; E. A. Locke, D. B. Feren, V. M. McCaleb, K. N. Shaw, and A. T. Denny, "The Relative Effectiveness of Four Methods of Motivating Employee Performance," in K. D. Duncan, M. M. Gruneberg, and D. Wallis (eds.), *Changes in Working Life* (London: Wiley, 1980), pp. 363–88; K. L. Miller and P. R. Monge, "Participation, Satisfaction, and Productivity: A Meta-Analytic Review," *Academy of Management Journal*, December 1986, pp. 727–53; J. A. Wagner III and R. Z. Gooding, "Effects of Societal Trends on Participation Research," *Administrative Science Quarterly*, June 1987, pp. 241–62; and J. A. Wagner III and R. Z. Gooding, "Shared Influence and Organizational Behavior: A Meta-Analysis of Situational Variables Expected to Moderate Participation-Outcome Relationships," *Academy of Management Journal*, September 1987, pp. 524–41.

Quality Circles

Currently, the most widely discussed form of participative management is the **quality circle**.[16] Originally begun in the United States and exported to Japan in the 1950's, the quality circle has been imported back to the United States. As it developed in Japan, the quality circle concept is frequently mentioned as one of the techniques that Japanese firms utilize that has allowed them to make better quality products at lower costs than their American counterparts can. In fact, this concept has grown so popular in Japan, one expert estimates that approximately one out of every nine Japanese workers is involved in a quality circle.[17]

What is a quality circle? It's a work group of eight to ten employees and supervisors who have a shared area of responsibility. They meet regularly—typically once a week, on company time and on company premises—to discuss their quality problems, investigate causes of the problems, recommend solutions, and take corrective actions. They take over the responsibility for solving quality problems, and they generate and evaluate their own feedback. But management typically retains control over the final decision regarding implementation of recommended solutions. Of course, it is not presumed that employees inherently have this ability to analyze and solve quality problems. Therefore, part of the quality circle concept includes teaching participating employees group communication skills, various quality strategies, and measurement and problem analysis techniques. Figure 7–3 describes a typical quality circle process.

Quality circle

A work group of employees who meet regularly to discuss their quality problems, investigate causes, recommend solutions, and take corrective actions.

Linking Participation and Motivation Theories

Participative management draws on a number of the motivation theories discussed in the previous chapter. For instance, Theory Y is consistent with participative management, while Theory X aligns with the more traditional autocratic style of managing people. In terms of motivation-hygiene theory, participative management could provide employees with intrinsic motivation by increasing opportunities for growth, responsibility, and involvement in the work itself. Similarly, the process of making and implementing a decision, and then seeing it work out can help satisfy an employee's needs for responsibility, achievement, recognition, growth, and enhance self-esteem. So participative management is compatible with ERG theory and efforts to stimulate the achievement need.

Participative Management in Practice

West Germany, France, Holland, and the Scandinavian countries have firmly established the principle of industrial democracy in Europe, and other nations

---

[16] See, for example, G. W. Meyer and R. G. Stott, "Quality Circles: Panacea or Pandora's Box?," *Organizational Dynamics*, Spring 1985, pp. 34–50; M. L. Marks, P. H. Mirvis, E. J. Hackett, and J. F. Grady, Jr., "Employee Participation in a Quality Circle Program: Impact on Quality of Work Life, Productivity, and Absenteeism," *Journal of Applied Psychology*, February 1986, pp. 61–69; and E. E. Lawler III and S. A. Mohrman, "Quality Circles: After the Honeymoon," *Organizational Dynamics*, Spring 1987, pp. 42–54.

[17] "A Quality Concept Catches on Worldwide," *Industry Week*, April 16, 1979, p. 125.

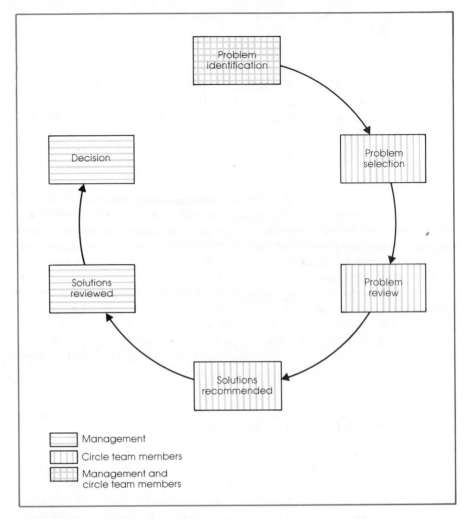

FIGURE 7–3
How a Typical Quality Circle Operates

like Japan, Israel, and Yugoslavia have traditionally practiced some form of participative decision making for decades.[18] But participation has been much slower to gain ground in U.S. organizations. The resistance doesn't come from operative employees; but rather from management—upper, middle, and lower.[19] So, in the U.S., when participation is implemented and proves effective, it tends to be at the operative level. Accepting participation in the management ranks runs counter to the authority-based and hierarchically-controlled characteristics of many, if not most, large organizations and even a substantial proportion of small ones. The higher managers go up in the organization, the harder it seems for them to shift to a participative style.[20] Moreover, much of what is

[18] W. E. Halal and B. S. Brown, "Participative Management," p. 21.
[19] B. Saporito, "The Revolt Against 'Working Smarter,' " p. 59.
[20] Ibid., p. 60.

called "participative management" in U.S. organizations is really "psuedo-partici-pation." Managers go through the motions of seeking out employees' ideas on problems and including them in the decision making process, but managers still retain almost complete control over the final choice.[21]

What about quality circles? How popular are they in practice? A 1982 study showed that 44 percent of all companies with more than 500 employees had quality circle programs. Further, it is estimated that over 90 percent of the *Fortune 500* companies use quality circles.[22] General Electric, for instance, has more than a thousand at plants across the United States.[23] But the success of quality circles has been far from overwhelming. As a case in point, one study of 176 companies that had adopted quality circles found that the manage-ment at 60 percent were lukewarm or unhappy about what, if anything, their circles were accomplishing.[24] It's not surprising, then, that some organizations have dropped them completely. Yet, in defense of the concept, undoubtedly much of this lack of enthusiasm is attributable to improper introduction of the technique, inadequate support for the circle concept, and/or unrealistic expectations by management in terms of productivity improvement.

PERFORMANCE-BASED COMPENSATION

Ken Iverson is chief executive officer of Nucor, a large steel company. His company had a bad year in 1986, and he "suffered" along with the stockholders. Because his compensation is determined by company profits, Iverson took a 41 percent pay cut to $252,642.[25]

Pay for performance is not reserved just for senior managers. Operative employees also can participate in such programs. Store employees at 60 Great Atlantic & Pacific Tea Co. (A&P) supermarkets in the Philadelphia area have taken a 25 percent pay cut in exchange for a cash bonus based on their store's sales. The program is given credit for having significantly increased labor pro-ductivity in these stores, while at the same time boosting employee overall wages.[26]

What Is Performance-Based Compensation?

Piece-rate, wage incentive plans, profit-sharing, and lump-sum bonuses are all forms of **performance-based compensation**. What differentiates these forms of pay from more traditional plans is that instead of paying a person for *time* on the job, their pay is adjusted to reflect some performance measure. That might

Performance-based compensation

Paying employees based on some performance measure.

[21] W. E. Halal and B. S. Brown, "Participative Management," p. 20.

[22] Cited in *Harvard Business Review*, January–February 1985, p. 66.

[23] J. Main, "The Trouble with Managing Japanese-Style," *Fortune*, April 2, 1984, p. 51.

[24] Ibid., p. 50.

[25] B. Brophy and M. Walsh, " 'Thanks for the Bonus, but Where's My Raise?' " *U.S. News & World Report*, July 20, 1987, p. 44.

[26] "How A&P Fattens Profits by Sharing Them," *Business Week*, December 22, 1986, p. 44.

be individual productivity, work group or departmental productivity, unit profitability, or the overall organization's profit performance. Two of the more widely used of the performance-based compensation plans are piece-rate wages for production workers and annual performance bonuses based on corporate profits for senior executives.

In **piece-rate pay plans**, workers are paid a fixed sum for each unit of production completed. When an employee gets no base salary and is paid only on what he or she produces, this is a pure piece-rate plan. People who work ball parks selling peanuts and soda pop frequently are paid this way. They might get to keep twenty-five cents for every bag of peanuts they sell. If they sell 200 bags during a game, they make $50. If they sell only 40 bags, their take is a mere $10. The harder they work and the more peanuts they sell, the more they earn. Many organizations use a modified piece-rate plan, where employees earn a base hourly wage plus a piece-rate differential. So a legal typist might be paid $5 an hour plus twenty cents per page. Such modified plans provide a floor under an employee's earnings, while still offering a productivity incentive.

For years, senior corporate executives received regular increases in their pay, regardless of their company's success or failure. More top executives than ever are now finding their compensation linked directly to corporate performance. When things go well for a firm, it is assumed that management had a large part in that outcome, so they should share in the good times. For example, David Margolis, who heads up Colt Industries, earns a base salary of $440,000. Because the company recently had a very strong year, he earned an additional $555,000 performance bonus—pushing his total pay close to $1 million.[27] Of course, in a bad year, executives may get no bonus at all.

Piece-rate pay plans

Workers are paid a fixed sum for each unit of production completed.

Linking Performance-Based Compensation and Expectancy Theory

Performance-based compensation is probably most compatible with expectancy theory predictions. Specifically, individuals should perceive a strong relationship between their performance and the rewards they receive if motivation is to be maximized. If rewards are allocated completely on nonperformance factors—such as seniority or job title—then employees are likely to reduce their effort.

The evidence supports the importance of this linkage, especially for operative employees working under piece-rate systems. For example, one study of 400 manufacturing firms found that those companies with wage incentive plans achieved 43 to 64 percent greater productivity than those without such plans.[28]

Performance-Based Compensation in Practice

"Pay-for-performance" is a concept that is rapidly replacing the annual cost-of-living raise. A recent study of 1,600 firms employing 9,000,000 workers found

[27] A. Bennett, "Executives Face Change in Awarding of Pay, Stock Options," *Wall Street Journal*, February 28, 1986, p. 27.

[28] M. Fein, "Work Measurement and Wage Incentives," *Industrial Engineering*, September 1973, pp. 49–51.

OB Close-Up

The Scanlon Plan

Scanlon Plans blend participative management and performance-based compensation. Originally a product of the late 1930s, created to save companies from financial collapse, they blend a Theory Y view of human nature and a participatory philosophy of management with a pay incentive system and a suggestion system.[29]

The philosophy underlying Scanlon Plans is that an organization should function as a single unit, that workers are capable of and willing to contribute ideas and suggestions, and that improvements should be shared with the workers.

The core of any Scanlon Plan is (1) a system of committees, and (2) a formula for determining and sharing the cost savings. Committees made up of worker and management representatives review employee-initiated proposals and implement the good ones. Committees also calculate the cost savings that result from these suggestions, using a formula based on a relationship of labor costs to the sales value of production. The cost savings are then typically divided up: 75 percent for the employee and 25 percent for management.

Scanlon Plans have met with both success and failure. The keys to making them effective appears to be a climate of trust between management and employees, and a strong commitment by all participants.[30]

that 75 percent used bonuses or rewards that differ from conventional raises and that a major proportion of these performance-based compensation plans had been installed since 1982. The most popular type of incentive is profit sharing, used by 32 percent, closely followed by lump-sum bonuses, used by 30 percent. Moreover, the study found that about 30 percent of the respondents were reducing or eliminating across-the-board pay increases and cost-of-living raises.[31] This trend appears to be even stronger in the upper management ranks where organizations are relying less on salary and more on bonuses tied directly to individual managers' performance or the overall organization's performance to reward executives.[32]

Scanlon plans

A blend of participative management and performance-based compensation that uses committees and a formula for determining and sharing of cost savings.

[29] F. G. Lesieur and E. S. Puckett, "The Scanlon Plan Has Proved Itself," *Harvard Business Review*, September–October 1969, pp. 109–19.

[30] C. Alderfer, "Group and Intergroup Relations," in J. R. Hackman and J. L. Suttle (eds.), *Improving Life at Work* (Santa Monica, CA: Goodyear, 1977), pp. 287–90.

[31] Cited in B. Brophy and M. Walsh, " 'Thanks for the Bonus,' " p. 43.

[32] A. Bennett, "Executives Face Change," p. 27.

Mike Evans and Jane Murphy both work for PepsiCo, but they have very different needs in terms of fringe benefits. Mike is married, has three young children, and a wife who is at home full-time. Jane, too, is married, but her husband has a high-paying job with the federal government, and they have no children. Mike is concerned about having a good medical plan and enough life insurance to support his family if he weren't around. In contrast, Jane's husband already has her medical needs covered on his plan, and life insurance is a low priority for both her and her husband. Rather, she is more interested in extra vacation time and long-term financial benefits like a tax-deferred savings plan.

What Are Flexible Benefits?

Flexible benefits

Employees tailor their benefit program to meet their personal needs by picking and choosing from among a menu of benefit options.

Flexible benefits allow employees to pick and choose from among a menu of benefit options. The idea is to allow each employee to choose a benefit package that is individually tailored to his or her own needs and situation. It replaces the traditional "one-benefit-plan-fits-all" programs that have dominated organizations for fifty years.[33]

The average organization provides fringe benefits worth approximately 40 percent of an employee's salary. But traditional benefit programs were designed for the typical employee of the 1950s—a male with a wife and two children at home. Less than 10 percent of employees now fit this stereotype. Twenty-five percent of today's employees are single and a third are part of two-income families without any children. As such, these traditional programs don't tend to meet the needs of today's more diverse workforce. Flexible benefits, however, do meet these diverse needs. An organization sets up a flexible spending account for each employee, usually based on some percentage of his or her salary, and then a price tag is put on each benefit. Options might include inexpensive medical plans with high deductibles; expensive medical plans with low or no deductibles; hearing, dental, and eye coverage; vacation options; extended disability; a variety of savings and pension plans; life insurance; college tuition reimbursement plans; and extended vacation time. Employees then select benefit options until they have spent the dollar amount in their account.

Linking Flexible Benefits and Expectancy Theory

Giving all employees the same benefits assumes all employees have the same needs. Of course, we know this assumption is false. So flexible benefits turn the benefits' expenditure into a motivator.

Consistent with expectancy theory's thesis that organizational rewards should be linked to each individual employee's goals, flexible benefits individual-

[33] See A. Bernstein, "Benefits Are Getting More Flexible—But *Caveat Emptor*," *Business Week*, September 8, 1986, pp. 64–66; and L. Reibstein, "To Each According to His Needs: Flexible Benefits Plans Gain Favor," *Wall Street Journal*, September 16, 1986, p. 33.

ize rewards by allowing each employee to choose the compensation package that best satisfies his or her current needs. That flexible benefits can turn the traditional homogeneous benefit program into a motivator was demonstrated at one company: 80 percent of the organization's employees changed their benefit packages when a flexible plan was put into effect.[34]

Flexible Benefits in Practice

In 1987, about 22 percent of large corporations had a flexible benefit program in place.[35] A major consulting firm estimated that, between 1986 and 1988, the number of flexible plans more than doubled among companies with more than 1,000 employees.[36] Clearly, flexible benefits is an idea whose time has come. Though it is more cumbersome for management to oversee—administrative costs are usually higher for managing flexible programs—it frequently produces savings for organizations. Many organizations use the introduction of flexible benefits to raise deductibles and premiums. Moreover, once in place, costly increases in things like health insurance premiums often have to be substantially absorbed by the employee.

TWO-TIER PAY SYSTEMS

Kathy Schwab and Kathy Knoop are both flight attendants for American Airlines. Their job descriptions are essentially the same. Schwab, however, earns $1,200 a month, while Knoop averages around $3,300 a month.[37] True, Knoop is a fifteen-year veteran and Schwab is in her first year on the job. But should this justify a 175 percent premium for *experience* in the *same* job? What's going on here? The answer is that American Airlines has negotiated a two-tier pay system with its flight attendants' union.

What Is a Two-Tier Pay System?

A **two-tier pay system** provides for new employees to be hired at significantly lower wage rates than those already employed in the same job. For instance, new machinists at Boeing start at $6.70 an hour while coworkers, hired before the two-tier contract, make a minimum of $11.38 an hour.[38]

There are two basic versions of the system. One establishes a temporary

Two-tier pay system

New employees are hired at significantly lower wage rates than those already employed and performing the same jobs.

---

[34] E. E. Lawler III, "Reward Systems," in *Improving Life at Work*, J. R. Hackman and J. L. Suttle (eds.), p. 182.

[35] "Flexible Benefits Are Offered by More Firms, Spurred by Tax Reform Act," *Wall Street Journal*, September 15, 1987, p. 1.

[36] L. Reibstein, "To Each According to His Needs."

[37] I. Ross, "Employers Win Big in the Move to Two-Tier Contracts," *Fortune*, April 29, 1985, p. 83.

[38] S. Flax, "Pay Cuts Before the Job Even Starts," *Fortune*, January 9, 1984, p. 75.

lower rate that catches up, in steps, to the higher level. Typically, contracts call for a three-to-ten year catch-up period. The other version keeps new employees permanently trailing the top-tier rate. American Airlines, as a case in point, negotiated a two-tier system for their pilots and flight attendants. Senior pilots, hired before the two-tier contract, can earn $127,900 a year. The lower tier, however, restricts new hires to only about half as much, regardless of how many years they fly.

Why would unions agree to a two-tier system? They would do so because it is an alternative to the pay cut that current employees would otherwise have to take. As a result of deregulation, nonunionized competitors, and low-cost foreign competition, many employers have had to find some way to significantly cut expenses. The two-tier pay system is such an alternative. It does drastically cut labor costs.

Linking Two-Tier Pay Systems and Equity Theory

A two-tier pay system may sound like a viable option for management, but it directly contradicts equity theory. In fact, based on equity theory predictions, you'd expect that to pay people such obviously different wages for doing essentially similar jobs would demotivate employees. Employees compare their input-outcome ratio against others. One of the most obvious "others" is co-workers. If you're doing the same job as someone else for significantly less money, yet feel your background and abilities are essentially similar, you're not likely to ignore this perceived discrepancy. The evidence suggests this to be the case.[39]

Two-tier pay systems build resentment among new hires, undermine employee loyalty, work against new employees exerting a high level of work effort, and increase the turnover rate among the newer hires.

Two-Tier Pay Systems in Practice

Two-tier systems were seen by many managers in the early 1980s as a quick and simple solution to high labor costs. But it hasn't turned out to be the instant panacea that management had hoped.[40] As noted earlier, it creates perceived inequities which, in turn, act to demotivate the newer, lower-paid employees. It appears that many two-tier programs included in previous union contracts will be dropped or significantly modified in future union-management negotiations.[41]

[39] R. A. White, "Employee Preferences for Nontaxable Compensation Offered in a Cafeteria Compensation Plan: An Empirical Study," *Accounting Review*, July 1983, pp. 539–61; M. Charlier and F. C. Brown III, "American Air Attendants Seek to Topple Two-Tier Pay," *Wall Street Journal*, March 25, 1987, p. 6; and J. E. Martin and M. M. Peterson, "Two-Tier Wage Structures: Implications for Equity Theory," *Academy of Management Journal*, June 1987, pp. 297–315.

[40] Ibid.

[41] See, for example, M. Charlier and F. C. Brown III, "American Air Attendants Seek to Topple Two-Tier Pay;" and D. Wessel, "Two-Tier Pay Spreads, but the Pioneer Firms Encounter Problems," *Wall Street Journal*, October 14, 1985, p. 1.

Susan Ross is your classic "morning person." She rises each day at 5 A.M. sharp, full of energy. On the other hand, as she puts it, "I'm usually ready for bed right after the 7 P.M. news."

Susan's work schedule as a claims processor at Hartford Insurance is flexible. It allows her some degree of freedom as to when she comes to work and when she leaves. Her office opens at 6 A.M. and closes at 7 P.M. It's up to her how she schedules her eight hour day within this thirteen hour period. Because Susan is a morning person and also has a seven-year-old son who gets out of school at 3 P.M. every day, Susan opts to work from 6 A.M. to 3 P.M. "My work hours are perfect. I'm at the job when I'm mentally most alert, and I can be home to take care of Sean after he gets out of school."

What Are Alternative Work Schedules?

Most people work an eight-hour day, five days a week.[42] They start at a fixed time and leave at a fixed time. But a number of organizations have introduced alternative work schedule options, such as the compressed workweek and flextime, as a way to improve employee motivation and to better utilize human resources.

The most popular form of **compressed workweek** is four ten-hour days. The 4–40 program was conceived to allow workers more leisure time and shopping time, and to permit them to travel to and from work at nonrush-hour times. Supporters suggested that such a program can increase employee enthusiasm, morale, and commitment to the organization; increase productivity and reduce costs; reduce machine downtime in manufacturing; reduce overtime, turnover, and absenteeism; and make it easier for the organization to recruit employees.

Compressed workweek

A four-day week, with employees working ten hours a day.

Proponents argue that the compressed workweek may positively affect productivity in situations in which the work process requires significant start-up and shutdown periods.[43] When start-up and shutdown times are a major factor, productivity standards take these periods into consideration in determining the time required to generate a given output. Consequently, in such cases, the compressed workweek will increase productivity even though performance of the workers is not affected, because the improved work scheduling reduces nonproductive time.

The evidence on 4–40 program performance is generally positive.[44] While some employees complain of fatigue near the end of the day, and about the difficulty of coordinating their jobs with their personal lives—the latter a problem

[42] S. J. Smith, "The Growing Diversity of Work Schedules," *Monthly Labor Review*, November 1986, pp. 7–13.

[43] E. J. Calvasina and W. R. Boxx, "Efficiency of Workers on the Four-Day Workweek," *Academy of Management Journal*, September 1975, pp. 604–10.

[44] See, for example, J. W. Seybolt and J. W. Waddoups, "The Impact of Alternative Work Schedules on Employee Attitudes: A Field Experiment," paper presented at the Western Academy of Management Meeting; Hollywood, CA, April 1987.

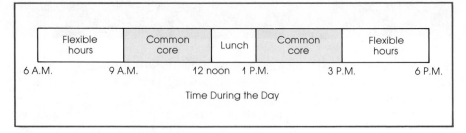

FIGURE 7–4
Example of a Flextime Schedule

especially for working mothers—most like the 4–40 program. In one study, for instance, when employees were asked whether they wanted to continue their 4–40 program, which had been in place for six months, or go back to a traditional five-day week, 78 percent wanted to keep the shorter workweek.[45]

The compressed workweek doesn't increase employee discretion. Management still sets the work hours. Flextime, however, is a scheduling option that allows employees, within specific parameters, to decide when to go to work. Susan Ross' work schedule at Hartford Insurance is an example of flextime. But what specifically is flextime?

Flextime

Employees work during a common core time period each day but have discretion in forming their total workday from a flexible set of hours outside the core.

Flextime is short for flexible work hours. It allows employees some discretion over when they arrive at work and leave. Employees have to work a specific number of hours a week, but they are free to vary the hours of work within certain limits. As shown in Figure 7–4, each day consists of a common core, usually six hours, with a flexibility band surrounding the core. For example, exclusive of a one-hour lunch break, the core may be 9:00 A.M. to 3:00 P.M., with the office actually opening at 6:00 A.M. and closing at 6:00 P.M. All employees are required to be at their jobs during the common core period, but they are allowed to accumulate their other two hours before and/or after the core time. Some flextime programs allow extra hours to be accumulated and turned into a free day off each month.

The benefits claimed for flextime are numerous. They include reduced absenteeism, increased productivity, reduced overtime expenses, a lessening in hostility toward management, reduced traffic congestion around work sites, elimination of tardiness, and increased autonomy and responsibility for employees that may increase employee job satisfaction.[46] But beyond the claims, what's flextime's record?

Telecommuting

Employees do their work at home on a computer that is linked to their office.

Most of the performance evidence stacks up favorably. Flextime tends to reduce absenteeism and frequently improves worker productivity,[47] probably

---

[45] J. C. Goodale and A. K. Aagaard, "Factors Relating to Varying Reactions to the 4-Day Work Week," *Journal of Applied Psychology*, February 1975, pp. 33–38.

[46] W. F. Glueck, "Changing Hours of Work: A Review and Analysis of the Research," *The Personnel Administrator*, March 1979, pp. 44–47.

[47] See, for example, D. A. Ralston and M. F. Flanagan, "The Effect of Flextime on Absenteeism and Turnover for Male and Female Employees," *Journal of Vocational Behavior*, April 1985, pp. 206–17; D. A. Ralston, W. P. Anthony, and D. J. Gustafson, "Employees May Love Flextime, but What Does It Do to the Organization's Productivity?," *Journal of Applied Psychology*, May 1985, pp. 272–79; and J. B. McGuire and J. R. Liro, "Flexible Work Schedules, Work Attitudes, and Perceptions of Productivity," *Public Personnel Management*, Spring 1986, pp. 65–73.

Telecommuting: The Ultimate Flextime?

It might be close to the ideal job for many people. No commuting, flexible hours, freedom to dress as you please, and little or no interruptions from colleagues. It's called **telecommuting,** and refers to employees who do their work at home on a computer that is linked to their office.[48] Currently, about two million people work at home doing things like taking orders over the phone, filling out reports and other forms, and processing or analyzing information. Forecasters predict that ten to twenty million people could be telecommuting by the year 2000.

Whether the forecasts prove accurate depends on some questions for which we do not yet have answers. Will people balk at losing the regular social contact that a formal office provides? Would employees who do their work at home be at a political disadvantage? Might they be less likely to be considered for salary increases and promotions? Is being out of sight equivalent to being out of mind? Will nonwork-related distractions like children, neighbors, and the close proximity of the refrigerator significantly reduce productivity? Will nontelecommuters in the organization feel discriminated against? As we answer questions such as these, the future of telecommuting will become far more clear.

for several reasons. Employees can schedule their work hours to align with personal demands, thus reducing tardiness and absences, and employees can adjust their work activities to those hours in which they are individually more productive.

Flextime's major drawback is that it's not applicable to every job. It works well with clerical tasks where an employee's interaction with people outside his or her department is limited. It is not a viable option for receptionists, sales personnel in retail stores, or similar jobs where comprehensive service demands that people be at their work stations at predetermined times.

Linking Alternative Work Schedules and Motivation Theories

Not everyone prefers the traditional fixed eight-hour day. The larger blocks of leisure time created by the compressed workweek, for example, may be very appealing to the employee with a boat, a weekend house in the country, or a long daily commute. Employees with young children or other responsibili-

[48] See, for example, C. Ansberry, "When Employees Work at Home, Management Problems Often Arise," *Wall Street Journal*, April 20, 1987, p. 25; K. Christensen, "A Hard Day's Work in the Electronic Cottage," *Across the Board*, April 1987, pp. 17–22; and C. A. Hamilton, "Telecommuting," *Personnel Journal*, April 1987, pp. 91–101.

ties that make unplanned demands on their time find that flextime allows them more freedom to balance their work and personal commitments.[49]

In terms of motivation theories, alternative work schedules respond to the diverse needs of the work force. Flextime, however, because it increases employee autonomy and responsibility, is likely to provide greater motivational properties than the compressed workweek. Flextime appeals to an individual's growth need (ERG theory) or desire for autonomy (motivation-hygiene theory).

Alternative Work Schedules in Practice

Alternatives to the traditional workweek have gained popularity over the past decade. The compressed workweek grew 4.5 times as fast as did total employment between 1973 and 1985.[50] But it still is used by a small percentage of organizations. It's also interesting that it has been estimated that about 28 percent of compressed workweek experiments end as failures.[51]

Flextime is more widely used and, where careful thought has been given to its applicability, is more successful. Twenty-eight percent of organizations now offer flexible time schedules.[52] Most of these, though, are small organizations, so the percentage of the total work force on flextime is lower—about 12 percent.[53] Based on current trends, you should expect to see more use of flextime in the coming years.

JOB DESIGN

"Every day was the same thing," Frank Greer began. "Put the right passenger seat into Jeeps as they came down the assembly line, pop in four bolts locking the seat frame to the car body, then tightening the bolts with my electric wrench. Thirty cars and 120 bolts an hour, eight hours a day. I didn't care that they were paying me $14 an hour, I was going crazy. I did it for almost a year-and-a-half. Finally, I just said to my wife this isn't going to be the way I'm going to spend the rest of my life. My brain was turning to Jello on that job. So I quit. Now I work in a print shop and I make less than $10 an hour. But let me tell you, the work I do now is really interesting. It challenges me! I look forward every morning to going to work again."

Jobs are different. Some are more interesting and challenging than others. Moreover, given what we know about perception and human needs, there is no reason to believe that everyone perceives given jobs similarly. What *you*

---

[49] R. B. Dunham, J. L. Pierce, and M. B. Castaneda, "Alternative Work Schedules: Two Field Quasi-Experiments," *Personnel Psychology*, Summer 1987, pp. 215–42.

[50] S. J. Smith, "The Growing Diversity of Work Schedules," p. 9.

[51] S. D. Nollen, *New Work Schedules in Practice: Managing Time in a Changing Society* (New York: Van Nostrand Reinhold, 1982).

[52] Cited in *USA Today*, June 27, 1986, p. B-1.

[53] E. F. Mellor, "Shift Work and Flextime: How Prevalent Are They?," *Monthly Labor Review*, November 1986, p. 19.

consider to be a routine and boring job, someone *else* may view as quite satisfying. So while Frank Greer didn't like his assembly-line job, and quit, many of his co-workers continue to do routine work without a complaint. They regularly come to work on time and put in a full day's effort. As one of Frank's former colleagues put it, "I really like my job here at Jeep. I've been on this same assembly-line for almost twenty years. I hope to be able to do it for twenty more."

This section looks at the design of jobs as a variable under management's control. Specifically, it looks at job design options and how they affect employee motivation.

From Job Simplification to QWL

Job design is concerned with the way that tasks are combined to form complete jobs. The content and design of jobs has interested engineers and economists for centuries. In its early years, job design was really nothing more than a synonym for job specialization or simplification. In 1776, for instance, Adam Smith articulated in his *Wealth of Nations* the economic efficiencies that could be achieved by dividing jobs into smaller and smaller pieces so each worker could perform a minute and specialized task. Undoubtedly one of the most important early efforts at job design was undertaken at the turn of this century by Frederick Taylor in what has become known as the scientific management movement.

Job design

The way that tasks are combined to form complete jobs.

Scientific Management   In the early 1900s, Frederick Taylor proposed **scientific management** principles designed to maximize production efficiency.[54] He sought to replace the seat-of-the-pants approach for determining each element of a worker's job with a scientific approach. The centerpiece of scientific management was the elimination of time and motion waste. This was done by carefully studying jobs to determine the most efficient way they could be completed. Jobs were partitioned into small and simple segments, and the workers were given specific instructions on how each segment was to be done.

Scientific management

A body of literature developed in the early 1900s concerned with incentives, selection, training, and the design of jobs to eliminate time and motion waste.

The results of Taylor's efforts—in economic terms—were nothing short of spectacular. He was consistently able to achieve productivity improvements in the range of 200 percent or more. Many workers, however, did not like the jobs designed according to the dictates of scientific management. They found the repetitive work depersonalized, boring, and unchallenging. Because their jobs often represented small "cogs" in a big "wheel," employees increasingly complained that their work was meaningless. To offset the boredom of their highly repetitive jobs, workers would do things that were not always in the best interest of the organization. They came to work late, they took three- or four-day weekends, and they quit to find more interesting work.

Probably one of the most publicized reactions to overspecialized jobs was the action by automobile assembly-line workers in the early 1970s at the Lordstown, Ohio, Chevrolet plant. Workers were found to be welding empty soda pop bottles inside doors, purposely gouging the paint on cars as they went by, and engaging in other dysfunctional behaviors. The Lordstown workers,

[54] F. W. Taylor, *Principles of Scientific Management* (New York: Harper and Brothers, 1911).

it was said, were frustrated and looking for ways to overcome the dull, repetitive, and unchallenging tasks they were assigned. Welding a bottle inside a door or putting a deep scratch into a car's paint without getting caught provided a diversionary outlet.

The Lordstown events occurred in the early 1970s, but the recognition that a good thing—work simplification—could be carried too far began to get attention in the late 1940s and early 1950s. As a result of insights from psychologists, sociologists, and other social scientists, attention began to shift to the human needs of people. The jobs themselves had been engineered to be efficiently performed by robotlike workers. But people are not robots. They have needs and feelings. No matter how well engineered a job is, if the design fails to consider the human element, the economies of specialization could be more than offset by the diseconomies of employee dissatisfaction. And on many jobs, this is exactly what was happening. So attention became increasingly focused on job design approaches that would make work less routine and more meaningful.

Job Rotation   An early and primitive effort at dealing with the routineness in work was the use of **job rotation**. When an activity no longer is challenging, the employee would be rotated to another job, at the same level, that has similar skill requirements. The shifts can include as few as two people—the rotation being merely an exchange of jobs. However, the organization can provide much more elaborate rotation designs where a dozen or more employees are involved.

The strength of job rotation is that it reduces boredom through diversifying the employee's activities. Of course, it can also have indirect benefits for the organization since employees with a wider range of skills give management more flexibility in scheduling work, adapting to changes, and filling vacancies. On the other hand, job rotation is not without its drawbacks. Training costs are increased, and productivity is reduced by moving a worker into a new position just when his or her efficiency at the prior job was creating organizational economies. Job rotation also creates disruptions. Members of the work group have to adjust to the new employee. The supervisor may also have to spend more time answering questions and monitoring the work of the recently rotated employee. Finally, job rotation can demotivate intelligent and ambitious trainees who seek specific responsibilities in their chosen specialty.

Job Enlargement   In the 1950s, the idea of expanding jobs horizontally, or what we call **job enlargement**, grew in popularity. Increasing the number and variety of tasks that an individual performed resulted in jobs with more diversity. Instead of only sorting the incoming mail by department, for instance, a mail sorter's job could be enlarged to include physically delivering the mail to the various departments or running outgoing letters through the postage meter.

Efforts at job enlargement met with less than enthusiastic results. As one employee who experienced such a redesign on his job remarked, "Before I had one lousy job. Now, through enlargement, I have three!"

So, while job enlargement attacked the lack of diversity in overspecialized jobs, it did little to instill challenge or meaningfulness to a worker's activities. Job enrichment was introduced to deal with the shortcomings of enlargement.

Job rotation

The periodic shifting of a worker from one task to another.

Job enlargement

The horizontal expansion of jobs.

Job Enrichment **Job enrichment** refers to the vertical expansion of jobs. It increases the degree to which the worker controls the planning, execution, and evaluation of his or her work. An enriched job organizes tasks so as to allow workers to do a complete activity, increases the employee's freedom and independence, increases responsibility, and provides feedback so individuals will be able to assess and correct their own performance.

Job enrichment

The vertical expansion of jobs.

Reports of organizations implementing job enrichment programs have been well publicized, and the importance of the concept requires that it be given an expanded discussion. Such a discussion will be undertaken later in this chapter. From an historical perspective, it is sufficient to note that job enrichment essentially developed in the 1960s as a response to employee dissatisfaction and productivity problems that excessive specialization created. The interest it initiated continues through to today.

Sociotechnical Systems Another job design innovation of the 1960s was the concept of **sociotechnical systems**. Like job enlargement and enrichment, this approach represented a response to the overly narrow scientific management view of job design.

Sociotechnical systems

A job design philosophy emphasizing both the technical and social aspects of work.

Sociotechnical systems is more a philosophy toward job design than a specific technique. Its central theme is that job design must address both the technical and the social aspects of the organization if work systems are to produce greater employee productivity and higher personal fulfillment for organization members. Every job has technological aspects. But technical tasks are performed in an environment influenced by a culture, a set of values, and generally acceptable organization practices. Redesign efforts that look only at the technical aspects of a job are likely to overlook critical factors that influence employee performance and satisfaction.

Advocates of sociotechnical systems provided no explicit guidance in exactly how the work, the social surroundings, and the organization interact. Their suggestions, however, did rely heavily on group-oriented approaches to work. The idea of work teams, which we shall discuss later in this section, evolved out of the sociotechnical systems philosophy.

Quality of Work Life Today, job design has become part of a larger effort to improve the quality of the work environment. The term **quality of work life** (QWL) describes a process by which an organization responds to employee needs by developing mechanisms to allow them to share fully in making the decisions that design their lives at work.[55] Redesigning jobs to increase diversity and autonomy and to allow workers more opportunities to grow and innovate; participative decision making; improved work group interactions; reduced supervision and increased self-management; and expanded employee-management collaboration are examples of QWL efforts. Obviously these approaches to job design would be consistent with many of our motivation theories—for example,

Quality of work life (QWL)

A process by which an organization responds to employee needs by developing mechanisms to allow them to share fully in making decisions that design their lives at work.

[55] See, for instance, R. E. Walton, "Quality of Working Life: What Is It?," *Sloan Management Review*, Fall 1973, pp. 11–21; D. A. Ondrack and M. G. Evans, "Job Enrichment and Job Satisfaction in Quality of Working Life and Nonquality of Working Life Sites," *Human Relations*, September 1986, pp. 871–89; and D. Buchanan, "Job Enrichment Is Dead: Long Live High-Performance Work Design," *Personnel Management*, May 1987, pp. 40–43.

Theory Y, motivation-hygiene, ERG, and expectancy. In three-quarters of a century, job design has gone from limiting an employee's involvement in his or her job through simplification, to widening that involvement to include the multitude of job-related factors that influence the overall quality of the employee's work life.

The Job Characteristics Model

What are the key dimensions to any job? How could management use that information to better design jobs? The best answers to these questions lie in the **job characteristics model** (JCM). As you'll see, the JCM can guide managers in evaluating jobs and help them to predict an employee's motivation, work performance, and job satisfaction.[56]

Job characteristics model

Identifies five job characteristics and their relationship to personal and work outcomes.

Core Dimensions   According to the JCM, any job can be described in terms of five core job dimensions, defined as follows:

1. **Skill variety**—the degree to which the job requires a variety of different activities so the worker can use a number of different skills and talents
2. **Task identity**—the degree to which the job requires completion of a whole and identifiable piece of work
3. **Task significance**—the degree to which the job has a substantial impact on the lives or work of other people
4. **Autonomy**—the degree to which the job provides substantial freedom, independence, and discretion to the individual in scheduling the work and in determining the procedures to be used in carrying it out
5. **Feedback**—the degree to which carrying out the work activities required by the job results in the individual obtaining direct and clear information about the effectiveness of his or her performance.

Skill variety

The degree to which the job requires a variety of different activities.

Task identity

The degree to which the job requires completion of a whole and identifiable piece of work.

Task significance

The degree to which the job has a substantial impact on the lives or work of other people.

Autonomy

The degree to which the job provides substantial freedom and discretion to the individual in scheduling the work and in determining the procedures to be used in carrying it out.

Feedback

The degree to which carrying out the work activities required by a job results in the individual obtaining direct and clear information about the effectiveness of his or her performance.

Table 7–1 offers examples of job activities that rate high and low for each characteristic.

Figure 7–5 presents the model. Notice how the first three dimensions—skill variety, task identity, and task significance—combine to create meaningful work. That is, if these three characteristics exist in a job, we can predict that the incumbent will view the job as being important, valuable, and worthwhile. Notice, too, that jobs that possess autonomy give the job incumbent a feeling of personal responsibility for the results and that, if a job provides feedback, the employee will know how effectively he or she is performing. From a motivational standpoint, the model says that internal rewards are obtained by an individual when he *learns* (knowledge of results) that he *personally* (experienced responsibility) has performed well on a task that he *cares* about (experienced meaningfulness).[57] The more that these three psychological states are

---

[56] J. R. Hackman and G. R. Oldham, "Development of the Job Diagnostic Survey," *Journal of Applied Psychology*, April 1975, pp. 159–70.

[57] J. R. Hackman, "Work Design," in J. R. Hackman and J. L. Suttle (eds.), *Improving Life at Work* (Santa Monica, CA: Goodyear, 1977), p. 129.

TABLE 7–1

Examples of High and Low Job Characteristics

Skill Variety	
High variety	The owner-operator of a garage who does electrical repair, rebuilds engines, does body work, and interacts with customers
Low variety	A body shop worker who sprays paint eight hours a day
Task Identity	
High identity	A cabinetmaker who designs a piece of furniture, selects the wood, builds the object, and finishes it to perfection
Low identity	A worker in a furniture factory who operates a lathe solely to make table legs
Task Significance	
High significance	Nursing the sick in a hospital intensive care unit
Low significance	Sweeping hospital floors
Autonomy	
High autonomy	A telephone installer who schedules his or her own work for the day, makes visits without supervision, and decides on the most effective techniques for a particular installation
Low autonomy	A telephone operator who must handle calls as they come according to a routine, highly specified procedure
Feedback	
High feedback	An electronics factory worker who assembles a radio and then tests it to determine if it operates properly
Low feedback	An electronics factory worker who assembles a radio and then routes it to a quality control inspector who tests it for proper operation, and makes needed adjustments

Source: G. Johns, *Organizational Behavior: Understanding Life at Work*, 2nd ed. (Glenview, IL: Scott, Foresman, 1988), p. 198. With permission.

present, the greater will be the employee's motivation, performance, and satisfaction, and the lower his or her absenteeism and likelihood of leaving the organization. As Figure 7–5 shows, the links between the job dimensions and the outcomes are moderated or adjusted by the strength of the individual's growth need, that is, by the employee's desire for self-esteem and self-actualization. This means that individuals with a high growth need are more likely to experience the psychological states when their jobs are enriched than are their counterparts with a low growth need. Moreover, they will respond more positively to the psychological states, when they are present, than will low-growth-need individuals.

Predictions from the Model   The core dimensions can be combined into a single predictive index, called the **motivating potential score** (MPS). Its computation is shown in Figure 7–6.

Jobs that are high on motivating potential must be high on at least one of the three factors that lead to experiencing meaningfulness, and they must be high on both autonomy and feedback. If jobs score high on motivating potential, the model predicts that motivation, performance, and satisfaction

Motivating potential score

A predictive index suggesting the motivation potential in a job.

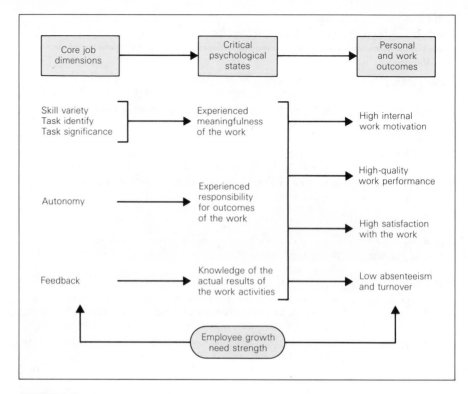

FIGURE 7–5
The Job Characteristics Model

Source: J. R. Hackman, "Work Design," in *Improving Life at Work*, eds. J. R. Hackman and J. L. Suttle (Santa Monica, CA: Scott, Foresman and Company, 1977), p. 129.

will be positively affected, while the likelihood of absence and turnover is lessened.

Research Evidence   The job characteristics model has been well researched. Most of the evidence supports the general framework of the theory—that is, there is a multiple set of job characteristics and these characteristics impact behavioral outcomes.[58] But there is still considerable debate around the five specific core dimensions in the JCM, the multiplicative properties of the MPS, and whether other moderating variables may not be as good or better than growth need strength.

There is some question whether task identity adds to the model's predictive

---

[58] See "Job Characteristics Theory of Work Redesign," in J. B. Miner, *Theories of Organizational Behavior* (Hinsdale, IL: Dryden Press, 1980), pp. 231–66; B. T. Loher, R. A. Noe, N. L. Moeller, and M. P. Fitzgerald, "A Meta-Analysis of the Relation of Job Characteristics to Job Satisfaction," *Journal of Applied Psychology*, May 1985, pp. 280–89; W. H. Glick, G. D. Jenkins, Jr., and N. Gupta, "Method Versus Substance: How Strong Are Underlying Relationships Between Job Characteristics and Attitudinal Outcomes?," *Academy of Management Journal*, September 1986, pp. 441–64; and Y. Fried and G. R. Ferris, "The Validity of the Job Characteristics Model: A Review and Meta-Analysis," *Personnel Psychology*, Summer 1987, pp. 287–322.

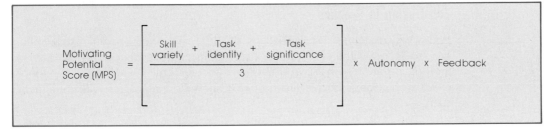

FIGURE 7–6
Computing a Motivating Potential Score

ability,[59] and there is evidence suggesting that skill variety may be redundant with autonomy.[60] Further, a number of studies have found that by adding all the variables in the MPS, rather than adding some and multiplying by others, the MPS becomes a better predictor of work outcomes.[61] Finally, while the strength of an individual's growth needs has been found to be a meaningful moderating variable in many studies,[62] other variables—such as the presence or absence of social cues, perceived equity with comparison groups, and propensity to assimilate work experience[63] —have also been found to moderate the job characteristics-outcome relationship. Given the current state of research on moderating variables, one should be cautious in unequivocally accepting growth-need strength as originally included in the JCM.

Where does this leave us? Given the current state of evidence, we can make the following statements with relative confidence: (1) People who work on jobs with high-core job dimensions are generally more motivated, satisfied, and productive than are those who do not; and (2) job dimensions operate through the psychological states in influencing personal and work outcome variables rather than influence them directly.[64]

[59] See R. B. Dunham, "Measurement and Dimensionality of Job Characteristics," *Journal of Applied Psychology*, August 1976, pp. 404–09; J. L. Pierce and R. B. Dunham, "Task Design: A Literature Review," *Academy of Management Review*, January 1976, pp. 83–97; and D. M. Rousseau, "Technological Differences in Job Characteristics, Employee Satisfaction, and Motivation: A Synthesis of Job Design Research and Sociotechnical Systems Theory," *Organizational Behavior and Human Performance*, October 1977, pp. 18–42.

[60] Ibid.; and Y. Fried and G. R. Ferris, "The Dimensionality of Job Characteristics: Some Neglected Issues," *Journal of Applied Psychology*, August 1986, pp. 419–26.

[61] Ibid.

[62] See, for instance, P. E. Spector, "Higher-Order Need Strength as a Moderator of the Job Scope—Employee Outcome Relationship: A Meta-Analysis," *Journal of Occupational Psychology*, June 1985, pp. 119–27; G. B. Graen, T. A. Scandura, and M. R. Graen, "A Field Experimental Test of the Moderating Effects of Growth Need Strength on Productivity," *Journal of Applied Psychology*, August 1986, pp. 484–91; and Y. Fried and G. R. Ferris, "The Validity of the Job Characteristics Model."

[63] C. A. O'Reilly and D. F. Caldwell, "Informational Influence as a Determinant of Perceived Task Characteristics and Job Satisfaction," *Journal of Applied Psychology*, April 1979, pp. 157–65; R. V. Montagno, "The Effects of Comparison Others and Prior Experience on Responses to Task Design," *Academy of Management Journal*, June 1985, pp. 491–98; and P. C. Bottger and I. K-H. Chew, "The Job Characteristics Model and Growth Satisfaction: Main Effects of Assimilation of Work Experience and Context Satisfaction," *Human Relations*, June 1986, pp. 575–94.

[64] Hackman, "Work Design," pp. 132–33.

Job Design in Practice

Following guidelines established by the JCM, what actions can management take to increase the skill variety, task significance, feedback and the like in their organization's jobs? Two answers are job enrichment and the use of autonomous work teams. In this section, we'll show how managers can implement each.

Job Enrichment How do you enrich an individual's job? The following suggestions specify the types of changes in jobs that are most likely to lead to improvements in each of the five core dimensions (see Figure 7–7).

1. *Combine tasks.* Managers should seek to take existing and fractionalized tasks and put them back together to form a new and larger module of work. This increases skill variety and task identity.

2. *Create natural work units.* The creation of natural work units means that the tasks an employee does form an identifiable and meaningful whole. This increases employee "ownership" of the work and improves the likelihood that employees will view their work as meaningful and important rather than as irrelevant and boring.

3. *Establish client relationships.* The client is the user of the product or service that the employee works on. Wherever possible, managers should try to establish direct relationships between workers and their clients. This increases skill variety, autonomy, and feedback for the employee.

4. *Expand jobs vertically.* Vertical expansion gives employees responsibilities and controls that were formerly reserved for management. It seeks to partially close the gap between the "doing" and the "controlling" aspects of the job, and it increases employee autonomy.

FIGURE 7–7
Guidelines for Enriching a Job

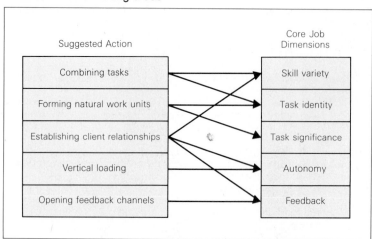

Source: From *Improving Life at Work* by J. R. Hackman and J. L. Suttle.
Copyright © 1977 by Scott, Foresman and Company. Reprinted by permission.

5. *Open feedback channels.* By increasing feedback, employees not only learn how well they are performing their jobs, but also whether their performance is improving, deteriorating, or remaining at a constant level. Ideally, this feedback about performance should be received directly as the employee does the job, rather than from management on an occasional basis.[65]

Travelers Insurance used the preceding suggestions to design a job enrichment program for its keypunch operators.[66] Management was displeased with their performance—output seemed low, the error rate high, and absenteeism excessive. The following changes were introduced:

1. The random assignment of work was replaced by assigning to each operator continuing responsibility for certain accounts.
2. Some planning and control functions were combined with the central task of keypunching.
3. Each operator was given several channels of direct contact with clients. When problems arose, the operator, not the supervisor, took them up with the client.
4. Operators were given the authority to set their own schedules, plan their daily work, and correct obvious coding errors on their own.
5. Incorrect cards were returned by the computer department to the operators who punched them, and the operators corrected their own errors. Weekly computer printouts of errors and productivity were sent directly to the operator rather than the supervisor.

These enrichment efforts led to some impressive results. Fewer keypunch operators were needed, output increased, error rates and absenteeism were reduced, and job attitudes improved. The changes reportedly saved Travelers over $90,000 a year.

Autonomous Work Teams **Autonomous work teams** represent job enrichment at the group level. Work groups are given a high degree of self-determination in the management of their day-to-day work. Typically this includes collective control over the pace of work, determination of work assignments, organization of breaks, and collective choice of inspection procedures. Fully autonomous work teams even select their own members and have the members evaluate each other's performance. As a result, supervisory positions take on decreased importance and may even be eliminated. Autonomous work teams draw from the job characteristics model. Self-managed work teams have three features: (1) employees with functionally interrelated tasks who collectively are responsible for end products; (2) individuals who have a variety of skills so they may undertake all or a large proportion of groups' tasks; and (3) feedback and evaluation in terms of the performance of whole groups.[67]

Autonomous work teams

Groups that are free to determine how the goals assigned to them are to be accomplished and how tasks are to be allocated.

---

[65] Ibid., pp. 136–40.

[66] J. R. Hackman, G. R. Oldham, R. Janson, and K. Purdy, "A New Strategy for Job Enrichment," *California Management Review*, Summer 1975, pp. 57–71.

[67] T. D. Wall, N. J. Kemp, P. R. Jackson, and C. W. Clegg, "Outcomes of Autonomous Workgroups: A Long-Term Field Experiment," *Academy of Management Journal*, June 1986, pp. 280–304.

Volvo began using autonomous work teams in the 1960s to build cars in Sweden.[68] The first major experiment with these self-managed teams in the U.S. was in the early 1970s, by General Foods, at a new pet food plant it built in Kansas.[69] Today, a number of organizations have implemented the concept. For instance, General Motors is using teams in its joint venture with Toyota in California to make Chevrolet Novas and Toyota Corollas.[70] Factory workers are divided into small teams that define their own jobs and monitor the quality of their output. The groups even conduct their own daily quality audits, a chore that once was relegated to a separate group of inspectors. They also have "stop-line" cords that allow them to shut down the line if they encounter a problem. GM is now attempting to transfer what they learned from their joint venture with Toyota to more than a third of their thirty-two car-and-truck assembly plants.

Clarifying Job Design Outcomes

By the early 1980s, it had generally been assumed that the move from job simplification toward QWL programs represented enlightened management practices. Job enrichment and autonomous work teams, for instance, were desirable because they positively influenced the five core dimensions in the job characteristics model. Very recently, however, this assumption has been shown to be a simplistic evaluation of job design efforts.[71] There are actually four different approaches to designing jobs. No one approach is more right than the others. Rather, each focuses on a different set of outcomes. So the approach that managers choose should reflect the objectives that they seek.

Table 7–2 proposes that there are four different schools of thought regarding job design. These are the industrial engineering approaches of scientific management and time-and-motion study, the psychological approaches of job enrichment and the JCM, the human-factors or ergonomics approach, and the biological approaches to work physiology. These four schools tend to focus on different sets of outcome variables and, not surprisingly, offer different recommendations for managers. As you'll see, this taxonomy demonstrates that there is no "one best way" to look at the design of jobs. What is "best" depends on the outcome variables with which you're concerned. This taxonomy can help to explain why the best design for reducing stress or improving safety may not at all be the best design for improving employee motivation.

---

[68] See R. E. Walton, "From Hawthorne to Topeka to Kalmar," in *Man and Work in Society*, ed. E. L. Cass and F. G. Zimmer (New York: Van Nostrand Reinhold, 1975), pp. 118–21.

[69] Ibid.

[70] "Why Image Counts: A Tale of Two Industries," *Business Week*, June 8, 1987, pp. 138–39; and "GM's Bootstrap Battle: The Factory-Floor View," *U.S. News & World Report*, September 21, 1987, pp. 52–53.

[71] M. A. Campion and P. W. Thayer, "Development and Field Evaluation of an Interdisciplinary Measure of Job Design," *Journal of Applied Psychology*, February 1985, pp. 29–43; and M. A. Campion and P. W. Thayer, "Job Design: Approaches, Outcomes, and Trade-Offs," *Organizational Dynamics*, Winter 1987, pp. 66–79.

TABLE 7-2
Four Schools of Thought on Job Design

School	Examples of Recommendations	Outcome Focus
Engineering	Use work simplification, specialization, and time-and-motion study	Efficiency
Psychological	Enhance autonomy, skill and task variety, and social interactions	Satisfaction
Ergonomics	Develop equipment and jobs that are simple, safe, and reliable, and that minimize mental requirements on the worker	System reliability
Biological	Improve seating positions, lessen strength demands, and reduce noise distractions	Employee comfort

The Engineering School   The **engineering school** takes a very mechanistic approach to job design. It relies on industrial engineering principles such as work simplification, specialization, and time-and-motion study, as advocated by Adam Smith and Frederick Taylor. This school, for instance, recommends that managers design jobs so as to make them as simple and repetitive as possible; to make extensive use of specialized tools and procedures; and to reduce unnecessary eye, hand, and body motions.

Given the engineering school's mechanistic approach to job design, we should expect implementation of its recommendations to lead to positive efficiency results. This would include higher personnel-utilization rates because of greater substitutability among workers, lower training requirements, and fewer accidents and errors. But these benefits come with costs. This focus on efficiency generally leads to lower employee satisfaction and higher absenteeism.

Engineering school of job design

A mechanistic approach that focuses on efficiency.

The Psychological School   The job-characteristics model, with its emphasis on increasing employee satisfaction, is probably the best example of the **psychological school** of job design. Proponents advocate enhancing autonomy, skill and task variety, social interactions, and similar aspects in a job. As one would expect, this approach does tend to lead to more satisfied and motivated workers, strong job performance for many, and less absenteeism. Ironically, this concern with employee satisfaction tends to get just the opposite benefits and drawbacks of the engineering school. That is, the psychological emphasis results in lower utilization levels, requires more training time, places more mental demands and stress on workers, and increases the likelihood of accidents and errors.

Psychological school of job design

Redesigning jobs to increase employee satisfaction and motivation.

The Ergonomics School   The **ergonomics school** strives to enhance the person-machine fit by seeking to develop equipment and jobs that are simple, safe, and reliable and minimize mental requirements on the worker. Its advocates suggest the need to ensure that the workplace has the proper lighting, visibility, and similar workplace-layout specifications. Consistent with its objectives, emphasis on ergonomics leads to fewer accidents and errors and less stress, work overload, and mental fatigue. Additionally, a good person-machine fit leads to less training time and higher utilization rates.

Ergonomics school of job design

Seeks to increase system reliability by developing equipment and jobs that are safe, simple, reliable, and that minimize mental requirements on the worker.

Biological school of job design

Job design efforts that focus on improving the comfort and physical well-being of the employee.

The Biological School   The final category focuses on the comfort and physical well-being of the worker. Concerns of the **biological school** include seating positions, endurance requirements, strength demands, noise and temperature levels, and similar variables that affect the worker's comfort. Where attention is paid to these variables, workers require less physical effort and experience fewer body aches and pains and fewer medical incidents.

Summary   There are at least four different emphases that job design can take. If you're concerned with improving efficiency, the engineering school's recommendations should be followed. If employee satisfaction is the primary concern, the psychological school provides the best direction. Following the advice of the ergonomics school should increase system reliability, reduce employee fatigue and stress, and lessen the probability of accidents. If increasing employee comfort is the objective, the biological school offers the best advice. Management needs to identify what it is that it wants to improve, and this will suggest which work-design variables should get attention.

Our interest in this chapter has been with designing jobs to increase employee motivation and satisfaction. This falls clearly into the psychological school. But there are trade-offs. Increasing motivational properties in a job may come at the expense of increased training time, lower utilization levels, greater likelihood of errors on the job, and greater chance of mental overload. Managers need to keep these trade-offs in mind when they make job redesign decisions.

IMPLICATIONS FOR PERFORMANCE AND SATISFACTION

There are a number of techniques and programs for applying motivation theories. In this chapter, we reviewed eight of them: management by objectives, OB Mod, participative management, performance-based compensation, flexible benefits, two-tier pay systems, alternative work schedules, and job design. While it is always dangerous to synthesize a large number of complex ideas into a few simple guidelines, the following suggestions tap the essence of what we know about applying motivation theories toward improving employee performance and satisfaction.

Recognize Individual Differences   Employees have different needs. Don't treat them all alike. Moreover, spend the time to understand what's important to each employee. This will allow you to individualize rewards, schedule work, and design jobs to align with individual needs.

Use Goals and Feedback   Employees should have hard, specific goals, as well as feedback on how well they fare in pursuit of those goals.

Allow Employees to Participate in Decisions that Affect Them   Employees can contribute to a number of decisions that affect them: setting work goals, choosing their own fringe benefit packages, selecting preferred work schedules, and the like. This can increase employee productivity, commitment to work goals, motivation, and job satisfaction.

Link Rewards to Performance   Rewards should be contingent on performance. Importantly, employees must perceive a clear linkage. Regardless of how closely rewards are actually correlated to performance criteria, if individuals perceive this correlation to be low, the result will be low performance, a decrease in job satisfaction, and an increase in turnover and absenteeism statistics.

Check the System for Equity   Rewards should also be perceived by employees as equating with the inputs they give. At a simplistic level, this should mean that experience, abilities, effort, and other obvious inputs should explain differences in performance and, hence, pay, job assignments, and other obvious rewards.

POINT

OBJECTIVE FACTORS DETERMINE TASK RESPONSE

People respond to the objective facets or attributes of their jobs. The job characteristics model, as a specific case in point, demonstrates how jobs that are high in attributes such as skill variety and autonomy lead to high levels of satisfaction, motivation, and performance, and to low levels of absenteeism and turnover among employees. This task attribute approach to job design began in the early 1960s as a result of the work of Turner and Lawrence.[1] It has reached its full development in the Job Characteristics Model.

Turner and Lawrence conducted a study of employees in a number of different manufacturing jobs in diverse geographical locations, to assess their response to different kinds of jobs. They broke jobs down into six attributes: (1) variety, (2) autonomy, (3) required social interaction, (4) opportunities for social interaction, (5) knowledge and skill requirements, and (6) responsibility. They argued that those jobs that had all of these six attributes could be considered complex and challenging. Further, they argued that employees would prefer such complex jobs to jobs that would score low on these attributes.

What Turner and Lawrence found partially supported their expectations. Employees who had jobs which scored high in the six attributes were absent less often. But they weren't significantly more satisfied. So the researchers reanalyzed their data and found an interesting explanation—employees in small towns responded differently to the six task attributes than those in large cities. Specifically, Turner and Lawrence found that there was a positive relationship between high scores on the attributes and satisfaction among workers from small towns, but not among those in the cities. The researchers concluded that complex and challenging jobs were more important to people in small towns, because their jobs were the central focus in their lives. In contrast, workers in large cities had a variety of nonwork interests to fill out their lives.

The Job Characteristics Model evolved out of the earlier work by Turner and Lawrence. As you'll remember, the JCM argues that there are five key attributes or dimensions that characterize jobs. The model proposes that jobs that score high on these five attributes lead to high employee performance and satisfaction. However, the model's predictions work best with employees that have a high growth need.

The common assumption in these approaches to job design is that jobs have objective and stable task characteristics that people perceive and respond to consistently and predictably. That assumption seems valid.

We can draw three conclusions based on the task attribute approach to motivation. First, the objective attributes of an individual's job are the primary determinant of his or her responses to tasks. So job characteristics are key predictors of employee performance and satisfaction. Second, when research fails to support a relationship between job characteristics and performance/satisfaction, it is possible that all relevant job characteristics have not been considered. There may be attributes, beyond the five identified in the JCM, that are important in explaining and predicting employee behavior. Finally, when research fails to support a relationship between job characteristics and performance/satisfaction, the other place to look is at individual differences. The logic of the JCM approach to motivation is valid. If results aren't supportive, the problem undoubtedly lies in identifying individual differences—like living in a large city or having low growth need strength—that lessen the importance of holding a complex and challenging job.

[1] See A. N. Turner and P. R. Lawrence, *Industrial Jobs and the Worker*. Boston: Harvard Graduate School of Business Administration, 1965.

COUNTERPOINT

SOCIAL FACTORS DETERMINE TASK RESPONSE

The characteristics of a job are not fixed and objective. Rather, they are socially constructed realities that are defined by signals or messages that an employee receives from others. Employees develop their perception of their job in large part from norms, roles, attitudes of friends at work and at home, and organizational messages from employers, labor unions, and relevant others. A social information processing view of job design would suggest that job satisfaction can be manipulated by such subtle actions as a co-worker or boss commenting on the existence or absence of features such as difficulty, challenge, or autonomy in the job.

It has been traditionally believed that people respond to the objective characteristics of the jobs that they do. But attributes like variety, identity, or autonomy are not fully objective. The same job may be perceived differently by different groups. Even the same attribute may be seen as positive in one setting and negative in another. It seems reasonable to suggest, therefore, that employees may respond to both informational influences and objective characteristics.

Interestingly, that is just what the research indicates. For example, in one study, investigators manipulated both the task characteristics and information cues in a simulated selection task. They found that informational cues had a greater impact on job satisfaction than the objective characteristics of the task itself. Similarly, when another set of investigators manip-

ulated task characteristics and information cues in a simulated routine clerical task, they too found that the informational cues were the dominant force determining job satisfaction.

An employee's attitudes reflect both objective characteristics of the job or task and the informational influence of others. Moreover, the communication that an employee receives from others in terms of informational cues may be a more powerful motivation force than the actual properties of the task. To generalize, it may be that the informational cues that we get on our job from bosses, coworkers, and subordinates are as important as goal setting, equitable compensation, or intrinsically meaningful tasks in creating high motivation, high productivity, and favorable attitudes about our work.

The implications of this approach should certainly not be lost on management. Given the importance that social cues play in molding an individual's perception of his or her job, managers should spend less effort on actually redesigning jobs to make them complex and challenging, and more time telling employees how interesting and important their jobs are. This approach is likely to increase employee motivation and satisfaction, while saving managers a lot of time and money.

This is based on J. Thomas and R. Griffin, "The Social Information Processing Model of Task Design: A Review of the Literature," *Academy of Management Review*, October 1983, pp. 672–82.

KEY TERMS

Autonomous Work Teams

Autonomy

Biological School of Job Design

Compressed Workweek

Engineering School of Job Design

Ergonomics School of Job Design

Feedback

Flexible Benefits

Flextime

Job Characteristics Model

Job Design

Job Enlargement

Job Enrichment

Job Rotation

Management by Objectives (MBO)

Motivating Potential Score

OB Mod

Participative Management

Performance-Based Compensation

Piece-Rate Pay Plans

Psychological School of Job Design

Quality Circle

Quality of Work Life (QWL)

Scanlon Plans

Scientific Management

Skill Variety

Sociotechnical Systems

Task Identity

Task Significance

Telecommuting

Two-Tier Pay System

FOR DISCUSSION

1. Relate goal-setting theory with the MBO process. How are they similar? Different?

2. What factors in public sector organizations might work against an effective MBO program?

3. How might a college instructor use OB Mod to improve learning in the classroom?

4. Do you think participative management is likely to be more effective in certain types of organization? With certain types of employees? Discuss.

5. Identify five different criteria by which organizations can compensate employees. Based on your knowledge and experience, do you think performance is the criterion most used in practice? Discuss.

6. What drawbacks, if any, do you see to implementing flexible benefits? (Consider this question from the perspectives of both the organization and the employee.)

7. If two-tier pay systems run counter to equity theory logic, why would intelligent managers seek to negotiate such programs? What other ways could management lower labor costs without the negative side-effects from two-tier systems?

8. Does flextime have an impact on any of the five core dimensions in JCM? Discuss.

9. Would you want a full-time job telecommuting? How do you think most of your friends would feel about such a job? Do you think telecommuting has a future?

10. What is *QWL*? Is it the same thing as job enrichment? Discuss.

11. "Employees should have jobs that give them autonomy and diversity." Build an argument to support this statement. Then negate your argument.

12. Students often complain about doing group projects in a class. Why is that? Relate your answer to autonomous work teams. Would you want to be a member of one? Discuss.

FOR FURTHER READING

BOWERS, M. H., and R. D. RODERICK, "Two-Tier Pay Systems: The Good, the Bad, and the Debatable," *Personnel Administrator*, June 1987, pp. 101–12. Assesses the costs and benefits to management in implementing a two-tier pay system.

FLAIM, P. O., "Work Schedules of Americans: An Overview of New Findings," *Monthly Labor Review*, November 1986, pp. 3–6. Highlights current status of work schedules, including workers who hold multiple jobs, percentage who work Saturdays and Sundays, evening employment, home-based work, flextime, and preferences for trading off hours of work for reduction in earnings.

GRIFFIN, R. W., "Toward an Integrated Theory of Task Design," in L. L. Cummings and B. M. Staw (eds.), *Research in Organizational Behavior*, Vol. 9 (Greenwich, CT: JAI Press, 1987), pp. 79–120. Reviews the literature on job design and then presents a conceptual framework to integrate various approaches.

KELLY, J. E., *Scientific Management, Job Redesign and Work Performance*. New York: Academic Press, 1982. Challenges many assumptions about job redesign and argues that many job redesign initiatives were achieved through changes in pay programs, control systems, and other traditional scientific management mechanisms rather than through changes in intrinsic motivation or worker attitudes.

MILLER, C. S., and M. H. SCHUSTER, "Gainsharing Plans: A Comparative Analysis," *Organizational Dynamics*, Summer 1987, pp. 44–67. Compares six gain-sharing or productivity-sharing plans and offers suggestions for choosing the best one for an organization's needs.

NADLER, D. A., and E. E. LAWLER III, "Quality of Work Life: Perspectives and Directions," *Organizational Dynamics*, Winter 1983, pp. 20–30. Clarifies definition and assesses which factors predict why some quality of work life efforts are more successful than others.

EXERCISE 7

ASSESSING YOUR JOB'S MOTIVATING POTENTIAL

Describe your present job (or a previous paid or unpaid job you've had) using the following questionnaire. Circle the number that best describes the job. Be as objective as possible in your answers.

1. How much *variety* is there in your job? That is, to what extent does the job require you to do many different things at work, using a variety of your skills and talents?

1 ---------------- 2 ---------------- 3 ---------------- 4 ---------------- 5 ---------------- 6 ---------------- 7

Very little; the job requires me to do the same routine things over and over again.

Moderate variety.

Very much; the job requires me to do many different things, using a number of different skills and talents.

2. To what extent does your job involve doing a *"whole"* and *identifiable piece of work*? That is, is the job a complete piece of work that has an obvious beginning and end, or is it only a small part of the overall piece of work, which is finished by other people or by machines?

1 ---------------- 2 ---------------- 3 ---------------- 4 ---------------- 5 ---------------- 6 ---------------- 7

My job is only a tiny part of the overall piece of work; the results of my activities cannot be seen in the final product or service.

My job is a moderate-sized "chunk" of the overall piece of work; my own contribution can be seen in the final outcome.

My job involves doing the whole piece of work, from start to finish; the results of my activities are easily seen in the final product or service.

3. In general, *how significant or important* is your job? That is, are the results of your work likely to significantly affect the lives or well-being of other people?

1 ---------------- 2 ---------------- 3 ---------------- 4 ---------------- 5 ---------------- 6 ---------------- 7

Not very significant; the outcomes of my work are *not* likely to have important effects on other people.

Moderately significant.

Highly significant; the outcomes of my work can affect other people in very important ways.

4. How much *autonomy* is there in your job? That is, to what extent does your job permit you to decide on *your own* how to go about doing the work?

1 ---------------- 2 ---------------- 3 ---------------- 4 ---------------- 5 ---------------- 6 ---------------- 7

Very little; the job gives me almost no personal "say" about how and when the work is done.

Moderate autonomy; many things are standardized and not under my control, but I can make some decisions about the work.

Very much; the job gives me almost complete responsibility for deciding how and when the work is done.

5. To what extent does doing *the job itself* provide you with information about your work performance? That is, does the actual *work itself* provide clues about how well you are doing—aside from any feedback co-workers or supervisors may provide?

1 ---------------- 2 ---------------- 3 ---------------- 4 ---------------- 5 ---------------- 6 ---------------- 7

| Very little; the job itself is set up so that I could work forever without finding out how well I am doing. | Moderately; sometimes doing the job provides feedback to me; sometimes it does not. | Very much; the job is set up so that I get almost constant feedback as I work about how well I am doing. |

Turn to page 563 for scoring directions and key.

Source: Based on J. R. Hackman and G. R. Oldham, *Work Redesign* (Reading, MA: Addison-Wesley, 1980).

CASE INCIDENT 7

CONTRASTING TWO JOBS

Richard Ebert has manned his toll booth at the Golden Gate Bridge toll plaza for twenty-six years. He is one of forty-six agents who sit in eleven 3 foot by 3 foot booths collecting tolls from about 110,000 drivers a day. He loves his job: "This place is like working at a national monument. It's just like Yosemite or the Grand Canyon!"

What's Ebert's job like? He conducts a new transaction, on average, about every six seconds. As the Golden Gate Bridge District describes the toll collector's job, all that is basically required is that he or she "remain alert, friendly, and accurate," eight hours a day, five days a week, week in and week out, year in, year out. Starting pay is $1,955 a month, but top of the scale is only $2,212 monthly. The hours are steady and the job is unusually secure. But the Bridge District is serious when it says it expects accuracy from its toll collectors. The margin for error is $1 per thousand, and collectors who exceed that figure are placed on three months probation, regardless of seniority. Incidentally, the job isn't as mundane as it may seem. There are different tolls for each type of vehicle, so there is some diversity in the job.

Do you think the Bridge District has difficulty filling vacancies for this job? If you answered "Yes," think again. The last time a position opened up, the District received more than 1,200 written applications. In the crowd that showed up, one employee recalls, a scuffle escalated to a "near riot."

Jane McKenna recently quit her job as a security screener at Los Angeles International Airport. She only worked for three months but, like so many people in this job, threw in the towel after only a short time. It is not unusual, in fact, for the job of security screener at a large international airport to have an annual turnover rate of 200 percent.

Jane described her job as "terribly boring and stressful. I'd sit in front of that black-and-white monitor for thirty minute stretches, looking for the outline of knives, guns, or bombs. Passengers, of course, were in a hurry. If I saw something suspicious and asked the person to open his or her suitcase, they'd get grouchy or even hostile. And the people behind 'em in line would start making nasty comments. Add to this the fact that FAA inspectors are regularly testing us to make sure we don't let anything suspicious get through, and that airlines are fined up to $1,000 for each failure to detect a mock weapon, and you understand why I quit."

How much did Jane McKenna earn as a security screener? The security firm that she worked for paid her $140 a week. She also got a $50 bonus when she caught mock weapons in luggage carried by FAA inspectors and $25 for weapons seized from regular passengers.

QUESTIONS

1. Explain the toll collector's job, as you would picture it, in terms of the JCM. What, if anything, could management do to raise this job's MPS?
2. Evaluate the security screener's job in terms of the JCM. What, if anything, could management do to raise its MPS?
3. While demand is high for the toll collector's job, airport security firms can't find and keep people in screening jobs. Can this difference be explained in terms of the JCM? Explain.
4. Would you be interested in these jobs as a career? Explain.
5. If the airport screening job paid the same as the toll collector job, would you expect the former's turnover problem to disappear? Discuss.

8

Foundations of Group Behavior

■ *Learning objectives*

Differentiate between formal and informal groups
Explain why people join groups
List the four stages of group development
Identify the key factors in explaining group behavior
Describe how role requirements change in different situations
Describe how norms exert influence on an individual's behavior
Summarize the importance of the Hawthorne studies to the understanding of behavior
List the benefits and disadvantages of cohesive groups

One of the truly remarkable things about work groups is that they can make 2 + 2 = 5. Of course, they also have the capability of making 2 + 2 = 3.

—— S.P.R.

Two facts make the contents of this chapter critical for your understanding of organizational behavior. First, the behavior of individuals in groups is something more than the sum total of each acting in his or her own way. In other words, when individuals are in groups, they act differently from when they are alone. Second, work groups are a vital part of almost every organization. Committees, task forces, project teams, work crews, staff groups, quality circles, and autonomous work teams are some of the more popular types of work groups that have become increasingly visible in organizations in recent years. This chapter defines groups, reviews the various reasons why people join them, describes how groups develop, and then presents a comprehensive model that will help you to explain work group behavior.

DEFINING AND CLASSIFYING GROUPS

Group

Two or more individuals, interacting and interdependent, who come together to achieve particular objectives.

Formal group

A designated work group defined by the organization's structure.

Informal group

A group that is neither formally structured nor organizationally determined; appears in response to the need for social contact.

Command group

A manager and his or her immediate subordinates.

A **group** is defined as two or more individuals, interacting and interdependent, who come together to achieve particular objectives. Groups can be either formal or informal. By **formal**, we mean defined by the organization's structure, with designated work assignments establishing tasks and work groups. In formal groups, the behaviors that one should engage in are stipulated by and directed toward organizational goals. In contrast, **informal groups** are alliances that are neither formally structured nor organizationally determined. These groups are natural formations in the work environment, which appear in response to the need for social contact.

It is possible to subclassify groups further as command, task, interest, or friendship groups.[1] Command and task groups are dictated by the formal organization, whereas interest and friendship groups are informal alliances.

The **command group** is determined by the organization chart. It is composed of the subordinates who report directly to a given manager. An elementary school principal and her twelve teachers form a command group, as do the director of postal audits and his five inspectors.

Task groups, also organizationally determined, represent those working

[1] L. R. Sayles, "Work Group Behavior and the Larger Organization," in C. Arensburg et al. (eds.), *Research in Industrial Relations* (New York: Harper & Row, 1957), pp. 131–45.

together to complete a job task. However, a task group's boundaries are not limited to its immediate hierarchical superior. It can cross command relationships. For instance, if a college student is accused of a campus crime, it may require communication and coordination among the Dean of Academic Affairs, the Dean of Students, the Registrar, the Director of Security, and the student's advisor. Such a formation would constitute a task group. It should be noted that all command groups are also task groups, but because task groups can cut across the organization, the reverse need not be true.

People who may or may not be aligned into common command or task groups may affiliate to attain a specific objective with which each is concerned. This is an **interest group**. Employees who band together to have their vacation schedule altered, to support a peer who has been fired, or to seek increased fringe benefits represent the formation of a united body to further their common interest.

Groups often develop because the individual members have one or more common characteristics. We call these formations **friendship groups**. Social allegiances, which frequently extend outside the work situation, can be based on similar age, support for "Big Red" Nebraska football, having attended the same college, or the holding of similar political views, to name just a few such characteristics.

Informal groups provide a very important service by satisfying their members' social needs. Because of interactions that result from the close proximity of workstations or task interactions, we find workers playing golf together, riding to and from work together, lunching together, and spending their breaks around the water cooler together. We must recognize that these types of interactions among individuals, even though informal, deeply affect their behavior and performance.

Task group

Those working together to complete a job task.

Interest group

Those working together to attain a specific objective with which each is concerned.

Friendship group

Those brought together because they share one or more common characteristics.

WHY DO PEOPLE JOIN GROUPS?

There is no single reason why individuals join groups. Since most people belong to a number of groups, it is obvious that different groups provide different benefits to their members. The most popular reasons for joining a group are related to our needs for security, status, self-esteem, affiliation, power, and goal achievement.

Security

"There's strength in numbers." By joining a group, we can reduce the insecurity of "standing alone"—we feel stronger, have fewer self-doubts, and are more resistant to threats. New employees are particularly vulnerable to a sense of isolation, and turn to the group for guidance and support. However, whether we are talking about new employees or those with years on the job, we can state that few individuals like to stand alone. We get reassurances from interacting with others and being part of a group. This often explains the appeal of unions—

if management creates an environment in which employees feel insecure, they are likely to turn to unionization to reduce their feelings of insecurity.

Status

"I'm a member of our company's running team. Last month, at the National Corporate Relays, we won the national championship. Didn't you see our picture in the company newsletter?" These comments demonstrate the role that a group can play in giving prestige. Inclusion in a group viewed as important by others provide recognition and status for its members.

Self-Esteem

"Before I was asked to pledge Phi Omega Chi, I felt like a nobody. Being in a fraternity makes me feel much more important." This quote demonstrates that groups can provide people with feelings of self-worth. That is, in addition to conveying status to those outside the group, membership can also give increased feelings of worth to the group members themselves. Our self-esteem is bolstered, for example, when we are accepted by a highly valued group. Being assigned to a task force whose purpose is to review and make recommendations for the location of the company's new corporate headquarters can fulfill one's needs for competence and growth, as well as for status.

Affiliation

"I'm independently wealthy, but I wouldn't give up my job. Why? Because I really like the people I work with!" This quote, from a $45,000-a-year purchasing agent who inherited several million dollars' worth of real estate, verifies that groups can fulfill our social needs. People enjoy the regular interaction that comes with group membership. For many people, these on-the-job interactions are their primary source for fulfilling their needs for affiliation. For almost all people, work groups significantly contribute to fulfilling their needs for friendships and social relations.

Power

"I tried for two years to get the plant management to increase the number of female restrooms on the production floor to the same number as the men have. It was like talking to a wall. But I got about fifteen other women who were production employees together and we jointly presented our demands to management. The construction crews were in here adding female restrooms within ten days!"

This episode demonstrates that one of the appealing aspects of groups is that they represent power. What often cannot be achieved individually becomes possible through group action. Of course, this power may not be sought only to make demands on others. It may be desired merely as a countermeasure.

Why Detroit Wants to Use Production Teams

General Motors, Ford, and Chrysler have been pushing hard in recent years to convince the United Auto Workers' union to accept a production system based on Japanese-style teams.[2] At the heart of this team concept is the idea of training workers to perform several jobs instead of just one and allowing workers greater control over the production process. Maybe not surprisingly, UAW leaders have resisted these changes. They see such changes as undermining the long standing job classification system and work rules that they spent decades negotiating into contracts.

What do the large automobile manufacturers hope to gain through the use of production teams? First, teams create a more flexible organization. Work team members learn several jobs, rather than just one, and thus can be reorganized as needed. Second, teams have demonstrated the ability to generate higher productivity. As job classifications are reduced from as many as 100 to as few as 2, and union work rules are loosened, output typically jumps by 20 to 40 percent. Third, teams increase employee satisfaction. Production workers have more control over their jobs, a greater variety of work, and participate in decisions previously made by foremen. Finally, the auto manufacturers see teams as a means of improving product quality. The traditional production-line job was designed to maximize speed. Mistakes would be caught at the end of the process by quality control inspectors. Production teams, on the other hand, take responsibility for the quality of their work. Members are encouraged to solve quality problems as they occur.

In order to protect themselves from unreasonable demands by management, individuals may align with others.

Informal groups additionally provide opportunities for individuals to exercise power over others. For individuals who desire to influence others, groups can offer power without a formal position of authority in the organization. As a group leader, you may be able to make requests of group members and obtain compliance without any of the responsibilities that traditionally go with formal managerial positions. So, for people with a high power need, groups can be a vehicle for fulfillment.

Goal Achievement

"I'm part of a three-person team studying how we can cut our company's transportation costs. They've been going up at over 30 percent a year for several

[2] "Detroit vs. the UAW: At Odds Over the Teamwork," *Business Week*, August 24, 1987, pp. 54–55.

years now so the corporate controller assigned representatives from cost accounting, shipping, and marketing to study the problem and make recommendations."

This task group was created to achieve a goal that would be considerably more difficult if pursued by a single person. There are times when it takes more than one person to accomplish a particular task—there is a need to pool talents, knowledge, or power in order to get a job completed. In such instances, management will rely on the use of a formal group.

STAGES OF GROUP DEVELOPMENT

Group development is a dynamic process. Most groups are in a continual state of change. But just because groups probably never reach complete stability doesn't mean that there isn't some general pattern that describes how most groups evolve. There is strong evidence that groups pass through a standard sequence of four stages.[3] As shown in Figure 8–1, these four stages have been labeled forming, storming, norming, and performing.

The first stage—*forming*—is characterized by a great deal of uncertainty about the group's purpose, structure, and leadership. Members are "testing the waters"—to determine what types of behavior are acceptable. This stage is complete when members have begun to think of themselves as part of a group.

The *storming* stage is one of intragroup conflict. Members accept the existence of the group, but there is resistance to the control that the group imposes on individuality. Additionally, there is conflict over who will control the group. When stage II is complete, there will be a relatively clear hierarchy of leadership within the group.

The third stage is one in which close relationships develop and the group demonstrates cohesiveness. There is now a strong sense of group identity and camaraderie. This *norming* stage is complete when there is a continuing structure for the group and the group has assimilated a common set of expectations of what defines correct member behavior.

The final stage is *performing*. The structure at this point is fully functional and accepted. Group energy has moved from getting to know and understand each other to the job of task performance.

Most of you have probably encountered each of these stages when you have had to do a group term project for a class. Group members are selected and then you meet for the first time. There is a "feeling out" to assess what the group is going to do and how it is going to do it. This is usually rapidly followed by the battle for control: Who is going to lead us? Once this is resolved and a hierarchy is agreed upon, the group moves to identifying specific activities of what needs to be done, who is going to do it, and dates by which the parts need to be completed. General expectations become set and agreed upon for each member. This forms the foundation for what you hope will be a coordinated group effort culminating in a project that group members and the instructor

[3] B. W. Tuckman, "Developmental Sequence in Small Groups," *Psychological Bulletin*, May 1965, pp. 384–99.

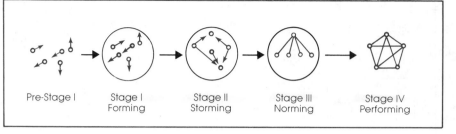

FIGURE 8–1
Stages of Group Development

agree is a job well done. Of course, groups occasionally don't get much beyond the first or second stage, which frequently results in projects and grades that are disappointing.

Should one assume from the foregoing that group effectiveness improves as progression is made through the four stages? While some argue that effectiveness of work units increases at advanced stages,[4] it is not that simple. While this assumption may be generally true, what makes a group effective is a complex issue. Under some conditions, high levels of conflict are conducive to high group performance. So we might expect to find situations where groups in stage II outperform those in stages III or IV. Similarly, movement through stages is not always clear. Sometimes, in fact, several stages are going on simultaneously—as when groups are storming and performing at the same time. Groups even occasionally regress to previous stages. Therefore, to assume that this developmental process is followed precisely by all groups or that stage IV is always the most preferable is likely to prove incorrect. It is better to think of this four-stage model as a general framework. It reminds you that groups are dynamic entities and can help you to better understand the problems and issues that are most likely to surface during a group's life.

TOWARD EXPLAINING WORK GROUP BEHAVIOR

Why are some group efforts more successful than others? The answer to that question is complex, but it includes variables such as the ability of the group's members, the size of the group, level of conflict, and internal pressures on members to conform to the group's norms. Figure 8–2 presents the major components that determine group performance and satisfaction.[5] It can help you sort out the key variables and their interrelationships.

[4] L. N. Jewell and H. J. Reitz, *Group Effectiveness in Organizations* (Glenview, IL: Scott, Foresman, 1981).

[5] This model is substantially based on the work of P. S. Goodman, E. Ravlin, and M. Schminke, "Understanding Groups in Organizations," in L. L. Cummings and B. M. Staw (eds.), *Research in Organizational Behavior*, Vol. 9 (Greenwich, CT: JAI Press, 1987), pp. 124–28; and J. R. Hackman, "The Design of Work Teams," in J. W. Lorsch (ed.), *Handbook of Organizational Behavior* (Englewood Cliffs, NJ: Prentice Hall, 1987), pp. 315–42.

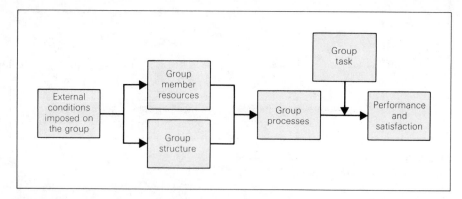

FIGURE 8–2
Group Behavior Model

Work groups don't exist in isolation. They are part of a larger organization. A design team in General Electric's appliance division, for instance, must live within the rules and policies dictated from the division's headquarters and GE's corporate offices. So every work group is influenced by external conditions imposed from outside it. The work group itself has a distinct set of resources determined by its membership. This includes things like intelligence and motivation of members. It also has an internal structure that defines member roles and norms. These factors—group member resources and structure—determine interaction patterns and other processes within the group. Finally, the group process-performance/satisfaction relationship is moderated by the type of task that the group is working on. In the following pages, we'll elaborate on each of the basic boxes identified in Figure 8–2.

EXTERNAL CONDITIONS IMPOSED ON THE GROUP

To begin understanding the behavior of a work group, you need to view it as a subsystem embedded in a larger system.[6] That is, when we realize that groups are a subset of a larger organization system, we can extract part of the explanation of the group's behavior from an explanation of the organization to which it belongs.

Organization Strategy

An organization has a strategy which defines what business it is in or wants to be in, and the kind of organization it is or wants to be. It is set by top management,

---

[6] F. Friedlander, "The Ecology of Work Groups," in J. W. Lorsch (ed.) *Handbook of Organizational Behavior*, pp. 301–14.

often in collaboration with lower-level managers. Strategy outlines the organization's goals and the means for attaining these goals. It might, for example, direct the organization toward reducing costs, improving quality, expanding market share, or shrinking the size of its overall operations. The strategy that an organization is pursuing, at any given time, will influence the power of various work groups which, in turn, will determine the resources that the organization's top management is willing to allocate to it for performing its tasks. To illustrate, an organization that is retrenching through selling off or closing down major parts of its business is going to have work groups with a shrinking resource base, increased member anxiety, and the potential for heightened intragroup conflict.[7]

Authority Structures

Organizations have authority structures that define who reports to whom, who makes decisions, and what decisions individuals or groups are empowered to make. This structure typically determines where a given work group is placed in the organization's hierarchy, the formal leader of the group, and formal relationships between groups. So while a work group might be led by someone who emerges informally from within the group, the formally designated leader—appointed by management—has authority that others in the group don't.

Formal Regulations

Organizations create rules, procedures, policies, and other forms of regulations to standardize employee behavior. If McDonald's has standard operating procedures for taking orders, cooking hamburgers, and filling soda containers, the discretion of work group members to set independent standards of behavior is severely limited. The more formal regulations that the organization imposes on all its employees, the more the behavior of work group members will be consistent and predictable.

Organizational Resources

Some organizations are large, profitable, with an abundance of resources. Their employees, for instance, will have modern and high quality tools and equipment to do their job. Other organizations aren't as fortunate. When organizations have limited resources, so do their work groups. What a group actually accomplishes is, to a large degree, determined by what it is capable of accomplishing. The presence or absence of resources such as money, time, raw materials, equipment—which are allocated to the group by the organization—have a large bearing on the group's behavior.

[7] See, for example, J. Krantz, "Group Processes under Conditions of Organizational Decline," *The Journal of Applied Behavioral Science*, Vol. 21, No. 1, 1985, pp. 1–17.

Personnel Selection Process

Members of any work group are first members of the organization of which the group is a part. Members of a cost-reduction task force at Boeing first had to be hired as employees of the company. So the criteria that an organization uses in its selection process will determine the kinds of people that will be in its work groups.

The selection factor becomes even more critical if a large segment of the organization's employees are unionized. In such cases, the terms of the union's collective bargaining contract will play a key part in specifying who is hired as well as acceptable and unacceptable behaviors of work group members.

Performance Evaluation and Reward System

Another organization-wide variable that affects all employees is the performance evaluation and reward system.[8] Does the organization provide employees with challenging, specific performance objectives? Does the organization reward the accomplishment of individual or group objectives? Since work groups are part of the larger organizational system, group members' behavior will be influenced by how the organization evaluates performance and what behaviors are rewarded.

Organizational Culture

Every organization has an unwritten culture that defines for employees standards of acceptable and unacceptable behavior. After a few months, most employees understand their organization's culture. They know things like how to dress for work, whether rules are rigidly enforced, what kinds of questionable behaviors are sure to get them into trouble and which are likely to be overlooked, the importance of honesty and integrity, and the like. While many organizations have subcultures—often created around work groups—with an additional or modified set of standards, they still have a dominant culture which conveys to all employees those values the organization holds dearest. Members of work groups have to accept the standards implied in the organization's dominant culture if they are to remain in good standing.

Physical Work Setting

Finally, we propose that the physical work setting that is imposed on the group by external parties has an important bearing on work group behavior.[9] Architects, industrial engineers, and office designers make decisions regarding the size and physical layout of an employee's work space, the arrangement of equipment, illumination levels, and the need for acoustics to cut down on noise distractions.

---

[8] J. R. Hackman, "The Design of Work Teams," pp. 325–26.

[9] See, for instance, G. R. Oldham and Y. Fried, "Employee Reactions to Workspace Characteristics," *Journal of Applied Psychology*, February 1987, pp. 75–80.

These create both barriers and opportunities for work group interaction. It's obviously a lot easier for employees to talk or "goof off" if their work stations are close together, there are no physical barriers between them, and their supervisor is in an enclosed office fifty yards away.

GROUP MEMBER RESOURCES

A group's potential level of performance is, to a large extent, dependent on the resources that its members individually bring to the group. In this section, we want to look at two resources that have received the greatest amount of attention: abilities and personality characteristics.

Abilities

Part of a group's performance can be predicted by assessing the task-relevant and intellectual abilities of its individual members. Sure, it's true that we occasionally read about the athletic team composed of mediocre players who, because of excellent coaching, determination, and precision teamwork, beat a far more talented group of players. But such cases make the news precisely because they represent an aberration. As the old saying goes, "The race doesn't always go to the swiftest nor the battle to the strongest, but that's the way to bet." Group performance is not merely the summation of its individual members' abilities. However, these abilities set parameters for what members can do and how effectively they will perform in a group.

What predictions can we make regarding ability and group performance? First, evidence indicates that individuals who hold crucial abilities for attaining the group's task tend to be more involved in group activity, generally contribute more, are more likely to emerge as the group leader, and are more satisfied if their talents are effectively utilized by the group.[10] Second, intellectual ability and task-relevant ability have both been found to be related to overall group performance. However, the correlation is not particularly high, suggesting that other factors such as the size of the group, the type of tasks being performed, the actions of its leader, and level of conflict within the group also influence performance.[11]

Personality Characteristics

There has been a great deal of research on the relationship between personality traits and group attitudes and behavior. The general conclusion is that attributes that tend to have a positive connotation in our culture tend to be positively

[10] A. D. Szilagyi, Jr. and M. J. Wallace, Jr., *Organizational Behavior and Performance*, 4th ed. (Glenview, IL: Scott, Foresman, 1987), p. 223.
[11] Ibid.

related to group productivity, morale, and cohesiveness. These include traits such as sociability, self-reliance, and independence. In contrast, negatively evaluated characteristics such as authoritarianism, dominance, and unconventionality tend to be negatively related to the dependent variables.[12] These personality traits affect group performance by strongly influencing how the individual will interact with other group members.

Is any one personality characteristic a good predictor of group behavior? The answer is "No." The magnitude of the effect of any *single* characteristic is small, but taken *together*, the consequences for group behavior are of major significance. We can conclude, therefore, that personality characteristics of group members play an important part in determining behavior in groups.

GROUP STRUCTURE

Work groups are not unorganized mobs. They have a structure which shapes the behavior of members and makes it possible to explain and predict a large portion of individual behavior within the group as well as the performance of the group itself. What are some of these structural variables? They include formal leadership, roles, norms, group size, and composition of the group.

Formal Leadership

Almost every work group has a formal leader. He or she is typically identified by titles such as unit or department manager, supervisor, foreman, project leader, task force head, committee chair, or the like. This leader can play an important part in the group's success; so much so, in fact, that we have devoted an entire chapter to the topic of leadership (see Chapter 10). As a sort of "coming attraction," let's highlight a few of the things we know about leadership and group performance.

Studies that have examined the effects of leader traits on group performance have generally provided inconclusive results. Far more promising findings have surfaced when situational variables, like the task structure in the jobs and characteristics of followers, have been used as moderating variables. In terms of achieving high group satisfaction, participative leadership seems to be more effective than an autocratic style. But participation doesn't necessarily lead to higher performance. In some situations, the group guided by a directive, autocratic leader will outperform its participative counterpart. The bulk of research studies in recent years have been focused on trying to identify the contingency variables associated with leader success. That is, *when* should a leader be democratic and *when* should a leader be autocratic? As previously noted, we'll provide some answers for you in Chapter 10.

---

[12] M. E. Shaw, *Contemporary Topics in Social Psychology* (Morristown, NJ: General Learning Press, 1976), pp. 350–51.

Roles

Shakespeare said, "All the world's a stage, and all the men and women merely players." Using the same metaphor, all group members are actors, each playing a **role**. By this term, we mean a set of expected behavior patterns attributed to someone occupying a given position in a social unit. The understanding of role behavior would be dramatically simplified if each of us chose one role and "played it out" regularly and consistently. Unfortunately, we are required to play a number of diverse roles, both on and off our jobs. As we shall see, one of the tasks in understanding behavior is grasping the role that a person is currently playing.

For example, on his job, Bill Patterson is a plant manager with Electrical Industries, a large electrical equipment manufacturer in Phoenix. He has a number of roles that he fulfills on that job—for instance, Electrical Industries employee, member of middle management, electrical engineer, and the primary company spokesperson in the community. Off the job, Bill Patterson finds himself in still more roles: husband, father, Catholic, Rotarian, tennis player, member of the Thunderbird Country Club, and president of his homeowners' association. Many of these roles are compatible; some create conflicts. For instance, how does his religious involvement influence his managerial decisions regarding layoffs, expense account padding, or providing accurate information to government agencies? A recent offer of promotion requires Bill to relocate, yet his family very much wants to stay in Phoenix. Can the role demands of his job be reconciled with the demands of husband and father roles?

The issue should be clear: Like Bill Patterson, we all are required to play a number of roles, and our behavior varies with the role we are playing. Bill's behavior when he attends church on Sunday morning is different from his behavior on the golf course later that same day. So different groups impose different role requirements on individuals.

Role Identity   There are certain attitudes and actual behaviors consistent with a role, and they create the **role identity**. People have the ability to shift roles rapidly when they recognize that the situation and its demands clearly require major changes. For instance, when union stewards were promoted to supervisory positions, it was found that their attitudes changed from pro-union to pro-management within a few months of their promotion. When these promotions had to be rescinded later because of economic difficulties in the firm, it was found that the demoted supervisors had once again adopted their pro-union attitudes.[13]

When the situation is more vague and the role one is to play less clear, people often revert to old role identities. An investigation of high school reunions verified this view.[14] At the reunions studied, even though participants had been away from high school and their peers for five, ten, or twenty or more years, they reverted back to their old roles. The "ins" replayed their former roles,

Role

A set of expected behavior patterns attributed to someone occupying a given position in a social unit.

Role identity

Certain attitudes and behaviors consistent with a role.

---

[13] S. Lieberman, "The Effects of Changes in Roles on the Attitudes of Role Occupants," *Human Relations*, November 1956, pp. 385–402.

[14] R. Keyes, *Is There Life After High School?* (New York: Warner Books, 1976).

as did the "outs." Even though entirely new criteria were being used in the real world for success, the former "jocks," student officers, and the cheerleaders acted as "ins" and the others expected them to. Despite the fact that some of the former losers were now winners by society's standards, they found it very difficult to deal with the winner's role when placed in an environment in which they had always been losers. With the role requirements ill-defined, identities became clouded, and individuals reverted back to old patterns of behavior.

Role perception

An individual's view of how he or she is supposed to act in a given situation.

Role Perception One's view of how one is supposed to act in a given situation is a **role perception**. Based on an interpretation of how we believe we are supposed to behave, we engage in certain types of behavior.

Where do we get these perceptions? We get them from stimuli all around us—friends, books, movies, television. Undoubtedly many of today's young surgeons formed their role identities from their perception of Hawkeye on "M.A.S.H.," while college instructors may be emulating the character of Professor Kingsfield in *The Paper Chase*. It also seems reasonable to conclude that many current police officers learned their roles from "Hill Street Blues" and "Miami Vice," and tomorrow's lawyers will have been influenced by "L.A. Law." Of course, the primary reason that apprenticeship programs exist in many trades and professions is to allow individuals to watch an "expert" so they can learn to act as they are supposed to.

Role expectations

How others believe a person should act in a given situation.

Role Expectations **Role expectations** are defined as how others believe you should act in a given situation. How you behave is determined, to a large part, by the role defined in the context in which you are acting. The role of a U.S. senator is viewed as having propriety and dignity, whereas a football coach is seen as aggressive, dynamic, and inspiring to his players. In the same context, we might be surprised to learn that the neighborhood priest moonlights during the week as a bartender, because our role expectations of priests and bartenders tend to be considerably different. When role expectations are concentrated into generalized categories, we have role stereotypes.

During the last several decades we have seen a major change in the general population's role stereotypes of females. In the 1950s, a woman's role was to stay home, take care of the house, raise children, and generally care for her husband. Today, most of us no longer hold this stereotype. Boys *can* play with Barbie Dolls and girls *can* play with G.I. Joes. Girls can aspire to be doctors, lawyers, and astronauts as well as the more traditional careers of nurse, school teacher, secretary, or housewife. In other words, many of us have changed our role expectations of women, and, similarly, many women carry new role perceptions.

Psychological contract

An unwritten agreement that sets out what management expects from the employee, and vice versa.

In the workplace, it can be helpful to look at the topic of role expectations through the perspective of the **psychological contract**. There is an unwritten agreement that exists between employees and their employer. This psychological contract sets out mutual expectations—what management expects from workers, and vice versa.[15] In effect, this contract defines the behavioral expectations that go with every role. Management is expected to treat employees justly,

[15] H. G. Baker, "The Unwritten Contract: Job Perceptions," *Personnel Journal*, July 1985, pp. 37–41.

provide acceptable working conditions, clearly communicate what is a fair day's work, and give feedback on how well the employee is doing. Employees are expected to respond by demonstrating a good attitude, following directions, and showing loyalty to the organization.

What happens when role expectations as implied in the psychological contract are not met? If management is derelict in keeping up its part of the bargain, we can expect negative repercussions on employee performance and satisfaction. When employees fail to live up to expectations, the result is usually some form of disciplinary action up to and including firing.

The psychological contract should be recognized as a "powerful determiner of behavior in organizations."[16] It points out the importance of accurately communicating role expectations. In Chapter 15, we shall discuss how organizations socialize employees in order to get them to play out their roles in the way management desires.

Role Conflict   When an individual is confronted by divergent role expectations, the result is **role conflict**. It exists when an individual finds that compliance with one role requirement may make more difficult the compliance with another. At the extreme it would include situations in which two or more role expectations are mutually contradictory.

Role conflict

A situation in which an individual is confronted by divergent role expectations.

Many believe that the topic of role conflict is the most critical role concept in attempting to explain behavior.[17] This, for example, is one of the classic problems of college presidents, a fact which became highly evident in the late 1960s. The college president is forced to reconcile diverse role expectations by faculty, students, board members, alumni, and other administrators. The behavior expectations that are perceived as acceptable by one group are often totally in disagreement with the expectations of other groups.[18]

Our previous discussion of the many roles Bill Patterson had to deal with included several role conflicts—for instance, Bill's attempt to reconcile the expectations placed on him as head of his family and as an executive with Electrical Industries. The former emphasizes stability and concern for the desire of his wife and children, as you will remember, to remain in Phoenix. Electrical Industries, on the other hand, expects its employees to be responsive to the needs and requirements of the company. Although it might be in Bill's financial and career interests to accept a relocation, the conflict comes down to choosing between family and career role expectations.

The issue of ethics in business demonstrates a well-publicized area of role conflict among corporate executives. For example, one study found that 57 percent of *Harvard Business Review* readers had experienced the dilemma of having to choose between what was profitable for their firms and what was ethical.[19]

---

[16] E. H. Schein, *Organizational Psychology*, 3rd ed. (Englewood Cliffs, NJ: Prentice Hall, 1980), p. 24.

[17] See, for instance, S. E. Jackson and R. S. Schuler, "A Meta-Analysis and Conceptual Critique of Research on Role Ambiguity and Role Conflict in Work Settings," *Organizational Behavior and Human Decision Processes*, August 1985, pp. 16–78.

[18] S. P. Robbins, *Positional Authority of Selected College and University Presidents as Perceived by Their Interacting Publics*, doctoral dissertation, University of Arizona, Tucson, 1971.

[19] S. N. Brenner and E. A. Molander, "Is the Ethics of Business Changing?" *Harvard Business Review*, January-February 1977, pp. 57–71.

All of us have faced and will continue to face role conflicts. The critical issue, from our standpoint, is how conflicts, imposed by divergent expectations within the organization, impact on behavior. Certainly they increase internal tension and frustration. There are a number of behavioral responses one may engage in. For example, one can give a formalized bureaucratic response. The conflict is then resolved by relying on the rules, regulations, and procedures that govern organizational activities. For example, a worker faced with the conflicting requirements imposed by the corporate controller's office and his own plant manager decides in favor of his immediate boss—the plant manager. Similarly, many college professors create a formal environment in class by calling their students "Mr." and "Ms.," and expecting to be called "Professor"— to avoid allowing friendships to interfere with the objective requirements of the professorial role. Other behavioral responses may include withdrawal, stalling, negotiation or, as we found in our discussion of dissonance in Chapter 5, redefining the facts or the situation to make them appear congruent.

An Experiment: Zimbardo's Simulated Prison   One of the more illuminating role experiments was done by Stanford University psychologist Philip Zimbardo and his associates.[20] They created a "prison" in the basement of the Stanford psychology building; hired at $15 a day two dozen emotionally stable, physically healthy, law-abiding students who scored "normal average" on extensive personality tests; randomly assigned them the role of either "guard" or "prisoner"; and established some basic rules. The experimenters then stood back to see what would happen.

At the start of the planned two-week simulation, there were no measurable differences between those individuals assigned to be guards and those chosen to be prisoners. Additionally, the guards received no special training in how to be prison guards. They were told only to "maintain law and order" in the prison and not to take any nonsense from the prisoners: Physical violence was forbidden. To simulate further the realities of prison life, the prisoners were allowed visits from relatives and friends, but while the mock guards worked eight-hour shifts, the mock prisoners were kept in their cells around the clock and were allowed out only for meals, exercise, toilet privileges, head count lineups, and work details.

It took the "prisoners" little time to accept the authority positions of the guards or the mock guards to adjust to their new authority roles. After the guards crushed a rebellion attempt on the second day, the prisoners became increasingly passive. Whatever the guards "dished out," the prisoners took. The prisoners actually began to believe and act as if they were, as the guards constantly reminded them, inferior and powerless. And every guard, at some time during the simulation, engaged in abusive, authoritative behavior. For example, one guard said, "I was surprised at myself . . . I made them call each other names and clean the toilets out with their bare hands. I practically considered the prisoners cattle, and I kept thinking: 'I have to watch out for them in case they try something.' " Another guard added, "I was tired of seeing the prisoners in their rags and smelling the strong odors of their bodies that filled the cells. I watched them tear at each other on orders given by us. They

[20] P. G. Zimbardo, C. Haney, W. C. Banks, and D. Jaffe, "The Mind Is a Formidable Jailer: A Pirandellian Prison," *The New York Times*, April 8, 1973, pp. 38–60.

didn't see it as an experiment. It was real and they were fighting to keep their identity. But we were always there to show them who was boss."

The simulation actually proved *too* successful in demonstrating how quickly individuals learn new roles. The researchers had to stop the experiment after only six days because of the pathological reactions that the participants were demonstrating. And remember, these were individuals chosen precisely for their normalcy and emotional stability.

What should you conclude from this prison simulation? The participants in this prison simulation had, like the rest of us, learned stereotyped conceptions of guard and prisoner roles from the mass media and their own personal experiences in power and powerlessness relationships gained at home (parent-child), in school (teacher-student), and in other situations. This, then, allowed them easily and rapidly to assume roles that were very different from their inherent personalities. In this case, we saw that people with no prior personality pathology or training in their roles could execute extreme forms of behavior consistent with the roles they were playing.

Norms

Did you ever notice that golfers don't speak while their partners are putting on the green or that employees don't criticize their boss in public? This is because of "**norms.**"

All groups have established norms, that is, acceptable standards of behavior that are shared by the group's members. Norms tell members what they ought or ought not to do under certain circumstances. From an individual's standpoint, they tell what is expected of you in certain situations. When agreed to and accepted by the group, norms act as a means of influencing the behavior of group members with a minimum of external controls. Norms differ among groups, communities, and societies, but they all have them.

Formalized norms are written up in organizational manuals, setting out rules and procedures for employees to follow. By far, the majority of norms in organizations are informal. You do not need someone to tell you that throwing paper airplanes or engaging in prolonged gossip sessions at the water cooler are unacceptable behaviors when the "big boss from New York" is touring the office. Similarly, we all know that when we are in an employment interview discussing what we did not like about our previous job, there are certain things we should not talk about (difficulty in getting along with co-workers or our supervisor), while it is very appropriate to talk about other things (inadequate opportunities for advancement or unimportant and meaningless work). Evidence suggests that even high school students recognize that in such interviews certain answers are more socially desirable than others.[21]

Students learn how to quickly assimilate classroom norms. Depending upon the environment created by the instructor, the norms may support unequivocal acceptance of the material suggested by the instructor, or, at the other extreme, students may be expected to question and challenge the instructor

Norms

Acceptable standards of behavior within a group that are shared by the group's members.

---

[21] A. Harlan, J. Kerr, and S. Kerr, "Preference for Motivator and Hygiene Factors in a Hypothetical Interview Situation: Further Findings and Some Implications for the Employment Interview," *Personnel Psychology*, Winter 1977, pp. 557–66.

on any point that is unclear. For example, in most classroom situations, the norms dictate that one not engage in loud, boisterous discussion that makes it impossible to hear the lecturer or humiliate the instructor by pushing him or her "too far," even if one has obviously located a weakness in something the instructor has said. Should some in the classroom group behave in such a way as to violate these norms, we can expect pressure to be applied against the deviant members so as to bring their behavior into conformity with group standards.

The Hawthorne Studies   It is generally agreed among behavioral scientists that full-scale appreciation of the importance norms play in influencing worker behavior did not occur until the early 1930s. This enlightenment grew out of a study undertaken at Western Electric Company's Hawthorne Works in Chicago between 1927 and 1932.[22] Conducted under the direction of Harvard psychologist Elton Mayo, the Hawthorne studies concluded that a worker's behavior and sentiments were closely related, that group influences were significant in affecting individual behavior, that group standards were highly effective in establishing individual worker output, and that money was less a factor in determining worker output than group standards, sentiments, and security. Let us briefly review the Hawthorne investigations and demonstrate the importance of these findings in explaining group behavior.

The Hawthorne researchers began by examining the relation between the physical environment and productivity. Illumination, temperature, and other working conditions were selected to represent this physical environment. The researchers' initial findings contradicted their anticipated results.

They began with illumination experiments with various groups of workers. The researchers manipulated the intensity of illumination upward and downward, while at the same time noting changes in group output. Results varied, but one thing was clear: In no case was the increase or decrease in output in proportion to the increase or decrease in illumination. So the researchers introduced a control group: An experimental group was presented with varying intensity of illumination, while the controlled unit worked under a constant illumination intensity. Again, the results were bewildering to the Hawthorne researchers. As the light level was increased in the experimental unit, output rose for each group. But to the surprise of the researchers, as the light level was dropped in the experimental group, productivity continued to increase in both. In fact, a productivity decrease was observed in the experimental group only when the light intensity had been reduced to that of moonlight. Mayo and his associates concluded that illumination intensity was only a minor influence among the many influences that affected an employee's productivity, but they could not explain the behavior they had witnessed.

As a follow-up to the illumination experiments, the researchers began a second set of experiments in the relay assembly test room at Western Electric. A small group of women was isolated from the main work group so that their behavior could be more carefully observed. They went about their job of assembling small telephone relays in a room laid out similar to their normal depart-

[22] Much of this description was adapted from "The Hawthorne Studies: A Synopsis," reported in E. L. Cass and F. G. Zimmer (eds.), *Man and Work in Society* (New York: Van Nostrand Reinhold, 1975), pp. 278–306.

ment. The only difference was the placement in the room of a research assistant who acted as an observer—keeping records of output, rejects, working conditions, and a daily log sheet describing everything that happened. Over a two-and-a-half-year period, this small group's output increased steadily as did its morale. The number of personal absences and those due to sickness were approximately one-third of those recorded by women in the regular production department. What became evident was that this group's performance was significantly influenced by its status of being a "special" group. The women in the test room thought that being in the experimental group was fun, that they were in sort of an elite group, and that management was concerned with their interest by engaging in such experimentation.

A third experiment in the bank wiring observation room was similar in design to the experiment in the relay test room, except that male workers were used. Additionally, a sophisticated wage incentive plan was introduced on the assumption that individual workers will maximize their productivity when they see that it is directly related to economic rewards. The most important finding coming out of this experiment was that employees did not individually maximize their outputs. Rather, their output became controlled by a group norm that determined what was a proper day's work. Output was not only being restricted, but individual workers were giving erroneous reports. The total for a week would check with the total week's output, but the daily reports showed a steady, level output regardless of actual daily production. What was going on?

Interviews determined that the group was operating well below its capability and was leveling output in order to protect itself. Members were afraid that if they significantly increased their output, the unit incentive rate would be cut, the expected daily output would be increased, layoffs might occur, or slower men would be reprimanded. So the group established its idea of a fair output—neither too much nor too little. They helped each other out to ensure that their reports were nearly level.

The norms that the group established included a number of "don'ts." *Don't* be a rate-buster, turning out too much work. *Don't* be a chiseler, turning out too little work. *Don't* be a squealer on any of your peers.

How did the group enforce these norms? Their methods were neither gentle nor subtle. They included sarcasm, name calling, ridicule, and even physical punches to the upper arm of members who violated the group's norms. Members would also ostracize individuals whose behavior was against the group's interest.

The Hawthorne studies made an important contribution to our understanding of group behavior—particularly the significant place that norms have in determining individual work behavior.

Common Classes of Norms   A work group's norms are like an individual's fingerprints—each is unique. Yet there are still some common classes of norms that appear in most work groups.[23]

Probably the most widespread norms deal with *performance-related processes*. Work groups typically provide their members with explicit cues on

[23] Adapted from P. S. Goodman, E. C. Ravlin, and M. Schminke, "Understanding Groups in Organizations," p. 159.

how hard they should work, how to get the job done, their level of output, appropriate communication channels, and the like. These norms are extremely powerful in affecting an individual employee's performance—they are capable of significantly modifying a performance prediction that was based solely on the employee's ability and level of personal motivation.

A second category of norms encompasses *appearance factors*. This includes things like appropriate dress attire, loyalty to the work group or organization, when to look busy, and when it's acceptable to goof off. Some organizations have formal dress codes. However, even in their absence, norms frequently develop to dictate the kind of clothing that should be worn to work. College seniors, interviewing for their first postgraduate job, pick up this norm quickly. Every spring on college campuses throughout the country, you can usually spot those interviewing for jobs—they're the ones walking around in the dark gray or blue pinstriped suits. They are enacting the dress norms they have learned are expected in professional positions. Presenting the appearance of loyalty is important in many work groups and organizations. For instance, in many organizations, especially among professional employees and those in the executive ranks, it is considered inappropriate to be openly looking for another job. This concern for demonstrating loyalty, incidentally, often explains why ambitious aspirants to top management positions in an organization willingly take work home at night, come in on weekends, and accept transfers to cities they would otherwise not prefer to live in.

Another class of norms concerns *informal social arrangements*. These norms come from informal work groups and primarily regulate social interactions within the group. With whom group members eat lunch, friendships on and off the job, social games, and the like are influenced by these norms. Many of the games and social patterns that Mayo and his associates found at the Hawthorne Works plant were dictated by informal social arrangement norms.

A final category of norms relates to *allocation of resources*. These norms can originate in the group or in the organization and cover things like pay, assignment of difficult jobs, and allocation of new tools and equipment. In some organizations, for example, new personal computers are distributed equally to all groups. So every department might get five, regardless of the number of people in the department or their need for the computers. In another organization, equipment is allocated to those groups who can make the best use of it. So some departments might get twenty computers and some none. These resource allocation norms can have a direct impact on employee satisfaction and an indirect effect on group performance.

The "How" and "Why" of Norms   *How* do norms develop? *Why* are they enforced? A review of the research allows us to answer these questions.[24]

Norms typically develop gradually as group members learn what behaviors are necessary for the group to function effectively. Of course, critical events in the group might short-circuit the process and act quickly to solidify new norms. Most norms develop in one or more of the following four ways: (1) *Explicit statements made by a group member*—often the group's supervisor or a powerful member. The group leader might, for instance, specifically say

---

[24] D. C. Feldman, "The Development and Enforcement of Group Norms," *Academy of Management Journal*, January 1984, pp. 47–53.

that no personal phone calls are allowed during working hours or that coffee breaks are to be kept to ten minutes. (2) *Critical events in the group's history.* These set important precedents. A bystander is injured while standing too close to a machine, and, from that point on, members of the work group regularly monitor each other to ensure that no one other than the operator gets within five feet of any machine. (3) *Primacy.* The first behavior pattern that emerges in a group frequently sets group expectations. Friendship groups of students often stake out seats near each other on the first day of class and become perturbed if an outsider takes "their" seats in a later class. (4) *Carry-over behaviors from past situations.* Group members bring expectations with them from other groups of which they have been members. This can explain why work groups typically prefer to add new members who are similar to current ones in background and experience. This is likely to increase the probability that the expectations they bring are consistent with those already held by the group.

But groups do not establish or enforce norms for every conceivable situation. The norms that the group will enforce tend to be those that are important to it. But what makes a norm important? (1) *If it facilitates the group survival.* Groups don't like to fail, so they look to enforce those norms that increase their chances for success. This means that they will try to protect themselves from interference from other groups or individuals. (2) *If it increases the predictability of group members' behaviors.* Norms that increase predictability enable group members to anticipate each other's actions and to prepare appropriate responses. (3) *If it reduces embarrassing interpersonal problems for group members.* Norms are important if they ensure the satisfaction of their members and prevent as much interpersonal discomfort as possible. (4) *If it allows members to express the central values of the group and clarify what is distinctive about the group's identity.* Norms that encourage expression of the group's values and distinctive identity help to solidify and maintain the group.

Conformity   As a member of a group, you desire acceptance by the group. Because of your desire for acceptance, you are susceptible to **conforming** to the group's norms. There is considerable evidence that groups can place strong pressures on individual members to change their attitudes and behaviors to conform to the group's standard.[25]

Conformity

Adjusting one's behavior to align with the norms of the group.

Do individuals conform to the pressures of all the groups they belong to? Obviously not, because people belong to many groups and their norms vary. In some cases, they may even have contradictory norms. So what do people do? They conform to the important groups to which they belong or hope to belong. The important groups have been referred to as *reference* groups and are characterized as ones where the person is aware of the others, the person defines himself or herself as a member, or would like to be a member, and the person feels that the group members are significant to him or her.[26] The implication, then, is that *all* groups do not impose equal conformity pressures on their members.

The impact that group pressures for conformity can have on an individual

[25] C. A. Kiesler and S. B. Kiesler, *Conformity* (Reading, MA: Addison-Wesley, 1969).
[26] Ibid., p. 27.

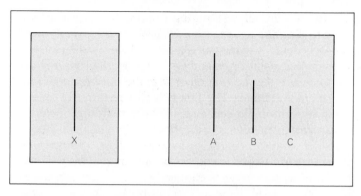

FIGURE 8–3
Examples of Cards Used in Asch Study

member's judgment and attitudes was demonstrated in the now classic studies by Solomon Asch.[27] Asch made up groups of seven or eight people, who sat in a classroom and were asked to compare two cards held by the experimenter. One card had one line, the other had three lines of varying length. As shown in Figure 8–3, one of the lines on the three-line card was identical to the line on the one-line card. Also, as shown in Figure 8–3, the difference in line length was quite obvious; under ordinary conditions, subjects made fewer than 1 percent errors. The object was to announce aloud which of the three lines matched the single line. But what happens if all the members in the group begin to give incorrect answers? Will the pressures to conform result in an unsuspecting subject (USS) altering his or her answer to align with the others? That was what Asch wanted to know. So he arranged the group so only the USS was unaware that the experiment was "fixed." The seating was prearranged: The USS was placed so as to be the last to announce his or her decision.

The experiment began with several sets of matching exercises. All the subjects gave the right answers. On the third set, however, the first subject would give an obviously wrong answer—for example, saying "C" in Figure 8–3. The next subject gave the same wrong answer, and so did the others until it got to the unknowing subject. He knew "B" was the same as "X," yet everyone had said "C." The decision confronting the USS is this: Do you state a perception publicly that differs from the preannounced position of the others? Or do you give an answer that you strongly believe is incorrect in order to have your response agree with the other group members?

The results obtained by Asch demonstrated that over many experiments and many trials, subjects conformed in about 35 percent of the trials; that is, the subjects gave answers that they knew were wrong but that were consistent with the replies of other group members.

What can we conclude from this study? The results suggest that there are group norms that press us toward conformity. We desire to be one of the group and avoid being visibly different. We can generalize further to say that when an individual's opinion of objective data differs significantly from that of

[27] S. E. Asch, "Effects of Group Pressure upon the Modification and Distortion of Judgments," in H. Guetzkow (ed.), *Groups, Leadership and Men* (Pittsburgh: Carnegie Press, 1951), pp. 177–90.

others in the group, he or she feels extensive pressure to align his or her opinions to conform with that of the others.

Size

Does the size of a group affect the group's overall behavior? The answer to this question is a definite "Yes," but the effect depends on what dependent variables you look at.[28]

The evidence indicates, for instance, that smaller groups are faster at completing tasks than are larger ones. However, if the group is engaged in problem solving, large groups consistently get better marks than their smaller counterparts. Translating these results into specific numbers is a bit more hazardous, but we can offer some parameters. Large groups—with a dozen or more members—are good for gaining diverse input. So if the goal of the group is fact-finding, larger groups should be more effective. On the other hand, smaller groups are better at doing something productive with that input. Groups of approximately seven members, therefore, tend to be more effective for taking action.

One of the most important findings related to the size of a group has been labeled **social loafing**. It directly challenges the logic that the productivity of the group as a whole should at least equal the sum of the productivity of each individual in that group.

Social loafing

Group size and individual performance are inversely related.

$$2 + 2 = 3$$

A common stereotype about groups is that the sense of team spirit spurs individual effort and enhances the group's overall productivity. In the late 1920s, a German psychologist named Ringelmann compared the results of individual and group performance on a rope-pulling task.[29] He expected that the group's effort would be equal to the sum of the efforts of individuals within the group. That is, three people pulling together should exert three times as much pull on the rope as one person, and eight people should exert eight times as much pull. Ringelmann's results, however, did not confirm his expectations. Groups of three people exerted a force only two-and-a-half times the average individual performance. Groups of eight collectively achieved less than four times the solo rate.

Replications of Ringelmann's research with similar tasks have generally supported his findings.[30] Increases in group size are inversely related to individual performance. More may be better in the sense that the total productivity of a group of four is greater than one or two, but the individual productivity of each group member declines.

What causes this social loafing effect? It may be due to a belief that others

---

[28] E. J. Thomas and C. F. Fink, "Effects of Group Size," *Psychological Bulletin*, July 1963, pp. 371–84; A. P. Hare, *Handbook of Small Group Research* (New York: Free Press, 1976); and M. E. Shaw, *Group Dynamics: The Psychology of Small Group Behavior*, 3rd ed. (New York: McGraw-Hill, 1981).

[29] W. Moede, "Die Richtlinien der Leistungs-Psychologie," *Industrielle Psychotechnik*, Vol. 4 (1927), pp. 193–207.

[30] See, for example, G. Jones, "Task Visibility, Free Riding, and Shirking: Explaining the Effect of Structure and Technology on Employee Behavior," *Academy of Management Review*, October 1984, pp. 684–95; and R. Albanese and D. D. Van Fleet, "Rational Behavior in Groups: The Free-Riding Tendency," *Academy of Management Review*, April 1985, pp. 244–55.

in the group are not pulling their own weight. If you see others as lazy or inept, you can reestablish equity by reducing your effort. Another explanation is the dispersion of responsibility. Because the results of the group cannot be attributed to any single person, the relationship between an individual's input and the group's output is clouded. In such situations, individuals may be tempted to become "free riders" and coast on the group's efforts. In other words, there will be a reduction in efficiency where individuals think that their contribution cannot be measured.

The implications for OB of this effect on work groups are significant. Where managers utilize collective work situations to enhance morale and teamwork, they must also provide means by which individual efforts can be identified. If this is not done, management must weigh the potential losses in productivity against any possible gains in worker satisfaction.[31]

The research on group size also leads us to two additional conclusions: (1) Groups with an odd number of members tend to be preferred over those with an even number, and (2) groups made up of five or seven members do a pretty good job of extracting the best elements of both small and large groups.[32] The preference of an odd number of members eliminates the possibility of ties. Groups made up of five or seven members are large enough to form a majority and allow for diverse input yet avoid the negative outcomes often associated with large groups, such as domination by a few members, development of subgroups, inhibited participation by some members, and excessive time taken to reach a decision.

Composition

Most group activities require a variety of skills and knowledge. Given this requirement, it would be reasonable to conclude that heterogeneous groups—those composed of dissimilar individuals—would be more likely to have diverse abilities and information and should be more effective. Research studies substantiate this conclusion.[33]

When a group is heterogeneous in terms of personality, opinions, abilities, skills, and perspectives, there is an increased probability that the group will possess the needed characteristics to complete its tasks effectively.[34] The group may be more conflict-laden and less expedient as diverse positions are introduced and assimilated, but the evidence generally supports the conclusion that heterogeneous groups perform more effectively than do those that are homogeneous.

A more specific offshoot of the composition issue has recently received

[31] B. Latane, K. Williams, and S. Harkins, "Social Loafing," *Psychology Today*, October 1979, p. 110.

[32] Thomas and Fink, "Effects of Group Size"; Hare, *Handbook*; Shaw, *Group Dyanmics*; and P. Yetton and P. Bottger, "The Relationships Among Group Size, Member Ability, Social Decision Schemes, and Performance," *Organizational Behavior and Human Performance*, October 1983, pp. 145–59.

[33] See, for example, P. S. Goodman, E. C. Ravlin, and L. Argote, "Current Thinking about Groups: Setting the Stage for New Ideas," in P. S. Goodman and Associates, *Designing Effective Work Groups* (San Francisco: Jossey-Bass, 1986), pp. 15–16.

[34] Shaw, *Contemporary Topics*, p. 356.

a great deal of attention by group researchers. This is the degree to which members of a group share a common demographic attribute such as age, sex, race, educational level, or length of service in the organization and the impact of these attributes on turnover. We'll call this variable "**group demography**."[35]

We discussed individual demographic factors in Chapter 3. Here we consider the same type of factors but in a group context—that is, it is not whether a person is male or female, or has been employed with the organization a year rather than ten years. What now becomes our focus of attention is the individual's attribute in relationship to the others with whom he or she works. Let's work through the logic of group demography, review the evidence, and then consider the implications.

Groups and organizations are composed of **cohorts**, which we define as individuals who hold a common attribute. For instance, everyone in a group born in 1960 is of the same age. This means they also have shared common experiences. People born in 1960 have experienced the women's movement but not the Korean conflict. People born in 1945 shared the Vietnam War but not the Great Depression. Women in organizations today who were born prior to 1945 matured prior to the women's movement and have substantially different experiences from women born after 1960. Group demography, therefore, suggests that such attributes as age or the date that someone joins a specific work group or organization should help us to predict turnover. How would this occur? Essentially the logic would go like this: Turnover will be greater among those with dissimilar experiences because communication is more difficult; conflict and power struggles more likely, and more severe when they occur. The increased conflict makes group membership less attractive, so employees are more likely to quit. Similarly, the losers in a power struggle are more apt to leave voluntarily or be forced out.

Several studies have sought to test this thesis, and the evidence is quite encouraging.[36] For example, in departments or separate work groups where a large portion of members entered at the same time, there is considerably more turnover among those outside this cohort. Also, where there are large gaps between cohorts, turnover is higher. People who enter together or at approximately the same time are more likely to associate with one another, have a similar perspective of the group or organization, and thus are more likely to stay. On the other hand, discontinuities or bulges in the group's date-of-entry distribution is likely to result in a higher turnover rate within that group.

The implications from this line of inquiry is that the composition of a group may be an important predictor of turnover. Differences, per se, may not predict turnover. But large differences in similarity within a single group will lead to turnover. If everyone is moderately dissimilar from everyone else in a group, the feelings of being an outsider are reduced. So, it's the degree of dispersion on an attribute, rather than the level, that matters most. We can speculate that variance within a group in respect to other attributes, such as

Group demography

The degree to which members of a group share a common demographic attribute such as age, sex, race, educational level, or length of service in the organization, and the impact of these attributes on turnover.

Cohorts

Individuals who, as part of a group, hold a common attribute.

---

[35] This term is adapted from J. Pfeffer, "Organizational Demography: Implications for Management," *California Management Review*, Fall 1985, pp. 67–81.

[36] B. E. McCain, C. A. O'Reilly III, and J. Pfeffer, "The Effects of Departmental Demography on Turnover: The Case of a University," *Academy of Management Journal*, December 1983, pp. 626–41; and W. G. Wagner, J. Pfeffer, and C. A. O'Reilly III, "Organizational Demography and Turnover in Top-Management Groups," *Administrative Science Quarterly*, March 1984, pp. 74–92.

social background, sex differences, or levels of education, might similarly create discontinuities or bulges in the distribution that will encourage some members to leave. To extend this even farther, the fact that a group member is a female, in itself, may mean little in predicting turnover. In fact, if the work group is made up of ten members, nine of which are women, we'd be more likely to predict that the lone male would leave. In the executive ranks of organizations, where females are the minority, we would predict this minority status to increase the likelihood that female managers would quit.

GROUP PROCESSES

The next component in our group behavior model considers the processes that go on within a work group—the communication patterns used by members to exchange information, group discussion processes, leader behavior, power dynamics, conflict interactions, and the like. Chapters 9 through 12 elaborate on many of these processes.

Why are processes important to understanding work group behavior? One way to answer this question is to return to the topic of social loafing. We found that one-plus-one-plus-one doesn't necessarily add up to three. In group tasks where the visibility of each member's contribution is unclear, there is a tendency for individuals to decrease their effort. Social loafing, in other words, illustrates a process loss as a result of using groups. But group processes can also produce positive results. That is, groups can create outputs greater than the sum of their inputs. Figure 8–4 illustrates how group processes can impact on a group's actual effectiveness.

Synergy is a term used in biology that refers to an action of two or more substances which results in an effect that is different from the individual summation of the substances. We can use the concept to better understand group processes.

Social loafing, for instance, represents negative synergy. The whole is *less* than the sum of the parts. Research teams, on the other hand, are often used in research laboratories, because they can pull on the diverse skills of various individuals to produce more meaningful research as a group than could be generated by each of the researchers working independently. That is, they produce positive synergy. Their process gains exceed their process losses.

Synergy

An action of two or more substances which results in an effect that is different from the individual summation of the substances.

$1 + 1 = 3$

FIGURE 8–4
Effects of Group Processes

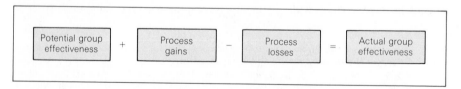

Imagine, for a moment, that there are two groups at a major oil company. The job of the first is to consider possible location sites for a new refinery. The decision is going to affect people in many areas of the company—production, engineering, marketing, distribution, personnel, purchasing, real estate development, and the like—so key people from each of these areas will need to provide input into the decision. The job of the second group is to coordinate the building of the refinery after the site has been selected, the design finalized, and the financial arrangements completed. Research on group effectiveness tells us that management would be well advised to use a larger group for the first task than for the second.[37] The reason is that large groups facilitate pooling of information. The addition of a diverse perspective to a problem-solving committee typically results in a process gain. But when a group's task is coordinating and implementing a decision, the process loss created by each additional member's presence is likely to be greater than the process gain he or she makes. So the size-performance relationship is moderated by the group's task requirements.

The preceding conclusions can be extended: The impact of group processes on the group's performance and member satisfaction is also moderated by the tasks that the group is doing. The evidence indicates that the complexity and interdependence of tasks influence the group's effectiveness.[38] Tasks can be generalized to be either simple or complex. Complex tasks are ones that tend to be novel or nonroutine. Simple ones are routine and standardized. We would hypothesize that the more complex the task, the more the group will benefit from discussion among members on alternative work methods. If the task is simple, group members don't need to discuss such alternatives. They can rely on standardized operating procedures for doing the job. Similarly, if there is a high degree of interdependence among the tasks that group members must perform, they'll need to interact more. Effective communication and minimal levels of conflict, therefore, should be more relevant to group performance when tasks are interdependent.

These conclusions are consistent with what we know about information-processing capacity and uncertainty.[39] Tasks that have higher uncertainty (which are those that are complex and interdependent) require more information processing. This, in turn, puts more importance on group processes. So just because a group is characterized by poor communication, weak leadership, high levels of conflict, and the like, does not necessarily mean that it will be low-performing. If the group's tasks are simple and require little interdependence among members, the group still may be effective.

[37] V. F. Nieva, E. A. Fleishman, and A. Rieck, "Team Dimensions: Their Identity, Their Measurement, and Their Relationships." Final Technical Report for Contract No. DAHC 19-C-0001. Washington, D.C.: Advanced Research Resources Organizations, 1978.

[38] See, for example, J. R. Hackman and C. G. Morris, "Group Tasks, Group Interaction Process and Group Performance Effectiveness: A Review and Proposed Integration," in L. Berkowitz (ed.), *Advances in Experimental Social Psychology* (New York: Academic Press, 1975), pp. 45–99.

[39] J. Galbraith, *Organizational Design* (Reading, MA: Addison-Wesley, 1977).

OB Close-Up

Office Automation and Work Groups

New computer programs may soon change the way groups of people work together.[40] Software, or what more aptly might be called **groupware,** will enable employees to collaborate across barriers of space and time to revolutionize the way people interact at work and, very importantly, to improve group productivity.

What does the future hold? Linked desktop terminals running the new software will coordinate schedules and route messages. New products will emerge as teams of employees share databases and interact from their computer work stations. Managers will confer with subordinates, peers, superiors, suppliers, and customers via computer networks. Meetings will take place among employees thousands of miles apart, with computer software guiding discussion and keeping the meeting on track. And to insure that misunderstandings are minimized, cameras connected to computers will record and store conversations.

How many years away is this groupware? A number of software programs to facilitate group effectiveness are already here. For example, a product called Coordinator is based on the assumption that business is essentially a set of action-oriented conversations such as requests, offers, counteroffers, and promises. The program lets a user compose a message on a personal computer, assign it to a conversation category, and transmit it via standard telephone lines to other users. The system then tracks every user's conversations, reminds each of his or her pending commitments, and keeps records of the status of group projects.

SHOULD MANAGEMENT SEEK COHESIVE GROUPS?

Cohesiveness

Degree to which group members are attracted to each other and share common goals.

It is often implied that effective work groups are cohesive. In this section we want to determine whether **cohesiveness,** as a group characteristic, is desirable. More specifically, should management actively seek to create work groups that are highly cohesive?

Intuitively, it would appear that groups in which there is a lot of internal disagreement and a lack of cooperative spirit would be relatively less effective in completing their tasks than would groups in which individuals generally agree and cooperate and where members like each other. Research to test this intuition has focused on the concept of group cohesiveness, defined as the degree to which members are attracted to one another and share the group's goals. That is, the more that members are attracted to each other and the more that the group's goals align with their individual goals, the greater

[40] L. S. Richman, "Software Catches the Team Spirit," *Fortune*, June 8, 1987, pp. 125–36.

the group's cohesiveness. In the following pages, we'll review the factors that have been found to influence group cohesiveness and then look at the effect of cohesiveness on group productivity.[41]

Determinants of Cohesiveness

What factors determine whether group members will be attracted to one another? Cohesiveness can be affected by such factors as time spent together, the severity of initiation, group size, external threats, and previous successes.

Time Spent Together   If you rarely get an opportunity to see or interact with other people, you're unlikely to be attracted to them. The amount of time that people spend together, therefore, influences cohesiveness. As people spend more time together, they become more friendly. They naturally begin to talk, respond, gesture, and engage in other interactions. These interactions typically lead to the discovery of common interests and increased attraction.[42]

The opportunity for group members to spend time together is dependent on their physical proximity. We would expect more close relationships among members who are located close to one another rather than far apart. People who live on the same block, ride the same car pool, or share a common office are more likely to become a cohesive group because the physical distance between them is minimal. For instance, among clerical workers in one organization it was found that the distance between their desks was the single most important determinant of the rate of interaction between any two of the clerks.[43]

Severity of Initiation   The more difficult it is to get into a group, the more cohesive that group becomes. The hazing through which fraternities typically put their pledges is meant to screen out those who don't want to "pay the price" and to intensify the desire of those who do to become fraternity actives. But group initiation needn't be as blatant as hazing. The competition to be accepted to a good medical school results in first-year medical school classes that are highly cohesive. The common initiation rites—applications, test taking, interviews, and the long wait for a final decision—all contribute to creating this cohesiveness. Similarly, the months or often years that an apprentice trade worker must put in to developing his or her skills before being advanced to journeyman status results in union journeymen generally being a cohesive group.

Group Size   If group cohesiveness tends to increase with the time members are able to spend together, it seems logical that cohesiveness should decrease as group size increases, since it becomes more difficult for a member to interact

Groupware

Computer software programs that allow employees to collaborate across barriers of space and time.

[41] For an excellent review of the group cohesiveness literature, see A. J. Lott and B. E. Lott, "Group Cohesiveness as Interpersonal Attraction: A Review of Relationships with Antecedent and Consequent Variables," October 1965, pp. 259–309.

[42] C. Insko and M. Wilson, "Interpersonal Attraction as a Function of Social Interaction," *Journal of Personality and Social Psychology*, December 1977, pp. 903–11.

[43] J. T. Gullahorn, "Distance and Friendship as Factors in the Gross Interaction Matrix," *Sociometry*, February–March 1952, pp. 123–34.

with all the members. This is generally what the research indicates.[44] As group size expands, interaction with all members becomes more difficult, as does the ability to maintain a common goal. Not surprisingly, too, as a single group's size increases, the likelihood of cliques forming also increases. The creation of groups within groups tends to decrease overall cohesiveness.

Evidence suggests that these size-cohesiveness conclusions may be moderated by the gender of the group members.[45] In experiments comparing groups of four and sixteen members, some made up of males only, some with females only, and others mixed, the small groups proved to be more cohesive than large ones as long as all the members were of the same sex. But when the groups were made up of both males and females, the larger groups were more cohesive. Members of both sexes liked the mixed groups more than the single-sex groups, and apparently the opportunity to interact with a larger set of both sexes increased cohesiveness. While it is dangerous to generalize from this study, we should nevertheless be aware of the possible moderating effect of sex on the size-cohesiveness relationship, especially nowadays as the work force becomes more equally divided between males and females.

External Threats   Most of the research supports the proposition that a group's cohesiveness will increase if the group comes under attack from external sources.[46] Management threats frequently bring together an otherwise disarrayed union. Efforts by management to redesign unilaterally even one or two jobs or to discipline one or two employees occasionally grab local headlines when the entire work force walks out in support of the abused few. These examples illustrate a cooperative phenomenon that can develop within a group when it is attacked from outside.

While a group generally moves toward greater cohesiveness when threatened by external agents, this does not occur under all conditions. If group members perceive that their group may not meet an attack well, then the group becomes less important as a source of security, and cohesiveness will not necessarily increase. Additionally, if members believe the attack is directed at the group merely because of its existence and that it will cease if the group is abandoned or broken up, there is likely to be a decrease in cohesiveness.[47]

Previous Successes   If a group has a history of previous successes, it builds an esprit de corps that attracts and unites members. Successful firms find it easier to attract and hire new employees. The same holds true for successful research groups, well-known and prestigious universities, and winning athletic teams. When Bill Bowerman was head track coach at the University of Oregon during the 1960s, he never had trouble attracting the country's top track and field athletes to his campus. The best athletes wanted to come to Oregon

[44] E. J. Thomas and C. F. Fink, "Effects of Group Size," *Psychological Bulletin*, July 1963, pp. 371–84.

[45] L. Libo, *Measuring Group Cohesiveness* (Ann Arbor: University of Michigan, Institute of Social Research, 1953).

[46] A. Stein, "Conflict and Cohesion: A Review of the Literature," *Journal of Conflict Resolution*, March 1976, pp. 143–72.

[47] A. Zander, "The Psychology of Group Processes," in M. R. Rosenzweig and L. W. Porter (eds.), *Annual Review of Psychology*, Vol 30 (Palo Alto, CA: Annual Reviews, 1979), p. 436.

because of Bowerman's highly successful program. In fact, Bowerman claims to never have initiated contact with an athlete. In contrast to track coaches at other major universities, if an athlete wanted to compete at Oregon, he had to prove genuine interest by taking the first step. Continuing with another university example, if you harbor ambitions of attending a top-quality graduate school of business, you should recognize that the success of these schools attracts large numbers of aspiring candidates—many have twenty or more applicants for every vacancy.

Effects of Cohesiveness on Group Productivity

The previous section indicates that, generally speaking, group cohesiveness is increased when members spend time together and undergo a severe initiation, when the group size is small, when external threats exist, and when the group has a history of previous successes. But is increased cohesiveness always desirable from the point of view of management? Is it related to increased productivity?

Research has generally shown that highly cohesive groups are more effective than those with less cohesiveness,[48] but the relationship is more complex than merely allowing us to say high cohesiveness is good. First, high cohesiveness is both a cause and outcome of high productivity. Second, the relationship is moderated by performance-related norms.

Cohesiveness influences productivity and productivity influences cohesiveness. Camaraderie reduces tension and provides a supportive environment for the successful attainment of group goals. But as already noted, the successful attainment of group goals, and the members' feelings of having been a part of a successful unit, can serve to enhance the commitment of members. Basketball coaches, for example, are famous for their endearment of teamwork. They believe that if the team is going to win games, members have to learn to play together. Popular coaching phrases include, "There are no individuals on this team" and "We win together, or we lose together." The other side of this view, however, is that winning reinforces camaraderie and leads to increased cohesiveness; that is, successful performance leads to increased intermember attractiveness and sharing.

More important has been the recognition that the relationship of cohesiveness and productivity depends on the performance-related norms established by the group.[49] The more cohesive the group, the more its members will follow its goals. If performance-related norms are high (for example, high output, quality work, cooperation with individuals outside the group), a cohesive group will be more productive than a less cohesive group. But if cohesiveness is high and performance norms are low, productivity will be low. If cohesiveness is low and performance norms are positive, productivity increases but less than in the high cohesiveness-high norms situation. Where cohesiveness and performance-related norms are both low, productivity will tend to fall into the low-to-moderate range. These conclusions are summarized in Figure 8–5.

[48] See, for example, L. Berkowitz, "Group Standards, Cohesiveness, and Productivity," *Human Relations*, November 1954, pp. 509–19.
[49] Nieva, Fleishman, and Rieck, "Team Dimensions," p. 17.

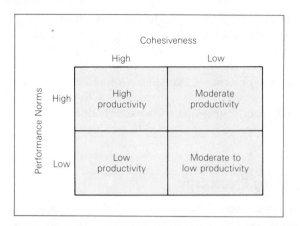

FIGURE 8–5
Relationship Between Group Cohesiveness,
Performance Norms, and Productivity

We've covered a lot of territory in this chapter. Since we essentially organized our discussion around the group behavior model in Figure 8–2, let's use this model to draw our conclusions regarding performance and satisfaction.

Performance

Any predictions about a group's performance must begin by recognizing that work groups are part of a larger organization and that factors like the organization's strategy, authority structure, selection procedures, and reward system can provide a favorable or unfavorable climate for the group to operate within. For example, if an organization is characterized by distrust between management and workers, it is more likely that work groups in that organization would develop norms to restrict effort and output than in an organization where trust is high. So don't look at any group in isolation. Rather, begin by assessing the degree of support external conditions provide the group. It is obviously a lot easier for any work group to be productive when the overall organization of which it is a part is growing, and it has both top management's support and abundant resources. Similarly, a group is more likely to be productive when its members have the requisite skills to do the group's tasks and the personality characteristics that facilitate working well together.

A number of structural factors show a relationship to performance. Among the more prominent are role perception, norms, the size of the group, and its demographic makeup.

There is a positive relationship between role perception and an employee's performance evaluation.[50] The degree of congruence that exists between an employee and his or her boss, in the perception of the employee's job, influences the degree to which that employee will be judged as an effective performer by the boss. To the extent that the employee's role perception fulfills the boss's role expectation, the employee will receive a higher performance evaluation.

Norms control group member behavior by establishing standards of right or wrong. If we know the norms of a given group, it can help us to explain the behaviors of its members. Where norms support high output, we can expect individual performance to be markedly higher than where group norms aim to restrict output. Similarly, acceptable standards of absence will be dictated by the group norms.

The impact of size on a group's performance depends upon the type of task in which the group is engaged. Larger groups are more effective in fact-finding activities. Smaller groups are more effective in action-taking tasks. Our knowledge of social loafing suggests that if management uses larger groups, efforts should be made to provide measures of individual performance within the group.

We found the group's demographic composition to be a key determinant of individual turnover. Specifically, the evidence indicates that group members who share a common age or date of entry into the work group are less prone to resign.

The primary contingency variable moderating the relationship between group processes and performance is the group's task. The more complex and interdependent the tasks, the more that inefficient processes will lead to reduced group performance.

Finally, we found that cohesiveness can play an important function in influencing a group's level of productivity. Whether or not it does depends on the group's performance-related norms.

Satisfaction

As with the role perception-performance relationship, high congruence between a boss and employee, as to the perception of the employee's job, shows a significant association with high employee satisfaction.[51] Similarly, role conflict is associated with job-induced tension and job dissatisfaction.[52]

The group size-satisfaction relationship is what one would intuitively expect: Larger groups are associated with lower satisfaction.[53] As size increases,

[50] T. P. Verney, "Role Perception Congruence, Performance, and Satisfaction," in D. J. Vredenburgh and R. S. Schuler (eds.), *Effective Management: Research and Application*, Proceedings of the 20th Annual Eastern Academy of Management, Pittsburgh, PA, May 1983, pp. 24–27.

[51] Ibid.

[52] M. Van Sell, A. P. Brief, and R. S. Schuler, "Role Conflict and Role Ambiguity: Integration of the Literature and Directions for Future Research," *Human Relations*, January 1981, pp. 43–71; and A. G. Bedeian and A. A. Armenakis, "A Path-Analytic Study of the Consequences of Role Conflict and Ambiguity," *Academy of Management Journal*, June 1981, pp. 417–24.

[53] Thomas and Fink, "Effects of Group Size"; Hare, *Handbook*; and Shaw, *Group Dynamics*.

opportunities for participation and social interaction decrease, as does the ability for members to identify with the group's accomplishments. At the same time, having more members also prompts dissension, conflict, and the formation of subgroups, which all act to make the group a less pleasant entity to be a part of.

Finally, we can make a set of predictions regarding both performance and satisfaction based on the impact of task as a moderating variable and research on the job characteristics model discussed in the previous chapter. A group can be expected to work especially hard on its tasks and members of that group are likely to be satisfied with their work when: (a) the group task requires members to use a variety of relatively high-level skills; (b) the group task is a whole and meaningful piece of work, with a visible outcome; (c) the outcomes of the group's work on the task have significant consequences for other people either inside or outside the organization; (d) the task provides group members with substantial autonomy for deciding about how they do the work; and (e) work on the task generates regular, trustworthy feedback about how well the group is performing.[54]

[54] J. R. Hackman, "The Design of Work Teams," p. 324.

POINT

DESIGNING JOBS AROUND GROUPS

It's time to take small groups seriously; that is, to use groups, rather than individuals, as the basic building blocks for an organization. I propose that we can design organizations from scratch around small groups rather than the way we have always done it—around individuals.

Why would management want to do such a thing? At least seven reasons can be identified. First, small groups seem to be good for people. They can satisfy important membership needs. They can provide a moderately wide range of activities for individual members. They can provide support in times of stress and crisis. They are settings in which people can learn not only cognitively but empirically to be reasonably trusting and helpful to one another. Second, groups seem to be good problem-finding tools. They seem to be useful in promoting innovation and creativity. Third, in a wide variety of decision situations, they make better decisions than individuals do. Fourth, they are great tools for implementation. They gain commitment from their members so that group decisions are likely to be willingly carried out. Fifth, they can control and discipline individual members in ways that are often extremely difficult through impersonal quasilegal disciplinary systems. Sixth, as organizations grow large, small groups appear to be useful mechanisms for fending off many of the negative effects of large size. They help to prevent communication lines from growing too long, the hierarchy from growing too steep, and the individual from getting lost in the crowd. There is also a seventh, but altogether different, kind of argument for taking groups seriously. Groups are natural phenomena, and facts of organizational life. They can be created, but their spontaneous development cannot be prevented.

Operationally, how would an organization function that was designed around groups? One answer to this question is merely to take the things that organizations do with individuals and apply them with groups. The idea would be to raise the level from the atom to the molecule and *select* groups rather than individuals, *train* groups rather than individuals, *pay* groups rather than individuals, *promote* groups rather than individuals, *design* jobs for groups rather than for individuals, *fire* groups rather than individuals, and so on down the list of activities that organizations have traditionally carried on in order to use human beings in their organizations.

In the past, the human group has been primarily used for patching and mending organizations that were built around the individual. The time is rapidly approaching, and it may already be here, for management to begin redesigning organizations around groups.

Adapted from H. J. Leavitt, "Suppose We Took Groups Seriously," in E. L. Cass and F. G. Zimmer (eds.), *Man and Work in Society* (New York: Van Nostrand Reinhold, 1975), pp. 67–77.

COUNTERPOINT
JOBS SHOULD BE DESIGNED AROUND INDIVIDUALS

The argument that organizations can and should be designed around groups might hold in a socialistic society, but not in the United States. The following response directly relates to the United States and American workers, although it is probably generalizable to other economically advanced capitalistic countries. In fact, given China's and Russia's recent successes in isolated experiments with profit-motivated businesses, the case for the individually oriented organization may be applicable throughout the world.

America was built on the individual ethic. This ethic has been pounded into us from birth. The result is that it is deeply embedded in the psyche of every American. We strongly value individual achievement. We praise competition. Even in team sports, we want to identify individuals for recognition. Sure, we enjoy group interaction. We like being part of a team, especially a winning team. But it is one thing to be a member of a work group while maintaining a strong individual identity and another to sublimate your identity to that of the group. The latter is inconsistent with the values of American life.

The American worker likes a clear link between his or her individual effort and a visible outcome. It is not happenstance that the United States, as a nation, has a considerably larger proportion of high achievers than exists in socialistic countries. America breeds achievers, and achievers seek personal responsibility. They would be frustrated in job situations where their contribution is commingled and homogenized with the contributions of others.

Americans want to be hired based on their individual talents. They want to be evaluated on their individual efforts. They also want to be rewarded with pay raises and promotions based on their individual performance. Americans believe in an authority and status hierarchy. They accept a system where there are bosses and subordinates. They are not likely to accept a group's decision on such issues as their job assignments and wage increases.

One of the more interesting illustrations of America's commitment to the individualistic ethic is research that has assessed the public's views on the American tax structure. We'd expect the rich to favor low tax rates on individuals with high incomes—$60,000 a year or more. But studies consistently find that Americans below the government's defined "poverty level" also strongly favor lower tax rates for high-income earners. A reasonable interpretation of these findings is that there is a very strong belief, held across the full range of economic levels, that anyone can make it in America. And when they make it, they don't want to be saddled with a heavy tax burden! Isn't this consistent with the stereotype of the individualistic American, motivated by his or her self-interest? Yes! Is this a worker who would be satisfied, and reach his or her full productive capacity, in a group-centered organization? Not likely!

KEY TERMS

Cohesiveness

Cohorts

Command Group

Conformity

Formal Group

Friendship Group

Group

Group Demography

Groupware

Informal Group

Interest Group

Norms

Psychological Contract

Role

Role Conflict

Role Expectations

Role Identity

Role Perception

Social Loafing

Synergy

Task Group

FOR DISCUSSION

1. Compare and contrast command, task, interest, and friendship groups.

2. What might motivate you to join a group?

3. How could you use the four-stage group development model to better understand group behavior?

4. What is the relationship between a work group and the organization of which it is a part?

5. Identify five roles you play. What behaviors do they require? Are any of these roles in conflict? If so, in what way? How do you resolve these conflicts?

6. How would it help you to know that a woman has to reconcile her roles of mother, Methodist, Democrat, Councilwoman, and warden of the Michigan State Penitentiary for Women?

7. What is the relationship between the psychological contract and role expectations?

8. Describe the Hawthorne studies. What is the importance of this research to understanding group behavior?

9. How do norms develop?

10. How can a group's demography help you to predict turnover?

11. What factors influence the degree to which group members will be attracted to each other?

12. "High cohesiveness in a group leads to higher group productivity." Do you agree or disagree? Explain.

FOR FURTHER READING

GIST, M. E., E. A. LOCKE, and M. S. TAYLOR, "Organizational Behavior: Group Structure, Process, and Effectiveness," *Journal of Management*, Summer 1987, pp. 237–57. Examines the role of groups in the organization, especially inputs such as group structure, strategies, leadership, and reward allocation to members.

GLADSTEIN, D. L., "Groups in Context: A Model of Task Group Effectiveness," *Administrative Science Quarterly*, December 1984, pp. 499–517. Tests a comprehensive model of group effectiveness with sales teams and finds that traditional theories account for 90 percent of the variance in team satisfaction and self-reported effectiveness, but none of the variance in the teams' sales performance.

GOODMAN, P. S. (ed.), *Designing Effective Work Groups*. San Francisco: Jossey-Bass, 1986. A collection of eleven articles that provides a fresh perspective on designing, managing, and maintaining more productive work groups.

KRACKHARDT, D., and L. W. PORTER, "When Friends Leave: A Structural Analysis of the Relationship Between Turnover and Attitudes," *Administrative Science Quarterly*, June 1985, pp. 242–61. Additional insights into the group demography phenomenon.

McGRATH, J. C., *Groups: Interaction and Performance*. Englewood Cliffs, NJ: Prentice Hall, 1984. Comprehensive review of the literature on different types of groups.

ZANDER, A., *Making Groups Effective*. San Francisco: Jossey-Bass, 1982. Summarizes how to make groups effective, by one of the founders of group dynamics.

GROUP EFFECTIVENESS CHECKLIST

The following twenty items provide a checklist for you to use in describing the effectiveness of a group or groups to which you belong. If you have been using groups to do role plays, cases, or other exercises in your OB class, use one of these groups as your point of reference.

	Mostly Yes	Mostly No
1. The atmosphere is relaxed and comfortable.		
2. Group discussion is frequent, and it is usually pertinent to the task at hand.		
3. Group members understand what they are trying to accomplish.		
4. People listen to each others' suggestions and ideas.		
5. Disagreements are tolerated and an attempt is made to resolve them.		
6. There is general agreement on most courses of action taken.		
7. The group welcomes frank criticism from inside and outside sources.		
8. When the group takes action, clear assignments are made and accepted.		
9. There is a well-established, relaxed working relationship among the members.		
10. There is a high degree of trust and confidence among the leader and subordinates.		
11. The group members strive hard to help the group achieve its goal.		
12. Suggestions and criticisms are offered and received with a helpful spirit.		
13. There is a cooperative rather than a competitive relationship among group members.		
14. The group goals are set high but not so high as to create anxieties or fear of failure.		
15. The leaders and members hold a high opinion of the group's capabilities.		
16. Creativity is stimulated within the group.		
17. There is ample communication within the group of topics relevant to getting the work accomplished.		
18. Group members feel confident in making decisions.		
19. People are kept busy but not overloaded.		
20. The leader of the group is well suited for the job.		

Turn to page 563 for scoring directions and key.

Source: A. J. DuBrin, *Contemporary Applied Management*. Plano, TX: Business Publications, Inc., 1985, pp. 169–70. With permission.

CASE INCIDENT 8

GAMES PEOPLE PLAY IN THE SHIPPING DEPARTMENT

The Science Fiction Book Club (SFBC) sells a large list of science fiction books, at discount prices, entirely by mail order. In 1988, the club shipped over 370,000 books and generated revenues of $5.4 million. Anyone familiar with the mail-order business realizes that it offers extremely high profit potential because, under careful management, inventory costs and overhead can be kept quite low. The biggest problems in mail-order businesses are filling orders, shipping the merchandise, and billing the customers. At SFBC, the Packing and Shipping (P&S) Department employs eight full-time people:

Ray, forty-four years old, has worked in P&S for seven years.

Al, forty-nine years old, has worked in P&S for nine years.

R. J., fifty-three years old, has worked in P&S for sixteen years. He had been head of the department for two years back in the late 1970s but stepped down voluntarily due to continuing stomach problems that doctors attributed to supervisory pressures.

Pearl, fifty-nine years old, was the original employee hired by the founder. She has been at SFBC for twenty-five years and in P&S for twenty-one years.

Margaret, thirty-one years old, is the newest member of the department. She has been employed less than a year.

Steve, twenty-seven years old, has worked in P&S for three years. He goes to college at nights and makes no effort to hide that he plans on leaving P&S and probably SFBC when he gets his degree next year.

George, forty-six years old, is currently head of P&S. He has been with SFBC for ten years, and in P&S for six.

Gary, twenty-five years old, has worked in P&S for two years.

The jobs in a shipping department are uniformly dull and repetitive. Each person is responsible for wrapping, addressing, and making the bills out on anywhere from 100 to 200 books a day. Part of George's responsibilities are to make allocations to each worker and to ensure that no significant backlogs occur. However, George spends less than 10 percent of his time in supervisory activities. The rest of the time he wraps, addresses, and makes out bills just like everyone else.

Apparently to deal with the repetitiveness of their jobs, the department members have created a number of games that they play among themselves. They seem almost childish, but it is obvious that the games mean something to these people. Importantly, each is played regularly. Some

of the ones that will be described are played at least once a day. All are played a minimum of twice a week.

"The Stamp Machine Is Broken" is a game that belongs to Al. At least once a day, Al goes over to the postage meter in the office and unplugs it. He then proceeds loudly to attempt to make a stamp for a package. "The stamp machine is broken again," he yells. Either Ray or Gary, or both, will come over and spend thirty seconds or so trying to "fix it," then "discover" that it's unplugged. The one who finds it unplugged then says "Al, you're a mechanical spastic" and others in the office join in and laugh.

Gary is the initiator of the game "Steve, There's a Call for You." Usually played in the late afternoon, an hour or so before everyone goes home, Gary will pick up the phone and pretend that there is someone on the line. "Hey, Steve, it's for you," he'll yell out. "It's Mr. Big [the president of SFBC]. Says he wants you to come over to his office right away. You're going to be the new vice-president!" The game is an obvious sarcastic jab at Steve's going to college and his frequent comments about someday being a big executive.

At least two or three times a day, Ray will go out of his way to walk by Margaret's desk. As he walks by, he sensuously runs his hand down her back and blows in her ear. She always jumps, though she knows he's coming. Ray's desk is two ahead of Margaret's and to get behind her he has to walk by her. The irony of this little flirtatious game is that Margaret obviously loves the attention, though she always plays "upset" by Ray's actions. In fact, when Ray was on vacation for two weeks last month, everyone noticed how Margaret seemed depressed. Could she actually be missing Ray?

R. J., though fifty-three years old, has never married and lives with his mother. The main interests in his life are telling stories and showing pictures of last year's vacation and planning for this year's vacation. Without exception, everyone finds R. J.'s vacation talk boring. But that doesn't stop Pearl or George from "setting him up" several times a week. "Hey R. J., can we see those pictures you took last year in Oregon again?" That question always gets R. J. to drop whatever he's doing and pull 75 to 100 pictures from his top drawer. "Hey, R. J., what are you planning to do on your vacation this year?" always gets R. J.'s eyes shining and invariably leads to the unfolding of maps he also keeps in his top drawer.

George's favorite game is "What's It Like to Be Rich?" which he plays with Pearl. Pearl's husband had been a successful banker and had died a half-dozen years earlier. He left her very well off financially. Pearl enjoys everyone knowing that she doesn't have to work, has a large lovely home, buys a new car every year, and includes some of the city's more prominent business people and politicians among her friends. George will mention the name of some big shot in town and Pearl never fails to take the bait. She proceeds to tell how he is a close friend of hers. George might also bring up money in some context in order to allow Pearl to complain about high taxes, the difficulty in finding good housekeepers, the high cost of traveling to Europe, or some other concern of the affluent.

QUESTIONS

1. Analyze the group's interactions using the group behavior model.
2. How do these games affect the department's performance?
3. Are these games functional? Dysfunctional? Explain.

9

Communication and Group Decision Making

■ *Chapter outline*

■ *Learning objectives*

Describe the process of communication
Outline barriers to effective communication
Summarize techniques for overcoming the barriers
List the benefits and disadvantages of each communication network
Identify factors affecting the use of the grapevine
List the advantages and disadvantages to group decision making

Every improvement in communication makes the bore more terrible.

—— F. M. COLBY

Probably the most frequently cited source of interpersonal conflict is poor communication.[1] Because we spend nearly 70 percent of our waking hours communicating—writing, reading, speaking, listening—it seems reasonable to conclude that one of the most inhibiting forces to successful group performance is a lack of effective communication.

No group can exist without **communication**: the transference of meaning among its members. It is only through transmitting meaning from one person to another that information and ideas can be conveyed. Communication, however, is more than merely imparting meaning. It must also be understood. In a group where one member speaks only German and the others do not know German, the individual speaking German will not be fully understood. Therefore, communication must include both the *transference and understanding of meaning*.

An idea, no matter how great, is useless until it is transmitted and understood by others. Perfect communication, if there were such a thing, would exist when a thought or idea was transmitted so that the mental picture perceived by the receiver was exactly the same as that envisioned by the sender. Although elementary in theory, perfect communication is never achieved in practice, for reasons we shall expand upon later.

Before making too many generalizations concerning communication and problems in communicating effectively, we need to review briefly the functions that communication performs and describe the communication process.

Communication

The transference and understanding of meaning.

FUNCTIONS OF COMMUNICATION

Communication serves four major functions within a group or organization: control, motivation, emotional expression, and information.[2]

Communication acts to *control* member behavior in several ways. Organizations have authority hierarchies and formal guidelines that employees are required to follow. When employees, for instance, are required to first communi-

---

[1] See, for example, K. W. Thomas and W. H. Schmidt, "A Survey of Managerial Interests with Respect to Conflict," *Academy of Management Journal*, June 1976, p. 317.

[2] W. G. Scott and T. R. Mitchell, *Organization Theory: A Structural and Behavioral Analysis* (Homewood, IL: Richard D. Irwin, 1976).

cate any job-related grievance to their immediate boss, to follow their job description, or to comply with company policies, communication is performing a control function. But informal communication also controls behavior. The Hawthorne experiments, discussed in the previous chapter, showed how the group maintained control by communicating—sometimes very explicitly—the norms that were to be followed.

Communication fosters *motivation* by clarifying to employees what is to be done, how well they are doing, and what can be done to improve performance if it's subpar. We saw this operating in our review of goal-setting and reinforcement theories in Chapter 6. The formation of specific goals, feedback on progress toward the goals, and reinforcement of desired behavior all stimulate motivation and require communication.

For many employees, their work group is a primary source for social interaction. The communication that takes place within the group is a fundamental mechanism by which members show their frustrations and feelings of satisfaction. Communication, therefore, provides a release for the *emotional expression* of feelings and for fulfillment of social needs.

The final function that communication performs relates to its role in facilitating decision making. It provides the *information* that individuals and groups need to make decisions by transmitting the data to identify and evaluate alternative choices.

No one of these four functions should be seen as being more important than the others. For groups to perform effectively, they need to maintain some form of control over members, stimulate members to perform, provide a means for emotional expression, and make decision choices. You can assume that almost every communication interaction that takes place in a group or organization performs one or more of these four functions.

THE COMMUNICATION PROCESS

Communication process

The steps between a source and a receiver that result in the transference of meaning.

Communication can be thought of as a process or flow. Communication problems occur when there are deviations or blockages in that flow. In this section, we will describe the **process** in terms of a communication model and then consider how distortions can disrupt the process.

A Communication Model

Before communication can take place, a purpose, expressed as a message to be conveyed, is needed. It passes between a source (the sender) and a receiver. The message is encoded (converted to symbolic form) and is passed by way of some medium (channel) to the receiver, who retranslates (decodes) the message initiated by the sender. The result is a transference of meaning from one person to another.[3]

---

[3] D. K. Berlo, *The Process of Communication* (New York: Holt, Rinehart and Winston, 1960), pp. 30–32.

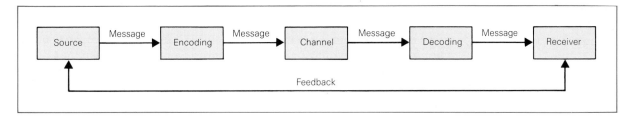

FIGURE 9–1
The Communication Process Model

Figure 9–1 depicts the communication process. This model is made up of seven parts: (1) the communication source, (2) encoding, (3) the message, (4) the channel, (5) decoding, (6) the receiver, and (7) feedback.

The source initiates a message by **encoding** a thought. Four conditions have been described that affect the encoded message: skill, attitudes, knowledge, and the social-cultural system.

Encoding
Converting a communication message to symbolic form.

My success in communicating to you is dependent upon my writing skills; in the writing of textbooks, if the authors are without the requisite skills, their messages will not reach students in the form desired. One's total communicative success includes speaking, reading, listening, and reasoning skills as well. As we discussed in Chapter 5, our attitudes influence our behavior. We hold predisposed ideas on numerous topics, and our communications are affected by these attitudes. Further, we are restricted in our communicative activity by the extent of our knowledge on the particular topic. We cannot communicate what we do not know, and should our knowledge be too extensive, it is possible that our receiver will not understand our message. Clearly, the amount of knowledge the source holds about his or her subject will affect the message he or she seeks to transfer. And, finally, just as attitudes influence our behavior, so does our position in the social-cultural system in which we exist. Your beliefs and values, all part of your culture, act to influence you as a communicative source.

The **message** is the actual physical product from the source encoding. "When we speak, the speech is the message. When we write, the writing is the message. When we paint, the picture is the message. When we gesture, the movements of our arms, the expressions on our face are the message."[4] Our message is affected by the code or group of symbols we use to transfer meaning, the content of the message itself, and the decisions that the source makes in selecting and arranging both codes and content.

Message
What is communicated.

The **channel** is the medium through which the message travels. It is selected by the source, who must determine which channel is formal and which one is informal. Formal channels are established by the organization and transmit messages that pertain to the job-related activities of members. They traditionally follow the authority network within the organization. Other forms of messages, such as personal or social, follow the informal channels in the organization.

Channel
The medium through which a communication message travels.

The receiver is the object to whom the message is directed. But before the message can be received, the symbols in it must be translated into a form

[4] Ibid., p. 54.

Decoding

Retranslating a sender's communication message.

that can be understood by the receiver. This is the **decoding** of the message. Just as the encoder was limited by his or her skills, attitudes, knowledge, and social-cultural system, so is the receiver equally restricted. Just as the source must be skillful in writing or speaking, the receiver must be skillful in reading or listening, and both must be able to reason. One's level of knowledge, attitudes, and cultural background influences one's ability to receive, just as it does the ability to send.

The final link in the communicative process is a **feedback loop**. "If a communication source decodes the message that he encodes, if the message is put back into his system, we have feedback."[5] Feedback is the check on how successful we have been in transferring our messages as originally intended. It determines whether understanding has been achieved.

Feedback loop

The final link in the communication process; puts the message back into the system as a check against misunderstandings.

Sources of Distortion

Unfortunately, most of the seven components in the process model have the potential to create distortion and, therefore, impinge upon the goal of communicating perfectly. These sources of distortion explain why the message that is decoded by the receiver is rarely the exact message that the sender intended.

If the encoding is done carelessly, the message decoded by the sender will have been distorted. The message itself can also cause distortion. The poor choice of symbols and confusion in the content of the message are frequent problem areas. Of course, the channel can distort a communication if a poor one is selected or if the noise level is high. The receiver represents the final potential source for distortion. His or her prejudices, knowledge, perceptual skills, attention span, and care in decoding are all factors that can result in interpreting the message somewhat differently than envisioned by the sender.

BARRIERS TO EFFECTIVE COMMUNICATION

We have noted the potential for distortion in the communication process. As illustrated in Table 9–1, what managers say can be different from what they mean and still different from a subordinate's interpretation. What causes such communication breakdown? In addition to the general distortions previously identified in the communication process, there are other barriers to effective communication of which you should be aware.

Filtering

Filtering

A sender's manipulation of information so that it will be seen more favorably by the receiver.

Filtering refers to a sender manipulating information so that it will be seen more favorably by the receiver. For example, when a manager tells his boss what he feels his boss wants to hear, he is filtering information. Does this

[5] Ibid., p. 103.

TABLE 9–1
How Communications Break Down

What the Manager Said	What the Manager Meant	What the Subordinate Heard
I'll look into hiring another person for your department as soon as I complete my budget review.	We'll start interviewing for that job in about three weeks.	I'm tied up with more important things. Let's forget about hiring for the indefinite future.
Your performance was below par last quarter. I really expected more out of you.	You're going to have to try harder, but I know you can do it.	If you screw up one more time, you're out.
I'd like that report as soon as you can get to it.	I need that report within the week.	Drop that rush order you're working on and fill out that report today.
I talked to the boss but at the present time, due to budget problems, we'll be unable to fully match your competitive salary offer.	We can give you 95 percent of that offer, and I know we'll be able to do even more for you next year.	If I were you, I'd take that competitive offer. We're certainly not going to pay that kind of salary to a person with your credentials.
We have a job opening in Los Angeles that we think would be just your cup of tea. We'd like you to go out there and look it over.	If you'd like that job, it's yours. If not, of course you can stay here in Denver. You be the judge.	You don't have to go out to L.A. if you don't want to. However, if you don't, you can kiss good-bye to your career with this firm.
Your people seem to be having some problems getting their work out on time. I want you to look into this situation and straighten it out.	Talk to your people and find out what the problem is. Then get with them and jointly solve it.	I don't care how many heads you bust, just get me that output. I've got enough problems around here without you screwing things up too.

Source: *Organizational Behavior: Theory and Practice* by S. Altman, E. Valenzi, and R. M. Hodgetts, copyright © 1985 by Harcourt Brace Jovanovich, Inc. Reproduced by permission of the publisher.

happen much in organizations? Sure! As information is passed up to senior executives, it has to be condensed and synthesized by underlings so those on top don't become overloaded with information. The personal interests and perceptions of what is important by those doing the synthesizing is going to result in filtering. As a former group vice-president of General Motors described it, the filtering of communications through levels at GM made it impossible for senior managers to get objective information because "lower-level specialists . . . provided information in such a way that they would get the answer they wanted. I know. I used to be down below and do it."[6]

The major determinant of filtering is the number of levels in an organiza-

[6]J. DeLorean, quoted in S. P. Robbins, *The Administrative Process* (Englewood Cliffs, NJ: Prentice Hall, 1976), p. 404.

tion's structure. The more vertical levels in the organization's hierarchy, the more opportunities there are for filtering.

Selective Perception

We have mentioned selective perception before in this book. It appears again because the receivers, in the communication process, selectively see and hear based on their needs, motivations, experience, background, and other personal characteristics. Receivers also project their interests and expectations into communications as they decode them. The employment interviewer who *expects* a female job applicant to put her family ahead of her career is likely to *see* that in female applicants, regardless of whether the applicants feel that way or not. As we said in Chapter 3, we don't see reality; rather, we interpret what we see and call it reality.

Emotions

How the receiver feels at the time of receipt of a communication message will influence how he or she interprets it. The same message received when you're angry or distraught is likely to be interpreted differently when you're in a neutral disposition. Extreme emotions—such as jubilation or depression— are most likely to hinder effective communication. In such instances, we are most prone to disregard our rational and objective thinking processes and substitute emotional judgments.

Language

Words mean different things to different people. "The meanings of words are *not* in the words; they are in us."[7] Age, education, and cultural background are three of the more obvious variables that influence the language a person uses and the definitions they give to words. The language of William F. Buckley, Jr., is clearly different from that of the typical high school-educated Burger King employee. The latter, in fact, would undoubtedly have trouble understanding much of Buckley's vocabulary (but then, so do a lot of people with graduate degrees!). The language problem, of course, goes both ways. Try your hand at the quiz in Table 9–2. If you are a black who was raised in an urban environment, you should be able to get ten or more of the items right. For rural whites, a score of three or four would be typical.

In an organization, employees usually come from diverse backgrounds. Additionally, the grouping of employees into departments creates specialists who develop their own jargon or technical language. In large organizations, members are also frequently widely dispersed geographically—even operating in different countries—and individuals in each locale will use terms and phrases that are unique to their area.

---

[7] S. I. Hayakawa, *Language in Thought and Action* (New York: Harcourt Brace Jovanovich, 1949), p. 292.

TABLE 9–2

Test Your Ability to Understand Black Street Language

What is:

1. Bad?	6. Hanging?	11. A natural?
2. A crib?	7. Humbuggin?	12. An oreo?
3. Fat-mouthing?	8. A jackleg?	13. Racking?
4. A fox?	9. Later?	14. A splib?
5. A grey-boy?	10. A Mack man?	15. Stepping?

ANSWERS: (1) Good, strong, or brave. (2) Where one lives; place of domicile. (3) Talking too much. (4) An attractive woman. (5) A white male. (6) Doing nothing. (7) Fighting. (8) An amateur. (9) Goodbye. (10) A pimp. (11) An Afro haircut. (12) A black person who thinks or acts like a white. (13) Studying. (14) A black person. (15) Dancing.

Source: Adapted from T. Kochman, " 'Rapping' in the Black Ghetto." *TransAction*, February 1969, pp. 26–34: *Rappin' and Stylin'Out: Communication in Urban Black America*, ed. T. Kochman (Urbana: University of Illinois Press, 1972); and W. Safire, "Getting Down," *The New York Times Magazine*, January 18, 1981, pp. 6, 8.

The existence of vertical levels can also cause language problems. For instance, differences in meaning with regard to words such as *incentives* and *quotas* have been found at different levels in management. Top managers often speak about the need for incentives and quotas, yet these terms imply manipulation and create resentment among many lower managers.

The point is that while you and I both speak a common language—English—our usage of that language is far from uniform. If we knew how each of us modified the language, communication difficulties would be minimized. The problem is that members in an organization usually don't know how others, with whom they interact, have modified the language. Senders tend to assume that the words and terms they use mean the same to the receiver as they do to them. This, of course, is often incorrect, thus creating communication difficulties.

OVERCOMING THE BARRIERS

Given that there are barriers to communication, what can individuals do to minimize problems and attempt to overcome these barriers? The following suggestions should be helpful in making communication more effective.

Use Feedback

Many communication problems can be attributed directly to misunderstandings and inaccuracies. These are less likely to occur if you ensure that the feedback loop is utilized in the communication process. We'll elaborate using verbal feedback as an illustration, but keep in mind that feedback can also be written or nonverbal.

If you ask a receiver, "Did you understand what I said?" the response to this question represents feedback. But the "yes" or "no" type of feedback can definitely be improved upon. A sender can ask a set of questions relating to the message in order to determine whether or not it was received as intended. Better yet, a sender can ask the receiver to restate the message, in his or her own words. If the sender then hears what was intended, understanding and accuracy should be enhanced. Feedback can also be more subtle than the direct asking of questions or the summarizing of the message by the receiver. General comments made by the receiver can give the sender a sense of the reaction to a message. Additionally, organizational processes and rewards—such as performance appraisals, salary reviews, job assignments, and promotion decisions—represent important, but more subtle, forms of feedback.

Simplify Language

Since language can be a barrier, the sender should seek to structure messages in ways that will make them clear and understandable. Words should be chosen carefully. The sender needs to simplify his or her language and consider the audience to whom a message is directed, so that the language will be compatible with the receiver. Remember, effective communication is achieved when a message is both received and *understood*. Understanding is improved by simplifying the language used in relation to the audience intended. This means, for example, that a hospital administrator should always try to communicate in clear and easily understood terms and that the language used for conveying messages to the surgical staff should be purposely different from that used with employees in the admissions office. Specialized vocabularies—jargon—can facilitate understanding when it is used with other group members who speak that "language," but it can cause innumerable problems when used outside that group. "Antecedent conditions," "beta weights," "single zero-order correlations," and "unstandardized regression coefficients" are examples of terms that facilitate communication among social scientists but are only likely to create confusion when used among those untrained in research and statistics.

Listen Actively

When someone talks, we hear. But, too often, we don't listen. Listening is an active search for meaning, whereas hearing is passive. When you listen, two people are thinking—the receiver and the sender.

Many of us are poor listeners, because listening is difficult and because it's usually more satisfying to be on the offensive. Listening, in fact, is often more tiring than talking. It demands intellectual effort. Unlike hearing, **active listening** demands total concentration. The average person speaks at a rate of about 150 words per minute, whereas we have the capacity to listen at the rate of over 1,000 words per minute. The difference creates idle brain time and opportunities for mind wandering.

Active listening is enhanced when the receiver develops empathy with the sender, that is, when the receiver tries to place himself or herself in the sender's position. Since senders differ in attitudes, interests, needs, and expectations, empathy makes it easier to understand the actual content of a message. An empathetic listener reserves judgment on the message's content and carefully

Active listening

The active search for meaning when one listens.

FIGURE 9–2

TABLE 9–3
Suggestions for Effective Listening

1. **Stop talking!**
   You cannot listen if you are talking.
   Polonius (*Hamlet*): "Give every man thine ear, but few thy voice."
2. **Put the talker at ease.**
   Help a person feel free to talk.
   This is often called a permissive environment.
3. **Show a talker that you want to listen.**
   Look and act interested. Do not read your mail while someone talks.
   Listen to understand rather than to oppose.
4. **Remove distractions.**
   Don't doodle, tap, or shuffle papers.
   Will it be quieter if you shut the door?
5. **Empathize with talkers.**
   Try to help yourself see the other person's point of view.
6. **Be patient.**
   Allow plenty of time. Do not interrupt a talker.
   Don't start for the door or walk away.
7. **Hold your temper.**
   An angry person takes the wrong meaning from words.
8. **Go easy on argument and criticism.**
   These put people on the defensive, and they may "clam up" or become angry.
   Do not argue: Even if you win, you lose.
9. **Ask questions.**
   This encourages a talker and shows that you are listening.
   It helps to develop points further.
10. **Stop talking!**
    This is first and last, because all other guides depend on it.
    You cannot do an effective listening job while you are talking.

   - Nature gave people two ears but only one tongue,
     which is a gentle hint that they should listen more than they talk.
   - Listening requires two ears,
     one for meaning and one for feeling.
   - Decision makers who do not listen
     have less information for making sound decisions.

Source: *Human Behavior at Work: Organizational Behavior*, Seventh Edition, by K. Davis and J.W. Newstrom © 1985 by McGraw-Hill, Inc. With permission.

listens to what is being said. The goal is to improve one's ability to receive the full meaning of a communication, without having it distorted by premature judgments or interpretations. Other suggestions for effective listening are offered in Table 9–3.

Constrain Emotions

It would be naive to assume that we always communicate in a fully rational manner. Yet we know that emotions can severely cloud and distort the transference of meaning. If we're emotionally upset over an issue, we're more likely to misconstrue incoming messages, and we may fail to express our outgoing messages clearly and accurately. The best approach is to refrain from further explicit communication until your composure is regained.

COMMUNICATION PATTERNS

Communication patterns encompass the directions that communications take in groups and organizations, as well as the channels by which communications flow. In this section, we'll describe downward, upward, and lateral communications, identify the five most common formal communication networks and assess the advantages of each, and conclude with a discussion of the informal network.

Directions of Communication

Communications can flow vertically or laterally. The vertical dimension can be further divided into downward and upward directions.[8]

Downward   Communication that flows from one level of a group or organization to a lower level is a downward communication. When we think of managers communicating with subordinates, the downward pattern is the one we usually think of. It is used by group leaders and managers to assign goals, provide job instructions, inform underlings of policies and procedures, point out problems that need attention, and offer feedback about performance. But downward communication doesn't have to be oral or face-to-face contact. When management sends letters to employees' homes to advise them of the organization's new sick leave policy, it is using downward communication.

Is downward communication an effective method for transmitting information? Its major problem lies in filtering. The more levels a message must go through to get to the bottom of the hierarchy, the more likely that a sizable portion of the original information will be lost or substantially distorted. This effect, however, can be substantially offset by relying on feedback provided by upward communication.

Upward   Upward communication flows to a higher level in the group or organization. It is used to provide feedback to higher-ups, inform them of progress toward goals, and relay current problems. Upward communication keeps managers aware of how employees feel about their jobs, coworkers, and the organization in general. Managers also rely on upward communication for ideas on how things can be improved.

Some organizational examples of upward communication include performance reports prepared by lower management for review by middle and top management, suggestion boxes, employee attitude surveys, grievance proce-

---

[8] R. L. Simpson, "Vertical and Horizontal Communication in Formal Organizations," *Administrative Science Quarterly*, September 1959, pp. 188–96; and B. Harriman, "Up and Down the Communications Ladder," *Harvard Business Review*, September–October 1974, pp. 143–51.

dures, superior-subordinate discussions, and informal "gripe" sessions where employees have the opportunity to identify and discuss problems with their boss or representatives of higher management.

Lateral   When communication takes place among members of the same work group, among members of work groups at the same level, among managers at the same level, or among any horizontally equivalent personnel, we describe it as lateral communications.

Why would there be a need for horizontal communications if a group or organization's vertical communications are effective? The answer is that horizontal communications are often necessary to save time and facilitate coordination. In some cases, these lateral relationships are formally sanctioned. Often, they are informally created to short-circuit the vertical hierarchy and expedite action. So lateral communications can, from management's viewpoint, be good or bad. Since strict adherence to the formal vertical structure for all communications can impede the efficient and accurate transfer of information, lateral communications can be beneficial. In such cases, they occur with the knowledge and support of superiors. But they can create dysfunctional conflicts when the formal vertical channels are breached, when members go above or around their superiors to get things done, or when bosses find out that actions have been taken or decisions made without their knowledge.

Communication Networks

Communication networks

Channels by which information flows.

The three directions just described can be combined into a variety of **communication networks**. Most studies of communication networks have taken place in groups created in a laboratory setting. As a result, the research conclusions have limited application because of the artificial settings and the small groups used. Five common networks are shown in Figure 9–3; these are the chain, "Y," wheel, circle, and all-channel. For our discussion purposes, let's think in an organizational context and assume that the organization has only five mem-

FIGURE 9–3
Common Communication Networks

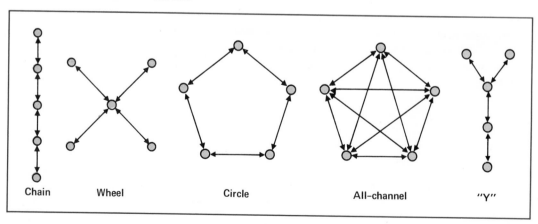

Chain   Wheel   Circle   All–channel   "Y"

TABLE 9-4

Networks and Evaluation Criteria

Criteria	Networks				
	Chain	Y	Wheel	Circle	All-Channel
Speed	Moderate	Moderate	Fast	Slow	Fast
Accuracy	High	High	High	Low	Moderate
Emergence of leader	Moderate	Moderate	High	None	None
Satisfaction	Moderate	Moderate	Low	High	High

Source: Adapted from A. Bavelas and D. Barrett, "An Experimental Approach to Organizational Communication," *Personnel*, March 1951, p. 370.

bers. While this obviously is a simplistic assumption, it will permit us to translate readily the networks in Figure 9–3 into their organizational equivalent.

The chain would represent a five-level hierarchy where communications cannot move laterally, only upward and downward. In a formal organization, this type of network would be found in direct-line authority relations with no deviations. For example, the payroll clerk reports to the payroll supervisor, who in turn reports to the general accounting manager, who reports to the plant controller, who reports to the plant manager. These five individuals would represent a chain network.

If we turn the "Y" network upside down, we can see two subordinates reporting to a supervisor, with two levels of hierarchy still above the supervisor. This is, in effect, a four-level hierarchy.

If we look at the wheel diagram in Figure 9–3 as if we were standing above the network, it becomes obvious that the wheel represents a supervisor with four subordinates. However, there is no interaction between the subordinates. All communications are channeled through the supervisor.

The circle network allows members to interact with adjoining members, but no farther. It would represent a three-level hierarchy in which there is communication between superiors and subordinates and lateral communication at the lowest level.

Finally, the all-channel network allows each of the subjects to communicate freely with the other four. Of the networks discussed, it is the least structured. While it is like the circle, in some respects, the all-channel network has no central position. However, there are no restrictions; all members are equal. This network is best illustrated by a committee, where no one member either formally or informally assumes a dominant or take-charge position. All members are free to share their viewpoints.

Evaluating Network Effectiveness   Is any one network better than the others? The answer to that depends on the dependent variable you are concerned about.

Table 9–4 summarizes the effectiveness of the various networks against four criteria—speed, accuracy, the probability that a leader will emerge, and level of satisfaction among members. One observation is immediately apparent: No single network will be best for all occasions. If speed is important, the wheel and all-channel networks are preferred. The chain, "Y," and wheel score high on accuracy. The structure of the wheel facilitates the emergence of a leader. The circle and all-channel networks are best if you are concerned with having high employee satisfaction.

The Informal Network   The previous discussion of networks emphasized formal communication patterns, but the formal system is not the only communication system in a group or organization. Let us, therefore, now turn our attention to the informal system—where information flows along the well-known **grapevine** and rumors can flourish.

A classic study of the grapevine was reported over thirty-five years ago.[9] The researcher investigated the communication pattern among sixty-seven managerial personnel in a small manufacturing firm. The basic approach used was to learn from each communication recipient how he first received a given piece of information and then trace it back to its source. It was found that, while the grapevine was an important source of information, only 10 percent of the executives acted as liaison individuals, that is, passed the information on to more than one other person. For example, when one executive decided to resign to enter the insurance business, 81 percent of the executives knew about it, but only 11 percent transmitted this information on to others.

Two other conclusions from this study are also worth noting. Information on events of general interest tended to flow between the major functional groups (that is, production, sales) rather than within them. Also, no evidence surfaced to suggest that any one group consistently acted as liaisons; rather, different types of information passed through different liaison persons.

An attempt to replicate this study among employees in a small state government office also found that only 10 percent act as liaison individuals.[10] This is interesting since the replication contained a wider spectrum of employees— including rank-and-file as well as managerial personnel. However, the flow of information in the government office took place within rather than between functional groups. It was proposed that this discrepancy might be due to comparing an executive-only sample against one which also included rank-and-file workers. Managers, for example, might feel greater pressure to stay informed and thus cultivate others outside their immediate functional group. Also, in contrast to the findings of the original study, the replication found that a consistent group of individuals acted as liaisons by transmitting information in the government office.

Is the information that flows along the grapevine accurate? The evidence indicates that about 75 percent of what is carried is accurate.[11] But what conditions foster an active grapevine? What gets the rumor mill rolling?

It is frequently assumed that rumors start because they make titillating gossip. Such is rarely the case. Rumors have at least four purposes: to structure

---

Grapevine

The informal communication channel.

---

[9] K. Davis, "Management Communication and the Grapevine," *Harvard Business Review*, September–October 1953, pp. 43–49.

[10] H. Sutton and L. W. Porter, "A Study of the Grapevine in a Governmental Organization," *Personnel Psychology*, Summer 1968, pp. 223–30.

[11] K. Davis, cited in R. Rowan, "Where Did *That* Rumor Come From?" *Fortune*, August 13, 1979, p. 134.

and reduce anxiety; to make sense of limited or fragmented information; to serve as a vehicle to organize group members, and possibly outsiders, into coalitions; and to signal a sender's status ("I'm an insider and, with respect to this rumor, you're an outsider") or power ("I have the power to make you into an insider").[12] Research indicates that rumors emerge as a response to situations that are *important* to us, where there is *ambiguity*, and under conditions that arouse *anxiety*.[13] Work situations frequently contain these three elements, which explains why rumors flourish in organizations. The secrecy and competition that typically prevail in large organizations—around such issues as the appointment of new bosses, the relocation of offices, and the realignment of work assignments—create conditions that encourage and sustain rumors on the grapevine. A rumor will persist either until the wants and expectations creating the uncertainty underlying the rumor are fulfilled or until the anxiety is reduced.

What can we conclude from this discussion? Certainly the grapevine is an important part of any group or organization's communication network and well worth understanding. It identifies for managers those confusing issues that employees consider important and anxiety provoking. It acts, therefore, as both a filter and a feedback mechanism, picking up the issues that employees consider relevant. Maybe more important, again from a managerial perspective, it seems possible to analyze grapevine information and to predict its flow, given that only a small set of individuals (around 10 percent) actively passes on information to more than one other person. By assessing which liaison individuals will consider a given piece of information to be relevant, we can improve our ability to explain and predict the pattern of the grapevine.

Can management entirely eliminate rumors? "No!" What management *can* do, however, is minimize the negative consequences of rumors by limiting their range and impact. Table 9–5 offers a few suggestions for minimizing those negative consequences.

TABLE 9–5
Suggestions for Reducing the Negative Consequences of Rumors

1. Announce timetables for making important decisions.
2. Explain decisions and behaviors that may appear inconsistent or secretive.
3. Emphasize the downside, as well as the upside, risks of current decisions and future plans.
4. Openly discuss worst case possibilities—it is almost never as anxiety provoking as the unspoken fantasy.

Source: Adapted from L. Hirschhorn, "Managing Rumors," in L. Hirschhorn (ed.), *Cutting Back* (San Francisco: Jossey-Bass, 1983), pp. 54–56. With permission.

[12] L. Hirschhorn, "Managing Rumors," in L. Hirschhorn (ed.), *Cutting Back* (San Francisco: Jossey-Bass, 1983), pp. 49–52.
[13] R. L. Rosnow and G. A. Fine, *Rumor and Gossip: The Social Psychology of Hearsay* (New York: Elsevier, 1976).

Managers Can Make Office Gossip Work for Them

Managers often view office gossip with mixed feelings. On one hand they see it as harmful, potentially undermining formal communication channels, especially when it conveys erroneous information. On the other hand, managers want to have access to the gossip chain. It gives them early warnings of others' plans and problems that may be brewing.

The best managers are selective in using gossip.[14] They keep their ears open to grapevine information. They recognize that gossip is a natural phenomenon whenever people get together. It helps bind people together, lets the powerless blow off steam, and conveys concerns of employees. But effective managers aren't perceived as part of the gossip chain. For instance, they may have a loyal subordinate or colleague who discreetly shares grapevine information with them. Then they only pass along news that is likely to improve relationships in the organization while, at the same time, they act quickly to stamp out gossip that might be harmful to specific individuals or to their unit's overall performance.

NONVERBAL COMMUNICATION

Nonverbal communication

Messages conveyed through body movements, the intonations or emphasis we give to words, facial expressions, and the physical distance between the sender and receiver.

Kinesics

The study of body motions.

Anyone who has ever paid a visit to a singles bar or a nightclub is aware that communication need not be verbal in order to convey a message. A glance, a stare, a smile, a frown, a provocative body movement—they all convey meaning. This example illustrates that no discussion of communication would be complete without a discussion of **nonverbal communications**. This includes body movements, the intonations or emphasis we give to words, facial expressions, and the physical distance between the sender and receiver.

The academic study of body motions has been labeled **kinesics**. It refers to gestures, facial configurations, and other movements of the body. But it is a relatively new field, and it has been subject to far more conjecture and popularizing than the research findings support. Hence, while we acknowledge that body movement is an important segment of the study of communication and behavior, conclusions must be necessarily guarded. Recognizing this qualification, let us briefly consider the ways in which body motions convey meaning.

It has been argued that every *body movement* has a meaning and that

---

[14] W. Kiechel III, "In Praise of Office Gossip," *Fortune*, August 19, 1985, pp. 253–56.

no movement is accidental.[15] For example, through body language,

We say, "Help me, I'm lonely. Take me, I'm available. Leave me alone, I'm depressed." And rarely do we send our messages consciously. We act out our state of being with nonverbal body language. We lift one eyebrow for disbelief. We rub our noses for puzzlement. We clasp our arms to isolate ourselves or to protect ourselves. We shrug our shoulders for indifference, wink one eye for intimacy, tap our fingers for impatience, slap our forehead for forgetfulness.[16]

While we may disagree with the specific meaning of these movements, body language adds to and often complicates verbal communication. A body position or movement does not by itself have a precise or universal meaning, but when it is linked with spoken language, it gives fuller meaning to a sender's message.

If you read the verbatim minutes of a meeting, you could not grasp the impact of what was said in the same way you could if you had been there or saw the meeting on video. Why? There is no record of nonverbal communication. The emphasis given to words or phrases is missing. To illustrate how *intonations* can change the meaning of a message, consider the student in class who asks the instructor a question. The instructor replies, "What do you mean by that?" The student's reaction will be different depending on the tone of the instructor's response. A soft, smooth tone creates a different meaning from an intonation that is abrasive with strong emphasis placed on the last word.

The facial expression of the instructor will also convey meaning. A snarled face says something different from a smile. Facial expressions, along with intonations, can show arrogance, aggressiveness, fear, shyness, and other characteristics that would never be communicated if you read a transcript of what had been said.

The way individuals space themselves in terms of *physical distance* also has meaning. What is considered proper spacing is largely dependent on cultural norms. For example, what is "businesslike" distance in some European countries would be viewed as "intimate" in many parts of North America. If someone stands closer to you than is considered appropriate, it may indicate aggressiveness or sexual interest. If farther away than usual, it may mean disinterest or displeasure with what is being said.

It is important for the receiver to be alert to these nonverbal aspects of communication. You should look for nonverbal cues as well as listen to the literal meaning of a sender's words. You should particularly be aware of contradictions between the messages. The boss may say that she is free to talk to you about that raise you have been seeking, but you may see nonverbal signals that suggest that this is *not* the time to discuss the subject. Regardless of what is being said, an individual who frequently glances at her wristwatch is giving the message that she would prefer to terminate the conversation. We misinform others when we express one emotion verbally, such as trust, but nonverbally communicate a contradictory message that reads, "I don't have confidence in you." These contradictions often suggest that "actions speak louder (and more accurately) than words."

[15] R. L. Birdwhistell, *Introduction to Kinesics* (Louisville, KY: University of Louisville Press, 1952).

[16] J. Fast, *Body Language* (Philadelphia: M. Evan, 1970), p. 7.

OB Close-Up

Beware of the Seven Deadly Sins of Management Communication

If you expect to be a successful manager, you need to be aware of the seven deadly sins.[17] Committing any one of them will lessen your effectiveness.

1. NOT REALIZING THAT YOUR MESSAGE MAY GET A DIFFERENT RESPONSE THAN YOU EXPECT. People see the world differently, based on their experiences, values, attitudes, and perceptions. Expect to be misunderstood and adjust your message anticipating ways your ideas could be misinterpreted.

2. IMPRESSING INSTEAD OF EXPRESSING. First and foremost, the objective of communication is to transfer information, not exert power. Too often, managers are more concerned with sounding impressive and appearing knowledgeable than in making sure the ideas get across.

3. CHOOSING THE WRONG MEDIUM. It's easy to get in the habit of using the same medium over and over again. You have choices: telephones, memos, letters, interviews, group meetings, electronic mail, etc. Use the one that will most effectively carry the message you want.

4. FAILING TO CLOSE THE FEEDBACK LOOP. Effective communication requires understanding by the recipient. Use feedback to insure that the message received is the message sent.

5. APPLYING A NONVERBAL VETO. Studies show that as much as 78 percent of meaning is transmitted nonverbally—through tone of voice, appearance, timing, and the like. Consider how these nonverbal messages might distort your intended message.

6. NOT HELPING YOUR READER OR LISTENER GET THE MESSAGE. Don't turn your communiqué into an Easter egg hunt. Clarify the more important points in your message. As the guide for public speaking reminds us, "Tell 'em what you're going to tell 'em; tell 'em, and then tell 'em what you told 'em."

7. VIEWING COMMUNICATION AS A FRINGE BENEFIT. Communication is the essence of a manager's job. It is not a morale booster or "icing on the cake." Good communication practices is not just a *desirable* quality, it's a *requirement* for effective management.

GROUP DECISION MAKING

One of the more obvious applications of communication concepts is in the area of group decision making. We communicate information, and information is used in the making of decisions. Moreover, group decisions require transmit-

---

[17] Reprinted from *Management World*, July 1984, with permission from AMS, Trevose, PA 19047. Copyright (1984) AMS.

ting of messages between members, and the effectiveness of this communication process will have a significant impact on the quality of the group's decisions.

The belief—characterized by juries—that two heads are better than one has long been accepted as a basic component of our legal system. This belief has expanded to the point that, today, many decisions in organizations are made by groups or committees. There are permanent executive committees that meet on a regular basis, special task forces created to analyze unique problems, temporary project teams used to develop new products, and "quality circles" made up of representatives from management and labor who meet to identify and solve production problems, to name a few of the more obvious examples.

Groups vs. the Individual

Decision making groups may be widely used in organizations, but does that imply that group decisions are preferable to those made by an individual alone? The answer to this question depends on a number of factors. Let's begin by looking at the advantages and disadvantages that groups afford.[18]

Advantages of Groups   Individual and group decisions each have their own set of strengths. Neither is ideal for all situations. The following identifies the major advantages that groups offer over individuals in the making of decisions:

1. *More complete information and knowledge.* By aggregating the resources of several individuals, we bring more input into the decision process.

2. *Increased diversity of views.* In addition to more input, groups can bring heterogeneity to the decision process. This opens up the opportunity for more approaches and alternatives to be considered.

3. *Increased acceptance of a solution.* Many decisions fail after the final choice has been made because people do not accept the solution. However, if people who will be affected by a decision and who will be instrumental in implementing it are able to participate in the decision itself, they will be more likely to accept it and encourage others to accept it. This translates into more support for the decision and higher satisfaction among those required to implement it.

4. *Increased legitimacy.* Our society values democratic methods. The group decision making process is consistent with democratic ideals and, therefore, may be perceived as being more legitimate than decisions made by a single person. When an individual decisionmaker fails to consult with others before making a decision, the decisionmaker's complete power can create the perception that the decision was made autocratically and arbitrarily.

Disadvantages of Groups   Of course, group decisions are not without drawbacks. Their major disadvantages include:

---

[18] N. R. F. Maier, "Assets and Liabilities in Group Problem Solving: The Need for an Integrative Function," *Psychological Review*, April 1967, pp. 239–49; and G. W. Hill, "Group Versus Individual Performance: Are $N + 1$ Heads Better than One?" *Psychological Bulletin*, May 1982, pp. 517–39.

1. *Time consuming*. It takes time to assemble a group. The interaction that takes place once the group is in place is frequently inefficient. The result is that groups take more time to reach a solution than would be the case if an individual were making the decision. This can limit management's ability to act quickly and decisively when necessary.

2. *Pressures to conform*. As noted in the previous chapter, there are social pressures in groups. The desire by group members to be accepted and considered as an asset to the group can result in squashing any overt disagreement, thus encouraging conformity among viewpoints.

3. *Domination by the few*. Group discussion can be dominated by one or a few members. If this dominant coalition is also composed of low- and medium-ability members, the group's overall effectiveness will suffer.

4. *Ambiguous responsibility*. Group members share responsibility, but who is actually accountable for the final outcome? In an individual decision, it is clear who is responsible. In a group decision, the responsibility of any single member is watered down.

Effectiveness and Efficiency   Whether groups are more effective than individuals depends on the criteria you use for defining effectiveness. In terms of *accuracy*, group decisions will tend to be more accurate. The evidence indicates that, on the average, groups make better quality decisions than individuals.[19] This doesn't mean, of course, that all groups will outperform *every* individual. Rather, group decisions have been found to be better than those that would be reached by the average individual in the group. However, they are seldom better than the performance of the best individual.[20]

If decision effectiveness is defined in terms of *speed*, individuals are superior. If *creativity* is important, groups tend to be more effective than individuals. And if effectiveness means the degree of *acceptance* the final solution achieves, the nod again goes to the group.

But effectiveness cannot be considered without also assessing efficiency. In terms of efficiency, groups almost always stack up as a poor second to the individual decision maker. With few exceptions, group decision making consumes more work hours than if an individual were to tackle the same problem alone. The exceptions tend to be those instances where, to achieve comparable quantities of diverse input, the single decision maker must spend a great deal of time reviewing files and talking to people. Because groups can include members from diverse areas, the time spent searching for information can be reduced. However, as we noted, these advantages in efficiency tend to be the exception. Groups are generally less efficient than individuals. In deciding whether to use groups, then, consideration should be given to assessing whether increases in effectiveness are more than enough to offset the losses in efficiency.

Summary   Groups offer an excellent vehicle for performing many of the steps in the decision making process. They are a source of both breadth and depth of input for information gathering. If the group is composed of individuals

---

[19] M. E. Shaw, *Group Dynamics*, 3rd ed. (New York: McGraw-Hill, 1981).

[20] See, for example, F. C. Miner, Jr., "Group Versus Individual Decision Making: An Investigation of Performance Measures, Decision Strategies, and Process Losses/Gains," *Organizational Behavior and Human Performance*, February 1984, pp. 112–24.

TABLE 9–6
The Group Decision: Its Assets and Liabilities

Assets	Liabilities
Breadth of information	Time consuming
Diversity of information	Conformity
Acceptance of solution	Domination of discussion
Legitimacy of process	Ambiguous responsibility

with diverse backgrounds, the alternatives generated should be more extensive and the analysis more critical. When the final solution is agreed upon, there are more people in a group decision to support and implement it. These pluses, however, can be more than offset by the time consumed by group decisions, the internal conflicts they create, or the pressures they generate toward conformity. Table 9–6 briefly outlines the group's assets and liabilities. It allows you to evaluate the net advantage or disadvantage that would accrue in a given situation when you have to choose between an individual or group decision.

Groupthink and Groupshift

Two by-products of group decison making have received a considerable amount of attention by researchers in OB. As we'll show, these two phenomena have the potential to affect the group's ability to appraise alternatives objectively and arrive at quality decision solutions.

The first phenomenon, called **groupthink**, is related to norms. It describes situations in which group pressures for conformity deter the group from critically appraising unusual, minority, or unpopular views. Groupthink is a disease that attacks many groups and can dramatically hinder their performance. The second phenomenon we shall review is called **groupshift**. It indicates that in discussing a given set of alternatives and arriving at a solution, group members tend to exaggerate the initial positions that they held. In some situations, caution dominates, and there is a conservative shift. More often, however, the evidence indicates that groups tend toward a risky shift. Let's look at each of these phenomena in more detail.

Groupthink A number of years ago I had a peculiar experience. During a faculty meeting, a motion was placed on the floor stipulating each faculty member's responsibilities in regard to counseling students. The motion received a second, and the floor was opened for questions. There were none. After about fifteen seconds of silence, the chairman asked if he could "call for the question" (fancy terminology for permission to take the vote). No objections were voiced. When the chairman asked for those in favor, a vast majority of the thirty-two faculty members in attendance raised their hands. The motion was passed, and the chairman proceeded to the next item on the agenda.

Nothing in the process seemed unusual, but the story is not over. About twenty minutes following the end of the meeting, a professor came roaring

Groupthink

Phenomenon in which the norm for consensus overrides the realistic appraisal of alternative courses of action.

Groupshift

A change in decision risk between the group's decision and the individual decision that members within the group would make; can be either toward conservatism or greater risk.

into my office with a petition. The petition said that the motion on counseling students had been rammed through and requested the chairman to replace the motion on the next month's agenda for discussion and a vote. When I asked this professor why he had not spoken up less than an hour earlier, he gave me a frustrated look. He then proceeded to tell me that in talking with people after the meeting, he realized there actually had been considerable opposition to the motion. He didn't speak up, he said, because he thought he was the only one opposed. Conclusion: The faculty meeting we had attended had been attacked by the deadly groupthink "disease."

Have you ever felt like speaking up in a meeting, classroom, or informal group, but decided against it? One reason may have been shyness. On the other hand, you may have been a victim of groupthink, the phenomenon that occurs when group members become so enamoured with seeking concurrence that the norm for consensus overrides the realistic appraisal of alternative courses of action and the full expression of deviant, minority, or unpopular views. It describes a deterioration in an individual's mental efficiency, reality testing, and moral judgments as a result of group pressures.[21]

We have all seen the symptoms of the groupthink phenomenon:

1. Group members rationalize any resistance to the assumptions they have made. No matter how strongly the evidence may contradict their basic assumptions, members behave so as to reinforce those assumptions continually.

2. Members apply direct pressures on those who momentarily express doubts about any of the group's shared views or who question the validity of arguments supporting the alternative favored by the majority.

3. Those members who have doubts or hold differing points of view seek to avoid deviating from what appears to be group consensus by keeping silent about misgivings and even minimizing to themselves the importance of their doubts.

4. There appears to be an illusion of unanimity. If someone does not speak, it is assumed that he or she is in full accord. In other words, abstention becomes viewed as a "Yes" vote.[22]

In studies of American foreign policy decisions, these symptoms were found to prevail when government policymaking groups failed: unpreparedness at Pearl Harbor in 1941, the U.S. invasion of North Korea, the Bay of Pigs fiasco, and the escalation of the Vietnam War by introduction of bombing during the Johnson administration. Importantly, these four groupthink characteristics could not be found where group policy decisions were successful: the Cuban missile crisis and the formulation of the Marshall Plan.[23]

Groupthink appears to be closely aligned with the conclusions Asch drew in his experiments with a lone dissenter. Individuals who hold a position that is different from the dominant majority are under pressure to suppress, withhold, or modify their true feelings and beliefs. As members of a group, we find it is

---

[21] I. L. Janis, *Victims of Groupthink* (Boston: Houghton Mifflin, 1972).
[22] Ibid.
[23] Ibid.

more pleasant to be in agreement—to be a positive part of the group—than to be a disruptive force, even if disruption is necessary to improve the effectiveness of the group's decisions.

Are all groups equally vulnerable to groupthink? The evidence suggests not. Researchers have focused in on three moderating variables—the group's cohesiveness, its leader's behavior, and its insulation from outsiders—but the findings have not been consistent.[24] At this point, the most valid conclusions we can make would be: (1) highly cohesive groups have more discussion and bring out more information but it's unclear whether such groups discourage dissent; (2) groups with impartial leaders who encourage member input generate and discuss more alternative solutions; (3) leaders should avoid expressing a preferred solution early in the group's discussion because this tends to limit critical analysis and significantly increases the likelihood that the group will adopt this solution as the final choice; and (4) insulation of the group leads to fewer alternatives being generated and evaluated.

Groupshift In comparing group decisions with the individual decisions of members within the group, evidence suggests that there are differences.[25] In some cases, the group decisions are more conservative than the individual decisions. More often, the shift is toward greater risk.[26]

What appears to happen in groups is that the discussion leads to a significant shift in the positions of members toward a more extreme position in the direction toward which they were already leaning before the discussion. So conservative types become more cautious and the more aggressive types take on more risk. The group discussion tends to *exaggerate* the initial position of the group.

The groupshift can be viewed as actually a special case of groupthink. The decision of the group reflects the dominant decision making norm that develops during the group's discussion. Whether the shift in the group's decision is toward greater caution or more risk depends on the dominant prediscussion norm.

The greater occurrence of the shift toward risk has generated several explanations for the phenomena.[27] It's been argued, for instance, that the discussion creates familiarization among the members. As they become more comfortable with each other, they also become more bold and daring. Another argument is that our society values risk, that we admire individuals who are willing to take risks, and that group discussion motivates members to show that they are at least as willing as their peers to take risks. The most plausible explanation of the shift toward risk, however, seems to be that the group diffuses responsibility. Group decisions free any single member from accountability for the group's

[24] C. R. Leana, "A Partial Test of Janis' Groupthink Model: Effects of Group Cohesiveness and Leader Behavior on Defective Decision Making," *Journal of Management*, Spring 1985, pp. 5–17; and G. Moorhead and J. R. Montanari, "An Empirical Investigation of the Groupthink Phenomenon," *Human Relations*, May 1986, pp. 399–410.

[25] D. G. Myers and H. Lamm, "The Group Polarization Phenomenon," *Psychological Bulletin*, July 1976, pp. 602–27.

[26] See, for example, N. Kogan and M. A. Wallach, "Risk Taking as a Function of the Situation, the Person, and the Group," in *New Directions in Psychology*, Vol. 3 (New York: Holt, Rinehart and Winston, 1967); and M. A. Wallach, N. Kogan, and D. J. Bem, "Group Influence on Individual Risk Taking," *Journal of Abnormal and Social Psychology*, Vol. 65 (1962), pp. 75–86.

[27] R. D. Clark III, "Group-Induced Shift Toward Risk: A Critical Appraisal," *Psychological Bulletin*, October 1971, pp. 251–70.

final choice. Greater risk can be taken because even if the decision fails, no one member can be held wholly responsible.

So how should you use the findings on groupshift? You should recognize that group decisions exaggerate the initial position of the individual members, that the shift has been shown more often to be toward greater risk, and that whether a group will shift toward greater risk or caution is a function of the members' prediscussion inclinations.

Group Decision Making Techniques

Interacting groups

Typical groups, where members interact with each other face to face.

The most common form of group decision making takes place in face-to-face **interacting groups**. But as our discussion of groupthink demonstrated, interacting groups often censor themselves and pressure individual members toward conformity of opinion. Brainstorming, nominal group, and Delphi techniques have been proposed as ways to reduce many of the problems inherent in the traditional interacting group. We'll discuss each in this section.

Brainstorming

An idea-generation process that specifically encourages any and all alternatives, while withholding any criticism of those alternatives.

Brainstorming   **Brainstorming** is meant to overcome pressures for conformity in the interacting group that retard the development of creative alternatives.[28] It does this by utilizing an idea-generation process that specifically encourages any and all alternatives while withholding any criticism of those alternatives.

In a typical brainstorming session, a half-dozen to a dozen people sit around a table. The group leader states the problem in a clear manner so that it is understood by all participants. Members then "free wheel" as many alternatives as they can in a given length of time. No criticism is allowed, and all the alternatives are recorded for later discussion and analysis. That one idea stimulates others and that judgment of even the most bizarre suggestions are withheld until later encourages group members to "think the unusual."

Brainstorming, however, is merely a process for generating ideas. The next two techniques go further by offering techniques for actually arriving at a preferred solution.[29]

Nominal Group Technique   The **nominal group technique** restricts discussion or interpersonal communication during the decision making process, hence, the term *nominal*. Group members are all physically present, as in a traditional committee meeting, but members operate independently. Specifically, a problem is presented and then the following steps take place:

1. Members meet as a group but, before any discussion takes place, each member independently writes down his or her ideas on the problem.
2. This silent period is followed by each member presenting one idea to the group. Each member takes his or her turn, going around the table, presenting a single idea until all ideas have been presented and recorded

Nominal group technique

A group decision method in which individual members meet face to face to pool their judgments in a systematic but independent fashion.

[28] A. F. Osborn, *Applied Imagination: Principles and Procedures of Creative Thinking* (New York: Scribners, 1941).

[29] The following discussion is based on A. L. Delbecq, A. H. Van deVen, and D. H. Gustafson, *Group Techniques for Program Planning: A Guide to Nominal and Delphi Processes* (Glenview, IL: Scott, Foresman, 1975).

(typically on a flip chart or chalkboard). No discussion takes place until all ideas have been recorded.

3. The group now discusses the ideas for clarity and evaluates them.

4. Each group member silently and independently rank orders the ideas. The final decision is determined by the idea with the highest aggregate ranking.

The chief advantage of the nominal group technique is that it permits the group to meet formally but does not restrict independent thinking as does the interacting group.

Delphi Technique   A more complex and time-consuming alternative is the **Delphi technique**. It is similar to the nominal group technique except that it does not require the physical presence of the group's members. In fact, the Delphi technique never allows the group members to meet face to face. The following steps characterize the Delphi techniques:

1. The problem is identified and members are asked to provide potential solutions through a series of carefully designed questionnaires.

2. Each member anonymously and independently completes the first questionnaire.

3. Results of the first questionnaire are compiled at a central location, transcribed, and reproduced.

4. Each member receives a copy of the results.

5. After viewing the results, members are again asked for their solutions. The results typically trigger new solutions or cause changes in the original position.

6. Steps 4 and 5 are repeated as often as necessary until consensus is reached.

Like the nominal group technique, the Delphi technique insulates group members from the undue influence of others. Because it does not require the physical presence of the participants, the Delphi technique can be used for decision making among geographically scattered groups. For instance, Sony could use the technique to query its managers in Tokyo, Brussels, Paris, London, New York, Toronto, Rio de Janeiro, and Melbourne as to the best worldwide price for one of the company's products. The cost of bringing the executives together at a central location is avoided. Of course, the Delphi technique has its drawbacks. Because the method is extremely time consuming, it is frequently not applicable where a speedy decision is necessary. Additionally, the method may not develop the rich array of alternatives that the interacting or nominal group technique does. The ideas that might surface from the heat of face-to-face interaction may never arise.

Summary: Evaluating Effectiveness   How do these various techniques stack up against the traditional interacting group? As we find so often, each technique has its own unique set of strengths and weaknesses. The choice of one technique over the others depends on the criteria you seek to emphasize. For instance, as Table 9–7 indicates, the interacting group is good for building group cohesiveness, brainstorming keeps social pressures to a minimum, and the Delphi tech-

Delphi technique

A group decision method in which individual members, acting separately, pool their judgment in a systematic and independent fashion.

TABLE 9–7
Evaluating Group Effectiveness

Effectiveness Criteria	Type of Group			
	Interacting	Brainstorming	Nominal	Delphi
Number of ideas	Low	Moderate	High	High
Quality of ideas	Low	Moderate	High	High
Social pressure	High	Low	Moderate	Low
Time/money costs	Moderate	Low	Low	High
Task orientation	Low	High	High	High
Potential for interpersonal conflict	High	Low	Moderate	Low
Feelings of accomplishment	High to low	High	High	Moderate
Commitment to solution	High	Not applicable	Moderate	Low
Builds group cohesiveness	High	High	Moderate	Low

nique minimizes interpersonal conflict. The "best" technique is defined by the criteria you use to evaluate the group.

IMPLICATIONS FOR PERFORMANCE AND SATISFACTION

A careful review of this chapter finds a common theme regarding the relationship between communication and employee satisfaction: The less the uncertainty, the greater the satisfaction. Distortions, ambiguities, and incongruities all increase uncertainty and, hence, have a negative impact on satisfaction.[30]

The less distortion that occurs in communication, the more that goals, feedback, and other management messages to employees will be received as they were intended.[31] This, in turn, should reduce ambiguities and clarify the group's task. Extensive use of vertical, lateral, and informal channels will increase communication flow, reduce uncertainty, and improve group performance and satisfaction. We should also expect incongruities between verbal and nonverbal communiqués to increase uncertainty and reduce satisfaction.

We cited how different networks influence satisfaction and performance. The evidence suggests that job satisfaction is highest in the circle and all-channel networks, where democracy was most simulated. These networks also proved

[30] See, for example, R. S. Schuler, "A Role Perception Transactional Process Model for Organizational Communication-Outcome Relationships," *Organizational Behavior and Human Performance*, April 1979, pp. 268–91.

[31] J. P. Walsh, S. J. Ashford, and T. E. Hill, "Feedback Obstruction: The Influence of the Information Environment on Employee Turnover Intentions," *Human Relations*, January 1985, pp. 23–46.

to generate more effective performance in the solution of complex problems. Where high performance requires close supervision and tight controls, the wheel was found to be most effective. Additionally, there is impressive evidence that communication networks have a significant impact on turnover.[32] Turnover does not occur randomly throughout a work group. Rather, it tends to be concentrated in patterns defined by whom people go to for help and advice. So there tends to be a snowball effect among employees who interact more often. Turnover itself causes more turnover among people who are in similar advice networks.

Findings in the chapter further suggest that the goal of perfect communication is unattainable. Yet, there is evidence that demonstrates a positive relationship between effective communication (which includes factors such as perceived trust, perceived accuracy, desire for interaction, top management receptiveness, and upward information requirements) and worker productivity.[33] Choosing the correct channel, clarifying jargon, and utilizing feedback may, therefore, make for more effective communication, but candidness requires the admission that the human factor generates distortions that can never be fully eliminated. The communication process represents an exchange of messages, but the outcome is meanings that may or may not approximate those that the sender intended. Whatever the sender's expectations, the decoded message in the mind of the receiver represents his or her reality. And it is this "reality" that will determine performance, along with the individual's level of motivation and his or her degree of satisfaction. The issue of motivation is critical, so we should briefly review how communication is central in determining an individual's degree of motivation.

You will remember from expectancy theory that the degree of effort an individual exerts depends on his or her perception of the effort-performance, performance-reward, and reward-goal satisfaction linkages. If individuals are not given the data necessary to make the perceived probability of these linkages high, motivation will be less than it could be. If rewards are not made clear, if the criteria for determining and measuring performance are ambiguous, or if individuals are not relatively certain that their effort will lead to satisfactory performance, then effort will be reduced. So communication plays a significant role in determining the level of motivation.

A final implication from the communication literature relates to predicting turnover. The use of realistic job previews acts as a communication device for clarifying role expectations. Employees who have been exposed to a realistic job preview have more accurate information about that job. Comparisons of turnover rates between organizations that use the realistic job preview versus either no preview or only presentation of positive job information show that those *not* using the realistic preview have almost 29 percent higher turnover on the average.[34] This makes a strong case for management conveying honest and accurate information about a job to applicants during the recruiting and selection process.

[32] D. Krackhardt and L. W. Porter, "The Snowball Effect: Turnover Embedded in Communication Networks," *Journal of Applied Psychology*, February 1986, pp. 50–55.

[33] S. A. Hellweg and S. L. Phillips, "Communication and Productivity in Organizations: A State-of-the-Art Review," in *Proceedings of the 40th Annual Academy of Management Conference*, Detroit, Michigan, 1980, pp. 188–92.

[34] R. R. Reilly, B. Brown, M. R. Blood, and C. Z. Malatesta, "The Effects of Realistic Previews: A Study and Discussion of the Literature," *Personnel Psychology*, Winter 1981, pp. 823–34.

POINT

MAKING JUDGMENTS IS THE MAJOR BARRIER TO COMMUNICATION

The major barrier to mutual interpersonal communication is our very natural tendency to judge, to evaluate, and to approve (or disapprove) the statements of the other person or the other group. Let me illustrate this view with a couple of simple examples. Suppose that someone, commenting on this discussion, says, "I didn't like what that man said." What will you respond? Almost invariably your reply will be either approval or disapproval of the attitude expressed. Either you respond, "I didn't either; I thought it was terrible," or else you tend to reply, "Oh, I thought it was really good." In other words, the primary reaction is to evaluate it from *your* point of view, your own frame of reference.

Or take another example. Suppose that I say with some feeling, "I think the Republicans are showing a lot of good sound sense these days." What is the response that arises in your mind? The overwhelming likelihood is that it will be evaluative. In other words, you will find yourself agreeing, or disagreeing, or making some judgment about me such as "He must be a conservative" or "He seems solid in his thinking."

Although the tendency to make evaluations is common in almost all interchange of language, it is greatly heightened in those situations where feelings and emotions are deeply involved. So the stronger our feelings, the more likely it is that there will be no mutual element in the communication. There will be just two ideas, two feelings, two judgments, missing each other in psychological space.

I am sure you recognize this from your own experience. When you have not been emotionally involved yourself and have listened to a heated discussion, you often go away thinking, "Well, actually they weren't talking about the same thing." And they were not. Each was making a judgment, an evaluation, from his or her own frame of reference. There was really nothing that could be called communication in any genuine sense. This tendency to react to any emotionally meaningful statement by forming an evaluation of it from our own point of view is, I repeat, the major barrier to interpersonal communication.

The solution to this evaluative tendency is to see the expressed idea and attitudes from the other person's point of view, to sense how it feels to him, or her, to achieve his or her frame of reference in regard to the thing about which he or she is talking. When each of the different parties comes to *understand* the other from the *other's* point of view rather than *judge* that point of view, the insincerities, the lies, and the "false fronts" drop away with astonishing speed.

Adapted from C. R. Rogers, in C. R. Rogers and F. J. Roethlisberger, "Barriers and Gateways to Communication," *Harvard Business Review*, August 1952, pp. 46–50.

COUNTERPOINT

THE SEARCH FOR IMPROVED COMMUNICATION IS THE PROBLEM

The major barrier to communication is the naive assumption that individuals actually want to *improve* communication. Most of us seem to overlook a very basic fact: It is often in the sender's and/or receiver's best interest purposely to keep communication ambiguous.

"Lack of communication" seems to have replaced original sin as the explanation for the ills of the world. We're continually hearing that problems would go away if we could "just communicate better." Some of the basic assumptions underlying this view need to be looked at carefully.

One assumption is the way in which poor communication resembles original sin: Both tend to get tangled up with control of the situation. If one defines communication as mutual understanding, this does not imply control for either party and certainly not for both. However, equating good communication with control appears in the assumption that better communication will necessarily reduce strife and conflict. Each individual's definition of better communication, like his or her definition of virtuous conduct, becomes that of having the other party accept his or her views, which would reduce conflict at that party's expense. A better understanding of the situation might serve only to underline the differences rather than to resolve them. Indeed, many of the techniques thought of as poor communication were apparently developed with the aim of bypassing or avoiding confrontation.

Another assumption that grows from this view is that when a conflict has existed for a long time and shows every sign of continuing, lack of communication must be one of the basic problems. Usually if the situation is examined more carefully, plenty of communication will be found; the problem is again one of equating communication with agreement.

Still a third assumption, somewhat related but less squarely based on the equation of communication with controls, is that it is always in the interest of at least one of the parties to an interaction and often of both to attain maximum clarity as measured by some more or less objective standard. Aside from the difficulty of setting up this standard—whose standard? and doesn't this give *him* or *her* control of the situation?—there are some sequences, and perhaps many of them, in which it is to the interests of both parties to leave the situation as fuzzy and undefined as possible. This is notably true in culturally or personally sensitive and taboo areas involving prejudices, preconceptions, and so on, but it can also be true when the area is merely a new one that could be seriously distorted by using old definitions and old solutions.

Too often we forget that keeping organizational communications fuzzy cuts down on questions, permits faster decision making, minimizes objections, reduces opposition, makes it easier to deny one's earlier statements, preserves freedom to change one's mind, helps to preserve mystique and hide insecurities, allows one to say several things at the same time, permits one to say "no" diplomatically, and helps to avoid confrontation and anxiety.

If you want to see the fine art of ambiguous communication up close, all you have to do is watch a television interview with a politician who is running for office. The interviewer attempts to get specific information, while the politician tries to retain multiple possible interpretations. Such ambiguous communications allow the politician to approach his or her ideal image of being "all things to all people."

Based on C. O. Kursh, "The Benefits of Poor Communication," *The Psychoanalytic Review*, Summer-Fall 1971, pp. 189–208; and E. M. Eisenberg and M. G. Witten, "Reconsidering Openness in Organizational Communication," *Academy of Management Review*, July 1987, pp. 418–26.

KEY TERMS

Active Listening

Brainstorming

Channel

Communication

Communication Networks

Communication Process

Decoding

Delphi Technique

Encoding

Feedback Loop

Filtering

Grapevine

Groupshift

Groupthink

Interacting Groups

Kinesics

Message

Nominal Group Technique

Nonverbal Communication

FOR DISCUSSION

1. "Communication is the transference of meaning among group members." Discuss this definition and indicate what is missing from this definition to ensure that communication is effective.

2. Describe the functions that communication provides within a group or organization. Give an example of each.

3. Describe the communication process, identifying its key components. Give an example of how this process operates with both oral and written messages.

4. "Ineffective communication is the fault of the sender." Do you agree or disagree? Discuss.

5. Describe the advantages and disadvantages of each of these networks: (a) all-channel, (b) chain, (c) circle, (d) wheel, and (e) "Y."

6. For each of the networks, indicate the conditions under which it will be most effective.

7. What can you do to improve the likelihood that your communiqués will be received and understood as you intend?

8. "Informal communication can facilitate a group's effectiveness." Do you agree or disagree? Discuss.

9. "Rumors start because something makes titillating gossip." Do you agree or disagree? Discuss.

10. What is groupthink? Is the concept applicable to the family unit as well as to organizations? Explain.

11. What can management do to improve group decision making effectiveness?

12. When are group decisions better than those made by individuals?

FOR FURTHER READING

Guzzo, R. A., "Group Decision Making and Group Effectiveness in Organizations," in P. S. Goodman and Associates, *Designing Effective Work Groups*. San Francisco: Jossey-Bass, 1986, pp. 34–71. Reviews current theoretical frameworks of group effectiveness, their relevance for understanding group decision making, and considers implications for practice.

Hatfield, J. D., and R. C. Huseman, "Perceptual Congruence about Communication as Related to Satisfaction: Moderating Effects of Individual Characteristics," *Academy of Management Journal*, June 1982, pp. 349–58. Shows how congruence about communication between supervisor and subordinate is significantly related to job satisfaction.

ROBERTS, K. H., *Communicating in Organizations*. Chicago: Science Research Associates, 1984. A forty-three-page booklet that discusses the essential issues in organizational communication.

SCHWEIGER, D. M., W. R. SANDBERG, and J. W. RAGAN, "Group Approaches for Improving Strategic Decision Making: A Comparative Analysis of Dialectical Inquiry, Devil's Advocacy, and Consensus," *Academy of Management Journal*, March 1986, pp. 51–71. Compares three approaches to strategic decision making in groups. Both dialectical inquiry and devil's advocacy were found to be more effective than consensus in generating high quality recommendations and testing underlying assumptions.

SNYDER, R. A., and J. H. MORRIS, "Organizational Communication and Performance," *Journal of Applied Psychology*, August 1984, pp. 461–65. This study found that two perceived communication variables—the quality of supervisory communication and information exchange within the peer work group—were strongly related to overall organization performance.

TOMPKINS, P. K., "The Functions of Human Communication in Organizations," in C. C. Arnold and J. W. Bowers (eds.), *Handbook of Rhetorical and Communication Theory*. Boston: Allyn & Bacon, 1984, pp. 659–719. Excellent summary of the recent literature in organizational communication.

EXERCISE 9
TEST YOUR MANAGEMENT COMMUNICATION SKILLS

Circle the answer that best describes what you would do in each situation.

1. Your boss's immediate supervisor asks you to lunch. When you return, you sense your boss is curious. Do you . . .
   a. give your boss a detailed description of the lunch?
   b. avoid telling your boss anything?
   c. mention the lunch casually—as though it really had no significance?
2. You're in the middle of an important meeting with your boss and there's a long-distance business call for you. Do you . . .
   a. ask the boss's secretary to say you're out of the office?
   b. accept the call and take as much time as it needs?
   c. tell the person you're in a meeting and ask when you may call back?
3. As you're ready to leave for a hard-to-get job interview, you discover a spot on your shirt. Do you . . .
   a. call to reschedule the interview?
   b. rush to the nearest store and buy a new shirt?
   c. decide that the spot is not very noticeable after all, and go to the interview "as is"?
4. You're conducting a staff meeting on new sales procedures. One employee keeps interrupting with questions not germane to the subject. Do you . . .
   a. request all employees to hold their questions until you're finished?
   b. accept the interruptions?
   c. tell the employee that interruptions are out of order?
5. You're asked, by someone outside the company, to write a recommendation for a former employee whose work record was not very satisfactory. Do you . . .
   a. write a letter that details your negative observations?
   b. write a letter emphasizing one or two positive points?
   c. decline the request?
6. A staff member comes to you to complain about the work habits of another. Do you say . . .
   a. "We'll have to discuss that later—there's too much else to do now"?
   b. "I'll be glad to talk with both of you—together, not separately"?
   c. "What's the problem . . . let's discuss it now"?
7. Your employees' Christmas party is underway when you arrive. Everybody seems well into the season's spirits—too well, in fact. Do you . . .
   a. try to be a "good guy" and join in the fun?
   b. leave immediately?
   c. tell the person in charge that the party is out-of-hand and suggest it be ended as soon as possible?
8. For the fourth consecutive Friday, a staff member asks to leave early. Do you say . . .
   a. "I can't keep giving you permission like this—others resent it"?
   b. "Not today—there may be a staff meeting at 4 o'clock"?
   c. "You're important to us—I need you to put in a full day, especially on Fridays"?
9. You've been quoted correctly and favorably by the writer of a national magazine article. Do you now . . .
   a. send the writer a gift?
   b. call and thank the writer for the publicity?
   c. write an appreciative note and offer to be of future help to the writer?

10. You've been hired from outside the company as director of a large department. You know several staff members thought they should have had the position. On the first day, do you . . .
   a. initiate individual conversations with those individuals about the situation?
   b. ignore the problem and hope it'll go away?
   c. recognize the problem but concentrate on your job and on getting to know everyone?
11. An employee says to you, "I shouldn't tell you this, but have you heard . . .?" Do you say . . .
   a. "I don't want to hear any office gossip"?
   b. "I'm interested only if it concerns our business"?
   c. "What's the latest—let me in on it"?
12. Your boss, in a customer meeting, makes an inaccurate statement. Do you . . .
   a. point out the mistake later to your boss—and expect him or her to correct the statement?
   b. correct your boss in front of the customer?
   c. try to handle it yourself with the customer—at another time?

Turn to page 564 for scoring directions and key.

Source: Communispond, Inc., as reproduced in Jacob's Ladder, *Baltimore Sun*, May 4, 1983, p. D1. With permission.

CASE INCIDENT 9
BRUSQUE OR EFFICIENT?

The people at WBFL had never seen anyone like Stan Moorhead before. WBFL is a television network affiliate in Buffalo, New York. Stan was the new station manager. He came to Buffalo after three years as manager of a smaller station in Memphis. In only two months, Stan has introduced a whole new management approach to WBFL. Maybe his most radical ideas relate to internal communications at the station. The following are a few examples (with selected quotes supplied by Stan):

"This place is memo crazy. In the first week I was here, I received over a dozen memos from staff members and the *shortest* was six pages long!" In response, Stan instituted a new rule: Any memo sent to him was not to exceed one page in length. Anything longer won't be read. "If these people can't make their point in 200 or 300 words, then they're not sure what they want to say."

"I told the people who report to me that they are well-paid professionals and I'm not their nursemaid. If they have a problem, fine, come to me and we'll discuss it. But here's the new catch: Don't come to me with a problem unless you've thoroughly thought it out and have a recommended solution to offer. It's not my job to make the decisions for my staff. I'm an advisor, not a dictator." Most of Stan's staff find this new procedure tough to follow. As the News Director noted, "I've been here for six years. When I had a problem in the past, I went to the station manager and he'd tell me how to handle it. This new policy makes my job twice as difficult. Now I have to review alternatives, select a solution, and be prepared to defend that solution to Stan. My job was a whole lot easier before Stan got here."

Maybe the most radical action Stan has taken was to remove all the chairs from his office, except for his own. "I learned this trick when I was in Memphis. People would come into my office, sit down, and what should have been a five-minute meeting turned into a thirty-minute B.S.-session. Once people sit down and get comfortable, they think they have a right to talk on forever. Well, my time is valuable and so is theirs! So I took out all the chairs. My door is open and I'm available when needed. But when anyone comes into my office, they stand up. Sure it's a little strange. It makes people feel ill at ease. But it sure cuts out the idle chit-chat. People say what they have to say and leave. And, of course, if I really want to pursue a conversation at length, we can move next door to my conference room where there are plenty of chairs."

QUESTIONS

1. Have Stan's new management methods improved communication or created additional barriers? Explain.
2. Stan is convinced his ideas make WBFL more efficient but many of his employees have resisted the changes. Does this suggest that employees resist ideas that make an organization more efficient? Does it suggest that Stan's changes may not really be increasing efficiency? Discuss.
3. What impact do you think Stan's new ideas have on decision making at WBFL?

10

Leadership

■ **Learning objectives**

Describe the nature of leadership

Summarize the conclusions of trait theories

Identify the limitations of behavioral theories

Describe Fiedler's contingency model

Summarize the path-goal theory

State the situational leadership theory

Explain leader-member exchange theory

Describe the leader-participation model

Explain why no leadership style is ideal in all situations

Define implicit leadership theories

Leadership is making people do what they don't want to do, and liking it.

—— H. S. TRUMAN

It has been accepted as a truism that good leadership is essential to business, to government, and to the countless groups and organizations that shape the way in which we live, work, and play.[1] If leadership is such an important factor, the critical issue is: What makes a great leader? The tempting answer is, great followers. While there is some truth to this response, the issue is far more complex.

WHAT IS LEADERSHIP?

Leadership

The ability to influence a group toward the achievement of goals.

Leadership is the ability to influence a group toward the achievement of goals. The source of this influence may be formal, such as that provided by the possession of managerial rank in an organization. Since management positions come with some degree of formally designated authority, an individual may assume a leadership role as a result of the position he or she holds in the organization. But not all leaders are managers or, for that matter, are all managers leaders. Just because an organization provides its managers with certain rights is no assurance that they will be able to lead effectively. We find that nonsanc-

FIGURE 10–1

Source: Reprinted by permission: Tribune Media Services, Inc.

[1] F. E. Fiedler, "Style or Circumstance: The Leadership Enigma," *Psychology Today*, March 1969, p. 39.

OB Close-Up

Leaders and Managers Are Different!

Abraham Zaleznik of the Harvard Business School argues that leaders and managers are very different kinds of people.[2] They differ in motivation, personal history, and in how they think and act.

Managers tend to adopt impersonal, if not passive, attitudes toward goals, whereas leaders adopt a personal and active attitude toward them.

Managers tend to view work as an enabling process involving some combination of people and ideas interacting to establish strategies and make decisions.

Leaders work from high-risk positions, indeed often are temperamentally disposed to seek out risk and danger, especially where opportunity and reward appear high.

Managers prefer to work with people; they avoid solitary activity because it makes them anxious. They relate to people according to the role they play in a sequence of events or in a decision making process, while leaders, who are concerned with ideas, relate in more intuitive and empathetic ways.

Managers need order in the face of the potential chaos that many fear in human relationships. In contrast, one often hears leaders referred to in adjectives rich in emotional content. Leaders tend to be people who feel separate from their environment, including other people. They may work in organizations, but they never belong to them. Their sense of who they are doesn't depend on memberships, work roles, or other social indicators of identity.

---

tioned leadership, that is, the ability to influence that arises outside of the formal structure of the organization, is as important or more important than formal influence. In other words, leaders can emerge from within a group as well as being formally appointed.

TRANSITION IN LEADERSHIP THEORIES

The leadership literature is voluminous, and much of it is confusing and contradictory. In order to make our way through this "forest," we shall consider four approaches to explaining what makes an effective leader. The first sought to find universal personality traits that leaders had to some greater degree than nonleaders. The second tried to explain leadership in terms of the behavior that a person engaged in. Both approaches have been described as "false starts,"

[2] A. Zaleznik, "Excerpts from 'Managers and Leaders: Are They Different?'" *Harvard Business Review*, May–June 1986, p. 54.

based on their erroneous and oversimplified conception of leadership.[3] The third looked to contingency models to explain the inadequacies of previous leadership theories in reconciling and bringing together the diversity of research findings. Most recently, attention has returned to traits, but from a different perspective. Researchers are now attempting to identify the set of traits that people implicitly refer to when they characterize someone as a leader. This line of thinking proposes that leadership is as much style—projecting the appearance of being a leader—as it is substance. In this chapter, we shall present the contributions and limitations of each of these four approaches and conclude by attempting to ascertain the value of the leadership literature in explaining and predicting behavior.

TRAIT THEORIES

If we were to describe a leader based on the general connotations presented in today's media, we might list qualities such as intelligence, charisma, decisiveness, enthusiasm, strength, bravery, integrity, self-confidence, and so on—possibly eliciting the conclusion that effective leaders must be one part Boy Scout and two parts Jesus Christ. The search for characteristics such as those listed that would differentiate leaders from nonleaders occupied the early psychologists who studied leadership.

Is it possible to isolate one or more personality, social, physical, or intellectual characteristics in individuals we generally acknowledge as leaders—Mahatma Gandhi, Martin Luther King, Jr., Joan of Arc, Adolph Hitler, Winston Churchill, General Douglas MacArthur, John F. Kennedy, Lee Iacocca, Ted Turner, Donald Trump—that nonleaders do not possess? We may agree that these individuals meet our definition of a leader, but they represent individuals with utterly different characteristics. If the concept of traits were to be proved valid, there must be specific characteristics that all leaders possess.

Research efforts at isolating these traits resulted in a number of dead ends. For instance, a review of twenty different studies identified nearly eighty leadership traits, but only five of these traits were common to four or more of the investigations.[4] If the search was intended to identify a set of traits that would always differentiate leaders from followers and effective from ineffective leaders, the search obviously failed. Perhaps it was a bit optimistic to believe that there could be consistent and unique traits that would apply across the board to all effective leaders no matter whether they were in charge of the Hell's Angels, the Mormon Tabernacle Choir, General Electric, the CIA, the Ku Klux Klan, or the Congress of Racial Equality.

If, however, the search was intended to identify traits that were consistently associated with leadership, the results can be interpreted in a more impressive light. For example, intelligence, dominance, self-confidence, high energy level,

---

[3] V. H. Vroom, "The Search for a Theory of Leadership," in J. W. McGuire (ed.), *Contemporary Management: Issues and Viewpoints* (Englewood Cliffs, NJ: Prentice Hall, 1974), p. 396.

[4] J. G. Geier, "A Trait Approach to the Study of Leadership in Small Groups," *Journal of Communication*, December 1967, pp. 316–23.

and task-relevant knowledge are five traits that show consistently positive correlations with leadership.[5] But "positive correlations" should not be interpreted to mean "definitive predictors." The correlations between these traits and leadership have generally been in the range of $+ 0.25$ to $+ 0.35$[6] —interesting results, but not earth shattering!

The results represent the conclusions based on seventy years of trait research. These modest correlations coupled with the inherent limitations of the trait approach—it overlooks the needs of followers, generally fails to clarify the relative importance of various traits, doesn't separate cause from effect (for example, are leaders self-confident or does success as a leader build self-confidence?), and ignores situational factors—naturally led researchers in other directions. Although there has been some resurgent interest in traits during the past decade,[7] a major movement away from traits began as early as the 1940s. Leadership research from the late 1940s through the mid-1960s emphasized the preferred behavioral styles that leaders demonstrated.

BEHAVIORAL THEORIES

The inability to strike "gold" in the trait mines led researchers to look at the **behaviors** that specific leaders exhibited. They wondered if there were something unique in the way that effective leaders behave. For example, do they tend to be more democratic than autocratic?

Behavioral theories

Theories proposing that specific behaviors differentiate leaders from nonleaders.

Not only, it was hoped, would the behavioral approach provide more definitive answers about the nature of leadership but, if successful, it would have practical implications quite different from those of the trait approach. If trait research had been successful, it would have provided a basis for *selecting* the "right" person to assume formal positions in groups and organizations requiring leadership. In contrast, if behavioral studies were to turn up critical behavioral determinants of leadership, we could *train* people to be leaders. The difference between trait and behavioral theories, in terms of application, lies in their underlying assumptions. If trait theories were valid, then leaders are basically born: You either have it or you do not. On the other hand, if there were specific behaviors that identified leaders, then we could teach leadership—we could design programs that implanted these behavioral patterns in individuals who desired to be effective leaders. This was surely a more exciting avenue for it would mean that the supply of leaders could be expanded. If training worked, we could have an infinite supply of effective leaders.

There were a number of studies that looked at behavioral styles. We shall briefly review the most popular: the Ohio State group and the University of Michigan group. Then we shall see how the concepts that these studies developed could be used to create a grid for looking at and appraising leadership styles.

[5] R. M. Stogdill, *Handbook of Leadership: A Survey of Theory and Research* (New York: Free Press, 1974).

[6] Ibid.

[7] See, for instance, D. A. Kenny and S. J. Zaccaro, "An Estimate of Variance Due to Traits in Leadership," *Journal of Applied Psychology*, November 1983, pp. 678–85.

Ohio State Studies

The most comprehensive and replicated of the behavioral theories resulted from research that began at Ohio State University in the late 1940s.[8] These studies sought to identify independent dimensions of leader behavior. Beginning with over a thousand dimensions, they eventually narrowed the list into two categories that substantially accounted for most of the leadership behavior described by subordinates. They called these two dimensions *initiating structure* and *consideration*.

Initiating structure

The extent to which a leader is likely to define and structure his or her role and those of subordinates in the search for goal attainment.

Initiating structure refers to the extent to which a leader is likely to define and structure his or her role and those of subordinates in the search for goal attainment. It includes behavior that attempts to organize work, work relationships, and goals. The leader characterized as high in initiating structure could be described in terms such as assigns group members to particular tasks, expects workers to maintain definite standards of performance, and emphasizes the meeting of deadlines.

Consideration

The extent to which a leader is likely to have job relationships characterized by mutual trust, respect for subordinates' ideas, and regard for their feelings.

Consideration is described as the extent to which a person is likely to have job relationships that are characterized by mutual trust, respect for subordinates' ideas, and regard for their feelings. He or she shows concern for his or her followers' comfort, well-being, status, and satisfaction. A leader high in consideration could be described as one who helps subordinates with personal problems, is friendly and approachable, and treats all subordinates as equals.

Extensive research, based on these definitions, found that leaders high in initiating structure and consideration (a "high-high" leader) tended to achieve high subordinate performance and satisfaction more frequently than those who rated low on either consideration, initiating structure, or both. However, the "high-high" style did not always result in positive consequences. For example, leader behavior characterized as high on initiating structure led to greater rates of grievances, absenteeism, and turnover and lower levels of job satisfaction for workers performing routine tasks. Other studies found that high consideration was negatively related to performance ratings of the leader by his superior. In conclusion, the Ohio State studies suggested that the "high-high" style generally resulted in positive outcomes, but enough exceptions were found to indicate that situational factors needed to be integrated into the theory.

University of Michigan Studies

Leadership studies undertaken at the University of Michigan's Survey Research Center, at about the same time as those being done at Ohio State, had similar research objectives: to locate behavioral characteristics of leaders that appeared to be related to measures of performance effectiveness.

The Michigan group also came up with two dimensions of leadership

[8] R. M. Stogdill and A. E. Coons (eds.), *Leader Behavior: Its Description and Measurement*, Research Monograph No. 88 (Columbus: Ohio State University, Bureau of Business Research, 1951). For an updated literature review of the Ohio State research, see S. Kerr, C. A. Schriesheim, C. J. Murphy, and R. M. Stogdill, "Toward a Contingency Theory of Leadership Based upon the Consideration and Initiating Structure Literature," *Organizational Behavior and Human Performance*, August 1974, pp. 62–82.

behavior that they labeled **employee oriented** and **production oriented.**[9] Leaders who were employee oriented were described as emphasizing interpersonal relations; they took a personal interest in the needs of their subordinates and accepted individual differences among members. The production-oriented leaders, in contrast, tended to emphasize the technical or task aspects of the job—their main concern was in accomplishing their group's tasks and the group members were a means to that end.

The conclusions arrived at by the Michigan researchers strongly favored the leaders who were employee oriented in their behavior. Employee-oriented leaders were associated with higher group productivity and higher job satisfaction. Production-oriented leaders tended to be associated with low group productivity and lower work satisfaction.

Employee-oriented leader

One who emphasizes interpersonal relations.

Production-oriented leader

One who emphasizes technical or task aspects of the job.

Managerial Grid

A nine-by-nine matrix outlining eighty-one different leadership styles.

The Managerial Grid

A graphic portrayal of a two-dimensional view of leadership style has been developed by Blake and Mouton.[10] They propose a **Managerial Grid®** based on the styles of "concern for people" and "concern for production," which essentially represent the Ohio State dimensions of consideration and initiating structure or the Michigan dimensions of employee oriented and production oriented.

The grid, depicted in Figure 10–2, has nine possible positions along each axis, creating eighty-one different positions in which the leader's style may fall. The grid does not show results produced but, rather, the dominating factors in a leader's thinking in regard to getting results.

Based on the findings of Blake and Mouton, managers perform best under a 9,9 style, as contrasted, for example, with a 9,1 (authority type) or the 1,9 (country-club type) leader.[11] Unfortunately, the grid offers a better framework for conceptualizing leadership style than for presenting any tangible new information in clarifying the leadership quandary since there is little substantive evidence to support the conclusion that a 9,9 style is most effective in all situations.[12]

Summary of Behavioral Theories

We have described the most popular and important of the attempts to explain leadership in terms of the behavior exhibited by the leader. There were other

[9] R. Kahn and D. Katz, "Leadership Practices in Relation to Productivity and Morale," D. Cartwright and A. Zander (eds.), *Group Dynamics: Research and Theory*, 2nd ed. (Elmsford, NY: Row, Paterson, 1960).

[10] R. R. Blake and J. S. Mouton, *The Managerial Grid* (Houston: Gulf, 1964).

[11] See, for example, R. R. Blake and J. S. Mouton, "A Comparative Analysis of Situationalism and 9,9 Management by Principle," *Organizational Dynamics*, Spring 1982, pp. 20–43.

[12] See, for example, L. L. Larson, J. G. Hunt, and R. N. Osborn, "The Great Hi-Hi Leader Behavior Myth: A Lesson from Occam's Razor," *Academy of Management Journal*, December 1976, pp. 628–41; and P. C. Nystrom, "Managers and the Hi-Hi Leader Myth," *Academy of Management Journal*, June 1978, pp. 325–31.

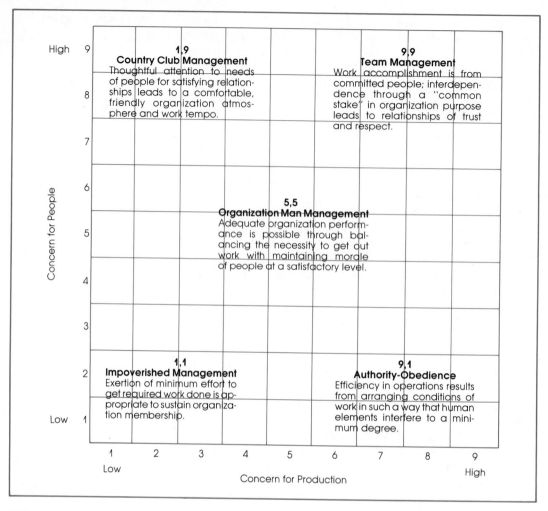

FIGURE 10–2
The Managerial Grid®

Source: R. R. Blake, J. S. Mouton, L. B. Barnes, and L. E. Greiner, "Breakthrough in Organization Development," *Harvard Business Review*, November-December 1964, p. 136. Copyright © by the President and Fellows of Harvard College; all rights reserved.

efforts,[13] but they faced the same problem that confronted the Ohio State and Michigan findings: They had very little success in identifying consistent relationships between patterns of leadership behavior and group performance. General statements could not be made because results would vary over different ranges of circumstances. What was missing was consideration of the situational factors that influence success or failure. For example, it seems unlikely that Jesse Jackson would have been a great leader of black causes at the turn of the century, yet he is in the 1980s. Would Ralph Nader have risen to lead a consumer

[13] See, for example, the three styles—autocratic, participative, and laissez-faire—proposed by K. Lewin and R. Lippitt, "An Experimental Approach to the Study of Autocracy and Democracy: A Preliminary Note," *Sociometry*, no. 1 (1938), pp. 292–380; or the 3-D theory proposed by W. J. Reddin, *Managerial Effectiveness* (New York: McGraw-Hill, 1970).

activist group had he been born in 1834 rather than 1934, or in Costa Rica rather than Connecticut? It seems quite unlikely, yet the behavioral approaches we have described could not clarify these situational factors.

It became increasingly clear to those who were studying the leadership phenomenon that the predicting of leadership success was more complex than isolating a few traits or preferable behaviors. The failure to obtain consistent results led to a focus on situational influences. The relationship between leadership style and effectiveness suggested that under condition a, style x would be appropriate, while style y would be more suitable for condition b, and style z for condition c. But what were the conditions a, b, c, and so forth? It was one thing to say that leadership effectiveness was dependent on the situation and another to be able to isolate those situational conditions.

There has been no shortage of studies attempting to isolate critical situational factors that affect leadership effectiveness. For instance, popular moderating variables used in the development of contingency theories include the degree of structure in the task being performed, the quality of leader-member relations, the leader's position power, subordinates' role clarity, group norms, information availability, subordinate acceptance of leader's decisions, and subordinate maturity.[14]

Several approaches to isolating key situational variables have proven more successful than others and, as a result, have gained wider recognition. We shall consider six of these: the autocratic-democratic continuum, the Fiedler model, Hersey and Blanchard's situational theory, leader-member exchange theory, and the path-goal and leader-participation models.

Autocratic-Democratic Continuum Model

If **autocratic** and **democratic** behavior were viewed only as two extreme positions, this model would be correctly labeled as a behavioral theory. However, they are merely two of many positions along a continuum. At one extreme the leader makes the decisions, tells his or her subordinates, and expects them to carry out that decision. At the other extreme, the leader fully shares his or her decision-making power with subordinates, allowing each member of the group to carry an equal voice—one person, one vote. Between these two extremes fall a number of leadership styles, with the style selected dependent upon forces in the leader, the operating group, and the situation. Although this represents a contingency theory, we shall find, upon investigating other contingency approaches, that it is quite primitive.

As depicted in Figure 10–3, there is a relationship between the degree of authority used and the amount of freedom available to subordinates in

Autocratic leader

One who dictates decisions down to subordinates.

Democratic leader

One who shares decision making with subordinates.

---

[14]J. P. Howell, P. W. Dorfman, and S. Kerr, "Moderating Variables in Leadership Research," *Academy of Management Review*, January 1986, pp. 88–102.

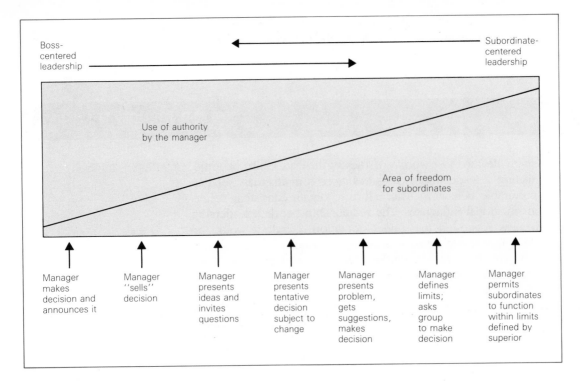

FIGURE 10–3
Leadership-Behavior Continuum

Source: R. Tannenbaum and W. H. Schmidt, "How to Choose a Leadership Pattern," *Harvard Business Review*, March-April 1958, p. 96. With permission. Copyright © 1958 by the President and Fellows of Harvard College; all rights reserved.

reaching decisions. This continuum is seen as a zero-sum game; as one gains, the other loses, and vice versa.[15] However, much of the research using this model has been concentrated on the extreme positions.

After reviewing eleven separate studies, Filley, House, and Kerr found seven to demonstrate that participative leadership has positive effects upon productivity while there were no significant effects in the other four. Although only three of the eleven investigations reported on participative leadership's effect on subordinate satisfaction, all showed positive results.[16]

Hamner and Organ reached a similar conclusion when they reviewed the research:

> Generally speaking, we find that participative leadership is associated with greater satisfaction on the part of subordinates than is nonparticipative leadership; or, at worst, that participation does not lower satisfaction. We cannot summarize so easily the findings with respect to productivity. Some studies find participative groups to be more productive; some find nonparticipative groups to be more

[15] R. Tannenbaum and W. H. Schmidt, "How to Choose a Leadership Pattern," *Harvard Business Review*, March–April 1958, pp. 95–101.

[16] A. C. Filley, R. J. House, and S. Kerr, *Managerial Process and Organizational Behavior*, 2nd ed. (Glenview, IL: Scott, Foresman, 1976), p. 223.

effective; and quite a few studied show no appreciable differences in productivity between autocratically versus democratically managed work groups.[17]

The preceding information suggests a clear link between participation or the democratic style of leadership and satisfaction, but the relationship of this style to productivity is less apparent. The research can be interpreted as saying that people like democracy, but that it will not necessarily result in higher productivity.

A contingency approach would recognize that neither the democratic nor autocratic extreme is effective in all situations. The following models more comprehensively appraise these situational characteristics.

Fiedler Model

The first comprehensive contingency model for leadership was developed by Fred Fiedler.[18] His model proposes that effective group performance depends upon the proper match between the leader's style of interacting with his or her subordinates and the degree to which the situation gives control and influence to the leader. Fiedler developed an instrument, which he called the least preferred co-worker (**LPC**) questionnaire, that purports to measure whether a person is task or relationship oriented. Further, he isolated three situational criteria—leader-member relations, task structure, and position power—that he believes can be manipulated so as to create the proper match with the behavioral orientation of the leader. In a sense, the Fiedler model is an outgrowth of trait theory, since the LPC questionnaire is a simple psychological test. However, Fiedler goes significantly beyond trait and behavioral approaches by attempting to isolate situations, relating his personality measure to his situational classification, and then predicting leadership effectiveness as a function of the two.

LPC

Least preferred co-worker questionnaire that measures task or relationship-oriented leadership style.

This description of the Fiedler model is somewhat abstract. Let us now look at the model more closely.

Fiedler believes a key factor in leadership success to be an individual's basic leadership style. So he begins by trying to find out what that basic style is. Fiedler created the LPC questionnaire for this purpose. It contains sixteen contrasting adjectives (such as pleasant-unpleasant, efficient-inefficient, open-guarded, supportive-hostile). The questionnaire then asks the respondent to think of all the co-workers they have ever had and to describe the one person they *least enjoyed* working with by rating him or her on a scale of 1 to 8 for each of the sixteen sets of contrasting adjectives. Fiedler believes that based on the respondents' answers to this LPC questionnaire, he can determine their basic leadership style. If the least preferred co-worker is described in relatively positive terms (a high LPC score), then the respondent is primarily interested in good personal relations with this co-worker. That is, if you essentially describe the person you are least able to work with in favorable terms, Fiedler would label you relationship oriented. In contrast, if the least preferred co-worker is seen in relatively unfavorable terms (a low LPC score), the respondent is primarily interested in productivity and thus would be labeled task oriented. About 16

---

[17] W. C. Hamner and D. W. Organ, *Organizational Behavior: An Applied Psychological Approach* (Dallas: Business Publications, 1978), pp. 396–97.

[18] F. E. Fiedler, *A Theory of Leadership Effectiveness* (New York: McGraw-Hill, 1967).

percent of respondents score in the middle range.[19] Such individuals cannot be classified as either relationship or task oriented and thus fall outside the theory's predictions. The rest of our discussion, therefore, relates to the 84 percent who score in either the high or low range of the LPC.

Fiedler assumes that an individual's leadership style is fixed. As we'll show in a moment, this is important because it means that if a situation requires a task-oriented leader and the person in that leadership position is relationship oriented, either the situation has to be modified or the leader removed and replaced if optimum effectiveness is to be achieved. Fiedler argues that leadership style is innate to a person—you *can't* change your style to fit changing situations!

After an individual's basic leadership style has been assessed through the LPC, it is necessary to match the leader with the situation. Fiedler has identified three contingency dimensions that, he argues, define the key situational factors that determine leadership effectiveness. These are **leader-member relations**, **task structure**, and **position power**. They are defined as follows:

1. *Leader-member relations*—the degree of confidence, trust, and respect subordinates have in their leader
2. *Task structure*—the degree to which the job assignments are procedurized (that is, structured or unstructured)
3. *Position power*—the degree of influence a leader has over power variables such as hiring, firing, discipline, promotions, and salary increases

So the next step in the Fiedler model is to evaluate the situation in terms of these three contingency variables. Leader-member relations are either good or poor, task structure either high or low, and position power either strong or weak.

Fiedler states the better the leader-member relations, the more highly structured the job, and the stronger the position power, the more control or influence the leader has. For example, a very favorable situation (where the leader would have a great deal of control) might involve a payroll manager who is well respected and whose subordinates have confidence in her (good leader-member relations), where the activities to be done—such as wage computation, check writing, report filing—are specific and clear (high task structure), and the job provides considerable freedom for her to reward and punish her subordinates (strong position power). On the one hand, an unfavorable situation might be the disliked chairman of a voluntary United Way fund-raising team. In this job, the leader has very little control. Altogether, by mixing the three contingency variables, there are potentially eight different situations or categories in which a leader could find himself or herself.

With knowledge of an individual's LPC and an assessment of the three contingency variables, the Fiedler model proposes matching them up to achieve maximum leadership effectiveness.[20] Based on Fiedler's study of over twelve hundred groups, where he compared relationship versus task-oriented leadership styles in each of the eight situational categories, he concluded that task-

Leader-member relations

The degree of confidence, trust, and respect subordinates have in their leader.

Task structure

The degree to which job assignments are procedurized.

Position power

Influence derived from one's formal structural position in the organization; includes power to hire, fire, discipline, promote, and give salary increases.

[19] S. Shiflett, "Is There a Problem with the LPC Score in LEADER MATCH?," *Personnel Psychology*, Winter 1981, pp. 765–69.

[20] F. E. Fiedler, M. M. Chemers, and L. Mahar, *Improving Leadership Effectiveness: The Leader Match Concept* (New York: John Wiley, 1977).

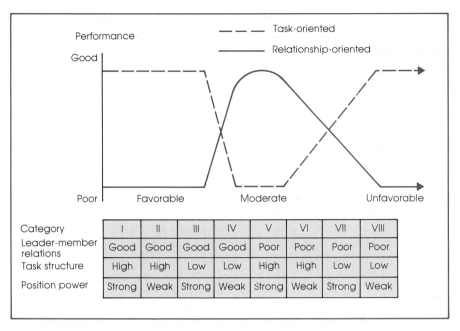

FIGURE 10–4
Findings from Fiedler Model

Category	I	II	III	IV	V	VI	VII	VIII
Leader-member relations	Good	Good	Good	Good	Poor	Poor	Poor	Poor
Task structure	High	High	Low	Low	High	High	Low	Low
Position power	Strong	Weak	Strong	Weak	Strong	Weak	Strong	Weak

oriented leaders tend to perform better in situations that were *very favorable* to them and in situations that were *very unfavorable* (see Figure 10–4). So Fiedler would predict that when faced with a category I, II, III, VII, or VIII situation, task-oriented leaders perform better. Relationship-oriented leaders, however, perform better in moderately favorable situations—categories IV through VI.

Given Fiedler's findings, how would you apply them? You would seek to match leaders and situations. Individuals' LPC scores would determine the type of situation for which they were best suited. That "situation" would be defined by evaluating the three contingency factors of leader-member relations, task structure, and position power. But remember that Fiedler views an individual's leadership style as being fixed. Therefore, there are really only two ways in which to improve leader effectiveness. First, you can change the leader to fit the situation. Analogous to a baseball game, management can reach into its "bullpen" and put in a right-handed pitcher or a left-handed pitcher, depending on the situational characteristics of the hitter. So, for example, if a group situation rates as highly unfavorable but is currently led by a relationship-oriented manager, the group's performance could be improved by replacing that manager with one who is task oriented. The second alternative would be to change the situation to fit the leader. That could be done by restructuring tasks or increasing or decreasing the power that the leader has to control factors such as salary increases, promotions, and disciplinary actions. To illustrate, assume a task-oriented leader were in a category IV situation. If this leader could increase his or her position power, then the leader would be operating in category III and the leader-situation match would be compatible for high group performance.

Do not surmise that Fiedler has closed all the gaps and put to rest all the questions underlying leadership effectiveness. Research finds that the Fiedler model predicts all except category II when laboratory studies are reviewed; however, when field studies are analyzed, the model produces supportive evidence for only categories II, V, VII, and VIII.[21] So we have conflicting results depending on the type of studies used.

As a whole, reviews of the major studies undertaken to test the overall validity of the Fiedler model lead to a generally positive conclusion. That is, there is considerable evidence to support the model.[22] But additional variables are probably needed if an improved model is to fill in some of the remaining gaps. Moreover, there are problems with the LPC and the practical use of the model that need to be addressed. For instance, the logic underlying the LPC is not well understood and studies have shown that respondents' LPC scores are not stable.[23] Also, the contingency variables are complex and difficult for practitioners to assess. It's often difficult in practice to determine how good the leader-member relations are, how structured the task is, and how much position power the leader has.[24]

Our conclusion is that Fiedler has clearly made an important contribution toward understanding leadership effectiveness. His model has been the object of much controversy and probably will continue to be. Field studies fall short of providing full support and the model could benefit by including additional moderating variables. But Fiedler's work continues to be a dominant input in the development of a contingency explanation of leadership effectiveness.

Hersey-Blanchard's Situational Theory

One of the most widely practiced leadership models is Paul Hersey and Ken Blanchard's situational leadership theory.[25] It has been used as a major training device at such *Fortune* 500 companies as BankAmerica, Caterpillar, IBM, Mobil Oil, and Xerox; it has also been widely accepted in all the military services.[26] Although the theory has not undergone extensive evaluation to test its validity, we include it here because of its wide acceptance and its strong intuitive appeal. Additionally, in defense of the theory, at this point in its development it's too early to dismiss it out of hand merely because researchers have not chosen to evaluate it more thoroughly.

---

[21] L. H. Peters, D. D. Hartke, and J. T. Pohlmann, "Fiedler's Contingency Theory of Leadership: An Application of the Meta-Analysis Procedures of Schmidt and Hunter," *Psychological Bulletin*, March 1985, pp. 274–85.

[22] Ibid.

[23] See, for instance, R. W. Rice, "Psychometric Properties of the Esteem for the Least Preferred Coworker (LPC) Scale," *Academy of Management Review*, January 1978, pp. 106–18; and C. A. Schriesheim, B. D. Bannister, and W. H. Money, "Psychometric Properties of the LPC Scale: An Extension of Rice's Review," *Academy of Management Review*, April 1979, pp. 287–90.

[24] See E. H. Schein, *Organizational Psychology*, 3rd ed. (Englewood Cliffs, NJ: Prentice Hall, 1980), pp. 116–17; and B. Kabanoff, "A Critique of Leader Match and Its Implications for Leadership Research," *Personnel Psychology*, Winter 1981, pp. 749–64.

[25] P. Hersey and K. H. Blanchard, "So You Want to Know Your Leadership Style?" *Training and Development Journal*, February 1974, pp. 1–15; and P. Hersey and K. H. Blanchard, *Management of Organizational Behavior: Utilizing Human Resources*, 4th ed. (Englewood Cliffs, NJ: Prentice Hall, 1982), pp. 150–61.

[26] Hersey and Blanchard, *Management of Organizational Behavior*, p. 171.

Situational leadership is a contingency theory that focuses on the followers. Successful leadership is achieved by selecting the right leadership style, which Hersey and Blanchard argue is contingent on the level of the followers' maturity. Before we proceed, we should clarify two points: why focus on the followers? and, what is meant by the term *maturity*?

The emphasis on the followers in leadership effectiveness reflects the reality that it is they who accept or reject the leader. Regardless of what the leader does, effectiveness depends on the actions of his or her followers. This is an important dimension that has been overlooked or underemphasized in most leadership theories.

The term **maturity**, as defined by Hersey and Blanchard, is the ability and willingness of people to take responsibility for directing their own behavior. It has two components: job maturity and psychological maturity. The first encompasses one's knowledge and skills. Individuals who are high in job maturity have the knowledge, ability, and experience to perform their job tasks without direction from others. Psychological maturity relates to the willingness or motivation to do something. Individuals high in psychological maturity don't need much external encouragement; they are already intrinsically motivated.

Maturity

The ability and willingness of people to take responsibility for directing their own behavior.

Situational leadership uses the same two leadership dimensions that Fiedler identified: task and relationship behaviors. However, Hersey and Blanchard go a step farther by considering each as either high or low and then combining them into four specific leadership styles: telling, selling, participating, and delegating. They are described as follows:

- *Telling* (high task–low relationship). The leader defines roles and tells people what, how, when, and where to do various tasks. It emphasizes directive behavior.
- *Selling* (high task–high relationship). The leader provides both directive behavior and supportive behavior.
- *Participating* (low task–high relationship). The leader and follower share in decision making, with the main role of the leader being facilitating and communicating.
- *Delegating* (low task–low relationship). The leader provides little direction or support.

The final component in Hersey and Blanchard's theory is defining four stages of maturity:

- *M1*. People are both unable and unwilling to take responsibility to do something. They are neither competent nor confident.
- *M2*. People are unable but willing to do the necessary job tasks. They are motivated but currently lack the appropriate skills.
- *M3*. People are able but unwilling to do what the leader wants.
- *M4*. People are both able and willing to do what is asked of them.

Figure 10–5 integrates the various components into the situational leadership model. As followers reach high levels of maturity, the leader responds by not only continuing to decrease control over activities, but also by continuing to decrease relationship behavior as well. At stage M1, followers need clear

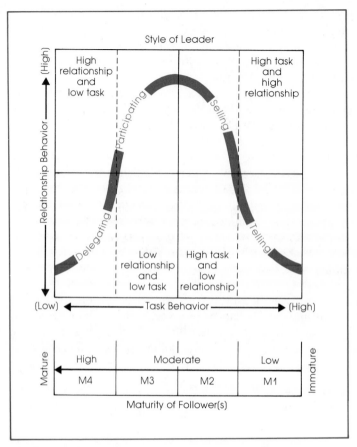

FIGURE 10–5
Situational Leadership Model

Source: Adapted from P. Hersey and K. Blanchard, *Management of Organizational Behavior: Utilizing Human Resources*, 4th ed. © 1982, p. 152. Reprinted by permission of Prentice-Hall Inc., Englewood Cliffs, N.J.

and specific directions. At stage M2, both high-task and high-relationship behavior is needed. The high-task behavior compensates for the followers' lack of ability, and the high-relationship behavior tries to get the followers psychologically to "buy into" the leader's desires. M3 creates motivational problems that are best solved by a supportive, nondirective, participative style. Finally, at stage M4, the leader doesn't have to do much because followers are both willing and able to take responsibility.

The astute reader might have noticed the high similarity between Hersey and Blanchard's four leadership styles and the four extreme "corners" in the Managerial Grid. The telling style equates to the 9,1 leader; selling equals 9,9; participating is equivalent to 1,9; and delegating is the same as the 1,1 leader. Is situational leadership, then, merely the Managerial Grid with one major difference—the replacement of the 9,9 ("one style for all occasions") contention with the recommendation that the "right" style should align with the maturity of the followers? Hersey and Blanchard say "No!"[27] They argue that the grid emphasizes *concern* for production and people, which are attitudinal dimensions. Situational leadership, in contrast, emphasizes task and relationship *behavior*. In spite of Hersey and Blanchard's claim, this is a pretty minute differentiation. Understanding of the situational leadership theory is probably enhanced by considering it as a fairly direct adaptation of the grid framework to reflect four stages of follower maturity.

Finally, we come to the critical question: Is there evidence to support situational leadership theory? As noted earlier, the theory has received little attention from researchers. Fewer than half-a-dozen studies have been undertaken to empirically test its validity, and most of these were not comprehensive.[28] Hence, any conclusions about situational leadership must be guarded. Probably the best summary statement we can currently make is that the present evidence provides partial support for the theory, especially for followers with low maturity (M1), but more research is clearly necessary.[29] Until additional, empirical research can more fully support the theory, any enthusiastic endorsement should be cautioned against.

Leader-Member Exchange Theory

For the most part, the leadership theories we've covered to this point have largely assumed that leaders treat all their subordinates in the same manner. But think about your experiences in groups. Did you notice that leaders often act very differently toward different subordinates? Did the leader tend to have favorites who made up his or her "in" group? If you answered "yes" to both these questions, you're acknowledging what George Graen and his associates have observed, which creates the foundation for their leader-member exchange theory (recently renamed from the vertical dyad linkage theory).[30]

The leader-member exchange (LMX) theory argues that because of time pressures, leaders establish a special relationship with a small group of their subordinates. These individuals make up the in-group—they are trusted, get a disproportionate amount of the leader's attention, and are more likely to receive special privileges. Other subordinates fall into the out-group. They get less of

[27] P. Hersey and K. H. Blanchard, "Grid Principles and Situationalism: Both! A Response to Blake and Mouton," *Group and Organization Studies*, June 1982, pp. 207–10.

[28] R. K. Hambleton and R. Gumpert, "The Validity of Hersey and Blanchard's Theory of Leader Effectiveness," *Group and Organization Studies*, June 1982, pp. 225–42; C. L. Graeff, "The Situational Leadership Theory: A Critical View," *Academy of Management Review*, April 1983, pp. 285–91; W. Blank, J. R. Weitzel, and S. G. Green, "Situational Leadership Theory: A Test of Underlying Assumptions," paper presented at the National Academy of Management Conference, Chicago, August 1986; and R. P. Vecchio, "Situational Leadership Theory: An Examination of a Prescriptive Theory," *Journal of Applied Psychology*, August 1987, pp. 444–51.

[29] R. P. Vecchio, "Situational Leadership Theory."

[30] F. Dansereau, J. Cashman, and G. Graen, "Instrumentality Theory and Equity Theory as Complementary Approaches in Predicting the Relationship of Leadership and Turnover Among Managers," *Organizational Behavior and Human Performance*, October 1973, pp. 184–200; and G. Graen, M. Novak, and P. Sommerkamp, "The Effects of Leader-Member Exchange and Job Design on Productivity and Satisfaction: Testing a Dual Attachment Model," *Organizational Behavior and Human Performance*, August 1982, pp. 109–31.

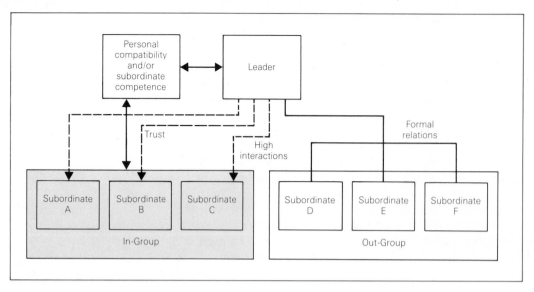

FIGURE 10–6
Leader-Member Exchange Theory

the leader's time, fewer of the preferred rewards that the leader controls, and have superior-subordinate relations based on formal authority interactions.

The theory proposes that early in the history of the interaction between a leader and a given subordinate, the leader implicitly categorizes the subordinate as an "in" or "out" and that relationship is relatively stable over time.[31] Just precisely how the leader chooses who falls into each category is unclear, but there is evidence that leaders tend to choose in-group members because they have personal characteristics (for example, age, sex, personality) that are compatible with the leader and/or a higher level of competence than out-group members.[32] (See Figure 10–6.) LMX theory predicts that subordinates with in-group status will have higher performance ratings, less turnover, and greater satisfaction with their superior.

Research to test LMX theory has been generally supportive.[33] More specifically, the theory and research surrounding it provide substantive evidence that leaders do differentiate among subordinates, that these disparities are far from

[31] G. Graen and J. Cashman, "A Role-Making Model of Leadership in Formal Organizations: A Development Approach," in J. G. Hunt and L. L. Larson (eds.), *Leadership Frontiers* (Kent, OH: Kent State University Press, 1975), pp. 143–65; and R. Liden and G. Graen, "Generalizability of the Vertical Dyad Linkage Model of Leadership," *Academy of Management Journal*, September 1980, pp. 451–65.

[32] D. Duchon, S. G. Green, and T. D. Taber, "Vertical Dyad Linkage: A Longitudinal Assessment of Antecedents, Measures, and Consequences," *Journal of Applied Psychology*, February 1986, pp. 56–60.

[33] See, for example, G. Graen, M. Novak, and P. Sommerkamp, "The Effects of Leader-Member Exchange;" T. Scandura and G. Graen, "Moderating Effects of Initial Leader-Member Exchange Status on the Effects of a Leadership Intervention," *Journal of Applied Psychology*, August 1984, pp. 428–36; and R. P. Vecchio and B. C. Gobdel, "The Vertical Dyad Linkage Model of Leadership: Problems and Prospects," *Organizational Behavior and Human Performance*, August 1984, pp. 5–20.

random, and that in-group and out-group status is related to employee performance and satisfaction.[34]

Path-Goal Theory

Currently, one of the most respected approaches to leadership is the path-goal theory. Developed by Robert House, path-goal theory is a contingency model of leadership that extracts key elements from the Ohio State leadership research on initiating structure and consideration and the expectancy theory of motivation.[35]

The essense of the theory is that it's the leader's job to assist his or her followers in attaining their goals and to provide the necessary direction and/ or support to ensure that their goals are compatible with the overall objectives of the group or organization. The term "path-goal" is derived from the belief that effective leaders clarify the path to help their followers get from where they are to the achievement of their work goals and make the journey along the path easier by reducing roadblocks and pitfalls.

According to path-goal theory, a leader's behavior is *acceptable* to subordinates to the degree that it is viewed by them as an immediate source of satisfaction or as a means of future satisfaction. A leader's behavior is *motivational* to the degree that it (1) makes subordinate need satisfaction contingent on effective performance and (2) provides the coaching, guidance, support, and rewards that are necessary for effective performance. To test these statements, House identified four leadership behaviors. The *directive leader* lets subordinates know what is expected of them, schedules work to be done, and gives specific guidance as to how to accomplish tasks. This closely parallels the Ohio State dimension of initiating structure. The *supportive leader* is friendly and shows concern for the needs of subordinates. This is essentially synonymous with the Ohio State dimension of consideration. The *participative leader* consults with subordinates and uses their suggestions before making a decision. The *achievement-oriented leader* sets challenging goals and expects subordinates to perform at their highest level. In contrast to Fiedler's view of a leader's behavior, House assumes that leaders are flexible. Path-goal theory implies that the same leader can display any or all of these behaviors depending on the situation.

As Figure 10–7 illustrates, path-goal theory proposes two classes of situational or contingency variables that moderate the leadership behavior-outcome relationship—those in the *environment* that are outside the control of the subordinate (task structure, the formal authority system, and the work group) and those that are part of the personal characteristics of the *subordinate* (locus of control, experience, and perceived ability). Environmental factors determine the type of leader behavior required as a complement if subordinate outcomes

---

[34] A. Jago, "Leadership: Perspectives in Theory and Research," *Management Science*, March 1982, pp. 331.

[35] R. J. House, "A Path-Goal Theory of Leader Effectiveness," *Administrative Science Quarterly*, September 1971, pp. 321–38; R. J. House and T. R. Mitchell, "Path-Goal Theory of Leadership," *Journal of Contemporary Business*, Autumn 1974, p. 86; and R. J. House, "Retrospective Comment," in L. E. Boone and D. D. Bowen, *The Great Writings in Management and Organizational Behavior*, 2nd ed. (New York: Random House, 1987), pp. 354–64.

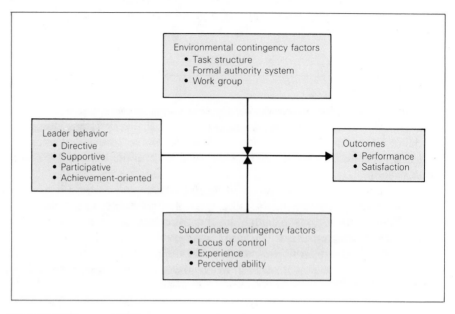

FIGURE 10–7
The Path-Goal Theory

are to be maximized, while personal characteristics of the subordinate determine how the environment and leader behavior are interpreted. So the theory proposes that leader behavior will be ineffective when it is redundant with sources of environmental structure or incongruent with subordinate characteristics.

The following are some examples of hypotheses that have evolved out of path-goal theory:

- Directive leadership leads to greater satisfaction when tasks are ambiguous or stressful than when they are highly structured and well laid out.

- Supportive leadership results in high employee performance and satisfaction when subordinates are performing structured tasks.

- Directive leadership is likely to be perceived as redundant among subordinates with high perceived ability or with considerable experience.

- The more clear and bureaucratic the formal authority relationships, the more leaders should exhibit supportive behavior and deemphasize directive behavior.

- Directive leadership will lead to higher employee satisfaction when there is substantive conflict within a work group.

- Subordinates with an internal locus of control (those who believe they control their own destiny) will be more satisfied with a participative style.

- Subordinates with an external locus of control will be more satisfied with a directive style.

- Achievement-oriented leadership will increase subordinates' expectancies that effort will lead to high performance when tasks are ambiguously structured.

Research to validate hypotheses such as these are generally encouraging.[36] The evidence supports the logic underlying the theory. That is, employee performance and satisfaction are likely to be positively influenced when the leader compensates for things lacking in either the employee or the work setting. However, the leader who spends time explaining tasks when those tasks are already clear or the employee has the ability and experience to handle them without interference, is likely to see such directive behavior as redundant or even insulting.

What does the future hold for path-goal theory? Its framework has been tested and appears to have moderate to high empirical support. We can, however, expect to see more research focused on refining and extending the theory by incorporating additional moderating variables.

Leader-Participation Model

One of the more recent additions to the contingency approach is the leader-participation model proposed by Victor Vroom and Phillip Yetton.[37] It relates leadership behavior and participation to decision making. Recognizing that task structures have varying demands for routine or nonroutine activities, these researchers suggest that leader behavior must adjust to reflect the task structure. Vroom and Yetton's model is normative—it provides a sequential set of rules that should be followed in determining the form and amount of participation in decision making, as determined by different types of situations. As shown in Figure 10–8, the model is a decision tree incorporating seven contingencies and five alternative leadership styles.

The model assumes that any of five behaviors may be feasible in a given situation—Autocratic I (AI), Autocratic II (AII), Consultative I (CI), Consultative II (CII), and Group II (GII):

- **AI.** You solve the problem or make a decision yourself using information available to you at that time.

- **AII.** You obtain the necessary information from subordinates and then decide on the solution to the problem yourself. You may or may not tell subordinates what the problem is in getting the information from them. The role played by your subordinates in making the decision is clearly one of providing the necessary information to you rather than generating or evaluating alternative solutions.

- **CI.** You share the problem with relevant subordinates individually, getting their ideas and suggestions without bringing them together as a group. Then *you* make the decision that may or may not reflect your subordinates' influence.

- **CII.** You share the problem with your subordinates as a group, collectively obtaining their ideas and suggestions. Then, you make the decision that may or may not reflect your subordinates' influence.

---

[36] J. Indik, "Path-Goal Theory of Leadership: A Meta-Analysis," paper presented at the National Academy of Management Conference, Chicago, August 1986.

[37] V. H. Vroom and P. W. Yetton, *Leadership and Decision-Making* (Pittsburgh: University of Pittsburgh Press, 1973).

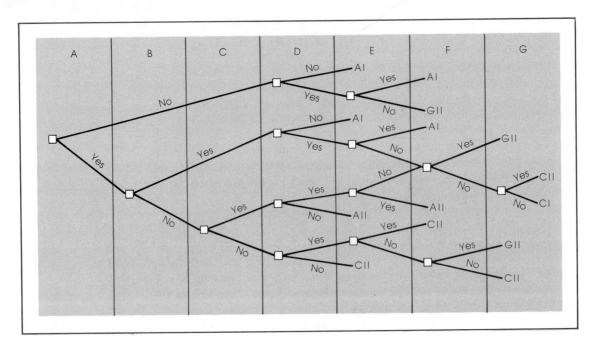

FIGURE 10–8
Leader-Participation Model

■ GII. You share the problem with your subordinates as a group. Together you generate and evaluate alternatives and attempt to reach an agreement (consensus) on a solution.

Although these five decision behaviors closely parallel the autocratic-democratic continuum depicted in Figure 10–3, the Vroom-Yetton model goes beyond that model by suggesting a specific way of analyzing problems by means of seven contingency questions. By answering "Yes" or "No" to these questions, the leader can arrive at which of the five decision behaviors is preferred—that is, how much participation should be used.

The seven questions must be answered in order from A to G:

A. Is there a quality requirement?

B. Do I have sufficient information to make a high quality decision?

C. Is the problem structured?

D. Is acceptance of the decision by subordinates critical to its implementation?

E. If I were to make the decision by myself, is it reasonably certain that it would be accepted by my subordinates?

F. Do subordinates share the organizational goals to be obtained in solving this problem?

G. Is conflict among subordinates likely in obtaining the preferred solution?

Again, referring to Figure 10–8, based on the answers to questions A through G, the leader follows the decision tree until reaching its end. The designation at the end of the branch (either AI, AII, CI, CII, or GII) tells the leader what to do.

To illustrate how the model would work, assume you're a manufacturing manager in a large electronics plant.[38] The company's management has always been searching for ways of increasing efficiency. They have recently installed new machines and put in a new simplified work system, but to the surprise of everyone, including yourself, the expected increase in productivity was not realized. In fact, production has begun to drop, quality has fallen off, and the number of employee resignations has risen.

You do not believe that there is anything wrong with the machines. You have had reports from other companies who are using them and they confirm this opinion. You have also had representatives from the firm that built the machines go over them and they report that they are operating at peak efficiency.

You suspect that some parts of the new work system may be responsible for the change, but this view is not widely shared among your immediate subordinates, who are four first-line supervisors, each in charge of a section, and your supply manager. The drop in production has been variously attributed to poor training of the operators, lack of an adequate system of financial incentives, and poor morale. Clearly, this is an issue about which there is considerable depth of feeling within individuals and potential disagreement between your subordinates.

This morning you received a phone call from your division manager. He had just received your production figures for the last six months and was calling to express his concern. He indicated that the problem was yours to solve in any way that you think best, but that he would like to know within a week what steps you plan to take.

You share your division manager's concern with the falling productivity and know that your employees are also concerned. The problem is to decide what steps to take to rectify the situation.

Referring back to Figure 10–8, what would you do? Answers to the seven questions would be: (A) Yes, (B) No, (C) No, (D) Yes, (E) No, (F) Yes, (G) Yes. Working along the model's flow chart, you arrive at the solution: GII. That is, you should share the problem with your subordinates and reach a consensus on a solution.

To date the research testing the leader-participation model has been encouraging,[39] but considerably more investigations are needed to test the model's normative propositions against effectiveness data. It does, however, confirm existing empirical evidence that leaders use participation (1) when the quality of the decision is important, (2) when it is important that subordinates accept the decision and it is unlikely that they will do so unless they are allowed to take part in it, and (3) when subordinates can be trusted to pay attention to the goals of the group rather than simply to their own preferences.

This model has also confirmed that leadership research should be directed

---

[38] From V. H. Vroom, "A New Look at Managerial Decision Making," *Organizational Dynamics*, Spring 1973, pp. 66–80. With permission.

[39] See, for example, V. H. Vroom and A. G. Jago, "On the Validity of the Vroom-Yetton Model," *Journal of Applied Psychology*, April 1978, pp. 151–62; C. Margerison and R. Glube, "Leadership Decision-Making: An Empirical Test of the Vroom and Yetton Model," *Journal of Management Studies*, February 1979, pp. 45–55; and R. H. G. Field, "A Test of the Vroom-Yetton Normative Model of Leadership," *Journal of Applied Psychology*, October 1982, pp. 523–32.

FIGURE 10–9

Source: Brant Parker and Johnny Hart, *Let There Be Reign* (Greenwich, CT: Fawcett Books, 1972).

at the situation rather than the person. It probably makes more sense to talk about autocratic and participative *situations* rather than autocratic and participative *leaders*. As did House in his path-goal theory, Vroom and Yetton argue against the notion that leader behavior is inflexible. The leader-participation model assumes that the leader can adjust his or her style to different situations.

The cartoon in Figure 10–9 proposes adjusting the individual to the coat, rather than vice versa. We can think of the "coat" as analogous to the "situation." In terms of leadership, if an individual's leadership style range is very narrow, as Fiedler proposes, we are required to place individuals into the appropriate "size of coat" if they are to lead successfully. If House and Vroom and Yetton are right, then all the leader has to do is assess the "coat" that is available and adjust his or her style accordingly. Whether we adjust the coat to fit the person or fix the person to fit the coat is an important issue. The answer is probably that it depends on the person. Individuals differ in terms of a personality

Self-monitoring

A personality trait that measures an individual's ability to adjust his or her behavior to external, situational factors.

trait that taps behavior flexibility. It's called **self-monitoring**.[40] Some people show considerable adaptability in adjusting their behavior to external, situational factors. They can behave differently in different situations. Others, however, exhibit high levels of consistency regardless of the situation. A person who is a high self-monitor should be more able to adjust his or her leadership style to changing situations.

---

[40] See, for instance, M. Snyder and N. Cantor, "Thinking about Ourselves and Others: Self-Monitoring and Social Knowledge," *Journal of Personality and Social Psychology*, August 1980, pp. 222–34; and D. F. Caldwell and C. A. O'Reilly III, "Boundary Spanning and Individual Performance: The Impact of Self-Monitoring," *Journal of Applied Psychology*, February 1982, pp. 124–27.

Sometimes Leadership Is Irrelevant!

In keeping with the contingency spirit, we want to conclude this section by offering this notion: the belief that *some* leadership style *will always* be effective *regardless* of the situation may not be true. Leadership may not always be important. Data from numerous studies collectively demonstrate that, in many situations, whatever behaviors leaders exhibit are irrelevant. Certain individual, job, and organizational variables can act as *substitutes* for leadership or *neutralize* the leader's effect to influence his or her subordinates.[41]

Neutralizers make it impossible for leader behavior to make any difference to subordinate outcomes. They negate the leader's influence. Substitutes, on the other hand, make a leader's influence not only impossible but also unnecessary. They act as a replacement for the leader's influence. For instance, characteristics of subordinates such as their experience, training, "professional" orientation, or need for independence can neutralize the effect of leadership. These characteristics can replace the need for a leader's support or ability to create structure and reduce task ambiguity. Jobs that are inherently unambiguous and routine or that are intrinsically satisfying may place fewer demands on the leadership variable. Organizational characteristics like explicit formalized goals, rigid rules and procedures, or cohesive work groups can act in the place of formal leadership.

This recent recognition that leaders don't always have an impact on subordinate outcomes should not be that surprising. After all, we have introduced a number of independent variables—attitudes, personality, ability, and group norms, to name but a few—that have been documented to have an impact on employee performance and satisfaction. Yet supporters of the leadership concept have tended to place an undue burden on this variable for explaining and predicting behavior. It is too simplistic to consider subordinates as guided to goal accomplishments based solely on the behavior of their leader. It is important, therefore, to recognize explicitly that leadership is merely another independent variable in our overall OB model. In some situations, it may contribute a lot to explaining employee productivity, absence, turnover, and satisfaction, but in other situations, it may contribute little toward that end.

LOOKING FOR COMMON GROUND: WHAT DOES IT ALL MEAN?

The topic of leadership certainly doesn't lack for theories. But from an overview perspective, what does it all mean? Let's try to identify commonalities among the leadership theories and attempt to determine what, if any, practical value the theories hold for application to organizations.

[41] S. Kerr and J. M. Jermier, "Substitutes for Leadership: Their Meaning and Measurement," *Organizational Behavior and Human Performance*, December 1978, pp. 375–403; J. P. Howell and P. W. Dorfman, "Substitutes for Leadership: Test of a Construct," *Academy of Management Journal*, December 1981, pp. 714–28; P. W. Howard and W. F. Joyce, "Substitutes for Leadership: A Statistical Refinement," paper presented at the 42nd Annual Academy of Management Conference, New York, August 1982; and J. P. Howell, P. W. Dorfman, and S. Kerr, "Leadership and Substitutes for Leadership," *Journal of Applied Behavioral Science*, Vol. 22, No. 1, 1986, pp. 29–46.

Careful examination discloses that the concepts of "task" and "people"—often expressed in more elaborate terms that hold substantially the same meaning—permeate most of the theories.[42] The task dimension is called just that by Fiedler, but it goes by the name of "initiating structure" for the Ohio State group, "directive leadership" by path-goal supporters, "production orientation" by the Michigan researchers, and "concern for production" by Blake and Mouton. The people dimension gets similar treatment going under such aliases as "consideration," "employee-oriented," "supportive," or "relationship-oriented" leadership. It seems clear that leadership behavior can be reduced to two dimensions—task and people—but researchers continue to differ as to whether the orientations are two ends of a single continuum (you could be high on one or the other but not both) or two independent dimensions (you could be high or low on both).

Although one well-known scholar argues that virtually every theory has also "wrestled with the question of how much a leader should share power with subordinates in decision making,"[43] there is far less support for this contention. The autocratic-participative continuum, the situational leadership theory, and the leadership-participation model address this issue, but the task-people dichotomy appears to be far more encompassing.

Leadership theorists don't agree on the issue of whether a leader's style is fixed or flexible. For example, Fiedler takes the former position, while Vroom and Yetton argue for the latter. Our position is that both are probably right—it depends on the leader's personality. High self-monitors are more likely to adjust their leadership style to changing situations than are low self-monitors. So the need to adjust the situation to the leader in order to improve the leader-situation match seems to be necessary only with low self-monitoring individuals.

How should we interpret the findings presented in this chapter? Some traits have shown, over time, to be modest predictors of leadership effectiveness. But that a manager possesses intelligence, dominance, self-confidence, or the like would by no means assure us that his or her subordinates would be productive and satisfied employees. The ability of these traits to predict leadership success is just not that strong.

The early task-people approaches (such as the Ohio State, Michigan, and Managerial Grid theories) also offer us little substance. The strongest statement one can make based on these theories is that leaders who rate high in people orientation should end up with satisfied employees. The research is too mixed to make predictions regarding employee productivity or the effect of a task orientation on productivity and satisfaction.

Controlled laboratory studies designed to test the Fiedler model, in aggregate, have generally supported the theory. But field studies provide more limited support. We suggest that when category II, V, VII, and VIII situations exist, the utilization of the LPC instrument to assess whether there is a leader-situation match and the use of that information to predict employee productivity and satisfaction outcomes seem warranted.

Hersey and Blanchard's situational leadership theory is straightforward,

---

[42] B. Karmel, "Leadership: A Challenge to Traditional Research Methods and Assumptions," *Academy of Management Review*, July 1978, pp. 477–79.

[43] Schein, *Organizational Psychology*, p. 132.

intuitively appealing, and important for its explicit recognition that the subordinate's ability and motivation are critical to the leader's success. Yet, in spite of its wide acceptance by practitioners, the limited amount of empirical support renders the theory, at least at this time, more speculative than substantive.

Leader-member exchange theory looks at leadership from a different angle. It focuses on in-groups and out-groups. Given the impressive evidence that in-group employees have higher performance and satisfaction than out-group members, the theory provides valuable insight for predicting leader effect as long as we know whether an employee is an "in" or "out."

The autocratic-participative continuum and its modern-day equivalent, the Vroom-Yetton leadership-participation model, offer a diversity of leadership styles. Although studies to validate the Vroom-Yetton model are still scarce, the early results are encouraging. One investigation, for example, found that leaders who were high in agreement with the model had subordinates with higher productivity and higher satisfaction than did those leaders who were in low agreement with the model.[44] A major reservation, in addition to the need for more confirming studies, is the complexity of the model itself. With five styles, seven contingency variables, and eighteen possible outcomes, it would be difficult to use as a guide for practicing managers. One might additionally question whether, under the stress of day-to-day activities, managers could be expected to follow the rational, conscious process the model requires. Of course, from our descriptive perspective, we might answer, "It doesn't matter." What does matter is that where we find leaders who follow the model, we should expect also to find productive and satisfied employees.

Finally, the path-goal model provides a framework for explaining and predicting leadership effectiveness that has developed a solid, empirical foundation. It recognizes that a leader's success depends on adjusting his or her style to the environment that the leader is placed in and the individual characteristics of followers. In a limited way, path-goal theory validates contingency variables in other leadership theories. For example, its emphasis on task structure is consistent with the Fiedler model and Vroom and Yetton (remember their question C: Is the problem structured?). Path-goal's recognition of individual characteristics is also consistent with Hersey and Blanchard's focus on the experience and ability of followers.

ANOTHER PERSPECTIVE: IMPLICIT THEORIES OF LEADERSHIP

Previously, we said that people like Gandhi, Hitler, Churchill, and Kennedy have generally been acknowledged as leaders. We suggested that they had some personal characteristics that made them leaders, yet trait studies offered us little guidance in explaining what was unique about these people. In recent years, some leadership researchers have returned to the "trait mines," but with a different twist. They openly acknowledge that it's not easy to dismiss the reality that the general public and media have shared expectations and stereotypes as to what makes an effective leader and what positive leadership

---

[44] Margerison and Glube, "Leadership Decision-Making."

OB Close-Up

The One Minute Manager: Anatomy of a Best-Seller

The One Minute Manager,[45] by Blanchard and Johnson, burst onto the *New York Times* bestseller list in the early 1980s and stayed there for over two years. While some academic reviewers were highly critical of its simple "how to" orientation, the book has sold millions of copies to practicing and aspiring managers. Why? It promises to make managers better and do it in one-minute installments. The authors argue that you can be an effective leader—"get very big results from people"—by following the three secrets to One Minute Management.

First, you set one minute goals with your subordinates. Specifically, you and each of your subordinates agree on the subordinates' work goals. The subordinates then write each goal on a single sheet of paper so you can read it in a minute or less, and these goals are checked regularly by the subordinates to see whether they are actually meeting them.

Second, you give one minute praisings. You praise people immediately and specifically when they do something right.

Third, you give one minute reprimands. Spend half of that minute telling the subordinate exactly what he or she did wrong and let them know how you feel about what they did wrong. Then spend the other thirty seconds telling the subordinate how much you value the rest of his or her work.

Simple? Yes! Simplistic? Maybe! Blanchard and Johnson's plan does not address contingency factors, but it is not inconsistent with the notion that leaders have both task and people responsibilities.

characteristics are like. The fact is, despite the sophisticated contingency models of leadership that have been developed over the past thirty years, most people use implicit theories to explain leader success and failure. In this section, we'll review two implicit theories of leadership. While it's still unclear whether they are very accurate in predicting actual leadership effectiveness, implicit leadership theories have an inherently intuitive appeal to us for no other reason than they look at leadership the way the average person "on the street" views the subject.

Attribution Theory of Leadership

In Chapter 4, we discussed attribution theory in relation to perception. Attribution theory has also been used to help explain the perception of leadership.

Attribution theory, as you remember, deals with people trying to make

[45] K. Blanchard and S. Johnson, *The One Minute Manager* (New York: William Morrow, 1982).

sense out of cause-effect relationships. When something happens, they want to attribute it to something. In the context of leadership, attribution theory says that leadership is merely an attribution that people make about other individuals.[46] Using the attribution framework, researchers have found that people characterize leaders with traits like intelligence, outgoing personality, strong verbal skills, aggressiveness, understanding, and industriousness.[47] Similarly, the high-high leader (high on both initiating structure and consideration) has been found to be consistent with attributions of what makes a good leader.[48] That is, regardless of the situation, a high-high leadership style tends to be perceived as best.

One of the more interesting themes in the attribution theory of leadership literature is the perception that effective leaders are generally considered consistent or unwavering in their decisions. That is, one of the explanations for why Lee Iacocca and Ronald Reagan (during his first term as President) were perceived as leaders was that both were fully committed, steadfast, and consistent in the decisions they made and the goals they set. Evidence indicates that a "heroic" leader is perceived as being someone who takes up a difficult or unpopular cause but, through determination and persistence, ultimately succeeds.[49]

Charismatic Leadership Theory

Charismatic leadership theory is an extension of attribution theory. It says that followers make attributions of heroic or extraordinary leadership abilities when they observe certain behaviors. Studies on charismatic leadership have, for the most part, been directed at identifying those behaviors that differentiate charismatic leaders from their noncharismatic counterparts.

There are two types of leaders.[50] The kind that most of our leadership theories have been talking about have been **transactional leaders**. They guide or motivate their followers in the direction of established goals by clarifying role and task requirements. But there is another type of leader who inspires followers to transcend their own self-interests for the good of the organization, and who is capable of having a profound and extraordinary effect on his or her followers. These are **transformational** or charismatic **leaders**. By the force of their personal abilities, they transform their followers by raising their sense of the importance and value of their tasks. "I'd walk through fire if my boss asked me to" is the kind of support that charismatic leaders inspire.

Charismatic leadership

Followers make attributions of heroic or extraordinary leadership abilities when they observe certain behaviors.

Transactional leaders

Leaders who guide or motivate their followers in the direction of established goals by clarifying role and task requirements.

Transformational leaders

Leaders who inspire followers to transcend their own self-interest for the good of the organization and who are capable of having a profound and extraordinary effect on their followers.

[46] See, for instance, J. C. McElroy, "A Typology of Attribution Leadership Research," *Academy of Management Review*, July 1982, pp. 413–17; and J. R. Meindl and S. B. Ehrlich, "The Romance of Leadership and the Evaluation of Organizational Performance," *Academy of Management Journal*, March 1987, pp. 91–109.

[47] R. G. Lord, C. L. DeVader, and G. M. Alliger, "A Meta-Analysis of the Relation Between Personality Traits and Leadership Perceptions: An Application of Validity Generalization Procedures," *Journal of Applied Psychology*, August 1986, pp. 402–10.

[48] G. N. Powell and D. A. Butterfield, "The 'High-High' Leader Rides Again!," *Group and Organization Studies*, December 1984, pp. 437–50.

[49] B. M. Staw and J. Ross, "Commitment in an Experimenting Society: A Study of the Attribution of Leadership from Administrative Scenarios," *Journal of Applied Psychology*, June 1980, pp. 249–60.

[50] B. M. Bass, *Leadership and Performance Beyond Expectations* (New York: Free Press, 1985).

Several authors have attempted to identify personal characteristics of the charismatic leader. Robert House (of path-goal fame) has identified three: extremely high confidence, dominance, and strong convictions in his or her beliefs.[51] Warren Bennis, after studying ninety of the most effective and successful leaders in the U.S., found that they had four common competencies: They had a compelling vision or sense of purpose; they could communicate that vision in clear terms that their followers could readily identify with; they demonstrated consistency and focus in the pursuit of their vision; and they knew their own strengths and capitalized on them.[52] The most recent and comprehensive analysis, however, has been completed by Conger and Kanungo at McGill University.[53] Among their conclusions, they propose that charismatic leaders have an idealized goal that they want to achieve; a strong personal commitment to their goal; are perceived as unconventional; are assertive, self-confident, and unconcerned with their followers' needs; and are perceived as agents of radical change rather than managers of the status quo. Table 10–1 summarizes the key characteristics that appear to differentiate charismatic leaders from noncharismatic ones.

What can we say about the charismatic leader's impact on his or her followers' attitudes and behavior? One study found that followers of charismatic leaders were more self-assured, experienced more meaningfulness in their work, reported more support from their leaders, worked longer hours, saw their leaders as more dynamic, and had higher performance ratings than the followers of the noncharismatic but effective leaders.[54] Another study—a laboratory experiment using House's three characteristics of charismatic leadership—found that people working under charismatic leaders were more productive and satisfied than those working under leaders who relied on the more traditional transactional behaviors of initiating structure and consideration.[55] Two studies, of course, provide a limited set of information to generalize from. We need more research on this subject. But the early evidence is encouraging.

A final thought before we conclude this section: Charismatic or transformational leadership may not always be needed to achieve high levels of employee performance. It may be most appropriate when the follower's task has an ideological component.[56] This may explain why, when charismatic leaders surface, it is more likely to be in politics, religion, wartime, or when a business firm is introducing a radically new product or facing a life-threatening crisis. Such conditions tend to involve ideological concerns. Franklin D. Roosevelt offered a vision out of the Great Depression. General MacArthur was unyielding in promoting his strategy for defeating the Japanese in World War II. Steve Jobs achieved unwavering loyalty and commitment from the technical staff he oversaw

---

[51] R. J. House, "A 1976 Theory of Charismatic Leadership," in J. G. Hunt and L. L. Larson (eds.), *Leadership: The Cutting Edge* (Carbondale: Southern Illinois University Press, 1977), pp. 189–207.

[52] W. Bennis, "The 4 Competencies of Leadership," *Training and Development Journal*, August 1984, pp. 15–19.

[53] J. A. Conger and R. N. Kanungo, "Toward a Behavioral Theory of Charismatic Leadership in Organizational Settings," *Academy of Management Review*, October 1987, pp. 637–47.

[54] B. J. Smith, *An Initial Test of a Theory of Charismatic Leadership Based on Responses of Subordinates*. Ph.D. thesis, University of Toronto, 1982.

[55] J. P. Howell, "A Laboratory Study of Charismatic Leadership." Paper presented at the National Academy of Management Conference, San Diego, CA, 1985.

[56] R. J. House, "A 1976 Theory of Charismatic Leadership."

TABLE 10–1
Key Characteristics of Charismatic Leaders

1. *Self-confident.* They have complete confidence in their judgment and ability.
2. *A vision.* This is an idealized goal that proposes a future better than the status quo. The greater the disparity between this idealized goal and the status quo, the more likely that followers will attribute extraordinary vision to the leader.
3. *Strong convictions in that vision.* Charismatic leaders are perceived as being strongly committed. They are perceived as willing to take on high personal risk, incurring high costs, and engaging in self-sacrifice to achieve their vision.
4. *Behave out of the ordinary.* Those with charisma engage in behavior that is perceived as novel, unconventional, and counter to norms. When successful, these behaviors evoke surprise and admiration in followers.
5. *Perceived as a change agent.* Charismatic leaders are perceived as agents of radical change rather than as caretakers of the status quo.

Based on J. A. Conger and R. N. Kanungo, "Toward a Behavioral Theory of Charismatic Leadership in Organizational Settings," *Academy of Management Review*, October 1987, pp. 637–47.

at Apple Computer during the late 1970s and early 1980s by articulating a vision of personal computers which would dramatically change the way people lived. Lee Iacocca inspired a new vision for Chrysler as it teetered on the verge of bankruptcy.

IMPLICATIONS FOR PERFORMANCE AND SATISFACTION

Leadership plays a central part in understanding group behavior, for it is the leader who usually provides the direction toward goal attainment. Therefore, a more accurate predictive capability should be valuable in improving group performance.

In this chapter we described a transition in approaches to the study of leadership—from the simple trait orientation to increasingly complex and sophisticated transactional models, such as path-goal and leader-participation models. With the increase in complexity has also come an increase in our ability to explain and predict behavior.

Predictive ability increased as a result of the recognition that inclusion of situational factors was critical. Recent efforts have moved beyond mere recognition toward specific attempts to isolate these situational variables. We can expect further progress to be made with leadership models, but in the last decade we have taken several large steps—large enough that we now can make moderately effective predictions as to who can best lead a group and explain under what conditions a given approach (such as task oriented or people oriented) is likely to lead to high performance and satisfaction.

In addition, the study of leadership has expanded to include implicit theories, especially the transformational or charismatic view of leadership. As we learn more about the personal characteristics that followers attribute to charismatic leaders and the conditions that facilitate its emergence, we should be increasingly able to predict situations when followers will exhibit extraordinary commitment and loyalty to their leaders and to their leaders' goals.

POINT

LEADERS MAKE A REAL DIFFERENCE!

There can be little question that the success of an organization, or any group within an organization, depends largely on the quality of its leadership. Whether in business, government, education, medicine, or religion, the quality of an organization's leadership determines the quality of the organization itself. Successful leaders anticipate change, vigorously exploit opportunities, motivate their followers to higher levels of productivity, correct poor performance, and lead the organization toward its objectives.

The importance relegated to the leadership function is well known. Rarely does a week go by that we don't hear or read about some leadership concern: "President Fails to Provide the Leadership America Needs!" "Lakers Win NBA Title on Magic Johnson's Leadership!" "The Democratic Party Searches for New Leadership!" "Sculley Leads Apple Turnaround!" A review of the leadership literature led two academics to conclude that the research shows "a consistent effect for leadership explaining 15 to 32 percent of the variance on relevant organizational outcomes."[*]

Why is leadership so important to an organization's success? The answer lies in the need for coordination and control. Organizations exist to achieve objectives that are either impossible or extremely inefficient to achieve if done by individuals acting alone. The organization itself is a coordination and control mechanism. Rules, policies, job descriptions, and authority hierarchies are illustrations of devices created to facilitate coordination and control. But leadership, too, contributes toward integrating various job activities, coordinating communication between organizational subunits, monitoring activities, and controlling deviations from standard. No amount of rules and regulations can replace the experienced leader who can make rapid and decisive decisions.

The importance of leadership is not lost on those who staff organizations. Corporations, government agencies, school systems, and institutions of all shapes and sizes cumulatively spend billions of dollars every year to recruit, select, evaluate, and train individuals for leadership positions. The best evidence, however, of the importance organizations place on leadership roles is exhibited in salary schedules. Leaders are routinely paid ten, twenty, or more times the salary of those in nonleadership positions. The head of General Motors earns approximately $1 million annually. The highest skilled auto worker, in contrast, earns under $40,000 a year. The president of this auto worker's union makes better than $75,000 a year. Police officers typically make around $25,000 to $30,000 a year. Their boss probably earns 25 percent more, and his boss another 25 percent more. The pattern is well established. The more responsibility a leader has, as evidenced by his or her level in the organization, the more he or she earns. Would organizations voluntarily pay their leaders so much more than their nonleaders if they didn't strongly believe that leaders make a real difference?

[*] D. V. Day and R. G. Lord, "Leadership and Organizational Performance: A Critical Review of Current Data and Theory." Paper presented at the National Academy of Management Conference; Chicago, August 1986.

COUNTERPOINT
LEADERS DON'T MAKE A DIFFERENCE!

Given the resources that have been spent on studying, selecting, and training leaders, you'd expect there to be clear evidence supporting the positive impact of leadership on a group or organization's performance. That evidence has failed to surface!

Analyses of leadership have frequently presumed that leadership style or leader behavior was an independent variable that could be selected or trained at will to conform to what research would find to be optimal. Even theorists who took a more contingent view of appropriate leadership behavior generally assumed that with proper training, appropriate behavior could be produced. Fiedler, noting how hard it is to change behavior, suggested changing the situational characteristics rather than the person, but this was an unusual suggestion in the context of prevailing literature that suggested that leadership style was something to be strategically selected according to the variables of the particular leadership theory.

But the leader is embedded in a social system, which constrains behavior. The leader has a role set, in which members have expectations for appropriate behavior and persons make efforts to modify the leader's behavior. Pressures to conform to the expectations of peers, subordinates, and superiors are all relevant in determining actual behavior.

Leaders, even in high-level positions, have unilateral control over fewer resources and fewer policies than might be expected. Investment decisions may require approval of others, while hiring and promotion decisions may be accomplished by committees. Leader behavior is constrained both by the demands of others in the role set and by organizationally prescribed limitations on the sphere of activity and influence.

Many factors that may affect organizational performance are outside a leader's control, even if he or she were to have complete discretion over major areas of organizational decision. For example, consider the executive in a home construction firm. Costs are largely determined by operation of commodities and labor markets, and demand is largely affected by interest rates, availablity of mortgage money, and economic conditions that are affected by governmental policies over which the executive has little control. School superintendents have little control over birth rates and community economic development, both of which profoundly affect school system budgets. While the leader may react to contingencies as they arise, or may be a better or worse forecaster, in accounting for variation in organizational outcomes, he or she may account for relatively little compared to external factors.

The leader's success or failure may also be partly due to circumstances unique to the organization but still outside his or her control. Leader positions in organizations vary in terms of the strength and position of the organization. The choice of a new executive does not fundamentally alter a market and financial position that has developed over years and affects the leader's ability to make strategic changes and the likelihood that the organization will do well or poorly. Organizations have relatively enduring strengths and weaknesses. The choice of a particular leader for a particular position has limited impact on these capabilities.

There is a basic myth associated with leadership. We believe in attribution—when something happens, we believe something has *caused* it. Leaders play that role in organizations. They take the credit for successes and the blame for failures. A more realistic conclusion would probably be that except in times of rapid growth, change, or crisis, leaders don't make much of a difference in an organization's performance.

Much of this argument is based on J. Pfeffer, "The Ambiguity of Leadership," *Academy of Management Review*, January 1977, pp. 104–11.

KEY TERMS

Autocratic Leader	LPC
Behavioral Theories	Managerial Grid
Charismatic Leadership	Maturity
Consideration	Position Power
Democratic Leader	Production-Oriented Leader
Employee-Oriented Leader	Self-monitoring
Initiating Structure	Task Structure
Leader-Member Relations	Transactional Leaders
Leadership	Transformational Leaders

FOR DISCUSSION

1. Trace the development of leadership research.
2. Discuss the strengths and weaknesses in the trait approach to leadership.
3. "Behavioral theories of leadership are static." Do you agree or disagree? Discuss.
4. What is the Managerial Grid? Contrast its approach to leadership with the Ohio State and Michigan groups.
5. Develop an example where you operationalize the Fiedler model.
6. Contrast the situational leadership theory with the Managerial Grid.
7. How do Hersey and Blanchard define *maturity*? Is this contingency variable included in any other contingency theory of leadership?
8. Develop an example where you operationalize path-goal theory.
9. Reconcile Hersey and Blanchard's situational leadership theory, path-goal theory, and substitutes for leadership.
10. Describe the leader-participation model. What are its contingency variables?
11. When might leaders be irrelevant?
12. What kind of activities could a college student pursue that might lead to the perception that he or she was a charismatic leader? In doing those activities, what might the student do to further enhance this perception of being charismatic?

FOR FURTHER READING

BEHLING, O., and C. F. RAUCH, JR., "A Functional Perspective on Improving Leadership Effectiveness," *Organizational Dynamics*, Spring 1985, pp. 51–61. The leader with a functional perspective uses structures within the larger organization to get people to accomplish important tasks and commit themselves to organizational goals.

GRIFFIN, R. W., K. D. SKIVINGTON, and G. MOORHEAD, "Symbolic and Interactional Perspectives on Leadership: An Integrative Framework," *Human Relations*, April 1987, pp. 199–218. Presents and discusses a symbolic interactional leadership model.

HUNT, J. G., "Organizational Leadership: The Contingency Paradigm and Its Challenges," in B. Kellerman (ed.), *Leadership: Multidisciplinary Perspectives*. Englewood Cliffs, NJ: Prentice Hall, 1984, pp. 113–38. Reviews the strengths and weaknesses in the contingency approaches to leadership.

KELLERMAN, B., *Leadership: Multidisciplinary Perspectives*. Englewood Cliffs, NJ: Prentice Hall, 1984. An edited volume with articles that reveal the diverse perspectives taken within the leadership literature.

KUHNERT, K. W., and P. LEWIS, "Transactional and Transformational Leadership: A Constructive/Developmental Analysis," *Academy of Management Review*, October 1987, pp. 648–57. Explains how critical personality differences in leaders lead to either transactional or transformational leadership styles.

SMITH, J. E., K. P. CARSON, and R. A. ALEXANDER, "Leadership: It Can Make a Difference," *Academy of Management Journal*, December 1984, pp. 765–76. A study of church ministers found that effective leadership was associated with improved organizational performance.

EXERCISE 10
COMPUTE YOUR LPC SCORE

Think of the person with whom you work least well. He or she may be someone you work with now, or may be someone you knew in the past. He or she does not have to be the person you like least well, but should be the person with whom you now have or have had the most difficulty in getting a job done. Describe this person as he or she appears to you by placing an "x" at that point which you believe best describes that person. Do this for each pair of adjectives.

	8	7	6	5	4	3	2	1	
Pleasant									Unpleasant
Friendly	8	7	6	5	4	3	2	1	Unfriendly
Rejecting	1	2	3	4	5	6	7	8	Accepting
Helpful	8	7	6	5	4	3	2	1	Frustrating
Unenthusiastic	1	2	3	4	5	6	7	8	Enthusiastic
Tense	1	2	3	4	5	6	7	8	Relaxed
Distant	1	2	3	4	5	6	7	8	Close
Cold	1	2	3	4	5	6	7	8	Warm
Cooperative	8	7	6	5	4	3	2	1	Uncooperative
Supportive	8	7	6	5	4	3	2	1	Hostile
Boring	1	2	3	4	5	6	7	8	Interesting
Quarrelsome	1	2	3	4	5	6	7	8	Harmonious
Self-assured	8	7	6	5	4	3	2	1	Hesitant
Efficient	8	7	6	5	4	3	2	1	Inefficient
Gloomy	1	2	3	4	5	6	7	8	Cheerful
Open	8	7	6	5	4	3	2	1	Guarded

Source: From *Leadership and Effective Management* by F. E. Fiedler and M. M. Chemers. Copyright © 1974 by Scott, Foresman & Co. Reprinted by permission.

Turn to page 564 for scoring directions and key.

In the summer of 1986, the American media had decided that then-President Ronald Reagan was the definitive role model of leadership. The following comments and analysis came from articles published by *Time* and *Fortune* at that time.*

Reagan was described as presiding over one of the longest economic recoveries in modern history, conquering inflation, and renewing confidence in America's future. Pollsters reported that Reagan had consistently higher approval ratings in polls, over a longer period, than any other two-term President since polling began.

To what did the media attribute Reagan's success? Certainly part of it was being in the right place at the right time. He came into office after a long depressive streak in American history that began with the assassination of John Kennedy and proceeded through the riots and other assassinations of the 1960s, the Vietnam War, Watergate, Nixon's resignation, the Arab oil embargo, and the Iranian hostage crisis. His recent predecessors had been labeled as "weak and devious." The previous incumbent, Jimmy Carter, had been described as seeing the future through pessimistic eyes.

One of Reagan's leadership qualities had been his optimistic outlook. He sincerely believed in America and its future. He also could use his superb communication skills to project this optimism. He was particularly adept at selling nostalgia. He brought Norman Rockwell's vision of America's bright and triumphant past to life. *Time* con-

cluded that Reagan was able to give Americans a pride in themselves and their country that had been absent since Kennedy's death. He restored self-assurance to the American people and to the office of the Presidency.

Reagan's themes were also singled out for his consistency and focus. He had a clear set of goals. He kept his agenda short and easy to understand: decrease taxes, reduce domestic spending, increase defense expenditures, and develop a tougher foreign policy. He used his previous acting experience and stage presence to sell his ideas. Reagan defined the issues he wanted considered and then set out to control the agenda to insure their implementation.

The following is an update on that earlier analysis:

By the end of his Presidency, it was generally acknowledged by the same media that Reagan had lost his leadership effectiveness. The last two years of his Presidency were characterized by a series of setbacks. The Iran-Contra Scandal, a soaring budget deficit, a stock market crash, and rejection of two Supreme Court nominees are a few of the more obvious. What had at one time looked like a textbook example of leadership effectiveness had, in a period of less than twenty-four months, collapsed. The new concern was with the leadership vacuum in the White House.

QUESTIONS

1. Review this case in light of the charismatic theory of leadership.
2. Does this case suggest that leadership effectiveness is more a result of luck than competence? Discuss.

---

* See, for instance, "Yankee Doodle Manager," *Time*, July 7, 1986, pp. 12–16; and "What Managers Can Learn from Manager Reagan," *Fortune*, September 15, 1986, pp. 33–41.

11

Power and Politics

■ *Learning objectives*

Define the four bases of power
Define the four sources of power
List seven power tactics and their contingencies
Explain how power is achieved
Clarify what creates dependency in power relationships
Describe the importance of a political perspective
List those individual and organizational factors that stimulate political behavior

You can get much farther with a kind word and a gun than you can with a kind word alone.

———— A. CAPONE

Power has been described as the last dirty word. It is easier for most of us to talk about money or even sex than it is to talk about power. People who have it deny it; people who want it, try not to appear to be seeking it; and those who are good at getting it, are secretive about how they got it.[1]

Ten years ago, we knew little about power. That's no longer true. During the past decade, we've gained considerable insights into the topic.[2] We can now make some fairly accurate predictions, for example, about what one should do if one wants to have power in a group or organization. In this chapter, we'll demonstrate that the acquisition and distribution of power is a natural process in any group or organization. Power determines the goals to be sought and how resources will be distributed. These, in turn, have important implications for member performance and satisfaction.

A DEFINITION OF POWER

Power refers to a capacity that A has to influence the behavior of B, so that B does something he or she would not otherwise do. This definition implies (1) a *potential* that need not be actualized to be effective, (2) a *dependence* relationship, and (3) the assumption that B has some *discretion* over his or her own behavior. Let's look at each of these points more closely.

Power may exist but not be used. It is, therefore, a capacity or potential. One can have power but not impose it.

Probably the most important aspect of power is that it is a function of **dependence**. The greater B's dependence on A, the greater is A's power in

Power

A capacity that A has to influence the behavior of B so that B does things he or she would not otherwise do.

Dependency

B's relationship to A when A possesses something that B requires.

[1] R. M. Kanter, "Power Failure in Management Circuits," *Harvard Business Review*, July–August 1979, p. 65.

[2] See, for example, D. Kipnis, *The Powerholders* (Chicago: University of Chicago Press, 1976); S. B. Bacharach and E. J. Lawler, *Power and Politics in Organizations* (San Francisco: Jossey-Bass, 1980); J. Pfeffer, *Power in Organizations* (Marshfield, MA: Pitman, 1981); and H. Mintzberg, *Power In and Around Organizations* (Englewood Cliffs, NJ: Prentice Hall, 1983).

the relationship. Dependence, in turn, is based on alternatives that B perceives and the importance that B places on the alternative(s) that A controls. A person can have power over you only if he or she controls something you desire. If you want a college degree, have to pass a certain course to get that degree, and your current instructor is the only faculty member in the college that teaches that course, he or she has power over you. Your alternatives are highly limited and you place a high degree of importance on obtaining a passing grade. Similarly, if you're attending college on funds totally provided by your parents, you probably recognize the power that they hold over you. You are dependent on them for financial support. But once you're out of school, have a job, and are making a solid income, your parents' power is reduced significantly. Who among us, though, has not known or heard of the rich relative who is able to control a large number of family members merely through the implicit or explicit threat of "writing them out of the will"?

For A to get B to do something he or she otherwise would not do means that B must have the discretion to make choices. At the extreme, if B's job behavior is so programmed that he is allowed no room to make choices, he obviously is constrained in his ability to do something other than what he is doing. For instance, job descriptions, group norms, organizational rules and regulations, as well as community laws and standards constrain people's choices. As a nurse, you may be dependent on your supervisor for continued employment. But in spite of this dependence, you're unlikely to comply with her request to perform heart surgery on a patient or steal several thousand dollars from petty cash. Your job description and laws against stealing constrain your ability to make these choices.

CONTRASTING LEADERSHIP AND POWER

A careful comparison of our description of power with our description of leadership in the previous chapter should bring the recognition that the two concepts are closely intertwined. Leaders use power as a means of attaining group goals. Leaders achieve goals, and power is a means of facilitating their achievement.

What differences are there between the two terms? One difference relates to goal compatibility. Power does not require goal compatibility, merely dependence. Leadership, on the other hand, requires some congruence between the goals of the leader and the led. A second difference relates to the direction of influence. Leadership focuses on the downward influence on one's subordinates. It ignores lateral and upward influence patterns. Power does not. Still another difference deals with research emphasis. Leadership research, for the most part, emphasizes style. It seeks answers to such questions as: How supportive should a leader be? How much decision making should be shared with subordinates? In contrast, the research on power has tended to encompass a broader area and focus on tactics for gaining compliance. It has gone beyond the individual as exerciser because power can be used by groups as well as by individuals to control other individuals or groups.

Where does power come from? What is it that gives an individual or group influence over others? The early answer to these questions was a five-category classification scheme identified by French and Raven.[3] They proposed that there were five bases or sources of power that they termed coercive, reward, expert, legitimate, and referent power. Coercive power depends on fear; reward power derives from the ability to distribute anything of value (typically money, favorable performance appraisals, interesting work assignments, friendly colleagues, and preferred work shifts or sales territories); expert power refers to influence that derives from special skills or knowledge; legitimate power is based on the formal rights one receives as a result of holding an authoritative position or role in an organization; and **referent power** develops out of others' admiration for one and their desire to model their behavior and attitudes after that person. While French and Raven's classification scheme provided an extensive repertoire of possible bases of power, their categories created ambiguity because they confused bases of power with sources of power.[4] The result was much overlapping. We can improve our understanding of the power concept by separating bases and sources so as to develop clearer and more independent categories.

Referent power

Influence held by A based on B's admiration and desire to model himself or herself after A.

Bases of power refers to what the powerholder has that gives him or her power. Assuming that you're the powerholder, your bases are what you control that enables you to manipulate the behavior of others. There are four power bases—coercive power, reward power, persuasive power, and knowledge power.[5] We'll expand on each in a moment.

How are sources of power different from bases of power? The answer is that sources tell us where the power holder gets his or her power bases. That is, sources refer to how you come to control the bases of power. There are four sources—the position you hold, your personal characteristics, your expertise, and the opportunity you have to receive and obstruct information.[6] Each of these will also be discussed in a moment.

Let us now consider the four bases of power.

Bases of Power

Coercive Power   The **coercive** base depends on fear. One reacts to this power out of fear of the negative ramifications that might result if one fails to comply. It rests on the application, or the threat of application, of physical sanctions such as infliction of pain, deformity, or death; the generation of frustration through restriction of movement; or the controlling through force of basic physiological or safety needs.

Coercive power

Power that is based on fear.

[3] J. R. P. French, Jr., and B. Raven, "The Bases of Social Power," in D. Cartwright (ed.), *Studies in Social Power* (Ann Arbor: University of Michigan, Institute for Social Research, 1959), pp. 150–67.

[4] Bacharach and Lawler, *Power and Politics*, pp. 34–36.

[5] Adapted from Ibid., and A. Etzioni, *Comparative Analysis of Complex Organizations* (New York: Free Press, 1961).

[6] Bacharach and Lawler, *Power and Politics*, pp. 34–36.

In the 1930s, when John Dillinger went into a bank, held a gun to the teller's head, and asked for the money, he was incredibly successful at getting compliance with his request. His power base? Coercive. A loaded gun gives its holder power because others are fearful that they will lose something that they hold dear—their lives.

> Of all the bases of power available to man, the power to hurt others is possibly most often used, most often condemned, and most difficult to control . . . the state relies on its military and legal resources to intimidate nations, or even its own citizens. Businesses rely upon the control of economic resources. Schools and universities rely upon their right to deny students formal education, while the church threatens individuals with loss of grace. At the personal level, individuals exercise coercive power through a reliance upon physical strength, verbal facility, or the ability to grant or withhold emotional support from others. These bases provide the individual with the means to physically harm, bully, humiliate, or deny love to others.[7]

At the organization level, A has coercive power over B if A can dismiss, suspend, or demote B, assuming that B values his or her job. Similarly, if A can assign B work activities that B finds unpleasant or treat B in a manner that B finds embarrassing, A possesses coercive power over B.

Reward Power   The opposite of coercive power is the power to reward. People comply with the wishes of another because it will result in positive benefits; therefore, one who can distribute rewards that others view as valuable will have power over them. Our definition of rewards is here limited to only material rewards. This would include salaries and wages, commissions, fringe benefits, and the like.

Persuasive power

The ability to allocate and manipulate symbolic rewards.

Persuasive Power   Persuasive power rests on the allocation and manipulation of symbolic rewards. If you can decide who is hired, manipulate the mass media, control the allocation of status symbols, or influence a group's norms, you have persuasive power. For instance, when a teacher uses the class climate to control a deviant student, or when a union steward arouses the members to use their informal power to bring a deviant member into line, you are observing the use of persuasive power.

Knowledge power

The ability to control unique and valuable information.

Knowledge Power   Knowledge, or access to information, is the final base of power. We can say that when an individual in a group or organization controls unique information, and when that information is needed to make a decision, that individual has knowledge-based power.

To summarize, the bases of power refer to what the powerholder controls that enables him or her to manipulate the behavior of others. The coercive base of power is the control of punishment, the reward base is the control of material rewards, the persuasive base is the control of symbolic rewards, and the knowledge base is the control of information. Table 11–1 offers some common symbols that would suggest a manager has developed strong power bases.

[7] Kipnis, *Powerholders*, pp. 77–78.

TABLE 11–1
Common Symbols of a Manager's Power

To what extent a manager can
- Intercede favorably on behalf of someone in trouble with the organization
- Get a desirable placement for a talented subordinate
- Get approval for expenditures beyond the budget
- Get above-average salary increases for subordinates
- Get items on the agenda at policy meetings
- Get fast access to top decision makers
- Get regular, frequent access to top decision makers
- Get early information about decisions and policy shifts

Source: Reprinted by permission of the *Harvard Business Review*. An exhibit from "Power Failure in Management Circuits," by Rosabeth M. Kanter (July/August 1979), p 67. Copyright © 1979 by the President and Fellows of Harvard College; all rights reserved.

Sources of Power

Position Power In formal groups and organizations, probably the most frequent access to one or more of the power bases is one's structural position. A teacher's position includes significant control over symbols, a secretary frequently is privy to important information, and the head coach of an NFL team has substantial coercive resources at his disposal. All of these bases of power are achieved as a result of the formal position each holds within their structural hierarchy.

Personal Power Personality traits were discussed in Chapter 3 and again in the previous chapter on leadership. They reappear within the topic of power when we acknowledge the fact that one's **personal** characteristics can be a source of power. If you are articulate, domineering, physically imposing, or possessing of that mystical quality called "charisma," you hold personal characteristics that may be used to get others to do what you want.

Personal power

Influence attributed to one's personal characteristics.

Expert Power Expertise is a means by which the powerholder comes to control specialized information (rather than the control itself, which we have discussed as the knowledge base of power). Those who have expertise in terms of specialized information can use it to manipulate others. Expertise is one of the most powerful sources of influence, especially in a technologically oriented society. As jobs become more specialized, we become increasingly dependent on "experts" to achieve goals. So, while it is generally acknowledged that physicians have expertise and hence **expert power**—when your doctor talks, you listen— you should also recognize that computer specialists, tax accountants, solar engineers, industrial psychologists, and other specialists are able to wield power as a result of their expertise.

Expert power

Influence based on special skills or knowledge.

Opportunity Power Finally, being in the right place at the right time can give one the **opportunity** to exert power.[8] One need not hold a formal position in a group or organization to have access to information that is important to

Opportunity power

Influence obtained as a result of being in the right place at the right time.

[8] D. J. Brass, "Being in the Right Place: A Structural Analysis of Individual Influence in an Organization," *Administrative Science Quarterly*, December 1984, pp. 518–39.

others or to be able to exert coercive influence. An example of how one can use an opportunity to create a power base is the story of former U.S. President, Lyndon Johnson, when he was a student at Southwestern Texas State Teachers College. He had a job as special assistant to the college president's personal secretary.

> As special assistant, Johnson's assigned job was simply to carry messages from the president to the department heads and occasionally to other faculty members. Johnson saw that the rather limited function of messenger had possibilities for expansion; for example, encouraging recipients of the messages to transmit their own communications through him. He occupied a desk in the president's outer office, where he took it upon himself to announce the arrival of visitors. These added services evolved from a helpful convenience into an aspect of the normal process of presidential business. The messenger had become an appointments secretary, and, in time, faculty members came to think of Johnson as a funnel to the president. Using a technique which was later to serve him in achieving mastery over the Congress, Johnson turned a rather insubstantial service into a process through which power was exercised.[9]

Johnson eventually broadened his informal duties to include handling the president's political correspondence, preparing his reports for state agencies, and even regularly accompanying the college president on his trips to the state capital—the president eventually relying on his young apprentice for political counsel. Certainly this represents an example of someone using an opportunity to redefine his job and to give himself power.

Summary

The foundation to understanding power begins by identifying where power comes from (sources) and, given that one has the means to exert influence, what it is that one manipulates (bases). Figure 11–1 visually depicts the relationship between sources and bases. Sources are the means. Individuals can use their position in the structure, rely on personal characteristics, develop expertise,

FIGURE 11–1
Sources and Bases of Power

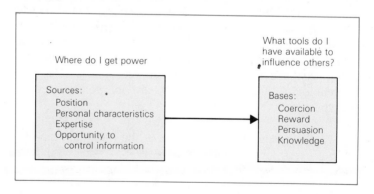

---

[9] D. Kearns, "Lyndon Johnson and the American Dream," *The Atlantic Monthly*, May 1976, p. 41.

Predictions About People with a High Need for Power

David McClelland and his associates have conducted nearly 100 studies on the power motive.[10] These studies provide convincing evidence that there is, in fact, something called a *need for power* (see Chapter 6), and that it allows for meaningful predictions of behavior. The following represent some of the more interesting findings related to individuals high in the need for power:

- They show partiality toward ingratiating followers.
- They inhibit group discussion when they are group leaders, resulting in the group considering fewer alternatives and having lower quality of decisions.
- They pursue occupations like teaching, psychology, journalism, and business that allow them to exert significant influence over others.
- High-power males report that they have more arguments, play competitive sports more, have less stable interpersonal relations, experience more emotional problems, and are more impulsively aggressive than low-power males.

or take advantage of opportunities to control information. Control of one or more of these sources allows the powerholder to manipulate the behavior of others via coercion, reward, persuasion, or knowledge bases. To reiterate, sources are *where* you get power. Bases are *what* you manipulate. Those who seek power must develop a source of power. Then, and only then, can they acquire a power base.

DEPENDENCY: THE KEY TO POWER

Earlier in this chapter it was said that probably the most important aspect of power is that it is a function of dependence. In this section, we'll show how an understanding of dependency is central to furthering your understanding of power itself.

The General Dependency Postulate

Let's begin with a general postulate: *The greater B's dependency on A, the greater power A has over B.* When you possess anything that others require

[10] D. C. McClelland, *Human Motivation* (Glenview, IL: Scott, Foresman, 1985).

but that you alone control, you make them dependent upon you and, therefore, you gain power over them.[11] Dependency, then, is inversely proportional to the alternative sources of supply. If something is plentiful, possession of it will not increase your power. If everyone is intelligent, intelligence gives no special advantage. Similarly, among the superrich, money is no longer power. But as the old saying goes, "in the land of the blind, the one-eyed man is king!" If you can create a monopoly by controlling information, prestige, or anything that others crave, they become dependent on you. Conversely, the more that you can expand your options, the less power you place in the hands of others. This explains, for example, why most organizations develop multiple suppliers rather than give their business to only one. It also explains why so many of us aspire to financial independence. Financial independence reduces the power that others can have over us.

Michael Milken provides an example of the role that dependency plays in a work group or an organization. He is the incredibly successful head of the corporate bond department at the New York brokerage firm of Drexel, Burnham, and Lambert. A native Californian, Milken grew disenchanted with New York and decided to return to southern California and a warmer climate. But Milken made so much money for his employer that the firm was not about to let him go. The solution: Rather than lose his skills to a competitor with West Coast connections, the company agreed to move its entire bond department to California. Milken and his staff were all moved to Los Angeles. The cost of setting up the office, moving employees and their families, and absorbing housing subsidies were all part of the price Drexel, Burnham, and Lambert was willing to pay to keep Milken's skills.[12]

Another example took place in professional basketball during the fall of 1981. Earvin "Magic" Johnson, the then twenty-two-year-old superstar on the Los Angeles Laker team, chose one Wednesday evening to blast his coach's system. He told the press that he could not continue to play under his coach, Paul Westhead, and demanded to be traded. Within twenty-four hours, the Lakers' owner fired Westhead.

Westhead's record was not in question. He had led the Lakers to the NBA championship during the 1979–80 season. At the time of his firing, the team was only half-a-game behind its conference leader with a 7–4 win-loss record. The issue really was: Who was dispensable? In the summer of 1981, Johnson had signed a twenty-five-year, $25 million contract with the Laker organization. Westhead, on the other hand, was operating under a far less lucrative four-year pact. Johnson was a major asset to the Laker team and his twenty-five-year contract made it almost impossible for him to be traded. No other team was willing to assume such a contractual obligation. The Laker owner had little choice but to fire the coach. Regardless of the fact that a professional coach is the formal boss over the team members, this example dramatizes that a player or any employee (who has no legitimate position power) can still be extremely influential if the "team's" options are severely restricted.

---

[11] R. E. Emerson, "Power-Dependence Relations," *American Sociological Review*, Vol. 27 (1962), pp. 31–41.

[12] S. Johnson, "Mohammed and the Mountain," *The New York Times*, January 29, 1978, p. F5.

What Creates Dependency?

Dependency is increased when the resource you control is *important*, *scarce*, and *nonsubstitutable*.[13]

Importance　　If nobody wants what you've got, it's not going to create dependency. To create dependency, therefore, the thing(s) you control must be perceived as being important. It's been found, for instance, that organizations actively seek to avoid uncertainty.[14] We should, therefore, expect that those individuals or groups who can absorb an organization's uncertainty will be perceived as controlling an important resource. For instance, a study of industrial organizations found that the marketing departments in these firms were consistently rated as the most powerful.[15] It was concluded by the researcher that the most critical uncertainty facing these firms was selling their products. This might suggest that during a labor strike, the organization's negotiating representatives have increased power or that engineers, as a group, would be more powerful at Apple Computer than at Procter & Gamble. These inferences appear to be generally valid. Labor negotiators do become more powerful within the personnel area and the organization as a whole during periods of labor strife. An organization such as Apple Computer, which is heavily technologically oriented, is highly dependent on its engineers to maintain its product quality. And, at Apple, engineers are clearly the most powerful group. At Procter & Gamble, marketing is the name of the game, and marketers are the most powerful occupational group. These examples support not only the view that the ability to reduce uncertainty increases a group's importance and, hence, its power but also that what's important is situational. It varies between organizations and undoubtedly also varies over time within any given organization.

Scarcity　　As noted previously, if something is plentiful, possession of it will not increase your power. A resource needs to be perceived as scarce to create dependency.

This can help to explain how low-ranking members in an organization, who have important knowledge not available to high-ranking members, gain power over the high-ranking members. Possession of a scarce resource—in this case, important knowledge—makes the high-ranking member dependent on the low-ranking member. This also helps to make sense out of behaviors of low-ranking members that, otherwise, might seem illogical, such as destroying the procedure manuals that describe how a job is done, refusing to train people in their job or even to show others exactly what they do, creating specialized language and terminology that inhibits others from understanding their jobs, or operating in secrecy so the activity will appear more complex and difficult than it really is.

The scarcity-dependency relationship can further be seen in the power of occupational categories. Individuals in occupations in which the supply of personnel is low relative to demand can negotiate compensation and benefit

---

[13] Mintzberg, *Power In and Around Organizations*, p. 24.

[14] R. M. Cyert and J. G. March, *A Behavioral Theory of the Firm* (Englewood Cliffs, NJ: Prentice Hall, 1963).

[15] C. Perrow, "Departmental Power and Perspective in Industrial Firms," in M. N. Zald (ed.), *Power in Organizations* (Nashville, TN: Vanderbilt University Press, 1970).

packages far more attractive than can those in occupations where there is an abundance of candidates. College administrators have no problem today finding English instructors. The market for business teachers, in contrast, is extremely tight—with demand high and the supply limited. The result is that the bargaining power of business faculty allows them to negotiate higher salaries, lighter teaching loads, and other benefits. Similarly, petroleum engineers were able to negotiate incredibly attractive deals with employers in the late 1970s. But by the mid- and late 1980s, when the demand for oil dropped and exploration projects were shelved, those same petroleum engineers found their bargaining power greatly reduced. There is nothing inherently magic about the skills of a petroleum engineer that allowed new college graduates in the field to earn 30 percent more than other engineering graduates in 1979—scarcity had temporarily created dependency, which, in turn, increased the bargaining power of petroleum engineers.

Nonsubstitutability   The more that a resource has no viable substitutes, the more power that control over that resource provides. This is illustrated in a concept we'll call the "**elasticity of power.**"

In economics, considerable attention is focused on the elasticity of demand, which is defined as the relative responsiveness of quantity demanded to change in price. This concept can be modified to explain the strength of power.

Elasticity of power is defined as the relative responsiveness of power to change in available alternatives. One's ability to influence others is viewed as being dependent on how these others perceive their alternatives.

As shown in Figure 11–2, assume that there are two individuals. Mr. A's power elasticity curve is relatively inelastic. This would describe, for example, an employee who believed that he had a large number of employment opportunities outside his current organization. Fear of being fired would have only a moderate impact on Mr. A., for he perceives that he has a number of other alternatives. Mr. A's boss finds that threatening A with termination has only a minimal impact on influencing A's behavior. A reduction in alternatives (from X to $X-1$) only increases the power of A's boss slightly (A' to A''). However, Mr. B's curve is relatively elastic. He sees few other job opportunities. His age, education, present salary, or lack of contacts may severely limit his ability to find a job somewhere else. As a result, Mr. B is dependent on his present organization and boss. If B loses his job (Y to $Y-1$), he may face prolonged unemployment, and it shows itself in the increased power of B's boss. As long as B perceives his options as limited and B's boss holds the power to terminate his employment, B's boss will hold considerable power over him. In such a situation, it is obviously important for B to get his boss to believe that his options are considerably greater than they really are. If this is not achieved, B places his fate in the hands of his boss and makes him captive to almost any demands the boss devises.

Higher education provides an excellent example of how this elasticity concept operates. In universities where there are strong pressures for the faculty to publish, we can say that a department head's power over a faculty member is inversely related to that member's publication record. The more recognition the faculty member receives through publication, the more mobile he or she is. That is, since other universities want faculty who are highly published and visible, there is an increased demand for his or her services. Although the

Elasticity of power

The relative responsiveness of power to change in available alternatives.

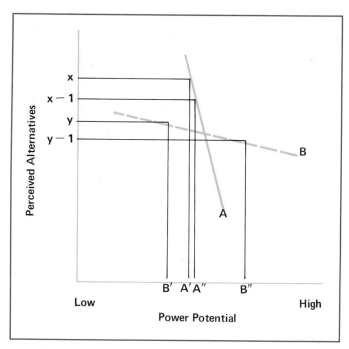

FIGURE 11–2
Elasticity of Power

concept of tenure can act to alter this relationship by restricting the department head's alternatives, those faculty members with little or no publications have the least mobility and are subject to the greatest influence from their superiors.

POWER TACTICS

This section is a logical extension of our previous discussions. We've reviewed *where* power comes from and *what* it is that powerholders manipulate. Now, we go the final step—to power tactics. Tactics tell us *how* to manipulate the bases. The following discussion will show you how employees translate their power bases into specific actions.

One of the few elements of power that has gone beyond anecdotal evidence or armchair speculation is the topic of tactics. Recent research indicates that there are standardized ways by which powerholders attempt to get what they want.[16]

When 165 managers were asked to write essays describing an incident

[16] See D. Kipnis, S. M. Schmidt, and I. Wilkinson, "Intraorganizational Influence Tactics: Explorations in Getting One's Way," *Journal of Applied Psychology*, August 1980, pp. 440–52; W. K. Schilit and E. A. Locke, "A Study of Upward Influence in Organizations," *Administrative Science Quarterly*, June 1982, pp. 304–16; and D. Kipnis, S. M. Schmidt, C. Swaffin-Smith, and I. Wilkinson, "Patterns of Managerial Influence: Shotgun Managers, Tacticians, and Bystanders," *Organizational Dynamics*, Winter 1984, pp. 58–67.

in which they influenced their bosses, co-workers, or subordinates, a total of 370 power tactics grouped into fourteen categories were identified. These answers were condensed, rewritten into a fifty-eight-item questionnaire, and given to over 750 employees. These respondents were not only asked how they went about influencing others at work but also the possible reasons for influencing the target person. The results, which are summarized here, give us considerable insight into power tactics—how managerial employees influence others and the conditions under which one tactic is chosen over another.[17]

The findings identified seven tactical dimensions or strategies:

- *Reason*—use of facts and data to make a logical or rational presentation of ideas
- *Friendliness*—use of flattery, creation of goodwill, acting humble, and being friendly prior to making a request
- *Coalition*—getting the support of other people in the organization to back up the request
- *Bargaining*—use of negotiation through the exchange of benefits or favors
- *Assertiveness*—use of a direct and forceful approach such as demanding compliance with requests, repeated reminders, ordering individuals to do what is asked, and pointing out that rules require compliance
- *Higher authority*—gaining the support of higher levels in the organization to back up requests
- *Sanctions*—use of organizationally derived rewards and punishments such as preventing or promising a salary increase, threatening to give an unsatisfactory performance evaluation, or withholding a promotion

The researchers found that employees do not rely on the seven tactics equally. However, as shown in Table 11–2, the most popular strategy was the use of reason, regardless of whether the influence was directed upward or downward. Additionally, the researchers uncovered four contingency variables that affect the selection of a power tactic: the manager's relative power, the manager's objectives for wanting to influence, the manager's expectation of the target person's willingness to comply, and the organization's culture.

A manager's relative power impacts the selection of tactics in two ways. First, managers who control resources that are valued by others, or who are perceived to be in positions of dominance, use a greater variety of tactics than do those with less power. Second, managers with power use assertiveness with greater frequency than do those with less power. Initially, we can expect that most managers will attempt to use simple requests and reason. Assertiveness is a backup strategy, used when the target of influence refuses or appears reluctant to comply with the request. Resistance leads to managers using more directive strategies. Typically, they shift from using simple requests to insisting that their demands be met. But the manager with relatively little power is more likely to stop trying to influence others when he or she encounters resistance, because he or she perceives the costs associated with assertiveness as unacceptable.

[17] This section is adapted from Kipnis, Schmidt, Swaffin-Smith, and Wilkinson, "Patterns of Managerial Influence."

TABLE 11-2
Usage of Power Tactics: From Most to Least Popular

	When Managers Influenced Superiors*	When Managers Influenced Subordinates
Most Popular	Reason	Reason
	Coalition	Assertiveness
	Friendliness	Friendliness
	Bargaining	Coalition
	Assertiveness	Bargaining
Least Popular	Higher authority	Higher authority
		Sanctions

* Sanctions is omitted in the scale that measures upward influence.

Source: Reprinted, by permission of the publisher, from "Patterns of Managerial Influence: Shotgun Managers, Tacticians, and Bystanders," by D. Kipnis et al. *Organizational Dynamics*, Winter 1984, p. 62. © 1984 Periodicals Division, American Management Associations, New York. All rights reserved.

Managers vary their power tactics in relation to their objectives. When managers seek benefits from a superior, they tend to rely on kind words and the promotion of pleasant relationships; that is, they use friendliness. In comparison, managers attempting to persuade their superiors to accept new ideas usually rely on reason. This matching of tactics to objectives also holds true for downward influence. For example, managers use reason to sell ideas to subordinates and friendliness to obtain favors.

The manager's expectations of success guides his or her choice of tactics. When past experience indicates a high probability of success, managers use simple requests to gain compliance. Where success is less preditable, managers are more tempted to use assertiveness and sanctions to achieve their objectives.

Finally, we know that cultures within organizations differ markedly—for example, some are warm, relaxed, and supportive; others are formal and conservative. The organizational culture in which a manager works, therefore, will have a significant bearing on defining which tactics are considered appropriate. Some cultures encourage the use of friendliness, some encourage reason, and still others rely on sanctions and assertiveness. So the organization itself will influence which subset of power tactics is viewed as acceptable for use by managers.

POWER IN GROUPS: COALITIONS

Those "out of power" and seeking to be "in" will first try to increase their power individually. Why spread the spoils if one doesn't have to? But if this proves ineffective, the alternative is to form a **coalition**. There is strength in numbers.

Coalition

Two or more individuals who combine their power to push for or support their demands.

The natural way to gain influence is to become a powerholder. Therefore, those who want power will attempt to build a personal power base. But, in many instances, this may be difficult, risky, costly, or impossible. In such cases, efforts will be made to form a coalition of two or more "outs" who, by joining together, can combine their resources to increase rewards for themselves.[18]

In the late 1960s, college students found that by joining together to form a "student power group," they could achieve ends that had been impossible individually. Historically, employees in organizations who were unsuccessful in bargaining on their own behalf with management resorted to labor unions to bargain for them. In recent years, even some managers have joined unions after finding it difficult to exert power individually to attain higher wages and greater job security.

What predictions can we make about coalition formation?[19] First, coalitions in organizations often seek to maximize their size. In political science theory, coalitions move the other way—they try to minimize their size. They tend to be just large enough to exert the power necessary to achieve their objectives. But legislatures are different from organizations. Specifically, decision making in organizations does not end with merely selection from among a set of alternatives. The decision must also be implemented. In organizations, the implementation of and commitment to the decision is at least as important as the decision itself. It's necessary, therefore, for coalitions in organizations to seek a broad constituency to support the coalition's objectives. This means expanding the coalition to encompass as many interests as possible. This coalition expansion to facilitate consensus building, of course, is more likely to occur in organizational cultures where cooperation, commitment, and shared decision making are highly valued. In autocratic and hierarchically controlled organizations, this search for maximizing the coalition's size is less likely to be sought.

Another prediction about coalitions relates to the degree of interdependence within the organization. More coalitions will likely be created where there is a great deal of task and resource interdependence. In contrast, there will be less interdependence among subunits and less coalition formation activity where subunits are largely self-contained or resources are abundant.

Finally, coalition formation will be influenced by the actual tasks that workers do. The more routine the task of a group, the greater the likelihood that coalitions will form. The more that the work that people do is routine, the greater their substitutability for each other and, thus, the greater their dependence. To offset this dependence, they can be expected to resort to a coalition. We see, therefore, that unions appeal more to low-skill and nonprofessional workers than to skilled and professional types. Of course, where the supply of skilled and professional employees is high relative to their demand or where organizations have standardized traditionally unique jobs, we would expect even these incumbents to find unionization attractive.

[18] P. P. Poole, "Coalitions: The Web of Power," in D. J. Vredenburgh and R. S. Schuler (eds.), *Effective Management: Research and Application*, Proceedings of the 20th Annual Eastern Academy of Management, Pittsburgh, May 1983, pp. 79–82.

[19] See Pfeffer, *Power in Organizations*, pp. 155–57.

When people get together in groups, power will be exerted. People want to carve out a niche from which to exert influence, to earn awards, and to advance their careers.[20] When employees in organizations convert their power into action, we describe them as engaged in politics. Those with good political skills have the ability to use their bases of power effectively.[21]

Definition

There have been no shortages of definitions for organizational politics. Essentially, however, they have focused on the use of power to affect decision making in the organization or on behaviors by members that are self-serving and organizationally nonsanctioned.[22] For our purposes, we shall define **political behavior** in organizations as *those activities that are not required as part of one's formal role in the organization, but that influence, or attempt to influence, the distribution of advantages and disadvantages within the organization.*[23]

This definition encompasses key elements from what most people mean when they talk about organizational politics. Political behavior is *outside* one's specified job requirements. The behavior requires some attempt to use one's *power* bases. Additionally, our definition encompasses efforts to influence the goals, criteria, or processes used for *decision making* when we state that politics is concerned with "the distribution of advantages and disadvantages within the organization." Our definition is broad enough to include such varied political behaviors as withholding key information from decision makers, whistleblowing, spreading rumors, leaking confidential information about organizational activities to the media, exchanging favors with others in the organization for mutual benefit, or lobbying on behalf of or against a particular individual or decision alternative.

A final comment relates to what has been referred to as the "legitimate-illegitimate" dimension in political behavior.[24] **Legitimate political behavior** refers to normal everyday politics—complaining to your supervisor, bypassing the chain of command, forming coalitions, obstructing organizational policies or decisions through inaction or excessive adherence to rules, and developing contacts outside the organization through one's professional activities. On the other hand, there are also **illegitimate** or extreme political behaviors that violate the implied "rules of the game." Those who pursue such activities are often

Political behavior

Those activities that are not required as part of one's formal role in the organization but that influence, or attempt to influence, the distribution of advantages and disadvantages within the organization.

Legitimate political behavior

Normal everyday politics.

Illegitimate political behavior

Extreme political behavior that violates the implied rules of the game.

---

[20] S. A. Culbert and J. J. McDonough, *The Invisible War: Pursuing Self-interest at Work* (New York: John Wiley, 1980), p. 6.

[21] Mintzberg, *Power In and Around Organizations*, p. 26.

[22] D. J. Vredenburgh and J. G. Maurer, "A Process Framework of Organizational Politics," *Human Relations*, January 1984, pp. 47–66.

[23] D. Farrell and J. C. Petersen, "Patterns of Political Behavior in Organizations," *Academy of Management Review*, July 1982, p. 405.

[24] Ibid., pp. 406–07.

OB Close-Up

Politics Is in the Eye of the Beholder

A behavior that one person labels as "organizational politics" is very likely to be characterized as an instance of "effective management" by another.[25] The fact is not that effective management is necessarily political, though in some cases it might be. Rather, a person's reference point determines what he or she classifies as organizational politics. Take a look at the following labels used to describe the same phenomenon. These suggest that politics, like beauty, is in the eye of the beholder.

"Political" label	*"Effective management" label*
1. Blaming others	1. Fixing responsibility
2. Ingratiation	2. Positive reinforcement
3. Creating obligations	3. Developing working relationships
4. Apple-polishing	4. Demonstrating loyalty
5. Passing the buck	5. Delegating authority
6. Coopting	6. Negotiation
7. Covering your rear	7. Documenting decisions
8. Creating conflict	8. Encouraging change and innovation
9. Forming coalitions	9. Facilitating teamwork
10. Whistleblowing	10. Improving efficiency

described as individuals who "play hardball." Illegitimate activities include sabotage, whistleblowing, and symbolic protests such as unorthodox dress, wearing protest buttons, or groups of employees cumulatively calling in sick.

The vast majority of all organizational political actions are of the legitimate variety. The reasons are pragmatic: the extreme illegitimate forms of political behavior pose a very real risk of loss of organizational membership or extreme sanctions against those who use them and then fall short in having enough power to insure they work.

The Importance of a Political Perspective

Those who fail to acknowledge political behavior ignore the reality that organizations are political systems. It would be nice if all organizations or formal groups

---

[25] Based on T. C. Krell, M. E. Mendenhall, and J. Sendry, "Doing Research in the Conceptual Morass of Organizational Politics." Paper presented at the Western Academy of Management Conference, Hollywood, CA, April 1987.

within organizations could be described in such terms as supportive, harmonious, trusting, collaborative, or cooperative. A nonpolitical perspective can lead one to believe that employees will always behave in ways consistent with the interests of the organization. In contrast, a political view can explain much of what may seem to be irrational behavior in organizations. It can help to explain, for instance, why employees withhold information, restrict output, attempt to "build empires," publicize their successes, hide their failures, distort performance figures to make themselves look better, and engage in similar activities that appear to be at odds with the organization's desire for effectiveness and efficiency.

Factors Contributing to Political Behavior

Recent research and observation has identified a number of factors that appear to be associated with political behavior. Some are individual characteristics, derived from the unique qualities of the people that the organization employs; others are a result of the organization's culture or internal environment.

Individual Factors   At the individual level, researchers have identified certain personality characteristics, needs, and other individual factors that are likely to be related to political behavior. Employees who are authoritarian, have a high-risking propensity, or possess an external locus of control have been shown to act politically with less regard for the consequences to the organization.[26] A high need for power, autonomy, security, or status has also been found to be a major contributor to an employee's tendency to engage in political behavior.[27]

Additionally, an individual's investment in the organization, perceived alternatives, and expectations of success will influence the degree to which he or she will pursue illegitimate means of political action.[28] The more that a person has invested in the organization in terms of expectations of increased future benefits, the more a person has to lose if forced out and the less likely he or she is to use illegitimate means. The more alternative job opportunities an individual has—due to a favorable job market, scarce skills or knowledge, prominent reputation, or influential contacts outside the organization—the more likely he or she is to risk illegitimate political actions. Last, if an individual places a low expectation of success in using illegitimate means, it is unlikely that he or she will attempt them. Conversely, high expectations of success—and use of illegitimate means—are most likely to be the province of experienced

[26] See, for example, B. T. Mayes and R. W. Allen, "Toward a Definition of Organizational Politics," *Academy of Management Review*, October 1977, pp. 672–78; D. J. Moberg, "Factors Which Determine the Perception and Use of Organizational Politics," paper presented at the 38th Annual Academy of Management Conference, San Francisco, 1978; and L. W. Porter, R. W. Allen, and H. L. Angle, "The Politics of Upward Influence in Organizations," in L. L. Cummings and B. M. Staw (eds.), *Research in Organizational Behavior*, Vol. 3 (Greenwich, CT: JAI Press, 1981), pp. 121–22.

[27] See, for example, J. E. Haas and T. E. Drabek, *Complex Organizations: A Sociological Perspective* (New York: Macmillan, 1973); R. T. Mowday, "The Exercise of Upward Influence in Organizations," *Administrative Science Quarterly*, March 1978, pp. 137–56; and D. L. Madison, R. W. Allen, L. W. Porter, P. A. Renwick, and B. T. Mayes, "Organizational Politics: An Exploration of Manager's Perceptions," *Human Relations*, February 1980, pp. 79–100.

[28] Farrell and Petersen, "Patterns of Political Behavior," p. 408.

"I have to take one three times a day to curb my insatiable appetite for power."

FIGURE 11–3

Source: Drawing by Dana Fradon; © 1977, The New Yorker Magazine, Inc.

and powerful individuals with polished political skills and inexperienced and naive employees who misjudge their probabilities of success.

Organizational Factors   Political activity is probably more a function of the organization's characteristics than of individual difference variables. Why? Because most organizations have a large number of employees with the individual characteristics we listed, yet the presence of political behavior varies widely.

   While we acknowledge the role that individual differences can play in fostering politicking, the evidence more strongly supports that certain situations and cultures promote politics. More specifically, when an organization's resources are declining or when the existing pattern of resources is changing, politics is more likely to surface.[29] In addition, cultures characterized by low trust, role ambiguity, unclear performance evaluation systems, zero-sum reward allocation practices, and democratic decision making will create opportunities for political activities to breed.[30]

[29] S. C. Goh and A. R. Doucet, "Antecedent Situational Conditions of Organizational Politics: An Empirical Investigation," paper presented at the Annual Administrative Sciences Association of Canada Conference, Whistler, B. C.; May 1986; and C. Hardy, "The Contribution of Political Science to Organizational Behavior," in J. W. Lorsch (ed.), *Handbook of Organizational Behavior* (Englewood Cliffs, NJ: Prentice Hall, 1987), p. 103.

[30] See, for example, Madison et al., "Organizational Politics"; Porter et al., "The Politics of Upward Influence in Organizations," pp. 113–20; Vredenburgh and Maurer, "A Process Framework of Organizational Politics"; and Farrell and Petersen, "Patterns of Political Behavior," p. 409.

When organizations cut back to improve efficiency, reductions in resources have to be made. Threatened with the loss of resources, people may engage in political actions to safeguard what they have. But any changes, especially those that imply significant reallocation of resources within the organization, are likely to stimulate conflict and increase politicking.

The less trust there is within the organization, the higher the level of political behavior and the more likely that the political behavior will be of the illegitimate kind. So high trust should suppress the level of political behavior in general and inhibit illegitimate actions in particular.

Role ambiguity means that the prescribed behaviors of the employee are not clear. There are fewer limits, therefore, to the scope and functions of the employee's political actions. Since political activities are defined as those not required as part of one's formal role, the greater the role ambiguity, the more one can engage in political activity with little chance of it being visible.

The practice of performance evaluation is far from a perfected science. The more that organizations use subjective criteria in the appraisal, emphasize a single outcome measure, or allow significant time to pass between the time of an action and its appraisal, the greater the likelihood that an employee can get away with politicking. Subjective performance criteria create ambiguity. The use of a single outcome measure encourages individuals to do whatever is necessary to "look good" on that measure, but often at the expense of performing well on other important parts of the job that are being appraised. The amount of time that elapses between an action and its appraisal is also a relevant factor. The longer the time period, the more unlikely that the employee will be held accountable for his or her political behaviors.

The more that an organization's culture emphasizes the zero-sum or win-lose approach to reward allocations, the more employees will be motivated to engage in politicking. The zero-sum approach treats the reward "pie" as fixed so that any gain one person or group achieves has to come at the expense of another person or group. If I win, you must lose! If $10,000 in annual raises is to be distributed among five employees, then any employee who gets more than $2,000 takes money away from one or more of the others. Such a practice encourages making others look bad and increasing the visibility of what you do.

In the last twenty-five years there has been a general move in North America toward making organizations less autocratic. While much of this trend has been more in theory than in practice, it is undoubtedly true that in many organizations, managers are being asked to behave more democratically. Managers are told that they should allow subordinates to advise them on decisions and that they should rely to a greater extent on group input into the decision process. Such moves toward democracy, however, are not necessarily desired by individual managers. Many managers sought their positions in order to have legitimate power so as to be able to make unilateral decisions. They fought hard and often paid high personal costs to achieve their influential positions. Sharing their power with others runs directly against their desires. The result is that managers may use the required committees, conferences, and group meetings in a superficial way—as arenas for maneuvering and manipulating.

Knowledge-based power is the most strongly and consistently related to effective performance. For example, in a study of five organizations, knowledge was the most effective base for getting others to perform as desired.[31] Competence appears to offer wide appeal, and its use as a power base results in high performance by group members.

In contrast, position power does *not* appear to be related to performance differences. In spite of position being the most widely given reason for complying with a superior's wishes, it does not seem to lead to higher performance, though the findings are far from conclusive. Among blue-collar workers, one researcher found significantly positive relations between position power and four to six production measures. However, position power was not related with average earnings or performance against schedule.[32] Another study could find no relationship between the use of position power and high efficiency ratings.[33] One's position is effective for exacting compliance, but there is little evidence to suggest that it leads to higher levels of performance. This may be explained by the fact that position power tends to be fairly constant, especially within a given organization.

The use of reward and coercive power has a significant inverse relationship to performance. People hold a negative view of reward and coercion as reasons for complying with a superior's requests. This view is reflected in the finding that these bases are associated with lower performance.[34] Further, research finds the use of coercive power to be negatively related to group effectiveness.[35]

We find that knowledge power is also strongly and consistently related to satisfaction. The evidence overwhelmingly indicates that this base is most satisfying to subjects of the power.[36] Knowledge-based power obtains both public and private compliance and avoids the problem of making subjects comply merely because the powerholder has the "right" to request compliance. Additionally, our value system is built on the idea of merit and competence, and knowledge power appears to align most closely with these values. If individuals find knowledge power to be most compatible with American values, it should logically give the greatest satisfaction.

---

[31] J. G. Bachman, D. G. Bowers, and P. M. Marcus, "Bases of Supervisory Power: A Comparative Study in Five Organizational Settings," in A. S. Tannenbaum (ed.), *Control in Organizations* (New York: McGraw-Hill, 1968), p. 236.

[32] K. Student, "Supervisory Influence and Work-Group Performance," *Journal of Applied Psychology*, June 1968, pp. 188–94.

[33] J. Ivancevich, "An Analysis of Control, Bases of Control, and Satisfaction in an Organizational Setting," *Academy of Management Journal*, December 1970, pp. 427–36.

[34] J. G. Bachman, "Faculty Satisfaction and the Dean's Influence: An Organizational Study of Twelve Liberal Arts Colleges," *Journal of Applied Psychology*, February 1968, pp. 55–61; and J. G. Bachman, C. G. Smith, and J. A. Slesinger, "Control, Performance and Satisfaction: An Analysis of Structure and Individual Effort," *Journal of Personality and Social Psychology*, August 1966, pp. 127–36.

[35] Bachman, Bowers, and Marcus, "Bases of Supervisory Power."

[36] Ibid.

Finally, the use of coercive power is inversely related to individual satisfaction. Coercion not only creates resistance, it is generally disliked by individuals. Studies of college teachers and sales personnel found coercion the least preferred power base.[37] A study of insurance company employees also drew the same conclusion.[38]

[37] See note 34.
[38] Ivancevich, "Analysis of Control."

POINT

SUCCESSFUL MANAGERS ARE POWER ORIENTED

What makes or motivates a good manager? This question is so enormous in scope that anyone trying to answer it has difficulty knowing where to begin. Some people might say that a good manager is one who is successful, and by now, most business researchers and business executives themselves know what motivates people who successfully run their own small businesses. The key to their success has turned out to be what psychologists call "the need for achievement," the desire to do something better or more efficiently than it has been done before.

But what does achievement motivation have to do with good management? There is no reason on theoretical grounds why a person who has a strong need to be more efficient should make a good manager. Rather, the manager's job seems to call more for someone who can influence people than for someone who does things better on his or her own. In motivational terms, then, we might expect the successful manager to have a greater "need for power" than a need to achieve.

To measure the motivations of managers, good and bad, we studied a number of individual managers from different U.S. corporations who were participating in management workshops designed to improve their managerial effectiveness. The general conclusion of these studies is that the top manager of a company must possess a high need for power, that is, a concern for influencing people. However, this need must be disciplined and controlled so that it is directed toward the benefit of the institution as a whole and not toward the manager's personal aggrandizement. Moreover, the top manager's need for power ought to be greater than his or her need for being liked by people.

In examining the motive scores of over fifty managers of both high- and low-morale units in all sections of the same large company, we found that most of the managers—over 70 percent—were high in power motivation compared with employees in general. This finding confirms that power motivation is important for management. (Remember that as we use the term "power motivation," it refers not to dictatorial behavior, but to a desire to have impact, to be strong and influential.) The better managers, as judged by the morale of those working for them, tended to score even higher in power motivation. But the most important determining factor of high morale turned out not to be how their power motivation compared to their need to achieve but whether it was higher than their need to be liked. This relationship existed for 80 percent of the better sales managers as compared with only 10 percent of the poorer managers. And the same held true for other managers in nearly all parts of the company.

In summary, the good manager in a large company does not have a high need for achievement, as we define and measure that motive, although there must be plenty of that motive somewhere in the organization. The top managers shown here have a high need for power and an interest in influencing others, both greater than their interest in being liked by people. The manager's concern for power should be socialized—controlled so that the institution as a whole, not only the individual, benefits. People and nations with this motive profile are empire builders; they tend to create high morale and to expand the organizations they head.

Adapted by permission of the *Harvard Business Review.* Excerpted from "Power Is the Great Motivator" by D. C. McClelland and D. H. Burnham (*Harvard Business Review*, March–April 1976). Copyright © 1976 by the President and Fellows of Harvard College; all rights reserved.

COUNTERPOINT

THE CASE FOR THE RELATIONAL MANAGER

Data from contemporary research indicate that people who now get to the top in management are strongly power motivated. They do not typically show strong needs for affiliation—for close, cozy groups. But the organizational world is not fixed; it is slowly changing. So it seems quite possible that researchers will "discover" some years from now that successful managers are more relational than they had believed and less competitive or power oriented.

Some relevant questions we have been worrying about include these:

Do competitive, power-driven people now succeed because of the inherent nature of organized work or because that's the way we set up our organizations in the old days and changing now is very painful?

Does the direct, competitive, power image of the executive at least partly reflect the rigid old organization's effort to attract people like itself from the shrinking population of young people who still share those standards?

Let us elaborate on the assertion that times are indeed changing in a direction calling for more *relational* managerial styles.

Consider the following findings and current trends:

1. Despite the widespread macho mythology about competitiveness in the executive suite, research points out that competitiveness does not seem to be the key to success. Other, more "intrinsic" styles called "work" (preference for getting on with the work) and "mastery" (an interest in mastering skills and the like) seem to play a far bigger role.

2. Young people are shifting their values and interests (not radically, but incrementally) away from careers as their central life focus and toward a concern about general "lifestyle."

3. The hunger for warm, affectionate relationships appears to be growing in the United States. Many of the traditional institutions that provided people with a sense of membership and community have been declining. And faith in them has been declining more rapidly.

4. Firms using strongly relational styles often are successful in the United States. Recent studies of American companies, derived from earlier observations of Japanese organizations, suggest the advantages, including the cost-effectiveness, of a relational milieu.

5. Women are moving into management. Organizations now have access to a large number of people in our society who traditionally have been trained to a very high level of relational orientation and skill.

6. More and more, the tasks of contemporary organizations (particularly in high-technology industries) require teamwork. Buying collections of individual stars does not necessarily produce great team performance unless those stars can be bonded together with some strong relational glue.

Taken together, these forces seem to dictate a prescription for incremental, modest, but real shifts toward more relational strategies.

Adapted by permission of the publisher, from "A Case for the Relational Manager" by H. J. Leavitt and J. Lipman-Blumen, *Organizational Dynamics*, Summer 1980 © 1980 by AMACOM, a division of American Management Associations, pp. 27–32. All rights reserved.

KEY TERMS

Coalition

Coercive Power

Dependency

Elasticity of Power

Expert Power

Illegitimate Political Behavior

Knowledge Power

Legitimate Political Behavior

Opportunity Power

Personal Power

Persuasive Power

Political Behavior

Power

Referent Power

FOR DISCUSSION

1. What is power? How is it different from leadership?

2. Contrast French and Raven's power classification to the bases and sources presented in this chapter.

3. What is the difference between a source of power and a base of power?

4. Contrast power tactics with power bases and sources. What are some of the key contingency variables that determine which tactic a powerholder is likely to use?

5. "Knowledge power and expert power are the same thing." Do you agree or disagree? Discuss.

6. What is a coalition? When is it likely to develop?

7. Based on the information presented in this chapter, what would you do as a new college graduate entering a new job to maximize your power and accelerate your career progress?

8. How are power and politics related?

9. "More powerful managers are good for an organization. It is the powerless, not the powerful, that are the ineffective managers." Do you agree or disagree with this statement? Discuss.

10. Define political behavior. Differentiate between legitimate and illegitimate political actions.

11. "Politicking in organizations is bad." Do you agree or disagree with this statement? Discuss.

12. What factors contribute to political activity?

FOR FURTHER READING

GANDZ, J., and V. V. MURRAY, "The Experience of Workplace Politics," *Academy of Management Journal*, June 1980, pp. 237–51. Reports from recent graduates of a business school on the impact that politics has in their organizations.

KOTTER, J. P., "Power, Dependence, and Effective Management," *Harvard Business Review*, July–August 1977, pp. 125–36. Describes common characteristics of managers who have been successful at acquiring considerable power and using it to manage their dependence on others.

MULDER, M., R. D. DE JONG, L. KOPPELAAR, and J. VERHAGE, "Power, Situation, and Leaders' Effectiveness: An Organizational Field Study," *Journal of Applied Psychology*, November 1986, pp. 566–70. Found that open consultation was judged to be used more often in noncrisis situations, while formal power, sanction power, and expert power were more prevalent in crisis situations.

PODSAKOFF, P. M. and C. A. SCHRIESHEIM, "Field Studies of French and Raven's Bases of Power: Critique, Reanalysis, and Suggestions for Future Research," *Psychological Bulle-*

tin, May 1985, pp. 387–411. Challenges much of the research on French and Raven's conceptualization of power.

VREDENBURGH, D. J., and J. G. MAURER, "A Process Framework of Organizational Politics," *Human Relations*, January 1984, pp. 47–66. Summarizes the literature, to date, on organizational politics and presents a model to facilitate understanding.

YUKL, G., and T. TABER, "The Effective Use of Managerial Power," *Personnel*, March–April 1983, pp. 37–44. Provides guidelines for managers in using five common types of leadership power.

EXERCISE 11

POWER ORIENTATION TEST

Instructions: For each statement, circle the number that most closely resembles your attitude.

Statement	DISAGREE A Lot	DISAGREE A Little	Neutral	AGREE A Little	AGREE A Lot
1. The best way to handle people is to tell them what they want to hear.	1	2	3	4	5
2. When you ask someone to do something for you, it is best to give the real reason for wanting it rather than giving reasons that might carry more weight.	1	2	3	4	5
3. Anyone who completely trusts anyone else is asking for trouble.	1	2	3	4	5
4. It is hard to get ahead without cutting corners here and there.	1	2	3	4	5
5. It is safest to assume that all people have a vicious streak, and it will come out when they are given a chance.	1	2	3	4	5
6. One should take action only when it is morally right.	1	2	3	4	5
7. Most people are basically good and kind.	1	2	3	4	5
8. There is no excuse for lying to someone else.	1	2	3	4	5
9. Most people forget more easily the death of their father than the loss of their property.	1	2	3	4	5
10. Generally speaking, people won't work hard unless they're forced to do so.	1	2	3	4	5

Source: R. Christie and F. L. Geis, *Studies in Machiavellianism.* © Academic Press 1970. Reprinted by permission.

Turn to page 565 for scoring directions and key.

Tom Brokaw comes from humble roots in South Dakota. But today, at the age of forty-eight, he earns approximately $2 million a year and is king of the hill at NBC News. As one colleague put it, "Tom Brokaw *is* NBC News, and will be as long as he wants to be." Our question: How did he do it?[39]

Tom Brokaw took over as sole anchor in 1983. NBC News was in disarray. The anchor chair had been passed from John Chancellor to Roger Mudd and Tom Brokaw together and finally to Brokaw alone; the news division had seen three presidents in five years. An atmosphere of confusion and malaise prevailed that inevitably affected the quality of the "Nightly News"—stories were missed, internal communications were faulty, the newscast lacked a clear sense of direction.

The nadir was reached with the Mudd-Brokaw debacle. They were supposed to be the Huntley-Brinkley of the '80s, but the ratings were awful and the anchors argued over assignments and airtime. After seventeen months, NBC gave up on the format and went with Brokaw over Mudd, partly because Brokaw was better at live coverage, partly because he was more willing to promote himself and NBC.

Once ensconced, he proceeded to banish any lingering shadows from the past by rebuilding the staff of the "Nightly News." Virtually all the key players have been replaced, mostly by people who had worked with Brokaw before. The newscast today has been essentially shaped by Brokaw and his people.

As a leader, Brokaw fosters a collegial atmosphere. He participates in discussions but doesn't dominate them, nor is he dogmatic in insisting how correspondents handle their stories. At the same time, there's no question he's become the proverbial 2000-pound gorilla. He's known to indulge in an occasional shouting fit in the newsroom, and although one or two senior editors will challenge him, for most of the staff, Brokaw's wish is their command. Colleagues say that he doesn't pull any of that "prima donna stuff," but it's pretty clear that when he conveys the direction he thinks things should go, people quickly start running that way.

From his base at the "Nightly News," Brokaw has gradually increased his sphere of influence into other areas of the news division. For instance, in June 1987, he took on the job of chief of correspondents. He is now to represent correspondents' interests within the network as a sort of ombudsman. He will also have a say in how correspondents are deployed, which correspondents are hired and which are fired. Brokaw describes his new position as "a watershed move" in the evolution of the anchorman's responsibilities, a step in "the institutional future of network news" that will last long after he is gone. His correspondents aren't so sure. As one put it, "How can I talk to Tom Brokaw when my problem is Tom Brokaw?"

Brokaw argues that one reason he needs to assume more management responsibility is to offset a perception of weakness in the leadership of Lawrence K. Grossman, the current president of NBC News. When Grossman first took over in 1984, he was respected for bringing a sense of stability and moral purpose to the division. Since then, however, many at the network, including Brokaw, have grown critical of the substance of Grossman's administration, feeling he's paid too much attention to cosmetics and too little to the fundamentals of news gathering.

Brokaw's style has worked well for him at NBC News. His forte is frank but discreet diplomacy. If he has a disagreement with someone, the differences are discussed in private. Colleagues say that when he has fits of temper, they are usually followed by private chats that serve to prevent long-lasting hard feelings.

Brokaw now faces what may be his greatest diplomatic challenge: how to deal with NBC's new owners, General Electric. GE is known for its unsentimental attachment to the bottom line, and it's been taking a hard look at the losses of NBC News. In dealing with GE, Brokaw has taken pains to portray himself as a realist. He admits network news has been guilty of extravagance and that some belt-tightening is in order. But he also wants to help determine how much is cut, and whom, so that the quality of the news isn't crippled. Some people at NBC News question how effective his subtle approach will be if GE starts decimating the news division at some point in the future. "It's going to be interesting," one correspondent said, "to see where Tom says, 'Enough is enough,' and decides to go for the fight."

QUESTIONS

1. What are Brokaw's sources of power?
2. What are Brokaw's bases of power?
3. Do you think a person has to have a high power need to reach a position such as a network anchor? To keep the position?
4. "Brokaw's power improves the effectiveness of NBC News." Do you agree or disagree? Discuss.

Based on D. Hill, "How Tom Brokaw Has Built His Power—And Uses It," *TV Guide,* October 24, 1987, pp. 7–11.

12

Conflict and Intergroup Relations

■ *Chapter outline*

■ *Learning objectives*

Differentiate between the traditional, human relations, and interactionist views of conflict

Outline the conflict process

Differentiate between functional and dysfunctional conflict

Summarize the sources of conflict

Describe five methods for reducing conflicts

List the benefits and disadvantages of conflict

Explain the factors that affect intergroup relations

Identify methods for managing intergroup relations

Part of my job as a coach is to keep the five guys who hate me away from the five guys who are undecided.

———— C. STENGEL

It has been proposed that conflict is a theme that has occupied the thinking of man more than any other—with the exception of God and love.[1] It has been only recently, though, that conflict has become a major area of interest and research for students of organizational behavior. The evidence suggests that this interest has been well placed—the type and intensity of conflict *does* affect group behavior.

In this chapter, we shall define conflict, review three different ways of looking at it, present a process model of conflict, and consider the impact of conflict on group behavior. Then we'll discuss an issue closely intertwined with conflict; that is, intergroup relations. In addition to defining and clarifying the importance of intergroup relations, we'll review the key factors that affect intergroup relations and methods for managing intergroup performance.

A DEFINITION OF CONFLICT

There has been no shortage of definitions for conflict.[2] In spite of the divergent meanings the term has acquired, several common themes underlie most definitions. Conflict must be *perceived* by the parties to it. Whether conflict exists or not is a perception issue. If no one is aware of a conflict, it is generally agreed that no conflict exists. Of course, conflicts perceived may not be real, while many situations that otherwise could be described as conflictive are not because the group members involved do not perceive the conflict. For a conflict to exist, therefore, it must be perceived. Additional commonalities among most conflict definitions are the concepts of *opposition*, *scarcity*, and *blockage* and the assumption that there are two or more parties whose interests or goals appear to be incompatible. Resources—whether money, jobs, prestige, power, or whatever—are not unlimited, and their scarcity encourages blocking behavior. The parties are therefore in opposition. When one party blocks the goal achievement of another, a conflict state exists.

Differences between definitions tend to center on *intent* and whether

---

[1] R. D. Luce and H. Raiffa, *Games and Decisions* (New York: John Wiley, 1957).

[2] C. F. Fink, "Some Conceptual Difficulties in the Theory of Social Conflict," *Journal of Conflict Resolution*, December 1968, pp. 412–60.

OB Close-Up

Is Conflict Different from Competition?

"Competition and conflict are the same thing!" "Competition is good but conflict isn't!" "Competition leads to conflict!" Which, if any, of these views are correct?

Competition and conflict are not synonymous terms. Competition is aimed at obtaining a goal without interference from another party. It is regulated by rules. When two athletes race against each other in a track meet, their behavior is governed by the rules of the game. Both wait for the gun before taking off, they stay in their proper lanes, and they do nothing to physically block the other. Conflict, on the other hand, is directed against another party. In conflict, one party purposely seeks to block the other's goal attainment. So it is possible for competition to occur without conflict, for conflict to exist without competition, and for both to take place simultaneously. Moreover, intense competition can lead to conflict. In our track meet example, if one of the athletes purposely cuts into the other's lane and this forces the competitor to break his stride, competitive behavior is likely to escalate to conflict. But just because conflict implies blockage does not mean that conflict is necessarily bad. As we'll point out, some conflicts are functional.

Conflict

A process in which an effort is purposely made by A to offset the efforts of B by some form of blocking that will result in frustrating B in attaining his or her goals or furthering his or her interests.

conflict is a term limited only to *overt acts*. The intent issue is a debate over whether blockage behavior must be a determined action or whether it could occur as a result of fortuitous circumstances. As to whether the conflict can only refer to overt acts, some definitions, for example, require signs of manifest fighting or open struggle as criteria for the existence of conflict.

Our definition of conflict acknowledges awareness (perception), opposition, scarcity, and blockage. Further, we assume it to be a determined action, which can exist at either the latent or overt level. We define **conflict** to be *a process in which an effort is purposely made by A to offset the efforts of B by some form of blocking that will result in frustrating B in attaining his or her goals or furthering his or her interests.*

While this definition may, at first glance, seem esoteric, the terms and concepts that are used will become increasingly clear later in this chapter when we describe the stages that lead to conflict.

TRANSITIONS IN CONFLICT THOUGHT

It is entirely appropriate to say that there has been "conflict" over the role of conflict in groups and organizations. One school of thought has argued that conflict must be avoided—that it indicates a malfunctioning within the group.

We call this the *traditional* view. Another school of thought, the *human relations* view, argues that conflict is a natural and inevitable outcome in any group and that it need not be evil, but rather has the potential to be a positive force in determining group performance. The third, and most recent perspective, proposes not only that conflict *can* be a positive force in a group but explicitly argues that some conflict is *absolutely necessary* for a group to perform effectively. We label this third school the *interactionist* approach. Let us take a closer look at each of these views.[3]

The Traditional View

The early approach to conflict assumed that all conflict was bad. Conflict was viewed negatively, and it was used synonymously with such terms as violence, destruction, and irrationality to reinforce its negative connotation. Conflict, by definition, was viewed as being harmful and was to be avoided.

The **traditional view** was consistent with the attitudes that prevailed about group behavior in the 1930s and 1940s. From findings provided by studies like those done at Hawthorne, it was argued that conflict was a dysfunctional outcome resulting from poor communication, a lack of openness and trust between people, and the failure of managers to be responsive to the needs and aspirations of their employees.

The view that all conflict is bad certainly offers a simple approach to looking at the behavior of people who create conflict. Since all conflict is to be avoided, we need merely direct our attention to the causes of conflict and correct these malfunctionings in order to improve group and organizational performance. Although research studies now provide strong evidence to dispute that this approach to conflict reduction results in high group performance, most of us still evaluate conflict situations utilizing this outmoded standard.

Traditional view

The belief that all conflict must be avoided.

The Human Relations View

The **human relations** position argued that conflict was a natural occurrence in all groups and organizations. Since conflict was inevitable, the human relations school advocated acceptance of conflict. They rationalized its existence: It cannot be eliminated, and there are even times when conflict may benefit a group's performance. The human relations view dominated conflict theory from the late 1940s through the mid-1970s.

Human relations view

The belief that conflict is a natural and inevitable outcome in any group.

The Interactionist View

The current view toward conflict is the **interactionist** perspective. While the human relations approach *accepted* conflict, the interactionist approach *encourages* conflict on the grounds that a harmonious, peaceful, tranquil, and cooperative group is prone to becoming static, apathetic, and nonresponsive to needs

Interactionist view

The belief that conflict is not only a positive force in a group but that it is absolutely necessary for a group to perform effectively.

[3] This section has been adapted from S. P. Robbins, *Managing Organizational Conflict: A Nontraditional Approach* (Englewood Cliffs, NJ: Prentice Hall, 1974), pp. 11–25.

for change and innovation. The major contribution of the interactionist approach, therefore, is encouraging group leaders to maintain an ongoing minimum level of conflict—enough to keep the group viable, self-critical, and creative.

Given the interactionist view, and it is the one we shall take in this chapter, it becomes evident that to say conflict is all good or bad is inappropriate and naive. Whether a conflict is good or bad depends on the type of conflict. Specifically, it's necessary to differentiate between functional and dysfunctional conflicts.

FUNCTIONAL VERSUS DYSFUNCTIONAL CONFLICT

Functional conflict

Conflict that supports the goals of the group and improves its performance.

Dysfunctional conflict

Conflict that hinders group performance.

The interactionist view does not propose that *all* conflicts are good. Rather, some conflicts support the goals of the group and improve its performance; these are **functional**, constructive forms of conflict. Additionally, there are conflicts that hinder group performance; these are **dysfunctional** or destructive forms.

Of course, it is one thing to argue that conflict can be valuable for the group, but how does one tell if a conflict is functional or dysfunctional?

The demarcation between functional and dysfunctional is neither clear nor precise. No one level of conflict can be adopted as acceptable or unacceptable under all conditions. The type and level of conflict that creates healthy and positive involvement toward one group's goals may, in another group or in the same group at another time, be highly dysfunctional.

The important criterion is group performance. Since groups exist to attain a goal or goals, it is the impact that the conflict has on the group, rather than on any singular individual, that defines functionality. The impact of conflict on the individual and on the group is rarely mutually exclusive, so the ways that individuals perceive a conflict may have an important influence on its effect on the group. However, this need not be the case, and when it is not, our orientation will be to the group. For us to appraise the impact of conflict on group behavior—to consider its functional and dysfunctional effects—we shall consider whether the individual group members perceive the conflict as being good or bad to be irrelevant. A group member may perceive an action as dysfunctional, in that the outcome is personally dissatisfying to him or her. However, for our analysis, it would be functional if it furthers the objectives of the group.

THE CONFLICT PARADOX

Conflict paradox

Conflict contributes to a group's performance but most groups and organizations try to eliminate it.

If some conflict has been proven to be beneficial to a group's performance, why do most of us continue to look at conflict as undesirable? The answer to this **conflict paradox** is that we live in a society that has been built upon the traditional view. Tolerance of conflict is counter to most cultures in developed nations. In North America, the home, school, and church are generally the most influential institutions during the early years when our attitudes are forming. These institutions, for the most part, have historically reinforced anticonflict values and emphasized the importance of getting along with others.

The home has historically reinforced the authority pattern through the parent figure. Parents knew what was right and children complied. Conflict between children or between parents and children has generally been actively discouraged. The traditional school systems in developed countries reflected the structure of the home. Teachers had *the* answers and were not to be challenged. Disagreements at all levels were viewed negatively. Examinations reinforced this view: Students attempted to get their answers to agree with those the teacher had determined were right. The last major influencing institution, the church, also has supported anticonflict values. The religious perspective emphasizes peace, harmony, and tranquility. Church doctrines, for the most part, advocate acceptance rather than argument. This is best exemplified by the teachings of the Roman Catholic Church. According to its beliefs, when the pope speaks officially (ex cathedra) on religious matters, he is infallible. Such dogma has discouraged questioning the teachings of the Church.

Should we be surprised, then, that the traditional view of conflict continues to receive wide support in spite of the evidence to the contrary?

Let us now proceed to move beyond definitions and philosophy, to describe and analyze the evolutionary process leading to conflict outcomes.

THE CONFLICT PROCESS

The conflict process can be seen as comprising four stages: potential opposition, cognition and personalization, behavior, and outcomes. The process is diagrammed in Figure 12–1.

Stage I: Potential Opposition

The first step in the conflict process is the presence of conditions that create opportunities for conflict to arise. They *need not* lead directly to conflict, but one of these conditions is necessary if conflict is to arise. For simplicity's sake, these conditions (which also may be looked at as causes or sources of conflict) have been condensed into three general categories: communication, structure, and personal variables.

Communication The communicative source represents those opposing forces that arise from semantic difficulties, misunderstandings, and "noise" in the communication channels. Much of this discussion can be related back to our comments on communication and communication networks in Chapter 9.

One of the major myths that most of us carry around with us is that poor communication is the reason for conflicts—"if we could just communicate with each other, we could eliminate our differences." Such a conclusion is not unreasonable, given the amount of time each of us spends communicating. But, of course, poor communication is certainly not the source of *all* conflicts,

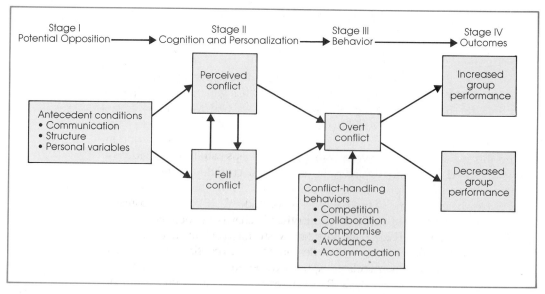

FIGURE 12–1
The Conflict Process

though there is considerable evidence to suggest that problems in the communication process act to retard collaboration and stimulate misunderstanding.

A review of the research suggests that semantic difficulties, insufficient exchange of information, and noise in the communication channel each are barriers to communication and potential antecedent conditions to conflict.[4] Specifically, evidence demonstrates semantic difficulties arise as a result of differences in training, selective perception, and inadequate information about others. Research has further demonstrated a surprising finding: The potential for conflict increases when either too little or too much communication takes place. Apparently, an increase in communication is functional up to a point, whereupon it is possible to overcommunicate with a resultant increase in the potential for conflict. Too much information as well as too little can lay the foundation for conflict. Further, the channel chosen for communicating can have an influence on stimulating opposition. The filtering process that occurs as information is passed between members and the divergence of communications from formal or previously established channels offer potential opportunities for conflict to arise.

Structure The term structure is used, in this context, to include variables such as size, degree of specialization in the tasks assigned to group members, jurisdictional clarity, member goal compatibility, leadership styles, reward systems, and the degree of dependence between groups.

Research indicates that size and specialization act as forces to stimulate conflict. The larger the group and the more specialized its activities, the greater the likelihood of conflict. Tenure and conflict have been found to be inversely related. The potential for conflict tends to be greatest where group members are younger and where turnover is high.

[4] Ibid., pp. 39–40.

The greater the ambiguity in precisely defining where responsibility for actions lies, the greater the potential for conflict to emerge. Such jurisdictional ambiguities increase intergroup fighting for control of resources and territory.

Groups within organizations have diverse goals. For instance, purchasing is concerned with the timely acquisition of inputs at low prices, marketing's goals concentrate on disposing of outputs and increasing revenues, quality control's attention is focused on improving quality and ensuring that the organization's products meet up to standard, and production units seek efficiency of operations by maintaining a steady production flow. This diversity of goals among groups is a major source of conflict. Where groups within an organization seek diverse ends, some of which—like sales and credit—are inherently at odds, there are increased opportunities for conflict.

There is some indication that a close style of leadership—tight and continuous observation with general control of the others' behaviors—increases conflict potential, but the evidence is not particularly strong. Too much reliance on participation may also stimulate conflict. Research tends to confirm that participation and conflict are highly correlated, apparently because participation encourages the promotion of differences. Reward systems, too, are found to create conflict when one member's gain is at another's expense. Finally, if a group is dependent on another group (in contrast to the two being mutually independent) or if interdependence allows one group to gain at another's expense, opposing forces are stimulated.[5]

Personal Variables   Personal factors include the individual value systems that each person has and the personality characteristics that account for individual idiosyncracies and differences.

The evidence indicates that certain personality types—for example, individuals who are highly authoritarian and dogmatic, and who demonstrate low esteem—lead to potential conflict. Most important, and probably the most overlooked variable in the study of social conflict, is differing value systems. Value differences, for example, are the best explanation of such diverse issues as prejudice, disagreements over one's contribution to the group and the rewards one deserves, or assessments of whether this particular book is any good. That John dislikes blacks and Dana believes John's position indicates his ignorance, that an employee thinks he is worth $30,000 a year but his boss believes him to be worth $24,000, and that Ann thinks this book is interesting to read while Jennifer views it as a "crock of . . ." are all value judgments. And differences in value systems are important sources for creating the potential for conflict.

Stage II: Cognition and Personalization

If the conditions cited in Stage I generate frustration, then the potential for opposition becomes actualized in the second stage. The antecedent conditions can only lead to conflict when one or more of the parties are affected by, and cognitive of, the conflict.

As we noted in our definition of conflict, perception is required. Therefore, one or more of the parties must be aware of the existence of the antecedent

[5] Ibid., pp. 49–50.

Perceived conflict

Awareness by one or more parties of the existence of conditions that create opportunities for conflict to arise.

Felt conflict

Emotional involvement in a conflict creating anxiety, tenseness, frustration, or hostility.

conditions. However, because a conflict is **perceived** does not mean that it is personalized. In other words, "A may be aware that B and A are in serious disagreement . . . but it may not make A tense or anxious, and it may have no effect whatsoever on A's affection towards B."[6] It is at the **felt** level, when individuals become emotionally involved, that parties experience anxiety, tenseness, frustration, or hostility.

Stage III: Behavior

We are in the third stage of the conflict process when a member engages in action that frustrates the attainment of another's goals or prevents the furthering of the other's interests. This action must be intended; that is, there must be a knowing effort to frustrate another. At this juncture, the conflict is out in the open.

Overt conflict covers a full range of behaviors—from subtle, indirect, and highly controlled forms of interference to direct, aggressive, violent, and uncontrolled struggle. At the low range, this overt behavior is illustrated by the student who raises his or her hand in class and questions a point the instructor has made. At the high range, strikes, riots, and wars come to mind.

Stage III is also where most conflict-handling behaviors are initiated. Once the conflict is overt, the parties will develop a method for dealing with the conflict. This does not exclude conflict-handling behaviors from being initiated in Stage II, but in most cases, these techniques for reducing the frustration are used when the conflict has become observable rather than as preventive measures.

Figure 12–2 represents one author's effort at identifying the primary conflict-handling orientations. Using two dimensions—*cooperativeness* (the degree to which one party attempts to satisfy the other party's concerns) and *assertiveness* (the degree to which one party attempts to satisfy his or her own concerns)—five conflict-handling orientations can be identified: *competition* (assertive and uncooperative), *collaboration* (assertive and cooperative), *avoidance* (unassertive and uncooperative), *accommodation* (unassertive and cooperative), and *compromise* (midrange on both assertiveness and cooperativeness).[7]

Competition

Rule-regulated efforts to obtain a goal without interference from another party.

Competition When one person seeks to achieve his or her goals or further his or her interests, regardless of the impact on the parties to the conflict, he or she **competes** and dominates. These win-lose struggles, in formal groups or in an organization, frequently utilize the formal authority of a mutual superior as the dominant force, and the conflicting individuals each will use their own power bases in order to resolve a victory in their favor.

Collaboration

A situation where the parties to a conflict each desire to satisfy fully the concern of all parties.

Collaboration When the parties to conflict each desire to satisfy fully the concern of all parties, we have cooperation and the search for a mutually beneficial outcome. In **collaboration**, the behavior of the parties is aimed at solving the

[6] L. R. Pondy, "Organizational Conflict: Concepts and Models," *Administrative Science Quarterly*, September 1967, p. 302.

[7] K. W. Thomas, "Conflict and Conflict Management," in M. Dunnette (ed.), *Handbook of Industrial and Organizational Psychology* (Chicago: Rand McNally, 1976), pp. 889–935.

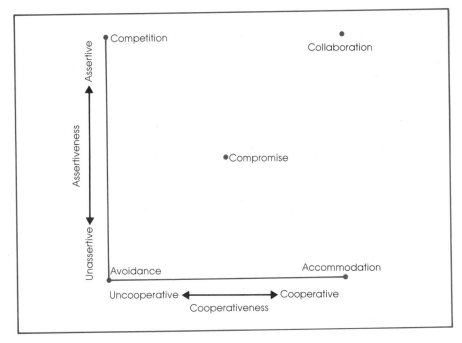

FIGURE 12–2
Dimensions of Conflict-Handling Orientations

Source: K. Thomas, "Conflict and Conflict Management," in M. D. Dunnette (ed.), *Handbook of Industrial and Organizational Psychology*, p. 900. Copyright © 1976 Rand McNally. Reprinted by permission of John Wiley & Sons, Inc.

problem, at clarifying the differences rather than accommodating various points of view. The participants consider the full range of alternatives, the similarities and differences in viewpoint become more clearly focused, and the causes or differences become outwardly evident. Because the solution sought is advantageous to all parties, collaboration is often thought of as a win-win approach to resolving conflicts. It is, for example, a frequent tool of marriage counselors. Behavioral scientists, who value openness, trust, authenticity, and spontaneity in relationships, are also strong advocates of a collaborative approach to resolving conflicts.

Avoidance   A person may recognize that a conflict exists but react by withdrawing or by suppressing the conflict. We call this **avoidance**. Indifference or the desire to evade overt demonstration of disagreement can result in withdrawal: The individuals acknowledge physical separation and each stakes out a territory that is distinct from the other's. If withdrawal is not possible or desirable, the individuals may suppress, that is, withhold, their differences. When group members are required to interact because of the interdependence of their tasks, suppression is a more probable outcome than withdrawal.

Accommodation   When the parties seek to appease their opponent, they may be willing to place their opponent's interests above their own. In order that the relationship can be maintained, one party is willing to be self-sacrificing. We refer to this behavior as **accommodation**. When husbands and wives have

Avoidance

Withdrawing from or suppressing conflict.

Accommodation

The willingness of one party in a conflict to place his or her opponent's interests above his or her own.

differences, it is not uncommon for one to accommodate the other by placing their spouse's interest above their own.

Compromise   When each party to the conflict must give up something, sharing occurs, resulting in a compromised outcome. In **compromise**, there is no clear

Compromise

A situation in which each party to a conflict must give up something.

TABLE 12–1
When to Use the Five Conflict-Handling Orientations

Conflict-Handling Orientation	Appropriate Situations
Competition	1. When quick, decisive action is vital 2. On important issues where unpopular actions need implementing 3. On issues vital to the organization's welfare and when you know you're right 4. Against people who take advantage of noncompetitive behavior
Collaboration	1. To find an integrative solution when both sets of concerns are too important to be compromised 2. When your objective is to learn 3. To merge insights from people with different perspectives 4. To gain commitment by incorporating concerns into a consensus 5. To work through feelings that have interfered with a relationship
Avoidance	1. When an issue is trivial, or more important issues are pressing 2. When you perceive no chance of satisfying your concerns 3. When potential disruption outweighs the benefits of resolution 4. To let people cool down and regain perspective 5. When gathering information supersedes immediate decision 6. When others can resolve the conflict more effectively 7. When issues seem tangential or symptomatic of other issues
Accommodation	1. When you find you are wrong—to allow a better position to be heard, to learn, and to show your reasonableness 2. When issues are more important to others than yourself—to satisfy others and maintain cooperation 3. To build social credits for later issues 4. To minimize loss when you are outmatched and losing 5. When harmony and stability are especially important 6. To allow subordinates to develop by learning from mistakes
Compromise	1. When goals are important, but not worth the effort or potential disruption of more assertive modes 2. When opponents with equal power are commited to mutually exclusive goals 3. To achieve temporary settlements to complex issues 4. To arrive at expedient solutions under time pressure 5. As a backup when collaboration or competition is unsuccessful

Source: K. W. Thomas, "Toward Multidimensional Values in Teaching: The Example of Conflict Behaviors," *Academy of Management Review*, July 1977, p. 487. With permission.

winner or loser. Rather, there is a rationing of the object of the conflict or, where the object is not divisible, one rewards the other by yielding something of substitute value. The distinguishing characteristic of compromise, therefore, is that it requires each party to give up something. Negotiations between unions and management represent a situation where compromise is required in order to reach a settlement and agree upon a labor contract.

No one conflict resolution mode is appropriate in all situations. But when is one preferable over another? Table 12–1 lists situations that tend to favor each. The use of this list, however, implies that individuals can adjust their conflict-resolution actions to the situation. This may not be accurate. In fact, research indicates that people have an underlying disposition to handle conflicts in certain ways.[8] More specifically, individuals have more or less preferred styles of conflict resolution, these styles tend to be relied upon quite consistently regardless of the conflict situation, and an individual's mode of conflict resolution can be predicted rather well from a combination of intellectual and personality characteristics. So it may be more appropriate to look at the five conflict-handling behaviors as relatively fixed rather than as a set of options from which individuals choose to fit the appropriate situation.

Stage IV: Outcomes

The interplay between the overt conflict behavior and conflict-handling behaviors result in consequences. As the model demonstrates, they may be functional in that the conflict has resulted in an improvement in the group's performance. Conversely, group performance may be hindered and we would describe the outcome as dysfunctional.

Functional Outcomes   How might conflict act as a force to increase group performance? It is hard to visualize a situation where open or violent aggression could be functional. But there are a number of instances where it is possible to envision how low or moderate levels of conflict could improve the effectiveness of a group. Because it is often difficult to think of instances where conflict can be constructive, let us consider some examples and then look at the research evidence.

Conflict is constructive when it improves the quality of decisions, stimulates creativity and innovation, encourages interest and curiosity among group members, provides the medium through which problems can be aired and tensions released, and fosters an environment of self-evaluation and change. The evidence suggests that conflict can improve the quality of decision making by allowing all points, particularly the ones that are unusual or held by a minority, to be weighed in important decisions.[9] Conflict is an antidote for groupthink. It does not allow the group passively to "rubber stamp" decisions that may be based on weak assumptions, inadequate consideration to relevant alternatives, or other

---

[8] R. J. Sternberg and L. J. Soriano, "Styles of Conflict Resolution," *Journal of Personality and Social Psychology*, July 1984, pp. 115–26.

[9] See, for instance, I. I. Mitroff and J. R. Emshoff, "On Strategic Assumptions Making: A Dialectical Approach to Policy and Planning," *Academy of Management Review*, January 1979, pp. 1–12; and R. A. Cosier, "Dialectical Inquiry in Strategic Planning: A Case of Premature Acceptance?," *Academy of Management Review*, October 1981, pp. 643–48.

debilities. Conflict challenges the status quo and therefore furthers the creation of new ideas, promotes reassessment of group goals and activities, and increases the probability that the group will respond to change.

Research studies in diverse settings confirm the functionality of conflict. Consider the following findings:

The comparison of six major decisions during the administration of four different U.S. presidents found that conflict reduced the chance that groupthink would overpower policy decisions. The comparisons demonstrated that conformity among presidential advisors was related to poor decisions, while an atmosphere of constructive conflict and critical thinking surrounded the well-developed decisions.[10]

The bankruptcy of the Penn Central Railroad has been generally attributed to mismanagement and a failure of the company's board of directors to question actions taken by management. The board was composed of outside directors who met monthly to oversee the railroad's operations. Few questioned decisions made by the operating management, though there was evidence that several board members were uncomfortable with many decisions made by the management. Apathy and a desire to *avoid* conflict allowed poor decisions to stand unquestioned.[11] This, however, should not be surprising since a review of the relationship between bureaucracy and innovation has found that conflict encourages innovative solutions.[12] The corollary of this finding also appears true: Lack of conflict results in a passive environment with reinforcement of the status quo.

Not only do better and more innovative decisions result from situations where there is some conflict, but there is evidence indicating that conflict can be positively related to productivity. It was demonstrated that, among established groups, performance tended to improve more when there was conflict among members than when there was fairly close agreement. The investigators observed that when groups analyzed decisions that had been made by the individual members of that group, the average improvement among the high-conflict groups was 73 percent greater than was that of those groups characterized by low-conflict conditions.[13] Others have found similar results: Groups composed of members with different interests tend to produce higher-quality solutions to a variety of problems than do homogeneous groups.[14]

Similarly, studies of professionals—systems analysts and research and development scientists—support the constructive value of conflict. An investigation of twenty-two teams of systems analysts found that the more incompatible groups

---

[10] I. L. Janis, *Victims of Groupthink* (Boston: Houghton Mifflin, 1972).

[11] P. Binzen and J. R. Daughen, *Wreck of the Penn Central* (Boston: Little, Brown, 1971).

[12] V. A. Thompson, "Bureaucracy and Innovation," *Administrative Science Quarterly*, March 1965, pp. 1–20.

[13] J. Hall and M. S. Williams, "A Comparison of Decision-Making Performances in Established and Ad-Hoc Groups," *Journal of Personality and Social Psychology*, February 1966, p. 217.

[14] R. L. Hoffman, "Homogeneity of Member Personality and Its Effect on Group Problem-Solving," *Journal of Abnormal and Social Psychology*, January 1959, pp. 27–32; and R. L. Hoffman and N. R. F. Maier, "Quality and Acceptance of Problem Solutions by Members of Homogeneous and Heterogeneous Groups," *Journal of Abnormal and Social Psychology*, March 1961, pp. 401–7.

were likely to be more productive.[15] Research and development scientists have been found to be most productive where there is a certain amount of intellectual conflict.[16]

Conflict can even be constructive on sports teams and in unions. Studies of sports teams indicate that moderate levels of group conflict contribute to team effectiveness and provide an additional stimulus for high achievement.[17] An examination of local unions found that conflict between members of the local was positively related to the union's power and to member loyalty and participation in union affairs.[18] These findings might suggest that conflict within a group indicates strength rather than, in the traditional view, weakness.

Dysfunctional Outcomes   The destructive consequences of conflict upon a group or organization's performance are generally well known. A reasonable summary might state: Uncontrolled opposition breeds discontent, which acts to dissolve common ties, and eventually leads to destruction of the group. And, of course, there is a substantial body of literature to document how conflict—the dysfunctional varieties—can reduce group effectiveness.[19] Among the more undesirable consequences are a retarding of communication, reductions in group cohesiveness, and subordination of group goals to the primacy of infighting between members. At the extreme, conflict can bring group functioning to a halt and potentially threaten the group's survival.

This discussion has again returned us to the issue of what is functional and what is dysfunctional. Research on conflict has yet to identify those situations where conflict is more likely to be constructive than destructive. However, the difference between functional and dysfunctional conflict is important enough for us to go beyond the substantive evidence and propose at least two hypotheses. The first is that extreme levels of conflict—exemplified by overt struggle or violence—are rarely, if ever, functional. Functional conflict is probably most often characterized by low to moderate levels of subtle and controlled opposition. Second, the type of group activity should be another factor determining functionality. We hypothesize that the more creative or unprogrammed the decision making tasks of the group, the greater the probability that internal conflict is constructive. Groups that are required to tackle problems requiring new and novel approaches—as in research, advertising, and other professional activities—will benefit more from conflict than groups performing highly programmed activities—for instance, those of work teams on an automobile assembly line.

[15] R. E. Hill, "Interpersonal Compatibility and Work Group Performance Among Systems Analysts: An Empirical Study," *Proceedings of the Seventeenth Annual Midwest Academy of Management Conference*, Kent, Ohio, April 1974, pp. 97–110.

[16] D. C. Pelz and F. Andrews, *Scientists in Organizations* (New York: John Wiley, 1966).

[17] H. Lenk, "Konflikt und Leistung in Spitzensportmannschafter: Isozometrische Strukturen von WettKämpfachtern in Ruden," *Soziale Welt*, Vol. 15 (1964), pp. 307–43.

[18] A. Tannenbaum, "Control Structure and Union Functions," *American Journal of Sociology*, May 1956, pp. 127–40.

[19] For an excellent source of studies that focus on the dysfunctional consequences of conflict, see the *Journal of Conflict Resolution*.

OB Close-Up

General Motors and the Price of Eliminating Conflict

H. Ross Perot is an outspoken superpatriot and a self-made billionaire. In 1984, he sold Electronic Data Systems, the Dallas-based computer services company he founded in the early 1960s, to General Motors for $2.5 billion and immediately became GM's largest stockholder and a member of the board.

GM's decision to buy EDS was motivated by the desire to improve its internal coordination. EDS had the people and experience to coordinate GM's massive information systems and to help GM achieve its goal of becoming a world leader in factory automation. GM's chairman, Roger Smith, also looked forward to having Perot's fiery spirit to reinvigorate GM's bureaucracy for the big battle with the Japanese.

Unfortunately, the marriage was not a happy one. Perot saw problems at GM and felt compelled to speak out.[20] He was particularly frustrated about how slow GM was in responding to the actions of competitors, as evidenced by these types of comments: "The first EDSer to see a snake kills it. At GM, the first thing you do is go hire a consultant on snakes. Then you get a committee on snakes, and then you discuss it for a couple of years." Or, "It takes this company [GM] four years to get a car from the drawing board to a showroom. Good Heavens, we won World War II in less time!" Or, "At GM the stress is not on getting results—on winning—but on bureaucracy, on conforming to the GM system. You get to the top of General Motors not by doing something, but by not making a mistake."

Perot's comments were not unfounded. GM is a rigid bureaucracy, strongly tradition-bound, that has failed to react to the changing world automobile market. For instance, its U.S. market share fell from 47 percent to 36 percent between 1976 and 1986. GM has been unwilling to change from the formula—established in the 1920s—that worked so well through the early 1970s.

Roger Smith had wanted Perot to act as an irritant inside GM—to shake things up. And that he did. Perot loudly and enthusiastically questioned many of GM's longstanding management practices. He went down to the factory floor to talk to workers about new ideas. He even anonymously shopped for cars at GM dealerships to assess customer service. But in December 1986, Smith had apparently had enough of Perot's criticism of GM practices. To silence Perot and get his resignation from GM's board, Smith agreed to pay Perot roughly double the market price—a whopping $750 million—for his stake in GM. GM had decided that it was worth the money to eliminate the conflict, whether it was functional or otherwise.

[20] For a few of Perot's opinions on GM, see "The GM System Is Like a Blanket of Fog," *Fortune*, February 15, 1988, pp. 48–49.

For the most part, the concepts from Chapter 8 on have dealt with *intra*group activities. For instance, the previous material in this chapter emphasized interpersonal and intragroup conflict. But we need to understand relationships between groups as well as within groups. In this section, we'll focus on *inter*group relationships. These are the coordinated bridges that link two distinct organizational groups.[21] As we'll show, the efficiency and quality of these relationships can have a significant bearing on one or both of the groups' performances and their members' satisfaction.

Factors Affecting Intergroup Relations

Successful intergroup performance is a function of a number of factors. The umbrella concept that overrides these factors is *coordination*. Each of the following can affect efforts at coordination.

Interdependence The first overriding question we need to ask is: Do the groups really need coordination? The answer to this question lies in determining the degree of interdependence that exists between the groups. That is, do the groups depend on each other and, if so, how much? The three most frequently identified types of interdependence are pooled, sequential, and reciprocal.[22] Each requires an increasing degree of group interaction (see Figure 12–3).

When two groups function with relative independence but their combined output contributes to the organization's overall goals, **pooled interdependence** exists. At a firm like Apple Computer, for instance, this would describe the relationship between the Product Development department and the Shipping department. Both are necessary activities if Apple is to develop new products and get those products into consumers' hands, but each is essentially separate and distinct from the other. All other things being equal, coordination requirements between groups linked by pooled interdependence are less than with sequential or reciprocal interdependence.

The Purchasing and Parts Assembly departments at Apple are **sequentially interdependent**. One group—Parts Assembly—depends on another—Purchasing—for its inputs, but the dependency is only one-way. Purchasing is not directly dependent on Parts Assembly for its inputs. In sequential interdependence, if the group that provides the input doesn't perform its job properly, the other group which is dependent on the first will be significantly affected. In our Apple example, if Purchasing fails to order an important component that goes into the assembly process, then the Parts Assembly department may have to slow down or temporarily close its assembly operations.

Pooled interdependence

Where two groups function with relative independence but their combined output contributes to the organization's overall goals.

Sequential interdependence

One group depends on another for its input but the dependency is only one way.

[21] J. M. Brett and J. K. Rognes, "Intergroup Relations in Organizations," in P. S. Goodman and associates (eds.), *Designing Effective Work Groups* (San Francisco: Jossey-Bass, 1986), p. 205.

[22] J. D. Thompson, *Organizations in Action* (New York: McGraw-Hill, 1967), pp. 54–55.

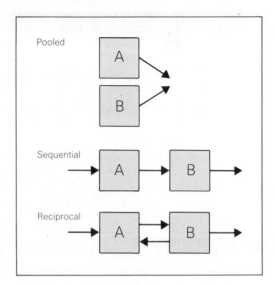

FIGURE 12–3
Types of Interdependence

Reciprocal interdependence

Where groups exchange inputs and outputs.

The most complex form of interdependence is **reciprocal**. In these instances, groups exchange inputs and outputs. For example, Sales and Product Developments groups at Apple are reciprocally interdependent. Sales people, in contact with customers, acquire information about their future needs. Sales then relays this back to Product Development so they can create new computer products. The long-term implications are that if Product Development doesn't come up with new products that potential customers find desirable, Sales personnel are not going to get orders. So there is high interdependence—Product Development needs Sales for information on customer needs so it can create successful new products, and Sales depends on the Product Development group to create products that it can successfully sell. This high degree of dependency translates into greater interaction and increased coordination demands.

Task Uncertainty   The next coordination question is: What type of tasks are the groups involved in? For simplicity's sake, we can think of a group's tasks as ranging from highly routine to highly nonroutine.[23] (See Figure 12–4.)

Highly routine tasks have little variation. Problems that group members face tend to contain few exceptions and are easy to analyze. Such group activities lend themselves to standardized operating procedures. For example, manufacturing tasks in a tire factory are made up of highly routine tasks. At the other extreme are nonroutine tasks. These are activities that are unstructured, with many exceptions and problems that are hard to analyze. Many of the tasks undertaken by marketing research and product development groups are of this variety. Of course, a lot of group tasks fall somewhere in the middle or combine both routine and nonroutine tasks.

Task uncertainty

The greater the uncertainty in a task, the more custom the response. Conversely, low uncertainty encompasses routine tasks with standardized activities.

The key to **task uncertainty** is that nonroutine tasks require considerably more processing of information. Tasks with low uncertainty tend to be standard-

[23] C. Perrow, "A Framework for the Comparative Analysis of Organizations," *American Sociological Review*, April 1967, pp. 194–208.

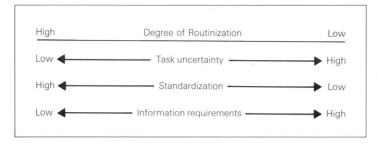

FIGURE 12–4
Task Continuum

ized. Further, groups that do such tasks do not have to interact much with other groups. In contrast, groups that undertake tasks that are high in uncertainty face problems that require custom responses. This, in turn, leads to a need for more and better information. We would expect the people in the marketing research department at Goodyear Tire & Rubber to interact much more with other departments and constituencies—marketing, sales, product design, tire dealers, advertising agencies, and the like—than would people in Goodyear's manufacturing group.

Time and Goal Orientation   How different are the groups in terms of their members' background and thinking? This is the third question relevant to the degree of coordination necessary between groups. Research demonstrates that a work group's perceptions of what is important may differ on the basis of the time frame that governs their work and their goal orientation.[24] This can make it difficult for groups with different perceptions to work together.

Why might work groups have different time and goal orientations? Top management divides work up by putting common tasks into common functional groups and assigning these groups specific goals. Then, people are hired with the appropriate background and skills to complete the tasks and help the group achieve its goals. This differentiation of tasks and hiring of specialists makes it easier to coordinate intragroup activities. But it makes it increasingly difficult to coordinate interaction between groups.

To illustrate how orientations differ between work groups, manufacturing personnel have a short-term time focus. They worry about today's production schedule and this week's productivity. In contrast, people in research and development focus on the long run. They're concerned about developing new products that may not be produced for several years. Similarly, work groups often have different goal orientations. Sales, as a case in point, wants to sell anything and everything. Their goals center on sales volume, and increasing revenue and market share. Their customers' ability to pay for the sales they make are not their concern. But people in the credit department want to ensure that sales are made only to credit-worthy customers. These differences in goals often make it difficult for sales and credit to communicate. It also makes it harder to coordinate their interactions.

---

[24] P. R. Lawrence and J. W. Lorsch, *Organization and Environment* (Homewood, IL: R. D. Irwin, 1969), pp. 34–39.

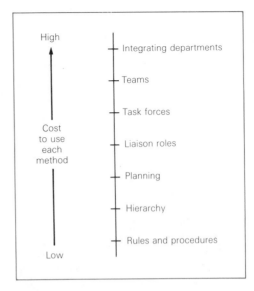

High

↑

Cost
to use
each
method

Low

— Integrating departments

— Teams

— Task forces

— Liaison roles

— Planning

— Hierarchy

— Rules and procedures

FIGURE 12–5
Methods for Managing Intergroup Relations

Methods for Managing Intergroup Relations

What coordination methods are available for managing intergroup relations? There are a number of options; the seven most frequently used are identified in Figure 12–5. These seven are listed on a continuum, in order of increasing cost.[25] They also are cumulative in the sense that succeeding methods higher on the continuum add to, rather than are substituted for, lower methods.

Rules and Procedures   The most simple and least costly method for managing intergroup relations is to establish, in advance, a set of formalized rules and procedures that will specify how group members are to interact with each other. In large organizations, for example, standard operating procedures are likely to specify that when additional permanent staff are needed in any department, a "request for new staff" form is to be filed with the personnel department. Upon receipt of this form, the personnel department begins a standardized process to fill the request. Notice that such rules and procedures minimize the need for interaction and information flow between the departments or work groups. The major drawback to this method is that it works well only when intergroup activities can be anticipated ahead of time and when they recur often enough to justify establishing rules and procedures for handling them.

Hierarchy   If rules and procedures are inadequate, the use of the organization's hierarchy becomes the primary method for managing intergroup relations. What this means is that coordination is achieved by referring problems to a common superior higher in the organization. In a college, if the chairpersons for the English and Speech Communication departments can't agree on where

[25] J. Galbraith, *Designing Complex Organizations* (Reading, MA: Addison-Wesley, 1973).

the new courses in debate will be taught, they can take the issue to the college dean for a resolution. The major limitation to this method is that it increases demands on the common superior's time. If all differences were resolved by this means, the organization's chief executive would be overwhelmed with resolving intergroup problems, leaving little time for other matters.

Planning   The next step up the continuum is the use of planning to facilitate coordination. If each work group has specific goals for which it is responsible, then each knows what it is supposed to do. Intergroup tasks that create problems are resolved in terms of the goals and contributions of each group. In a state motor vehicle office, the various work groups—testing and examinations, driving permits, vehicle registration, cashiering, and the like—each have a set of goals which define their area of responsibility and acts to reduce intergroup conflicts. Planning tends to break down as a coordination device where work groups don't have clearly defined goals or where the volume of contacts between groups is high.

Liaison Roles   Liaison roles refers to individuals with specialized roles designed to facilitate communication between two interdependent work units. In one organization where accountants and engineers had a long history of conflict, management hired an engineer with an MBA degree and several years of experience in public accounting. This person could speak the language of both groups and understood their problems. As a result of this new liaison role, conflicts that had previously made it difficult for the accounting and engineering departments to coordinate their activities were significantly reduced. The major drawback to this coordination device is that there are limits to any liaison person's ability to handle information flow between interacting groups, especially where the groups are large and interactions are frequent.

Task Forces   A task force is a temporary group made up of representatives from a number of departments. It exists only long enough to solve the problem it was created to handle. After a solution is reached, task force participants return to their normal duties.

  Task forces are an excellent device for coordinating activities when the number of interacting groups is more than two or three. For example, when Audi began receiving numerous complaints about its cars accelerating when the transmission was put in reverse, even when drivers swore their foot was firmly on the brake, the company created a task force to assess the problem and develop a solution. Representatives from design, production, legal, and engineering departments were brought together. After a solution was determined, the task force was disbanded.

Teams   As tasks become more complex, additional problems arise during the act of execution. Previous coordination devices are no longer adequate. If the delays in decisions become long, lines of communication become extended, and top managers are forced to spend more time on day-to-day operations, the next response is to use permanent teams. They are typically formed around frequently occurring problems—with team members maintaining a dual responsibility to their primary functional department and to the team. When the team has accomplished its task, each member returns full time to his or her functional assignment.

This form of coordination device is popular in aerospace firms. There are functional departments based on common functions. Teams are formed around the major problem areas or projects that the firm is working on. So, for instance, manufacturing operations might have a wing team located in one place in the plant (see Figure 12–6), with members coming from the various functional areas.

Integrating Departments   When intergroup relations become too complex to be coordinated through plans, task forces, teams, and the like, organizations may create integrating departments. These are permanent departments with members formally assigned to the task of integration between two or more groups. While they're permanent and expensive to maintain, they tend to be used when an organization has a number of groups with conflicting goals, nonroutine problems, and intergroup decisions that have a significant impact on the organization's total operations. They are also excellent devices to manage intergroup conflicts for organizations facing long-term retrenchments. When organizations are forced to shrink in size—as has recently occurred in industries such as steel, mining, and oil exploration—conflicts over how cuts are to be distributed and how the smaller resource pie is to be allocated become major and ongoing dilemmas. The use of integrating departments in such cases can be an effective means for managing these intergroup relations.

FIGURE 12–6
Example of a Team Intergroup-Coordination Device

Source: J. R. Galbraith, *Organization Design* (Reading, MA: Addison-Wesley, 1977), p. 117.

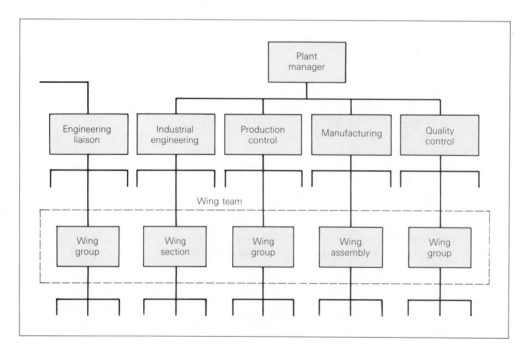

Summary It may help to put this discussion in perspective by considering methods for managing intergroup relations in terms of effectiveness.

Researchers state that the effectiveness of intergroup relations can be evaluated in terms of efficiency and quality.[26] Efficiency considers the costs to the organization of transforming an intergroup conflict into actions agreed to by the groups. Quality refers to the degree to which the outcome results in a well-defined and enduring exchange agreement. Using these definitions, the seven methods introduced in this section were presented, in order, from most efficient to least efficient. That is, ignoring outcomes for a moment, rules and procedures are less costly to implement than hierarchy, hierarchy is less costly than planning, and so forth. But, of course, keeping costs down is only one consideration. The other element of effectiveness is quality, or how well the coordination device works in facilitating interaction and reducing dysfunctional conflicts. As we've shown, the least costly alternative may not be adequate. So managers have a number of options at their disposal for managing intergroup relations. But since they tend to be cumulative, with costs rising as you move up the continuum in Figure 12–6, the most effective coordination device will be the one lowest on the continuum that facilitates an enduring integrative exchange.

IMPLICATIONS FOR PERFORMANCE AND SATISFACTION

Many people assume that conflict is related to lower group and organizational performance. This chapter has demonstrated that this assumption is frequently fallacious. Conflict can be either constructive or destructive to the functioning of a group or unit. As shown in Figure 12–7, levels of conflict can be either too high or too low. Either extreme hinders performance. An optimal level is where there is enough conflict to prevent stagnation, stimulate creativity, allow tensions to be released, and initiate the seeds for change; yet not so much as to be disruptive or deter coordination of activities.

Inadequate or excessive levels of conflict can hinder the effectiveness of a group or an organization, resulting in reduced satisfaction of group members, increased absence and turnover rates, and eventually lower productivity. On the other hand, when conflict is at an optimal level, complacency and apathy should be minimized, motivation should be enhanced through the creation of a challenging and questioning environment with a vitality that makes work interesting, and there should be the needed turnover to rid the organization of misfits and poor performers.

Intergroup conflicts can also affect an organization's performance. Emphasis at this level, however, has tended to focus on dysfunctional conflicts and methods for managing them. Where organizational performance depends on effective group relations and where there is high interdependence between groups, management needs to insure that the proper integrative device is put in place. However, consistent with the interactionist perspective on conflict,

---

[26] Brett and Rognes, "Intergroup Relations in Organizations," p. 212.

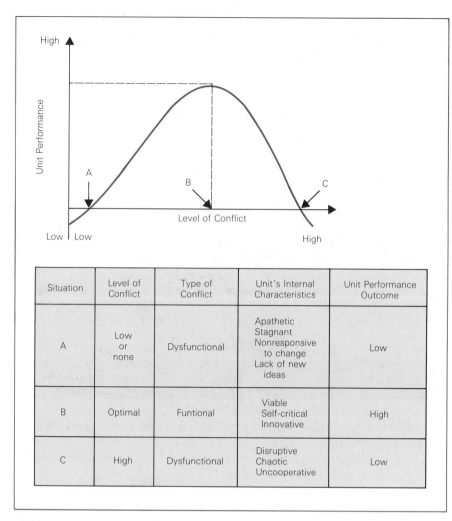

FIGURE 12–7
Conflict and Unit Performance

Situation	Level of Conflict	Type of Conflict	Unit's Internal Characteristics	Unit Performance Outcome
A	Low or none	Dysfunctional	Apathetic Stagnant Nonresponsive to change Lack of new ideas	Low
B	Optimal	Funtional	Viable Self-critical Innovative	High
C	High	Dysfunctional	Disruptive Chaotic Uncooperative	Low

there is no reason to believe that *all* intergroup conflicts are dysfunctional. Some minimal levels of conflict can facilitate critical thinking among group members, make a group more responsive to the need for change, and provide similar benefits that can enhance group and organizational performance.

POINT

CONFLICT IS GOOD FOR AN ORGANIZATION

We've made considerable progress in the last fifteen years toward overcoming the negative stereotype given to conflict. Most behavioral scientists and an increasing number of practitioners now accept that the goal of effective management is not to eliminate conflict. Rather, it is to create the right intensity of conflict so as to reap its functional benefits.

Since conflict can be good for an organization, it is only logical to acknowledge that there may be times when managers will purposely want to increase its intensity. Let's briefly review how stimulating conflict can provide benefits to the organization.

Conflict is a means by which to bring about radical change. It is an effective device by which management can change drastically the existing power structure, current interaction patterns, and entrenched attitudes.

Conflict facilitates group cohesiveness. While conflict increases hostility between groups, external threats tend to cause a group to pull together as a unit. Intergroup conflicts raise the extent to which members identify with their own group and increase feelings of solidarity, while, at the same time, internal differences and irritations dissolve.

Conflict improves group and organizational effectiveness. The stimulation of conflict initiates the search for new means and goals and clears the way for innovation. The successful solution of a conflict leads to greater effectiveness, to more trust and openness, to greater attraction of members for each other, and to depersonalization of future conflicts. In fact, it has been found that as the number of minor disagreements increases, the number of major clashes decreases.

Conflict brings about a slightly higher, more constructive level of tension. This enhances the chances of solving the conflicts in a way satisfactory to all parties concerned. When the level of tension is very low, the parties are not sufficiently motivated to do something about a conflict.

These points are clearly not comprehensive. As noted in the chapter, conflict provides a number of benefits to an organization. However, groups or organizations devoid of conflict are likely to suffer from apathy, stagnation, groupthink, and other debilitating diseases.

The points presented here were influenced by E. Van de Vliert, "Escalative Intervention in Small-Group Conflicts," *Journal of Applied Behavioral Science*, Vol. 21, No. 1, 1985, pp. 19–36.

COUNTERPOINT

ALL CONFLICTS ARE DYSFUNCTIONAL!

It may be true that conflict is an inherent part of any group or organization. It may not be possible to eliminate it completely. However, just because conflicts exist is no reason to deify them. *All* conflicts are dysfunctional, and it is one of management's major responsibilities to keep conflict intensity as low as humanly possible. A few points will support my case.

The negative consequences from conflict can be devastating. The list of negatives associated with conflict are awesome. The most obvious include increased turnover, decreased employee satisfaction, inefficiencies between work units, sabotage, labor grievances and strikes, and physical aggression.

Effective managers build teamwork. A good manager builds a coordinated team. Conflict works against such an objective. A successful work group is like a successful sports team; each member knows his or her role and supports his or her teammates. When a team works well, the whole becomes greater than the sum of the parts. Management creates teamwork by minimizing internal conflicts and facilitating internal coordination.

Competition is good for an organization, but not conflict. Competition and conflict should not be confused with each other. *Conflict* is behavior directed against another party, whereas *competition* is behavior aimed at obtaining a goal without interference from another party. Competition is healthy; it is the source of organizational vitality. Conflict, on the other hand, is destructive.

Managers who accept and stimulate conflict don't survive in organizations. The whole argument on the value of conflict may be moot as long as senior executives in organizations view conflict from the traditional view. In the traditional view, *any* conflict will be seen as bad. Since the evaluation of a manager's performance is made by higher-level executives, those managers who do not succeed in eliminating conflicts are likely to be appraised negatively. This, in turn, will reduce opportunities for advancement. Any manager who aspires to move up in such an environment will be wise to follow the traditional view and eliminate any outward signs of conflict. Failure to follow this advice might result in the premature departure of the manager.

KEY TERMS

Accommodation

Avoidance

Collaboration

Competition

Compromise

Conflict

Conflict Paradox

Dysfunctional Conflict

Felt Conflict

Functional Conflict

Human Relations View

Interactionist View

Perceived Conflict

Pooled Interdependence

Reciprocal Interdependence

Sequential Interdependence

Task Uncertainty

Traditional View

FOR DISCUSSION

1. Define conflict.

2. How does *conflict* differ from *competition*?

3. Name, discuss, and contrast three views on conflict.

4. What is the difference between functional and dysfunctional conflict? What determines functionality?

5. Under what conditions might conflict be beneficial to a group?

6. Identify various types of conflict.

7. What are the components in the conflict process model? From your own experiences, give an example of how a conflict proceeded through the four stages.

8. Discuss five conflict resolution techniques. What are the strengths and weaknesses of each?

9. "The larger the group, the greater the likelihood of conflict." Do you agree or disagree? Discuss.

10. "Units within an organization will always have divergent goals; therefore, all organizations will be characterized by the presence of conflict." Do you agree or disagree? Discuss.

11. "Participation is an excellent method for identifying differences and resolving conflicts." Do you agree or disagree? Discuss.

12. How do you assess the effectiveness of intergroup relations?

FOR FURTHER READING

Blake, R. R., and J. S. Mouton, *Solving Costly Organizational Conflicts*. San Francisco: Jossey-Bass, 1984. Describes a method for resolving conflicts and establishing trust and cooperation among groups, departments, and divisions that must work together.

Brewer, M. B., and R. M. Kramer, "The Psychology of Intergroup Attitudes and Behavior," in M. R. Rosenzweig and L. W. Porter (eds.), *Annual Review of Psychology*, Vol. 36. Palo Alto, CA: Annual Reviews, Inc., 1985, pp. 219–43. Reviews recent intergroup research related to processes and outcomes.

Cliff, G., "Managing Organizational Conflict," *Management Review*, May 1987, pp. 51–53. Argues that the potential for friction between an organization's functions or departments is on the rise. Describes external and internal forces increasing friction and how to keep them from becoming destructive.

Rahim, M. A., "A Strategy for Managing Conflict in Complex Organizations," *Human Relations*, January 1985, pp. 81–89. Describes diagnosis and intervention methods designed to attain and maintain a moderate amount of conflict.

SCHNEER, J. A., and M. N. CHANIN, "Manifest Needs as Personality Predispositions to Conflict-Handling Behavior," *Human Relations*, September 1987, pp. 575–90. Researchers found a relationship between the need for dominance and affiliation and conflict-handling mode preference.

SHOCKLEY-ZALABAK, P. S., "Current Conflict Management Training: An Examination of Practices in Ten Large American Organizations," *Group and Organization Studies*, December 1984, pp. 491–507. Reviews conflict management training programs in a selected number of organizations to determine content taught, cost, and other factors.

Think of disagreements you have encountered in a particular task situation with your immediate supervisor. Then indicate below how frequently you engage in each of the described behaviors. For each item select the number that represents the behavior you are MOST LIKELY to exhibit. There are no right or wrong answers. Please respond to all items on the scale. The alternative responses (1–7) are:

1	2	3	4	5	6	7
Always	Very Often	Often	Sometimes	Seldom	Very Seldom	Never

1. I blend my ideas with my supervisor to create new alternatives for resolving a disagreement.   1 2 3 4 5 6 7
2. I shy away from topics which are sources of disputes with my supervisor.   1 2 3 4 5 6 7
3. I make my opinion known in a disagreement with my supervisor.   1 2 3 4 5 6 7
4. I suggest solutions which combine a variety of viewpoints.   1 2 3 4 5 6 7
5. I steer clear of disagreeable situations.   1 2 3 4 5 6 7
6. I give in a little on my ideas when my supervisor also gives in.   1 2 3 4 5 6 7
7. I avoid my supervisor when I suspect that he or she wants to discuss a disagreement.   1 2 3 4 5 6 7
8. I integrate arguments into a new solution from the issues raised in a dispute with my supervisor.   1 2 3 4 5 6 7
9. I will go 50-50 to reach a settlement with my supervisor.   1 2 3 4 5 6 7
10. I raise my voice when I'm trying to get my supervisor to accept my position.   1 2 3 4 5 6 7
11. I offer creative solutions in discussions of disagreements.   1 2 3 4 5 6 7
12. I keep quiet about my views in order to avoid disagreements.   1 2 3 4 5 6 7
13. I give in if my supervisor will meet me halfway.   1 2 3 4 5 6 7
14. I downplay the importance of a disagreement.   1 2 3 4 5 6 7
15. I reduce disagreements by making them seem insignificant.   1 2 3 4 5 6 7
16. I meet my supervisor at a mid-point in our differences.   1 2 3 4 5 6 7
17. I assert my opinion forcefully.   1 2 3 4 5 6 7
18. I dominate arguments until my supervisor understands my position.   1 2 3 4 5 6 7
19. I suggest we work together to create solutions to disagreements.   1 2 3 4 5 6 7
20. I try to use my supervisor's ideas to generate solutions to problems.   1 2 3 4 5 6 7
21. I offer trade-offs to reach solutions in a disagreement.   1 2 3 4 5 6 7
22. I argue insistently for my stance.   1 2 3 4 5 6 7
23. I withdraw when my supervisor confronts me about a controversial issue.   1 2 3 4 5 6 7
24. I side-step disagreements when they arise.   1 2 3 4 5 6 7
25. I try to smooth over disagreements by making them appear unimportant.   1 2 3 4 5 6 7
26. I insist my position be accepted during a disagreement with my supervisor.   1 2 3 4 5 6 7
27. I make our difference seem less serious.   1 2 3 4 5 6 7

1	2	3	4	5	6	7
Always	Very Often	Often	Sometimes	Seldom	Very Seldom	Never

28. I hold my tongue rather than argue with my supervisor.   1 2 3 4 5 6 7
29. I ease conflict by claiming our differences are trivial.   1 2 3 4 5 6 7
30. I stand firm in expressing my viewpoints during a disagreement with my supervisor.   1 2 3 4 5 6 7

Turn to page 565 for scoring directions and key.

Source: The Organizational Communication Conflict Instrument (OCCI), Form B, was developed by L. L. Putnam and C. Wilson. Reprinted by permission of the authors and Sage Publications, Inc.

Republic Avionics designs and manufactures sophisticated electronic devices for aerospace use. More than 90 percent of Republic's work evolves out of subcontracting for major aerospace firms like Boeing, General Dynamics, Lockheed, and McDonnell-Douglas. Founded in the late 1940s, the company grew to fifteen hundred employees by the mid-1960s and has been stable at this size ever since.

Republic's organization is designed around projects. When a contract is obtained, it is assigned to a project manager who, in turn, is supported by one or more assistant project managers. A typical project manager may oversee five or six projects at a time. The actual manufacturing of the electronic devices is done in the company's manufacturing division, which is headed by the director of manufacturing, Frank West. The director of manufacturing and project managers all report to a common boss—the vice-president of operations. Currently the vice-president of operations is Rob McDowell.

If each contract is to meet its time and quality objectives and come within budget, the project manager must work closely with manufacturing. The importance of each is recognized at Republic. While the vice-president of manufacturing's annual salary of $120,000 is well above the average project manager's salary of $70,000, project managers earn more than second-level managers in the production function responsible for the manufacturing of the various components.

John Wilson had been hired by Republic in August 1987 to be a project manager. An engineer by training, he had established an impressive research record in the aerospace industry and Republic's top management considered itself lucky to have hired Wilson away from Zaron Industries, where he was a senior researcher in its elec-tronic laboratories. Wilson was charged at Republic with supervising a number of projects, including a multimillion dollar subcontract for General Dynamics. Wilson was supported by Dave Brown, a twenty-six-year-old industrial engineer with an M.B.A. who had recently been hired out of a prestigious graduate school of business. Dave Brown impressed a large number of people at Republic as being bright and extremely ambitious.

In February 1988, Rob McDowell was informed by the auditing department that Wilson's project for General Dynamics was well behind schedule and running 14 percent over cost estimates. When McDowell confronted Wilson, the latter was obviously surprised. "I've had no knowledge that the project is off schedule. My assistant, Dave Brown, had mentioned that he's had to stay on top of the production people to make sure our project gets high priority. In fact, he's written several rather strong letters under my signature to Frank West to keep him aware of our concern. But Dave's always said everything was O.K. and that he just had to push those guys over in manufacturing a bit more than they have become accustomed to." An inquiry by McDowell to Frank West got a curt reply, "Tell John Wilson to get off my rear. I've got over three dozen manufacturing projects to get done and his letters and those nasty phone calls from his assistant have caused my people to give his projects lowest priority."

QUESTIONS

1. How does Republic Avionics manage intergroup relations?
2. What is the source of this conflict?
3. Has anyone done anything wrong? Explain.
4. What should McDowell do to deal with the current problem?

13

Foundations of Organization Structure

■ *Learning objectives*

Describe the three components that make up organization structure
Summarize the factors that determine structure
Differentiate between mechanistic and organic structures
List the conditions that favor different organization structures
Explain the moderating factors that influence the structure-performance/satisfaction relationship

One man's red tape is another man's system.

—— D. WALDO

Michele and Tony Chen are twins. Both grew up in Seattle, attended the University of Washington, and graduated with degrees in computer science in 1986. Upon graduation, Michele joined a San Francisco consulting firm as a systems specialist. Tony went to work for a Boston firm that writes computer software programs. At a recent family Thanksgiving dinner, the two spent some time comparing their job impressions.

"Did I ever make a mistake," began Tony. "I had four job offers and I took the one I did because it was a well-known company, provided me the opportunity to specialize in writing expert systems programs, and the promotion potential looked good because there were a number of levels of management. Well, there are many opportunities to move up here, but there's also a lot of competition. Of course, I've never been afraid of competition. It's just that jobs are so specialized and top management so removed from the daily routine that no one seems to notice what I do. I'm just a cog in this wheel. I'm a number—employee number HO 397, to be exact—and except for my boss and a few people in adjoining cubicles, no one even knows my name. It couldn't be more impersonal. You wouldn't believe the umpteen-zillion rules and regulations we have to follow. The company's policy manual has over 500 pages! I spent my first four weekends with the firm in my office reading that manual. The actual work I do is really interesting and I've learned a lot of technical aspects about programming. But I hate this feeling of alienation I have. This company, day-by-day, is stripping me of my identity. I've begun making a few calls to some of our old college friends to let them know I'm back in the job market and to let me know if they hear of anything interesting. But maybe it's me. Maybe all companies are like this. What's your firm like?"

"It's nothing like yours," was Michele's reply. "Managers are purposely given a large number of people to supervise. This cuts down on the number of managers and minimizes the number of levels from the top of the company to the bottom. The place is really very informal. No policy manuals, no job descriptions, no complex chain of command. If I have a question or problem, I can take it up with anyone. We're all treated as equals. Even all the offices are exactly the same size—twelve feet by ten feet—including those of the three owners. I'm on a first-name basis with everyone, including the president. They ask for my ideas on projects. And my ideas are often accepted and implemented. We're all supposed to be professionals, and we're treated as such."

Tony and Michele work in organizations with very different structures. And as their comments suggest, these structures have a bearing on each twin's attitudes and behavior. In this chapter, we'll define the key dimensions of an organization's structure, show how these dimensions can be mixed and matched to create various organization designs, explain the factors that influence the type of structure an organization has, and then consider how structural variables have a specific impact on employee behavior.

WHAT IS STRUCTURE?

Organizations create structure to facilitate the coordination of activities and to control the actions of their members. Structure, itself, is made up of three components. The first has to do with the degree to which activities within the organization are broken up or differentiated. We call this *complexity*. Second, is the degree to which rules and procedures are utilized. This component is referred to as *formalization*. The third component of structure is *centralization*, which considers where decision-making authority lies. Combined, these three components make up an organization's structure.[1] Some organizations, like General Electric or the U.S. Department of Defense, are rigidly structured. They have lots of differentiated units, a great number of vertical levels between top management and the workers at the bottom, numerous rules and regulations that members are required to follow, and elaborate decision making networks. At the other extreme are organizations that are loosely structured—few differentiated units, only a couple levels of management hierarchy, little in terms of formalized regulations to restrict employees, and a simple system for making decisions. Of course, in between these two extremes lie a number of structural combinations. But while organizations differ in the ways they are structured, our primary interest is what impact these structural differences have on employee attitudes and behavior. First, however, let's briefly elaborate on the three components we have identified to ensure we have a common understanding of what is meant when we use the term **organization structure**.

Organization structure

The degree of complexity, formalization, and centralization in the organization.

Complexity

The degree of vertical, horizontal, and spatial differentiation in an organization.

Horizontal differentiation

The degree of differentiation between units based on the orientation of members, the nature of the tasks they perform, and their education and training.

Complexity

Complexity encompasses three forms of differentiation: horizontal, vertical, and spatial. **Horizontal differentiation** considers the degree of horizontal separation between units. The larger the number of different occupations within an organization that require specialized knowledge and skills, the more horizontally complex that organization is, because diverse orientations make it more difficult for organizational members to communicate and more difficult for management to coordinate their activities. When organizations have coordination problems because the cost accountants can't understand the priorities of the industrial

[1] S. P. Robbins, *Organization Theory: Structure, Design, and Applications,* 2nd ed. (Englewood Cliffs, NJ: Prentice Hall, 1987), Chapter 3.

engineers or because marketing and credit personnel have conflicting goals, the source of the problems is horizontal differentiation.

Vertical differentiation refers to the depth of the organizational hierarchy. The more levels that exist between top management and the operatives, the more complex the organization is. This is because there is a greater potential for communication distortion, it's more difficult to coordinate the decisions of managerial personnel, and it's harder for top management to oversee closely the actions of operatives where there are more vertical levels. For example, it's a lot more likely that information having to go through eight or ten levels of management hierarchy will become distorted or misinterpreted than if that information had to move through only two or three levels.

Spatial differentiation encompasses the degree to which the location of an organization's physical facilities and personnel are geographically dispersed. As spatial differentiation increases so does complexity, because communication, coordination, and control become more difficult. Coordinating Sheraton's hundreds of hotels, located around the world, is a far more complex undertaking than coordinating the dozen New York City hotels that make up the Helmsley chain.

Vertical differentiation

The number of hierarchical levels in the organization.

Spatial differentiation

The degree to which the location of an organization's offices, plants, and personnel are geographically dispersed.

Formalization

The second component of structure is **formalization**. This term refers to the degree to which jobs within the organization are standardized. If a job is highly formalized, then the job incumbent has a minimum amount of discretion over what is to be done, when it is to be done, and how he or she should do it. Employees can be expected always to handle the same input in exactly the same way, resulting in a consistent and uniform output. There are explicit job descriptions, lots of organizational rules, and clearly defined procedures covering work processes in organizations where there is high formalization. Where formalization is low, job behaviors are relatively nonprogrammed and employees have a great deal of freedom to exercise discretion in their work. Since an individual's discretion on the job is inversely related to the amount of behavior that is preprogrammed by the organization, the greater the standardization, the less input the employee has into how his or her work is to be done. Standardization not only eliminates the possibility of employees engaging in alternative behaviors, but it even removes the need for employees to consider alternatives.

Formalization

The degree to which jobs within the organization are standardized.

The degree of formalization can vary widely between organizations and within organizations. Certain jobs, for instance, are well known to have little formalization. College book travelers—the representatives of publishers who call on professors to inform them of their company's new publications—have a great deal of freedom in their jobs. They have no standard sales "spiel," and the extent of rules and procedures governing their behavior may be little more than the requirement that they submit a weekly sales report and some suggestions on what to emphasize for the various new titles. At the other extreme, there are clerical and editorial positions in the same publishing houses where employees are required to "clock in" at their workstation by 8:00 A.M. or be docked a half-hour of pay and, once at that workstation, to follow a set of precise procedures dictated by management.

Centralization

Centralization

The degree to which decision making is concentrated at a single point in the organization.

In some organizations, top managers make all the decisions. Lower-level managers merely carry out top management's directives. At the other extreme, there are organizations where decision making is pushed down to those managers who are closest to the action. The former case is called **centralization**; the latter is decentralization.

The term centralization refers to the degree to which decision making is concentrated at a single point in the organization. The concept includes only formal authority, that is, the rights inherent in one's position. Typically, it is said that if top management makes the organization's key decisions with little or no input from lower-level personnel, then the organization is centralized. In contrast, the more that lower-level personnel provide input or are actually given the discretion to make decisions, the more decentralized the organization.

An organization characterized by centralization is an inherently different structural animal from one that is decentralized. In a decentralized organization, action can be taken more quickly to solve problems, more people provide input into decisions, and employees are less likely to feel alienated from those who make the decisions that affect their work lives.

CLASSIFYING ORGANIZATION STRUCTURES

Concepts like complexity, formalization, and centralization often seem abstract to the typical reader or, for that matter, the average employee in an organization. In this section, we want to develop a simple classification scheme that can help you to describe organizations better. Then, we will offer a more detailed discussion of four specific structural designs that are now widely utilized.

Mechanistic and Organic Structures

Mechanistic structure

A structure characterized by high complexity, high formalization, and centralization.

Organic structure

A structure characterized by low complexity, low formalization, and decentralization.

An organization's overall structure generally falls into one of two designs. One is the **mechanistic structure**. It's characterized by high complexity (especially a great deal of horizontal differentiation), high formalization, a limited information network (mostly downward communication), and little participation by low-level members in decision making. At the other extreme is the **organic structure**. It is low in complexity and formalization, it possesses a comprehensive information network (utilizing lateral and upward communication as well as downward), and it involves high participation in decision making. As Figure 13–1 depicts, mechanistic structures are rigid, relying on authority and a well-defined hierarchy to facilitate coordination. The organic structure, on the other hand, is flexible and adaptive. Coordination is achieved through constant communication and adjustment.

The mechanistic-organic dichotomy is a useful designation device for generalizing about organization structures. The world of organizations, of course, is not so neatly defined. We can, however, introduce two specific structural forms that capture the essential ingredients of mechanistic and organic designs.

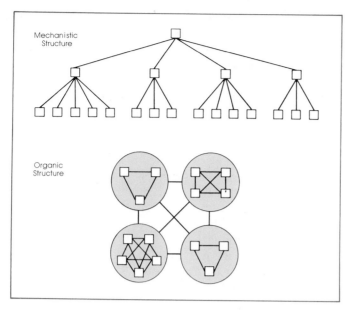

FIGURE 13-1
Two Diverse Structural Designs

You've undoubtedly heard the term **bureaucracy** to describe certain organizations. The bureaucratic structure has most of the characteristics associated with the mechanistic model. **Adhocracy**, or the adhocratic structure, combines most of the features we've described in the organic model.

To many, the term bureaucracy conjures up a host of attributes implying inefficiency—red tape, paper shuffling, rigid application of rules, and redundance of effort. That is not what we mean by the term. When we talk of bureaucracy, we refer to a structural design that German sociologist Max Weber has described as having the following characteristics:

- *Division of labor*—Each person's job is broken down into simple, routine, and well-defined tasks.

- *Well-defined authority hierarchy*—There is a multilevel formal structure, with a hierarchy of positions or offices. Each lower office is under the supervision and control of a higher one.

- *High formalization*—To ensure uniformity and to regulate the behavior of jobholders, there is heavy dependence on formal rules and procedures.

- *Impersonal nature*—Sanctions are applied uniformly and impersonally to avoid involvement with individual personalities and personal preferences of members.

- *Employment decisions based on merit*—Selection and promotion decisions are based on technical qualifications, competence, and performance of the candidate.

- *Career tracks for employees*—Members are expected to pursue a career in the organization. In return for this career commitment, employees are given permanent employment; that is, they are retained even if they "burn out" or their skills become obsolete.

Bureaucracy

A structure characterized by high complexity, high formalization, impersonality, career tracks, employment decisions based on merit, and separation of members' organizational and personal lives.

Adhocracy

A structure that is flexible, adaptive, and responsive; organized around unique problems to be solved by groups of relative strangers with diverse professional skills.

- *Distinct separation of members' organizational and personal lives*—To prevent the demands and interests of personal affairs from interfering with the rational impersonal conduct of the organization's activities, the two are kept completely separate.[2]

While these characteristics represent the ideal or perfect bureaucracy, cumulatively they are a fairly accurate description of most large organizations. Whether you are describing the structure of Mobil Oil, the American Broadcasting Company, Bristol-Myers, the New York City school system, or the U.S. Army, these organizations and thousands of others substantially meet all the characteristics we attribute to bureaucracy. In structural terms, they are highly complex and highly formalized. Whether they are centralized or decentralized typically depends on the type of people they employ. If employees are professionals or hold specialized skills, the bureaucracy will be decentralized. Otherwise, authority is typically kept centralized.

What bureaucracy is to the mechanistic form, adhocracy is to the organic. The term "adhocracy" refers to any structure that is essentially a flexible, adaptive, responsive system organized around unique problems to be solved by groups of relative strangers with diverse professional skills. In terms of our structural dimensions, adhocracies would be characterized as having moderate to low complexity, low formalization, and decentralized decision making.

As we'll show a bit later in this chapter, you're most likely to run into an adhocracy in a small organization or as an "attachment" to a bureaucracy in the form of project groups or task forces. For instance, Procter & Gamble is essentially a bureaucracy. But when P&G wants to develop a new product, say, a toothpaste, it will rely on an adhocratic structure. Personnel with expertise in finance, marketing, manufacturing, cost accounting, product design, research, and other relevant areas will be tapped from their functional departments and temporarily assigned the task of creating the product, designing its package, determining its market, computing its manufacturing costs, and assessing its profit margin. Once the problems have been fully worked out of the product and it is ready to be produced in quantity, the adhocratic structure is disbanded and the toothpaste is integrated into the permanent functional structure.

But some large organizations make use of the adhocracy form as their prime structural design. For instance, Digital Equipment Corporation (DEC) employs 100,000 employees and has annual sales of $7.6 billion, but there's a minimal amount of hierarchy and rule books. There are also no dress codes, fancy titles, or other trappings of bureaucracy.[3] The company's main offices in Maynard, Massachusetts look more like a large college student union than a corporate headquarters. Only the top half-dozen executives have sizable offices. Everyone else makes do with small, doorless cubicles. Engineers have essentially the same status as managers. Many have flexible hours and can work from computer modems in their homes. Technical decisions are typically made at the lowest levels by members of design teams. When someone has an idea at

---

[2] M. Weber, *The Theory of Social and Economic Organizations*, ed. T. Parsons and trans. A. M. Henderson and T. Parsons (New York: Free Press, 1947).

[3] D. Machan, "DEC's Democracy," *Forbes,* March 23, 1987, pp. 154–56.

Balancing Creativity and Efficiency

Organic structures facilitate flexibility, interaction among members, and creativity. But they tend to be inefficient. Mechanistic structures, in contrast, are well-oiled efficiency machines. They can provide standardized goods and services at lower costs than their organic counterparts. One of their major drawbacks, however, is that they stifle creativity. Narrowly defined jobs, high specialization, formal communication channels, and standardized operating procedures discourage trying new things or pursuing novel ideas. When asked why they do things a certain way, employees in mechanistic structures tend to respond with answers like: "Well, that's just the way we do things around here."

How do managers resolve the creativity-efficiency conflict? There is no easy answer. It is, in fact, a delicate balancing act. Apple Computer, however, provides an illustration of how the conflicting objectives can be achieved.[4]

Under cofounder Steve Jobs, Apple was a "one man show." He gave engineers tremendous freedom. New product development was going on all over the place in "skunkworks"—isolated and autonomous groups of employees working on a specific project. Research teams would work on projects in secret. After developing a product in their "back room," the team would show it to the marketing and management people, who often said, "That's not what we want." The project would then be canceled or sent back for modification. This system stimulated several revolutionary products— the Apple IIc, IIe, and the Macintosh—but it was an inefficient structure for a rapidly growing company that was facing increased competition from the likes of IBM, AT&T, and Compaq.

Since Jobs' departure in 1985, John Sculley (Apple's chairman and president) has sought to keep the creative juices flowing by institutionalizing the company's inventiveness. His goal: to produce a steady stream of new products. The primary structural change that Sculley introduced was to consolidate development efforts of all Apple's product lines into a single group. New managers have reined in unauthorized skunkworks and included marketing and manufacturing people early in the product development process. This has cut down on false starts and facilitated the development of more coherent families of computer products. At the same time, employees are still encouraged to pursue new ideas and not to fear consequences from failures.

Sculley's structural change seems to be working. In 1987 alone, Apple announced more new products than the firm had developed in its total previous ten year history. Also, in 1987, revenues and profits were expanding at a record pace.

[4] B. R. Schlender, "Apple Computer Tries to Achieve Stability but Remain Creative," *Wall Street Journal,* July 16, 1987, pp. 1 & 6.

DEC, they think nothing of jumping several levels of authority to gain support for it. Maybe most importantly, this structure works for DEC. Net income has consistently outpaced its competitors and employee turnover is less than half the industry average. Of course, adhocracy isn't for every organization. After we've looked at a few of the more widely used specific applications of the mechanistic and organic designs, we'll try to assess why the right structure for Digital Equipment Corporation may not be the right structure for an IBM or Motorola.

The Simple Structure

Simple structure

A structure characterized by low complexity, low formalization, and authority centralized in a single person.

What do a small retail store, an electronics firm run by a hard-driving entrepreneur, and the reelection campaign office for a city councilman in Eugene, Oregon have in common? They probably all have **simple structures**.

Most small organizations, or new ones that are just starting out, utilize the simple structure. In terms of absolute number, most organizations in North America are probably simple structures.

Simple structures are characterized most by what they're not rather than what they are.[5] The simple structure is *not* elaborated. It is low in complexity, has little formalization, and has authority centralized in a single person. Overall, it is more organic than mechanistic.

Figure 13–2 shows an example of the simple structure: the Fashion Flair retail stores. Notice that this organization is flat or low on vertical differentiation. Decision making is basically informal—all important decisions are centralized in the hands of the senior executive who, because of the organization's low complexity, is able readily to obtain key information and can act rapidly when required. The senior executive is the owner-manager at Fashion Flair.

The Functional Structure

Functional structure

A structure characterized by grouping similar and related occupational specialties together.

Pick up copies of the organization charts for most *Fortune* 500 companies and take a close look at how their organizations are designed. The probability is very high that the designs will encompass the **functional structure**.

The distinguishing feature of the functional structure is that similar and related occupational specialties are grouped together. Activities such as marketing, accounting, manufacturing, and personnel are grouped under a functional head who reports to a central headquarters. Figure 13–3 shows a typical functional structure for a manufacturing firm.

The functional structure is extremely popular, undoubtedly due to its compatibility with the bureaucratic structure. That is, the functional structure maximizes the economics from specialization. Putting like specialties together affords economies of scale and reduces duplication of personnel and equipment, and employees are likely to feel comfortable and satisfied because they are part of a homogeneous group where their peers all talk "the same language."

[5] H. Mintzberg, "Structure in 5's: A Synthesis of the Research on Organization Design," *Management Science,* March 1980, p. 331.

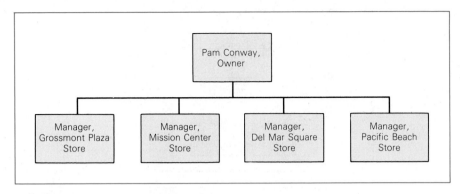

FIGURE 13–2
Simple Structure of Fashion Flair Stores

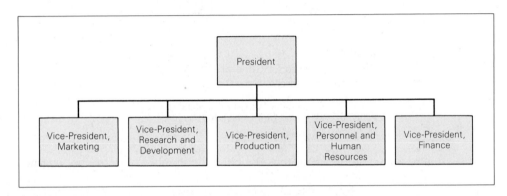

FIGURE 13–3
Functional Structure in a Manufacturing Organization

The Product Structure

In addition to organizing by function, you can structure an organization around product lines. Figure 13–4 shows a simplified version of the **product structure** developed by General Motors for its North American Automotive Operations. Created in 1984, this structure has two integrated car groups, each operating as a self-contained business unit. Each car group is responsible for its own product, including engineering, manufacturing, assembly, and marketing.

The major advantage to the product form is accountability. The product manager is responsible for all facets surrounding the product. Instead of having the marketing manager oversee fifteen different product lines, each product structure will have its own marketing manager with sole responsibility for marketing his or her division's product. In this way, product control is centralized with the product manager. The drawbacks, of course, are the need to coordinate activities between product structures and the duplication of functions within the various structures. Whereas in the functional structure a department of five people might be able to handle the entire organization's purchasing activities, if that organization is structured around ten product divisions, each will probably

Product structure

A structure characterized by grouping activities together that relate to a specific product.

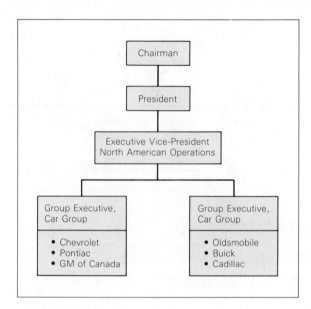

FIGURE 13–4
Product Structure for General Motors' North American Automotive Operations

Source: General Motors Corp., 1984 General Motors Public Interest Report (April 1984), p. 7. With permission.

require a purchasing agent, thus doubling the number of personnel engaged in purchasing.

The Matrix Structure

Matrix structure

A structure that creates dual lines of authority; combines the functional and product structures.

One of the more recent organizational design innovations is the **matrix structure**. Essentially, the matrix combines the functional and product structures. Ideally, it seeks to gain the strengths of each, while avoiding their weaknesses. That is, the strength of the functional structure lies in putting like specialists together, which minimizes the number necessary, and it allows the pooling and sharing of specialized resources across products. Its major disadvantage is the difficulty of coordinating the tasks of diverse functional specialists so that their activities are completed on time and within budget. The product structure, on the other hand, has exactly the opposite benefits and disadvantages. It facilitates the coordination among specialties to achieve on-time completion and meet budget targets. Further, it provides clear responsibility for all activities related to a product, but with duplication of activities and costs.

Figure 13–5 shows the matrix form as used in a College of Business Administration. The academic departments of accounting, economics, marketing, and so forth are functional units. Additionally, specific programs (that is, products) are overlaid on the functions. In this way, members in a matrix structure have a dual assignment: to their functional department and to their product group. For instance, a professor of accounting teaching an undergraduate course reports to the director of undergraduate programs as well as to the chairman

Programs / Academic Departments	Undergraduate	Master's	Ph. D.	Research	Executive Programs	Community-Service Programs
Accounting						
Administrative Studies						
Economics						
Finance						
Marketing						
Organizational Behavior						
Quantitative Methods						

FIGURE 13–5
Matrix Structure for a College of Business Administration

of the accounting department. Note, however, the potential for conflict and power struggles because professors have multiple superiors. Employees in a matrix structure, especially those who have a low tolerance for ambiguity, are likely to become frustrated if they find themselves having to satisfy conflicting directions from their functional and product bosses.

WHY DO STRUCTURES DIFFER?

We've described two general structural designs—the mechanistic and organic—and their counterparts in practice—bureaucracy and adhocracy. Then we briefly described four specific structural designs that you're likely to encounter. But why are some organizations structured along more mechanistic lines while others follow organic characteristics? What are the forces that influence the form that is chosen? In the following pages, we shall present the major forces that researchers have identified as causes or determinants of an organization's structure.

Strategy

An organization's structure is a means to help management achieve its objectives. Since objectives are derived from the organization's overall strategy, it is only logical that strategy and structure should be closely linked. More specifically, structure should follow strategy. If management makes a significant change in its organization's strategy, structure will need to be modified to accommodate and support this change.[6]

The primary research supporting this strategy-structure relationship was a study of close to 100 large U.S. companies conducted by Alfred Chandler. Tracing the development of these organizations over a period of fifty years, and compiling extensive case histories of companies such as DuPont, General Motors, Standard Oil of New Jersey, and Sears, Roebuck, Chandler concluded that changes in corporate strategy precede and lead to changes in an organization's structure. Chandler found that organizations usually begin with a single product or line. They do only one thing, like manufacturing, sales, or warehousing. The simplicity of the strategy requires only a simple, or loose, form of structure to execute it. Decisions can be centralized in the hands of a single senior manager, while complexity and formalization will be low.

As organizations grow, their strategies become more ambitious and elaborated. From the single product line, companies often expand their activities within their industry. This vertical integration strategy makes for increased interdependence between organizational units and creates the need for a more complex coordination device. This is achieved by redesigning the structure to form specialized units based on functions performed.

Finally, if growth proceeds further into product diversification, structure needs to be adjusted again to gain efficiency. A product diversification strategy demands a structural form that allows for the efficient allocation of resources, accountability for performance, and coordination between units. This can be achieved best by creating many independent divisions, each responsible for a specified product line.

In summary, the structure-follows-strategy thesis argues that as strategies move from single product, to vertical integration, to product diversification, management will need to develop more elaborate structures to maintain effectiveness. They'll begin with something that looks a lot like an adhocracy and move, over time, to a more structured bureaucracy.

Organization Size

Organization size

The number of people employed in an organization.

A quick glance at the organizations we deal with regularly in our lives would lead most of us to conclude that **size** would have some bearing on an organization's structure. The more than 800,000 employees of the U.S. Postal Service, for example, do not neatly fit into one building, or into several departments supervised by a couple of managers. It's pretty hard to envision 800,000 people being organized in any manner other than one that contained a great deal of horizontal, vertical, and spatial differentiation, used a large number of procedures and regulations to ensure uniform practices, and followed a high degree of decentralized decision making. On the other hand, a local messenger service that employs ten people and generates less than $300,000 a year in service fees is not likely to need decentralized decision making or formalized procedures and regulations.

A little more thought suggests that the same conclusion—size influences

---

[6] A. D. Chandler, Jr., *Strategy and Structure: Chapters in the History of the Industrial Enterprise* (Cambridge, MA: MIT Press, 1962).

structure—can be arrived at through a more sophisticated reasoning process. As an organization hires more operative employees, it will attempt to take advantage of the economic benefits from specialization. The result will be increased horizontal differentiation. Grouping like functions together will facilitate intragroup efficiencies, but will cause intergroup relations to suffer as each performs its different activities. Management, therefore, will need to increase vertical differentiation to coordinate the horizontally differentiated units. This expansion in size is also likely to result in spatial differentiation. All of this increase in complexity will reduce top management's ability to directly supervise the activities within the organization. The control achieved through direct surveillance, therefore, will be replaced by the implementation of formal rules and regulations. This increase in formalization may also be accompanied by still greater vertical differentiation as management creates new units to coordinate the expanding and diverse activities of organizational members. Finally, with top management further removed from the operating level, it becomes difficult for senior executives to make rapid and informative decisions. The solution is to substitute decentralized decision making for centralization. Following this reasoning, we see changes in size leading to major structural changes.

But does it actually happen this way? Does structure change directly as a result in a change in the total number of employees? A review of the evidence indicates that size has a significant influence on some but certainly not all elements of structure.

Size appears to have a decreasing rate of impact on complexity.[7] That is, increases in organization size are accompanied by initially rapid and subsequently more gradual increases in differentiation. The biggest effect, however, is on vertical differentiation.[8] As organizations increase their number of employees, more levels are added, but at a decreasing rate.

The evidence is quite strong linking size and formalization.[9] There is a logical connection between the two. Management seeks to control the behavior of its employees. This can be achieved by direct surveillance or by the use of formalized regulations. While not perfect substitutes for each other, as one increases, the need for the other should decrease. Because surveillance costs should increase very rapidly as an organization expands in size, it seems reasonable to expect that it would be less expensive for management to substitute formalization for direct surveillance as size increases.

There is also a strong inverse relationship between size and centralization.[10] In small organizations, it's possible for management to exercise control by keeping decisions centralized. As size increases, management is physically unable to maintain control in this manner and, therefore, is forced to decentralize.

[7] P. M. Blau, "A Formal Theory of Differentiation in Organizations," *American Sociological Review*, April 1970, pp. 201–18.

[8] D. S. Mileti, D. F. Gillespie, and J. E. Haas, "Size and Structure in Complex Organizations," *Social Forces*, September 1977, pp. 208–17.

[9] W. A. Rushing, "Organizational Size, Rules, and Surveillance," in J. A. Litterer (ed.), *Organizations: Structure and Behavior*, 3rd ed. (New York: John Wiley, 1980), pp. 396–405; and Y. Samuel and B. F. Mannheim, "A Multidimensional Approach Toward a Typology of Bureaucracy," *Administrative Science Quarterly*, June 1970, pp. 216–28.

[10] See, for example, P. M. Blau and R. A. Schoenherr, *The Structure of Organizations* (New York: Basic Books, 1971); and J. Child and R. Mansfield, "Technology, Size, and Organization Structure," *Sociology*, September 1972, pp. 369–93.

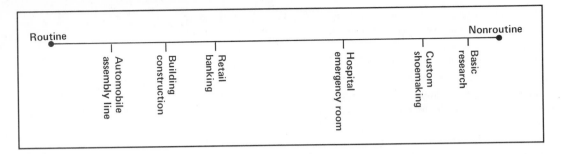

FIGURE 13–6
Technology Classification with Representative Examples

Technology

The term **technology** refers to how an organization transfers its inputs to outputs. Every organization has one or more technologies for converting financial, human, and physical resources into products or services. The Ford Motor Company, for instance, predominantly uses an assembly-line process to make its products. On the other hand, colleges may use a number of instruction technologies—the ever-popular formal lecture method, the case analysis method, the experiential exercise method, the programmed learning method, and so forth.

There is no agreement on a universal technology classification.[11] If there is a common denominator among those classifications that attempts to describe the processes or methods that organizations use to transform inputs into outputs, it is the *degree of routineness*. By this we mean that technologies tend toward either routine or nonroutine activities. The former are characterized by automated and standardized operations. This describes such diverse processes as mass-production assembly lines or repetitive clerical tasks. Nonroutine activities are customized. They include such varied operations as furniture restoring, custom shoemaking, or NASA's efforts at developing a space station. As shown in Figure 13–6, we can think of all technologies as falling somewhere along a routine-nonroutine continuum.

Some researchers argue that there is a *technological imperative*, that is, that technology *causes* structure.[12] A more moderate position is that technology *constrains* managers. If managers have a considerable degree of choice over their organization's technology, then there is little basis for the imperative argument. Technology would only control structure to the degree that managers chose a technology that demanded certain structural dimensions. For instance, it has been argued that organizations choose the domain in which they will operate and, hence, the activities in which they will engage.[13] If an organization decides to offer consulting advice tailored to the needs of its clients, it is not likely to use the routine-oriented mass-production technology. Similarly, the

---

[11] The most frequently referenced technology categories have been offered by J. Woodward, *Industrial Organization: Theory and Practice* (London: Oxford University Press, 1965); C. Perrow, "A Framework for the Comparative Analysis of Organizations," *American Sociological Review*, April 1967, pp. 194–208; and J. D. Thompson, *Organizations in Action* (New York: McGraw-Hill, 1967). For a review of these contributions, see Robbins, *Organization Theory*, pp. 126–37.

[12] Woodward, *Industrial Organization*: and Perrow, *Framework*.

[13] J. Pfeffer, *Organizational Design* (Arlington Heights, IL: AHM, 1978), p. 99.

fact that Honda of America chose to build a manufacturing facility in Ohio that could produce at least four hundred cars a day that could, in turn, retail in the $9,000–15,000 price range pretty well eliminated any technology other than one relying heavily on routinized mass-production activities. Had Honda decided to produce only four cars a day at that plant and charge $100,000 or more apiece for each car (which more accurately describes the production facility at Rolls Royce), then routine mass production might not be at all appropriate. The point is that "choice of domain, and a set of activities and tasks, tend to constrain the organization's technology, but the domain is still chosen."[14] The counterpoint, of course, is that even though domain is chosen, technology is still a major influence on structure. For instance, research laboratories are typically low in formalization, whereas claims departments in insurance companies are typically high on this structural dimension. A good part of this structural difference can be traced to the fact that research labs use nonroutine technologies and claims departments activities are standardized and routine.

What relationships have been found between technology and structure? Although the relationship is not overwhelmingly strong, we do find that routine tasks are associated with high complexity. Repetition essentially encourages increased horizontal and vertical differentiation, which leads to taller and more complex structures.[15]

The technology-formalization relationship is stronger. Studies consistently show routineness to be associated with the presence of rule manuals, job descriptions, and other formalized documentation.[16]

Finally, the technology-centralization relationship is less straightforward. It seems logical that routine technologies would be associated with a centralized structure, whereas nonroutine technologies, which rely more heavily on the knowledge of specialists, would be characterized by delegated decision authority. This position has met with some support.[17] However, a more generalizable conclusion is that the technology-centralization relationship is moderated by the degree of formalization.[18] Formal regulations and centralized decision making are both control mechanisms and management can substitute them for each other. Routine technologies should be associated with centralized control if there is a minimum of rules and regulations. However, if formalization is high, routine technology can be accompanied by decentralization. So, we would predict that routine technology would lead to centralization, but only if formalization is low.

Environment

An organization's **environment** represents anything outside the organization itself. The problem of defining an organization's environment, however, is

Environment

Anything outside the organization itself.

[14] Ibid.

[15] J. Hage and M. Aiken, "Routine Technology, Social Structure, and Organizational Goals," *Administrative Science Quarterly*, September 1969, pp. 366–77.

[16] D. Gerwin, "Relationships Between Structure and Technology at the Organizational and Job Levels," *Journal of Management Studies*, February 1979, pp. 70–79.

[17] A. Van De Ven, A. Delbecq, and R. Koenig, Jr., "Determinants of Coordination Modes Within Organizations," *American Sociological Review*, April 1976, pp. 322–38.

[18] J. Hage and M. Aiken, "Relationship of Centralization to Other Structural Properties," *Administrative Science Quarterly*, June 1967, pp. 72–92.

OB Close-Up

How Computers Can Change Organization Structures

When organizations introduce sophisticated, computer-based management information systems, they are changing technology. For instance, a computer-based MIS lessens the need to depend on direct supervision and staff reports as control mechanisms. A senior executive can monitor what's going on on the operating floor or in the accounts payable department by simply pushing a few keys on his or her desktop terminal. And such changes in technology have a very real effect on the organization's structure.[19] The most obvious result: Organizations become flatter and more organic.

Computer-based information systems allow managers to handle more subordinates because computer control substitutes for personal supervision. As a result, managers can effectively oversee more people and the organization will require fewer managers and, hence, there will be fewer levels in the hierarchy. The need for staff support is also reduced with a computer-based information system. Managers can tap information directly which makes large staff support groups redundant. Both forces—wider spans of supervision and reduced staff—lead to flatter organizations.

One of the more interesting phenomena created by sophisticated information systems is that they have allowed management to make organizations more organic without any loss in control.[20] Management can lessen formalization and become more decentralized—thus making their organizations more organic—without giving up control. Why? An MIS substitutes computer control for rules and decision discretion. Computer technology rapidly apprises top managers of the consequences of any decision and allows them to take corrective action if the decision is not to their liking. Thus there's the appearance of decentralization without any commensurate loss of control.

often quite difficult. "Nature has neatly packaged people into skins, animals into hides, and allowed trees to enclose themselves with bark. It is easy to see where the unit is and where the environment is. Not so for social organizations."[21] We'll define the environment as composed of those institutions or forces that affect the performance of the organization, but over which the organization has little control. These typically include suppliers, customers, government regulatory agencies, and the like. But keep in mind that it is not always clear who or what is included in any specific organization's relevant environment.

[19] See, for instance, "Management Discovers the Human Side of Automation," *Business Week*, September 29, 1986, pp. 70–75.

[20] Robbins, *Organization Theory*, pp. 399–400.

[21] J. Pfeffer and G. R. Salancik, *The External Control of Organizations: A Resource Dependence Perspective* (New York: Harper & Row, 1978), p. 29.

The environment-structure relationship has received a large amount of attention.[22] The reason for this attention is quite simple: Organizations must adapt to their environments if they are to succeed because organizations are dependent on their environments if they are to survive. They must identify and follow their environments, sense changes in those environments, and make appropriate adjustments as necessary. But changing environments produce uncertainty if management can't predict in what ways their environments are moving. And management doesn't like uncertainty. As a result, management will try to eliminate or at least minimize the impact of environmental uncertainty. Alterations in the organization's structural components are a major tool that management has for controlling environmental uncertainty. The environmental imperative would propose, therefore, that the degree of environmental uncertainty is *the* determinant of structure. If uncertainty is high, the organization will be designed along flexible lines in order to adapt to rapid changes, that is, as an organic structure. If uncertainty is low, management will opt for a structure that will be most efficient and offer the highest degree of managerial control—the mechanistic structure.

Does the evidence support these predictions? The answer is "Yes." Environmental uncertainty and organizational complexity are inversely related. This is particularly true for departments within organizations.[23] Those departments within the organization that are most dependent on the environment—such as marketing or research and development—are typically the lowest in complexity.

Similarly, formalization and environmental uncertainty are inversely related.[24] That is, certain and stable environments lead to high formalization. Why? Because stable environments create a minimal need for rapid response and economies exist for organizations that standardize their activities.

Centralization is also affected by the environment. If the environment is large and multifaceted, it becomes difficult for management to monitor. As a result, the structure tends to become decentralized.[25] This explains why the marketing function in organizations is typically decentralized. If a firm has a large number of customers and the needs of these customers are prone to rapid changes, management must be able to respond rapidly if it is to keep its customers satisfied. This can best be achieved by pushing key decisions down to the local marketing managers who are closest to the customer. Decentralization allows for more rapid response.

[22] The effects of environment on structure were recognized in the 1960s by T. Burns and G. M. Stalker, *The Management of Innovation* (London: Tavistock, 1961); F. E. Emery and E. L. Trist, "The Causal Texture of Organizational Environments," *Human Relations*, February 1965, pp. 21–32; and P. Lawrence and J. W. Lorsch, *Organization and Environment: Managing Differentiation and Integration* (Boston: Division of Research, Harvard Business School, 1967). For a review of these contributions, see Robbins, *Organization Theory*, pp. 153–59.

[23] P. Lawrence and J. W. Lorsch, *Organization and Environment*.

[24] See, for example, R. B. Duncan, "Characteristics of Organizational Environments and Perceived Environmental Uncertainty," *Administrative Science Quarterly*, September 1972, pp. 313–27.

[25] H. Mintzberg, *The Structuring of Organizations* (Englewood Cliffs, NJ: Prentice Hall, 1979), pp. 273–76.

Power-Control

Power-control

An organization's structure is the result of a power struggle by internal constituencies who are seeking to further their interests.

An increasingly popular and insightful approach to the question of what causes structure is to look to a political explanation. Strategy, size, technology, and environment—even when combined—can at best explain only 50 to 60 percent of the variability in structure.[26] There is a growing body of evidence that suggests that power and control can explain a good portion of the residual variance. More specifically, the **power-control** explanation states that an organization's structure is the result of a power struggle by internal constituencies who are seeking to further their interests.[27] Like all decisions in an organization, the structural decision is not fully rational. Managers do not necessarily choose those alternatives that will maximize the organization's interest. They choose criteria and weight them so that the "best choice" will meet the minimal demands of the organization, and also satisfy or enhance the interests of the decision maker. Strategy, size, technology, and environmental uncertainty act as constraints by establishing parameters and defining how much discretion is available. Almost always, within the parameters, there is a great deal of room for the decision maker to maneuver. The power-control position, therefore, argues that those in power will choose a structure that will maintain or enhance their control. Consistent with this perspective, we should expect structures to change very slowly, if at all. Significant changes would occur only as a result of a political struggle in which new power relations evolve. But this rarely occurs. Transitions in the executive suite are usually peaceful. They are evolutionary rather than revolutionary. However, major shake-ups in top management occasionally do occur. Not surprisingly. they are typically followed by major structural changes.

Predictions based on the power-control viewpoint differ from those based on the four previous approaches in that those approaches were basically contingency models: Structures change to reflect changes in strategy, size, technology, or environmental uncertainty. The power-control approach, however, is essentially noncontingent. It assumes little change within the organization's power coalition. Hence, it would propose that structures are relatively stable over time. More important, power-control advocates would predict that after taking into consideration strategy, size, technology, and environmental factors, those in power would choose a structure that would best serve their personal interests. What type of structure would that be? Obviously one that would be low in complexity, high in formalization, and centralized. These structural dimensions will most likely maximize control in the hands of senior management. A structure with these properties becomes the single "one best way" to organize. Of course, *best* in this context refers to "maintenance of control" rather than enhancement of organizational performance.

Is the power-control position an accurate description? The evidence suggests that it explains a great deal of why organizations are structured the way they are.[28] The dominant structural forms in organizations today are essentially mechanistic. Organic structures have received a great deal of attention by acade-

---

[26] J. Child, "Organization Structure, Environment and Performance: The Role of Strategic Choice," *Sociology*, January 1972, pp. 1–22; and D. S. Pugh, "The Management of Organization Structures: Does Context Determine Form?" *Organizational Dynamics*, Spring 1973, pp. 19–34.

[27] Pfeffer, *Organizational Design*.

[28] Ibid.

micians, but the vast majority of real organizations, especially those that employ several hundred or more employees, are mechanistic. Even the simple structure, though low in formalization, maintains control by consolidating decision making power in the hands of the senior executive.

Applying the Contingency Factors

Under what conditions would each of the contingency factors we've introduced—strategy, organization size, technology, and environment—be the dominant determinant of an organization's structure? More specifically, when should we expect to find mechanistic structures and when should organic structures be most prevalent?

Strategy   The strategy-determines-structure thesis argues that managers change their organization's structure to align with changes in strategy. Based on Chandler's research, we would expect single product firms to have a simple structure. As they expanded through vertical integration, they would adopt a functional structure. If product diversification continued, management would create a number of independent divisions with each responsible for a specific product line.

Follow-up studies generally support that strategy influences structure at the top levels of business firms.[29] But strategy undoubtedly has less impact on the structure of sub-units within the overall organization. Additionally, it is not clear how the strategy-structure relationship operates in service businesses or among not-for-profit organizations like hospitals, educational institutions, and government agencies.

Organization Size   The larger an organization's size, in terms of the number of members it employs, the more likely it is to use the mechanistic structure. The creation of extensive rules and regulations only makes sense when there is a large number of people to be coordinated. Similarly, given the fact that a manager's ability to supervise a set of subordinates directly has some outside limit, as more people are hired to do the work, more managers will be needed to oversee these people. This creates increased complexity.

We should not, however, expect the size-structure relationship to be linear over a wide range. This is because once the organization becomes relatively large—having 1,500 to 2,000 employees or more—it will tend to have already acquired most of the properties of a mechanistic structure. So the addition of 500 employees to an organization that has only 100 employees is likely to lead to significantly increased levels of complexity and formalization. Yet adding 500 employees to an organization that already employs 10,000 is likely to have little or no impact on that organization's structure.

Technology   The evidence demonstrates that routine technologies are associated with mechanistic structures, whereas organic structures are best for dealing with the uncertainties inherent with nonroutine technologies. But we shouldn't expect technology to affect all parts of the organization equally.

[29] For a review of the research, see Robbins, *Organization Theory*, p. 90.

The closer a department or unit within the organization is to the operating core, the more it will be affected by technology and, hence, the more technology will act to define structure. The primary activities of the organization take place at the operating core. State motor vehicle divisions, for example, process driver's license applications as well as distribute vehicle license plates and monitor the ownership of vehicles within their state. Those departments within the motor vehicle division that are at the operating core—giving out driver's tests, collecting fees for plates, and so on—will be significantly affected by technology. But as units become removed from this core, technology will play a less important role. The structure of the executive offices at the motor vehicle division, for instance, are not likely to be affected much by technology. So, to continue with the motor vehicle example, the use of routine technology at the operating core should result in the units at the core being high in both complexity and formalization. As units within the division move farther away from activities at the operating core, technology will become less of a constraint on structural choices.

Environment   Will a dynamic and uncertain environment always lead to an organic structure? Not necessarily. Whether environment is a major determinant of an organization's structure depends on the degree of dependence of the organization on its environment.

IBM operates in a highly dynamic environment—the result of a continual stream of new competitors introducing products to compete against theirs. But IBM's size, reputation for quality and service, and marketing expertise act as potent forces to lessen the impact of this uncertain environment on IBM's performance. IBM's ability to lessen its dependence on its environment results in a structure that is much more mechanistic in design than would be expected given the uncertain environment within which it exists. In contrast, firms like Apple Computer and Digital Equipment Corporation have been far less successful in managing their dependence on their environment. Environment, therefore, is a much stronger influence on Apple and DEC's structure than at IBM.

KEY STRUCTURAL VARIABLES AND THEIR RELEVANCE TO OB

Now we move to the crux of our concern: relating structure to performance and satisfaction. This is no trivial task. The research on the structure-performance relationship, for instance, has been described as "among the most vexing and ambiguous in the field of management and organizational behavior."[30] Six structural variables have received the bulk of the attention. As a result, the following analysis reviews the evidence as it relates only to these variables.[31]

[30] D. R. Dalton, W. D. Todor, M. J. Spendolini, G. J. Fielding, and L. W. Porter, "Organization Structure and Performance: A Critical Review," *Academy of Management Review*, January 1980, p. 60.

[31] This section has drawn on the findings and insights provided in L. W. Porter and E. E. Lawler III, "Properties of Organization Structure in Relation to Job Attitudes and Job Behavior," *Psychological Bulletin*, July 1965, pp. 23–51; L. R. James and A. P. Jones, "Organization Structure: A Review of Structural Dimensions and Their Conceptual Relationships with Individual Attitudes

This is not a major shortcoming, however, since these six include the essence of what we have called "organization structure."

Organization Size

If we look at the organization as a whole, there is increasing evidence to suggest that job satisfaction tends to decrease with size. This is intuitively logical since larger size results in fewer opportunities for individuals to participate in decision making, less proximity and identification with organizational goals, and less clarity between individual effort and an identifiable outcome. Increased organizational size also appears to lead to higher absenteeism, though not necessarily greater turnover. The larger size offers less opportunity for an employee to identify with his or her organization, but evidence suggests that larger organizations tend to pay better than smaller ones. The result is that individuals do not leave the larger organization but they do have a propensity to absent themselves more frequently from work. Interestingly, these findings may be moderated by the degree of decentralization. If increased size is accompanied by increased delegation of authority, the negative impact of size tends to be reduced.

The attention paid to the impact of size on performance and attitudes has not been focused solely at the level of the total organization. Concern has also been given to subunit size, that is, to the size of intraorganizational work units. There appears to be a definite positive relationship between subunit size and both absenteeism and turnover. This is in contrast to total organization size, which, as we noted, tends to be related only to absenteeism. Regarding job satisfaction, there seems to be no systematic and consistent relationship attributable to subunit size.

Organizational Level

Is satisfaction or performance affected by an employee's position in the vertical hierarchy? For instance, are senior executives more satisfied with their jobs than operatives or low-level supervisors?

and Behavior," *Organizational Behavior and Human Performance*, June 1976, pp. 74–113; C. J. Berger and L. L. Cummings, "Organizational Structure, Attitudes, and Behaviors," B. M. Staw (ed.), *Research in Organizational Behavior*, Vol. 1 (Greenwich, CT: JAI Press, 1979), pp. 169–208; Dalton et al., "Organization Structure," pp. 49–64; J. S. Ebeling and M. King, "Hierarchical Position in the Work Organization and Job Satisfaction: A Failure to Replicate," *Human Relations*, July 1981, pp. 567–72; G. Stephenson, C. Brotherton, G. Delafield, and M. Skinner, "Size of Organization, Attitudes to Work and Job Satisfaction," *Industrial Relations Journal*, Summer 1983, pp. 28–40; W. Snizek and J. H. Bullard, "Perception of Bureaucracy and Changing Job Satisfaction: A Longitudinal Analysis," *Organizational Behavior and Human Performance*, October 1983, pp. 275–87; D. J. Brass, "Technology and the Structuring of Jobs: Employee Satisfaction, Performance, and Influence," *Organizational Behavior and Human Decision Processes*, April 1985, pp. 216–40; M. D. Zalesny, R. V. Farace, and R. Kurchner-Hawkins, "Determinants of Employee Work Perceptions and Attitudes: Perceived Work Environment and Organizational Level," *Environment and Behavior*, September 1985, pp. 567–92; M. Roznowski and C. L. Hulin, "Influences of Functional Specialty and Job Technology on Employees' Perceptual and Affective Responses to Their Jobs," *Organizational Behavior and Human Decision Processes*, October 1985, pp. 186–208; and P. G. Benson, T. L. Dickinson, and C. O. Neidt, "The Relationship Between Organizational Size and Turnover: A Longitudinal Investigation," *Human Relations*, January 1987, pp. 15–30.

In terms of structural variables, the most frequently investigated characteristic has been level in the organizational hierarchy. Although the evidence is far from conclusive, the bulk of the evidence finds that as we go up the hierarchy, we generally find more satisfied employees. Although one can debate causality, it seems unlikely that satisfied employees are getting more promotions than grumpy employees. It is far more logical to conclude that as one moves up in the organization, pay, formal authority, status accoutrements, and other rewards increase and, with them, job satisfaction.

Span of Control

The term **span of control** refers to the number of subordinates who report directly to a manager. Does this variable influence employee performance or satisfaction?

A review of the research indicates that it is probably safe to say that there is no evidence to support a relationship between span of control and performance. While it is intuitively attractive to argue that large spans might lead to higher employee performance because these spans provide more distant supervision and more opportunity for personal initiative, the research fails to support this notion. At this point it is impossible to state that any particular span of control is best for producing high performance or high satisfaction among subordinates. The most we can say is that there is some, but slight, evidence that a *manager's* job satisfaction increases as the number of subordinates he or she supervises increases.

Horizontal Differentiation

There have not been many studies that have looked at the horizontal differentiation-performance relationship. The preponderance of evidence suggests a positive relationship—that is, the greater the specialization, the higher the performance—but because the measures of performance tend to be questionable and several studies find no association, a realistic conclusion would be that the relationship between horizontal differentiation and performance has not been clearly demonstrated.

Evidence for the impact of horizontal differentiation on satisfaction is only a little more encouraging. Horizontal differentiation has generally been regarded as leading to lower satisfaction in that a large segment of the work force is turned off and alienated by having to do narrowly defined and repetitive tasks. However, this conclusion must be moderated by individual differences. Some people prefer structured and narrowly defined work tasks, while others value autonomy and freedom. Again, a clear relationship between horizontal differentiation and satisfaction has not been demonstrated.

Vertical Differentiation

Are there significant differences in terms of employee performance and satisfaction in tall organizations (with many vertical levels) versus flat organizations? There are mixed findings on the performance dimension. Both positive and negative relationships are reported in reviews of the research, making it difficult to generalize. On the satisfaction dimension, it appears that vertical differentiation does matter. High-level managers in tall organizations and lower-level managers in flat organizations experience more satisfaction than their opposites.

Centralization

The last independent variable we shall look at is centralization. Although we must qualify our generalizations, there do seem to be some meaningful relationships between centralization and our dependent variables.

The evidence supports the conclusion that centralization is negatively related with performance. Although these studies were done with managerial and professional personnel—therefore limiting our ability to generalize to blue-collar and nonprofessional employees—the evidence is nevertheless consistent.

There is limited evidence that—for a large segment of the work force—decentralization generates less job alienation, less dissatisfaction with work, greater satisfaction with supervision, and greater communication frequency among co-workers at the same level in the organization. Yet, even though centralization and satisfaction appear to be inversely related, this conclusion is likely to be moderated by individual differences and the type of tasks that employees perform. For instance, we would predict that this inverse relationship is likely to be stronger among professionals than among blue-collar workers.

ARE ORGANIZATION STRUCTURES REAL OR IN PEOPLE'S MINDS?

Complexity, formalization, and centralization are objective structural components that can be measured by organizational researchers. Every organization can be evaluated as to the degree to which it is high or low in all three. But employees don't objectively measure these components. They observe things around them in an unscientific fashion and then form their own implicit models of what the organization's structure is like. How many different people did they have to interview with before they were offered their job? How many people work in their department and building? How visible is the organization's policy manual, if one exists? Is everyone given a copy? If not, is one readily available? Is it referred to frequently? How is the organization and its top management described in newspapers and periodicals? Answers to questions such as these, when combined with an employee's past experiences and comments made by peers, leads members to form an overall subjective image of what their organization's structure is like. This image, though, may in no way resemble the organization's actual objective structural characteristics.

The importance of implicit models of organization structure should not be overlooked. As we noted in Chapter 4, people respond to their perceptions rather than to objective reality. We know that the relationship between many structural variables (for example, span of control, horizontal differentiation, vertical differentiation) and subsequent levels of performance or job satisfaction are inconsistent. Some of this was explained as being attributable to individual preferences. Some employees, for instance, prefer narrowly defined and routine jobs; others abhor such characteristics. Additionally, however, a contributing cause to these inconsistent findings may be diverse perceptions of the objective characteristics. Researchers have focused on actual levels of the various structural components, but these may be irrelevant if people interpret similar components differently. The bottom line, therefore, is to understand how employees interpret their organization's structure. That should prove a more meaningful predictor of their behavior than the objective characteristics themselves.

IMPLICATIONS FOR PERFORMANCE AND SATISFACTION

This chapter has defined organization structure, explained its causes, presented a number of different ways in which structures may be designed, and then reviewed the evidence linking organization structure to performance and satisfaction. Our position is that an organization's internal structure contributes to explaining and predicting behavior. That is, in addition to individual differences and group factors, the structural relationships in which people work have an important bearing on employee attitudes and behavior.

What is the basis for our argument that structure has an impact on both attitudes and behavior? To the degree that an organization structure reduces ambiguity for an employee and clarifies concerns such as "What am I supposed to do?" "How am I supposed to do it?" "Who do I report to?" and "Who do I go to if I have a problem?" it shapes their attitudes and facilitates and motivates employees to higher levels of performance. Of course, structure also constrains employees to the extent that it limits and controls what they do.[32]

In spite of our claim that structure is important, much of the research from which we have drawn our conclusions has fatal flaws. For instance, measures of performance and satisfaction are frequently open to question, as are definitions and instruments used to measure such variables as size and centralization. Additionally, some studies include only professionals, while others include only blue-collar workers. It is not surprising, therefore, that we find conflicting results and qualified conclusions.

Figure 13–7 visually depicts what we have discussed in this chapter. Strategy, size, technology, environment, and power-control determine the type of structure an organization will have. Complexity, formalization, and centralization represent the structural components that can be mixed and matched to form various structural designs. For the most part, structural designs fall into one of two categories: mechanistic or organic. But common structural components do not necessarily have a uniform impact on every employee's level of performance and satisfaction. The impact of objective structural characteristics on members of the organization is moderated by the employees' individual preferences and their subjective interpretation of the objective characteristics. Let us now offer some general thoughts.

For a large proportion of the population, high structure—that is, high complexity, high formalization, and centralization—leads to reduced job satisfac-

---

[32] D. A. Nadler, J. R. Hackman, and E. E. Lawler III, *Managing Organizational Behavior* (Boston: Little, Brown, 1979), pp. 182–84.

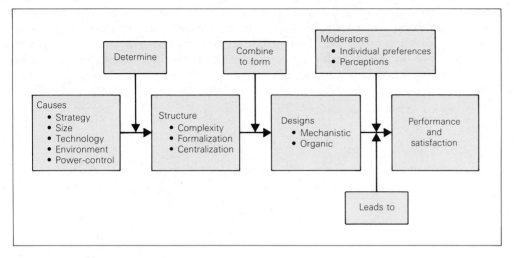

FIGURE 13–7
Organization Structure Model

tion. High vertical differentiation tends to alienate lower-level employees because vertical communication becomes more difficult and one can feel like "low man on the totem pole." On the other hand, upper management undoubtedly finds that the rewards that go with *their* positions enhance job satisfaction.

Specialization would also tend to be inversely related to satisfaction, especially where jobs have been divided into extremely minute tasks. This conclusion would have to be moderated to reflect individual differences among employees. While most prefer autonomy, not *all* do.

For individuals who value autonomy and self-actualization, large size, when accompanied by high centralization, results in lower satisfaction. As we have noted, there are fewer opportunities to participate in decision making, less proximity and identification with organizational goals, and less feeling that individual effort is linked to an identifiable outcome. In other words, the larger the organization, the more difficult it is for the individual to see the impact of his or her contribution to the final goods or service produced.

Organic structures increase cohesiveness among unit members and more closely align their authority with the responsibility for completion of a particular assignment. For certain types of activities, these structures are undoubtedly superior from management's standpoint. For instance, if tasks are nonroutine and there exists a great deal of environmental uncertainty, the organization can be more responsive when structured along organic rather than mechanistic lines. But these more responsive structures provide both advantages and disadvantages to employees. They rarely have restrictive job descriptions or excessive rules and regulations, and they do not require workers to obey commands that are issued by distant executives. But they usually have overlapping layers of responsibility and play havoc with individuals who need the security of doing standardized tasks. To maximize employee performance and satisfaction, individual differences should be taken into account.[33] Individuals with a high

[33] P. M. Nemiroff and D. L. Ford, Jr., "Task Effectiveness and Human Fulfillment in Organizations: A Review and Development of a Conceptual Contingency Model," *Academy of Management Review*, October 1976, pp. 69–82.

degree of bureaucratic orientation tend to place a heavy reliance on higher authority, prefer formalized and specific rules, and prefer formal relationships with others on the job. These people are better suited to mechanistic structures. Those individuals with a low degree of bureaucratic orientation would be better suited to organic structures.[34]

[34] Ibid., p. 74.

POINT

BUREAUCRACIES ARE A DYING STRUCTURAL BREED

Every age develops an organizational form appropriate for its time. Bureaucracy was the most efficient form for the first two-thirds of this century. However, it is now fading fast from the scene.

The bureaucratic "machine model" was developed as a reaction against the personal subjugation, nepotism and cruelty, and the capricious and subjective judgments that passed for managerial practices during the early days of the Industrial Revolution. Bureaucracy emerged out of the organizations' need for order and precision and the workers' demands for impartial treatment. It was an organization ideally suited to the values and demands of the Victorian era. And just as bureaucracy emerged as a creative response to a radically new age, so today new organizational shapes are surfacing before our eyes.

There are at least four relevant threats to bureaucracy:

1. *Rapid and unexpected change.* Bureaucracy's strength is its capacity to manage efficiently the routine and predictable events in human affairs. Bureaucracy, with its nicely defined chain of command, its rules, and its rigidities, is ill adapted to the rapid change the environment now demands.

2. *Growth in size.* While, in theory, there may be no natural limit to the height of a bureaucratic pyramid, in practice the element of complexity is almost invariably introduced with great size.

3. *Increasing diversity.* Today's activities require persons of very diverse, highly specialized competence.

Hurried growth, rapid change, and increase in specialization pit these three factors against the components of the pyramid structure, and we should expect the pyramid of bureaucracy to begin crumbling.

4. *Change in managerial behavior.* There is a subtle but perceptible change in the philosophy underlying management behavior. Real change seems under way because of:

   a. A new concept of human nature, based on increased knowledge of complex and shifting needs, which replaces an oversimplified, innocent, pushbutton idea of human nature.

   b. A new concept of power, based on collaboration and reason, which replaces a model of power based on coercion and threat.

   c. A new concept of organizational values, based on humanistic-democratic ideals, which replaces the depersonalized mechanistic value system of bureaucracy.

The real push for these changes stems from the need not only to humanize the organization, but to use it as a stimulus for personal growth and development of self-realization. Bureaucracies are a dying organizational form. They are, and will continue to be, replaced by adhocracies—adaptive, rapidly changing temporary structures—that more closely align with the tasks that today's organizations are attempting to achieve and the type of personnel they employ to accomplish those tasks.

Adapted from Warren G. Bennis, "The Coming Death of Bureaucracy," *Think*, November-December 1966, pp. 30–35. Reprinted by permission from *Think* Magazine, published by IBM, Copyright 1966 by International Business Machine Corp.

COUNTERPOINT

BUREAUCRACIES ARE ALIVE, WELL, AND FLOURISHING

There is no doubt that organizations are changing. But are these changes leaving bureaucracy behind? Nothing could be farther from the truth! Bureaucracies are alive, well, and flourishing.

The perspective of all modern scholars on the subject of bureaucracy is probably conditioned by the extent of their exposure to the pioneering work of Max Weber. Genius though he was, Weber did not have a crystal ball. He could not have foreseen all the many forms that the essence of bureaucracy could take. His formulation of bureaucracy has provided an invaluable tool for the analysis of organizational problems in a society that is making the adjustment to industrialization. However, rather than making the superficial assumption that "postindustrial" means "postbureaucratic," it might be wiser for today's students to inquire whether bureaucracy can adjust to the new age that, so the sociologists and economists insist, we have recently entered. Some believe that the transition in administrative thought from mechanical to organic models will be fatal to bureaucracy. But is bureaucracy restricted to the mechanical? In many cases, it would appear that external bureaucratic constraints have simply been replaced by more subtle influences on the individual. The end result in either case is the same: a high degree of predictability about human behavior within the large complex organization.

For Weber, the essence of bureaucracy was to make affairs of individuals more amenable to rational calculation. Given the administrative technology of the nineteenth century and his familiarity with the authoritarian tendencies of the Germans, it is little wonder that Weber described the bureaucratic instrument as he did. He would hardly have been surprised, however, to learn that more sophisticated means of controlling behavior had been invented. Weber's main scholarly concern, then, was with the progressive rationalization of the world and its impact on human relationships.

The current, postbureaucratic system is nothing more than the Weberian model with all the more sophisticated modifications. Despite all the contortions that management specialists have subjected themselves to in the twentieth century, the remarkable fact remains that there has been no substantial change in their basic premises. The guiding belief is still that regularities exist that, on one level or another, may be learned and acted upon. Whether the knowledge is embodied in the "bounded rationality" of a formal bureaucratic structure or in the professional's internalized determinants of behavior, administration is nothing more than the pursuit of a limited concept of rational discipline.

In reviewing the literature of a half-century of management science, one comes to the conclusion not that bureaucracy is dead but, rather, that the most controversial element of the Weberian model is gradually being replaced by a less artificial and more effective variation. To find specific elements of Weber's model of bureaucracy poorly adjusted to our times is a reasonable concession to the fact that conditions do change. But this is not the same as eliminating bureaucracy, for, in the most profound sense, bureaucracy will be with us as long as people insist that there is only one perception of reality by which rationality can be measured.

Adapted from Robert D. Miewald, "The Greatly Exaggerated Death of Bureaucracy," © 1970 by the Regents of the University of California. Reprinted from *California Management Review*, Vol. 13, No. 2, pp. 65–69 by permission of the Regents.

KEY TERMS

Adhocracy

Bureaucracy

Centralization

Complexity

Environment

Formalization

Functional Structure

Horizontal Differentiation

Matrix Structure

Mechanistic Structure

Organic Structure

Organization Size

Organization Structure

Power-Control

Product Structure

Simple Structure

Spatial Differentiation

Span of Control

Technology

Vertical Differentiation

FOR DISCUSSION

1. What is meant by the term "organization structure"?

2. Describe the factors that determine how complex an organization is.

3. Which one of the following *most* determines structure: strategy, size, technology, environment, or power-control? Explain.

4. Define and give examples of what is meant by the terms *technology* and *environment*.

5. Define a bureaucracy. Identify its key components. How prevalent do you think this structural form is?

6. Which one of the following structures is least centralized: simple, bureaucratic, or product? Why?

7. Under what conditions would management likely choose (a) a mechanistic structure? (b) an organic structure?

8. What is a matrix structure? What are its advantages? Disadvantages?

9. "Employees prefer to work in flat, decentralized organizations." Do you agree or disagree? Discuss.

10. What is the relationship between each of the following and employee performance and satisfaction: (a) size? (b) organizational level? (c) span of control? (d) horizontal differentiation? (e) vertical differentiation? (f) centralization?

11. Do you think most employees prefer high formalization? Support your position.

12. What is the importance of the statement: "Employees form implicit models of organization structure"?

FOR FURTHER READING

BLAU, P. M., and M. W. MEYER, *Bureaucracy in Modern Society*, 3rd ed. New York: Random House, 1987. Reviews theory and development of bureaucracy. Considers dysfunctions of bureaucracy and the relationship of bureaucratic administration to democratic governance.

HALL, R. H., *Organizations: Structure, Processes, and Outcomes*, 4th ed. Englewood Cliffs, NJ: Prentice Hall, 1987. Presents a thorough and up-to-date review of organization structure and design from a sociological perspective.

JOYCE, W. F., "Matrix Organization: A Social Experiment," *Academy of Management Journal*, September 1986, pp. 536–61. Presents an experiment to assess the effects of the matrix structure on organizational processes, role perceptions, and work attitudes.

KOLARSKA, L., "Centralization and Decentralization as Organizational Myths," *International*

Studies of Management and Organization, Fall, 1983, pp. 144–63. Provocative article that argues that centralization/decentralization is an ideological concept caught up in perception, power, and political processes.

MINTZBERG, H., *Structure in Fives*. Englewood Cliffs, NJ: Prentice Hall, 1983. Describes the primary structural designs available to management and the strengths and weaknesses of each.

PERROW, C., *Complex Organizations: A Critical Essay*, 3rd ed. New York: Random House, 1986. Provides a developmental overview of the major schools of organization thought and a close examination of recent approaches.

BUREAUCRATIC ORIENTATION TEST

Instructions.   For each statement, check the response (either mostly agree or mostly disagree) that best represents your feelings.

	MOSTLY AGREE	MOSTLY DISAGREE
1. I value stability in my job.	——	——
2. I like a predictable organization.	——	——
3. The best job for me would be one in which the future is uncertain.	——	——
4. The U.S. Army would be a nice place to work.	——	——
5. Rules, policies, and procedures tend to frustrate me.	——	——
6. I would enjoy working for a company that employed 85,000 people worldwide.	——	——
7. Being self-employed would involve more risk than I'm willing to take.	——	——
8. Before accepting a job, I would like to see an exact job description.	——	——
9. I would prefer a job as a freelance house painter to one as a clerk for the Department of Motor Vehicles.	——	——
10. Seniority should be as important as performance in determining pay increases and promotion.	——	——
11. It would give me a feeling of pride to work for the largest and most successful company in its field.	——	——
12. Given a choice, I would prefer to make $30,000 per year as a vice-president in a small company to $35,000 as a staff specialist in a large company.	——	——
13. I would regard wearing an employee badge with a number on it as a degrading experience.	——	——
14. Parking spaces in a company lot should be assigned on the basis of job level.	——	——
15. If an accountant works for a large organization, he or she cannot be a true professional.	——	——
16. Before accepting a job (given a choice), I would want to make sure that the company had a very fine program of employee benefits.	——	——
17. A company will probably not be successful unless it establishes a clear set of rules and procedures.	——	——
18. Regular working hours and vacations are more important to me than finding thrills on the job.	——	——
19. You should respect people according to their rank.	——	——
20. Rules are meant to be broken.	——	——

Turn to page 566 for scoring directions and key.

Source: A. J. DuBrin, *Human Relations: A Job Oriented Approach* © 1978, pp. 687–88. Reprinted with permission of Reston Publishing Co., a Prentice-Hall Co., 11480 Sunset Hills Road, Reston, Va. 22090.

CASE INCIDENT 13

IN SEARCH OF A 50 PERCENT INCREASE IN EFFICIENCY

Bill Richards was beaming. An organizational analyst for a major oil company, he had just put the finishing touches on a report he was sure would save the corporation a lot of money and give him the kind of visibility at the head office that he felt he deserved.

Bill's proposal argued that the current usage of secretaries at the head office was inefficient. The report showed that in 1987, the corporation had 1,440 secretarial positions. This category had four subclasses—from entry-level typists (Secretary I) earning $810 to $1,240 a month, up to executive secretaries (Secretary IV), which paid $1,930 to $2,525 a month. The breakdown within classes found the following numbers at each level: Secretary I, 685; Secretary II, 517; Secretary III, 210; and Secretary IV, 28.

The total compensation cost, in 1987, for Secretary I through IV positions was $23.8 million. Bill's proposal basically restructures the use of secretaries. Secretaries III and IV would continue to be assigned to individual executives, but the first two levels would be reassigned from individual managers to a secretarial pool. Bill's analysis shows that a pool would increase efficiency by 50 percent. Specifically, he argues that the same amount of work could be handled by fewer than half of the 1,200 individuals currently at Secretary I and II levels. In dollars and cents, he calculates that the company would save between $8 and $9 million a year.

Bill's proposal and recommendations were received by his superiors with great enthusiasm. A three-month timetable was established in which the restructuring would occur. Consistent with company personnel policies, every effort would be made to protect all employees with more than one year of service. They would be offered transfers to one of the six production facilities or two marketing offices located within thirty miles of the company's head office.

Rumor of what soon became known as "The Richards Report" spread rapidly. Before top management even approved the document, detailed word of the report's contents had reached every secretary. The response by the secretaries was less than enthusiastic. Some said they would quit before being relegated to a secretarial pool. Many commented on losing the continuity of working for a single manager. Those with the lowest seniority complained of not wanting to be transferred to openings in the company's facilities out in the suburbs.

A year after restructuring began, Bill Richards submitted a follow-up report that included the following information:

Secretarial compensation had been reduced by $8.7 million a year.

625 Secretary I and II employees were transferred or voluntarily resigned during the first three months of the program.

Absences increased from an average of 0.7 days per employee per month before the restructuring to 1.8 afterward.

Voluntary turnover increased from 1.7 per 100 employees per month before the restructuring to 6.1 afterward.

Comments from management indicate no significant loss in quality of secretarial support, but a definite improvement in the speed in which requests are completed.

QUESTIONS

1. The savings due to restructuring are far less than $8.7 million. What other costs must be deducted to get a true figure? Estimate these costs and compute the actual savings.
2. Explain how changes in technology may be able to offer insights into the secretaries' behavior.

14

Human Resource Policies and Practices

■ *Learning objectives*

Define the purposes of job analysis

Explain when to use interviews in selection

List the advantages of performance simulation tests over written tests

Define three skill categories

Summarize the four stages in a career

Describe the activities in an effective career counseling program

Explain the purposes of performance evaluation

Identify the advantages to using behaviors rather than traits in performance evaluation

Describe potential problems in evaluation and actions that can correct these problems

Outline the various types of rewards

Clarify how the existence of a union affects employee behavior

I failed to get this job I wanted because I answered one of the questions on the application wrong. The question asked "Do you advocate the overthrow of the United States government by revolution or violence?" I chose violence!

—— D. CAVETT

Jan Faust spent four years in convention sales at a large hotel but decided she could make a lot more money as a securities broker. After contacting more than a dozen security firms, she found one that would hire her. She went through their six month training program but after two-and-a-half years on the job, she was fired. The reason was that she was consistently ranked among the lowest sales performers. Her office manager's appraisal of the problem: "We blew it by hiring her. Jan was just not cut out for this type of job."

Nick Spanos works for the same brokerage firm as a research analyst. While Nick's job isn't in jeopardy, his performance is not at the level it once was. He attributes his lower performance to boredom. "I've been responsible for analyzing the same ten stocks in the pharmaceutical industry for over four years. I know these stocks backwards and forwards. I'm ready for new challenges. But management doesn't seem the least bit interested in my concerns. Do they honestly think I'll be content doing the same job forever?"

Margo Holcomb works as a registered nurse at a veteran's hospital in Toronto, Canada. She told me that she liked her job a lot but really valued the security she has. "We're unionized here. My pay and working conditions are determined in collective bargaining. I don't have to kiss-up to the administration like my friends who work in non-union jobs. If I think I'm being treated unfairly, I file a grievance. Come good times or bad times, my job is safe. I've got twenty-two years seniority!"

The previous scenarios dramatize the role that an organization's human resource policies and practices can play in affecting employee attitudes and behavior. While OB has traditionally addressed human resources management issues like performance evaluation, reward systems, and career development, it has relegated the discussion of topics such as selection practices, training and development programs, and union–management relations to separate courses in personnel and human resource management. I would argue that in doing so it omits several important pieces of the puzzle in the quest to explain and predict employee behavior. In this chapter, we'll provide an in-depth discussion on performance evaluation, reward systems, and career development. But, in addition, we'll introduce several other pertinent human resource management issues and briefly demonstrate what impact they have on employee attitudes and behavior.

TABLE 14–1
Popular Job Analysis Methods

1. **Observation Method.** An analyst watches employees directly or reviews films of workers on the job.
2. **Individual Interview Method.** Selected job incumbents are extensively interviewed, and the results of a number of these interviews are combined into a single job analysis.
3. **Group Interview Method.** Same as individual except that a number of job incumbents are interviewed simultaneously.
4. **Structured Questionnaire Method.** Workers check or rate the items they perform in their jobs from a long list of possible task items.
5. **Technical Conference Method.** Specific characteristics of a job are obtained from "experts," who typically are supervisors with extensive knowledge of the job.
6. **Diary Method.** Job incumbents record their daily activities in a diary.

SELECTION PRACTICES

The objective of effective selection is to match individual characteristics (ability, experience, etc.) with the requirements of the job. When management fails to get a proper match, both employee performance and satisfaction suffer. In this search to achieve the right individual-job fit, where does management begin? The answer is to assess the demands and requirements of the job. The process of assessing the activities within a job is called job analysis.

Job Analysis

Job analysis involves developing a detailed description of the tasks involved in a job, determining the relationship of a given job to other jobs, and ascertaining the knowledge skills, and abilities necessary for an employee to successfully perform the job.[1]

How is this information attained? Table 14–1 describes the more popular job analysis methods.

Information gathered by using one or more of the job analysis methods results in the organization being able to create a **job description** and **job specification**. The former is a written statement of what a jobholder does, how it is done, and why it is done. It should accurately portray job content, environment, and conditions of employment. The job specification states the minimum acceptable qualifications that an employee must possess to perform a given job successfully. It identifies the knowledge, skills, and abilities needed to do the job effectively. So job descriptions identify characteristics of the job, while job specifications identify characteristics of the successful job incumbent.

Job analysis

Developing a detailed description of the tasks involved in a job, determining the relationship of a given job to other jobs, and ascertaining the knowledge, skills, and abilities necessary for an employee to perform the job.

Job description

A written statement of what a jobholder does, how it is done, and why it is done.

[1] See, for example, J. V. Ghorpade, *Job Analysis: A Handbook for the Human Resource Director* (Englewood Cliffs, NJ: Prentice Hall, 1988).

Job specification

States the minimum acceptable qualifications that an employee must possess to perform a given job successfully.

The job description and specification are important documents for guiding the selection process. The job description can be used to describe the job to potential candidates. The job specification keeps the attention of those doing the selection on the list of qualifications necessary for an incumbent to perform a job and assists in determining whether or not candidates are qualified.

Selection Devices

What do application forms, interviews, employment tests, background checks, and personal letters of recommendation have in common? Each is a device for obtaining information about a job applicant that can help the organization determine whether the applicant's skills, knowledge, and abilities are appropriate for the job in question. In this section, we review the more important of these selection devices—interviews, written tests, and performance simulation tests.

Interviews   Do you know anyone who has gotten a job without at least one interview? You may have an acquaintance who got a part-time or summer job through a close friend or relative without having to go through an interview, but such instances are rare. There is little doubt that the interview is the most widely used selection device that organizations rely upon to differentiate candidates. Few employees are hired without one or more interviews. With a bit less certainty, we can also say that the interview seems to carry a great deal of weight. That is, not only is it widely used, its results tend to carry a disproportionate amount of influence in the selection decision. The candidate who performs poorly in the employment interview is likely to be cut from the applicant pool, regardless of his or her experience, test scores, or letters of recommendation.

These findings are important because, to many people's surprise, the interview is a poor selection device for most jobs.[2] Why? Because the data gathered from interviews are often biased and unrelated to future job performance. Research indicates that prior knowledge about an applicant biases the interviewer's evaluation, that interviewers tend to favor applicants who share their attitudes, that the order in which applicants are interviewed influences evaluations, that negative information is given unduly high weight, and that an applicant's ability to do well in an interview is irrelevant in most jobs.[3] On this last point: What relevance does "good interviewing skills" have for successful performance as a bricklayer, drillpress operator, or data-entry operator? The answer is: "Little or none!" These jobs don't require this skill. Yet employers typically use the interview as a selection device for such jobs. The evidence suggests that interviews are good for assessing an applicant's intelligence, level of motivation, and interpersonal skills. Since these are attributes that are most likely to be relevant qualities for upper managerial positions, the interview

[2] See R. D. Arvey and J. E. Campion, "The Employment Interview: A Summary and Review of Recent Research," *Personnel Psychology*, Summer 1982, pp. 281–322; E. D. Webster, *The Employment Interview: A Social Judgment Process* (Ontario, Canada: S.I.P., 1982); and J. E. Hunter and R. F. Hunter, "Validity and Utility of Alternative Predictors of Job Performance," *Psychological Bulletin*, January 1984, pp. 72–98.

[3] Ibid.

makes sense for the selection of senior executives. Its use in identifying "good performers" for most lower-level jobs appears unfounded.

Written Tests   Typical written tests include tests of intelligence, aptitude, ability, and interest. Long popular as selection devices, there has been a marked decline in their use since the late 1960s. The reason is that such tests have frequently been characterized as discriminating, and many organizations have not, or cannot, validate such tests as being job related.

Tests in intellectual ability, spatial and mechanical ability, perceptual accuracy, and motor ability have shown to be moderately valid predictors for many semiskilled and unskilled operative jobs in industrial organizations.[4] Intelligence tests are reasonably good predictors for supervisory positions.[5] But the burden is on management to demonstrate that any test used is job related. Since the characteristics that many of these tests tap are considerably removed from the actual performance of the job itself, getting high validity coefficients has often been difficult. The result has been a decreased use of traditional written tests and increased interest in performance simulation tests.

Performance Simulation Tests   What better way to find out if an applicant can do a job successfully than by having him or her do it? The logic of this question has resulted in increased usage of performance simulation tests. Undoubtedly the enthusiasm for these tests lies in the fact that they are based on job analysis data and, therefore, should more easily meet the requirement of job relatedness than do written tests. Performance simulation tests are made up of actual job behaviors rather than surrogates, as are written tests.

The two best known performance simulation tests are work sampling and assessment centers. The former is suited to routine jobs, whereas the latter is relevant for the selection of managerial personnel.

Work sampling is an effort to create a miniature replica of a job. Applicants demonstrate that they possess the necessary talents by actually doing the tasks. By carefully devising work samples based on job analysis data, the knowledge, skills, and abilities needed for each job are determined. Then each work sample element is matched with a corresponding job performance element. For instance, a work sample for a job that involves computations on an electronic calculator would require the applicant to make similar computations.

The results from work sample experiments are impressive. One review of the literature showed that work samples have almost always yielded validities superior to those yielded by traditional tests.[6] Another review similarly found work samples to be better than written aptitude, personality, or intelligence tests.[7]

Work sampling

Creating a miniature replica of a job to evaluate the performance abilities of job candidates.

---

[4] E. E. Ghiselli, "The Validity of Aptitude Tests in Personnel Selection," *Personnel Psychology*, Winter 1973, p. 475.

[5] G. Grimsley and H. F. Jarrett, "The Relation of Managerial Achievement to Test Measures Obtained in the Employment Situation: Methodology and Results," *Personnel Psychology*, Spring 1973, pp. 31–48; and A. K. Korman, "The Prediction of Managerial Performance: A Review," *Personnel Psychology*, Summer 1968, pp. 295–322.

[6] M. D. Dunnette and W. C. Borman, "Personnel Selection and Classification Systems," in M. R. Rosenzweig and L. W. Porter (eds.), *Annual Review of Psychology*, Vol. 30 (Palo Alto: CA: Annual Reviews, 1974), p. 513.

[7] J. J. Asher and J. A. Sciarrino, "Realistic Work Sample Tests: A Review," *Personnel Psychology*, Winter 1974, pp. 519–33.

A more elaborate set of performance simulation tests, specifically designed to evaluate a candidate's managerial potential, is administered in **assessment centers**. In assessment centers, line executives, supervisors, and/or trained psychologists evaluate candidates as they go through two to four days of exercises that simulate real problems that they would confront on the job. Based on a list of descriptive dimensions that the actual job incumbent has to meet, activities might include interviews, inbasket problem-solving exercises, group discussions, and business decision games.

The evidence on the effectiveness of assessment centers is extremely impressive. They have consistently demonstrated results that predict later job performance in managerial positions.[8] Although they are not cheap—AT&T, which has assessed more than 200,000 employees, computes its assessment costs at $800 to $1,500 per employee—the selection of an ineffective manager is unquestionably far more costly.

TRAINING AND DEVELOPMENT PROGRAMS

Competent employees will not remain competent forever. Their skills can deteriorate; technology may make their skills obsolete; the organization may move into new areas, changing the type of jobs that exist and the skills necessary to do them. This reality has not been overlooked by management. It has been estimated, for instance, that U.S. business firms spend an astounding $30 billion a year on formal courses and training programs to build workers' skills.[9] Of course, managers themselves can benefit from skill development efforts. Let's look at the type of skills that training can improve; then review skill training methods, as well as career development programs that can prepare employees for a future that's different from today.

Skill Categories

We can dissect skills into three categories: technical, interpersonal, and problem solving. Most training activities seek to modify one or more of these skills.

Technical   Most training is directed at upgrading and improving an employee's technical skills. This applies as much to white-collar jobs as to blue-collar. Jobs change as a result of new technologies and improved methods. Postal sorters have had to undergo technical training in order to learn to operate automatic sorting machines. Many auto repair personnel have had to undergo extensive training to fix and maintain recent models with front-wheel-drive trains, electronic ignitions, diesel engines, and other innovations. Not many clerical personnel during the past decade have been unaffected by the computer.

[8] B. B. Gaugher, D. B. Rosenthal, G. C. Thornton III, and C. Bentson, "Meta-Analysis of Assessment Center Validity," *Journal of Applied Psychology*, August 1987, pp. 493–511.

[9] "Corporate Training Has Itself Become Big Business," *Wall Street Journal*, August 5, 1986, p. 1.

Literally millions of such employees have had to be trained to operate and interface with a computer terminal.

Interpersonal   Almost all employees belong to a work unit. To some degree, their work performance depends on their ability to effectively interact with their co-workers and their boss. Some employees have excellent interpersonal skills. But others require training to improve theirs. This includes learning how to be a better listener, how to communicate ideas more clearly, and how to reduce conflict.

One employee who had had a history of being difficult to work with found that a three-hour group session in which she and co-workers openly discussed how each perceived the others significantly changed the way she interacted with her peers. Her coworkers were unanimous in describing her as arrogant. They all interpreted her requests as sounding like orders. Unaware of this tendency, she began to make conscious efforts to change the tone and content of her requests, and had very positive results in her relationships with her colleagues.

Problem Solving   Managers, as well as many employees who perform nonroutine tasks, have to solve problems on their job. When people require these skills, but are deficient, they can participate in problem-solving training. This would include activities to sharpen their logic, reasoning, and skills at defining problems, assessing causation, developing alternatives, analyzing alternatives, and selecting solutions.

Training Methods

Most training takes place on the job. This can be attributed to the simplicity of such methods and their usually lower cost. However, on-the-job training can disrupt the workplace and result in an increase in errors as learning proceeds. Also, some skill training is too complex to learn on the job. In such cases, it should take place outside the work setting.[10]

On-the-Job Training   Popular on-the-job training methods include job rotation and understudy assignments. *Job rotation* involves lateral transfers that enable employees to work at different jobs. Employees get to learn a wide variety of jobs and gain increased insight into the interdependency between jobs and a wider perspective on organizational activities. New employees frequently learn their jobs by understudying a seasoned veteran. In the trades, this is usually called an *apprenticeship*. In white-collar jobs, it is called a *coaching*, or *mentor*, relationship. In each, the understudy works under the observation of an experienced worker, who acts as a model whom the understudy attempts to emulate.

Both job rotation and understudy assignments apply to the learning of technical skills. Interpersonal and problem-solving skills are acquired more effectively by training that takes place off the job.

---

[10] For an extended discussion of on-the-job and off-the-job training methods, see D. DeCenzo and S. P. Robbins, *Personnel/Human Resource Management*, 3rd ed. (Englewood Cliffs, NJ: Prentice Hall, 1988), pp. 248–51, 255–61.

Off-the-Job Training   There are a number of off-the-job training methods that managers may want to make available to employees. The more popular are classroom lectures, films, and simulation exercises. *Classroom lectures* are well suited for conveying specific information. They can be used effectively for developing technical and problem-solving skills. *Films* can also be used to explicitly demonstrate technical skills that are not easily presented by other methods. Interpersonal and problem-solving skills may be best learned through *simulation exercises* such as case analyses, experiential exercises, role playing, and group interaction sessions. However, complex computer models, such as those used by airlines in the training of pilots, are another kind of simulation exercise, which in this case is used to teach technical skills. So, too, is *vestibule training*, in which employees learn their jobs on the same equipment they will be using, only the training is conducted away from the actual work floor. Many large department stores train cashiers how to operate their new computer cash registers in specially created vestibule labs that simulate the actual checkout environment. This way, mistakes result in learning experiences rather than irate customers.

Career Development

Career development or career planning is a means by which an organization can sustain or increase its employees' current productivity, while, at the same time, prepare employees for a changing world.

Career

A sequence of positions occupied by a person during the course of a lifetime.

Career stages

The four steps most people go through in their careers: exploration, establishment, midcareer, and late career.

Career Stages   A **career** is a "sequence of positions occupied by a person during the course of a lifetime."[11] This definition does not imply advancement or success or failure. Any work, paid or unpaid, pursued over an extended period of time, can constitute a career. In addition to formal job work, it may include schoolwork, homemaking, or volunteer work.[12]

Careers can be more easily understood if we think of them as proceeding through **stages**.[13] Most of us have or will go through four stages: exploration, establishment, midcareer, and late career.

Exploration begins prior to even entering the work force on a paid basis and ends for most of us in our mid-twenties as we make the transition from school to our primary work interest. It's a time of self-exploration and an assessment of alternatives. The *establishment* stage includes being accepted by our peers, learning the job, and gaining tangible evidence of successes or failures in the "real world." Most people don't face their first severe career dilemmas until they reach the *midcareer* stage, a stage that is typically reached between the ages of thirty-five and fifty. This is a time where one may continue to improve one's performance, level off, or begin to deteriorate. At this stage, the first dilemma is accepting the fact that you're no longer seen as a "learner."

[11] D. E. Super and D. T. Hall, "Career Development Exploration and Planning," in M. R. Rosenzweig and L. W. Porter (eds.), *Annual Review of Psychology*, Vol. 29 (Palo Alto: Annual Reviews, 1978), p. 334.

[12] D. T. Hall, *Careers in Organizations* (Santa Monica, CA: Goodyear, 1976), pp. 3–4.

[13] See, for example, D. E. Super, *The Psychology of Careers* (New York: Harper & Row, 1957); and E. H. Schein, "The Individual, the Organization, and the Career: A Conceptual Scheme," *Journal of Applied Behavioral Science*, August 1971, pp. 401–26.

Mistakes carry greater penalties. At this point in a career, you are expected to have moved beyond apprenticeship to journeyman status. For those who continue to grow through the midcareer stage, the *late career* usually is a pleasant time when you are allowed the luxury to relax a bit and enjoy playing the part of the elder statesman. For those who have stagnated or deteriorated during the previous stage, the late career brings the reality that they will not have an everlasting impact or change the world as they once thought. It is a time when individuals recognize that they have decreased work mobility and may be locked into their current jobs. They begin to look forward to retirement and the opportunities of doing something different.

If employees are to remain productive, career development and training programs need to be available that can support an employee's task and emotional needs at each stage. Table 14–2 identifies the more important of these needs.

Effective Career Development Practices   What kind of practices would characterize an organization that understood the value of career development? The following summarizes a few of the more effective practices.

There is an increasing body of evidence indicating that employees who

TABLE 14–2
Training Needs within Career Stages

Stage	Task Needs	Emotional Needs
Exploration	1. Varied job activities 2. Self-exploration	1. Make preliminary job choices 2. Settling down
Establishment	1. Job challenge 2. Develop competence in a speciality area 3. Develop creativity and innovation 4. Rotate into new area after three to five years	1. Deal with rivalry and competition; face failures 2. Deal with work/family conflicts 3. Support 4. Autonomy
Midcareer	1. Technical updating 2. Develop skills in training and coaching others (younger employees) 3. Rotation into new job requiring new skills 4. Develop broader view of work and own role in organization	1. Express feelings about midlife 2. Reorganize thinking about self in relation to work, family, community 3. Reduce self-indulgence and competitiveness
Late career	1. Plan for retirement 2. Shift from power role to one of consultation and guidance 3. Identify and develop successors 4. Begin activities outside the organization	1. Support and counseling to see one's work as a platform for others 2. Develop sense of identity in extraorganizational activities

Source: Adapted from D. T. Hall and M. Morgan, "Career Development and Planning," in K. Perlman, F. L. Schmidt, and W. C. Hamner, *Contemporary Problems in Personnel* (3rd ed.). Copyright © 1983 by John Wiley & Sons. Reprinted by permission of John Wiley & Sons.

receive especially *challenging job assignments* early in their careers do better on later jobs.[14] More specifically, the degree of stimulation and challenge in a person's initial job assignment tends to be significantly related to later career success and retention in the organization.[15] Apparently, initial challenges, particularly if they are successfully met, stimulate a person to perform well in subsequent years.

To provide information to all employees about job openings, job opportunities should be posted. *Job postings* list key job specification data—abilities, experience, and seniority requirements to qualify for vacancies—and are typically communicated through bulletin board displays or organizational publications.

One of the most logical parts to career development is *career counseling*. An effective program will cover the following issues with employees:

1. The employee's career goals, aspirations, and expectations for five years or longer

2. Opportunities available within the organization and the degree to which the employee's aspirations are realistic and match the opportunities available

3. Identification of what the employee would have to do in the way of further self-development to qualify for new opportunites

4. Identification of the actual next steps in the form of plans for new development activities or new job assignments that would prepare the employee for further career growth[16]

Organizations can offer group *workshops* to facilitate career development. By bringing together groups of employees with their supervisors and managers, problems and misperceptions can be identified and, it is hoped, resolved. These workshops can be general, or they can be designed to deal with problems common to certain groups of employees—new members, minorities, older workers, and so forth.

Periodic job changes can prevent obsolescence and stimulate career growth.[17] The changes can be lateral transfers, vertical promotions, or temporary assignments. The important element in periodic job changes is that they give the employee a variety of experiences that offer diversity and new challenges.

PERFORMANCE EVALUATION AND FEEDBACK SYSTEMS

Would you study differently or exert a different level of effort in a college course graded on a pass-fail basis than one where letter grades from A to F

---

[14] D. E. Berlew and D. T. Hall, "The Socialization of Managers: Effects of Expectations on Performance," *Administrative Science Quarterly*, September 1966, pp. 207–23; and D. W. Bray, R. J. Campbell, and D. L. Grant, *Formulative Years in Business: A Long-Term AT&T Study of Managerial Lives* (New York: John Wiley, 1974).

[15] See Super and Hall, "Career Development: Exploration and Planning," p. 362.

[16] J. Van Maanen and E. H. Schein, "Career Development," in J. R. Hackman and J. L. Suttle (eds.), *Improving Life at Work* (Santa Monica: CA: Goodyear, 1977), p. 87.

[17] H. G Kaufman, *Obsolescence and Professional Career Development* (New York: AMACOM, 1974).

are used? When I ask that question of students, I usually get an affirmative answer. Students typically tell me that they study harder when letter grades are at stake. Additionally, they tell me that when they take a course on a pass-fail basis, they tend to do just enough to ensure a passing grade.

This finding illustrates how performance evaluation systems influence behavior. Major determinants of your in-class behavior and out-of-class studying effort in college are the criteria and techniques your instructor uses to evaluate your performance. Of course, what applies in the college context also applies to employees at work. In this section, we'll show how the choice of a performance evaluation system and the way it's administered can be an important force influencing employee behavior.

Purposes of Performance Evaluation

Performance evaluation serves a number of purposes in organizations (see Table 14-3 for survey results on primary uses of evaluations). Management uses evaluations for general *personnel decisions*. Evaluations provide input into such important decisions as promotions, transfers, and terminations. Evaluations *identify training and development needs*. They pinpoint employee skills and competencies that are currently inadequate but for which programs can be developed to remedy. Performance evaluations can be used as a *criterion against which selection and development programs are validated*. Newly hired employees who perform poorly can be identified through performance evaluation. Similarly, the effectiveness of training and development programs can be determined by assessing how well those employees who have participated do on their performance evaluation. Evaluations also fulfill the purpose of *providing feedback to employees* on how the organization views their performance. Further, performance evaluations are used as the *basis for reward allocations*. Decisions as to who gets merit pay increases and other rewards are frequently determined by performance evaluations.

TABLE 14-3
Primary Uses of Performance Evaluations

Use	Percent[a]
Compensation	85.6
Performance feedback	65.1
Training	64.3
Promotion	45.3
Personnel planning	43.1
Retention/discharge	30.3
Research	17.2

[a] Based on responses from 600 organizations.

Source: Based on "Performance Appraisal: Current Practices and Techniques," *Personnel,* May-June 1984, p. 57.

Each of these functions of performance evaluation is important. Yet their importance to us depends on the perspective we're taking. Several are clearly relevant to personnel management decisions. But our interest is in organizational behavior. As a result, we shall be emphasizing performance evaluation in its role as a mechanism for providing feedback and as a determinant of reward allocations.

Performance Evaluation and Motivation

In Chapter 6, considerable attention was given to the expectancy model of motivation. We argued that this model currently offers one of the best explanations of what conditions the amount of effort an individual will exert on his or her job. A vital component of this model is performance, specifically the effort-performance and performance-reward linkages. Do people see effort leading to performance and performance to the rewards that they value? Clearly, they have to know what is expected of them. They need to know how their performance will be measured. Further, they must feel confident that if they exert an effort within their capabilities, it will result in a satisfactory performance as defined by the criteria by which they are being measured. Finally, they must feel confident that if they perform as they are being asked, they will achieve the rewards they value.

In brief, if the objectives that employees are expected to achieve are unclear, if the criteria for measuring those objectives are vague, and if the employees lack confidence that their efforts will lead to a satisfactory appraisal of their performance or believe that there will be an unsatisfactory payoff by the organization when their performance objectives are achieved, we can expect individuals to work considerably below their potential.

What Do We Evaluate?

The criteria or criterion that management chooses to evaluate, when appraising employee performance, will have a major influence on what employees do. Two examples illustrate this:

In a public employment agency, which served workers seeking employment and employers seeking workers, employment interviewers were appraised by the number of interviews they conducted. Consistent with the thesis that the evaluating criteria influence behavior, interviewers emphasized the *number* of interviews conducted rather than the *placements* of clients in jobs.[18]

A management consultant specializing in police research noticed that, in one community, officers would come on duty for their shift, proceed to get into their police cars, drive to the highway that cut through the town, and speed back and forth along this highway for their entire shift. Clearly this fast cruising had little to do with good police work, but this behavior made considerably more sense once the consultant learned that the community's City Council used mileage on police vehicles as an evaluative measure of police effectiveness.[19]

[18] P. M. Blau, *The Dynamics of Bureaucracy*, rev. ed. (Chicago: University of Chicago Press, 1963).

[19] "The Cop-Out Cops," *National Observer*, August 3, 1974.

These examples demonstrate the importance of criteria in performance evaluation. This, of course, begs the question: What should management evaluate? The three most popular sets of criteria are individual task outcomes, behaviors, and traits.

① **Individual Task Outcomes**   If ends count, rather than means, then management should evaluate an employee's task outcomes. Using task outcomes, a plant manager could be judged on criteria such as quantity produced, scrap generated, and cost per unit of production. Similarly, a salesperson could be assessed on overall sales volume in his or her territory, dollar increase in sales, and number of new accounts established.

② **Behaviors**   In many cases, it's difficult to identify specific outcomes that can be directly attributable to an employee's actions. This is particularly true of personnel in staff positions and individuals whose work assignments are intrinsically part of a group effort. In the latter case, the group's performance may be readily evaluated, but the contribution of each group member may be difficult or impossible to identify clearly. In such instances, it is not unusual for management to evaluate the employee's behavior. Using the previous examples, behaviors of a plant manager that could be used for performance evaluation purposes might include promptness in submitting his or her monthly reports or the leadership style that the manager exhibits. Pertinent salesperson behaviors could be average number of contact calls made per day or sick days used per year.

③ **Traits**   The weakest set of criteria, yet one that is still widely used by organizations, is individual traits. We say they are weaker than either task outcomes or behaviors because they are farthest removed from the actual performance of the job itself. Traits such as having "a good attitude," showing "confidence," being "intelligent" or "friendly," "looking busy," or possessing "a wealth of experience" may or may not be highly correlated with positive task outcomes, but only the naive would ignore the reality that such traits are frequently used in organizations as criteria for assessing an employee's level of performance.

Methods of Performance Evaluation

The previous section explained *what* we evaluate. Now we ask: *How* do we evaluate an employee's performance? That is, what are the specific techniques for evaluation? The following reviews the major performance evaluation methods.

Written Essays   Probably the simplest method of evaluation is to write a narrative describing an employee's strengths, weaknesses, past performance, potential, and suggestions for improvement. The written essay requires no complex forms or extensive training to complete. But the results often reflect the ability of the writer. A good or bad appraisal may be determined as much by the evaluator's writing skill as by the employee's actual level of performance.

Critical incidents

Evaluating those behaviors that are key in making the difference between executing a job effectively or ineffectively.

Critical Incidents   **Critical incidents** focus the evaluator's attention on those behaviors that are key in making the difference between executing a job effectively or ineffectively. That is, the appraiser writes down anecdotes that describe what the employee did that was especially effective or ineffective. The key here is that only specific behaviors, and not vaguely defined personality traits, are cited. A list of critical incidents provides a rich set of examples from which the employee can be shown those behaviors that are desirable and those that call for improvement.

Graphic rating scales

An evaluation method where the evaluator rates performance factors on an incremental scale.

Graphic Rating Scales　　One of the oldest and most popular methods of evaluation is the use of **graphic rating scales**. In this method, a set of performance factors, such as quantity and quality of work, depth of knowledge, cooperation, loyalty, attendance, honesty, and initiative, are listed. The evaluator then goes down the list and rates each on incremental scales. The scales typically specify five points, so a factor like *job knowledge* might be rated 1 ("poorly informed about work duties") to 5 ("has complete mastery of all phases of the job").

Why are graphic ratings scales so popular? Though they don't provide the depth of information that essays or critical incidents do, they are less time-consuming to develop and administer. They also allow for quantitative analysis and comparison.

Behaviorally anchored rating scales

An evaluation method where actual job related behaviors are rated along a continuum.

Behaviorally Anchored Rating Scales　　Behaviorally anchored rating scales have received a great deal of attention in recent years. These scales combine major elements from the critical incident and graphic rating scale approaches: The appraiser rates the employees based on items along a continuum, but the points are examples of actual behavior on the given job rather than general description or traits.

Behaviorally anchored rating scales specify definite, observable, and measurable job behavior. Examples of job-related behavior and performance dimensions are found by asking participants to give specific illustrations of effective and ineffective behavior regarding each performance dimension. These behavioral examples are then translated into a set of performance dimensions, each dimension having varying levels of performance. The results of this process are behavioral descriptions, such as anticipates, plans, executes, solves immediate problems, carries out orders, and handles emergency situations.

Multi-Person Comparisons　　Multi-person comparisons evaluate one individual's performance against one or more others. It is a relative rather than an absolute measuring device. The three most popular comparisons are group order ranking, individual ranking, and paired comparisons.

Group order ranking

An evaluation method that places employees into a particular classification such as quartiles.

The **group order ranking** requires the evaluator to place employees into a particular classification, such as top one-fifth or second one-fifth. This method is often used in recommending students to graduate schools. Evaluators are asked to rank the student in the top 5 percent, the next 5 percent, the next 15 percent, and so forth. But when used by managers to appraise employees, managers deal with all their subordinates. Therefore, if a rater has twenty subordinates, only four can be in the top fifth and, of course, four must also be relegated to the bottom fifth.

Individual ranking

An evaluation method that rank orders employees from best to worst.

The **individual ranking** approach rank orders employees from best to worst. If the manager is required to appraise thirty subordinates, this approach assumes that the difference between the first and second employee is the same as that between the twenty-first and twenty-second. Even though some of the employees may be closely grouped, this approach allows for no ties. The result is a clean ordering of employees, from the highest performer down to the lowest.

The **paired comparison** approach compares each employee with every other employee and rates each as either the superior or the weaker member of the pair. After all paired comparisons are made, each employee is assigned a summary ranking based on the number of superior scores he or she achieved. This approach ensures that each employee is compared against every other, but it can obviously become unwieldy when many employees are being compared.

Multi-person comparisons can be combined with one of the other methods to blend the best from both absolute and relative standards. For example, a college might use the graphic rating scale and the individual ranking method to provide more accurate information about its students' performance. The student's relative rank in the class could be noted next to an absolute grade of A, B, C, D, or F. A prospective employer or graduate school could then look at two students who each got a "B" in their different financial accounting courses and draw considerably different conclusions about each where next to one grade it says "ranked 4th out of 26," while the other says "ranked 17th out of 30." Obviously, the latter instructor gives out a lot more high grades!

Paired comparison

An evaluation method that compares each employee with every other employee and assigns a summary ranking based on the number of superior scores that the employee achieves.

Potential Problems

While organizations may seek to make the performance evaluation process free from personal biases, prejudices, or idiosyncracies, a number of potential problems can creep into the process. To the degree that the following factors are prevalent, an employee's evaluation is likely to be distorted.

Single Criterion   The typical employee's job is made up of a number of tasks. An airline flight attendant's job, for example, includes welcoming passengers, seeing to their comfort, serving meals, and offering safety advice. If performance on this job were assessed by a single criterion measure—say the time it took to provide food and beverages to a hundred passengers—the result would be limited evaluation of that job. More important, flight attendants whose performance evaluation included assessment on only this single criterion would be motivated to ignore those other tasks in their job. Similarly, if a football quarterback were appraised only on his percentage of completed passes, he would be likely to throw short passes and only in situations where he felt assured that they will be caught. Our point is that where employees are evaluated on a single job criterion, and where successful performance on that job requires good performance on a number of criteria, employees will emphasize the single criterion to the exclusion of other job-relevant factors.

Leniency Error   Every evaluator has his or her own value system that acts as a standard against which appraisals are made. Relative to the true or actual performance an individual exhibits, some evaluators mark high and others low. The former is referred to as positive **leniency error**, and the latter as negative leniency error. When evaluators are positively lenient in their appraisal, an individual's performance becomes overstated, that is, rated higher than it

Leniency error

The tendency to evaluate a set of employees too high (positive) or too low (negative).

Does Physical Attractiveness Affect Performance Evaluations?

A recent research study examined whether a person's physical attractiveness affected his or her performance evaluation.[20] The results are interesting, although a bit disturbing.

Thirty-four graduate business students received a set of four relatively equivalent performance review forms that presented information varying according to the job, sex, and appearance of the employee being evaluated. The students were asked to evaluate present performance, predict future success, and indicate the appropriateness of various personnel actions.

The results showed that attractiveness was advantageous for women in nonmanagerial positions and disadvantageous for women in managerial ones. But appearance had no effect whatsoever on evaluations of men. Apparently, the student evaluators believed that attractiveness enhanced the perceived femininity of females but did not enhance the perceived masculinity of the males. Moreover, the students may be assuming that femininity is inconsistent with managerial effectiveness. We described these findings as disturbing because they illustrate the possibility that sexual stereotypes may cloud an appraiser's judgment and result in biased evaluations.

actually should be. Similarly, a negative leniency error understates performance, giving the individual a lower appraisal.

If all individuals in an organization were appraised by the same person, there would be no problem. Although there would be an error factor, it would be applied equally to everyone. The difficulty arises when we have different raters with different leniency errors making judgments. For example, assume that Jones and Smith are performing the same job for different supervisors, but they have absolutely identical job performance. If Jones' supervisor tends to err toward positive leniency, while Smith's supervisor errs toward negative leniency, we might be confronted with two dramatically different evaluations.

Halo Error   The halo effect or error, as we noted in Chapter 4, is the tendency for an evaluator to let the assessment of an individual on one trait influence his or her evaluation of that person on other traits. For example, if an employee tends to be dependable, we might become biased toward that individual to the extent that we will rate him or her high on many desirable attributes.

People who design teaching appraisal forms for college students to fill

[20] M. E. Heilman and M. H. Stopeck, "Being Attractive, Advantage or Disadvantage? Performance-Based Evaluations and Recommended Personnel Actions as a Function of Appearance, Sex, and Job Type," *Organizational Behavior and Human Decision Processes*, April 1985, pp. 202–15.

out in evaluating the effectiveness of their instructor each semester must confront the halo effect. Students tend to rate a faculty member as outstanding on all criteria when they are particularly appreciative of a few things he or she does in the classroom. Similarly, a few bad habits—like showing up late for lectures, being slow in returning papers, or assigning an extremely demanding reading requirement—might result in students' evaluating the instructor as "lousy" across the board.

Similarity Error   When evaluators rate other people giving special consideration to those qualities that they perceive in themselves, they are making a **similarity error**. For example, the evaluator who perceives himself as aggressive may evaluate others by looking for aggressiveness. Those who demonstrate this characteristic tend to benefit, while others are penalized.

Similarity error

Giving special consideration when rating others to those qualities that the evaluator perceives in himself or herself.

Again, this error would tend to wash out if the same evaluator appraised all the people in the organization. However, interrater reliability obviously suffers when various evaluators are utilizing their own similarity criteria.

Low Differentiation   It is possible that, regardless of whom the appraiser evaluates and what traits are used, the pattern of evaluation remains the same. It is possible that the evaluator's ability to appraise objectively and accurately has been impeded by social differentiation, that is, the evaluator's style of rating behavior.

It has been suggested that evaluators may be classified as (1) high differentiators, who use all or most of the scale, or (2) low differentiators, who use a limited range of the scale.[21]

Low differentiators tend to ignore or suppress differences, perceiving the universe as more uniform than it really is. High differentiators, on the other hand, tend to utilize all available information to the utmost extent and thus are better able to perceptually define anomalies and contradictions than low differentiators.[22]

This finding tells us that evaluations made by low differentiators need to be carefully inspected and that the people working for a low differentiator have a high probability of being appraised as significantly more homogenous than they really are.

Forcing Information to Match Nonperformance Criteria   While rarely advocated, it is not an infrequent practice to find the formal evaluation taking place *following* the decision as to how the individual has been performing. This may sound illogical, but it merely recognizes that subjective, yet formal, decisions are often arrived at prior to the gathering of objective information to support that decision. For example, if the evaluator believes that the evaluation should not be based on performance, but rather seniority, he or she may be unknowingly adjusting each "performance" evaluation so as to bring it into line with the employee's seniority rank. In this and other similar cases, the evaluator is increasing or decreasing performance appraisals to align with the nonperformance criteria actually being utilized.

[21] A. Pizam, "Social Differentiation—A New Psychological Barrier to Performance Appraisal," *Public Personnel Management*, July—August 1975, pp. 244–47.

[22] Ibid., pp. 245–46.

Overcoming the Problems

That organizations can encounter problems with performance evaluations should not lead managers to give up on the process. Some things can be done to overcome most of the problems we have identified.

Use Multiple Criteria   Since successful performance on most jobs requires doing a number of things well, all those "things" should be identified and evaluated. The more complex the job, the more criteria that will need to be identified and evaluated. But everything need not be assessed. The critical activities that lead to high or low performance are the ones that need to be evaluated.

Deemphasize Traits   Many traits often considered to be related to good performance may, in fact, have little or no performance relationship. For example, traits like loyalty, initiative, courage, reliability, and self-expression are intuitively appealing as desirable characteristics in employees. But the relevant question is: Are individuals who are evaluated as high on those traits higher performers than those who rate low? We can't answer this question. We know that there are employees who rate high on these characteristics and are poor performers. We can find others who are excellent performers but do not score well on traits such as these. Our conclusion is that traits like loyalty and initiative may be prized by managers, but there is no evidence to support that certain traits will be adequate synonyms for performance in a large cross section of jobs.

Another weakness in traits is the judgment itself. What is "loyalty"? When is an employee "reliable"? What you consider "loyalty," I may not. So traits suffer from weak interrater agreement.

Use Multiple Evaluators   As the number of evaluators increases, the probability of attaining more accurate information increases. If rater error tends to follow a normal curve, an increase in the number of appraisers will tend to find the majority congregating about the middle. You see this approach being used in athletic competitions in such sports as diving and gymnastics. A multiple set of evaluators judges a performance, the highest and lowest scores are dropped, and the final performance evaluation is made up from the cumulative scores of those remaining. The logic of multiple evaluators applies to organizations as well.

If an employee has had ten supervisors, nine having rated her excellent and one poor, we can discount the value of the one poor evaluation. Therefore, by moving employees about within the organization so as to gain a number of evaluations, we increase the probability of achieving more valid and reliable evaluations.

The U.S. Army has made good use of this technique. For individuals who have been evaluated by ten or fifteen officers during their first five or six years in the service, there is less chance that one or two "slanted" evaluations will seriously influence decisions made on the basis of these performance appraisals.

Evaluate Selectively   It has been suggested that appraisers should evaluate in only those areas in which they have some expertise.[23] If raters make evaluations

---

[23] W. C. Borman, "The Rating of Individuals in Organizations: An Alternate Approach," *Organizational Behavior and Human Performance*, August 1974, pp. 105–24.

on *only* those dimensions on which they are in a good position to rate, we increase the interrater agreement and make the evaluation a more valid process. This approach also recognizes that different organizational levels often have different orientations toward ratees and observe them in different settings. In general, therefore, we would recommend that appraisers should be as close as possible, in terms of organizational level, to the individual being evaluated. Conversely, the more levels that separate the evaluator and evaluatee, the less opportunity the evaluator has to observe the individual's behavior and, not surprisingly, the greater the possibility for inaccuracies.

The specific application of these concepts would result in having immediate supervisors or co-workers as the major input into the appraisal and having them evaluate those factors that they are best qualified to judge. For example, it has been suggested that when professors are evaluating secretaries within a university, they use such criteria as judgment, technical competence, and conscientiousness, whereas peers (other secretaries) use such criteria as job knowledge, organization, cooperation with co-workers, and responsibility.[24] Such an approach appears both logical and more reliable, since people are appraising only those dimensions on which they are in a good position to make judgments.

Train Evaluators If you can't *find* good evaluators, the alternative is to *make* good evaluators. There is evidence to support that training evaluators can make them more accurate raters.[25]

Common errors such as halo and leniency have been minimized or eliminated in workshops where managers can practice observing and rating behaviors. These workshops would typically run from one to three days, but allocating many hours to training may not always be necessary. One case has been cited where both halo and leniency errors were decreased immediately after exposing evaluators to explanatory training sessions lasting only five minutes.[26] But the effects of training do appear to diminish over time.[27] This suggests the need for regular training refresher sessions.

Performance Feedback

A few years back, a nationwide motel chain advertised that, when it came to motel rooms, "the best surprise is no surprise." This logic also holds for performance evaluations. Employees like to know how they are doing. They expect feedback. This is typically done in the "annual review." But this review frequently creates problems. In some cases, it's a problem merely because managers put off such reviews. This is particularly likely if the appraisal is negative. But the annual review is additionally troublesome if the manager "saves up" performance-related information and unloads it during the appraisal review. In such

[24] Ibid.

[25] G. P. Latham, K. N. Wexley, and E. D. Pursell, "Training Managers to Minimize Rating Errors in the Observation of Behavior," *Journal of Applied Psychology*, October 1975, pp. 550–55.

[26] H. J. Bernardin, "The Effects of Rater Training on Leniency and Halo Errors in Student Rating of Instructors," *Journal of Applied Psychology*, June 1978, pp. 301–08.

[27] Ibid.; and J. M. Ivancevich, "Longitudinal Study of the Effects of Rater Training on Psychometric Error in Ratings, *Journal of Applied Psychology*, October 1979, pp. 502–08.

instances, it is not surprising that the manager may try to avoid addressing stressful issues that, even if confronted, may only be denied or rationalized by the employee.[28] Much of this problem can be avoided by sharing feedback information with employees on an ongoing basis, for example, providing daily output reports with comparative data on actual units produced and the goal for the day or bringing up problems as they occur rather than allowing them to accumulate for the annual review.

Regardless of whether feedback is provided annually or on an ongoing basis, management needs to offer performance feedback to employees. Yet, appraising another person's performance is one of the most emotionally charged of all management activities. The impression the subordinate receives about his assessment has a strong impact on his self-esteem and, importantly, on his subsequent performance. Of course, conveying good news is considerably less difficult for both the manager and the subordinate than revealing that performance has been below expectations. In this context, the discussion of the evaluation can have negative as well as positive motivational consequences. Statistically speaking, half of all employees are below the median, yet evidence tells us that the *average* employee's estimate of her own performance level generally falls around the seventy-fifth percentile.[29] A survey of over 800,000 high school seniors also found that people seem to see themselves as better than average. Seventy percent rated themselves above average on leadership, and when asked to rate themselves on "ability to get along with others," none rated himself or herself below average, 60 percent rated themselves in the top 10 percent, and 25 percent saw themselves among the top 1 percent. Similarly, a survey of 500 clerical and technical employees found that 58 percent rated their own performance as falling in the top 10 percent of their peers doing comparable jobs and a total of 81 percent placed themselves in the top 20 percent.[30]

Accordingly, the subordinate's perception of his or her own performance often overstates the manager's appraisal. Thus, to the extent that evaluation influences the behavior of organizational members, an organization's performance evaluation process can demotivate those employees who perceive the evaluation as unjust.

REWARD SYSTEMS

Our knowledge of motivation tells us that people do what they do to satisfy needs. Before they do anything, they look for the payoff or reward. Many of these rewards—salary increases, employee benefits, preferred job assignments—are organizationally controlled. While we previously discussed some organizational reward programs in Chapter 7, we should spend a moment to describe

---

[28] W. F. Cascio, *Applied Psychology in Personnel Management*, 3rd ed. (Englewood Cliffs, NJ: Prentice Hall, 1987), p. 102.

[29] R. J. Burke, "Why Performance Appraisal Systems Fail," *Personnel Administration*, June 1972, pp. 32–40.

[30] "How Do I Love Me? Let Me Count the Ways," *Psychology Today*, May 1980, p. 16.

OB Close-Up

Benefit Programs *May* Have an Impact on Employee Attitudes and Behavior

Most organizations provide their employees with an array of benefits. Today, benefits add, on average, about 40 percent to an employee's direct compensation.[31] So the $30,000 a year accountant actually represents a cost to an employer of something closer to $42,000.

What's included in this additional 40 percent? To begin with, certain benefits must be supplied by an organization for its employees, regardless of whether it wants to or not. With only a few exceptions, the hiring of any employee will require an organization to pay Social Security premiums, unemployment compensation, worker's compensation, and state disability premiums. To this, many employers provide basic paid leaves for rest periods, holidays, vacations, and absences due to illness; and pay part or all of the contributions for health insurance and a pension plan. But because these benefits are required by law or are necessary to initially attract job candidates, they are not likely to play much of a role in explaining and predicting behavior. So we'll assume the organization provides a foundation of basic benefits. It's the benefit programs beyond this basic level—where employers have discretion and differences between organizations is considerable—that can have implications on employee attitudes and behavior. Some examples might include flexible workhours, paternity leaves, paid sabbaticals, and on-site health facilities.

One benefit option that has been getting a lot of attention recently has been employer-sponsored child care. Currently, about 3,000 organizations in the U.S. provide some form of child-care support, with about 150 having day-care centers at or near their offices.[32] Proponents argue that employer-sponsored child care can lower turnover and absenteeism, improve productivity and satisfaction, and help to attract the best workers. Whether such programs actually achieve these ends are, at least at this time, still unclear.[33]

rewards that are under managerial discretion and the important role they can play in influencing employee behavior.

The types of rewards that an organization can allocate are more complex than is generally thought. Obviously, there is direct compensation. But there are also indirect compensation and nonfinancial rewards. Each of these types of rewards can be distributed on an individual, group, or organizationwide basis. Figure 14–1 presents a structure for looking at rewards.

[31] *Wall Street Journal*, June 10, 1980, p. 1.

[32] C. Trost, "Child-Care Center at Virginia Firm Boosts Worker Morale and Loyalty," *Wall Street Journal*, February 12, 1987, p. 25.

[33] T. I. Miller, "The Effects of Employee-Sponsored Child Care on Employee Absenteeism, Turnover, Productivity, Recruitment or Job Satisfaction: What Is Claimed and What Is Known," *Personnel Psychology*, Summer 1984, pp. 277–89.

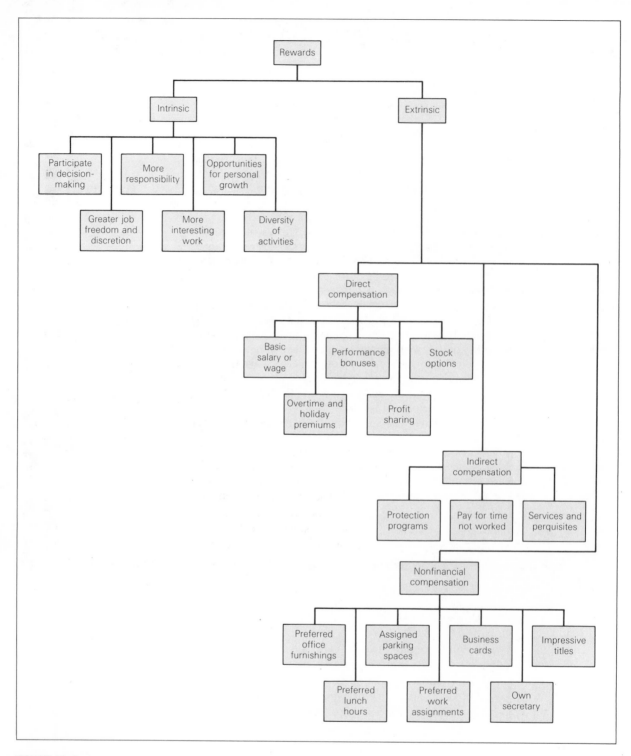

FIGURE 14–1
Types of Rewards

Intrinsic rewards are those that individuals receive for themselves. They are largely a result of the worker's satisfaction with his or her job. As we noted in Chapter 7, techniques like job enrichment or any efforts to redesign or restructure work to increase personal worth to the employee may make his or her work more intrinsically rewarding.

Extrinsic rewards include direct compensation, indirect compensation, and nonfinancial rewards. Of course, an employee expects some form of direct compensation: a basic wage or salary, overtime and holiday premium pay, bonuses based on performance, profit sharing, and/or possibly opportunities to purchase stock options. Employees will expect their direct compensation generally to align with their assessment of their contribution to the organization and, additionally, will expect it to be comparable to the direct compensation given to other employees with similar abilities and performance.

The organization will provide employees with indirect compensation: insurance, pay for holidays and vacations, services, and perquisites. Inasmuch as these are generally made uniformly available to all employees at a given job level, regardless of performance, they are really not motivating rewards. However, where indirect compensation is controllable by management and is used to reward performance, then it clearly needs to be considered as a motivating reward. To illustrate, if a company-paid membership in a country club is not available to all middle- and upper-level executives, but only to those who have shown particular performance ratings, then it is a motivating reward. Similarly, if company-owned automobiles and aircraft are made available to certain employees based on their performance rather than their "entitlement," we should view these indirect compensations as motivating rewards for those who might deem these forms of compensation as attractive.

As with direct compensation, indirect compensation may be viewed in an individual, group, or organizational context. However, if rewards are to be linked closely with performance, we should expect individual rewards to be emphasized. On the other hand, if a certain group of managers within the organization has made a significant contribution to the effective performance of the organization, a blanket reward such as a membership in a social club might be appropriate. Again, it is important to note that since rewards achieve the greatest return when they are specifically designed to meet the needs of each individual, and since group and organizational rewards tend to deal in homogeneity—that is, they tend to treat all people alike—these types of rewards must, by definition, be somewhat less effective than individual rewards. The only exceptions to that statement are those instances where there is a high need for cohesiveness and group congeniality. In such instances, individuals may find group rewards more personally satisfying than individual rewards.

The classification of nonfinancial rewards tends to be a smorgasbord of desirable "things" that are potentially at the disposal of the organization. The creation of nonfinancial rewards is limited only by managers' ingenuity and ability to assess "payoffs" that individuals with the organization find desirable and that are within the managers' discretion.

The old saying "One man's food is another man's poison" certainly applies to rewards. What one employee views as highly desirable, another finds superfluous. Therefore *any* reward may not get the desired result; however, where selection has been done assiduously, the benefits to the organization by way of higher worker performance should be impressive.

Intrinsic rewards

The pleasure or value one receives from the content of a work task.

Extrinsic rewards

Rewards received from the environment surrounding the context of the work.

Some workers are very status conscious. A paneled office, a carpeted floor, a large walnut desk, or a private bathroom may be just the office furnishing that stimulates an employee toward top performance. Status-oriented employees may also value an impressive job title, their own business cards, their own secretary, or a well-located parking space with their name clearly painted underneath the "Reserved" sign.

Some employees value having their lunch at, say, 1 P.M. to 2 P.M. If lunch is normally from 11 A.M. to 12 noon, the benefit of being able to take their lunch at another, more desirable time can be viewed as a reward. Having a chance to work with congenial colleagues or achieving a desired work assignment or an assignment where the worker can operate without close supervision are all rewards that are within the discretion of management and, when carefully aligned to individual needs, can provide stimulus for improved performance.

THE UNION-MANAGEMENT INTERFACE

Labor unions

An organization, made up of employees, that acts collectively to protect and promote employee interests.

Labor unions are a vehicle by which employees act collectively to protect and promote their interests. Currently, in the United States, approximately 18 percent of the work force belongs to and is represented by a union. For this segment of the labor force, wage levels and conditions of employment are explicitly articulated in a contract that is negotiated, through collective bargaining, between representatives of the union and the organization's management. But the impact of unions on employees is broader than their 18 percent representation figure might imply. This is because nonunionized employees benefit from the gains that unions make. There is a spillover effect so that the wages, benefits, and working conditions provided nonunionized employees tend to mirror—with some time lag—those negotiated for union members.

Labor unions influence a number of organizational activities.[34] Recruitment sources, hiring criteria, work schedules, job design, redress procedures, safety rules, and eligibility for training programs are examples of activities that are influenced by unions. The most obvious and pervasive area of influence, of course, is wage rates and working conditions. Where unions exist, performance evaluation systems tend to be less complex because they play a relatively small part in reward decisions. Wage rates, when determined through collective bargaining, emphasize seniority and downplay performance differences.

Figure 14–2 shows what impact a union has on an employee's performance and job satisfaction. The union contract affects motivation through determination of wage rates, seniority rules, layoff procedures, promotion criteria, and security provisions. Unions can influence the competence with which employees perform their jobs by offering special training programs to their members, by requiring apprenticeships, and by allowing members to gain leadership experience through union organizational activities. The actual level of employee performance will be further influenced by collective bargaining restrictions placed

[34] This material was adapted from T. H. Hammer, "Relationship Between Local Union Characteristics and Worker Behavior and Attitudes," *Academy of Management Journal*, December 1978, pp. 560–77.

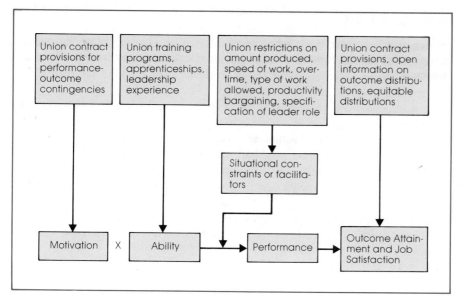

FIGURE 14–2

The Union's Impact on Employee Performance and Job Satisfaction

Source: T. H. Hammer, "Relationships Between Local Union Characteristics and Worker Behavior and Attitudes," *Academy of Management Journal*, December 1978, p. 573.

on the amount of work produced, the speed with which work can be done, overtime allowances per worker, or the kind of tasks a given employee is allowed to perform.

Are union members more satisfied with their jobs than their nonunion counterparts? The answer to this question is more complicated than a simple "Yes" or "No." The evidence consistently demonstrates that unions have only indirect effects on job satisfaction.[35] They increase pay satisfaction, but negatively affect satisfaction with the work itself (by decreasing job scope perceptions), satisfaction with co-workers and supervision (through less favorable perceptions of supervisory behavior), and satisfaction with promotions (through the lower importance placed on promotions).

IMPLICATIONS FOR PERFORMANCE AND SATISFACTION

An organization's human resource policies and practices represent important forces for shaping employee behavior and attitudes. In this chapter, we specifically discussed the influence of selection practices, training and development programs, performance evaluation systems, reward systems, and the existence of a union.

[35] See, for example, C. J. Berger, C. A. Olson, and J. W. Boudreau, "Effects of Unions on Job Satisfaction: The Role of Work-Related Values and Perceived Rewards," *Organizational Behavior and Human Performance*, December 1983, pp. 289–324.

Selection Practices

An organization's selection practices will determine who gets hired. If properly designed, it will identify competent candidates and accurately match them to the job. The use of the proper selection device will increase the probability that the right person will be chosen to fill a slot.

While employee selection is far from a science, some organizations fail to design their selection systems so as to maximize the likelihood that the right person-job fit will be achieved. When errors are made, the chosen candidate's performance may be less than satisfactory. Training may be necessary to improve the candidate's skills. At the worst, the candidate will prove unacceptable and a replacement will need to be found. Similarly, where the selection process results in the hiring of less qualified candidates or individuals who don't fit into the organization, those chosen are likely to feel anxious, tense, and uncomfortable. This, in turn, is likely to increase dissatisfaction with the job.

Training and Development Programs

Training programs can affect work behavior in two ways. The most obvious is by directly improving the skills necessary for the employee to successfully complete his or her job. An increase in ability improves the employee's potential to perform at a higher level. Of course, whether that potential becomes realized is largely an issue of motivation.

A second benefit from training is that it increases an employee's self-efficacy. **Self-efficacy** is a person's expectation that he or she can successfully execute the behaviors required to produce an outcome.[36] For employees, those behaviors are work tasks and the outcome is effective job performance. Employees with high self-efficacy have strong expectations about their abilities to perform successfully in new situations. They're confident and expect to be successful. Training, then, is a means to positively affect self-efficacy. In so doing, employees may be more willing to undertake job tasks and exert a high level of effort. Or in expectancy terms (see Chapter 6), individuals are more likely to perceive their effort as leading to performance.

We also discussed career development programs in this chapter. Organizations that provide formal career development activities and match them to needs that employees experience at various stages in their careers reduce the likelihood that productivity will decrease as a result of obsolescence or that job frustrations will create reduced satisfaction.[37]

In today's job environment—with increasing competition for many jobs and limited promotion opportunities in many others—employees will increas-

Self-efficacy

A person's expectation that he or she can successfully execute behaviors required to produce an outcome.

[36] A. Bandura, "Self-Efficacy: Towards a Unifying Theory of Behavioral Change," *Psychological Review*, March 1977, pp. 191–215.

[37] M. K. Mount, "Managerial Career Stage and Facets of Job Satisfaction," *Journal of Vocational Behavior*, June 1984, pp. 340–54; and C. S. Granrose and J. D. Portwood, "Matching Individual Career Plans and Organizational Career Management," *Academy of Management Journal*, December 1987, pp. 699–720.

ingly confront the reality of career plateauing. Out of frustration, employees may look for other jobs. Organizations that have well-designed career programs will have employees with more realistic expectations and career tracking systems that will lessen the chance that good employees will leave because of inadequate opportunities.

Performance Evaluation and Feedback Systems

A major goal of performance evaluation is to assess accurately an individual's performance contribution as a basis for making reward allocation decisions. If the performance evaluation process emphasizes the wrong criteria or inaccurately appraises actual job performance, employees will be over- or underrewarded. As equity theory demonstrated in Chapter 6, this can lead to negative consequences such as reduced effort, increases in absenteeism, or search for alternative job opportunities.

Inadequate or improper feedback was shown to decrease satisfaction and be a potential cause of reduced performance. The evaluation of an employee's performance typically affects the employee following his or her receipt of feedback information (or lack of same) rather than at the time the information is actually being gathered.

Reward Systems

If employees perceive that their efforts will be accurately appraised, and if they further perceive that the rewards they value are closely linked to their evaluations, the organization will have optimized the motivational properties from its evaluation and reward procedures and policies. More specifically, based on the contents of this chapter and our discussion of motivation in Chapters 6 and 7, we can conclude that rewards are likely to lead to high employee performance and satisfaction when they are (1) perceived as being equitable by the employee, (2) tied to performance, and (3) tailored to the needs of the individual. These conditions should foster a minimum of dissatisfaction among employees, reduce withdrawal patterns, and increase organizational commitment. If these conditions do not exist, the probability of withdrawal behavior increases, and the prevalence of marginal or barely adequate performance increases. If workers perceive that their efforts are not recognized or rewarded, and if they view their alternatives as limited, they may continue working, but perform at a level considerably below their capability.

Employee benefits like flexible workhours, paternity leaves, and day care centers may be most relevant for the impact they have on reducing absenteeism and improving job satisfaction. These rewards reduce barriers that many employees—particularly those with significant responsibilities outside the job—find get in the way of being at work on time or even making it to work at all. To the degree that these benefits lessen an employee's worries over outside responsibilities, they may increase satisfaction with the job and the organization.

Union-Management Interface

The existence of a union in an organization adds another variable in our search to explain and predict employee behavior. The union has been found to be an important contributor to employees' perceptions, attitudes, and behavior.

The power of the union surfaces in the collective bargaining agreement that it negotiates with the organization's management. Much of what an employee can and cannot do on the job is formally stipulated in this agreement. In addition, the informal norms that union cohesiveness fosters can encourage or discourage high productivity, organizational commitment, and morale.

POINT

COLLEGE STUDENTS SHOULDN'T BE ASKED TO GRADE THEIR TEACHERS

The evaluation of teacher performance by students is now a fixture of campus life. The results have become an important factor in faculty promotion and retention decisions. In practice, this translates into faculty members with higher student evaluation scores receiving more favorable consideration.

Treating student evaluations as though they were a straightforward measure of good teaching invites abuse. Most important, it fails to recognize the applicability of the "journeyman principle" to college faculty members. This principle acknowledges that those who wish to be practitioners of a skilled trade or profession must undergo rigorous training. Those who complete the training are known as journeymen and are assumed competent to perform satisfactorily the range of tasks ordinarily required. They are not required to prove competence, since journeymen status itself attests to such competence. It is the judgment of incompetence that is made on the basis of special evidence.

Use of this principle would result in a radically different approach to the evaluation of good teaching: It would no longer be important to obtain a fine measurement of the teaching performance of every faculty member. Small distinctions among the ranks of the competent would cease to be important, because they are insignificant with respect to the work. For example, any journeyman plumber can fix your sink, any competent pediatrician can diagnose a child's ear infection, and any competent mathematician can teach calculus. Following the journeyman principle, attention would be focused on identifying those at the extremes. It is important to detect the incompetent—those who cannot be trusted to perform the ordinary tasks properly. It is equally important to detect the exceptional—those who can handle the extraordinary tasks.

Do college faculty members fit the definition of journeyman? There are several reasons to suggest they do. Members of a college faculty have usually successfully completed some amount of graduate training, which may be taken to certify a certain high level of intellectual competence and mastery of subject matter. The ability to present material in a clear and organized fashion is generally a prerequisite for successfully completing a graduate degree. There is, additionally, the process of self-selection: Those who dislike teaching, or feel inarticulate or uncomfortable addressing groups, tend to avoid choosing teaching as a profession.

We may fairly conclude that college faculty members are intelligent, know their subject matter, express themselves reasonably well, and care about teaching. They are a highly selected sample who are, with a few exceptions, clustered at the upper end of the competence continuum. The current idea that it is important to evaluate the teaching performance of every faculty member so as to obtain proof of competence seems to derive from the contrary notion that college teachers are uniformly distributed over the whole continuum of competence.

Adapted from M. J. Rodin, "By a Faculty Member's Yardstick, Student Evaluations Don't Measure Up," *Chronicle of Higher Education*, May 3, 1982, p. 63.

COUNTERPOINT

CHALLENGES TO THE ASSUMPTION OF COMPETENCE

The journeyman principle is thought-provoking, but it is vulnerable on at least four points: (1) Teaching students is not like fixing a leaking sink; (2) most college teachers' apprenticeships don't emphasize teaching skills; (3) competence, even if demonstrated at one point in time, need not hold constant for an indefinite time period; and (4) the overt evidence that there is a good deal of bad teaching out there can't be ignored.

Teaching is not a routine task in the way sink repair may be considered routine. Every student is different. A standardized approach isn't likely to succeed in meeting the various learning styles and needs of students.

The successful completion of a graduate degree program is no assurance that a teacher can teach. Graduate study emphasizes research. Most graduate students are not required to teach in order to obtain their degree, and those who do so are evaluated infrequently, if at all. Sure, subject matter competence is needed to complete a graduate degree, but knowledge of a subject is no assurance that one can teach that material.

Even if we assumed that all faculty members were competent teachers at the time they were hired, why should we believe that competence will remain a constant over a teaching career? In many fields, subject matter is rapidly made obsolete and displaced. The knowledge held by the teacher of information processing in 1969 would be totally inadequate in 1989. And teaching ability can change over time. Changes in college administrative policy, salary levels, and colleagues can alter the teach-er's motivation. The faculty member's interests may also change over his or her career. Thirty years or more of tenure-protected job security (a luxury not offered those in the plumbing profession) can further act to deter a faculty member's motivation to keep up in his or her field or put in the extra effort to make classroom lectures interesting.

Finally, you can't ignore the reality that college teachers *aren't* "clustered at the upper end of the competence continuum." College teachers, like most populations on most competence scales, tend to be distributed along a bell-shaped curve. Some are excellent and some are poor, with most centered around the median. Without student evaluation information, faculty members are deprived of the kind of feedback that is necessary to assess their strengths and weaknesses and work toward reducing those weaknesses.

College faculty, in spite of superior academic qualifications, are not beyond evaluation. To follow the journeyman analogy would suggest, for instance, that a bridge should never be inspected since both the contractor who built it and the architects and engineers who designed it have met the journeyman requirement. The journeyman principle assumes that all teachers are competent when they enter the profession and that that competence is maintained throughout one's teaching career. These assumptions just are not valid.

Ideas expressed here were influenced by "Letters to the Editor," *Chronicle of Higher Education*, June 2, 1982, p. 25.

KEY TERMS

Assessment Centers

Behaviorally Anchored Rating Scales

Career

Career Stages

Critical Incidents

Extrinsic Rewards

Graphic Rating Scales

Group Order Ranking

Individual Ranking

Intrinsic Rewards

Job Analysis

Job Description

Job Specification

Labor Unions

Leniency Error

Paired Comparison

Self-Efficacy

Similarity Error

Work Sampling

FOR DISCUSSION

1. What is job analysis? How is it related to those the organization hires?

2. If you were a dean of a college of business, how would you determine which job candidates would be effective teachers?

3. Describe several *on-the-job* training methods and several *off-the-job* methods.

4. What would an effective career development program look like?

5. If you were a dean of a college of business, how would you evaluate the performance of your faculty members?

6. What relationship, if any, is there between job analysis and performance evaluation?

7. Why do organizations evaluate employees?

8. What are the advantages and disadvantages of the following performance evaluation methods: (1) written essays, (b) graphic rating scales, and (c) behaviorally anchored rating scales?

9. How can an organization's performance evaluation system affect employee behavior?

10. If the average employee believes that he is performing at the seventy-fifth percentile, what does this imply for employee performance reviews?

11. Some organizations have a personnel policy that pay information be kept secret. Not only is pay information not given out by management but employees are also discouraged from talking about their pay with co-workers. How do you think this practice affects employee behavior?

12. What impact do unions have on an organization's reward system?

FOR FURTHER READING

CASCIO, W. F., *Applied Psychology in Personnel Management*, 3rd ed. Englewood Cliffs, NJ: Prentice Hall, 1987. Applies psychological research and theory to the problems of organizational human resource utilization.

LARSON, J. R., "The Performance Feedback Process: A Preliminary Model," *Organizational Behavior and Human Performance*, February 1984, pp. 42–76. Outlines a model of the overall feedback process that focuses on the factors that influence supervisors' performance feedback as well as the effects that giving feedback can have on both the subordinate and supervisor.

OGILVIE, J. R., "The Role of Human Resource Management Practices in Predicting Organizational Commitment," *Group and Organization Studies*, December 1986, pp. 335–59. Research study finds that human resource management practices are more strongly related to commitment than demographic, job characteristics, social environment, or supervisory variables.

PEARCE, J. L., and L. W. PORTER, "Employee Responses to Formal Performance Appraisal Feedback," *Journal of Applied Psychology*, May 1986, pp. 211–18. Research study finds a significant drop in organizational commitment among employees receiving feedback that their performance is satisfactory but not outstanding.

SCHNEIDER, B., "The People Make the Place," *Personnel Psychology*, Autumn 1987, pp. 437–52. Provocatively argues that different kinds of organizations attract, select, and retain different kinds of people. Therefore, recruitment and selection—not the external environment or organizational structure—largely determine organizational behavior.

SCHNEIER, C. E., R. W. BEATTY, and L. S. BAIRD, "How to Construct a Successful Performance Appraisal System," *Training and Development Journal*, April 1986, pp. 38–42. Provides a clear and straightforward guide to developing a valid and reliable performance evaluation system.

Complete the following questionnaire by circling the answer that best describes your feelings about each statement. For each item, circle your response according to the following:

SA = Strongly Agree, A = Agree, D = Disagree, SD = Strongly Disagree.

1. I would leave my company rather than be promoted out of my area of expertise. SA A D SD
2. Becoming highly specialized and highly competent in some specific functional or technical area is important to me. SA A D SD
3. A career that is free from organization restriction is important to me. SA A D SD
4. I have always sought a career in which I could be of service to others. SA A D SD
5. A career that provides a maximum variety of types of assignments and work projects is important to me.
6. To rise to a position in general management is important to me. SA A D SD
7. I like to be identified with a particular organization and the prestige that accompanies that organization. SA A D SD
8. Remaining in my present geographical location rather than moving because of a promotion is important to me. SA A D SD
9. The use of my skills in building a new business enterprise is important to me. SA A D SD
10. I would like to reach a level of responsibility in an organization where my decisions really make a difference. SA A D SD
11. I see myself more as a generalist as opposed to being committed to one specific area of expertise. SA A D SD
12. An endless variety of challenges in my career is important to me.
13. Being identified with a powerful or prestigious employer is important to me. SA A D SD
14. The excitement of participating in many areas of work has been the underlying motivation behind my career. SA A D SD
15. The process of supervising, influencing, leading, and controlling people at all levels is important to me. SA A D SD
16. I am willing to sacrifice some of my autonomy to stabilize my total life situation. SA A D SD
17. An organization that will provide security through guaranteed work, benefits, a good retirement, and so forth, is important to me. SA A D SD
18. During my career I will be mainly concerned with my own sense of freedom and autonomy. SA A D SD
19. I will be motivated throughout my career by the number of products that I have been directly involved in creating. SA A D SD
20. I want others to identify me by my organization and job. SA A D SD
21. Being able to use my skills and talents in the service of an important cause is important to me. SA A D SD
22. To be recognized by my title and status is important to me. SA A D SD
23. A career that permits a maximum of freedom and autonomy to choose my own work, hours, and so forth, is important to me. SA A D SD
24. A career that gives me a great deal of flexibility is important to me. SA A D SD
25. To be in a position in general management is important to me. SA A D SD
26. It is important for me to be identified by my occupation. SA A D SD
27. I will accept a management position only if it is in my area of expertise. SA A D SD
28. It is important for me to remain in my present geographical location rather than move because of a promotion or new job assignment. SA A D SD

29. I would like to accumulate a personal fortune to prove to myself and others that I am competent. SA   A   D   SD

30. I want to achieve a position that gives me the opportunity to combine analytical competence with supervision of people. SA   A   D   SD

31. I have been motivated throughout my career by using my talents in a variety of different areas of work. SA   A   D   SD

32. An endless variety of challenges is what I really want from my career. SA   A   D   SD

33. An organization that will give me long-run stability is important to me. SA   A   D   SD

34. To be able to create or build something that is entirely my own product or idea is important to me. SA   A   D   SD

35. Remaining in my specialized area, as opposed to being promoted out of my area of expertise, is important to me. SA   A   D   SD

36. I do not want to be constrained by either an organization or the business world. SA   A   D   SD

37. Seeing others change because of my efforts is important to me. SA   A   D   SD

38. My main concern in life is to be competent in my area of expertise. SA   A   D   SD

39. The chance to pursue my own life-style and not be constrained by the rules of an organization is important to me. SA   A   D   SD

40. I find most organizations to be restrictive and intrusive. SA   A   D   SD

41. Remaining in my area of expertise, rather than being promoted into general management, is important to me. SA   A   D   SD

42. I want a career that allows me to meet my basic needs through helping others. SA   A   D   SD

43. The use of my interpersonal and helping skills in the service of others is important to me. SA   A   D   SD

44. I like to see others change because of my efforts. SA   A   D   SD

Turn to page 566 for scoring direction and key.

Adapted, by permission of the publisher, from "Reexamining the Career Anchor Model", by T. J. Delong, *PERSONNEL*, May-June 1982, pp. 56–57. © 1982 AMACOM, a division of American Management Associations, New York. All rights reserved.

Dana Ruff, manager for women's lingerie at the Macy's department store in San Francisco, always dreads November 1. That's the day that all managers are required to turn in performance evaluations on their employees. These evaluations become the major determinant of salary increases, decisions that are made in December and go into effect January 1.

"I can't think of any activity I dislike more in this job than doing the annual performance reviews," Dana related. "I see them as a no-win proposition. My poor performers fight the evaluations. They complain that I'm prejudiced, unobjective, overly picky. You name it, I've heard it all. They want to put the blame on anyone but themselves. And since I make the appraisals, I'm usually the target for most of the bitching. My good performers know they're doing a good job. There is nothing positive I can tell them that they don't expect. Their complaints are usually that I don't give them *enough* recognition. So, like I said, I can't win."

One of Dana's newer employees is one of her biggest problems. Shannon Hersch has been working for Dana and Macy's for seven months. In that short time, she has openly argued with Dana on a number of occasions, has badmouthed Dana within the department, and has made two formal complaints to the personnel office about the way Dana has treated her. As self-protection, Dana has taken to keeping a daily diary describing both the good and bad behaviors Shannon exhibits on the job.

Dana has been getting complaints from several of her people about Shannon. They say she is disruptive. She's negative about her job and even comments negatively on Macy's as a place to work. But Shannon has several friends in the department and she appears to be having an impact on them. Based on what she sees and hears down on the floor, Dana believes that Shannon is developing a coalition of marginal workers—those who have received negative appraisals. She notices that Shannon and three peers in the department regularly take coffee breaks and lunch together.

Dana is aware that her boss is watching her more closely as a result of the complaints made to personnel. She has eight full-time and ten part-time employees. It's October 25. Dana's evaluations of her employees are due within the week. Of course, Dana's own evaluation by her boss is due at the same time.

QUESTIONS

1. How do performance evaluations affect behavior?
2. Should Dana talk with her boss?
3. Should Dana talk with Shannon?
4. What do you think Shannon's strategy is?
5. How can Dana find out what impact Shannon is having on departmental performance and morale?

15

Cultural Systems

■ *Learning objectives*

Describe the common characteristics making up organizational culture
Explain the factors determining an organization's culture
List the factors that maintain an organization's culture
Clarify how culture is transmitted to employees
Outline the various socialization alternatives available to management
List the eight cross-national cultural clusters
Describe the four dimensions inherent in a nation's culture
Summarize U.S. culture using these four dimensions

In any organization, there are the ropes to skip and the ropes to know.

——— R. RITTI AND G. FUNKHOUSER

"This is a very different place to work in today than it was in 1983," commented Mike McManus, an engineer and twenty-year veteran at AT&T. "Our research engineering department used to have a staff of over 150. We were the seat of power in this company. We had a relatively free hand to design the best equipment possible and cost be damned! Our only guiding principle was to make it the best we could. Since deregulation in 1984, our department has shrunk to fewer than eighty people. We now take a clear back seat to marketing. And as I'm reminded at almost every weekly staff meeting, we no longer are driven by what *we think* is best for the customer. Now we design and build products to meet the *needs* of our customers, whatever that might be. And those products had better be cost-competitive because the days when we had no competition will never be seen again. Our old manufacturing-oriented culture encouraged taking too much time to make a product and at too high a price. Our new marketing culture is geared to supply customers with what they need quickly, and if that includes lower-quality telecommunications products with a host of superfluous options, so be it! And let me tell you something else: No one in this company has *not* been affected by this cultural change."[1]

The preceding quote illustrates that organizations have internal cultures and that these cultures influence the behavior of their members. But organizations are not islands unto themselves. They're part of their environment. And one of the more crucial elements of that environment, in terms of effect on employee behavior, is the national culture in which the employee works. Japan's culture, for instance, is different from that of the U.S., and those differences have an impact on organizational practices and employee behaviors. As a case in point, it is not unusual for unknowing U.S. executives to offend high-ranking Japanese managers when the former visit Japan. Accustomed to relating managerial authority to the size and furnishings of one's office, Americans often assume that a Japanese manager who has a small and sparsely furnished office is a low-level decision maker. American executives would likely behave differently if they knew that the offices of top Japanese managers do not flaunt the status accoutrements that their American counterparts do.[2]

This chapter introduces culture as a variable affecting organizational behavior. We'll start by looking inside an organization at what has become known

---

[1] Related to the author. Source's name changed.
[2] D. A. Ricks, M. Y. C. Fu, and J. S. Arpas, *International Business Blunders* (Columbus, OH: Grid, 1974).

as corporate or organizational culture. Then we'll move to the international scene and compare national cultures. We'll demonstrate that variations exist across national cultures, that these variations follow systematic patterns, and that an understanding of these patterns can help us to better explain and predict employee behavior within a given country.

ORGANIZATIONAL CULTURE

There is a famous story that IBM employees tell and retell of a plant security supervisor who challenged Thomas Watson, Jr., who, at the time of the story, was the all-powerful chairman of IBM's board. The supervisor, a twenty-two-year-old woman, was required to make certain that people entering security areas wore the correct clearance identification. One day, surrounded by his usual entourage, Watson approached the doorway to an area where the supervisor was on guard. He wore an orange badge acceptable elsewhere in the plant, but not the green badge, which alone permitted entrance at her door. Although the supervisor knew who Watson was, she told him what she had been instructed to say to anyone without proper clearance: "You cannot enter. Your admittance is not recognized." The people accompanying Watson were taken aback. Would this young security guard be fired on the spot? "Don't you know who he is?" someone asked. Watson raised his hand for silence while one of the party strode off and returned with the appropriate badge.[3]

This story conveys a message to IBM employees: No matter who you are, you obey the rules. That this story is well known among IBM employees attests that, in every organization, there are appropriate and inappropriate ways to do things. One common attribute held by those organizational members that are perceived as "good employees" is an understanding of "the way things are done around here"; that is, they know their organization's culture.

Institutionalization: A Forerunner of Culture

The idea of viewing organizations as cultures—where there is a system of shared meaning among members—is a relatively recent phenomenon. Fifteen years ago, organizations were, for the most part, simply thought of as rational means by which to coordinate and control a group of people. They had vertical levels, departments, authority relationships, and so forth. But organizations are more. They have personalities too, just like individuals. They can be rigid or flexible, unfriendly or supportive, innovative or conservative. General Electric offices and people *are* different from the offices and people at General Mills. Harvard and MIT are in the same business—education—and separated only by the width of the Charles River, but each has a unique feeling and character beyond its structural characteristics. Organizational theorists, in recent years, have begun to acknowledge this by recognizing the important role that culture plays in the lives of organization members. Interestingly, though, the origin

[3] W. Rodgers, *Think* (New York: Stein & Day, 1969), pp. 153–54.

of culture as an independent variable affecting an employee's attitudes and behavior can be traced back forty years ago to the notion of **institutionalization**.[4]

When an organization becomes institutionalized, it takes on a life of its own, apart from any of its members. The Internal Revenue Service, Chrysler Corporation, and Timex Corporation are examples of organizations that exist, and have existed, beyond the life of any one member. Additionally, when an organization becomes institutionalized, it becomes valued for itself, not merely for the goods or services it produces. It acquires immortality. If its original goals are no longer relevant, it doesn't go out of business. Rather, it redefines itself. When the demand for Timex's watches declined, the company merely redirected itself into the consumer electronics business—making, in addition to watches, clocks, computers, and health care products like digital thermometers and blood pressure testing devices. Timex took on an existence that went beyond its original mission to manufacture low-cost mechanical watches.

Institutionalization operates to produce common understandings among members about what is appropriate and, fundamentally, meaningful behavior.[5] So when an organization takes on institutional permanence, acceptable modes of behavior become largely self-evident to its members. As we'll see, this is essentially the same thing that organizational culture does. So an understanding of what makes up an organization's culture, and how it is created, sustained, and learned will enhance our ability to explain and predict the behavior of people at work.

Institutionalization

When an organization takes on a life of its own, apart from any of its members, and acquires immortality.

What Is Organizational Culture?

Organizational culture is one of those topics about which many people will say, "Oh, yeah, I know what you mean," but one that is quite difficult to define in any specific form. In this section, we'll propose a specific definition and review several peripheral issues that revolve around this definition.

A Definition   There seems to be wide agreement that **organizational culture** refers to a system of shared meaning held by members that distinguishes the organization from other organizations.[6] This system of shared meaning is, on closer analysis, a set of key characteristics that the organization values. There appear to be ten characteristics that, when mixed and matched, tap the essence of an organization's culture.[7]

Organizational culture

A common perception held by the organization's members; a system of shared meaning.

---

[4] P. Selznick, "Foundations of the Theory of Organizations," *American Sociological Review*, February 1948, pp. 25–35.

[5] L. G. Zucker, "Organizations as Institutions," in S. B. Bacharach (ed.), *Research in the Sociology of Organizations* (Greenwich, CT: JAI Press, 1983), pp. 1–47; and A. J. Richardson, "The Production of Institutional Behaviour: A Constructive Comment on the Use of Institutionalization Theory in Organizational Analysis," *Canadian Journal of Administrative Sciences*, December 1986, pp. 304–16.

[6] See, for example, H. S. Becker, "Culture: A Sociological View," *Yale Review*, Summer 1982, pp. 513–27; and E. H. Schein, *Organizational Culture and Leadership* (San Francisco: Jossey-Bass, 1985), p. 168.

[7] Based on G. G. Gordon and W. M. Cummins, *Managing Management Climate* (Lexington, MA: Lexington Books, 1979); and C. A. Betts and S. M. Halfhill, "Organization Culture: Theory, Definitions, and Dimensions," presented at the National American Institute of Decision Sciences' Conference, Las Vegas, November 1985.

1. *Individual initiative*: the degree of responsibility, freedom, and independence that individuals have

2. *Risk tolerance*: the degree to which employees are encouraged to be aggressive, innovative, and risk-seeking

3. *Direction*: the degree to which the organization creates clear objectives and performance expectations

4. *Integration*: the degree to which units within the organization are encouraged to operate in a coordinated manner

5. *Management support*: the degree to which managers provide clear communication, assistance, and support to their subordinates

6. *Control*: the number of rules and regulations, and the amount of direct supervision that is used to oversee and control employee behavior

7. *Identity*: the degree to which members identify with the organization as a whole rather than with their particular work group or field of professional expertise

8. *Reward system*: the degree to which reward allocations (that is, salary increases, promotions) are based on employee performance criteria in contrast to seniority, favoritism, and so on

9. *Conflict tolerance*: the degree to which employees are encouraged to air conflicts and criticisms openly

10. *Communication patterns*: the degree to which organizational communications are restricted to the formal hierarchy of authority

Each of these characteristics exists on a continuum from low to high. By appraising the organization on these ten characteristics, then, a composite picture of the organization's culture is formed. This picture becomes the basis for feelings of shared understanding that members have about the organization, how things are done in it, and the way members are supposed to behave. Table 15–1 demonstrates how these characteristics can be mixed to create highly diverse organizations.

Culture Is a Descriptive Term   Organizational culture is concerned with how employees perceive the ten characteristics, not whether they like them or not. That is, it is a descriptive term. This is important because it differentiates this concept from that of job satisfaction. Research on organizational culture has sought to measure how employees see their organization: Are there clear objectives and performance expectations? Does the organization reward innovation? Does it stifle conflict? In contrast, job satisfaction seeks to measure affective responses to the work environment. It is concerned with how employees feel about the organization's expectations, reward practices, methods for handling conflict, and the like. Although the two terms undoubtedly have characteristics that overlap, keep in mind that the term organizational culture is descriptive, while job satisfaction is evaluative.

Do Organizations Have Uniform Cultures?   Organizational culture represents a common perception held by the organization's members. This was made explicit when we defined culture as a system of *shared* meaning. We should expect, therefore, that individuals with different backgrounds or at different levels in

TABLE 15–1
Two Highly Diverse Organizational Cultures

Organization A	Organization B
This organization is a manufacturing firm. There are extensive rules and regulations that employees are required to follow. Every employee has specific objectives to achieve in his or her job. Managers supervise employees closely to ensure there are no deviations. People are allowed little discretion on their jobs. Employees are instructed to bring any unusual problem to their superior, who will then determine the solution. All employees are required to communicate through formal channels. Because management has no confidence in the honesty or integrity of its employees, it imposes tight controls. Managers and employees alike tend to be hired by the organization early in their careers, rotated into and out of various departments on a regular basis, and are generalists rather than specialists. Effort, loyalty, cooperation, and avoidance of errors are highly valued and rewarded.	This organization is also a manufacturing firm. Here, however, there are few rules and regulations. Employees are seen as hardworking and trustworthy, thus supervision is loose. Employees are encouraged to solve problems themselves, but to feel free to consult with their supervisors when they need assistance. Top management downplays authority differences. Employees are also encouraged to develop their unique specialized skills. Interpersonal and interdepartmental differences are seen as natural occurrences. Managers are evaluated not only on their department's performance but on how well their department coordinates its activities with other departments in the organization. Promotions and other valuable rewards go to employees who make the greatest contribution to the organization, even when those employees have strange ideas, unusual personal mannerisms, or unconventional work habits.

the organization will tend to describe the organization's culture in similar terms.

Acknowledgment that organizational culture has common properties does not mean, however, that there cannot be subcultures within any given culture. Most large organizations have a dominant culture and numerous sets of subcultures.[8]

A **dominant culture** expresses the core values that are shared by a majority of the organization's members. When we talk about an *organization's* culture, we are referring to its dominant culture. It is this macro view of culture that gives an organization its distinct personality. **Subcultures** tend to develop in large organizations to reflect common problems, situations, or experiences that members face. These subcultures are likely to be defined by department designations and geographical separation. The purchasing department, for example, can have a subculture that is uniquely shared by members of that department. It will include the **core values** of the dominant culture plus additional values unique to members of the purchasing department. Similarly, an office or unit of the organization that is physically separated from the organization's main operations may take on a different personality. Again, the core values are essentially retained but modified to reflect the separated unit's distinct situation.

If organizations had no dominant culture and were composed only of

Dominant culture

Expresses the core values that are shared by a majority of the organization's members.

Subcultures

Minicultures within an organization, typically defined by department designations and geographical separation.

Core values

The primary or dominant values that are accepted throughout the organization.

[8] See, for example, K. L. Gregory, "Native-View Paradigms: Multiple Cultures and Culture Conflicts in Organizations," *Administrative Science Quarterly*, September 1983, pp. 359–76.

numerous subcultures, the value of organizational culture as an independent variable would be significantly lessened, because there would be no uniform interpretation of what represented appropriate or inappropriate behavior. It is the "shared meaning" aspect of culture that makes it such a potent device for guiding and shaping behavior. But we cannot ignore the reality that many organizations also have subcultures that can influence the behavior of members.

Strong vs. Weak Cultures   It has become increasingly popular to differentiate between strong and weak cultures.[9] The argument here is that strong cultures have a greater impact on employee behavior and are more directly related to reduced turnover.

Strong cultures

Cultures where the core values are intensely held and widely shared.

A **strong culture** is characterized by the organization's core values being both intensely held and widely shared. The more members that accept the core values and the greater their commitment to those values, the stronger the culture is. Consistent with this definition, a strong culture will obviously have a greater influence on the behavior of its members. Religious organizations, cults, and Japanese companies are examples of organizations that have very strong cultures.[10] When a James Jones can entice nine hundred members of his Guyana cult to commit mass suicide, we see a behavioral influence considerably greater than that typically attributed to leadership. The culture of Jonestown had a degree of sharedness and intensity that allowed for extremely high behavioral control. Of course, the same strong cultural influence that can lead to the tragedy of a Jonestown can be directed positively to create immensely successful organizations like IBM, Mary Kay Cosmetics, and Sony.

A specific result of a strong culture should be lower employee turnover. A strong culture demonstrates high agreement among members about what the organization stands for. Such unanimity of purpose builds cohesiveness, loyalty, and organizational commitment. These, in turn, lessen the propensity for employees to leave the organization.[11]

Culture vs. Formalization   A strong organizational culture increases behavioral consistency. In this sense, we should recognize that a strong culture can act as a substitute for formalization.

In Chapter 13, we discussed how formalization's rules and regulations act to regulate employee behavior. High formalization in an organization creates predictability, orderliness, and consistency. Our point is that a strong culture achieves the same end without the need for written documentation. Therefore, we should view formalization and culture as two different roads to a common destination. The stronger an organization's culture, the less management need be concerned with developing formal rules and regulations to guide employee behavior. Those guides will have been internalized in employees when they accept the organization's culture.

---

[9] T. E. Deal and A. A. Kennedy, *Corporate Cultures*; and T. J. Peters and R. H. Waterman, Jr., *In Search of Excellence* (New York: Harper & Row, 1982).

[10] C. A. O'Reilly III, "Corporations, Cults and Organizational Culture: Lessons from Silicon Valley Firms," paper presented at the 42nd Annual Meeting of the Academy of Management, Dallas, 1983.

[11] R. T. Mowday, L. W. Porter, and R. M. Steers, *Employee-Organization Linkages: The Psychology of Commitment, Absenteeism, and Turnover* (New York: Academic Press, 1982).

OB Close-Up

There Are No "Right" Cultures!

A few years back, largely due to the tremendous commercial success and general acceptance of Tom Peters and Robert Waterman's book *In Search of Excellence*[12] (the book sold more than 5 million copies), many practicing managers thought that successful organizations had a set of common cultural characteristics. Peters and Waterman argued that well-managed or "excellent" companies like IBM, DuPont, 3M, McDonald's, and Procter & Gamble had common characteristics such as a bias for action, autonomy and entrepreneurship, and increased productivity through employee involvement.[13] Moreover, to quote Peters and Waterman, "without exception, the dominance and coherence of culture proved to be an essential quality of the excellent companies."[14]

While the idea that there might be a set of "right" cultural characteristics that differentiate successful from unsuccessful organizations is intuitively appealing, the evidence does not stack up that way.[15] What defines excellence in an organization is far from clear. Additionally, what was excellent yesterday is not necessarily excellent today. For instance, Peters and Waterman included firms such as Caterpillar Tractor, Schlumberger, and Wang Labs in their set of forty-three excellent firms, but each has had serious declines in financial performance since the publication of their book. Maybe most damning is the reality that there are undoubtedly hundreds, maybe thousands, of organizations that equal or exceed the performance of Peters and Waterman's excellent companies but have few, if any, of the "right" cultural characteristics.

To construe culture as a set of specific shared values implies that there are "right" cultures and "wrong" ones. Such a perspective misrepresents the concept of organizational culture and misdirects attention from *understanding what is* toward *prescribing what should be*. At this time, it is clearly presumptuous to state that we know the cultural characteristics prevalent in "excellent" organizations.

What Does Culture Do?

We've alluded to organizational culture's impact on behavior. We've also explicitly argued that a strong culture should be associated with reduced turnover.

---

[12] T. J. Peters and R. H. Waterman, *In Search of Excellence*.

[13] Ibid.

[14] Ibid., p. 75.

[15] See, for instance, "Who's Excellent Now?," *Business Week*, November 5, 1984, pp. 76–78; K. E. Aupperle, W. Acar, and D. E. Booth, "An Empirical Critique of *In Search of Excellence*: How Excellent Are the Excellent Companies?," *Journal of Management*, Winter 1986, pp. 499–512; and M. A. Hitt and R. D. Ireland, "Peters and Waterman Revisited: The Unended Quest for Excellence," *Academy of Management Executive*, May 1987, pp. 91–98.

In this section, we will more carefully review the functions that culture performs and assess whether culture can be a liability for an organization.

Culture's Functions   Culture performs a number of functions within an organization. First, it has a boundary defining role; that is, it creates distinctions between one organization and others. Second, it conveys a sense of identity for organization members. Third, culture facilitates the generation of commitment to something larger than one's individual self-interest. Fourth, it enhances social system stability. Culture is the social glue that helps hold the organization together by providing appropriate standards for what employees should say and do. Finally, culture serves as a sense-making and control mechanism that guides and shapes the attitudes and behavior of employees. It is this last function that is of particular interest to us. As the following quote makes clear, culture defines the rules of the game:

> Culture by definition is elusive, intangible, implicit, and taken for granted. But every organization develops a core set of assumptions, understandings, and implicit rules that govern day-to-day behavior in the workplace. . . . Until newcomers learn the rules, they are not accepted as full-fledged members of the organization. Transgressions of the rules on the part of high-level executives or front-line employees result in universal disapproval and powerful penalties. Conformity to the rules becomes the primary basis for reward and upward mobility.[16]

As we'll show later in this chapter, who is made job offers to join the organization, who is appraised as a high performer, and who gets the promotions are strongly influenced by the individual-organization "fit"—that is, whether the applicant or employee's attitudes and behavior are compatible with the culture. It is not a coincidence that employees at Disneyland and Disney World appear to be almost universally attractive, clean, wholesome-looking, with bright smiles. That's the image Disney seeks. The company selects employees who will maintain that image. And once on the job, both the informal norms and formal rules and regulations ensure that Disney employees will act in a relatively uniform and predictable way.

Culture as a Liability   We are treating culture in a nonjudgmental manner. We haven't said that it's good or bad, only that it exists. Many of its functions, as outlined, are valuable for both the organization and the employee. Culture enhances organizational commitment and increases the consistency of employee behavior. These are clearly benefits to an organization. From an employee's standpoint, culture is valuable because it reduces ambiguity. It tells employees how things are done and what's important. But we shouldn't ignore the potentially dysfunctional aspects of culture, especially a strong one, on an organization's effectiveness.

Culture is a liability where the shared values are not in agreement with those that will further the organization's effectiveness. This is most likely to occur when the organization's environment is dynamic. When the environment is undergoing rapid change, the organization's entrenched culture may no longer be appropriate. So consistency of behavior is an asset to an organization when it faces a stable environment. It may, however, burden the organization

---

[16] T. E. Deal and A. A. Kennedy, "Culture: A New Look Through Old Lenses," *Journal of Applied Behavioral Science*, November 1983, p. 501.

and make it difficult to respond to changes in the environment. This helps to explain the challenges AT&T has had adapting to a deregulated environment.[17] Its strong service and technology-oriented culture, which originated in the nineteenth century, was amazingly effective as long as the company remained in the telephone business and held a monopoly there. But after deregulation, AT&T chose to compete in the telecommunications and computer industries against the likes of IBM, Xerox, and the Japanese. AT&T has had a difficult time adjusting to its new environment, largely due to the fact that it has had to try to create a new, more market-driven culture and that its pre-deregulation culture was so strong.

Creating and Sustaining Culture

An organization's culture doesn't pop out of thin air. Once established, it rarely fades away. What forces influence the creation of a culture? What reinforces and sustains these forces once they are in place? We'll answer both of these questions in this section.

How a Culture Begins   An organization's current customs, traditions, and general way of doing things are largely due to what it has done before and the degree of success it had with those endeavors. This leads us to the ultimate source of an organization's culture: its founders.

The founders of an organization traditionally have a major impact in establishing the early culture. They have a vision or mission of what the organization should be. They are unconstrained by previous customs of doing things or ideologies. The small size that typically characterizes any new organization further facilitates the founders' imposing their vision on all organizational members. Because the founders have the original idea, they also typically have biases on how to get the idea fulfilled. The organization's culture results from the interaction between (1) the founders' biases and assumptions, and (2) what the original members that the founders initially employ learn subsequently from their own experiences.[18]

Henry Ford at the Ford Motor Company, Thomas Watson at IBM, J. Edgar Hoover at the FBI, Thomas Jefferson at the University of Virginia, Walt Disney at Disney Productions, Ray Kroc at McDonald's, David Packard at Hewlett-Packard, and Steven Jobs and Stephen Wozniak at Apple Computer are just a few obvious examples of individuals who have had immeasurable impact in shaping their organization's culture. For instance, Watson's views on research and development, product innovation, employee dress attire, and compensation policies are still evident at IBM, though he died in 1956. Disney Production continues to focus on Walt Disney's original vision of a company that created fantasy entertainment. McDonald's commitment to the values of quality, service, and cleanliness were originally proposed by Ray Kroc. The formality found today

[17] M. Langley, "AT&T Has Call for a New Corporate Culture," *The Wall Street Journal*, February 28, 1984, p. 24; and S. P. Feldman, "Culture and Conformity: An Essay on Individual Adaptation in Centralized Bureaucracy," *Human Relations*, April 1985, pp. 341–56.

[18] E. H. Schein, "The Role of the Founder in Creating Organizational Culture," *Organizational Dynamics*, Summer 1983, pp. 13–28.

OB Close-Up

Wal-Mart Personifies Sam Walton

Sam Walton may be the richest person in America—he's worth an estimated $6.5 billion—but the sixty-nine-year-old founder and chairman of Wal-Mart Stores' attitudes and life-style project the values that have made Wal-Mart the fourth largest U.S. retailer and closing fast on number three, J. C. Penney.[19]

Mr. Sam, as employees call the boss, drives a 1984 Ford pick-up, and his Bentonville, Arkansas office, covered in bargain-basement paneling, is appointed mostly with strewn-about books and computer printouts. He wears flannel shirts and khaki pants to work, lives in a modest brick-and-wood ranch-style house, and eats his breakfast each morning at the Ramada Inn coffee shop. He pays $5 for a haircut (with no tip) and a "night on the town" with his wife is typically a dinner of ribs and cheesecake at Fred's Hickory Inn. Not exactly the kind of opulence that will bring Robin Leach and his "Lifestyles of the Rich and Famous" crew to Bentonville, Arkansas!

Yet it's exactly this lifestyle that Mr. Sam has transferred to his Wal-Mart discount chain. Like its founder, Wal-Mart has a culture that values frugality, simplicity, and humility. Sam Walton has created a culture for Wal-Mart that has allowed it to effectively dominate retail shopping in small towns throughout the Sunbelt and Midwest.

---

at the University of Virginia is due, in large part, to the original culture created by its founder, Thomas Jefferson. Apple's informal and creative culture was established by Steve Jobs.

Keeping a Culture Alive Once a culture is in place, there are practices within the organization that act to maintain it by giving employees a set of similar experiences. For example, many of the human resource practices discussed in the previous chapter reinforce the organization's culture. The selection process, performance evaluation criteria, reward practices, training and career development activities, and promotion procedures ensure that those hired fit in with the culture, reward those who support it, and penalize (and even expel) those who challenge it. Three forces play a particularly important part in sustaining a culture—selection practices, the actions of top management, and socialization methods. Let's take a closer look at each.

The explicit goal of the *selection process* is to identify and hire individuals who have the knowledge, skills, and abilities to perform the jobs within the organization successfully. But, typically, more than one candidate will be identified who meets any given job's requirements. When that point is reached, it

---

[19] "Make That Sale, Mr. Sam," *Time,* May 18, 1987, pp. 54–55.

would be naive to ignore that the final decision as to who is hired will be significantly influenced by the decision maker's judgment of how well the candidates will fit into the organization. This attempt to ensure a proper match, whether purposely or inadvertently, results in the hiring of people who have common values (ones essentially consistent with those of the organization) or at least a good portion of those values.[20] Additionally, the selection process provides information to applicants about the organization. Candidates learn about the organization, and, if they perceive a conflict between their values and those of the organization, they can self-select themselves out of the applicant pool. Selection, therefore, becomes a two-way street, allowing either employer or applicant to abrogate a marriage if there appears to be a mismatch. In this way, the selection process sustains an organization's culture by selecting out those individuals who might attack or undermine its core values.

Applicants for entry-level positions in brand management at Procter & Gamble experience an exhaustive application and screening process. Their interviewers are part of an elite cadre who have been selected and trained extensively via lectures, video tapes, films, practice interviews, and role plays to identify applicants who will successfully fit in at P&G. Applicants are interviewed in depth for such qualities as their ability to "turn out high volumes of excellent work," "identify and understand problems," and "reach thoroughly substantiated and well reasoned conclusions that lead to action." P&G values rationality and seeks applicants who think that way. College applicants receive two interviews and a general knowledge test on campus, before being flown back to Cincinnati for three more one-on-one interviews and a group interview at lunch. Each encounter seeks corroborating evidence of the traits that the firm believes correlate highly with "what counts" for success at P&G.[21] Applicants for positions at Compaq Computer are carefully chosen for their ability to fit into the company's teamwork-oriented culture. As one executive put it, "We can find lots of people who are competent . . . The No. 1 issue is whether they fit into the way we do business."[22] At Compaq, that means job candidates who are easy to get along with and feel comfortable with the company's consensus management style. To increase the likelihood that loners and those with big egos get screened out, it's not unusual for a new hire to interview with fifteen people who represent all departments of the company and a variety of seniority levels.[23]

The actions of *top management* also have a major impact on the organization's culture.[24] Through what they say and how they behave, senior executives establish norms that filter down through the organization as to whether risk taking is desirable; how much freedom managers should give their subordinates; what is appropriate dress; what actions will pay off in terms of pay raises, promotions, and other rewards; and the like.

[20] G. Salaman, "The Sociology of Assessment: The Regular Commissions Board Assessment Procedure," in *People and Organizations: Media Booklet II* (Milton Keynes, England: Open University Press, 1974).

[21] R. Pascale, "The Paradox of 'Corporate Culture': Reconciling Ourselves to Socialization," *California Management Review*, Winter 1985, pp. 26–27.

[22] "Who's Afraid of IBM?," *Business Week*, June 29, 1987, p. 72.

[23] Ibid.

[24] D. C. Hambrick and P. A. Mason, "Upper Echelons: The Organization as a Reflection of Its Top Managers," *Academy of Management Review*, April 1984, pp. 193–206.

For example, look at Xerox Corp.[25] Its chief executive from 1961 to 1968 was Joseph C. Wilson. An aggressive, entrepreneurial type, he oversaw Xerox's staggering growth on the basis of its 914 copier, one of the most successful products in American history. Under Wilson, Xerox had an entrepreneurial environment, with an informal, high-camaraderie, innovative, bold, risk-taking culture. Wilson's replacement as CEO was C. Peter McColough, a Harvard MBA with a formal management style. He instituted bureaucratic controls and a major change in Xerox's culture. When McColough stepped down in 1982, Xerox had become stodgy and formal, with lots of politics and turf battles and layers of watchdog managers. Today, Xerox's CEO is David T. Kearns. He believed the culture he inherited hindered Xerox's ability to compete. To increase the company's competitiveness, Kearns has trimmed Xerox down by cutting 15,000 jobs, delegated decision making downward, and refocused the organization's culture around a simple theme: boosting the quality of Xerox products and services. By his actions and those of his senior managerial cadre, Kearns is conveying to everyone at Xerox that the company values and rewards quality, innovative thinking, efficiency, and staying on top of the competition.

No matter how good a job the organization does in recruiting and selection, new employees are not fully indoctrinated in the organization's culture. Maybe most important, because they are least familiar with the organization's culture, new employees are potentially most likely to disturb the beliefs and customs that are in place. The organization will, therefore, want to help new employees adapt to its culture. This adaptation process is called **socialization**.[26]

Socialization

The process that adapts employees to the organization's culture.

All Marines must go through boot camp, where they "prove" their commitment. Of course, at the same time, the Marine trainers are indoctrinating new recruits in the "Marine way." The success of any cult depends on effective socialization. New Moonies undergo a "brainwashing" ritual that substitutes group loyalty and commitment for family. New Morgan Guaranty bank employees go through a one year training program that tests their intellect, endurance, and that requires teamwork as an essential factor of survival. The reason is that Morgan Guaranty wants to mold new members into the firms collegial style.

As we discuss socialization, keep in mind that the most critical socialization stage is at the time of entry into the organization. This is when the organization seeks to mold the outsider into an employee in "good standing." Those employees who fail to learn the essential or pivotal role behaviors risk being labeled "nonconformists" or "rebels," which often leads to expulsion. But the organization will be socializing every employee, though maybe not as explicitly, throughout his or her entire career in the organization. This further contributes to sustaining the culture.

Socialization can be conceptualized as a process made up of three stages: prearrival, encounter, and metamorphosis.[27] The first stage encompasses all the learning that occurs before a new member joins the organization. In the

[25] "Culture Shock at Xerox," *Business Week*, June 22, 1987, pp. 1, 6–10.

[26] See, for instance, J. E. Hebden, "Adopting an Organization's Culture: The Socialization of Graduate Trainees," *Organizational Dynamics*, Summer 1986, pp. 54–72; and G. R. Jones, "Socialization Tactics, Self-Efficacy, and Newcomers' Adjustments to Organizations," *Academy of Management Journal*, June 1986, pp. 262–79.

[27] J. Van Maanen and E. H. Schein, "Career Development," in J. R. Hackman and J. L. Suttle (eds.), *Improving Life at Work* (Santa Monica, CA: Goodyear, 1977), pp. 58–62.

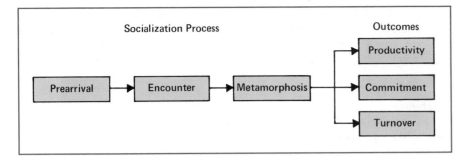

FIGURE 15–1
A Socialization Model

second stage, the new employee sees what the organization is really like and confronts the likelihood that expectations and reality may diverge. In the third stage, the relatively long-lasting changes take place. The new employee masters the skills required for his or her job, successfully performs his or her new roles, and makes the adjustments to his or her work group's values and norms.[28] This three-stage process impacts on the new employee's work productivity, commitment to the organization's objectives, and his or her decision to stay with the organization. Figure 15–1 depicts this process.

The **prearrival stage** explicitly recognizes that each individual arrives with a set of values, attitudes, and expectations. These cover both the work to be done and the organization. For instance, in many jobs, particularly professional work, new members will have undergone a considerable degree of prior socialization in training and in school. One major purpose of a business school, for example, is to socialize business students to the attitudes and behaviors that business firms want. If business executives believe that successful employees value the profit ethic, are loyal, will work hard, desire to achieve, and willingly accept directions from their superiors, they can hire individuals out of business schools who have been premolded in this pattern. But prearrival socialization goes beyond the specific job. The selection process is used in most organizations to inform prospective employees about the organization as a whole. In addition, as noted previously, the selection process also acts to ensure the inclusion of the "right type"—those who will fit in. "Indeed, the ability of the individual to present the appropriate face during the selection process determines his ability to move into the organization in the first place. Thus, success depends on the degree to which the aspiring member has correctly anticipated the expectations and desires of those in the organization in charge of selection."[29]

Upon entry into the organization, the new member enters the **encounter stage**. Here the individual confronts the possible dichotomy between her expectations—about her job, her co-workers, her boss, and the organization in general—and reality. If expectations prove to have been more or less accurate, the encounter stage merely provides for a reaffirmation of the perceptions gained earlier. However, this is often not the case. Where expectations and reality differ, the new employee must undergo socialization that will detach

Prearrival stage

The period of learning in the socialization process that occurs before a new employee joins the organization.

Encounter stage

The stage in the socialization process in which a new employee sees what the organization is really like and confronts the likelihood that expectations and reality may diverge.

[28] D. C. Feldman, "The Multiple Socialization of Organization Members," *Academy of Management Review*, April 1981, p. 310.

[29] Van Maanen and Schein, "Career Development," p. 59.

her from her previous assumptions and replace these with another set that the organization deems desirable. At the extreme, a new member may become totally disillusioned with the actualities of her job and resign. Proper selection should significantly reduce the probability of the latter occurrence.

TABLE 15–2
Entry Socialization Options

Formal or Informal? New employees may be put directly into their jobs, with no effort made to differentiate them from those who have been doing the job for a considerable length of time. Such cases represent examples of informal socialization—it takes place on the job and the new member gets little or no special attention. In contrast, socialization can be formal. The more formal the program, the more the new employee is segregated from the ongoing work setting and differentiated in some way to make explicit the newcomer's role. The more formal a socialization program, the more likely it is that management has participated in its design and execution and, hence, the more likely that the recruit will experience the learning that management desires. In contrast, the more informal the program, the more success will depend on the new employee selecting the correct socialization agents.

Individual or Collective? Another choice to be made by management is whether to socialize new members individually or to group them together and process them through an identical set of experiences. The individual approach is likely to develop far less homogeneous views than collective socialization. As with the informal structure, individual socializing is more likely to preserve individual differences and perspectives.

Fixed or Variable Time Period? A third major consideration for management is whether the transition from outsider to insider should be done on a fixed or variable time period. A fixed schedule reduces uncertainty for the new member since transition is standardized. Successful completion of certain standardized steps means that he or she will be accepted to full-fledged membership. Variable schedules, in contrast, give no advanced notice of their transition timetable. Variability characterizes the socialization for most professionals and managerial personnel.

Serial or Disjunctive? When an experienced organizational member, familiar with the new member's job, guides or directs a new recruit, this is serial socialization. In this process, the experienced member acts as a tutor and model for the new employee. When the recruit does not have predecessors available to offer guidance or a model for behavior, this is disjunctive socialization. Serial socialization maintains traditions and customs. It is preferred by organizations that seek to minimize the possibility of change over time. On the other hand, disjunctive socialization is likely to produce more inventive and creative employees because recruits are not burdened by traditions.

Investiture or Divestiture? Does management seek to confirm or dismantle the incoming identity of the new member? Investiture rites ratify the usefulness of the characteristics that the person brings to the new job. These individuals have been selected on the basis of what they can bring to the job. The organization does not want to change these recruits, so entry is made as smooth and trouble free as possible. If this is the goal, socialization efforts concentrate on reinforcing that "we like you just the way you are." Far more often there is a desire to strip away certain entering characteristics of a recruit. The selection process identified the candidate as a potential high performer; now it is necessary to make those minor modifications to improve the fit between the candidate and the organization. This fine-tuning may take the shape of requiring the recruit to sever old friendships; accepting a different way of looking at his or her job, peers, or the organization's purpose; doing a number of demeaning jobs to prove commitment; or even undergoing harassment and hazing by more experienced personnel to verify that he or she fully accepts his or her role in the organization.

Source: Adapted from J. Van Maanen, "People Processing: Strategies of Organizational Socialization," *Organizational Dynamics,* Summer 1978 (New York: AMACOM, a division of American Management Associations), pp. 19–36.

Finally, the new member must work out any problems discovered during the encounter stage. This may mean going through changes—hence, we call this the **metamorphosis stage**. The choices presented in Table 15–2 are alternatives designed to bring about the desired metamorphosis. But what is a desirable metamorphosis? We can say that metamorphosis is complete, and the entry socialization process, when the new member has become comfortable with the organization and his or her job. She has internalized the norms of the organization and her work group, and understands and accepts these norms. The new member feels accepted by her peers as a trusted and valued individual, is self-confident that she has the competence to complete the job successfully, and understands the system—not only her own tasks, but the rules, procedures, and informally accepted practices as well. Finally, she knows how she will be evaluated, that is, what criteria will be used to measure and appraise her work. She knows what is expected, and what constitutes a job "well done." As Figure 15–1 shows, successful metamorphosis should have a positive impact on the new employee's productivity and her commitment to the organization, and reduce her propensity to leave the organization.

Summary: How Cultures Form   Figure 15–2 summarizes how an organization's culture is established and sustained. The original culture is derived from the founder's philosophy. This, in turn, strongly influences the criteria used in hiring. The actions of the current top management set the general climate of what is acceptable behavior and what is not. How employees are to be socialized will depend on the degree of success achieved in matching new employee's values to those of the organization's in the selection process and top management's preference for socialization methods.

How Employees Learn Culture

Culture is transmitted to employees in a number of forms—the most potent being through stories, rituals, material symbols, and language.

Stories   In 1983, I spoke to a group of senior executives with the Electronic Data Systems Corporation, when the firm was run by H. Ross Perot, who later sold it to General Motors. One of EDS' more well-known stories is how, in 1979, Perot put together a team of six EDS managers in the United States and

FIGURE 15–2
How Organization Cultures Form

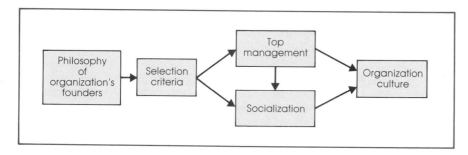

smuggled them into Iran in order to free two company executives being held in jail by the Khomeini regime for unsubstantiated charges of wrongdoing by the corporation. The team went into immediate training, developed an elaborate scheme to get into Iran, and upon their arrival succeeded in finding where the EDS executives were being held and initiating a mob to storm their prison. These two were freed along with 13,000 other prisoners. The team then led the two executives to safety by way of a sophisticated escape plan through Afghanistan.

I asked the more than 150 executives during my talk how many had been hired after that raid on the Iranian prison. About forty hands went up. Then I asked this group if anyone had *not* heard this story before. They had all heard it. (This was before this story became immortalized in a book[30] and a television movie.) I then inquired when they heard it. All but three had been told the story during the interview process with EDS. The rest heard it within their first few days on the job. I then asked all the EDS executives to tell me what they thought the meaning of this story was. They quickly honed in on things like "This company stands behind its people;" "Loyalty goes two ways—we're loyal to EDS and they're loyal to us;" "No barrier is too great to stop Ross Perot or EDS from achieving a goal once it's set;" and "EDS is one big family. When someone is in trouble, they can depend on their family for help."

Stories such as this circulate through many organizations, though they are rarely as dramatic. They typically contain a narrative of events about the organization's founders, rule-breaking, rags-to-riches successes, reductions in the workforce, relocation of employees, reactions to past mistakes, and organizational coping.[31] These stories anchor the present in the past and provide explanations and legitimacy for current practices.[32]

Rituals

Rituals
Repetitive sequences of activities that express and reinforce the key values of the organization, what goals are most important, which people are important and which are expendable.

Rituals   Rituals are repetitive sequences of activities that express and reinforce the key values of the organization, what goals are most important, which people are important and which are expendable.[33]

College faculty members undergo a lengthy ritual in their quest for permanent employment—tenure. Typically, the faculty member is on probation for six years. At the end of that period, the member's colleagues must make one of two choices: extend a tenured appointment or issue a one-year terminal contract. What does it take to obtain tenure? It usually requires satisfactory teaching performance, service to the department and university, and scholarly activity. But, of course, what satisfies the requirements for tenure in one department at one university may be appraised as inadequate in another. The key is that the tenure decision, in essence, asks those who are tenured to assess whether the candidate has demonstrated, based on six years of performance, whether he or she fits in. Colleagues who have been socialized properly will have proved themselves worthy of being granted tenure. Every year, hundreds of faculty members at colleges and universities are denied tenure. In some

---

[30] K. Follett, *On Wings of the Eagles* (New York: William Morrow, 1983).

[31] J. Martin, M. S. Feldman, M. J. Hatch, and S. B. Sitkin, "The Uniqueness Paradox in Organizational Stories," *Administrative Science Quarterly*, September 1983, pp. 438–53.

[32] A. M. Pettigrew, "On Studying Organizational Cultures," *Administrative Science Quarterly*, December 1979, p. 576.

[33] Ibid.

cases, this action is a result of poor performance across the board. More often, however, the decision can be traced to the faculty member's not doing well in those areas that the tenured faculty believe are important. The instructor who spends dozens of hours each week preparing for class, achieves outstanding evaluations by students, but neglects his or her research and publication activities, may be passed over for tenure. What has happened, simply, is that the instructor has failed to adapt to the norms set by the department. The astute faculty member will assess early on in the probationary period what attitudes and behaviors his or her colleagues want and will then proceed to give it to them. And, of course, by doing so the tenured faculty have made significant strides toward standardizing tenure candidates.

One of the best-known corporate rituals is Mary Kay Cosmetics' annual award meeting.[34] Looking like a cross between a circus and a Miss America pageant, the meeting takes place over a couple of days in a large auditorium, on a stage in front of a large, cheering audience, with all the participants dressed in glamorous evening clothes. Saleswomen are rewarded with an array of flashy gifts—gold and diamond pins, fur stoles, pink Cadillacs—based on success in achieving sales quota. This "show" acts as a motivator by publicly recognizing outstanding sales performance. In addition, the ritual aspect reinforces Mary Kay's personal determination and optimism that enabled her to overcome personal hardships, found her own company, and achieve material success. It conveys to her salespeople that reaching their sales quota is important and through hard work and encouragement they too can achieve success.

Material Symbols   Tandem Computers' headquarters in Cupertino, California, doesn't look like your typical head office operation. It has jogging trails, a basketball court, space for dance and yoga classes, and a large swimming pool—all for its employees' enjoyment. Every Friday afternoon at 4:30, employees partake in the weekly beer bust, courtesy of the company.[35] This informal corporate headquarters conveys to employees that Tandem values openness and equality.

Some corporations provide their top executives with chauffeur-driven limousines and, when they travel by air, unlimited use of the corporate jet. Others may not get to ride in limousines or private jets but they might still get a car and air transportation paid for by the company. Only, the car is a Chevrolet (with no driver) and the jet seat is in the economy section of a commercial airliner.

The layout of corporate headquarters, the types of automobiles top executives are given, and the presence or absence of corporate aircraft are a few examples of material symbols. Others include the size and layout of offices, the elegance of furnishings, executive perks, and dress attire. These material symbols convey to employees who is important, the degree of egalitarianism desired by top management, and the kinds of behavior (for example, risk-taking, conservative, authoritarian, participative, individualistic, social) that are appropriate.

[34] Cited in J. M. Beyer and H. M. Trice, "How an Organization's Rites Reveal Its Culture," *Organizational Dynamics*, Spring 1987, p. 15.

[35] M. Magnet, "Managing by Mystique at Tandem Computers," *Fortune*, June 28, 1982, pp. 84–91.

OB Close-Up

Cultural Compatibility in Acquisition Decisions

When acquisitions succeed or fail, cultural compatibility has increasingly been looked to for an explanation. While a favorable financial statement or product synergy may be the initial attraction to an acquisition candidate, whether the acquisition actually works may have more to do with how well the two organizations' cultures match up. A few examples can illustrate.

In 1984, General Motors purchased the computer services firm Electronic Data Systems Corp. for $2.5 billion. GM is a large, impersonal bureaucracy, with a strong culture that emphasizes loyalty, keeping a low profile and risk-aversion. EDS was a much smaller firm, with an equally strong culture that valued discipline, determination, competitiveness, risk-taking, and a twenty-four-hour-a-day commitment from its employees. EDS also was fully a reflection of its founder and CEO, Ross Perot. The merger was likened to a Green Beret outfit joining up with the Social Security Administration. EDS claimed its greatest asset was its people, while GM claimed its greatest asset was its cars. Not surprisingly, the EDS-GM marriage has been a rough one.[36] GM data-processing workers resented their transfer to EDS and scorned EDS's rules banning beards and drinking at lunch. EDS workers, meanwhile, viewed GM employees as lazy bureaucrats who couldn't make decisions. In 1986, GM tried unsuccessfully to sell EDS to AT&T. Currently, the car maker continues to deal with the problems of integrating EDS into its operations.

In 1983, BankAmerica Corp. purchased the discount brokerage firm of Charles Schwab & Co. Again, the companies were a mismatch from the beginning. BofA was conservative. Schwab, on the other hand, built its reputation on aggressiveness. It sought out and hired only outgoing and what some might call "flashy" brokers. One of the most obvious symbols of the differences between these two firms was in the cars their executives drove. BofA executives were provided with four-door, American-made sedans. Top executives at Schwab also drove company cars but theirs were Ferraris, Porsches, and BMWs. This mismatch was corrected in 1987, when Charles Schwab bought his company back from BankAmerica.

Acquisitions are much more likely to succeed when, as at Hershey Foods, care is taken to find appropriate candidates with a compatible culture. "It's like a marriage," says Hershey's CEO. "If the core values of two individuals or companies don't mesh, then the match should never take place—no matter how attractive it might seem from other angles."[37] Hershey's values boil down to four: people orientation, consumer- and quality-consciousness, honesty and integrity, and results-orientation. As Hershey's management has acquired firms like the Friendly Restaurant chain and San Giorgio-Skinner pasta, an understanding of its own culture and its compatibility with the cultures of its takeover candidates has resulted in an uninterrupted string of acquisition successes.

---

[36] "General Motors' Move to Sell EDS Fails, Highlights Problems of Integrating Unit," *The Wall Street Journal*, November 24, 1986, p. 3 and 20.

[37] S. J. Blank, "Hershey: A Company Driven by Values," *Personnel*, February 1987, p. 46.

Language Many organizations and units within organizations use language as a way to identify members of a culture or subculture. By learning this language, members attest to their acceptance of the culture and, in so doing, help to preserve it.

The kitchen personnel in a large hotel use terminology foreign to hotel people outside this area. Members of the U.S. Army sprinkle their language liberally with jargon that readily identifies its members. Many organizations, over time, develop unique terms to describe equipment, offices, key personnel, suppliers, customers, or products that relate to its business. New employees are frequently overwhelmed with acronyms and jargon that, after six months on the job, have become fully part of their language. But once assimilated, this terminology acts as a common denominator that unites members of a given culture or subculture.

NATIONAL CULTURE

The vast majority of research studies that have provided the basis for the conclusions made in this book were conducted in the United States with American subjects. If people in all the nations of the world were similar, our U.S. findings would be generalizable to employees in any country. Unfortunately, there is a growing body of evidence to indicate that **national cultures** differ widely and the result is marked differences in behavior patterns worldwide. A comparison between the United States and Japan can illustrate this point.

National culture

The primary values and practices that characterize a particular country.

American children are taught early the values of individuality and uniqueness. In contrast, Japanese children are indoctrinated to be "team players," to work within the group, and to conform. A significant part of an American student's education is to learn to think, analyze, and question. Their Japanese counterparts are rewarded for recounting facts. These different socialization practices result in different types of employees. The average U.S. worker is more competitive and self-focused than is the Japanese worker. Predictions of employee behavior, based on samples of U.S. workers, are likely to be off target when they are applied to a population of employees—like the Japanese— who prefer and perform better in standardized tasks, as part of a work team, with group-based decisions and rewards.

Cultural Clusters

The world is far from homogeneous. There are cultural differences between countries. Yet, each country is not completely unique. In recent years, considerable progress has been made in the area of cultural analysis. Research has demonstrated that countries can be grouped into meaningful categories or clusters, based on geography, shared language, and similar religions.[38] Figure 15–3 shows eight **cultural clusters** encompassing forty-two different countries. Those eight clusters are Near Eastern, Nordic, Germanic, Anglo-American, Latin

Cultural clusters

Grouping countries into meaningful categories based on geography, shared language, and similar religions.

[38] S. Ronen and O. Shenkar, "Clustering Countries on Attitudinal Dimensions: A Review and Synthesis," *Academy of Management Review*, July 1985, pp. 435–54.

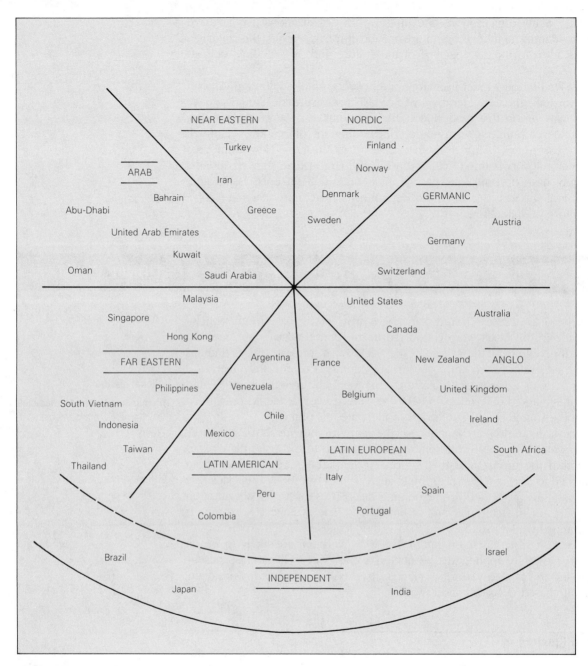

FIGURE 15–3
A Synthesis of Cultural Clusters

Source: S. Ronen and O. Shenkar, "Clustering Countries on Attitudinal Dimensions: A Review and Synthesis," *Academy of Management Review*, July 1985, p. 449.

European, Latin American, Far Eastern, and Arab. Countries are rated within each cluster by their per capita GNP. The most economically developed countries are closest to the center in Figure 15–3. Note that four countries—Brazil, Japan, India, and Israel—failed to fall into any cluster and thus were excluded.

What can we say about countries in common clusters? Essentially, their people share common values, attitudes, norms, and expectations. Work behaviors, then, should be more homogeneous among employees within clusters than across clusters. A German executive, for example, is more likely to be successful in managing an operation in Switzerland than a French or Italian manager because both Germany and Switzerland are in the Germanic cluster.

Cultural Dimensions

The concept of cultural clusters is important, but it would be valuable if we could narrow our focus a bit and identify the key dimensions that differentiate specific countries. Then we could make specific suggestions on how OB concepts we've discussed in this book might be modified for different countries. This is now possible, thanks to an illuminating cross-cultural study done by Geert Hofstede.[39] He surveyed 160,000 employees in sixty countries who all worked for a single multinational corporation. What did he find? His huge data base indicated that national culture had a major impact on employees' work-related values and attitudes. In fact, it explained more of the differences than did age, sex, profession, or position in the organization. More important, Hofstede found that managers and employees vary on four dimensions of national culture: (1) individualism versus collectivism, (2) power distance, (3) uncertainty avoidance, and (4) masculinity versus femininity.

Individualism vs. Collectivism **Individualism** refers to a loosely knit social framework in which people are supposed to look after their own interests and those of their immediate family. This is made possible because of the large amount of freedom that such a society allows individuals. Its opposite is **collectivism**, which is characterized by a tight social framework in which people expect others in groups of which they are a part (such as an organization) to look after them and protect them when they are in trouble. In exchange for this, they feel they owe absolute loyalty to the group.

Hofstede found that the degree of individualism in a country is closely related to that country's wealth. Rich countries like the United States, Great Britain, and the Netherlands are very individualistic. Poor countries like Colombia, Pakistan, and Taiwan are very collectivist.

Power Distance People naturally vary in terms of physical and intellectual abilities. This, in turn, creates differences in wealth and power. How does a society deal with these inequalities? Hofstede used the term **power distance** as a measure of the extent to which a society accepts the fact that power in institutions and organizations is distributed unequally. A high power distance society accepts wide differences in power in organizations. Employees show a great deal of respect for those in authority. Titles, rank, and status carry a lot of weight. When negotiating in high power distance countries, companies find it helps to send representatives with titles at least as high as those with whom they're bargaining. Countries high in power distance include the Philippines,

Individualism

A national culture attribute describing a loosely knit social framework in which people emphasize only the care of themselves and their immediate family.

Collectivism

A national culture attribute that describes a tight social framework in which people expect others in groups of which they are a part to look after them and protect them.

Power distance

A national culture attribute describing the extent to which a society accepts that power in institutions and organizations is distributed unequally.

[39] G. Hofstede, *Culture's Consequences: International Differences in Work-Related Values* (Beverly Hills, CA: Sage Publications, 1980); and G. Hofstede, "The Cultural Relativity of Organizational Practices and Theories," *Journal of International Business Studies*, Fall 1983, pp. 75–89.

Venezuela, and India. In contrast, a low power distance society plays down inequalities as much as possible. Superiors still have authority, but employees are not fearful or in awe of the boss. Denmark, Israel, and Austria are examples of countries with low power distance scores.

Uncertainty Avoidance We live in a world of uncertainty. The future is largely unknown and always will be. Societies respond to this uncertainty in different ways. Some socialize their members into accepting it with equanimity. People in such societies are more or less comfortable with risks. They're also relatively tolerant of behavior and opinions that differ from their own because they don't feel threatened by them. Hofstede describes such societies as having low **uncertainty avoidance**. That is, people feel relatively secure. Countries that fall into this category include Singapore, Hong Kong, and Denmark.

A society high in uncertainty avoidance is characterized by an increased level of anxiety among its people, which manifests itself in greater nervousness, stress, and aggressiveness. Because people feel threatened by uncertainty and ambiguity in these societies, mechanisms are created to provide security and reduce risk. Their organizations are likely to have more formal rules, there will be less tolerance for deviant ideas and behaviors, and members will strive to believe in absolute truths. Not surprisingly, in organizations in countries with high uncertainty avoidance, employees demonstrate relatively low job mobility, and lifetime employment is a widely practiced policy. Countries in this category include Japan, Portugal, and Greece.

Masculinity vs. Femininity The fourth dimension, like individualism and collectivism, represents a dichotomy. Hofstede called it masculinity versus femininity. Though his choice of terms is unfortunate (as you'll see, he gives them a strong sexist connotation), to maintain the integrity of his work we'll use his labels.

According to Hofstede, some societies allow both men and women to take many different roles. Others insist that people behave according to rigid sex roles. When societies make a sharp division between male and female activities, Hofstede claims "the distribution is always such that men take more assertive and dominant roles and women the more service-oriented and caring roles."[40] Under the category **masculinity** he puts societies that emphasize assertiveness and the acquisition of money and material things, while deemphasizing caring for others. In contrast, under the category **femininity** he puts societies that emphasize relationships, concern for others, and the overall quality of life. Where femininity dominates, members put human relationships before money and are concerned with the quality of life, preserving the environment, and helping others.

Hofstede found Japan to be the most masculine country. In Japan, almost all women are expected to stay home and take care of children. At the other extreme, he found the Nordic countries and the Netherlands to be the most feminine. There it's common to see men staying home as househusbands while their wives work; and working men are offered paternity leave to take care of newborn children.

Uncertainty avoidance

A national culture attribute describing the extent to which a society feels threatened by uncertain and ambiguous situations and tries to avoid them.

Masculinity

A national culture attribute describing the extent to which the dominant societal values are characterized by assertiveness, acquistion of money and things, and not caring for others or for the quality of life.

Femininity

A national culture attribute that emphasizes relationships, concern for others, and the overall quality of life.

---

[40] Hofstede, "The Cultural Relativity of Organizational Practices and Theories," p. 85.

Contrasting the U.S. and Other Nations

Comparing the forty countries on the four dimensions, Hofstede found the U.S. culture to rank as follows:

- Individualism/collectivism = Highest among the forty countries on individualism
- Power distance = Below average
- Uncertainty avoidance = Well below average
- Masculinity/femininity = Well above average on masculinity

The results are not inconsistent with the world image of the United States. The below-average score on power distance aligns with what one might expect from a representative type of government with democratic ideals. In this category, the United States would rate below nations with a small ruling class and a large, powerless set of subjects, and above those nations with very strong commitments to egalitarian values. The well-below-average ranking on uncertainty avoidance is also consistent with a representative type of government having democratic ideals. Americans perceive themselves as being relatively free from threats of uncertainty. The individualistic ethic is one of the most frequently used stereotypes to describe Americans, and, based on Hofstede's research, the stereotype seems well founded. The United States was ranked as the single most individualistic country in his entire set. Finally, the well-above-average score on masculinity is no surprise. Capitalism—which values aggressiveness and materialism—is consistent with Hofstede's masculine characteristics.

We haven't the space to review the results Hofstede obtained for each of the forty countries, although some examples of extreme scores are presented in Table 15–3. Since our concern is essentially with identifying similarities and differences among cultures, let's briefly identify those countries that are most like and least like the United States on the four dimensions.

The United States is strongly individualistic but low on power distance. This same pattern was exhibited by Great Britain, Australia, Canada, the Netherlands, and New Zealand. Those least similar to the United States on these dimensions were Venezuela, Colombia, Pakistan, Singapore, and the Philippines.

The United States scored low on uncertainty avoidance and high on masculinity. The same pattern was shown by Ireland, Great Britain, Philippines, Canada, New Zealand, Australia, India, and South Africa. Those least similar to the United States on these dimensions were Chile, Yugoslavia, and Portugal.

National Culture and Organizational Behavior

The implications of the previous findings are relevant to a number of the concepts introduced in this text. To illustrate this point, we can speculate on how motivation, leadership, and organization design theories might be modified when attempting to explain and predict the behavior of employees outside the United States.

Motivation   A good illustration of national differences can be seen through Maslow's hierarchy of needs. The hierarchy argues that people start at the

TABLE 15–3

Examples of Cultural Differences Among World Nations

Individualism	Collectivism
United States	Colombia
Australia	Venezuela
Great Britain	Pakistan
Canada	Peru

High Power Distance	Low Power Distance
Philippines	Austria
Mexico	Israel
Venezuela	Denmark
Yugoslavia	New Zealand

High Uncertainty Avoidance	Low Uncertainty Avoidance
Greece	Singapore
Portugal	Denmark
Belgium	Sweden
Japan	Hong Kong

High Masculinity	High Femininity
Japan	Sweden
Austria	Norway
Venezuela	Yugoslavia
Italy	Denmark

physiological level and then move progressively up the hierarchy in this order: physiological, safety, love, esteem, and self-actualization. This hierarchy, if it has any application at all, aligns with American culture. In countries like Japan, Greece, or Mexico, where uncertainty avoidance characteristics are strong, security needs would be on top of the need hierarchy. Countries that score high on femininity characteristics—Denmark, Sweden, Norway, the Netherlands, and Finland—would have social needs on top.[41] We would predict, for instance, that group work will motivate employees more when the country's cultures score high on the femininity criterion.

Another motivation concept that clearly has a U.S. bias is the achievement need. The view that a high achievement need acts as an internal motivator presupposes two cultural characteristics—a willingness to accept a moderate degree of risk (which excludes countries with strong uncertainty avoidance characteristics) and a concern with performance (countries with strong masculine characteristics). This combination is found exclusively in countries in the Anglo-American group and in some of their former colonies.[42]

MBO was introduced in Chapter 7 as a motivation technique. But MBO

[41] G. Hofstede, "Motivation, Leadership, and Organization: Do American Theories Apply Abroad?," *Organizational Dynamics*, Summer 1980, p. 55.

[42] Ibid.

is culture-bound. It is well adapted to the United States because its key components align reasonably well with U.S. culture.[43] MBO assumes that subordinates will be reasonably independent (not too high a score on power distance), that managers and subordinates will seek challenging goals (low in uncertainty avoidance), and that performance is considered important by both (high in masculinity). Countries in which the opposite conditions exist (such as Yugoslavia, Portugal, and Chile) are unlikely to accept MBO.

The use of work teams as a motivation device, also discussed in Chapter 7, should be more prevalent in cultures like Japan and less prevalent in places like India. Our reasoning follows Hofstede's findings. There are opposing forces operating in the U.S. culture working for and against group designs at the same time. You remember that the United States ranked below average on power distance and very high on individualism. The power distance ranking would suggest the use of groups to equalize power, while the high score on individualism would suggest the opposite. In countries such as Japan, where collectivism values are much stronger than those in the United States, employees will prefer work team designs. In contrast, employees in India—where power distance values are high—are likely to perform poorly in teams.

Leadership   Our review of the leadership literature in Chapter 10 concluded that effective leaders don't use a single style. They adjust their style to the situation. While not mentioned explicitly in our earlier discussion, certainly national culture—as well as the internal organizational culture—is an important situational variable determining which leadership style will be most effective.

National culture impacts on leadership by way of the subordinate. A leader cannot choose his or her style at will: "What is feasible depends to a large extent on the cultural conditioning of a leader's subordinates."[44] For example, a manipulative or autocratic style is compatible with high power distance, and we find high power distance scores in Latin American and Mediterranean countries. Power distance rankings should also be good indicators of employee willingness to accept participative leadership. Participation is likely to be most effective in low power distance cultures.

The implications of cross-cultural research for predicting leadership style are fairly straightforward. Effective leaders in high power distance cultures will tend to behave more autocratically, while effective leaders in very low power distance cultures will rely on a participative style.

Organization Design   Strategy, size, technology, and environment were shown in Chapter 13 as major factors influencing the structural design an organization has. Environment, of course, would include differences across national cultures.

In a country with a large power distance rating, people prefer that decisions be centralized.[45] Similarly, uncertainty avoidance characteristics relate to formalization. High uncertainty avoidance relates to high formalization.[46] Based on these relationships, we find certain patterns. The French and Italians tend to create rigid bureaucracies, high in both centralization and formalization. In

[43] Ibid, p. 58.
[44] Ibid., p. 57.
[45] Ibid., p. 60.
[46] Ibid.

India, preference is given to centralization and low formalization. Germans prefer formalization with decentralization.[47]

Cultural differences might also be used to predict the acceptance or rejection of innovative structural designs. For instance, the matrix's dual command structure requires greater tolerance for ambiguity, so cultures high in uncertainty avoidance characteristics may be less receptive to this structural design.

IMPLICATIONS FOR PERFORMANCE AND SATISFACTION

Cultural systems impose internal and external forces on employees. We call these forces organizational culture and national culture, respectively. Let's look at how each affects employee performance and satisfaction.

Organizational Culture

Figure 15–4 depicts organizational culture as an intervening variable. Employees form an overall subjective perception of the organization based on factors such as degree of autonomy, structure, reward orientation, warmth and support provided by managers, and willingness of management to tolerate conflict. This overall perception becomes, in effect, the organization's culture or personality. These favorable or unfavorable perceptions then affect employee performance and satisfaction, with the impact being greater for stronger cultures.

Does culture have an equal impact on both employee performance and satisfaction? The evidence says "No." There is a relatively strong relationship between culture and satisfaction, but this is moderated by individual differences.[48] In general, we propose that satisfaction will be highest when there is congruence between individual needs and the culture. For instance, an organization whose culture would be described as low in structure, having loose supervision, and rewarding people for high achievement is likely to have more satisfied employees if those employees have a high achievement need and prefer autonomy. Our conclusion, therefore, is that job satisfaction often varies according to the employee's perception of the organization's culture.

The relationship between culture and performance is less clear, although a number of studies find the two related.[49] But the relationship is moderated by the organization's technology.[50] Performance will be higher when the culture suits the technology. If the culture is informal, creative, and supports risk taking and conflict, performance will be higher if the technology is nonroutine. The more formally structured organizations that are risk aversive, that seek to eliminate conflict, and that are prone to more task-oriented leadership will achieve higher performance when routine technology is utilized.

[47] Ibid., and "Europe's New Managers," *Business Week*, May 24, 1982, p. 117.

[48] D. Hellriegel and J. W. Slocum, Jr., "Organizational Climate: Measures, Research, and Contingencies," *Academy of Management Journal*, June 1974, pp. 225–80.

[49] Ibid.

[50] J. W. Lorsch and J. J. Morse, *Organizations and Their Members* (New York: Harper & Row, 1974).

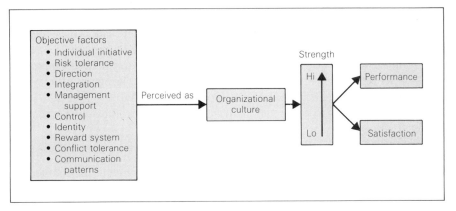

FIGURE 15–4
How Organizational Culture Impacts Performance and Satisfaction

We should not overlook the influence socialization has on employee performance. An employee's performance depends to a considerable degree on knowing what he should or should not do. Understanding the right way to do a job indicates proper socialization. Further, the appraisal of an individual's performance includes how well the person fits into the organization. Can he or she get along with co-workers? Does he or she have acceptable work habits, and demonstrate the right attitude? These qualities differ between jobs and organizations. For instance, on some jobs, employees will be evaluated higher if they are aggressive and outwardly indicate that they are ambitious. On another job, or on the same job in another organization, such an approach may be evaluated negatively. As a result, proper socialization becomes a significant factor in influencing both actual job performance and how it's perceived by others.

National Culture

The findings and conclusions presented in this book are, for the most part, based on research studies conducted in countries within the Anglo-American cluster. As long as you're concerned with trying to understand the behavior of employees born and raised in countries like the United States, Canada, Great Britain, and Australia, you should find it unnecessary to consider national culture as a confounding variable. It's not that national culture doesn't affect these individuals; it's just that the concepts we've discussed in this text already reflect this influence.

An understanding of differences between cultures should be particularly valuable for individuals who were born and raised in a non-Anglo-American cluster nation, those who plan on living and working in another country, or anyone who works with or manages people whose cultural backgrounds are different from his or her own.

If you fall into one of these groups, how do you use the information provided in the latter part of this chapter? First, determine from what country the person or persons whose behavior you're trying to understand comes. Second, evaluate the country of that person's origin in terms of Hofstede's four cultural dimensions. Third, compare this against the data for the United States (discussed in this chapter) and identify relevant differences. This is necessary because this text's frame of reference is essentially the United States. Finally, modify the concepts you've learned for explaining and predicting employee behavior to reflect these differences. Based on what we know about cultural differences, we should expect minimal modifications when the person whose behavior you're trying to understand is from a country within the Anglo-American cluster.

POINT

THE CASE AGAINST CULTURAL CHANGE

That an organization's culture is made up of relatively stable characteristics would imply that culture is very difficult for management to change. Such a conclusion would be correct.

An organization's culture develops over many years and is rooted in deeply held values to which employees are strongly committed. In addition, there are several forces continually operating to maintain a given culture. These would include written statements about the organization's mission and philosophy, the design of physical spaces and buildings, the dominant leadership style, hiring criteria, past promotion practices, entrenched rituals, popular stories about key people and events, the organization's historic performance evaluation criteria, and the organization's formal structure.

Selection and promotion policies are particularly important devices that work against cultural change. Employees chose the organization because they perceived their values to be a "good fit" with the organization. They become comfortable with that fit and will strongly resist efforts to disturb the equilibrium. Those in control will also select senior managers who will continue the current culture. Even attempts to change a culture by going outside the organization to hire a new chief executive are unlikely to be effective. The evidence indicates that the culture is more likely to change the executive than the other way around. Why? It's too entrenched, and change becomes a potential threat to member self-interest. In fact, a more pragmatic view of the relationship between an organization's culture and its chief executive would be to note that the practice of filling senior-level management positions from current managerial employees ensures that those who run the organization have been fully indoctrinated in the organization's culture. Promoting from within provides stability and lessens uncertainty. When Exxon's board of directors selects as a new chief executive officer an individual who has spent thirty years in the company, it virtually guarantees that the culture will continue unchanged.

Our argument, however, should not be viewed as saying that culture can never be changed. In the unusual case when an organization confronts a survival-threatening crisis—a crisis that is universally acknowledged as a true life-or-death situation—all members of the organization will be responsive to efforts at cultural change. But anything less is unlikely to be effective.

COUNTERPOINT

HOW TO CHANGE AN ORGANIZATION'S CULTURE

Changing an organization's culture is extremely difficult, but cultures *can* be changed. For example, Lee Iacocca came to Chrysler Corp. in 1978, when the company appeared to be only weeks away from bankruptcy. It took him about five years but, in what is now a well-worn story, he took Chrysler's conservative, inward-looking, and engineering-oriented culture and changed it into an action-oriented, market-responsive culture.

The evidence suggests that cultural change is most likely to take place when most or all of the following conditions exist:

A dramatic crisis. This is the shock that undermines the status quo and calls into question the relevance of the current culture. Examples of these crises might be a surprising financial setback, the loss of a major customer, or a dramatic technological breakthrough by a competitor.

Turnover in leadership. New top leadership, which can provide an alternative set of key values, may be perceived as more capable of responding to the crisis. This would definitely be the organization's chief executive but also might need to include all senior management positions.

Young and small organization. The younger the organization is, the less entrenched its culture will be. Similarly, it's easier for management to communicate its new values when the organization is small.

Weak culture. The more widely held a culture is and the higher the agreement among members on its values, the more difficult it will be to change. Conversely, weak cultures are more amendable to change than strong ones.

If conditions support cultural change, you should consider the following suggestions:

1. Have top management people become positive role models, setting the tone through their behavior.

2. Create new stories, symbols, and rituals to replace those currently in vogue.

3. Select, promote, and support employees who espouse the new values that are sought.

4. Redesign socialization processes to align with the new values.

5. Change the reward system to encourage acceptance of a new set of values.

6. Replace unwritten norms with formal rules and regulations that are tightly enforced.

7. Shake up current subcultures through extensive use of job rotation.

8. Work to get peer group consensus through utilization of employee participation and creation of a climate with a high level of trust.

Implementing most or all of these suggestions will not result in an immediate or dramatic shift in the organization's culture. Cultural change is a lengthy process—measured in years rather than months. But if the question is, "*Can* culture be changed?" the answer is "Yes!"

KEY TERMS

Collectivism	National Culture
Core Values	Organizational Culture
Cultural Clusters	Power Distance
Dominant Culture	Prearrival Stage
Encounter Stage	Rituals
Femininity	Socialization
Individualism	Strong Cultures
Institutionalization	Subcultures
Masculinity	Uncertainty Avoidance
Metamorphosis Stage	

FOR DISCUSSION

1. Contrast individual personality and organizational culture. How are they similar? How are they different?

2. What is the relationship between institutionalization, formalization, and organizational culture?

3. Can an employee survive in an organization if he or she rejects its core values? Explain.

4. What forces might contribute toward making a culture strong or weak?

5. How is an organization's culture maintained?

6. What benefits can socialization provide for the organization? For the new employee?

7. If management sought a culture characterized as innovative and autonomous, what might its socialization program look like?

8. If management sought a culture characterized as formalized and conflict free, what might its socialization program look like?

9. "We should be opposed to the manipulation of individuals for organizational purposes but a degree of social uniformity enables organizations to work better." Do you agree or disagree with this statement? Discuss.

10. Describe the U.S. culture in terms of the four major criteria by which cultures tend to differ.

11. How could you use Hofstede's research if you were an American manager transferred to Mexico?

12. In which countries are employees *most* like those in the United States? *Least* like those in the United States?

FOR FURTHER READING

ADLER, N. J., *International Dimensions of Organizational Behavior*. Boston: Kent Publishing, 1986. Discusses the impact of culture on organizations, managing cultural diversity, and managing international transitions.

FROST, P. J., L. F. MOORE, M. R. LOUIS, C. C. LUNDBERG, and J. MARTIN (eds.), *Organizational Culture*. Beverly Hills, CA: Sage Publications, 1985. An edited volume that discusses various perspectives on organizational culture, whether or not it can be managed, how it should be studied and how organizational cultures and the wider cultural context are linked.

GAGLIARDI, P., "The Creation and Change of Organizational Cultures: A Conceptual Framework," *Organization Studies*, Vol. 7, No. 2, 1986, pp. 117–34. When organizations find themselves with the wrong culture they can pursue cultural change, cultural revolution, or cultural incrementalism.

HARRIS, P. R., and R. T. MORAN, *Managing Cultural Differences*, 2nd ed. Houston: Gulf Publishing, 1987. A practical guide on cross-cultural training.

KILMANN, R. H., M. J. SAXTON, R. SERPA, *Gaining Control of the Corporate Culture*. San Francisco: Jossey-Bass, 1985. A collection of articles devoted to discussing methods for managing and changing cultures.

WILKINS, A. L., and N. J. BRISTOW, "For Successful Organization Culture, Honor Your Past," *Academy of Management Executive*, August 1987, pp. 221–28. The authors argue that for an organization to change its culture, it should build on its cultural roots and not blindly copy so-called "successful" organizations.

The following are a set of work issues that might be affected by national culture:

1. Role of women in organizations
2. Authority and decision making
3. Leadership style
4. Motivation techniques
5. Dealing with conflicts
6. Communication patterns

Take out a sheet of paper and make a matrix. Along the top, set up columns for each of the following countries: United States, Mexico, Canada, Sweden, and Pakistan. Along the left side, set up rows for each of the issues cited above. Now, as best you can, consider the behavioral implications from each of the six issues for working in the various countries.

After you've completed your matrix, form a group with two or three other people. Compare your analyses. Where your implications differ, discuss how you came to your conclusions.

CASE INCIDENT 15

NORDSTROM: WHERE SERVICE IS A SERIOUS BUSINESS

Nordstrom employees are fond of this story: When this specialty retail chain was in its infancy, a customer came in and wanted to return a set of automobile tires. The sales clerk was a bit uncertain how to handle the problem. As the customer and sales clerk spoke, Mr. Nordstrom walked by and overheard the conversation. He immediately interceded, asking the customer how much he paid for the tires. Mr. Nordstrom then instructed the clerk to take the tires back and provide a full cash refund. After the customer had received his refund and left, the perplexed clerk looked at the boss. "But, Mr. Nordstrom, we don't sell tires!" "I know," replied the boss, "but we do whatever we need to do to make the customer happy. I mean it when I say we have a no-questions-asked return policy." Nordstrom then picked up the telephone and called a friend in the auto parts business to see how much he could get for the tires.[51]

Without sacrificing style, variety, or value, Nordstrom distinguishes itself from its competition by its service. Cheerful Nordstrom employees are readily available to help customers and they will go to incredible lengths to make a sale. It is not unusual, for example, for a sales person to call a Nordstrom store hundreds of miles away to see if they have the item a customer wants. If they do, they have it shipped. Upon its arrival, the sales person may personally deliver the item to the customer's home.

In contrast to many retailers, every Nordstrom execu-tive started on the selling floor. Nordstrom rewards its salespeople with a salary, commission, and profit sharing package that is among the highest in its industry. College graduates start at $20,000 a year, and store managers can earn in excess of $100,000. The firm's rapid growth has meant rapid promotions for those who produce. The com-pany, which began in Seattle, now has fifty stores on the West Coast, has just opened its first stores on the East Coast, and is scouting for locations in the Midwest and South. Specialty retailers in these areas, many of whom have cut services to improve their profit margins, shiver at the thought of competing against Nordstrom. They know Nordstrom has a service culture that works. It also makes plenty of money. The company has the highest sales per square foot of any department store—more than 100 per-cent above the industry average. And profit growth ranks in retailing's top tier.

QUESTIONS

1. Compare Nordstrom's culture with the culture at a large department store you're familiar with. How do they com-pare?
2. What is the impact of the Nordstrom culture on its employ-ees?
3. If the Nordstrom culture has proven so successful, why don't competitors copy it?

[51] This case is partially based on T. Peters, "The Store Where the Action Is," *U.S. News & World Report*, May 12, 1986; and "Why Rivals Are Quaking as Nordstrom Heads East," *Business Week*, June 15, 1987, pp. 99–100.

16

Work Stress

■ *Learning objectives*

Describe potential sources of stress
Explain individual difference variables that moderate the stress-outcome relationship
Define stress consequences
Outline individual stress management strategies
List organizational stress management strategies

Ulcers? I give 'em, I don't get 'em.

Dawn Blackstone, Frank Greer, and Lynn Fleming talk about work stress.

Dawn: "I really loved my job as director of advertising. The pay was super and I had a great support staff. But I just couldn't take the pressure. Top management was constantly pushing me to increase our advertising revenues. The more I got, the more they wanted. I gave it my best for two years. Then my doctor told me I had ulcers. My stomach was hurting all the time. I was having trouble sleeping, too. Finally, I realized I had to get out. My new job has a lot less responsibility, and I'm making almost $10,000 a year less. But I'm sleeping nights again."

Frank: "I only got out of law school four years ago. I received an offer to join Cadwalader, Wickersham & Taft. $67,000 a year to start. What an opportunity! You know the Cadwalader law firm goes back to 1792? Well, I never worked so hard in my life. Harvard Law was a snap compared to practicing corporate law. I quit last month. I think I'm burned out. I'm going to take a few months off. Then maybe I'll get a contractor's license and begin building houses for a living."

Lynn: "I work a fourteen-hour day. I haven't taken a vacation in six years. Some people think investment banking is a pressure-cooker job. I don't. Sure, I put in lots of hours and there's a lot on the line—money-wise. But it's a real high. I try to get into the office by 6 A.M. As I come up on that elevator in the morning I can feel the excitement building inside me. When the doors open on my floor, I walk out primed and ready. It's like my days on the diving team in college. I used the pressure of competition to get myself psyched-up and then to get a peak performance. It's the same thing now. Except every day is the NCAA finals!"

Dawn, Frank, and Lynn's comments tell us that stress can have consequences for individuals and organizations. It may be negative, as experienced by Dawn and Frank. But as described by Lynn, stress can be constructive. In this chapter, we'll consider what causes stress, how it affects people differently, and ways individuals and organizations can manage stress.

The topic of stress and its relationship to worker behavior has only recently become a topic of interest to organizational researchers. Until about a dozen years ago, research on stress was essentially confined to its effect on health and was conducted by individuals in the medical profession. Why the recent concern with stress as an OB topic? First, stress appears to be linked to employee performance and satisfaction, so the topic is a relevant independent variable.

500   *Part IV   The Organization System*

Second, there is an implicit obligation of management to improve the quality of organizational life for employees. Because stress has been directly linked to coronary heart disease, a reduction in stress can increase both the general health and longevity of an organization's work force. Of course, this too can have performance implications.

One point of clarification is necessary before we proceed. The point is that the topic of stress has individual and group-level relevance as well as organization system implications. As we will show, an individual's stress level can be increased by such varied factors as his or her personality, role conflicts, or job's design. So work stress, while presented in this book's section on the organization system, is a multilevel concept.

WHAT IS STRESS?

Stress is a dynamic condition in which an individual is confronted with an opportunity, constraint, or demand related to what he or she desires and for which the outcome is perceived to be both uncertain and important.[1] This is a complicated definition. Let's look at its components more closely.

Stress is not necessarily bad in and of itself. While stress is typically discussed in a negative context, it also has positive value. It is an opportunity when it offers potential gain. Consider, for example, the superior performance that an athlete or stage performer gives in "clutch" situations. Such individuals often use stress positively to rise to the occasion and perform at or near their maximum.

More typically, stress is associated with **constraints** and **demands**. The former prevent you from doing what you desire. The latter refers to the loss of something desired. So when you take a test at school or you undergo your annual performance review at work, you feel stress because you confront opportunities, constraints, and demands. A good performance review may lead to a promotion, greater responsibilities, and a higher salary. But a poor review may prevent you from getting the promotion. An extremely poor review might even result in your being fired.

Two conditions are necessary for potential stress to become actual stress.[2] There must be uncertainty over the outcome and the outcome must be important. Regardless of the conditions, it is only when there is doubt or uncertainty regarding whether the opportunity will be seized, the constraint removed, or the loss avoided that there is stress. That is, stress is highest for those individuals who perceive that they are uncertain as to whether they will win or lose and lowest for those individuals who think that winning or losing is a certainty. But importance is also critical. If winning or losing is an unimportant outcome, there is no stress. If keeping your job or earning a promotion doesn't hold any importance to you, you have no reason to feel stress over having to undergo a performance review.

Stress

A dynamic condition in which an individual is confronted with an opportunity, constraint, or demand related to what he or she desires and for which the outcome is perceived to be both uncertain and important.

Constraints

Forces that prevent individuals from doing what they desire.

Demands

The loss of something desired.

[1] Adapted from R. S. Schuler, "Definition and Conceptualization of Stress in Organizations," *Organizational Behavior and Human Performance*, April 1980, p. 189.

[2] Ibid., p. 191.

IS WORK STRESS WIDESPREAD?

Whether work stress is actually a widespread problem depends on your definition of "widespread." There are no reliable statistics on stress intensity at work or the percentage of the work population suffering serious stress symptoms. However, we can approach the question from several other directions.

First, a lot of people in general seem to suffer from stress symptoms. For instance, the American Academy of Family Physicians estimates that two-thirds of office visits to its members are attributable to stress-related symptoms.[3]

Second, some stress seems to come with every job. Can you name three or four jobs that are stress-free? It's not as easy at it seems. Most of us can identify jobs that are high in stress—air traffic controllers, police officers, fire fighters, emergency room physicians. These are consistent with research that tells us that high stress jobs are those where incumbents have little control over their work, are under relentless time pressures, face threatening physical conditions, or have major responsibilities for financial or human resources.[4] But low-stress or, better yet, no-stress jobs are harder to identify. Jobs that are considered low on stress—farm laborer, household worker, stock handler, college professor[5] —are certainly not stress-free.

Third, the dramatic changes that have taken place in the economy—corporate raiders, increased foreign competition, deregulation, new technological innovations, and the like—have resulted in large layoffs in many organizations (especially the large ones) and the restructuring of jobs. The security provided by working for an AT&T, General Motors, or large government agency has been replaced with a reality that no one's job is totally safe. When co-workers or friends are losing their jobs and you fear for your own, stress levels are naturally going to increase.

Returning to our question—Is work stress widespread?—the answer would seem to be "yes." We're not saying that this stress level is necessarily high or even that it is seriously hindering most people in their work. A national survey of managers found that 65 percent believed that their jobs were more stressful than the average job.[6] But as Table 16–1 illustrates, the stressors that created above-average stress were factors like interruptions, role conflicts, and workload demands. And the ratings on these factors indicate that they were nowhere near the "always stressful" point (4 on a scale of 1 to 4).

UNDERSTANDING STRESS AND ITS CONSEQUENCES

What causes stress? What are its consequences for individual employees? Why is it that the same set of conditions that creates stress for one person seems

[3] C. Wallis, "Stress: Can We Cope?," *Time*, June 6, 1983.

[4] C. L. Cooper and R. Payne, *Stress at Work* (London: John Wiley, 1978).

[5] As reported in *U.S. News & World Report*, March 13, 1978, pp. 80–81.

[6] M. A. Tipgos, "The Things That Stress Us," *Management World*, June-August 1987, pp. 17–18.

TABLE 16-1

The Impact of Workplace Stressors
on Managerial Respondents
(n = 315)

Stressor	Average Rating of All Respondents*
Interruptions	2.8
Role conflict (conflicting demands on time by others)	2.7
Work load	2.6
Managing time on the job	2.4
Organizational politics	2.3
Finding time for outside activities	2.3
Responsibility for subordinates	2.3
Firing someone	2.3
Reprimanding or disciplining	2.3
Balancing personal life with worklife	2.2
Dealing with upper management	2.1
Reviewing performance	2.0
Role ambiguity (uncertainty of what others expect)	2.0
Pay/compensation	1.8
Interviewing and hiring	1.8
Overtime	1.7
Working with budgets	1.7
Working with computers	1.5
Travel	1.4

* On a scale of 1 to 4, where 1 means never or rarely stressful and 4 means always stressful.

Source: Reprinted from *Management World,* June–August 1987, with permission from AMS, Trevose, PA 19047. Copyright (1987) AMS.

to have little or no effect on another person? Figure 16–1 (on page 505) provides a model that can help to answer questions such as these.[7]

The model identifies three sets of factors—environmental, organizational, and individual—that act as *potential* sources of stress. Whether they become *actual* stress depends on individual differences such as job experience and personality. When stress is experienced by an individual, its symptoms can surface as physiological, psychological, and behavioral outcomes.

In the remainder of this chapter, we'll consider this model in more detail by reviewing the potential sources of stress, key individual difference variables, and stress consequences. Then we'll focus on stress management strategies that individuals themselves and organizations can utilize to help people cope with dysfunctional stress levels.

[7] This model is based on D. F. Parker and T. A. DeCotiis, "Organizational Determinants of Job Stress," *Organizational Behavior and Human Performance,* October 1983, p. 166; S. Parasuraman and J. A. Alutto, "Sources and Outcomes of Stress in Organizational Settings: Toward the Development of a Structural Model," *Academy of Management Journal,* June 1984, p. 333; and C. L. Cooper, "The Stress of Work: An Overview," *Aviation, Space, and Environmental Medicine,* July 1985, p. 628.

OB Close-Up

Is Stress Killing Off Many of Japan's Corporate Chiefs?

The chief executives of at least twelve major Japanese companies—including Seiko Epson, Kawasaki Steel, and All Nippon Airways—all died suddenly during the first seven months of 1987.[8] Coincidence? Maybe. But most were in their fifties and sixties, quite young to die in a country where the average male lives to age seventy-five. Many experts think that stress may be a prime contributor to the death of these executives.

From mid-1985 to mid-1987, the value of the Japanese yen rose 40 percent. This made Japanese products more expensive and reduced exports. The result was that many Japanese companies suffered slipping sales and profits.

Business executives in every country face downturns now and then. But in Japan, such downturns put extraordinary stress on top executives. Japanese managers are very competitive. Because they tend to spend their entire careers with a single company, they personally identify very closely with their firm's performance. Their company's success is their success. Their company's setbacks are also their setbacks. Additionally, the typical Japanese executive doesn't leave the office behind at the end of the day. Top executives have to attend a party or two after work almost every day, where they eat high-calorie food, drink a lot, and continue to talk business. Combine these workaholic tendencies with the added stress in economic hardtimes, and you have the ingredients for physiological disaster.

Interestingly, research indicates that there may be a pattern to the relationship between downturns in the Japanese economy and increased stress levels (as evidenced by sudden deaths among corporate executives) that goes beyond the problems in 1987. As a case in point, the incidence of heart attacks among Japanese managers was nearly four times as high during the oil crises of 1974 and 1979 as in the high-growth period of 1966–1968.[9]

POTENTIAL SOURCES OF STRESS

As the model in Figure 16–1 shows, there are three categories of potential stressors: environmental, organizational, and individual. Let's take a look at each.[10]

---

[8] J. M. Horowitz, "A Puzzling Toll at the Top," *Time*, August 3, 1987, p. 46.

[9] Ibid.

[10] This section is adapted from C. Cooper and R. Payne, *Stress at Work*; and S. Parasuraman and J. A. Alutto, "Sources and Outcomes of Stress in Organizational Settings," pp. 330–50.

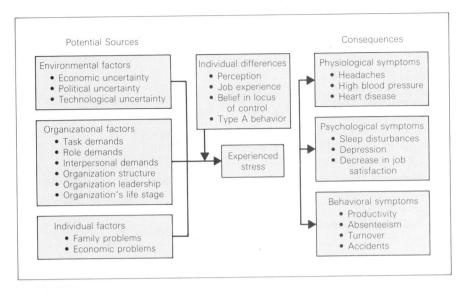

FIGURE 16–1
A Model of Stress

Environmental Factors

Just as environmental uncertainty influences the design of an organization's structure, it also influences stress levels among employees in that organization.

Changes in the business cycle create *economic uncertainties*. When the economy is contracting, people become increasingly anxious about their security. It was not a chance occurrence that suicide rates skyrocketed during the Great Depression of the 1930s. Minor recessions, too, increase stress levels. Downward swings in the economy are often accompanied by permanent reductions in force, temporary layoffs, reduced pay, shorter work weeks, and the like. The October 1987 stock market crash and the attendant speculation that another economic depression might be close at hand is a recent illustration of economic uncertainty raising anxiety levels among individuals.

Political uncertainties don't tend to create stress among North American employees as they do for employees in countries like Nicaragua or Iraq. The obvious reason is that the United States and Canada have stable political systems where change is typically implemented in an orderly manner. Yet political threats and changes, even in countries like the U.S. and Canada, can be stress-inducing. This is especially true when voters oust a political party from power. For instance, back in 1976, the Parti Québecois (PQ) was elected to power in the province of Quebec, Canada, replacing the thirty-year reign of the Liberal Party. Elected on the platform of separating Quebec from the rest of Canada, the PQ immediately made French the official language of the province, set new policies limiting English education, and arranged for an election to allow the citizens of Quebec to vote on separation. The political uncertainties that went with the election of the PQ caused considerable stress among the people of Quebec, particularly those with little or no skills in the French language.

New innovations can make an employee's skills and experience obsolete in a very short period of time. *Technological uncertainty*, therefore, is a third type of environmental factor that can cause stress. Computers, robotics, automation, and other forms of technological innovations are a threat to many people and cause them stress.

Organizational Factors

There are no shortages of factors within the organization that can cause stress: Pressures to avoid errors or complete tasks in a limited time period, work overload, a demanding and insensitive boss, and unpleasant co-workers are a few examples. We've categorized these factors around task, role, and interpersonal demands; organization structure; organizational leadership; and the organization's life stage.

Task demands are factors related to a person's job. They include the design of the individual's job (autonomy, task variety, degree of automation), working conditions, and the physical work layout. Assembly lines can put pressure on people when their speed is perceived as excessive. The more interdependence between a person's tasks and the tasks of others, the more potential stress there is. Autonomy, on the other hand, tends to lessen stress. Jobs where temperatures, noise, or other working conditions are dangerous or undesirable can increase anxiety. So, too, can working in an overcrowded room or in a visible location where interruptions are constant.

Role demands relate to pressures placed on a person as a function of the particular role he or she plays in the organization. Role conflicts create expectations that may be hard to reconcile or satisfy. Role overload is experienced when the employee is expected to do more than time permits. Role ambiguity is created when role expectations are not clearly understood and the employee is not sure what he or she is to do.

Interpersonal demands are pressures created by other employees. Lack of social support from colleagues and poor interpersonal relationships can cause considerable stress, especially among employees with a high social need.

Organization structure defines the level of differentiation in the organization, the degree of rules and regulations, and where decisions are made. Excessive rules and lack of participation in decisions that affect an employee are examples of structural variables that might be potential sources of stress.

Organizational leadership represents the managerial style of the organization's senior executives. Some chief executive officers create a culture characterized by tension, fear, and anxiety. They establish unrealistic pressures to perform in the short run, impose excessively tight controls, and routinely fire employees who don't "measure up." For instance, when Harold Geneen was chairman and CEO at ITT, division executives had to formally present their annual business plan to Geneen and his senior staff group. Each division executive would then be interrogated about every number in every graph, exhibit, and analysis in the plan. The exercise was known to put fear in the hearts of all the division executives and to occasionally bring tears to some of their eyes.

Organizations go through a cycle. They're established, they grow, become mature, and eventually decline. An *organization's life stage*—that is, where it is in this four stage cycle—creates different problems and pressures for employees. The establishment and decline stages are particularly stressful. The former is characterized by a great deal of excitement and uncertainty, while the latter typically requires cutbacks, layoffs, and a different set of uncertainties. Stress tends to be least in maturity where uncertainties are at their lowest ebb.

Individual Factors

The typical individual only works about forty hours a week. The experiences and problems that people encounter in those other 128 nonwork hours each week can spill over to the job. Our final category, then, encompasses factors that comprise the employee's personal life. Primarily, this focuses on family and personal economic problems.

National surveys consistently show that people hold *family* and personal relationships dear. Marital difficulties, the breaking off of a relationship, and discipline troubles with children are examples of relationship problems that create stress for employees and which aren't left at the front door when they arrive at work.

Economic problems created by individuals overextending their financial resources is another set of personal troubles that can create stress for employees and distract their attention from their work. Regardless of income level—people who make $50,000 a year seem to have as much trouble handling their finances as those who earn $15,000—some people are poor money managers or have wants that always seem to exceed their earning capacity.

Table 16–2 lists more than forty life events that, according to research, create stress for individuals.[11] The mean value given to each life event represents its relative weight or importance. Higher numbers create greater stress and require more adaptive or coping behavior. Notice, for example, how four out of the first five are problems related to family and relationships. Notice, too, that life change events typically characterized as positive—marriage, outstanding personal achievements, vacations, Christmas—are stress-creating.

Most of the research using the scale in Table 16–2 has been to establish relationships between individual scores and later health problems. The logic underlying the scale is that the accumulation of life change events lowers the body's resistance and enhances the probability of illness, injuries, and related health problems. Researchers have found that individuals who report life change scores totalling less than 150 points in the previous year are in generally good health a year later. If the total score is above 150 but less than 300, individuals have about a 50 percent chance of developing a serious illness in the following year. For those in the high-risk category—300 points or above—the chance of developing a serious illness rises to 70 percent.[12]

Stressors Are Additive

As the life change events scale illustrates, and which tends to be overlooked when stressors are reviewed individually, stress is an additive phenomenon.[13]

---

[11] T. H. Holmes and R. H. Rahe, "The Social Readjustment Rating Scale," *Journal of Psychosomatic Research*, August 1967, pp. 213–18.

[12] Ibid.

[13] H. Selye, *The Stress of Life*, rev. ed. (New York: McGraw-Hill, 1956).

TABLE 16–2
Life Change Events and Their Rating

Rank	Life Event	Mean Value
1. Death of spouse		100
2. Divorce		73
3. Marital separation from mate		65
4. Detention in jail or other institution		63
5. Death of a close family member		63
6. Major personal injury or illness		53
7. Marriage		50
8. Being fired at work		47
9. Marital reconciliation with mate		45
10. Retirement from work		45
11. Major change in the health or behavior of a family member		44
12. Pregnancy		40
13. Sexual difficulties		39
14. Gaining a new family member (e.g., through birth, adoption, oldster moving in, etc.)		39
15. Major business readjustment (e.g., merger, reorganization, bankruptcy, etc.)		39
16. Major change in financial state (e.g., a lot worse off or a lot better off than usual)		38
17. Death of a close friend		37
18. Changing to a different line of work		36
19. Major change in the number of arguments with spouse (e.g., either a lot more or a lot less than usual regarding child-rearing, personal habits, etc.)		35
20. Taking out a mortgage or loan for a major purchase (e.g., for a home, business, etc.)		31
21. Foreclosure on a mortgage or loan		30
22. Major change in responsibilities at work (e.g., promotion, demotion, lateral transfer)		29
23. Son or daughter leaving home (e.g., marriage, attending college, etc.)		29
24. Trouble with in-laws		29
25. Outstanding personal achievement		28
26. Wife beginning or ceasing work outside the home		26
27. Beginning or ceasing formal schooling		26
28. Major change in living conditions (e.g., building a new home, remodeling, deterioration of home or neighborhood)		25
29. Revision of personal habits (dress, manners, associations, etc.)		24
30. Trouble with the boss		23
31. Major change in working hours or conditions		20
32. Change in residence		20
33. Changing to a new school		20
34. Major change in usual type and/or amount of recreation		19
35. Major change in church activities (e.g., a lot more or a lot less than usual)		19
36. Major change in social activities (e.g., clubs, dancing, movies, visiting, etc.).		18
37. Taking out a mortgage or loan for a lesser purchase (e.g., for a car, TV, freezer, etc.)		17

TABLE 16–2 (*Continued*)

Rank	Life Event	Mean Value
38.	Major change in sleeping habits (a lot more or a lot less sleep, or change in part of day when asleep)	16
39.	Major change in number of family get-togethers (e.g., a lot more or a lot less than usual)	15
40.	Major change in eating habits (a lot more or a lot less food intake, or very different meal hours or surroundings)	15
41.	Vacation	13
42.	Christmas	12
43.	Minor violations of the law (e.g., traffic tickets, jaywalking, disturbing the peace, etc.)	11

Source: Adapted from T. H. Holmes and R. H. Rahe, "The Social Readjustment Scale," *Journal of Psychosomatic Research,* 11 (1967), p. 216. With permission from Pergamon Press, Ltd.

It builds up. Each new and persistent stressor adds to an individual's stress level. A single stressor, in and of itself, may seem relatively unimportant, but if it is added to an already high level of stress, it can be "the straw that breaks the camel's back." If we want to appraise the total amount of stress an individual is under, we have to sum up his or her opportunity stresses, constraint stresses, and demand stresses.

INDIVIDUAL DIFFERENCES

Not *everyone* who scores over 300 points on the life change events scale has a serious illness. On the other hand, some individuals who have incredibly stable and secure lives go to pieces when the smallest problem arises. Some people thrive on stressful situations, while others are totally overwhelmed by them. What is it that differentiates people in terms of their ability to deal with stress? What individual difference variables moderate the relationship between *potential* stressors and *experienced* stress? At least four variables—perception, job experience, belief in locus of control, and Type A behavior—have been found to be relevant moderators.

Perception

In Chapter 4, we demonstrated that employees react in response to their perception of reality rather than reality itself. Perception, therefore, will moderate the relationship between a potential stress condition and an employee's reaction to it. One person's fear that he'll lose his job because his company is laying off personnel may be perceived by another as an opportunity to get a large severance allowance and start his own business. Similarly, what one employee perceives as an efficient and challenging work environment may be viewed as threatening and demanding by others. So the stress potential in environmental, organizational, and individual factors doesn't lie in their objective condition. Rather, it lies in an employee's interpretation of those factors.

Job Experience

Experience is said to be a great teacher. It can also be a great stress-reducer. Think back to your first date or your first few days in college. For most of us, the uncertainty and newness of these situations created stress. But as we gained experience, that stress disappeared or at least significantly decreased. The same phenomenon seems to apply to work situations. That is, experience on the job tends to be negatively related to work stress. Two explanations have been offered.[14] First is the idea of selective withdrawal. Voluntary turnover is more probable among people who experience more stress. Therefore, people who remain with the organization longer are those with more stress-resistant traits; or at least more resistant to the stress characteristics of their organization. Second, people eventually develop coping mechanisms to deal with stress. Because this takes time, senior members of the organization are more likely to be fully adapted and should experience less stress.

Belief in Locus of Control

Locus of control was introduced in Chapter 3 as a personality attribute. Those with an internal locus of control believe they control their own destiny. Those with an external locus believe their lives are controlled by outside forces. Evidence indicates that internals perceive their jobs to be less stressful than do externals.[15]

When internals and externals confront a similar stressful situation, the internals are likely to believe that they can have a significant effect on the results. They, therefore, act in ways to take control of events. Externals are more likely to be passive and defensive. Rather than do something to reduce the stress, they acquiesce. So externals, who are more likely to feel helpless in stressful situations, are also more likely to experience stress.

Type A Behavior

Type A behavior

Aggressive involvement in a chronic, incessant struggle to achieve more and more in less and less time and, if necessary, against the opposing efforts of other things or other people.

A great deal of attention in recent years has been directed at what has become known as **Type A behavior**.[16] It is undoubtedly the most frequently used moderating variable related to stress.

[14] S. J. Motowidlo, J. S. Packard, and M. R. Manning, "Occupational Stress: Its Causes and Consequences for Job Performance," *Journal of Applied Psychology*, November 1987, pp. 619–20.

[15] See, for instance, G. R. Gemmill and W. J. Heisler, "Fatalism as a Factor in Managerial Job Satisfaction, Job Strain, and Mobility," *Personnel Psychology*, Summer 1972, pp. 241–50; and C. R. Anderson, D. Hellriegel, and J. W. Slocum, Jr., "Managerial Response to Environmentally Induced Stress," *Academy of Management Journal*, June 1977, pp. 260–72.

[16] M. Friedman and R. H. Rosenman, *Type A Behavior and Your Heart* (New York: Alfred A. Knopf, 1974).

Type A behavior is characterized by feeling a chronic sense of time urgency and by an *excessive* competitive drive. A Type A individual is "*aggressively* involved in a *chronic, incessant* struggle to achieve more and more in less and less time, and if required to do so, against the opposing efforts of other things or other persons."[17] In the North American culture, such characteristics tend to be highly prized and positively correlated with ambition and the successful acquisition of material goods. Type A's

1. are always moving, walking, and eating rapidly,
2. feel impatient with the rate at which most events take place,
3. strive to think or do two or more things simultaneously,
4. cannot cope with leisure time, and
5. are obsessed with numbers; success is measured in terms of how much of everything they acquire.

The opposite of Type A is **Type B behavior**. Type B's are "rarely harried by the desire to obtain a wildly increasing number of things or participate in an endless growing series of events in an ever decreasing amount of time."[18] Type B's

Type B behavior

Rarely harried by the desire to obtain a wildly increasing number of things or participate in an endlessly growing series of events in an ever decreasing amount of time.

1. never suffer from a sense of time urgency with its accompanying impatience,
2. feel no need to display or discuss either their achievements or accomplishments unless such exposure is demanded by the situation,
3. play for fun and relaxation, rather than to exhibit their superiority at any cost, and
4. can relax without guilt.

Obviously, Type A's are more likely to experience stress on and off the job. They subject themselves to more or less continuous time pressure, creating for themselves a life of deadlines. About 50 percent of the North American population are Type A's, though the proportion of Type A's among male managers is higher—in the 61 to 76 percent range.[19] You can gain some insight into your propensity to exhibit Type A behavior by completing the exercise at the end of this chapter.

STRESS CONSEQUENCES

Stress shows itself in a number of ways. For instance, an individual who is experiencing a high level of stress may develop high blood pressure, ulcers, irritability, difficulty in making routine decisions, loss of appetite, accident prone-

[17] Ibid., 84.
[18] Ibid., 84–85.
[19] A. P. Brief, R. S. Schuler, and M. Van Sell, *Managing Job Stress* (Boston: Little, Brown and Co., 1981).

ness, and the like. These can be subsumed under three general categories: physiological, psychological, and behavioral symptoms.[20]

Physiological Symptoms

Physiological symptoms

Changes in an individual's health as a result of stress.

Most of the early concern with stress was directed at **physiological symptoms.** This was predominately due to the fact that the topic was researched by specialists in the health and medical sciences. This research led to the conclusion that stress could create changes in metabolism, increase heart and breathing rates, increase blood pressure, bring on headaches, and induce heart attacks.

The link between stress and particular physiological symptoms is not clear. There are few, if any, consistent relationships.[21] This is attributed to the complexity of the symptoms and the difficulty of objectively measuring them. But of greater relevance is the fact that physiological symptoms have the least direct relevance to students of OB. Our concern is with behaviors and attitudes. Therefore, the two other symptoms of stress are more important to us.

Psychological Symptoms

Psychological symptoms

Changes in an individual's attitudes and disposition due to stress.

Stress can cause dissatisfaction. Job-related stress can cause job-related dissatisfaction. Job dissatisfaction, in fact, is "the simplest and most obvious psychological effect" from stress.[22] But stress shows itself in other **psychological** states—for instance, tension, anxiety, irritability, boredom, and procrastination.

The evidence indicates that when people are placed in jobs that make multiple and conflicting demands or in which there is a lack of clarity as to the incumbent's duties, authority, and responsibilities, both stress and dissatisfaction are increased.[23] Similarly, the less control people have over the pace of their work, the greater the stress and dissatisfaction. While more research is needed to clarify the relationship, the evidence suggests that jobs that provide a low level of variety, significance, autonomy, feedback, and identity to incumbents create stress and reduce satisfaction and involvement in the job.[24]

Behavioral Symptoms

Behavioral symptoms

Changes in an individual's behavior—including productivity, absence, and turnover—as a result of stress.

Behaviorally related stress symptoms include changes in productivity, absence, and turnover, as well as changes in eating habits, increased smoking or consumption of alcohol, rapid speech, fidgeting, and sleep disorders.

[20] Schuler, "Definition and Conceptualization of Stress," pp. 200–205.

[21] T. A. Beehr and J. E. Newman, "Job Stress, Employee Health, and Organizational Effectiveness: A Facet Analysis, Model, and Literature Review," *Personnel Psychology*, Winter 1978, pp. 665–99.

[22] Ibid., p. 687.

[23] C. L. Cooper and J. Marshall, "Occupational Sources of Stress: A Review of the Literature Relating to Coronary Heart Disease and Mental Ill Health," *Journal of Occupational Psychology*, Vol. 49, No. 1 (1976), pp. 11–28.

[24] J. R. Hackman and G. R. Oldham, "Development of the Job Diagnostic Survey," *Journal of Applied Psychology*, April 1975, pp. 159–70.

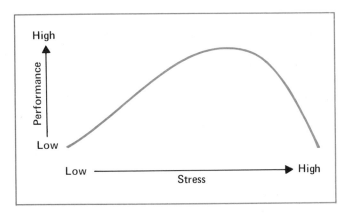

FIGURE 16–2
Relationship Between Stress and Job Performance

There has been a significant amount of research investigating the stress-performance relationship. The most thoroughly documented pattern in the stress-performance literature is the inverted-U relationship.[25] This is shown in Figure 16–2.

The logic underlying the inverted-U is that low to moderate levels of stress stimulate the body and increase its ability to react. Individuals then often perform their tasks better, more intensely, or more rapidly. But too much stress places unattainable demands or constraints on a person, which results in lower performance. This inverted-U pattern may also describe the reaction to stress over time, as well as to changes in stress intensity. That is, even moderate levels of stress can have a negative influence on performance over the long term as the continued intensity of the stress wears down the individual and saps his or her energy resources. An athlete may be able to use the positive effects of stress to obtain a higher performance during every Saturday's game in the fall season. Or a sales executive may be able to psych herself up for her presentation at the annual national meeting. But moderate levels of stress experienced continually over long periods of time—as typified by the emergency room staff in a large urban hospital—can result in lower performance. This may explain why emergency room staffs at such hospitals are frequently rotated and why it is unusual to find individuals who have spent the bulk of their career in such an environment. In effect, to do so would expose the individual to the risk of "career burnout."

Considerable attention has also been focused on how the Type A–Type B dichotomy affects job performance. Studies tend to find significant differences between Type A's and Type B's in quality of performance and effort exerted at the job.[26] But whether A's outperform B's or vice-versa seems to depend

---

[25] See, for instance, J. E. McGrath, "Stress and Behavior in Organizations," in M. D. Dunnette (ed.), *Handbook of Industrial and Organizational Psychology* (Chicago: Rand McNally, 1976); J. M. Ivancevich and M. T. Matteson, *Stress and Work* (Glenview, IL: Scott, Foresman, 1981); and R. D. Allen, M. A. Hitt, and C. R. Greer, "Occupational Stress and Perceived Organizational Effectiveness in Formal Groups: An Examination of Stress Level and Stress Type," *Personnel Psychology*, Summer 1982, pp. 359–70.

[26] See, for instance, K. A. Matthews, "Psychological Perspectives on the Type A Behavior Pattern," *Psychological Bulletin*, March 1982, pp. 293–323; and M. Jamal, "Type A Behavior and Job Performance: Some Suggestive Findings," *Journal of Human Stress*, Summer 1985, pp. 60–68.

on the type of job the person is doing. Type A's are fast workers. They go for quantity rather than quality. Not surprisingly, we find that Type A's outperform Type B's on simple tasks and in those jobs calling for persistance or endurance. On the other hand, Type B's outperform Type A's on tasks that require slow, careful response and broad focus of attention.

What about performance in managerial positions? Type A managers demonstrate their competitiveness by working long hours and, not infrequently, making poor decisions because they make them too fast. Type A's are also rarely creative. Because of their concern with quantity and speed, they rely on past experiences when faced with problems. They will not allocate the time that is necessary to develop unique solutions to new problems. They rarely vary in their responses to specific challenges in their milieu; hence their behavior is easier to predict than that of Type B's. In spite of the Type A's hard work, the Type B's are the ones who appear to make it to the top. Great salespeople are usually Type A's, while senior executives are usually Type B's. Why? The answer lies in the tendency of Type A's to trade off quality of effort for quantity:

> promotion and elevation, particularly in corporate and professional organizations, usually go to those who are wise rather than to those who are merely hasty, to those who are tactful rather than to those who are hostile, and to those who are creative rather than to those who are merely agile in competitive strife.[27]

The Type A–Type B dichotomy offers us some insight into the impact of personality characteristics on the stress-performance relationship. Where high energy alone is a major determinant in job success, Type A's should be highly effective. In those jobs where originality, thought, and care are important, the Type B personality should be more successful.

Job burnout

Experiencing physical, mental, and emotional exhaustion.

STRESS MANAGEMENT STRATEGIES

From the organization's standpoint, management may not be concerned when employees experience low-to-moderate levels of stress. The reason, as we showed earlier, is that such levels of stress can be functional and lead to higher employee performance. But high levels of stress or even low levels sustained over long periods of time can lead to reduced employee performance and, thus, require action by management.

While a limited amount of stress may benefit an employee's performance, don't expect employees to see it that way. From the individual's standpoint, even low levels of stress are likely to be perceived as undesirable. It's not unlikely, therefore, for employees and management to have different notions of what constitutes an acceptable level of stress on the job. What management may consider as "a positive stimulus that keeps the adrenalin running" is very likely to be seen as "excessive pressure" by the employee. Keep this in mind as we discuss individual and organizational approaches toward managing stress.[28]

---

[27] Friedman and Rosenman, *Type A Behavior*, p. 86.

[28] The following discussion has been strongly influenced by J. E. Newman and T. A. Beehr, "Personal and Organizational Strategies for Handling Job Stress," *Personnel Psychology*, Spring

OB Close-Up

Job Burnout and Professional Employees

People have undoubtedly suffered the symptoms of **job burnout** for decades: physical, mental, and emotional exhaustion. But burnout has only recently gained the attention of health specialists and behavioral scientists.[29]

Burnout seems to occur most often among professionals whose jobs require them to deal with other people—accountants, lawyers, managers, nurses, police officers, teachers, and the like. Though no reliable figures are available regarding the prevalence of job burnout, it has been estimated that about 20 percent of owners, managers, professionals, and technical personnel in the United States suffer from it.[30]

What conditions lead to job burnout? First, there is the existence of organizational or individual stressors like role ambiguity, performance pressures, interpersonal conflicts, or personal economic problems. Second, the burnout candidate tends to hold unrealistic expectations or ambitions. These combine to create stress, fatigue, frustration, and feelings of helplessness and guilt for the person.[31] When burnout sets in, the person finds that he or she has difficulty coping with the demands of the job. The eventual result is reduced productivity, satisfaction, and motivation.

The combination of stress and acceptance that many job problems have no clear-cut solution may explain why some professionals drop out of the careers that they've spent years in and for which they underwent extensive training. The decision by many nurses and secondary school teachers, for instance, to switch to other careers after only ten or fifteen years in these professions is probably somewhat a response to job burnout. Some of the strategies we discuss in the next section for managing stress can also help reduce the causes and symptoms of burnout.

Individual Approaches

An employee can take personal responsibility for reducing his or her stress level. Individual strategies that have proven effective include implementing

1979, pp. 1–38; A. P. Brief, R. S. Schuler, and M. Van Sell, *Managing Job Stress*; R. L. Rose and J. F. Veiga, "Assessing the Sustained Effects of a Stress Management Intervention on Anxiety and Locus of Control," *Academy of Management Journal*, March 1984, pp. 190–98; E. R. Kemery, A. G. Bedeian, K. W. Mossholder, and J. Touliatos, "Outcomes of Role Stress: A Multisample Constructive Replication," *Academy of Management Journal*, June 1985, pp. 363–75; N. S. Bruning and D. R. Frew, "Effects of Exercise, Relaxation, and Management Skills Training on Physiological Stress Indicators: A Field Experiment," *Journal of Applied Psychology*, November 1987, pp. 515–21; and F. Jordan, "Taking Control of Your Stress," *Management World*, June-August 1987, pp. 13–16.

[29] See, for instance, B. Perlman and E. A. Hartman, "Burnout: Summary and Future Research," *Human Relations*, April 1982, pp. 284–92; and O. I. Niehouse, "Controlling Burnout: A Leadership Guide for Managers," *Business Horizons*, July-August 1984, pp. 80–82.

[30] D. P. Rogers, "Helping Employees Cope with Burnout," *Business*, October-December 1984, pp. 3–7.

[31] Ibid.

time management techniques, increasing physical exercise, relaxation training, and expanding the social support network.

Time Management   Many people manage their time poorly. The things they have to accomplish in any given day or week are not necessarily beyond completion if they manage their time properly. The well-organized employee, like the well-organized student, can often accomplish twice as much as the person who is poorly organized. So an understanding and utilization of basic time management principles can help individuals better cope with job demands. A few of the more well-known time management principles include: (1) making daily lists of activities to be accomplished; (2) prioritizing activities by importance and urgency; (3) scheduling activities according to the priorities set; and (4) knowing your daily cycle and handling the most demanding parts of your job during the high part of your cycle when you are most alert and productive.[32]

Physical Exercise   Noncompetitive physical exercise like aerobics, race walking, jogging, swimming, and riding a bicycle have long been recommended by physicians as a way to deal with excessive stress levels. These forms of exercise increase heart capacity, lower at-rest heart rate, provide a mental diversion from work pressures, and offer a means to "let off steam."

Relaxation Training   Individuals can teach themselves to relax through techniques such as meditation, hypnosis, and biofeedback. The objective is to reach a state of **deep relaxation**, where one feels physically relaxed, somewhat detached from the immediate environment, and detached from body sensations.[33] Fifteen or twenty minutes a day of deep relaxation releases tension and provides a person with a pronounced sense of peacefulness. Importantly, significant changes in heart rate, blood pressure, and other physiological factors result from achieving the deep relaxation condition.

Deep relaxation

A state of physical relaxation, where the individual is somewhat detached from the immediate environment and detached from body sensations.

Social Support   Having friends, family, or work colleagues to talk to provides an outlet when stress levels become excessive. Expanding your social support network, therefore, can be a means for tension reduction. It provides you with someone to hear your problems and a more objective perspective on the situation. Research also demonstrates that social support moderates the stress-burnout relationship.[34] That is, high support reduces the likelihood that heavy work stress will result in job burnout.

Organizational Approaches

Several of the factors that cause stress—particularly task and role demands, and organization structure—are controlled by management. As such, they can be modified or changed. Strategies that management might want to consider

---

[32] See, for example, M. E. Haynes, *Practical Time Management: How to Make the Most of Your Most Perishable Resource* (Tulsa, OK: PennWell Books, 1985).

[33] H. Benson, *The Relaxation Response* (New York: William Morrow, 1975).

[34] D. Etzion, "Moderating Effects of Social Support on the Stress-Burnout Relationship," *Journal of Applied Psychology*, November 1984, pp. 615–22.

include improved personnel selection and job placement, use of realistic goal setting, redesigning of jobs, improved organizational communication, and establishment of corporate wellness programs.

Selection and Placement   While certain jobs are more stressful than others, we learned earlier in this chapter that individuals can differ in their response to stress situations. We know, for example, that individuals with little experience, an external locus of control, or Type A behavior tend to be more stress-prone. Selection and placement decisions should take these facts into consideration. While management shouldn't restrict hiring to only experienced individuals with an internal locus and who exhibit Type B behavior, such individuals may adapt better to high stress jobs and perform those jobs more effectively.

Goal Setting   We discussed goal setting in Chapter 6. Based on an extensive amount of research, we concluded that individuals perform better when they have specific and challenging goals and receive feedback on how well they are progressing toward these goals. The use of goals can reduce stress as well as provide motivation. Specific goals that are perceived as attainable clarify performance expectations. Additionally, goal feedback reduces uncertainties as to actual job performance. The result is less employee frustration, role ambiguity, and stress.

Job Redesign   Redesigning jobs to give employees more responsibility, greater participation in decision making, more meaningful work, more autonomy, and increased feedback can reduce stress, because these factors give the employee greater control over work activities and lessen dependence on others. But as we noted in our discussion of job design in Chapter 7, not all employees want enriched jobs. The right job redesign, then, for employees with a low need for growth might be less responsibility and increased division of labor. If individuals prefer structure and routineness, reducing skill variety should also reduce uncertainties and stress levels.

Organizational Communication   Increasing formal communication with employees reduces uncertainty by lessening role ambiguity and role conflict. Given the importance that perceptions play in moderating the stress-response relationship, management can also use effective communications as a means to shape employee perceptions. Remember that what employees categorize as demands, threats, or opportunities are merely an interpretation, and that interpretation can be affected by the symbols and actions communicated by management.

Wellness Programs   Our final suggestion is to offer organizationally-supported **wellness programs**. These programs focus on the employee's total physical and mental condition.[35] For example, they typically provide workshops to help people quit smoking, control alcohol use, lose weight, improve their diet, and develop a regular exercise program. The assumption underlying most wellness programs is that employees need to take personal responsibility for

Wellness programs

Organizationally supported programs that focus on the employee's total physical and mental condition.

[35] R. Kreitner, "Personal Wellness: It's Just Good Business," *Business Horizons*, May-June 1982, pp. 28–35.

their physical and mental health. The organization is merely a vehicle to facilitate this end.

Organizations, of course, aren't altruistic. They expect a payoff from their investment in wellness programs. A number of large corporations—including Campbell Soup, General Motors, IBM, Control Data, Burlington Industries, and Johnson & Johnson—report substantial reductions in stress-related illnesses and associated health problems as a result of their wellness programs.[36]

IMPLICATIONS FOR PERFORMANCE AND SATISFACTION

A number of factors (environmental, organizational, and individual), moderated by individual differences, cause employees to feel stressed. The more frequently these factors occur and the more intensely stressful they are for the employee, the greater the stress that he or she experiences. How intensely stressful the work situation is for a particular employee depends in part on his or her perceptions, job experience, belief in locus of control, and the extent to which he or she exhibits Type A behavior.

The existence of work stress, in and of itself, does not imply lower performance. The evidence indicates that stress can be either a positive or negative influence on employee performance. For many people, low-to-moderate amounts of stress enable them to perform their jobs better, by increasing their work intensity, alertness, and ability to react. However, a high level of stress or even a moderate level sustained over a long period of time eventually takes its toll and performance declines.

As stress increases, so typically does absenteeism. Alcohol and drug abuse, for example, cost employers billions of dollars each year in lost work time. A substantial part of this loss is undoubtedly a reaction to personal and work-related stress. It's interesting to note that studies demonstrate that women suffer more stress than men and have higher absentee rates.[37] But this is certainly largely due to role conflicts created by being career woman, homemaker, and parent. As we noted in Chapter 3, as traditional male and female roles at home are redefined toward greater sharing of home and parenting responsibilities, these differences between the sexes on absentee rates should disappear.

The impact of stress on satisfaction is pretty straightforward. Job-related tension tends to decrease general job satisfaction.[38] Even though low-to-moderate levels of stress may improve job performance, employees find stress dissatisfying.

[36] S. W. Hartman and J. Cozzetto, "Wellness in the Workplace," *Personnel Administrator*, August 1984, pp. 108–17.

[37] T. D. Jick and L. F. Mitz, "Sex Differences in Work Stress," *Academy of Management Review*, July 1985, pp. 408–20; and R. D. Hackett, "A Multiple Case Study of Employee Absenteeism," paper presented at the 1986 ASAC Conference, Whistler, British Columbia.

[38] See, for example, E. R. Kemery, A. G. Bedeian, K. W. Mossholder, and J. Touliatos, "Outcomes of Role Stress."

POINT

EMPLOYEE STRESS ISN'T A MANAGEMENT PROBLEM!

The recent attention given employee stress by behavioral scientists has been blown totally out of proportion. There is undoubtedly a small proportion of the working population which suffers from stress. These people have ongoing headaches, ulcers, high blood pressure, and the like. They may even turn to alcohol and drugs as an outlet to deal with their stress. But if there is a problem, it's a medical one. It is *not* a management problem. In support of this position, I'll argue that (1) stress is not that important because human beings are highly adaptive; (2) most stress that employees experience is of the positive type; and (3) even if the first two points weren't relevant, a good portion of what causes excessive work stress tends to be uncontrollable by management anyway.

Those who seem to be so concerned about employee stress forget that people are more adaptable than we traditionally give them credit for. They are amazingly resilient. Most successfully adjust to illnesses, misfortune, and other changes in their life. All through their school years, they adapted to the demands that dozens of teachers put on them. They survived the trials of puberty, dating, beginning and ending relationships, and leaving home—to name a few of the more potentially stressful times we have all gone through. By the time individuals enter the work force, they have experienced many difficult situations and, for the most part, they have adjusted to each. There is no reason to believe that this ability to adapt to changing or uncomfortable conditions breaks down once people begin their working careers.

Stress, like conflict, has a positive as well as a negative side. But that positive side tends to be overshadowed by concern with the negative. A life without stress is a life without challenge, stimulation, or change. As Table 16–2 so clearly illustrates, many positive and exciting life events—marriage, the birth of a child, inheriting a large sum of money, buying a new home, a job promotion, vacations—create stress. Does that mean that these positive events should be avoided? The answer is obviously no. Unfortunately, when most people talk about stress and the need to reduce it, they tend to overlook its positive side.

Finally, there is the reality that many sources of employee stress are outside the control of management. Management can't control environmental factors. Most individual factors, too, are outside management's influence. Even if stresses created by such individual factors as family and economic problems can be influenced by managerial actions, there remains the ethical question: Does management have the right to interfere in an employee's personal life? Undoubtedly a good portion of any employee's total stress level is created by factors that are uncontrollable by management—marital problems; divorce; children who get into trouble; poor personal financial management; uncertainty over the economy; societal norms to achieve and acquire material symbols of success; pressures of living in a fast-paced, urban world, and the like. The actions of management didn't create these stressors. Most are just part of modern living. More importantly, there is little that employers can do to lessen these stressors without extending their influence beyond the organization and into the employee's personal life. That's something that most of us would agree is outside the province of the employer-employee relationship.

COUNTERPOINT
STRESS CREATES REAL COSTS TO ORGANIZATIONS

For those who think management should ignore the problem of employee stress, they need to take a look at what stress is costing organizations.[*]

The total cost of work-related accidents in the United States is approximately $32 billion per year. It is estimated that at least three-quarters of all industrial accidents are caused by the inability of employees to cope with emotional distress.

Stress-related absenteeism, organizational medical expenses, and lost productivity are estimated to cost between $50 billion and $75 billion per year or an average of about $750 per worker. Stress-related headaches are the leading cause of lost work time in U.S. industry.

Coronary heart disease is a leading killer of Americans. Over one million Americans suffer heart attacks each year, and half of them are fatal. One out of every five average, healthy male Americans will suffer a heart attack before he reaches the age of sixty-five. Heart disease causes an annual loss of more than 135 million workdays. The premature loss of valued employees means the loss of experienced personnel and the additional cost of replacing these people. These facts are important because there now exists a wealth of research that links stress to heart disease.

More than 60 percent of long-term disability is related to psychological or psychosomatic problems often brought on or made worse by stress. State workers' compensation boards are increasingly awarding compensation for physical- and mental-stress claims. A single claim for permanent total disability can cost in excess of $250,000. Since each employer's workers' compensation costs are based on claims against that employer, any increase in awards is an added cost of doing business.

Two facts about stress cannot be ignored. First, people get sick from stress at work. Second, the costs associated with stress are significant to every employer. They include lost time, increased accidents, higher insurance premiums and health care costs, and lower productivity. The only natural conclusion one can draw is that managers cannot ignore the stress issue and must actively seek to do something about it. It is in management's self-interest to take an active stance because, if for no other reason, it provides a basis for defending the organization against claims that its jobs and working conditions are stress-creating and the primary cause for compensable emotional problems.

[*] These figures come from K. Albrecht, *Stress and the Manager* (Englewood Cliffs, NJ: Prentice Hall, 1979), pp. 33–34; "Stress: Can We Cope?," *Time*, June 6, 1983, pp. 48–54; J. W. Jones, "A Cost Evaluation for Stress Management," *EAP Digest*, November-December 1984, p. 34; and "Stress Claims Are Making Business Jumpy," *Business Week*, October 14, 1985, pp. 152–54.

KEY TERMS

Behavioral Symptoms
Constraints
Deep Relaxation
Demands
Job Burnout
Physiological Symptoms

Psychological Symptoms
Stress
Type A Behavior
Type B Behavior
Wellness Programs

FOR DISCUSSION

1. How are opportunities, constraints, and demands related to stress? Give an example of each.
2. How prevalent is work-related stress?
3. Describe the three sources of potential stress. Which of these are controllable by management?
4. What turns potential stress into actual stress?
5. Contrast Type A and Type B behavior. Are Type B individuals less effective employees than Type A's?
6. Do you think the proportion of Type A's in a society differs between countries? Explain.
7. What are the symptoms of stress?
8. What is the relationship between stress and performance?
9. What can individuals do to reduce their stress levels?
10. What can organizations do to reduce employee stress?
11. Some people say living in Los Angeles, New York, or other large, urban centers creates stresses on employees that don't exist in rural or small town communities. Is this a potential source of work stress? If so, where would it go in Figure 16–1?
12. Studies regularly show that "fear of nuclear war" is one of the greatest concerns among people today. Would increased "Cold War" tensions between the United States and the U.S.S.R. affect employee stress? Explain.

FOR FURTHER READING

BRIEF, A. P., and J. M. ATIEH, "Studying Job Stress: Are We Making Mountains Out of Molehills?," *Journal of Occupational Behavior*, April 1987, pp. 115–26. Argues that it is not safe to assume that job conditions that have an adverse impact on affective reactions to the job will also have a negative impact on overall subjective well-being.

JAMAL, M., "Relationship of Job Stress to Job Performance: A Study of Managers and Blue-Collar Workers," *Human Relations*, May 1985, pp. 409–24. In contrast to research that supports an inverted U-shaped relationship between stress and performance, this study found a negative linear relationship between job stress and supervisory ratings of performance.

JAMAL, M., "Job Stress, Stress-Prone Type A Behaviour, and Personal and Organizational Consequences," *Canadian Journal of Administrative Sciences*, December 1985, pp. 360–74. Research study finds that job stressors were significantly related to employees' psychosomatic complaints, job satisfaction, unproductive time at the job, and absenteeism. Type A behavior was found to be an important moderator of the stress-outcome relationship.

KAUFMANN, G. M., and T. A. BEEHR, "Interactions Between Job Stressors and Social Support: Some Counterintuitive Results," *Journal of Applied Psychology*, August 1986, pp. 522–26. In contrast to most models of job stress, this study found that social support strengthened the positive relationship between stressors and strains.

SHARIT, J., and G. SALVENDY, "Occupational Stress: Review and Reappraisal," *Human Factors*, April 1982, pp. 129–62. Reviews the measurements, sources, and management of stress as well as the relationship between stress and coronary heart disease.

TETRICK, L. E., and J. M. LaROCCO, "Understanding, Prediction, and Control as Moderators of the Relationships Between Perceived Stress, Satisfaction, and Psychological Well-Being," *Journal of Applied Psychology*, November 1987, pp. 538–43. Study finds that the ability to understand and control events in the work environment has moderating effects on the relationship between perceived stress and satisfaction.

EXERCISE 16

ARE YOU A TYPE A?

To determine your Type A or Type B profile, circle the number on the scale below that best characterizes your behavior for each trait.

1. Casual about appointments	1 2 3 4 5 6 7 8	Never late
2. Not competitive	1 2 3 4 5 6 7 8	Very competitive
3. Never feel rushed even under pressure	1 2 3 4 5 6 7 8	Always rushed
4. Take things one at a time	1 2 3 4 5 6 7 8	Try to do many things at once, think about what I am going to do next.
5. Slow doing things	1 2 3 4 5 6 7 8	Fast (eating, walking, etc.)
6. Express feelings	1 2 3 4 5 6 7 8	"Sit" on feelings
7. Many interests	1 2 3 4 5 6 7 8	Few interests outside work

Turn to page 568 for scoring directions and key.

Source: Adapted from R. W. Bortner, "Short Rating Scale as a Potential Measure of Pattern A Behavior," *Journal of Chronic Diseases*, June 1969, pp. 87–91. With permission.

K	D
6	7
8	7
6	6
5	4
6	1
5	4
1	1
37	30

CASE INCIDENT 16

THE "STRESS FOR SUCCESS" DILEMMA

Amy Redding was sitting in her office reviewing a speech she would be making the next day when Scott Oletta appeared at her doorway. Amy is head of research for a major securities and brokerage firm. Scott is an industry analyst who works for Amy. He is one of Amy's most valued analysts.

"Amy," Scott began, "I need to talk to you. You know I've been in this job for nearly four years. You hired me right out of graduate school. I thought the job would be challenging and it's been everything I had hoped for. I spend long hours here—I regularly put in twelve-hour days and have worked every Saturday for the past three months. But I'm not complaining. I love it. It's really challenging. But I've got no personal life. I was joking the other day with Nick in the mail room about not knowing what a love life is. The trouble is it's not a joke! Every time I meet someone and a relationship begins to develop, she gives me an ultimatum: 'It's either me or your work.' Women expect me to be free in the evenings and on weekends. And that just won't fly in this job. It consumes me.

"I weighed 170 pounds when I got out of school. This morning I weighed in at 205! I never smoked more than a pack a week in college. Did you know I'm up to three packs a day now? But what's got me really concerned is my drinking. For the past six months or so, I've had trouble sleeping. To help relax before bed, I began making myself a martini. Well, it worked, except I've been increasing the quantity lately. This morning, when I woke up, I looked at the vermouth bottle. It had been unopened until last night. It was half-empty. I figured out I had at least eight drinks last night! Amy, I'm scared. This job is my life, but the pressure to produce my industry reports and come up with continual recommendations at the rate we're expected to is getting to me.

"I called my sister down in Florida this morning and I ended up talking to her for an hour-and-a-half. She thinks I'm on a self-destructing course. She wants me to quit and come live with her for awhile. I'm afraid I'd go crazy without a job to consume me. You know I don't have any other interests. And I have to keep busy or I go crazy. There's so much I want to accomplish, career-wise, and I get frustrated that there are only twenty-four hours in the day.

"Amy, I don't know what to do. I think the best thing to do is quit this rat race and see if I can find a job with less pressure. I've written up my letter of resignation." Handing it to Amy, Scott said, "I'm not sure this is the answer, but I don't know what is."

QUESTIONS

1. What are the major stressors in Scott's life at the present time?
2. What stress symptoms is Scott displaying?
3. If you were Amy, how would you handle this situation?

17

Organizational Change and Development

■ *Learning objectives*

State how change encompasses almost all OB concepts
Summarize why some people resist change
Explain the change process
Describe OD values
Identify the OD consultation process
Clarify the political implications in a change intervention
Explain how OD interventions can reduce employee freedom and privacy
Describe the importance of aligning OD values and national culture
List various techniques available for introducing behavioral change

Most people hate any change that doesn't jingle in their pockets.

—— ANONYMOUS

The major U.S. automobile manufacturers like GM and Ford are currently spending tens of billions of dollars remodeling their plants and installing state-of-the-art robotics to compete more successfully against imports. One area currently receiving attention by these auto companies is computerized quality control. Sophisticated computer-controlled equipment is being put in place to significantly improve the ability to find and correct defects. This new equipment is changing the jobs of the people working in the quality control area, and the management of the auto firms have been seeking ways to reduce the resistance that quality control personnel are showing to these changes.

Innovation is the essence of long-term survival for many companies. At 3M Co., for instance, management explicitly seeks to get 25 percent of the firm's sales from products less than five years old. Such an ambitious goal *demands* the development of a continual stream of new ideas.

The last decade has seen many organizations shrink in size. These have included AT&T, Exxon, General Electric, Polaroid, B.F. Goodrich, and Caterpillar Tractor, to name just a few of the more visible. The downsizing of an organization can be a difficult experience for employees. There is high uncertainty, key people quit to pursue better opportunities elsewhere, and morale suffers. Yet, if management fails to help employees cope with this change, productivity and efficiency are sure to suffer.

The foregoing illustrates just three contemporary problems—acceptance of automation, the implementation of innovations, and the downsizing of an organization—that impose changes upon employees. More and more organizations today face a dynamic environment that requires adaptation. For instance, there is increased international competition, deregulation, threats from corporate raiders, mergers, growth in information technology, and changing societal values that impact customer preferences and employee expectations. Failure to adapt may threaten the organization's survival. But the topic of change runs wider than merely adapting to a changing environment. The need for change has been implied throughout this text. "A casual reflection on change should indicate that it encompasses almost all our concepts in the organizational behavior literature. Think about leadership, motivation, organizational environment, and roles. It is impossible to think about these and other concepts without inquiring about change."[1] This chapter is about what can be done to make change interventions in organizations more successful.

SOME DEFINITIONS

Let's begin with a few brief definitions. **Change** is concerned with making things different. **Change intervention** is a planned action to make things different. The person (or persons) who acts as catalyst, and assumes the responsibility for managing the change process, is the **change agent. Organizational development (OD)** is a popular term used to describe a systems-oriented approach to change. Several of these definitions deserve some elaboration.

Change agents can be managers or nonmanagers, employees of the organization, or outside consultants. For major change efforts, internal management often will hire the services of outside consultants to provide advice and assistance. Because they are from the outside, these individuals can offer an objective perspective often missing from insiders. However, outside consultants are disadvantaged because they usually have an inadequate understanding of the organization's history, culture, operating procedures, and personnel. Outside consultants also may be prone to initiating more drastic changes—which can be a benefit or a disadvantage—because they do not have to live with the repercussions after the change is implemented. In contrast, internal staff specialists or managers, when acting as the change agent, may be more thoughtful (and possibly cautious) because they must live with the consequences of their actions.

Organizational development is a term used for a variety of change-oriented activities. To some, it is merely a catchy name given to small-group discussion methods. At the other extreme, it has been defined in such a general way as to encompass almost the entire management process. For example, OD has been described as "a complex network of events that enhances the ability of organizational members to manage the culture of their organization, to be creative in solving problems, and to assist their organization in adapting to the external environment."[2] Our conclusion is that OD is not really a definable, single concept, but rather a convenient term used to encompass a variety of activities for managing change. It encompasses a broad range of interventions—from organization-wide changes in structure and systems to psychotherapeutic counseling sessions with groups and individuals—undertaken in response to changes in the external environment, that seek to improve organizational effectiveness and employee well-being.[3] We'll come back to discussing OD later in this chapter.

Change

Making things different.

Change intervention

A planned action to make things different.

Change agent

The person (or persons) who acts as catalyst, and assumes the responsibility for managing the change process.

Organizational development (OD)

A systems-oriented approach to change.

---

[1] P. S. Goodman and L. B. Kurke, "Studies of Change in Organizations: A Status Report," in P. S. Goodman (ed.), *Change in Organizations* (San Francisco: Jossey-Bass, 1982), pp. 1–2.

[2] W. French, *The Personnel Management Process*, 3rd ed. (Boston: Houghton Mifflin, 1974), p. 56.

[3] M. Beer and A. E. Walton, "Organization Change and Development," in M. R. Rosenzweig and L. W. Porter (eds.), *Annual Review of Psychology*, Vol. 38 (Palo Alto, CA: Annual Reviews, Inc., 1987), pp. 339–40.

Most people believe that people resist change. But do they?

Does an employee resist an upward change in pay rate or vacation allowance? Does a homemaker resist the replacement of a cranky old dishwasher for a new one? Does a manager resist an imposed schedule change that requires him to represent his division at an important reception for the new company president rather than finishing his quarterly budget? All these changes are likely to be welcomed warmly and to be implemented with great cooperation from the people concerned. What distinguishes these changes from the changes that people resist strongly is the fact that their nature and effects are relatively well-known and are enthusiastically desired. The degree of people's resistance to change depends on the kind of change involved and how well it is understood. What people resist is not change but loss, or the possibility of loss.[4]

People are likely to resist change for one of two reasons: loss of the known and tried, or concern over personal loss.[5]

Changes substitute ambiguity and uncertainty for the known. Regardless of how much you may dislike attending college, at least you know what is expected of you. But when you leave college and venture out into the world of full-time employment, regardless of how desirous you are to get out of college, you have to trade the known for the unknown. Employees in organizations hold the same dislike for uncertainty. If, for example, the introduction of word processors means that departmental secretaries will have to learn to operate these new pieces of equipment, some of the secretaries may fear that they will be unable to do so. They may, therefore, develop a negative attitude toward working with word processors or behave dysfunctionally if required to use them.

The other cause of resistance is fear of personal loss of something already possessed. Change threatens the "investment" one has already made in the status quo. The more people have invested in the current system, the more resistant they tend to be toward change. They fear the loss of status, money, authority, friendships, personal convenience, or other benefits they value. This explains why older employees tend to resist change more than younger ones. Older employees have generally invested more in the current system and, therefore, have more to lose by adapting to a change. If you have spent twenty years of your adult life as a mail sorter with the post office, you are likely to resist automatic letter sorters more actively than would a recent high school graduate who has been performing the job for only six months. The latter has less personal investment in the old system and is less threatened by automation.

Resistance to change doesn't necessarily surface in standardized ways. Resistance can be overt, implicit, immediate, or deferred.[6] It is easiest for management to deal with resistance when it is overt and immediate. For instance, a

---

[4] W. W. Burke, *Organization Development: Principles and Practices* (Boston: Little, Brown, 1982), pp. 51–52.

[5] Ibid.

[6] E. F. Huse, *Organizational Development and Change*, 2nd ed. (St. Paul, MN: West Publishing, 1980), p. 118.

change is proposed and employees quickly respond by voicing complaints, engaging in a work slowdown, threatening to go on strike, or the like. The greater challenge is managing resistance that is implicit or deferred. Implicit resistance efforts are more subtle—the loss of loyalty to the organization, loss of motivation to work, increased errors or mistakes, increased absenteeism due to "sickness"—and hence more difficult to recognize. Similarly, deferred actions cloud the link between the source of the resistance and reaction to it. A change may produce what appears to be only a minimal reaction at the time it is initiated but surfaces weeks, months, or even years later. Or a single change, in and of itself, has little impact. But it becomes the straw that breaks the camel's back. Reactions to change can build up and then explode in some response that seems totally out of proportion to the change action it follows. The resistance, of course, has merely been deferred and stockpiled. What surfaces is a response to an accumulation of previous changes.

A final point regarding resistance to change: It's not *always* dysfunctional. It provides a vehicle for employees to release pent-up frustrations. Rather than let those frustrations fester, overt resistance allows employees to bring their feelings to the surface. Management can then address employee concerns, help them to understand the change better, and lessen its threat. Employee resistance also may bring to light problems in a change proposal that management had overlooked. In an odd way, employee resistance is a form of checks-and-balances on management, and acts to preserve the organization's culture. It is a stability-reinforcing mechanism. For organizations that have a strong and effective culture, employee resistance signals to management that a given change action may act to undermine the shared values that have worked in the past.

THE CHANGE PROCESS

When resistance to change is seen as dysfunctional, what actions can be taken? Reducing resistance to change can best be understood by considering the complexity inherent in the change process (see Figure 17–1).

Successful change requires **unfreezing** the status quo, *movement* to a new state, and **refreezing** the new change to make it permanent.[7] Implicit in this three-step process is the recognition that the mere introduction of change does not ensure either the elimination of the prechange condition or the permanence of the change.

The management of a large oil company decided to reorganize its marketing function in the western United States. The firm had three divisional offices in the west, located in Seattle, San Francisco, and Los Angeles. The decision was made to consolidate the divisions into a single regional office to be located in San Francisco. The reorganization meant transferring over 150 employees, the elimination of some duplicate managerial positions, and the institution of a new hierarchy of command. As you might guess, a move of this magnitude was difficult to keep secret. The rumor of its occurrence preceded the announcement by several months. The decision itself was made unilaterally. It came

Unfreezing

Change efforts to overcome the pressures of both individual resistance and group conformity.

Refreezing

Stabilizing a change intervention by balancing driving and restraining forces.

[7] K. Lewin, *Field Theory in Social Science* (New York: Harper & Row, 1951).

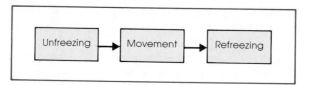

FIGURE 17–1
Change Process

from the executive offices in New York. Those people affected had no say whatsoever in the choice. For those in Seattle or Los Angeles, who may have disliked the decision and its consequences—the problems inherent in transferring to another city, pulling youngsters out of school, making new friends, having new co-workers, undergoing the reassignment of responsibilities—their only recourse was to quit. This actual case of an organizational change will be used to illustrate the unfreezing-movement-refreezing model.

The status quo can be considered an equilibrium state. To move from this equilibrium—to overcome the pressures of both individual resistance and group conformity—unfreezing is necessary. It can be achieved in one of three ways. (See Fig. 17–2.) The **driving forces**, which direct behavior away from the status quo, can be increased. The **restraining forces**, which hinder movement from the existing equilibrium, can be decreased. A third alternative is to *combine the first two approaches.*

Using the reorganization example cited, management can expect employee resistance to the consolidation. To deal with that resistance, management can use positive incentives to encourage employees to accept the change. For in-

Driving forces

Forces that direct behavior away from the status quo.

Restraining forces

Forces that hinder movement from the status quo.

FIGURE 17–2
Unfreezing the Status Quo

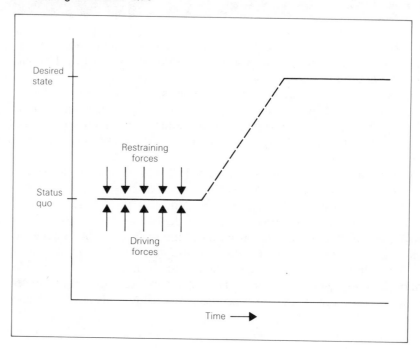

stance, increases in pay can be offered to those who accept the transfer. Very liberal moving expenses can be paid by the company. Management might offer low-cost mortgage funds to allow employees to buy new homes in San Francisco. Of course, management might choose to unfreeze acceptance of the status quo by removing restraining forces. Employees could be counseled individually. Each employee's concerns and apprehensions could be heard and clarified specifically. Assuming that most of the fears are unjustified, the counselor could assure the employees that there was nothing to fear and then demonstrate, through tangible evidence, that restraining forces are unwarranted. If resistance is extremely high, management may have to resort to both reducing resistance and increasing the attractiveness of the alternative if the unfreezing is to be successful.

Once unfreezing has been accomplished, the change itself can be implemented. In reality, there is no clear line separating unfreezing and moving. Many of the efforts made to unfreeze the status quo may, in and of themselves, introduce movement. So the tactics for dealing with resistance that the change agent uses may work on unfreezing and/or moving.

Six tactics have been suggested for use by change agents in dealing with resistance to change.[8] Let us review them briefly.

1. *Education and communication.* Resistance can be reduced through communicating with employees to help them see the logic of a change. This tactic basically assumes that the source of resistance lies in misinformation or poor communication: If employees receive the full facts and get any misunderstandings cleared up, resistance will subside. This can be achieved through one-on-one discussions, memos, group presentations, or reports. Does it work? It does, provided that the source of resistance is inadequate communication and that management-employee relations are characterized by mutual trust and credibility. If these conditions do not exist, the change is unlikely to succeed. Additionally, the time and effort that this tactic involves must be considered against its advantages, particularly when the change affects a large number of people.

2. *Participation.* It's difficult for individuals to resist a change decision in which they participated. Prior to making a change, those opposed can be brought into the decision process. Assuming that the participants have the expertise to make a meaningful contribution, their involvement can reduce resistance, obtain commitment, and increase the quality of the change decision. However, against these advantages are the negatives: potential for a poor solution and great time consumption.

3. *Facilitation and support.* Change agents can offer a range of supportive efforts to reduce resistance. When employee fear and anxiety are high, employee counseling and therapy, new skills training, or a short paid leave of absence may facilitate adjustment. The drawback of this tactic is that, as with the others, it is time consuming. Additionally, it is expensive, and its implementation offers no assurance of success.

4. *Negotiation.* Another way for the change agent to deal with potential

---

[8] J. P. Kotter and L. A. Schlesinger, "Choosing Strategies for Change," *Harvard Business Review*, March-April 1979, pp. 106–14.

OB Close-Up

Harwood Manufacturing: A Classic Study in Participative Change

One of the most famous studies on organizational change took place in the late 1940s at a plant of the Harwood Manufacturing Co., where pajamas were made.[9]

The plant employed about 500 people and had a long history of disruptions every time changes were made in the way work was conducted. Although the changes were typically minor—for instance, pajama folders who formerly folded tops with prefolded pants would be required to fold the pants as well—the employees resisted. They would complain and some would openly refuse to make the changes. Production decreased, and grievances, absenteeism, and job turnover would increase.

The usual way that Harwood's management made changes was autocratically. Management made the decision, then would call a group meeting where they would announce the changes to employees and explain why they were necessary. The changes would then be implemented. But, as we said, employees continued to resist these changes in their jobs. So Harwood's executives brought in a consultant as an outside change agent to help with the problem. As an experiment, the consultant arranged for the next change to be conducted in three groups using three different methods. In the first group, the change was initiated in the usual manner—autocratically. This was the control group. The second involved employee participation through elected representatives. These representatives, with management, worked out the details of the change; then tried the new methods and trained others in the new procedures. In the third group, there was full participation. All employees shared in the designing of new methods with management.

The consultant gathered data over a forty day period and what he found strongly supported the value of participation. In the control group, resistance occurred as before. Seventeen percent of the employees quit their jobs during the forty-day period, and grievances and absenteeism increased. However, in the representative and full participation groups, there were no quits, only one grievance, and no absenteeism. Moreover, participation was positively related to productivity. In the control group, output actually dropped from an average of sixty units per hour to forty-eight units during the experimental period. The participation-by-representation group generated sixty-eight units per hour and the total participation group averaged seventy-three units per hour.

resistance to change is to exchange something of value for a lessening of the resistance. For instance, if the resistance is centered in a few powerful individuals, a specific reward package can be negotiated that will meet their individual

---

[9]L. Coch and J. R. P. French, Jr., "Overcoming Resistance to Change," *Human Relations*, Vol. 1, No. 4 (1948), pp. 512–32.

needs. In the oil company's reorganization, acceptance of the transfer and reshuffling of duties by several highly valued middle managers was "bought" by providing them with larger staffs in their new jobs and by allowing them to live on company expense for nearly six months while they and their spouses "looked" for acceptable permanent housing accommodations. Negotiation, as a tactic, may be necessary when resistance comes from a powerful source. Yet one cannot ignore its potentially high costs. Additionally, there is the risk that, once a change agent negotiates to avoid resistance, he or she is open to the possibility of being blackmailed by other individuals in positions of power.

5. *Manipulation and cooptation.* Manipulation refers to covert influence attempts. Twisting and distorting facts to make them appear more attractive, withholding undesirable information, or creating false rumors to get employees to accept a change are all examples of manipulation. If corporate management threatens to close down a particular manufacturing plant if that plant's employees fail to accept an across-the-board pay cut, and if the threat is actually untrue, management is using manipulation. Cooptation, on the other hand, is a form of both manipulation and participation. It seeks to "buy off" the leaders of a resistance group by giving them a key role in the change decision. The leaders' advice is sought, not to seek a better decision, but to get their endorsement. Both manipulation and cooptation are relatively inexpensive and easy ways to gain the support of adversaries, but the tactics can backfire if the targets become aware that they are being tricked or used. Once discovered, the change agent's credibility may drop to zero.

6. *Coercion.* Last on the list of tactics is coercion, that is, the application of direct threats or force upon the resisters. If the corporate management mentioned in the previous discussion were really determined to close the manufacturing plant if employees did not acquiesce to a pay cut, then coercion would be the label attached to their change tactic. Other examples of coercion include threats of transfer, loss of promotions, negative performance evaulations, or a poor letter of recommendation. The advantages and drawbacks of coercion are approximately the same as those mentioned for manipulation and cooptation.

Assuming that a change has been implemented, if it is to be successful, the new situation needs to be refrozen so that it can be sustained over time. Unless this last step is taken, there is a very high chance that the change will be short lived and that employees will attempt to revert to the previous equilibrium state. The objective of refreezing, then, is to stabilize the new situation by balancing the driving and restraining forces.

How is refreezing done? Basically, it requires systematic replacement of the temporary forces with permanent ones. It may mean formalizing the driving or restraining forces, for instance, a permanent upward adjustment of salaries or the permanent removal of time clocks to reinforce a climate of trust and confidence in employees. The formal rules and regulations governing behavior of those affected by the change should be revised to reinforce the new situation. Over time, of course, the group's own norms will evolve to sustain the new equilibrium. But until that point is reached, the change agent will have to rely on more formal mechanisms.

Organizational development and planned change are not synonymous terms. All change activities are not necessarily subsumed under the OD label. In this section, we want to elaborate more fully on why all change activities aren't part of organizational development by clarifying OD's values and objectives.

OD interventions are typically built on humanistic-democratic values. The change agent may be directive in OD; however, there is a strong emphasis on collaboration. Concepts like power, authority, control, conflict, and coercion are held in relatively low esteem among OD change agents. The following briefly identifies the underlying values in most OD efforts:

1. *Respect for people.* Individuals are perceived as being responsible, conscientious, and caring. They should be treated with dignity and respect.

2. *Trust and support.* The effective and healthy organization is characterized by trust, authenticity, openness, and a supportive climate.

3. *Power equalization.* Effective organizations deemphasize hierarchical authority and control.

4. *Confrontation.* Problems shouldn't be swept under the rug. They should be openly confronted.

5. *Participation.* The more that people who will be affected by a change are involved in the decisions surrounding that change, the more they will be committed to implementing those decisions.

Table 17–1 summarizes the positive outcomes that can result from successful OD interventions.

THE OD CONSULTATION PROCESS

The unfreezing-movement-refreezing of planned change has been elaborated upon to orient it more specifically to the needs of the OD practitioner or consultant.[10] The process can be described as composed of seven phases: (1) entry, (2) contracting, (3) diagnosis, (4) feedback, (5) planning change, (6) intervention, and (7) evaluation. Keep in mind, as we describe each of these seven phases, that the consultant can be an insider as well as an outsider. That is, OD interventions can be implemented by trained professionals who work for the organization on a full-time basis and need not be someone brought in from the outside. Most large organizations—for example, almost all *Fortune* 500 firms, many federal and state agencies, and an increasing number of hospitals and school districts—have OD specialists on their staff to provide expertise to line managers. These specialists may be housed in separate OD departments

---

[10] See D. Kolb and A. Frohman, "An Organization Development Approach to Consulting," *Sloan Management Review*, Fall 1970, pp. 51–65; and W. W. Burke, *Organization Development*, pp. 158–64. This section is based on the discussion in the latter book.

TABLE 17–1
Ten Positive Results from OD

1. Improved organizational effectiveness (increased productivity and morale; more effective goal setting, planning, and organizing; clearer goals and responsibilities; better utilization of human resources; and bottom-line improvements)
2. Better management from top to bottom
3. Greater commitment and involvement from organizational members in making the organization successful
4. Improved teamwork within and between groups
5. A better understanding of an organization and its strengths and weaknesses
6. Improvement in communications, problem solving, and conflict resolution skills, resulting in increased effectiveness and less wasted time from communications break-downs, game playing, and win-lose confrontations
7. Efforts to develop a work climate that encourages creativity and openness, provides opportunities for personal growth and development, and rewards responsible and healthy behavior
8. A significant decrease in dysfunctional behavior
9. Increased personal and organizational awareness that improves the organization's ability to adapt to a continuously changing environment and to continue to grow, learn, and stay competitive
10. The ability to attract and keep healthy and productive people

Source: *MODMAN: Managing Organization Change and Development* by D. D. (Don) Warrick, p. 10. Copyright © Science Research Associates, Inc., 1984. Reprinted by permission of the publisher.

or be part of the organization's personnel/human resource management function.

Entry Contact between a consultant and a client/manager can be precipitated by either party. For an external consultant, the contact is likely to result from the manager's initiative. Internal consultants respond to requests from managers as well as initiating contact on their own when they see a problem in the organization where they think they can make a contribution.

What signs might signal to a manager that his or her unit is in need of OD expertise? The clearest sign is probably when the same kinds of problems keep recurring. No sooner does a problem get solved than another just like it surfaces. Another sign is when the manager's efforts at improving employee productivity, morale, attendance, or other performance concerns don't seem to be working. Still another is when employee morale is low in a unit but the manager is at a loss to identify any single cause.[11] Of course, any problem that seems particularly troublesome for a manager and which seems to be substantially affecting his or her employees, may be a candidate for the OD consultant's brand of expertise. After contact has been made, the consultant and manager will explore whether the former's skills are appropriate for the problem at hand.

Contracting Assuming that the consultant is willing to accept the task and that the manager believes the consultant can help with the problem, the next phase in the process is negotiating a contract. Essentially, this is merely a

[11] W. W. Burke, *Organization Development*, p. 10.

statement of agreement that clarifies what the consultant agrees to do. However, in contrast to most other types of contracts, the OD contract focuses more on process than content. Rather than tie the consultant down by defining precisely what he or she will do, it tends to set out the ground rules under which the parties will operate. Anything much beyond that would be inappropriate since the consultant has yet to objectively diagnose the problem which, of necessity, must precede any determination of what the proper intervention "solution" might be. This also explains why the methodological model for OD is often called **action research**. Data on the nature of a problem is systematically collected (the research aspect) and then the action is based on what the analyzed data indicates.[12]

Action research

The systematic collection of data and selection of a change intervention based on the data collected.

Diagnosis   There are two steps within the diagnostic phase: gathering information and summarizing it. The consultant gathers subjective data through observations, intuitions, and feelings. For the well-trained and experienced consultant, this is not irrelevant information. But the more substantive data are gathered through interviews, questionnaires, summaries of organizational documents, and other systematic methods.

One of the more well-known diagnostic instruments is the "Profile of Organizational Characteristics" developed by Rensis Likert[13] and shown in Figure 17–3. Likert was a strong proponent of participative management and developed this profile to diagnose the degree to which participative values permeate six areas: leadership, motivation, communication, decisions, goals, and control. These, in turn, are broken down into eighteen dimensions. Respondents then rate their organization on each of these dimensions using a twenty-point scale. For instance, organizational members would place the letter N at the place on the scale that best describes their assessment of the organization on a given dimension and an I to indicate their opinion of the ideal state. All the N's would be connected to form a profile of current perceptions, and by connecting all the I's, the consultant would have a profile of the ideal. Using this format, and by averaging members' responses to each question, Likert could categorize organizations as one of four types: System 1—autocratic, exploitive management; System 2—benevolent authoritative; System 3—consultative; and System 4—participative management. Because Likert favored participation, he argued that the most effective organizations were System 4 types. That may or may not be true, but that isn't our point here. Rather, the Profile of Organizational Characteristics illustrates one means for diagnosing change, although it's a limited tool applicable to those situations where participative management is a change goal.

Once the data are gathered, the consultant puts the information together, summarizes it, and organizes it in a form that can be readily understood and digested by the client/manager.

Feedback   This phase consists of the consultant meeting with the client system; that is, all those individuals who may be involved in the problem and its eventual solution. This obviously includes the manager who was involved from the

---

[12] Ibid., p. 8

[13] R. Likert, *The Human Organization* (New York: McGraw-Hill, 1967).

	SYSTEM 1	SYSTEM 2	SYSTEM 3	SYSTEM 4
LEADERSHIP How much confidence is shown in subordinates?	None	Condescending	Substantial	Complete
How free do they feel to talk to superiors about job?	Not at all	Not very	Rather free	Fully free
Are subordinates' ideas sought and used, if worthy?	Seldom	Sometimes	Usually	Always
MOTIVATION Is predominant use made of 1) fear, 2) threats, 3) punishment, 4) rewards, 5) involvement?	1,2,3 occasionally	4, some 3	4, some 3 and 5	5, 4, based on group set goals
Where is responsibility felt for achieving organization's goals?	Mostly at top	Top & middle	Fairly general	At all levels
COMMUNICATION How much communication is aimed at achieving organization's objectives?	Very little	Little	Quite a bit	A great deal
What is the direction of information flow?	Downward	Mostly downward	Down and up	Down, up and sideways
How is downward communication accepted?	With suspicion	Possibly with suspicion	With caution	With an open mind
How well do superiors know problems faced by subordinates?	Know little	Some knowledge	Quite well	Very well
DECISIONS At what level are decisions formally made?	Mostly at top	Policy at top	Broad policy at top, more delegation	Throughout but well integrated
What is the origin of technical and professional knowledge used in decision making?	Top management	Upper & middle	To a certain extent, throughout	To a great extent throughout
Are subordinates involved in decisions related to their work?	Not at all	Occasionally consulted	Generally consulted	Fully involved
What does decision-making process contribute to motivation?	Nothing, often weakens it	Relatively little	Some contribution	Substantial contribution
GOALS How are organizational goals established?	Orders issued	Orders, some comment invited	After discussion, by order	By group action (except in crisis)
How much covert resistance to goals is present?	Strong resistance	Moderate resistance	Some resistance at times	Little or none
CONTROL How concentrated are review and control functions?	Highly at top	Relatively highly at top	Moderate delegation to lower levels	Quite widely shared
Is there an informal organization resisting the formal one?	Yes	Usually	Sometimes	No—same goals as formal
What are cost, productivity, and other control data used for?	Policing, punishment	Reward and punishment	Reward - some self-guidance	Self-guidance problem-solving

FIGURE 17–3
Profile of Organizational Characteristics (Short Form)

Source: R. Likert, *The Human Organization* (New York: McGraw-Hill, 1975). With permission.

beginning. It might also include his or her immediate subordinates and any other levels of management that might be affected.

In these feedback sessions, the consultant will provide a summary of the data collected and some preliminary analysis. Discussion and debate then focuses on what the problems seem to be. The feedback is complete when the client group has accurately diagnosed the situation and reached a general consensus on the problems.

Planning Change   Once the diagnosis is understood and deemed correct, the appropriate intervention options begin to become clear. The consultant works collaboratively with the client system, primarily by presenting the different types of interventions that might be effective and the potential consequences of each. The relevant interventions, of course, should reflect the diagnosis. Some examples of interventions at the individual level are job redesign, training and management development, and techniques for changing attitudes and improving individual decision-making. At the group level, interventions might include team building, process consultation, and techniques for improving group decision making and managing conflicts. Organization-level interventions might include structural redesign, improving human resource systems, quality-of-work-life programs, intergroup development, and techniques for managing cultural change. A discussion of some of these options will be covered later in this chapter.

The final decision regarding which intervention will be used and how it will be implemented resides with the client. At this point, the OD consultant's job is merely to act as a resource person. The client can tap his or her expertise for advice and guidance. But the final decision belongs to the client/manager for he or she will have to be actively involved in its implementation and will have to live with its consequences.

Intervention   The next phase is implementing the intervention. This is the action part of action research. Whichever intervention is chosen, the OD consultant continues to work with the client to help make the intervention successful. In this phase, a major responsibility of the consultant is to help the client anticipate and plan for those unanticipated consequences the client might overlook but which can undermine the change effort.

Evaluation   No OD intervention is complete unless there is an evaluation of the change effort. Did it work? Was it successful in eliminating the problems identified in the diagnosis? As we'll discuss later in this chapter, evaluations of OD interventions can range from anecdotal data ("We all enjoyed the experience and thought we got a lot out of it") to methodologically rigorous research designs employing tight controls and objective measures of organizational performance. Ideally, the latter forms are more desirable. Nevertheless, the evaluation phase is important because it is the primary means by which the manager can judge the consequences of his or her change effort.

IMPLEMENTATION ISSUES IN OD

Why do some well-conceived and worthwhile change interventions fail? Can change intervention programs impinge on individual rights? Do change intervention strategies need to be modified to reflect the national culture in the country where it is being introduced? These questions relate to four current issues in

OD. First, OD values don't fit into all organizational cultures. Second, many OD endeavors fail because the change agent doesn't understand the politics of change. Third, OD has ethical implications. Efforts to humanize organizations can create a dilemma between the goals of freedom and equality. Finally, consistent with our discussion of cultural systems in Chapter 15, appropriate OD interventions should reflect the values and societal norms of the country where they are being implemented. In this section, we'll look at OD and organizational cultures, the politics of change, the ethics of control, and the need to choose or modify interventions to reflect differences in national cultures.

Differences in Organizational Cultures

OD values are not compatible with every organization's culture. OD embraces the values of collaboration, confrontation, authenticity, trust, support, and openness. These, however, are at odds with cultures that are characterized as risk aversive, low in integration, low in management support, high in control, and intolerant of conflict.

OD is clearly more compatible with organic structures and Theory Y assumptions (see Chapters 13 and 6, respectively) about human nature than mechanistic designs and Theory X assumptions. Of course, a large proportion of organizations in North America are bureaucratically structured, with extensive formalization and centralized decision power. These organizations might benefit most from having OD programs yet, paradoxically, they are also the type of organizations that are also most likely to resist OD values and make interventions difficult, if not impossible. Our point is that OD success is, to a large degree, dependent on the mesh between OD's values and those of the organization. Efforts to impose OD values in an alien culture are very likely to result in failure.

The Politics of Change

In Chapter 11, we described organizations as political systems with individuals and groups vying for power. Political dynamics, however, escalate during times of change,[14] because any significant change has the potential to disrupt the current balance of power among groups. Uncertainty and ambiguity surface. The result is that individuals and groups in the organization can be expected to use what power they have to protect their vested interests and insure that any change maintains or improves their current position.

The reality of organizational politics means that effective change agents should approach any change intervention by assessing how it might threaten the current power distribution. This perspective, incidentally, often disturbs many OD advocates. They would prefer to view organizations as cooperative systems, devoid of power struggles, self-serving coalitions, strategic maneuvering, and the like. But to ignore politics and the impact that change interventions

---

[14] V. E. Schein, "Organizational Realities: The Politics of Change," *Training and Development Journal*, February 1985, pp. 37–41; and G. K. Kenny, P. Morgan, and B. Hinings, "The Protection of Interests: Organizational Change in the Australian Services Canteens Organization," *Asian Pacific Journal of Management*, September 1986, pp. 11–23.

can have on the balance of power within an organization is naive at best and, at worst, may predestine the change effort to faliure.

Can a change agent do anything beyond recognizing the potential for resistance and being on the lookout for actions that seem to block the change? Yes.[15] First, the change agent can develop his or her power sources and bases. The possession of expertise, information, contacts, the ability to allocate rewards, and similar skills and resources can help convince others to go along with the change effort. Next, the change agent should assess the situation and key players. Who will be affected by the change? How powerful are they? Who has a positive, negative, or neutral stake in the change? How determined might those threatened by the change be in using their power to undermine the change effort? Remember, change cannot succeed unless there is a critical mass of support.[16]

After this assessment is complete, the change agent can select the proper power strategies. Table 17–2 describes a number of possible strategies for implementing change. In many cases, the change agent will want to use several of these strategies. But which one he or she chooses should reflect the political dynamics of the situation.

The Ethics of Control

We previously noted that OD interventions are typically based on humanistic-democratic values. They rely heavily on processes such as participation, collaboration, and confrontation. OD interventions are viewed as effective to the degree to which they increase openness, trust, risk-taking, autonomy, respect for people, and equalize power within the organization. The assumption by OD proponents is that these outcomes are desirable and lead to more effective organizational performance. Some writers have correctly noted, however, that when OD change agents use humanistic processes to achieve democratic outcomes, they are imposing their values on organizational participants.[17] For example, if employees in a given department have had trouble working with each other over a fairly long period of time, an OD change agent might recommend that the department members get together in an informal session and openly discuss their perceptions of each other, the sources of their disagreements, and similar issues. But not everyone feels comfortable participating in a process that requires them to be open about their feelings and attitudes. For such individuals, OD interventions that demand openness reduce their privacy and freedom. Even if participation is voluntary, the decision not to participate might carry negative connotations, result in lower performance appraisals, and have adverse career effects. Moreover, what if an employee does participate, is authentically open, reveals to the group some very personal fears and concerns, and then someone in the group uses this information vindictively against that employee at some later date? Hasn't the employee's privacy and freedom been compromised?

[15] V. E. Schein, "Organizational Realities."

[16] D. A. Nadler, "The Effective Management of Organizational Change," in J. W. Lorsch (ed.), *Handbook of Organizational Behavior* (Englewood Cliffs, NJ: Prentice Hall, 1987), p. 362.

[17] See, for example, C. R. Rogers, "Some Issues Concerning the Control of Human Behavior: A Symposium," *Science,* November 30, 1956, pp. 1060–64; and G. A. Walter, "Organizational Development and Individual Rights," *Journal of Applied Behavioral Science,* November 1984, pp. 423–39.

TABLE 17–2
Strategies for Implementing Change

- *Present a nonthreatening image.* When attempting to introduce innovative programs, it may be effective to be perceived as being conservative and essentially nonthreatening to existing organizational activities.
- *Present arguments in terms of the client's interests.* Don't distort information, but cast arguments for change proposals in terms of the benefits that will accrue to the client.
- *Diffuse opposition and bring out conflict.* Rather than stifle opposition, diffuse it through an open discussion of ideas. Conflicts that develop can be dealt with by engaging the opposition in legitimate discussion, answering objections, and allaying fears and facts. Open discussion can also spotlight any die-hard resistors, reducing opportunities for them to covertly thwart the change effort.
- *Align with powerful others.* In addition to gaining top management's approval, it can be beneficial to build alliances with operating or line managers who are directly affected by the change.
- *Bargain and make trade-offs.* Change is an on-going activity. Resistors may reduce their resistance if they are assured that other changes, which they favor, will be forthcoming.
- *Begin as an experiment.* Resistance may be lessened by introducing the change as an experiment. When something is viewed as temporary, it is less threatening. Having the change made permanent is easier once it is already in place.
- *Begin small.* Start small and slowly expand the change project. If an "all-or-nothing" stance has a reasonable chance of failing, it may be more effective to "get your foot in the door" and then expand the project slowly.

Source: Based on V. E. Schein, "Organizational Realities: The Politics of Change," *Training and Development Journal,* February 1985, pp. 39–40.

Even voluntary participation in an OD intervention implies control by the change agent over participants. Of course, you might say that managers attempt to control employees all the time and that doesn't seem to generate concerns about ethics. Why should OD interventions? The answer is twofold. First, employees understand that they give up some freedom when they accept employment. There is a trade-off—they give up forty hours a week for fifty or so weeks a year and, in turn, they receive a paycheck and an assortment of valuable benefits. Second, OD interventions control people by seeking to make them more open, trusting, authentic, and the like. How can you rail against outcomes such as these? The answer is, you can't. You're not likely to impress your bosses by arguing that mutual avoidance, closed communication, and distrusting relationships are O.K. because "they protect my privacy." So employees are under pressure to participate. They must surrender some of their freedoms and privacy or be labeled as "uncooperative." Consider some typical OD interventions: (1) Employees are asked to complete questionnaires and participate in interviews to determine their satisfaction with their job, their immediate supervisor, and the organization itself. The focus is on identifying problems that management may not be aware of so they can be corrected. (2) A manager and his or her subordinates are asked to look at the former's leadership style. The manager describes his or her style, then subordinates provide feedback. The change focus is on getting the manager to understand the dysfunctions of autocratic leadership and the superiority of participative management. (3) Group members with a history of interpersonal problems are asked to reveal personal frustrations, insecurities, and explain why they have difficulty working with each other. The change focus is on understanding others, improving communication, reducing conflicts, and improving work group performance. Employees can't easily decline participation in such apparently "worthwhile" change efforts.

Is something ethical if it promotes the greatest good for the greatest number? If so, OD interventions that reduce some employee rights might be considered ethical. But one can argue that management is unethical if it interferes with even one employee's freedoms. Does management have the right to even implicitly coerce employees to participate in an OD program "for the good of the organization?" This is not easy to answer. At the extreme, management could avoid all OD activities associated with the loss of employee freedom. But this might make planned change impossible. Why? Because changes don't occur unless there is some unfreezing of the status quo. And participation, confrontation, and similar OD processes contain risks for participants. These risks, in turn, stimulate the forces of change. If OD interventions minimize individual risk, the climate may be so bland as to have no effect on the change process. So the challenge for management in using OD interventions is to find the proper balance—where employees' rights and well-being are weighed against improvements in the organization's effectiveness.

Differences in National Cultures

We know that effective motivational practices, leadership styles, and organization designs differ across national boundaries. Why, then, shouldn't OD interventions? The answer, as several recent studies demonstrate, is that they should.[18]

It has been argued that OD's values match well with countries who score low on power distance, low on uncertainty avoidance, low on masculinity, and moderate on individualism (see Chapter 15 for a description of these terms).[19] Countries with this profile value equality, confrontation, willingness to take risks, open expression of feelings, and collaboration rather than competition. It seems logical that the greater the match between OD's values and a country's cultural dimensions, the greater the potential for acceptance and success of OD interventions.

A review of the research comparing countries on their cultural dimensions allows us to make several predictions. First, OD interventions that emphasize openness, equality and the like are most likely to be accepted in countries such as Denmark, Norway, and Sweden where the match between OD values and cultural dimensions is very high. Second, these forms of OD interventions are not likely to succeed in countries such as Colombia, Mexico, Italy, and Japan where the match is low. Third, and somewhat surprising given that a large proportion of OD enthusiasts come from American behavioral scientists, the United States' cultural dimensions don't align particularly well with those

[18] See R. Tainio and T. Santalainen, "Some Evidence for the Cultural Relativity of Organizational Development Programs," *Journal of Applied Behavioral Science*, May 1984, pp. 93–111; N. J. Adler, "The Future of Organization Development in Canada," *Canadian Journal of Administrative Sciences*, June 1984, pp. 122–32; and A. M. Jaeger, "Organization Development and National Culture: Where's the Fit?," *Academy of Management Review*, January 1986, pp. 178–90.

[19] The following discussion is based on A. M. Jaeger, "Organization Development and National Culture."

of general OD values. This may explain why OD has had some problems of acceptance and success in the U.S., especially the more radical interventions that strive to democratize American bureaucracies. It can also provide insights into why Great Britain, where security, stability, and class structure are deeply-rooted values, has difficulty accepting OD interventions that focus on risk-taking and equality; or why interventions that seek to increase employee assertiveness would be inappropriate in Japan because success would only produce organizational deviants.

The following five steps have been recommended to increase the likelihood that any OD intervention is in harmony with the country where it is being considered for introduction:[20]

1. Evaluate the ranking of the dimensions of culture in the given situation.
2. Make a judgment as to which values are the most deeply held and unlikely to change.
3. Evaluate interventions in terms of their harmony with the culture identified in Step 1.
4. Choose the intervention that would clash least with the most rigidly held values.
5. Incorporate process modifications in the proposed intervention to fit with the given cultural situation.

OD INTERVENTIONS

What are some of the OD techniques for bringing about change? In this section, we'll review the more popular intervention techniques. For simplicity and clarity, they have been categorized as either structural or human process.[21]

Structural Techniques

The OD techniques that fall within the structural category affect work content and relationships among workers. To review these techniques in detail would repeat concepts discussed previously, but a quick overview may be helpful.

Planned changes in the organization's formal structure—that is, altering its degree of complexity, formalization, and centralization—represent structural OD interventions. For instance, departmental responsibilities can be combined, vertical layers removed, and spans of control widened so as to make the organization flatter and less bureaucratic. The number of rules and procedures can be reduced to increase employee autonomy. An increase in decentralization can be made to speed up the decision making process.

---

[20] Ibid., p. 189.

[21] This categorization was adapted from F. Friedlander and L. D. Brown, "Organizational Development," in M. R. Rosenzweig and L. W. Porter (eds.), *Annual Review of Psychology* (Palo Alto, CA: Annual Reviews, 1974), pp. 313–41.

In Chapter 7, we presented job design as an application of motivation concepts. In our discussion, we suggested that jobs could be made more challenging, interesting, and motivating by combining tasks, forming natural work units, establishing client relationships, vertical loading, and opening feedback channels. These guidelines, of course, could just as accurately be considered as suggestions for implementing a job redesign OD intervention.

Human resource programs in training and career development might also be broadly interpreted to be structural OD techniques. Finally, efforts to modify an organization's culture—through creating new rituals, redesigning socialization processes, or changing the reward system—could be labeled as structural interventions.

Human Process Techniques

The vast majority of OD intervention efforts have been directed at changing the attitudes and behavior of organization members through the processes of communication, decision making, and problem solving. The five most popular techniques are sensitivity training, survey feedback, process consultation, team building, and intergroup development. For the most part, each emphasizes participation and collaboration.

Sensitivity training

Training groups that seek to change behavior through unstructured group interaction.

Sensitivity Training It can go by a variety of names—laboratory training, **sensitivity training**, encounter groups, or T-groups (training groups)—but all refer to a method of changing behavior through unstructured group interaction. Members are brought together in a free and open environment in which participants discuss themselves and their interactive processes, loosely directed by a professional behavioral scientist. The group is process oriented, which means that individuals learn through observing and participating rather than being told. The professional creates the opportunity for participants to express their ideas, beliefs, and attitudes. He or she does not accept—in fact, overtly rejects—any leadership role.

The objectives of the T-groups are to provide the subjects with increased awareness of their own behavior and how others perceive them, greater sensitivity to the behavior of others, and increased understanding of group processes. Specific results sought include increased ability to empathize with others, improved listening skills, greater openness, increased tolerance of individual differences, and improved conflict resolution skills.

If individuals lack awareness of how others perceive them, then the successful T-group can effect more realistic self-perceptions, greater group cohesiveness, and a reduction in dysfunctional interpersonal conflicts. Further, it will ideally result in a better integration between the individual and the organization.

Survey feedback

The use of questionnaires to identify discrepancies among member perceptions; discussion follows and remedies are suggested.

Survey Feedback One tool for assessing attitudes held by organizational members, identifying discrepancies among member perceptions, and solving these differences is the **survey feedback** approach.

Everyone in an organization can participate in survey feedback, but of key importance is the organizational family—the manager of any given unit and those employees who report directly to him or her. A questionnaire is usually completed by all members in the organization or unit. Organization members may be asked to suggest questions or may be interviewed to determine what issues are relevant. The questionnaire typically asks members for their perceptions and attitudes on a broad range of topics—such as decision making practices; communication effectiveness; coordination between units; and satisfaction with the organization, job, peers, and their immediate supervisor.

The data from this questionnaire are tabulated with data pertaining to an individual's specific "family" and to the entire organization and distributed to employees. These data then become the springboard for identifying problems and clarifying issues that may be creating difficulties for people. In some cases, the manager may be counseled by an external change agent about the meaning of the responses to the questionnaire and may even be given suggested guidelines for leading the organizational family in group discussion of the results. Particular attention is given to the importance of encouraging discussion and ensuring that discussions focus on issues and ideas and not on attacking individuals.

Finally, group discussion in the survey feedback approach should result in members identifying possible implications of the questionnaire's findings. Are people listening? Are new ideas being generated? Can decision making, interpersonal relations, or job assignments be improved? Answers to questions like these, it is hoped, will result in the group agreeing upon commitments to various actions that will remedy the problems that are identified.

Process Consultation   No organization operates perfectly. Managers often sense that their unit's performance can be improved, but they are unable to identify what can be improved and how it can be improved. The purpose of **process consultation** is for an outside consultant to assist a client, usually a manager, "to perceive, understand, and act upon process events" with which he or she must deal.[22] These might include work flow, informal relationships among unit members, and formal communication channels.

Process consultation (PC) is similar to sensitivity training in its assumption that organizational effectiveness can be improved by dealing with interpersonal problems, and in its emphasis on involvement. But PC is more task directed than sensitivity training.

Consultants in PC are there to "give the client 'insight' into what is going on around him, within him, and between him and other people"[23] They do not solve the organization's problems. Rather, the consultant is a guide or coach who advises on the process to help the client solve his or her own problems.

The consultant works with the client in *jointly* diagnosing what processes need improvement. The emphasis is on "jointly," because the client develops a skill at analyzing processes within his or her unit that can be continually called on long after the consultant is gone. Additionally, by having the client actively participate in both the diagnosis and the development of alternatives, there will be greater understanding of the process and the remedy and less resistance to the action plan chosen.

Importantly, the process consultant need not be an expert in solving the particular problem that is identified. The consultant's expertise lies in diagnosis

Process consultation

Consultant gives a client insight into what is going on around him or her, within him or her, and between him or her and other people; identifies processes that need improvement.

---

[22] E. H. Schein, *Process Consultation: Its Role in Organizational Development* (Reading, MA: Addison-Wesley, 1969), p. 9.

[23] Ibid.

and developing a helping relationship. If the specific problem uncovered requires technical knowledge outside the client and consultant's expertise, the consultant helps the client to locate such an expert and then instructs the client in how to get the most out of this expert resource.

Team Building Organizations are made up of people working together to achieve some common end. Since people are frequently required to work in groups, considerable attention has been focused in OD on **team building**.[24]

Team building

High interaction among group members to increase trust and openness.

Team building can be applied within groups or at the intergroup level where activities are interdependent. For our discussion, we shall emphasize the intragroup level and leave intergroup development to the next section. As a result, our interest concerns applications to organizational families (command groups), as well as communities, project teams, and task groups.

Not all group activity has interdependence of functions. To illustrate, consider a football team and a track team:

> Although members on both teams are concerned with the team's total output they function differently. The football team's output depends synergistically on how well each player does his particular job in concert with his teammates. The quarterback's performance depends on the performance of his linemen and receivers, and ends on how well the quarterback throws the ball, and so on. On the other hand, a track team's performance is determined largely by the mere addition of the performances of the individual members.[25]

Team building is applicable to the case of interdependence, such as in football. The objective is to improve coordinative efforts of team members which will result in increasing the group's performance.

The activities considered in team building typically include goal setting, development of interpersonal relations among team members, role analysis to clarify each member's role and responsibilities, and team process analysis. Of course, team building may emphasize or exclude certain activities depending on the purpose of the development effort and the specific problems with which the team is confronted. Basically, however, team building attempts to use high interaction among group members to increase trust and openness.

It may be beneficial to begin by having members attempt to define the goals and priorities of the group. This will bring to the surface different perceptions of what the group's purpose may be. Following this, members can evaluate the group's performance—how effective are they in structuring priorities and achieving their goals? This should identify potential problem areas. This self-critique discussion of means and ends can be done with members of the total group present or, where large size impinges on a free interchange of views, may initially take place in smaller groups followed up by the sharing of their findings with the total group.

Team building can also address itself to clarifying each member's role in the group. Each role can be identified and clarified. Previous ambiguities

---

[24] See, for instance, K. P. DeMeuse and S. J. Liebowitz, "An Empirical Analysis of Team-Building Research," *Group and Organization Studies*, September 1981, pp. 357–78; S. J. Liebowitz and K. P. DeMeuse, "The Application of Team-Building," *Human Relations*, January 1982, pp. 1–18; and D. Eden, "Team Development: A True Field Experiment at 3 levels of Rigor," *Journal of Applied Psychology*, February 1985, pp. 94–100.

[25] N. Margulies and J. Wallace, *Organizational Change: Techniques and Applications* (Glenview, IL: Scott, Foresman, 1973), pp. 99–100.

can be brought to the surface. For some individuals, it may offer one of the few opportunities they have had to think through thoroughly what their job is all about and what specific tasks they are expected to carry out if the group is to optimize its effectiveness.

Still another team building activity can be similar to that performed by the process consultant, that is, to analyze key processes that go on within the team to identify the way work is performed and how these processes might be improved to make the team more effective.

Intergroup Development   A major area of concern in OD is the dysfunctional conflict that exists between groups. As a result, this has been a subject to which change efforts have been directed.

Intergroup development seeks to change the attitudes, stereotypes, and perceptions that groups have of each other. For example, in one company the engineers saw the accounting department as composed of shy and conservative types, and the personnel department as having a bunch of "smiley types who sit around and plan company picnics." Such stereotypes can have an obvious negative impact on the coordinative efforts between the departments.

Although there are several approaches for improving intergroup relations,[26] a popular method emphasizes problem solving.[27] In this method, each group meets independently to develop lists of its perception of themselves, the other group, and how they believe the other group perceives them. The groups then share their lists, after which similarities and differences are discussed. Differences are clearly articulated, and the groups look for the causes of the disparities.

Are the groups' goals at odds? Were perceptions distorted? On what basis were stereotypes formulated? Have some differences been caused by misunderstandings of intentions? Have words and concepts been defined differently by each group? Answers to questions like these clarify the exact nature of the conflict. Once the causes of the difficulty have been identified, the groups can move to the integration phase—working to develop solutions that will improve relations between the groups.

Subgroups, with members from each of the conflicting groups, can now be created for further diagnosis and to begin to formulate possible alternative actions that will improve relations.

Intergroup development

OD efforts to improve interactions between groups.

EVALUATING OD EFFECTIVENESS

Do OD interventions work? Let's first review the research results and then look at the quality of the research that the findings are based upon.

---

[26] See, for example, E. H. Neilsen, "Understanding and Managing Intergroup Conflict," in J. W. Lorsch and P. R. Lawrence (eds.), *Managing Group and Intergroup Relations* (Homewood, IL: Irwin-Dorsey, 1972), pp. 329–43.

[27] R. R. Blake, J. S. Mouton, and R. L. Sloma, "The Union-Management Intergroup Laboratory: Strategy for Resolving Intergroup Conflict," *Journal of Applied Behavioral Science*, No. 1 (1965), pp. 25–57.

Review of the Research

Consistent with the previous section's emphasis on human process techniques, we'll focus our attention on how effective these techniques are in achieving their objectives.

Sensitivity Training   Research investigations into sensitivity training indicate that it can effectively change individual behavior. However, the impact of these changes on performance is inconclusive.[28] and the technique is not devoid of psychological risks. There have been cases reported of personality damage to those who were not adequately screened prior to participation. One study found that 19 percent, almost one out of five, of group participants suffered from negative psychological effects some six to eight months after the group met and nearly one out of ten had suffered serious psychological harm.[29]

"The evidence, though still limited, is reasonably convincing that T-group training and the laboratory method do induce behavioral changes in the 'back-home' setting."[30] But behavioral change means little unless we know what kind of change will be achieved. It has been argued by some, for instance, that there is no "typical" pattern of change; rather, there is a unique response for each individual.[31]

> If this is true, the present lack of knowledge about how individual differences variables interact with training program variables makes it nearly impossible for anyone to spell out ahead of time the outcomes to be expected from any given development program. That is, if training outcomes are truly unique and unpredictable, no basis exists for judging the potential worth of T-group training from an institutional or organizational point of view. Instead, its success or failure must be judged by each individual trainee in terms of his own personal goals.[32]

To summarize the results from sensitivity training, we find that the process changes behavior. Just specifically what that change means, however, in terms of on-the-job behavior, is still the subject of considerable debate.

Survey Feedback   What does the general evidence demonstrate about survey feedback? We find that survey feedback meetings can lead to attitudinal changes by participants. Satisfaction, positive attitudes toward work and one's supervisor, and involvement in the organization have been shown to increase as a result of group discussion surrounding the survey results.[33] However, the manager

---

[28] J. P. Campbell and M. D. Dunnette, "Effectiveness of T-Group Experience in Managerial Training and Development," *Psychological Bulletin*, August 1968, pp. 73–104.

[29] M. A. Lieberman, I. D. Yalom, and M. B. Miles, "Encounter: The Leader Makes a Difference," *Psychology Today*, March 1973, pp. 69–76.

[30] J. P. Campbell, M. D. Dunnette, E. E. Lawler III, and K. E. Weick, Jr., *Managerial Behavior, Performance, and Effectiveness* (New York: McGraw-Hill, 1970), p. 323.

[31] D. R. Bunker, "Individual Applications of Laboratory Training," *Journal of Applied Behavioral Science*, April–June 1965, pp. 131–47.

[32] Campbell et al., *Managerial Behavior*, p. 323.

[33] See, for example, D. G. Bowers, "O.D. Techniques and Their Results in 23 Organizations; the Michigan ICL Study," *Journal of Applied Behavioral Science*, January-February 1973, pp. 21–43; L. D. Brown, "Research Action: Organizational Feedback, Understanding, and Change," *Journal of Applied Behavioral Science*, November-December 1972, pp. 697–774; and J. M. Nicholas, "The Comparative Impact of Organization Development Interventions on Hard Criteria Measures," *Academy of Management Review*, October 1982, pp. 535–36.

of the organizational family can undermine the process. If the results are perceived as threatening, it has been suggested that managerial peer groups be formed to review and discuss findings before meeting with their subordinates in family groups.[34]

While the survey feedback approach changes attitudes, long-term changes in behavior have not resulted from mere group discussion of the results. There is, in fact, "little evidence that survey feedback alone leads to changes in individual behavior or organizational performance,"[35] Discussion and involvement will not bring about the desired changes if the discussion fails to initiate follow-up actions.[36]

Process Consultation   A review of six applications of the process consultation intervention found strong, but not overwhelming, support.[37] One of the applications achieved highly positive results. Three obtained mixed results; however, there was a definite balance to the positive side. The remaining applications split between "no appreciable effects" and a "negative impact." So while the effects ranged from highly positive to negative, two-thirds of the interventions demonstrated positive results.

Team Building   A review of fifty-six team building interventions found encouraging results—90 percent of the interventions obtained positive effects.[38] Other reports indicate that team building is effective in increasing member involvement and participation in group activities and in improving the effectiveness of meetings.[39] While participant attitudes are positively affected by team building, researchers suggest that it is unclear "what effects group development has on actual task performance."[40]

Intergroup Development   The final intervention, intergroup development, shows generally positive effects—better than 83 percent of these interventions got favorable evaluations—but 11 percent were negative.[41] Most of the positive results relate to attitudes, and we need to be careful about concluding the effects of intergroup development activities on individual behaviors or organization performance.[42]

---

[34] C. P. Alderfer and R. Ferriss, "Understanding the Impact of Survey Feedback," in W. W. Burke and H. A. Hornstein (eds.), *The Social Technology of Organizational Development* (Fairfax, VA: NTL Learning Resource Corp., 1972), pp. 234–43.

[35] Friedlander and Brown, "Organizational Development," p. 327.

[36] M. G. Miles, et al., "The Consequences of Survey Feedback: Theory and Evaluation," in W. G. Bennis, K. D. Benne, R. Chin (eds.), *The Planning of Change*, 2nd ed. (New York: Holt, Rinehart and Winston, 1969), pp. 456–68.

[37] R. T. Golembiewski, C. W. Proehl, Jr., and D. Sink, "Estimating the Success of OD Applications," *Training and Development Journal*, April 1982, p. 91.

[38] Ibid.

[39] Friedlander and Brown, "Organizational Development," p. 328.

[40] Ibid., p. 329.

[41] Golembiewski, et al., "Estimating the Success of OD Applications."

[42] Friedlander and Brown, "Organizational Development," p. 330.

Is the Research Tainted?

While the previous research is generally positive in its evaluation of OD interventions, there is growing concern that the research studies have not given a balanced appraisal of OD's effectiveness. The focus of this concern has essentially been directed at the diversity of methodological rigor used in the research reports. This has led one reviewer to argue that the more rigorous the research, the more likely the results are to show negative findings.[43] In other words, one of the possible explanations for most of the positive findings regarding OD interventions may be the predominance of weak or loose methodologies.

Evaluations of OD programs can be categorized as either "hard" or "soft" depending on the criteria used to assess effectiveness. Hard criteria are quantitative measures of job behavior or organizational performance. In contrast, soft criteria include anecdotal data, observational information, and measures of job satisfaction. Soft criteria appear to be more widely used in evaluation of OD programs, which can have the effect of biasing the results toward the positive side. It may well be that OD's success record is based more on the tendency of OD change agents to evaluate the results of their efforts by using anecdotes and attitude measures than the actual value of the interventions themselves.

If it's true that there is a bias toward positive findings in OD research, what's the cause? OD efforts may be more readily connected to satisfaction than hard measures of performance. Change agents may favor soft-positive results rather than hard-negative ones because they want to continue to sell their OD programs to clients, and positive results are a lot easier to sell. Still another possibility is that the bias lies in what gets published. Papers reporting positive findings are more likely to be published even if they contain some methodological shortcomings, while studies finding nonsignificant or negative results need to demonstrate a strong design to be considered for publication.[44]

Further investigation of this positive-bias phenomenon is certainly necessary. In the meantime, it's probably a good idea to look critically at the results of OD interventions to assess how these results were achieved and, specifically, the effectiveness criteria chosen in evaluating the changes.[45]

[43] D. E. Terpstra, "Relationship Between Methodological Rigor and Reported Outcomes in Organization Development Evaluation Research," *Journal of Applied Psychology*, October 1981, pp. 541–43.

[44] B. M. Bass, "Issues Involved in Relations Between Methodological Rigor and Reported Outcomes in Evaluations of Organizational Development," *Journal of Applied Psychology*, February 1983, pp. 197–99; and R. J. Bullock and D. J. Svyantek, "Positive-Findings Bias in Positive-Findings Bias Research," *Proceedings of the Academy of Management*, New York: August 1983, pp. 221–24.

[45] J. M. Nicholas and M. Katz, "Research Methods and Reporting Practices in Organization Development: A Review and Some Guidelines," *Academy of Management Review*, October 1985, pp. 737–49; and R. W. Woodman and S. J. Wayne, "An Investigation of Positive-Finding Bias in the Evaluation of Organization Development Intervention," *Academy of Management Journal*, December 1985, pp. 889–913.

Changes occur outside organizations that require internal adaptation. Deregulation in the airline industry, for example, is dramatically changing the rules of the game at places like Delta, TWA, and Continental Airlines. Cable television, VCRs, and nationally syndicated programming is rapidly producing new competitors for the three traditional television networks: ABC, CBS, NBC. If organizations fail to implement changes to adapt to their environments, their future survival can be at stake. Similarly, internal forces—like modifications in the organization's strategy, the makeup of its work force, or the introduction of new equipment—requires the implementation of planned change. Employees must adapt to these changes or their performance will suffer.

Organizational development relies on change interventions that emphasize collaboration, respect for people, trust and support, power equalization, confrontation, and participation. OD interventions are most likely to be effective when they are applied in organizations with strong humanistic cultures, where the intervention chosen reflects comprehensive diagnosis (including the national culture), and the rights of employees are balanced against the interests of improved organizational effectiveness. Moreover, the effective change agent recognizes the political dynamics in introducing change and selects an implementation strategy that reflects his or her own power and those of others that will be potentially affected by the change.

We've discussed, in this chapter, structural and behavioral techniques for bringing about change, as well as offering suggestions on how organizations can better process change. Unfortunately, a lot of the evaluative studies of OD interventions lack rigor—relying heavily on case studies and anecdotal data for support. If we acknowledge that research in this area is far from flawless, what *can* we say about OD in its relation to behavior and attitudes?

The best answer, at this time, is offered by a review of 207 intervention studies published between 1971 and 1981.[46] The reviewers placed these studies into eleven program categories (see Table 17–3). The common denominator among these categories is that they all were concerned with introducing change. But as Table 17–3 illustrates, they focused on different types of intervention programs.

The results, in aggregate, are impressive. While some of the results are distorted because of the small number of studies identified, you can't ignore the general direction of the findings: 86 percent of the measures of productivity showed improvement, 75 percent of the measures of withdrawal showed positive effects, and 75 percent noted more favorable attitudes toward work. So although the strength of effects vary by type of intervention and choice of dependent variable, change intervention programs overall appear to generally have a positive impact on employee behavior and attitudes.

[46] R. A. Katzell and R. A. Guzzo, "Psychological Approaches to Productivitiy Improvement," *American Psychologist*, April 1983, pp. 468–72; and R. A. Guzzo, R. D. Jette, and R. A. Katzell, "The Effects of Psychologically Based Intervention Programs on Worker Productivity: A Meta-Analysis," *Personnel Psychology*, Summer 1985, pp. 275–92.

TABLE 17–3
Effectiveness of Eleven Intervention Programs

	Percent Indicating Positive Effect On		
Program	Productivity	Absenteeism and Turnover	Attitudes
Recruitment and selection	NS	50	100
Training and instruction	92	71	78
Appraisal and feedback	93	60	67
Goal setting	95	67	70
Financial compensation	90	78	75
Work redesign	88	80	70
Supervisory methods	92	92	100
Organization structure	100	100	NS
Decision making techniques	100	NS	0
Work schedules	61	73	78
Sociotechnical systems redesign	95	70	100

NS = No studies identified

Adapted from R. A. Katzell and R. A. Guzzo, "Psychological Approaches to Productivity Improvement," *American Psychologist,* April 1983, p. 469.

Maybe one of the strongest cases for the effectiveness of OD values is a review of more than 500 studies, covering tens of thousands of employees, where change agents moved organizations from having authoritarian to participative climates.[47] One to two years after the change, productivity and earnings in the organizations improved 15 to 40 percent, while control organizations that didn't undergo the change interventions failed to generate such improvements.

[47] R. Likert, "Past and Future Perspectives on System 4," *Proceedings of the Academy of Management*, Orlando, Florida, 1977.

POINT

TRADITIONAL METHODS OF ORGANIZATIONAL CHANGE

It is possible to identify six types of traditional change programs if we examine their strategic rationale: (1) exposition and propagation, (2) elite corps, (3) psychoanalytic insight, (4) staff, (5) scholarly consultations, and (6) circulation of ideas to the elite.

Exposition and propagation. Knowledge is power. Those with the ideas—particularly philosophers like Marx, Keynes, and Darwin—change the world. So philosophers, rather than social scientists, induce social changes by their general thoughts and theories.

Elite corps. Like the previous view, the elite corps recognizes that knowledge is power. But the previous view assumes that the elitists (who have the ideas) can communicate their ideas to policy makers. The elite corps perspective assumes that policy makers and people in power can't communicate with each other. The solution, then, is to get some of the people who have knowledge into positions of power as policy makers.

Psychoanalytic insight. This view is similar to the elite corps idea in that it depends upon people in power. Its difference lies in the type of knowledge it requires of its elite. Rather than science, it emphasizes self-insight and psychiatric wisdom; thus we have effective change occurring through the well-analyzed executive. According to this view, corps of elite have special powers, but the specialty is psychoanalysis rather than science.

Staff. This fourth view is that social scientists should take responsibility for providing advice. They observe, analyze, and then plan rationally policy reactions to events of a government, an interest organization, or a business firm. Rather than lean on the detached scholar, the organization employs the scholar as staff.

Scholarly consultations. This is a procedure whereby science can be made useful to clients. It includes exploratory inquiry, scholarly understanding, scholarly confrontation, discovery of solutions, and scientific advice to the client. The social scientist accepts the problem more or less as stated by the client and attempts to deduce solutions from combinations of sociological laws. Little or no research is conducted, except that which is needed to clarify the problem. Finally, as a doctor advises a patient, the scholarly consultant tells the client what to do.

Circulation of ideas of the elite. This final view argues that if you want to change things, then you get your ideas to the people with power or to people who influence someone who can influence someone in power. Those who write position papers or articles in the newspapers which are read by the elite corps influence change.

Although the six strategies differ in objectives, in values, in means of influence, and although each has its own programmatic implications, they are similar in wanting to use knowledge to gain some socially desirable end.

Source: Adapted from W. G. Bennis, "A New Role for the Behavioral Sciences: Effecting Organizational Change," *Administrative Science Quarterly*, September 1963, pp. 130–34.

COUNTERPOINT

OD: A SIGNIFICANT DEPARTURE FROM TRADITION

Each of the six strategies shows a bias or an emphasis which can be questioned and which weakens its full impact. Four biases are particularly significant:[1]

Rationalistic bias: no program. Present to a greater or less degree in all the schemes is the belief that knowledge equals power. Obviously there is some truth in this. But knowledge about something does not necessarily lead to intelligent action.

Technocratic bias: no collaboration. Related to the rationalistic bias is the assumption that if a program is presented, the client can carry it out with dispatch. But this engineering approach to planned change rarely works without some form of collaboration between the change agent and the client.

Elite bias: no organizational strategy. Several of the strategies have an elite bias. They assume that if people in power possess the right ideas they will act in accordance with those ideas. This undoubtedly has some truth to it, but the elite bias accepts the notion of a unified and willfully coordinated power elite. It also accepts by implication the idea of a stagnant middle level and a fragmented mass society. These are questionable assumptions. This bias also ignores organizational forces and norms operating on the person in power; most specifically, role requirements. Remember, roles can corrupt.

Insight bias: no manipulability. There is a bias held by most clinical psychologists that

Insight bias: no manipulability. There is a bias held by most clinical psychologists that insight leads to more effective functioning. One needn't quarrel with the notion that insight equals change, though this could be challenged. Rather, short of some form of psychotherapy, just how does an executive learn to become a preventive, remedial, and diagnostic agent?

Organizational development efforts depart substantially from the six methods of change presented.[2] The OD consultant does not make recommendations in the traditional sense; his or her end product is not a written report to top management, concluding with recommendations for the solutions of substantive problems. The client organization, however, is assisted in the way it goes about solving problems.

There are seven characteristics that differentiate OD interventions from more traditional interventions:

1. an emphasis on the work team as the key unit for addressing issues and learning more effective modes of organizational behavior,

2. an emphasis, although not exclusively so, on group, intergroup, and organizational processes in contrast to substantive content,

3. the use of the action research model,

4. an emphasis on the collaborative management of work-team culture, including temporary teams,

5. an emphasis on the management of the culture of the total system, including intergroup culture,

6. attention to the management of system ramifications, and

7. a view of the change effort as an ongoing process.

[1] W. G. Bennis, "A New Role for the Behavioral Sciences: Effecting Organizational Change," *Administrative Science Quarterly*, September 1963, pp. 135–38.

[2] This section adapted from W. L. French and C. H. Bell, Jr., *Organization Development: Behavioral Science Interventions for Organization Improvement*, 3rd ed. (Englewood Cliffs, NJ:Prentice Hall, 1984), p. 22.

KEY TERMS

Action Research

Change

Change Agent

Change Intervention

Driving Forces

Intergroup Development

Organizational Development (OD)

Process Consultation

Refreezing

Restraining Forces

Sensitivity Training

Survey Feedback

Team Building

Unfreezing

FOR DISCUSSION

1. What is the relationship between OD and organizational adaptability?

2. Explain the statement, "Initiating change is no assurance that it will be accepted," in terms of the change process.

3. Why do people resist change?

4. What can a change agent do to deal with change resistance?

5. What differentiates OD from any change activity?

6. What is the "OD consultation process"? Contrast the roles of consultant and client in this process.

7. What impact does an organization's culture have in determining whether OD will be successful?

8. What impact does national culture have in determining whether OD will be successful?

9. What can the politically astute change agent do to increase the probability that an intervention will succeed?

10. Are some organizations more likely to require planned change interventions than others? If so, why?

11. What is sensitivity training? How effective is it in changing attitudes and job behavior?

12. What criticism might you lodge against those who argue that there are numerous research studies to support the effectiveness of OD interventions?

FOR FURTHER READING

BEER, M., and A. E. WALTON, "Organization Change and Development," in M. R. Rosenzweig and L. W. Porter (eds), *Annual Review of Psychology*, Vol. 38, pp. 339–67. Palo Alto, CA: Annual Reviews, 1987. Updates the OD literature with discussions of trends in general management and human resource management.

FRENCH, W. L., and C. H. BELL, JR., *Organizational Development: Behavioral Science Interventions for Organization Improvement*, 3rd edition. Englewood Cliffs, NJ: Prentice Hall, 1984. A popular introductory text that reviews OD theory and practice.

LIPPITT, G., R. LIPPITT, and C. LAFFERTY, "Cutting Edge Trends in Organization Development," *Training and Development Journal*, July 1984, pp. 59–62. A survey of 300 OD professionals identifies fifteen major trends that are likely to affect OD practice during the next decade.

PORRAS, J. I., and S. J. HOFFER, "Common Behavior Changes in Successful Organization Development Efforts," *Journal of Applied Behavioral Science*, November 1986, pp. 477–94. Survey of forty-two leaders in the field of organizational change found nine behavior changes common in successful OD efforts for individuals at all levels and five common behavior changes for managers.

Sashkin, M., and W. W. Burke, "OD in the 1980s," *Journal of Management*, Summer 1987, pp. 393–418. Reviews current state of OD and offers three possible scenarios for the future.

Warrick, D. D., and J. T. Thompson, "Still Crazy After All These Years," *Training and Development Journal*, April 1980, pp. 16–22. Notes discrepancies between traditional OD values and theories and what happens in practice.

For each of the following, indicate the degree to which your opinion agrees or disagrees
with the statement by circling one of the six responses.

	Response					
Statement	Agree very much	Agree on the whole	Agree a little	Disagree a little	Disagree on the whole	Disagree very much
1. In this complicated world of ours, the only way we can know what's going on is to rely on leaders or experts who can be trusted.	1	2	3	4	5	6
2. My blood boils whenever a person stubbornly refuses to admit he or she is wrong.	1	2	3	4	5	6
3. There are two kinds of people in this world: those who are for the truth and those who are against the truth.	1	2	3	4	5	6
4. Most people just don't know what's good for them.	1	2	3	4	5	6
5. Of all the different philosophies which exist in this world, there is probably only one which is correct.	1	2	3	4	5	6
6. The highest form of government is a democracy and the highest form of democracy is a government run by those who are most intelligent.	1	2	3	4	5	6
7. The main thing in life is for a person to want to do something important.	1	2	3	4	5	6
8. I'd like it if I could find someone who would tell me how to solve my personal problems.	1	2	3	4	5	6
9. Most of the ideas which get printed nowadays aren't worth the paper they are printed on.	1	2	3	4	5	6
10. Man on his own is a helpless and miserable creature.	1	2	3	4	5	6
11. It is only when a person devotes himself or herself to an ideal or cause that life becomes meaningful.	1	2	3	4	5	6
12. Most people just don't give a damn for others.	1	2	3	4	5	6
13. To compromise with our political opponents is dangerous because it usually leads to the betrayal of our own side.	1	2	3	4	5	6
14. It is often desirable to reserve judgment about what's going on until one has had a chance to hear the opinions of those one respects.	1	2	3	4	5	6
15. The *present* is all too often full of un-						

Statement	Response					
	Agree very much	Agree on the whole	Agree a little	Disagree a little	Disagree on the whole	Disagree very much
happiness. It is only the *future* that counts.	1	2	3	4	5	6
16. The United States and the U.S.S.R. have just about nothing in common.	1	2	3	4	5	6
17. In a discussion I often find it necessary to repeat myself several times to make sure I am being understood.	1	2	3	4	5	6
18. While I don't like to admit this even to myself, my secret ambition is to become a great person, like Einstein, or Beethoven, or Shakespeare.	1	2	3	4	5	6
19. Even though freedom of speech for all groups is a worthwhile goal, it is unfortunately necessary to restrict the freedom of certain political groups.	1	2	3	4	5	6
20. It is better to be a dead hero than to be a live coward.	1	2	3	4	5	6

Turn to page 568 for scoring directions and key.

Source: Adapted from V. C. Troldahl and F. A. Powell, "A Short-Form Dogmatism Scale for Use in Field Studies," *Social Forces*, December 1965, p. 213.

IMPLEMENTING CHANGE AT THE SCARBOROUGH DAILY NEWS

The *Scarborough Daily News* is a local newspaper published in a growing suburban community of Toronto, Canada. The paper's new publisher is Ian Robertson.

Ian had spent fifteen years at the much larger *Toronto Star*, rising to the position of senior national editor. But he decided he'd never get to the top at the *Star* and decided to accept the position of publisher of the *Daily News*. As publisher, he assumed complete responsibility for the paper's operation. Ian reported to J. William McDougall, chief executive officer of CFI Publishing Ltd., which owned and operated over a dozen Canadian newspapers.

The *Scarborough Daily News* was founded in 1955 and had grown over the years to a daily circulation of nearly 100,000. The paper currently employs approximately 300 people.

Ian knew the *Daily News* had serious problems when he accepted the job. In fact, he only agreed to take the job after McDougall offered a five-year guaranteed contract and carte blanche authority to make whatever changes were necessary.

One of the first things Ian is concerned with is the paper's financial performance. Profits are half the industry standard and have been flat for three years in a row. Even though circulation has been growing at a respectable six percent a year, expenses have been expanding at better than ten percent annually. Ian's initial thinking is that the paper is overstaffed. Possibly by reorganizing the four editorial departments (national, local, sports, and financial) and the three business areas (circulation, classified, and advertising), a significant reduction in staff could be achieved. But Ian is also greatly concerned about the work culture at the *Daily News*. The previous publisher, Claude Forte, was an easy-going guy who was more concerned with being liked than getting the job done. He hated confrontation and avoided making any decisions that might upset someone. For instance, Ian had looked through nearly 200 performance appraisals from last year and he couldn't find one negative comment in the batch. But he knew better. After only six weeks on the job, Ian was aware of at least two department heads who clearly were ineffective in their jobs. And the overall staff seemed lackadaisical and unprofessional. Ian was convinced that most of these people had the ability to be productive but that the culture encouraged mediocrity and complacency. Under Ian's new leadership, he was determined this could not continue.

QUESTIONS

1. Where should Ian start in his effort to turn the *Scarborough Daily News* around?
2. What steps should be taken to implement the necessary changes?
3. What methods would you recommend he use? Why?

Appendix: Scoring Keys for Exercises

Exercise 1. What Do You Know About Human Behavior?

The correct answers to this exercise are as follows:

1. T	6. F	11. F	16. T
2. F	7. T	12. T	17. T
3. F	8. F	13. F	18. F
4. F	9. F	14. F	19. F
5. F	10. T	15. F	20. F

How well did you do? Most people get between twelve and sixteen right. Did you beat the average?

The value of this exercise is to dramatize that some of what you know about human behavior is erroneous. The systematic study of OB will help you to sort out fact from fiction regarding the behavior of people at work.

Exercise 2. How Do You Feel About Your Present Job?

For questions 1, 2, 5, 7, 9, 12, 13, 15, and 17, score your answers as follows: Strongly agree = 5; Agree = 4; Undecided = 3; Disagree = 2; Strongly disagree = 1. The remaining questions are scored in the reverse manner: Strongly agree = 1; Agree = 2, and so forth. Now sum up your scores for the eighteen items on the questionnaire. The larger your total score, the higher your job satisfaction. For comparative purposes, you might be interested to know that this questionnaire has been administered to individuals in a wide variety of jobs, including managers, civil service office employees, clerical workers, taxi drivers, nurses, and part-time graduate students. Eleven different studies found the range of mean scores to be between 56.79 and 76.51, with the mean of the means at 64.32. How did your score compare?

Exercise 3. Who Controls Your Life?

This exercise is designed to measure your locus of control. Give yourself 1 point for each of the following selections: 1B, 2A, 3A, 4B, 5B, 6A, 7A, 8A, 9B, and 10A. Scores can be interpreted as follows:

8–10 = High internal locus of control

6–7 = Moderate internal locus of control

5 = Mixed

3–4 = Moderate external locus of control

1–2 = High external locus of control

The higher your internal score, the more you believe that you control your own destiny. The higher your external score, the more you believe that what happens to you in your life is due to luck or chance.

Exercise 4. Assumptions on Perceptions

Actual occupations of the four individuals are:

- R. B. Red (female) - Computer operations manager.
- W. C. White (male) - Truck driver.
- G. A. Green (male) - Army general.
- B. E. Brown (female) - Labor negotiator.

Exercise 5. Value Assessment Test

Each item in the value assessment exercise is coded in the following manner:

- A = theoretical dimension
- B = economic-political dimension
- C = aesthetic dimension
- D = social dimension

Total scores for each dimension are calculated by adding the number associated with the response on the dimension items for each "Yes" response. For example, in the B items (economic-political), if you replied "Yes" only to 31, 34, and 76, your total score on the economic-political dimension would be 23 (5 + 8 + 10). When a sample of 389 females and 352 males was taken, the following percentile norms were developed.

	Percentile	Theoretical	Economic-Political	Aesthetic	Social
	100	110	110	110	110
	90	74	70	96	96
	80	60	54	88	88
	70	48	46	79	82
	60	40	39	69	77
Female	50	32	32	62	72
(N = 389)	40	25	25	54	67
	30	19	21	46	59
	20	14	17	36	52
	10	8	11	22	39
	1	0	1	3	0

	Percentile	Theoretical	Economic-Political	Aesthetic	Social
	100	110	110	110	110
	90	85	89	83	90
	80	74	76	69	80
	70	66	67	60	73
	60	54	56	47	65
Male	50	45	49	39	56
(N = 352)	40	39	38	32	47
	30	31	30	26	39
	20	21	21	20	33
	10	11	12	12	25
	1	0	0	0	4

If you scored high on any dimension, the meaning is indicated below.[*]

Theoretical. A high score indicates that you prefer and consider most worthwhile those activities that involve a problem-solving attitude and are related to investigation, research, and scientific curiosity.

Economical-political. A high score indicates that you prefer and consider most worthwhile those activities that involve the accumulation of money and the securing of executive power.

Aesthetic. A high score indicates that you prefer and consider most worthwhile those activities that involve art, music, dance, and literature.

Social. A high score indicates that you prefer and consider most worthwhile those activities that involve service and help to people; you exhibit a definite desire to respond and be with people socially.

[*]The scoring instruction information was taken from J. R. Robinson and P. R. Shaver, *Measures of Social Psychological Attitudes*, rev. ed. (Ann Arbor, University of Michigan, Institute for Social Research, 1973), pp. 510–11.)

Exercise 6. Needs Test

- Growth needs are items 2, 5, 8, 11.
- Relatedness needs are items 1, 4, 7, 10.
- Existence needs are items 3, 6, 9, 12.

Add the scores for each need set (for example, the summation of your scores on items 2, 5, 8, and 11 represent your growth need total). If you considered all four items within a need category to be very important, you would obtain the maximum total of twenty points.

College students typically rate growth needs highest. However, you may currently have little income and consider existence needs as most important. For instance, one student of mine scored 20, 10, and 15 for growth, relatedness, and existence needs, respectively. This should be interpreted to mean that her relatedness needs are already substantially satisfied. Her growth needs, on the other hand, are substantially unsatisfied.

Note that a low score may imply that a need is unimportant to you or that it is substantially satisfied. The implication, however, is that *everyone* has these needs. So a low score is usually taken to mean that this need is substantially satisfied.

Exercise 7. Assessing Your Job's Motivating Potential

This questionnaire allows you to calculate your Motivating Potential Score from the Job Characteristics Model. The MPS represents a summary score indicating how motivating is the job you have described. Insert your scores from the questionnaire (the numbers 1 through 7) into the following formula to calculate your MPS:

$$\text{MPS} = \left(\frac{\text{Skill variety} + \text{Task identity} + \text{Task significance}}{3}\right) \times \text{Autonomy} \times \text{Feedback}$$

The higher your score, the higher your job's motivating potential. National norms are as follows: Skill variety = 4.7; Task identity = 4.7; Task significance = 5.5; Autonomy = 4.9; Feedback = 4.9, and MPS = 128. How does your (past or present) job compare to the national norms? What could be done to improve your job's MPS?

Exercise 8. Group Effectiveness Checklist

This checklist is designed to help you assess a group's effectiveness. The greater the number of statements to which you answered "Mostly Yes," the more likely the group is productive and its members are satisfied. You can also use this checklist as a development tool. If you want to improve a group's effectiveness, emphasize achieving the twenty qualities described in the checklist.

Exercise 9. Test Your Management Communication Skills[*]

CORRECT ANSWERS:

1a. Never forget who your boss is—and where your loyalty lies. If you tell him or her nothing, or if you tell him or her casually, you plant seeds of mistrust.

2c. Honesty and courtesy are the best policies. It's never right to lie. And it's never smart to waste your boss's time.

3b. Keeping appointments and looking your best are basic business principles. No one appreciates a last-minute cancellation of an appointment. You'd be surprised at what good eyes an interviewer has.

4a. Controlling the meeting starts with your setting the ground rules—up front. To feed one person's self-interest is not productive, or fair.

5c. This is the only practical answer. To detail negative observations could lead to legal action; to stress only positive points is to tell a half-truth.

6c. It's best to nip problems in the bud. Procrastination is a sin. And you must first talk with one employee to determine if there's a need to talk with two.

7c. Place the responsibility where it belongs. To be a "good guy" or to leave immediately is not facing up to the problem.

8c. Project a positive thought as you make your position clear. Blaming others is passing the buck; hiding behind a "maybe" meeting is a sign of weakness.

9c. This answer establishes you as an authority for future stories. To send a gift is unwarranted and tasteless. And to the writer, the story is not "publicity"—it's "news coverage."

10c. Take no action, particularly on your first day. To ignore the problem is foolish; to initiate conversations is a greater folly.

11b. Keep the conversation on a business level. It's your responsibility to stop office gossip, not encourage it.

12a. This action is prudent and professional. You don't want to embarrass your boss and customer. Nor do you want to be in an awkward position afterward.

Exercise 10. Compute Your LPC Score

Your score on the LPC scale is a measure of your leadership style. More specifically, it indicates your primary motivation or goal in a work setting.

To determine your LPC score, add up the points (1 through 8) for each of the sixteen items. If your score is 64 or above, you're a *high* LPC person or *relationship*-oriented. If your score is 57 or below, you're a *low* LPC person or *task*-oriented. If your score falls between 58 and 63, you'll need to determine for yourself in which category you belong.

[*]Communispond, Inc., 485 Lexington Avenue, New York, N.Y. 10017. With permission.

According to Fiedler, knowing your LPC score can allow you to find a situational match and, therefore, help you to be a more effective leader.

Exercise 11. Power Orientation Test

This test is designed to compute your Machiavellianism (Mach) score. To obtain your score, add the number you have checked on questions 1, 3, 4, 5, 9, and 10. For the other four questions, reverse the numbers you have checked: 5 becomes 1, 4 is 2, 2 is 4, 1 is 5. Total your ten numbers to find your score. The National Opinion Research Center, which used this short form of the scale in a random sample of American adults, found that the national average was 25.

The results of research using the Mach test have found that (1) men are generally more Machiavellian than women, (2) older adults tend to have lower Mach scores than younger adults, (3) there is no significant difference between high Machs and low Machs on measures of intelligence or ability, (4) Machiavellianism is not significantly related to demographic characteristics such as educational level or marital status, and (5) high Machs tend to be in professions that emphasize the control and manipulation of individuals—for example, managers, lawyers, psychiatrists, and behavioral scientists.

Exercise 12. How Do You Handle Conflict?

Putnam and Wilson's research found that the five conflict-handling approaches described in Chapter 12 collapsed into three conflict strategies: nonconfrontational (which includes avoidance and accommodation), solution-oriented (collaboration and compromise), and control (synonymous with competition).

To calculate your mean score, sum up the total score you made in each of the three categories and divide by the number of items measuring the strategy. Then subtract each score from seven.

Items 1, 4, 6, 8, 9, 11, 13, 16, 19, 20, 21 = Solution-oriented
Items 2, 5, 7, 12, 14, 15, 23, 24, 25, 27, 28, 29 = Nonconfrontational
Items 3, 10, 17, 18, 22, 26, 30 = Control

From a study conducted by Putnam and Wilson, 360 participants scored as follows:

Solution-orientation = 3.73
Control = 2.43
Nonconfrontational = 2.42

You may want to break into small groups and compare your score patterns. Discuss issues such as: Did individual scores align with previous images that these individuals had of their conflict-handling style? Is there a common pattern among group members' scores? If so, why? If not, why not? Do you think your group's results are generalizable to all students? How about successful managers?

Exercise 13. Bureaucratic Orientation Test

Give yourself one point for each statement for which you responded in the bureaucratic direction:

1. Mostly agree	11. Mostly agree
2. Mostly agree	12. Mostly disagree
3. Mostly disagree	13. Mostly disagree
4. Mostly agree	14. Mostly agree
5. Mostly disagree	15. Mostly disagree
6. Mostly disagree	16. Mostly agree
7. Mostly agree	17. Mostly disagree
8. Mostly agree	18. Mostly agree
9. Mostly disagree	19. Mostly agree
10. Mostly agree	20. Mostly disagree

A very high score (15 or over) would suggest that you would enjoy working in a bureaucracy. A very low score (5 or lower) would suggest that you would be frustrated by working in a bureaucracy, especially a large one.

Do you think your score is representative of most college students in your major? Discuss.

Exercise 14. Career Assessment Test

Score your responses by writing the number that corresponds to your response (SA = 4, A = 3, D = 2, SD = 1) to each question in the space next to the item number.

1 ___	2 ___	3 ___	4 ___	5 ___	6 ___
7 ___	8 ___	9 ___	10 ___	11 ___	12 ___
13 ___	14 ___	15 ___	16 ___	17 ___	18 ___
19 ___	20 ___	21 ___	22 ___	23 ___	24 ___
25 ___	26 ___	27 ___	28 ___	29 ___	30 ___
31 ___	32 ___	33 ___	34 ___	35 ___	36 ___
37 ___	38 ___	39 ___	40 ___	41 ___	42 ___
43 ___	44 ___				

Now obtain subscale scores by adding your scores on the items indicated and then divide by the number of items in the scale, as shown:

Technical Competence		
	÷ 6 = _____	
	#1, 2, 27, 35, 38, 41	

Technical Competence _____ ÷ 6 = _____
#1, 2, 27, 35, 38, 41

Autonomy _____ ÷ 6 = _____
#3, 18, 23, 36, 39, 40

Service _____ ÷ 6 = _____
#4, 21, 37, 42, 43, 44

Identity _____ ÷ 5 = _____
#7, 13, 20, 22, 26

Variety _____ ÷ 6 = _____
#5, 12, 14, 24, 31, 32

Managerial Competence _____ ÷ 6 = _____
#6, 10, 11, 15, 25, 30

Security _____ ÷ 5 = _____
#8, 16, 17, 28, 33

Creativity _____ ÷ 4 = _____
#9, 19, 29, 34

The preceding identifies your career anchors or "a syndrome of motives, values, and self-perceived competencies which function to guide and constrain an individual's career." Briefly, the eight career anchors mean the following:

- *Technical competence.* You organize your career around the challenge of the actual work you're doing.
- *Autonomy.* You value freedom and independence.
- *Service.* You're concerned with helping others or working on an important cause.
- *Identity.* You're concerned with status, prestige, and titles in your work.
- *Variety.* You seek an endless variety of new and different challenges.
- *Managerial competence.* You like to solve problems and want to lead and control others.
- *Security.* You want stability and career security.
- *Creativity.* You have a strong need to create something of your own.

The higher your score on a given anchor, the stronger your emphasis. You'll function best when your job fits with your career anchor. Lack of fit between anchor and a job can cause you to leave the organization or suffer excessive stress.

Ask yourself now: On which anchor did I receive the highest score? What jobs fit best with this anchor? You can use your analysis to help you select the right job and career for you.

Exercise 15. What's It Like to Work in Another Country?

Form groups and compare your analyses. Did your answers reflect Hofstede's research on cultural dimensions?

Exercise 16. Are You a Type A?

Total your score on the seven questions. Now mutliple it by 3. A total of 120 or more indicates you're a hard-core Type A. Scores below 90 indicate you're a hard-core Type B. The following gives you more specifics:

Points	Personality type
120 or more	A+
106–119	A
100–105	A−
90–99	B+
Less than 90	B

Exercise 17. How Receptive Are You to Change?

This questionnaire is designed to test dogmatism. To calculate your dogmatism score, write +1, +2, +3 or −1, −2, −3 next to each of the 20 statements depending on how you responded.

+1: Agree a little	−1: Disagree a little
+2: Agree on the whole	−2: Disagree on the whole
+3: Agree very much	−3: Disagree very much

Dogmatism is a form of close-mindedness. People who score high on this scale stubbornly hold on to their attitudes against all apparent reason and evidence. They are quick to reject opposing attitudes, even at the risk of being illogical or inconsistent. The higher your score on this scale, the less receptive to change you're likely to be.

How do your results align with your image of your willingness to accept change?

Glossary

The number in parentheses following each term indicates the chapter in which the term was defined.

Ability (3). An individual's capacity to perform the various tasks in a job.

Absenteeism (2). Failure to report to work.

Accommodation (12). The willingness of one party in a conflict to place his or her opponent's interests above his or her own.

Action research (17). The systematic collection of data and selection of a change intervention based on the data collected.

Active listening (9). The active search for meaning when one listens.

Adhocracy (13). A structure that is flexible, adaptive, and responsive; organized around unique problems to be solved by groups of relative strangers with diverse professional skills.

Affiliation need (6). The desire for friendly and close interpersonal relationships.

Assessment centers (14). A set of performance simulation tests designed to evaluate a candidate's managerial potential.

Attitudes (5). Evaluative statements or judgments concerning objects, people, or events.

Attitude surveys (5). Eliciting responses from employees through questionnaires about how they feel about their jobs, work groups, supervisors, and/or the organization.

Attribution theory (4). When individuals observe behavior, they attempt to determine whether it is internally or externally caused.

Authoritarianism (3). The belief that there should be status and power differences among people in organizations.

Autocratic leader (10). One who dictates decisions down to subordinates.

Autonomous work teams (7). Groups that are free to determine how the goals assigned to them are to be accomplished and how tasks are to be allocated.

Autonomy (7). The degree to which the job provides substantial freedom and discretion to the individual in scheduling the work and in determining the procedures to be used in carrying it out.

Avoidance (12). Withdrawing from or suppressing conflict.

Behaviorally anchored rating scales (14). An evaluation method where actual job-related behaviors are rated along a continuum.

Behavioral symptoms of stress (16). Changes in an individual's behavior—including productivity, absence, and turnover—as a result of stress.

Behavioral theories of leadership (10). Theories proposing that specific behaviors differentiate leaders from nonleaders.

Biographical characteristics (3). Personal characteristics—such as age, sex, and marital status—that are objective and easily obtained from personnel records.

Biological school of job design (7). Job design efforts that focus on improving the comfort and physical well-being of the employee.

Bounded rationality (4). Individuals make decisions by constructing simplified models that extract the essential features from problems without capturing all their complexity.

Brainstorming (9). An idea-generation process that specifically encourages any and all alternatives, while withholding any criticism of those alternatives.

Bureaucracy (13). A structure characterized by high complexity, high formalization, impersonality, career tracks, employment decisions based on merit, and separation of members' organizational and personal lives.

Career (14). A sequence of positions occupied by a person during the course of a lifetime.

Career stages (14). The four steps most people go through in their careers: exploration, establishment, midcareer, and late career.

Case study (2). An in-depth analysis of one setting.

Causality (2). The implication that the independent variable causes the dependent variable.

Caused behavior (1). Behavior that is directed toward some end; not random.

Centralization (13). The degree to which decision making is concentrated at a single point in the organization.

Change (17). Making things different.

Change agent (17). The person (or persons) who acts as a catalyst, and assumes the responsibility for managing the change process.

Change intervention (17). A planned action to make things different.

Channel (9). The medium through which a communication message travels.

Charismatic leadership (10). Followers make attributions of heroic or extraordinary leadership abilities when they observe certain behaviors.

Classical conditioning (3). A type of conditioning where an individual responds to some stimulus that would not invariably produce such a response.

Coalition (11). Two or more individuals who combine their power to push for or support their demands.

Coercive power (11). Power that is based on fear.

Cognitive dissonance (5). Any incompatibility between two or more attitudes or between behavior and attitudes.

Cognitive evaluation theory (6). Extrinsic rewards allocated for behavior that had been previously intrinsically rewarded tends to decrease the overall level of motivation.

Cohesiveness (8). Degree to which group members are attracted to each other and share common goals.

Cohorts (8). Individuals who, as part of a group, hold a common attribute.

Collaboration (12). A situation where the parties to a conflict each desire to satisfy fully the concern of all parties.

Collectivism (15). A national culture attribute that describes a tight social framework in which people expect others in groups of which they are a part to look after them and protect them.

Command group (8). A manager and his or her immediate subordinates.

Communication (9). The transference and understanding of meaning.

Communication networks (9). Channels by which information flows.

Communication process (9). The steps between a source and a receiver that result in the transference of meaning.

Competition (12). Rule-regulated efforts to obtain a goal without interference from another party.

Complexity (13). The degree of vertical, horizontal, and spatial differentiation in an organization.

Compressed workweek (7). A four-day week, with employees working ten hours a day.

Compromise (12). A situation in which each party to a conflict must give up something.

Conflict (12). A process in which an effort is purposely made by A to offset the efforts of B by some form of blocking that will result in frustrating B in attaining his or her goals or furthering his or her interests.

Conflict paradox (12). Conflict contributes to a group's performance but most groups and organizations try to eliminate it.

Conformity (8). Adjusting one's behavior to align with the norms of the group.

Conformity values (5). A low tolerance for ambiguity, having difficulty in accepting people with different values, and a desire that others accept one's values.

Consideration (10). The extent to which a leader is likely to have job relationships characterized by mutual trust, respect for subordinates' ideas, and regard for their feelings.

Constraints of stress (16). Forces that prevent individuals from doing what they desire.

Contingency variables (1). Those variables that moderate the relationship between the independent and dependent variables and improve the correlation.

Continuous reinforcement (3). A desired behavior is reinforced each and every time it is demonstrated.

Core values (15). The primary or dominant values that are accepted throughout the organization.

Correlation coefficient (2). Indicates the strength of a relationship between two or more variables.

Critical incidents (14). Evaluating those behaviors that are key in making the difference between executing a job effectively or ineffectively.

Cultural clusters (15). Grouping countries into meaningful categories based on geography, shared language, and similar religions.

Decoding (9). Retranslating a sender's communication message.

Deep relaxation (16). A state of physical relaxation, where the individual is somewhat detached from the immediate environment and detached from body sensations.

Delphi technique (9). A group decision method in which individual members, acting separately, pool their judgment in a systematic and independent fashion.

Demands of stress (16). The loss of something desired.

Democratic leader (10). One who shares decision making with subordinates.

Dependency (11). B's relationship to A when A possesses something that B requires.

Dependent variable (2). A response that is affected by an independent variable.

Dominant culture (15). Expresses the core values that are shared by a majority of the organization's members.

Driving forces (17). Change forces that direct behavior away from the status quo.

Dysfunctional conflict (12). Conflict that hinders group performance.

Effectiveness (2). Achievement of goal.

Efficiency (2). The ratio of effective output to the input required to achieve it.

Egocentrism values (5). The belief in rugged individualism and selfishness.

Elasticity of power (11). The relative responsiveness of power to changes in available alternatives.

Employee-oriented leader (10). One who emphasizes interpersonal relations.

Encoding (9). Converting a communication message to symbolic form.

Encounter stage (15). The stage in the socialization process in which a new employee sees what the organization is really like and confronts the likelihood that expectations and reality may diverge.

Engineering school of job design (7). A mechanistic approach that focuses on efficiency.

Environment (13). Anything outside the organization itself.

Equity theory (6). Individuals compare their job inputs and outcomes with those of others and then respond so as to eliminate any inequities.

ERG theory (6). There are three groups of core needs: existence, relatedness, and growth.

Ergonomics school of job design (7). Seeks to increase system reliability by developing equipment and jobs that are safe, simple, reliable, and that minimize mental requirements on the worker.

Escalation of commitment (5). An increased commitment to a previous decision in spite of negative information.

Existential values (5). A high tolerance for ambiguity and individuals with differing values.

Exit (5). Dissatisfaction expressed through behavior directed toward leaving the organization.

Expectancy theory (6). The strength of a tendency to act in a certain way depends on the strength of an expectation that the act will be followed by a given outcome and on the attractiveness of that outcome to the individual.

Expert power (11). Influence based on special skills or knowledge.

Externals (3). Individuals who believe that what happens to them is controlled by outside forces such as luck or chance.

Extrinsic rewards (14). Rewards received from the environment surrounding the context of the work.

Feedback (7). The degree to which carrying out the work activities required by a job results in the individual obtaining direct and clear information about the effectiveness of his or her performance.

Feedback loop (9). The final link in the communication process; puts the message back into the system as a check against misunderstandings.

Felt conflict (12). Emotional involvement in a conflict creating anxiety, tenseness, frustration, or hostility.

Femininity (15). A national culture attribute that emphasizes relationships, concern for others, and the overall quality of life.

Field experiment (2). A controlled experiment conducted in a real organization.

Field survey (2). Questionnaire or interview responses are collected from a sample, analyzed, and then inferences are made about the larger population from which the sample is representative.

Filtering (9). A sender's manipulation of information so that it will be seen more favorably by the receiver.

Fixed-interval schedule (3). Rewards are spaced at uniform time intervals.

Fixed-ratio schedule (3). Rewards are initiated after a fixed or constant number of responses.

Flexible benefits (7). Employees tailor their benefit program to meet their personal needs by picking and choosing from among a menu of benefit options.

Flextime (7). Employees work during a common core time period each day but have discretion in forming their total workday from a flexible set of hours outside the core.

Formal group (8). A designated work group defined by the organization's structure.

Formalization (13). The degree to which jobs within the organization are standardized.

Friendship group (8). Those brought together because they share one or more common characteristics.

Functional conflict (12). Conflict that supports the goals of the group and improves its performance.

Functional structure (13). A structure characterized by grouping similar and related occupational specialties together.

Fundamental attribution error (4). The tendency to underestimate the influence of external factors and overestimate the influence of internal factors when making judgments about the behavior of others.

Generalizability (2). The degree to which results of a research study are applicable to groups of individuals other than those who participate in the original study.

Goal-setting theory (6). The theory that specific and difficult goals lead to higher performance.

Grapevine (9). The informal communication channel.

Graphic rating scales (14). An evaluation method where the evaluator rates performance factors on an incremental scale.

Group (8). Two or more individuals, interacting and interdependent, who come together to achieve particular objectives.

Group demography (8). The degree to which members of a group share a common demographic attribute such as age, sex, race, educational level, or length of service in the organization, and the impact of these attributes on turnover.

Group order ranking (14). An evaluation method that places employees into a particular classification such as quartiles.

Groupshift (9). A change in decision risk between the group's decision and the individual decision that members within the group would make; can be either toward conservatism or greater risk.

Groupthink (9). Phenomenon in which the norm for consensus overrides the realistic appraisal of alternative courses of action.

Groupware (8). Computer software programs that allow employees to collaborate across barriers of space and time.

Halo effect (4). Drawing a general impression about an individual based on a single characteristic.

Hierarchy of needs theory (6). There is a hierarchy of five needs—physiological, safety, love, esteem, and self-actualization—and as each need is sequentially satisfied, the next need becomes dominant.

Higher-order needs (6). Needs that are satisfied internally; needs for love, esteem, and self-actualization.

Horizontal differentiation (13). The degree of differentiation between units based on the orientation of members, the nature of the tasks they perform, and their education and training.

Human relations view of conflict (12). The belief that conflict is a natural and inevitable outcome in any group.

Hygiene factors (6). Those factors—such as company policy and administration, supervision, and salary—that, when present in a job, placate workers. When these factors are present, people will not be dissatisfied.

Hypothesis (2). A tentative explanation about the relationship between two or more variables.

Illegitimate political behavior (11). Extreme political behavior that violates the implied rules of the game.

Implicit favorite model (4). A decision making model where the decision maker implicitly selects a preferred alternative early in the decision process and biases the evaluation of all other choices.

Independent variable (2). The presumed cause of some change in the dependent variable.

Individual ranking (14). An evaluation method that rank orders employees from best to worst.

Individualism (15). A national culture attribute describing a loosely knit social framework in which people emphasize only the care of themelves and their immediate family.

Informal group (8). A group that is neither structured nor organizationally determined; appears in response to the need for social contact.

Initiating structure (10). The extent to which a leader is likely to define and structure his or her role and those of subordinates in the search for goal attainment.

Institutionalization (15). When an organization takes on a life of its own, apart from any of its members, and acquires immortality.

Intellectual ability (3). That required to do mental activities.

Interacting groups (9). Typical groups, where members interact with each other face to face.

Interactionist view of conflict (12). The belief that conflict is not only a positive force in a group but that it is absolutely necessary for a group to perform effectively.

Interest group (8). Those working together to attain a specific objective with which each is concerned.

Intergroup development (17). OD efforts to improve interactions between groups.

Intermittent reinforcement (3). A desired behavior is reinforced often enough to make the behavior worth repeating, but not every time it is demonstrated.

Internals (3). Individuals who believe that they control what happens to them.

Intrinsic rewards (14). The pleasure or value one receives from the content of a work task.

Intuition (1). A feeling not necessarily supported by research.

Job analysis (14). Developing a detailed description of the tasks involved in a job, determining the relationship of a given job to other jobs, and ascertaining the knowledge, skills, and abilities necessary for an employee to perform the job successfully.

Job burnout (16). Experiencing physical, mental, and emotional exhaustion.

Job characteristics model (7). Identifies five job characteristics and their relationship to personal and work outcomes.

Job description (14). A written statement of what a jobholder does, how it is done, and why it is done.

Job design (7). The way that tasks are combined to form complete jobs.

Job enlargement (7). The horizontal expansion of jobs.

Job enrichment (7). The vertical expansion of jobs.

Job involvement (5). The degree to which a person identifies with his or her job, actively participates in it, and considers his or her performance important to his or her sense of self-worth.

Job rotation (7). The periodic shifting of a worker from one task to another.

Job satisfaction (2). A general attitude toward one's job; the difference between the amount of rewards workers receive and the amount they believe they should receive.

Job specification (14). States the minimum acceptable qualifications that an employee must possess to perform a given job successfully.

Kinesics (9). The study of body motions.

Knowledge power (11). The ability to control unique and valuable information.

Labor unions (14). A formal group of employees that acts collectively to protect and promote employee interests.

Laboratory experiment (2). In an artificial environment, the researcher manipulates an independent variable under controlled conditions, and then concludes that any change in the dependent variable is due to the manipulation or change imposed on the independent variable.

Leader-member relations (10). The degree of confidence, trust, and respect subordinates have in their leader.

Leadership (10). The ability to influence a group toward the achievement of goals.

Learning (3). Any relatively permanent change in behavior that occurs as a result of experience.

Legitimate political behavior (11). Normal everyday politics.

Leniency error (14). The tendency to evaluate a set of employees too high (positive) or too low (negative).

Locus of control (3). The degree to which people believe they are masters of their own fate.

Lower-order needs (6). Needs that are satisfied externally; physiological and safety needs.

Loyalty (5). Dissatisfaction expressed by passively waiting for conditions to improve.

LPC (10). Least preferred co-worker questionnaire that measures task or relationship-oriented leadership style.

Machiavellianism (3). Degree to which an individual is pragmatic, maintains emotional distance, and believes that ends can justify means.

Management (1). A field of study devoted to determining how best to attain goals in organizations.

Management by objectives (MBO) (7). A program that encompasses specific goals, participatively set, for an explicit time period, with feedback on goal progress.

Managerial Grid (10). A nine-by-nine matrix outlining eighty-one different leadership styles.

Manipulative values (5). Individuals who value striving to achieve their goals by manipulating things and people.

Masculinity (15). A national culture attribute describing the extent to which the dominant societal values are characterized by assertiveness, acquisition of money and things, and not caring for others or for the quality of life.

Matrix structure (13). A structure that creates dual lines of authority; combines the functional and product structures.

Maturity (10). The ability and willingness of people to take responsibility for directing their own behavior.

Mechanistic structure (13). A structure characterized by high complexity, high formalization, and centralization.

Message (9). What is communicated.

Metamorphosis stage (15). The stage in the socialization process in which a new employee adjusts to his or her work group's values and norms.

Model (2). Abstraction of reality; simplified representation of some real-world phenomenon.

Moderating variable (2). Abates the effect of the independent variable on the dependent variable; also known as contingency variable.

Motivating potential score (7). A predictive index suggesting the motivation potential in a job.

Motivation (6). The willingness to exert high levels of effort toward organizational goals, conditioned by the effort's ability to satisfy some individual needs.

Motivation-hygiene theory (6). Intrinsic factors are related to job satisfaction, while extrinsic factors are associated with dissatisfaction.

N ach (3). Need to achieve or strive continually to do things better.

National culture (15). The primary values and practices that characterize a particular country.

Neglect (5). Dissatisfaction expressed through allowing conditions to worsen.

Nominal group technique (9). A group decision method in which individual members meet face to face to pool their judgments in a systematic but independent fashion.

Nonverbal communication (9). Messages conveyed through body movements, the intonations or emphasis we give to words, facial expressions, and the physical distance between the sender and receiver.

Norms (8). Acceptable standards of behavior within a group that are shared by the group's members.

OB Mod (7). A program where managers identify performance-related employee behaviors and then implement an intervention strategy to strengthen desirable performance behaviors and weaken undesirable behaviors.

Operant conditioning (3). A type of conditioning in which desired voluntary behavior leads to a reward or prevents a punishment.

Opportunity power (11). Influence obtained as a result of being in the right place at the right time.

Opportunity to perform (6). High levels of performance are partially a function of an absence of obstacles that constrain the employee.

Optimizing model (4). A decision making model that describes how individuals should behave in order to maximize some outcome.

Organic structure (13). A structure characterized by low complexity, low formalization, and decentralization.

Organization size (13). The number of people employed in an organization.

Organization (1). A consciously coordinated social unit, composed of two or more people, that functions on a relatively continuous basis to achieve a common goal or set of goals.

Organizational behavior (OB) (1). A field of study that investigates the impact that individuals, groups, and structure have on behavior within organizations for the purpose of applying such knowledge toward improving an organization's effectiveness.

Organizational commitment (5). An individual's orientation toward the organization in terms of loyalty, identification, and involvement.

Organizational culture (15). A common perception held by the organization's members; a system of shared meaning.

Organizational development (OD) (17). A systems-oriented approach to change.

Organization structure (13). The degree of complexity, formalization, and centralization in the organization.

Paired comparison (14). An evaluation method that compares each employee with every other employee and assigns a summary ranking based on the number of superior scores that the employee achieves.

Participative management (7). A process where subordinates share a significant degree of decision making power with their immediate superiors.

Perceived conflict (12). Awareness by one or more parties of the existence of conditions that create opportunities for conflict to arise.

Perception (4). A process by which individuals organize and interpret their sensory impressions in order to give meaning to their environment.

Performance-based compensation (7). Paying employees based on some performance measure.

Personal power (11). Influence attributed to one's personal characteristics.

Personality (3). The sum total of ways in which an individual reacts and interacts with others.

Personality traits (3). Enduring characteristics that describe an individual's behavior.

Persuasive power (11). The ability to allocate and manipulate symbolic rewards.

Physical ability (3). That required to do tasks demanding stamina, dexterity, strength, and similar skills.

Physiological symptoms of stress (16). Changes in an individual's health as a result of stress.

Piece-rate pay plans (7). Workers are paid a fixed sum for each unit of production completed.

Political behavior (11). Those activities that are not required as part of one's formal role in the organization but that influence, or attempt to influence, the distribution of advantages and disadvantages within the organization.

Pooled interdependence (12). Where two groups function with relative independence but their combined output contributes to the organization's overall goals.

Position power (10). Influence derived from one's formal structural position in the organization: includes power to hire, fire, discipline, promote, and give salary increases.

Power (11). A capacity that A has to influence the behavior of B so that B does things he or she would not otherwise do.

Power-control view of structure (13). An organization's structure is the result of a power struggle by internal constituencies who are seeking to further their interests.

Power distance (15). A national culture attribute describing the extent to which a society accepts that power in institutions and organizations is distributed unequally.

Power need (6). The desire to make others behave in a way that they would not otherwise have behaved in.

Prearrival stage (15). The period of learning in the socialization process that occurs before a new employee joins the organization.

Process consultation (17). Consultant gives a client insights into what is going on around him or her, within him or her, and between him or her and other people; identifies processes that need improvement.

Production-oriented leader (10). One who emphasizes technical or task aspects of the job.

Productivity (2). A performance measure including effectiveness and efficiency.

Product structure (13). A structure characterized by grouping activities together that relate to a specific product.

Projection (4). Attributing one's own characteristics to other people.

Psychological contract (8). An unwritten agreement that sets out what management expects from the employee, and vice versa.

Psychological school of job design (7). Redesigning jobs to increase employee satisfaction and motivation.

Psychological symptoms of stress (16). Changes in an individual's attitudes and disposition due to stress.

Quality circle (7). A voluntary work group of employees who meet regularly to discuss their quality problems, investigate causes, recommend solutions, and take corrective actions.

Quality of worklife (QWL) (7). A process by which an organization responds to employee needs by developing mechanisms to allow them to share fully in making the decisions that affect their lives at work.

Rationality (4). Actions that are consistent and value maximizing.

Reactive values (5). Individuals who value basic physiological needs and are unaware of themselves or others as human beings.

Realistic job previews (4). Job applicants receive both unfavorable and favorable information about the job.

Reciprocal interdependence (12). Where groups exchange inputs and outputs.

Referent power (11). Influence held by A based on B's admiration and desire to model himself or herself after A.

Refreezing (17). Stabilizing a change intervention by balancing driving and restraining forces.

Reinforcement theory (6). Behavior is a function of its consequences.

Reliability (2). Consistency of measurement.

Research (2). The systematic gathering of information.

Restraining forces (17). Forces that hinder movement from the status quo.

Rituals (15). Repetitive sequences of activities that express and reinforce the key values of the organization, what goals are most important, which people are important and which are expendable.

Role (8). A set of expected behavior patterns attributed to someone occupying a given position in a social unit.

Role conflict (8). A situation in which an individual is confronted by divergent role expectations.

Role expectations (8). How others believe a person should act in a given situation.

Role identity (8). Certain attitudes and behavior consistent with a role.

Role perception (8). An individual's view of how he or she is supposed to act in a given situation.

Satisficing model (4). A decision making model where a decision maker chooses the first solution that is "good enough"; that is, satisfactory and sufficient.

Scanlon plans (7). A blend of participative management and performance-based compensation that uses committees and a formula for determining and sharing of cost savings.

Scientific management (7). A body of literature developed in the early 1900s concerned with incentives, selection, training, and the design of jobs to eliminate time and motion waste.

Selective perception (4). People interpret what they see based on their interests, background, experience, and attitudes.

Self-actualization (6). The drive to become what one is capable of becoming.

Self-efficacy (14). A person's expectation that he or she can successfully execute behaviors required to produce an outcome.

Self-monitoring (10). A personality trait that measures an individual's ability to adjust his or her behavior to external, situational factors.

Self-perception theory (5). Attitudes are used, after the fact, to make sense out of action (behavior) that has already occurred.

Self-serving bias (4). The tendency for individuals to attribute their successes to internal factors while putting the blame for failures on external factors.

Sensitivity training (17). Training groups that seek to change behavior through unstructured group interaction.

Sequential interdependence (12). One group depends on another for its input but the dependency is only one way.

Shaping behavior (3). Systematically reinforcing each successive step that moves an individual closer to the desired response.

Similarity error (14). Giving special consideration when rating others to those qualities that the evaluator perceives in himself or herself.

Simple structure (13). A structure characterized by low complexity, low formalization, and authority centralized in a single person.

Skill variety (7). The degree to which the job requires a variety of different activities.

Socialization (15). The process that adapts employees to the organization's culture.

Social learning theory (3). People can learn through observation and direct experience.

Social loafing (8). Group size and individual performance are inversely related.

Sociocentric values (5). The belief that it is more important to be liked and to get along with others than to get ahead.

Sociotechnical systems (7). A job design philosophy emphasizing both the technical and social aspects of work.

Spatial differentiation (13). The degree to which the location of an organization's offices, plants, and personnel are geographically dispersed.

Span of control (13). The number of subordinates who report directly to a manager.

Stereotyping (4). Judging someone on the basis of the perception of the group to which that person belongs.

Stress (16). A dynamic condition in which an individual is confronted with an opportunity, constraint, or demand related to what he or she desires and for which the outcome is perceived to be both uncertain and important.

Strong cultures (15). Cultures where the core values are intensely held and widely shared.

Subcultures (15). Minicultures within an organization, typically defined by department designations and geographical separation.

Survey feedback (17). The use of questionnaires to identify discrepancies among member perceptions; discussion follows and remedies are suggested.

Synergy (8). An action of two or more substances which results in an effect that is different from the individual summation of the substances.

Systematic study (1). Looking at relationships, attempting to attribute causes and effects, and drawing conclusions based on scientific evidence.

Task group (8). Those working together to complete a job task.

Task identity (7). The degree to which the job requires completion of a whole and identifiable piece of work.

Task significance (7). The degree to which the job has a substantial impact on the lives or work of other people.

Task structure (10). The degree to which job assignments are procedurized.

Task uncertainty (12). The greater the uncertainty in a task, the more custom the response. Conversely, low uncertainty encompasses routine tasks with standardized activities.

Team building (17). High interaction among group members to increase trust and openness.

Technology (13). How an organization transfers its inputs into outputs.

Telecommuting (7). Employees do their work at home on a computer that is linked to their office.

Theory (2). A set of systematically interrelated concepts or hypotheses that purport to explain and predict phenomena.

Theory X (6). The assumption that employees dislike work, are lazy, dislike responsibility, and must be coerced to perform.

Theory Y (6). The assumption that employees like work, are creative, seek responsibility, and can exercise self-direction.

Three needs theory (6). Achievement, power, and affiliation are three important needs that help to understand motivation.

Traditional view of conflict (12). The belief that all conflict must be avoided.

Transactional leadership (10). Leaders who guide or motivate their followers in the direction of established goals by clarifying role and task requirements.

Transformational leadership (10). Leaders who inspire followers to transcend their own self-interest for the good of the organization and who are capable of having a profound and extraordinary effect on their followers.

Tribalistic values (5). The belief in tradition and power exerted by authority figures.

Turnover (2). Voluntary and involuntary permanent withdrawal from the organization.

Two-tier pay system (7). New employees are hired at significantly lower wage rates than those already employed and performing the same jobs.

Type A behavior (16). Aggressive involvement in a chronic, incessant struggle to achieve more and more in less and less time and, if necessary, against the opposing efforts of other things or other persons.

Type B behavior (16). Rarely harried by the desire to obtain a wildly increasing number of things or participate in an endlessly growing series of events in an ever-decreasing amount of time.

Uncertainty avoidance (15). A national culture attribute describing the extent to which a society feels threatened by uncertain and ambiguous situations and tries to avoid them.

Unfreezing (17). Change efforts to overcome the pressures of both individual resistance and group conformity.

Validity (2). The degree to which a research study is actually measuring what it claims to be measuring.

Values (5). Basic convictions that a specific mode of conduct or end state of existence is personally or socially preferable to an opposite or converse mode of conduct or end state of existence.

Value system (5). A ranking of individual values according to their relative importance.

Variable (2). Any general characteristic that can be measured and that changes in either amplitude, intensity, or both.

Variable-interval schedule (3). Rewards are distributed in time so that reinforcements are unpredictable.

Variable-ratio schedule (3). The reward varies relative to the behavior of the individual.

Vertical differentiation (13). The number of hierarchical levels in the organization.

Voice (5). Dissatisfaction expressed through active and constructive attempts to improve conditions.

Wellness programs (16). Organizationally-supported programs that focus on the employee's total physical and mental condition.

Work sampling (14). Creating a miniature replica of a job to evaluate the performance abilities of job candidates.

Name Index

Capwell, D. F., 134
Carnegie, D., 157
Carroll, S. J., 186
Carson, K. P., 335
Carson, T., 121
Carsten, J. M., 136
Carter, J., 337
Cartwright, D., 307, 341
Cascio, W. F., 30, 448, 459
Cashman, J., 317–18
Cass, E. L., 214, 242, 259
Castaneda, M. B., 204
Caston, R. J., 154
Cattell, R. B., 55
Cavender, J. W., 134–35
Cavett, D., 430
Chadwick-Jones, J. K., 47
Chaiken, S., 142
Chancellor, J., 365
Chandler, A. D., Jr., 408, 415
Chandler, P., 114
Chanin, M. N., 392
Charlier, M., 200
Chelte, A. F., 132
Chemers, M. M., 312, 336
Chen, M., 397
Chen, T., 397
Cherrington, D. J., 121
Chew, I. K-H., 211
Child, J., 409, 414
Chin, R., 549
Christ, J., 304
Christensen, K., 203
Christie, R., 59, 364
Churchill, W., 304, 327
Cidambi, R., 123
Clark, R. D., III, 289
Clausen, J. A., 73, 132–33
Clegg, C. W., 213
Cliff, G., 391
Coch, L., 532
Colby, F. M., 267
Condie, S. J., 121
Conger, J. A., 330–31
Converse, P. E., 133
Coons, A. E., 306
Cooper, C. L., 180, 502–4, 512
Cooper, E. A., 164
Cooper, M. R., 142
Cosier, R. A., 377
Costello, T. W., 67
Cotton, J. L., 192
Cozzetta, J., 518
Crockett, W. H., 134, 136
Culbert, S. A., 353
Cummings, L. L., 78, 141, 154, 160,
    176–77, 221, 355, 417
Cummins, W. M., 467
Cyert, R. M., 347

D

Daft, R. L., 38
Dalton, D. R., 30, 37, 39, 416–17
Dansereau, F., 317
Darwin, C., 553
Daughen, J. R., 378
Davis, K., 276, 280
Day, D. V., 332
Deal, T. E., 470, 472
Dearborn, D. C., 89
DeCenzo, D., 435
de Charms, R., 158
Deci, E. L., 158
DeCotiis, T. A., 503
DeJong, R. D., 362
Delafield, G., 417
Delbecq, A. L., 290, 411
Delong, T. J., 462
Delorean, J., 271
DeMeuse, K. P., 546
Denisi, A. S., 91
Denny, A. T., 192
DeVader, C. L., 329
Dickerson, E., 167
Dickinson, T. L., 417
Dillinger, J., 342
Disney, W., 473
Dispenzieri, A., 44
Distefano, M. K., Jr., 134
Doherty, F., 145
Doherty, J., 145
Dorfman, P. W., 309, 325
Dorsett, T., 167
Dossett, D. L., 48
Doucet, A. R., 356
Drabek, T. E., 355
Driver, M. J., 7
Drucker, P. F., 185
DuBrin, A. J., 263, 427
Duchon, D., 318
Duncan, K. D., 178, 192
Duncan, R. B., 413
Dunham, R. B., 123, 204, 211
Dunnette, M. D., 59, 131, 374–75,
    433, 513, 548
Dyer, L., 167

E

Earley, P. C., 161–62
Ebeling, J. S., 417
Ebert, R., 224
Eden, D., 546
Ehrlich, S. B., 329
Eisenberg, E. M., 295
Eisenberg, J., 44
Emerson, R. E., 346

Emery, F. E., 413
Emshoff, J. R., 377
England, J. L., 121
Erez, M., 162
Etzion, D., 516
Etzioni, A., 341
Evans, M. G., 180, 198, 207
Eysenck, H. J., 55

F

Farace, R. V., 417
Farrell, D., 136, 353, 355–56
Farris, G., 123
Fast, J., 283
Faulkner, W., 90
Faust, J., 430
Fazio, R. H., 128, 142
Federico, J. M., 46–47
Federico, P., 46–47
Feild, H. S., 48
Fein, M., 196
Feldman, D. C., 48, 133, 244, 477
Feldman, M. S., 480
Feldman, S. P., 473
Feren, D. B., 192
Ferris, G. R., 210–11
Ferriss, R., 549
Festinger, L., 124–25
Fiedler, F. E., 302, 311–14, 326–27,
    333, 336
Field, R. H. G., 323
Fielding, G. J., 416
Filley, A. C., 310
Fine, G. A., 281
Fink, C. F., 247–48, 254, 257, 367
Fitzgerald, M. P., 210
Fitzgibbons, W. J., 47
Flaim, P. O., 221
Flanagan, M. F., 202
Flanagan, R. J., 46
Flax, S., 199
Fleishman, E. A., 50, 251, 255
Fleming, L., 500
Foley, P. M., 142
Follett, K., 480
Ford, C. H., 187–88
Ford, D. L., Jr., 421
Ford, H., 473
Ford, R. C., 187
Forester, J., 101
Forte, C., 559
Fournet, G. P., 134
Fradon, D., 356
Frantzve, J. L., 112
Freeman, R. B., 132, 137
French, J. R. P., Jr., 341, 532
French, W. L., 527, 554–55
Frew, D. R., 515

O'Reilly, C. A., III, 162, 211, 249, 324, 470
Organ, D. W., 310–11
Ormsby, J. G., 69
Osborn, A. F., 290
Osborn, R. N., 307

P

Packard, D., 473
Packard, J. S., 510
Parasuraman, S., 503–4
Parker, D. F., 167, 503
Parsons, T., 402
Pascale, R., 475
Patterson, B., 237, 239
Pavlov, I. P., 63–64
Payne, R., 502, 504
Peacock, A. C., 78
Pearce, J. L., 460
Pearlstein, S., 132
Pearson, J., 163–64
Pedalino, E., 69
Pelz, D. C., 379
Perlman, B., 515
Perlman, K., 437
Perot, H. R., 380, 479–80, 482
Perrow, C., 347, 382, 410, 426
Perry, J., 123
Peters, L. H., 173, 314
Peters, T., 41, 470–71, 498
Petersen, J. C., 353, 355–56
Peterson, M. M., 200
Peterson, R. O., 134
Pettigrew, A. M., 480
Petty, M. M., 134–35
Pfeffer, J., 249, 333, 339, 352, 410, 412, 414
Phillips, S. L., 293
Pierce, J. L., 123, 204, 210
Pinder, C. C., 180
Pizam, A., 445
Podsakoff, P. M., 39, 362
Pohlmann, J. T., 314
Pondy, L. R., 374
Poole, P. P., 352
Pooyan, A., 77
Popovich, P., 93
Popp, P. O., 47
Porac, J., 158
Porras, J. I., 555
Porter, L. W., 6, 14, 20, 43, 47, 53, 78, 123, 142, 150, 156, 163, 167, 172, 181, 254, 262, 280, 293, 355, 391, 416, 433, 436, 460, 470, 527, 543, 555
Portwood, J. D., 454
Powell, F. A., 558
Powell, G. N., 45, 329

Powell, M. C., 142
Power, D. J., 103
Premack, S. L., 93
Prest, W., 161
Price, J. L., 130, 136, 181
Pringle, C. D., 173–74
Pritchard, R. D., 158
Proehl, C. W., Jr., 549
Pryer, M. W., 134
Puckett, E. S., 197
Pugh, D. S., 414
Purdy, K., 213
Pursell, E. D., 447
Putnam, L. L., 394

Q

Quinn, R. P., 46, 132

R

Rabinowitz, S., 123
Rados, D. L., 100
Raelin, J. A., 121
Ragan, J. W., 297
Rahe, R. H., 507–9
Rahim, M. A., 391
Raiffa, H., 367
Ralston, D. A., 202
Rauch, C. F., Jr., 334
Rauschenberger, J., 149
Raven, B., 341
Ravlin, E. C., 142, 231, 243, 248
Raynor, J. O., 156
Reagan, R. W., 329, 337
Reddin, W. J., 308
Redding, A., 524
Reibstein, L., 129, 198–99
Reilly, R. R., 293
Reinharth, L., 167
Reitz, H. J., 231
Renwick, P. A., 355
Rhode, J. G., 3
Rhodes, S. R., 43–44, 47
Rice, R. W., 314
Richards, B., 428
Richardson, A. J., 467
Richman, L. S., 252
Ricks, D. A., 465
Rieck, A., 251, 255
Ringelmann, 247
Ritti, R., 465
Robbins, S. P., 226, 239, 271, 369, 398, 410, 412–13, 415, 435
Roberts, K. H., 297
Robertson, I., 180, 559
Rockwell, N., 337
Roderick, R. D., 220

Rodgers, W., 466
Rodin, M. J., 457
Roethlisberger, F. J., 294
Rogers, C. R., 294, 540
Rogers, D. P., 515
Rogers, J. F., 70
Rognes, J. K., 381, 387
Rokeach, M., 117, 122
Ronen, S., 164, 483–84
Roosevelt, F. D., 330
Rorer, L. G., 78
Rose, R. L., 515
Rosenman, R. H., 510, 514
Rosenthal, D. B., 434
Rosenzweig, M. R., 14, 20, 53, 78, 142, 150, 172, 254, 391, 433, 436, 527, 543, 555
Rosnow, R. L., 281
Ross, I., 199
Ross, J., 329
Ross, S., 201
Rothe, H. F., 40
Rotter, J. B., 39, 79
Rousseau, D. M., 211
Rowan, R., 280
Rowe, A. J., 111
Roznowski, M., 136, 417
Rubin, I. M., 157
Rudolf, C. J., 173
Ruff, D., 463
Rusbult, C., 136–37
Rushing, W. A., 409

S

Saari, L. M., 161–62
Safire, W., 273
Salaman, G., 475
Salancik, G. R., 160–61, 166, 412
Salvendy, G., 522
Samuel, Y., 409
Sandberg, W. R., 297
Santalainen, T., 542
Saporito, B., 191, 194
Sashkin, M., 192, 556
Saxton, M. J., 496
Sayles, L. R., 226
Scandura, T. A., 211, 318
Scarpello, V., 131
Schein, E. H., 239, 314, 326, 436, 438, 467, 473, 476–77, 545
Schein, V. E., 539–41
Schlender, B. R., 403
Schlesinger, L. A., 531
Schlitt, W. K., 349
Schmidt, F. L., 437
Schmidt, S. M., 349–50
Schmidt, W. H., 267, 310
Schminke, M., 231, 243

W

Waddoups, J. W., 201
Wagner, J. A., III, 192
Wagner, W. G., 249
Wahba, M. A., 150, 167, 172
Waldman, D. A., 44
Waldo, D., 397
Wallace, M. J., Jr., 235
Walker, H., 167
Wall, T. D., 213
Wallace, J., 546
Wallach, M. A., 60, 289
Wallis, C., 502
Wallis, D., 178, 192
Walsh, J. P., 292
Walsh, M., 195, 197
Walter, G. A., 540
Walton, A. E., 527, 555
Walton, R. E., 207, 214
Walton, S., 474
Wanous, J. P., 93, 156
Warren, J. R., 53
Warrick, D. D., 535, 556
Waterman, R., 41, 470–71
Watson, C. J., 46
Watson, T., 473
Watson, T., Jr., 466
Wayne, S. J., 550

Weaver, C. N., 154
Weber, M., 402, 424
Webster, E. C., 93, 432
Weick, K. E., Jr., 548
Weinberg, R., 4
Weiss, H. M., 78
Weitzel, J. R., 317
Weschler, I. R., 192
Wessel, D., 200
West, F., 395
Westhead, P., 346
Wexley, K. N., 447
White, G., 16
White, R. A., 200
Whyte, W. F., 14
Wicker, A. W., 127
Widiger, T. A., 78
Wiener, Y., 47
Wigdor, L. A., 154
Wilbur, E. R., 44
Wilkins, A. L., 496
Wilkinson, I., 349
Williams, C. R., 37
Williams, K., 248
Williams, M. S., 378
Williams, R., 48
Willings, D., 70
Wilson, C., 394
Wilson, E. O., 13

Wilson, J., 395
Wilson, J. C., 476
Wilson, M., 253
Winter, D. G., 157
Witten, M. G., 295
Wojnaroski, P., 161
Woodman, R. W., 550
Woodward, J., 410
Wozniak, S., 473
Wright, J., 132

Y–Z

Yalom, I. D., 548
Yetton, P., 248, 321–24, 327
York, D. R., 130
Yukl, G. A., 161–63
Zaccaro, S. J., 305
Zald, M. N., 347
Zalesny, M. D., 417
Zaleznik, A., 303
Zalkind, S. S., 67
Zander, A., 254, 262, 307
Zanna, M. P., 128
Zimbardo, P. G., 240
Zimmer, F. G., 214, 242, 259
Zucker, L. G., 467
Zwany, A., 156

Subject Index

Proximity, influence on perception, 85
Psychological:
    contract, 238–39
    school of job design, 215–16
Psychology, 7, 9
Punishment, 66

Q

Quality circles, 193–94
Quality of work life, 207–8

R

Ranking, performance evaluation, 442–43
Rationality, 99, 101, 108–9
Realistic job previews, 93
Reality vs. perception, 82
Referent power, 341
Reinforcement:
    continuous, 67
    extinction, 66
    negative, 66
    positive, 64–65, 66
    punishment, 66
    schedules, 67–68
    shaping, 66
    theory, 163, 175–76, 190
Relatedness needs, 155
Relational managers, 361
Reliability, 22
Republic Avionics, 395
Research:
    defined, 19
    designs, 22–26
    evaluation of, 22
    in organizational development, 547–50
    purpose of, 19
    variables, 20
Resistance to change, 528–29
Resource allocation norms, 244
Reward(s):
    equity in, 131
    extrinsic, 451
    impact on group, 234
    influence on behavior, 455
    intrinsic, 451
    and performance, 217
    power, 342
    types of, 449–52
Risk-taking personality, 59–60
Rituals, 480–81
Role(s):
    ambiguity, 357
    conflict, 239–40

defined, 237
expectations, 238–39
identity, 237–38
influence on behavior, 256–57
perception, 238
Rolls Royce, 411
Roman Catholic Church, 371
Rules, 233, 384
Rumors, 280–82

S

Safety needs, 149
San Giorgio-Skinner, 482
Satisfaction (*see* Job satisfaction)
Satisficing decision model, 101–03
Scanlon plans, 197
Scarborough Daily News, 559
Schlumberger, 471
Science Fiction Book Club, 264
Scientific management, 205–6
Sears, Roebuck, 135, 408
Security need, 227–28
Seiko Epson, 504
Selection:
    culture, role in, 474–75
    devices, 432–34, 454
    process, impact on group, 234
Selective perception, 89–90, 272
Self-actualization need, 149
Self-efficacy, 454
Self-esteem need, 228
Self-monitoring, 324
Self-perception theory, 128
Self-serving bias, 88–89
Seniority, as an independent variable, 47–48
Sensitivity training, 544, 548
Sex, as a biographical characteristic, 44–46, 72
Sex-role stereotypes, 90–91
Shaping behavior, 65–68
Shock experiment, 24–25
Sick pay, 70
Similarity:
    error, 445
    in perception, 85–86
Simple structure, 404–5
Situational approach (*see* Contingency)
Situational leadership theory, 314–17
Size (*see* Group size *and* Organization size)
Skills, people, 6
Skill training, 434–35
Skill variety, 208–11
Social desirability (*see* Conformity)
Socialization, 476–79

Social:
    learning, 65
    loafing, 247–48, 250
    norms, 244
    psychology, 8–9
    science, 12
Sociobiology, 13
Sociology, 7–9
Sociotechnical systems, 207
Sony, 291, 470
Southwestern Texas State Teachers College, 344
Span of control, influence on behavior, 418
Stages of group development, 230–31
Standard Oil of New Jersey, 408
Standard Oil of Ohio, 190
Standardization, 233
Status need, 228
Stereotypes, 90–91
Stories, 479–80
Strategy, effect on:
    group, 232–33
    structure, 407–8, 415
Stress (*see* Work stress)
Structure (*see* Organization structure)
Students as research subjects, 26
Subcultures, 469
Survey feedback, 544–45, 548–49
Surveys, attitude, 129–30
Symbols:
    cultural, 481
    power, 343
Synergy, 250
Systematic study, 4
System 4, 536

T

Tandem Computers, 481
Task:
    design (*see* Job design)
    forces, 385
    identity, 208–11
    oriented leaders, 326
    significance, 208–11
    structure, 311–14
    uncertainty, 382–83
Teaching evaluations, 457–58
Team building, 546–47, 549
Teams:
    integrating device, 385–86
    production, 229
Technical skill training, 434–35
Technology, determinant of structure, 410–11, 415–16